COMMAND	SHORTCUT
Insert date	Ctrl-;
Insert time	Ctrl-:
Format Number (general)	Ctrl-Shift-~
Format Number (#,##0.00)	Ctrl-Shift-!
Format Number (h:mm AM/PM)	Ctrl-Shift-@
Format Number (d-mmm-yy)	Ctrl-Shift-#
Format Number (($#,##0.00_);($#,##0.00))	Ctrl-Shift-$
Format Number (0%)	Ctrl-Shift-%
Format Number (0.00E+00)	Ctrl-Shift-^
Format Font (default)	Ctrl-1
Format Font (bold)	Ctrl-2
Format Font (italic)	Ctrl-3
Format Font (underline)	Ctrl-4
Format Font (strikeout)	Ctrl-5
Format Border (outline)	Ctrl-Shift-&
Format Border (no border)	Ctrl-Shift-_
Format Row Height (hide)	Ctrl-9
Format Row Height (unhide)	Ctrl-Shift-F9
Format Column Width (hide)	Ctrl-0
Format Column Width (unhide)	Ctrl-Shift-0
Options Display Formulas	Ctrl-`
Options Display (Outline Symbols)	Ctrl-8
Options Display (Show All/Show Placeholders/Hide All)	Ctrl-6
Options Calculation (Calc Now)	F9 or Ctrl-=
Options Calculation Calc Document	Shift-F9
Window Show Info	Ctrl-F2

Computer users are not all alike.
Neither are SYBEX books.

We know our customers have a variety of needs. They've told us so. And because we've listened, we've developed several distinct types of books to meet the needs of each of our customers. What are you looking for in computer help?

If you're looking for the basics, try the **ABC's** series. You'll find short, unintimidating tutorials and helpful illustrations. For a more visual approach, select **Teach Yourself,** featuring full-color screen-by-screen illustrations of how to use the latest software.

Learn Fast! books are really two books in one: a tutorial, to get you off to a fast start, followed by a command reference, to answer more advanced questions.

Mastering and **Understanding** titles offer you a step-by-step introduction, plus an in-depth examination of intermediate-level features, to use as you progress.

Our **Up & Running** series is designed for computer-literate consumers who want a no-nonsense overview of new programs. Just 20 basic lessons, and you're on your way.

We also publish two types of reference books. Our **Instant References** provide quick access to each of a program's commands and functions. SYBEX **Encyclopedias**, **Desktop References** and **A to Z** books provide a *comprehensive reference* and explanation of all of the commands, features, and functions of the subject software.

Sometimes a subject requires a special treatment that our standard series don't provide. So you'll find we have titles like **Advanced Techniques, Handbooks, Tips & Tricks,** and others that are specifically tailored to satisfy a unique need.

We carefully select our authors for their in-depth understanding of the software they're writing about, as well as their ability to write clearly and communicate effectively. Each manuscript is thoroughly reviewed by our technical staff to ensure its complete accuracy. Our production department makes sure it's easy to use. All of this adds up to the highest quality books available, consistently appearing on best-seller charts worldwide.

You'll find SYBEX publishes a variety of books on every popular software package. Looking for computer help? Help Yourself to SYBEX.

For a complete catalog of our publications:

SYBEX Inc.
2021 Challenger Drive, Alameda, CA 94501
Tel: (510) 523-8233/(800) 227-2346 Telex: 336311
Fax: (510) 523-2373

SYBEX

SYBEX is committed to using natural resources wisely to preserve and improve our environment. As a leader in the computer book publishing industry, we are aware that over 40% of America's solid waste is paper. This is why we have been printing the text of books like this one on recycled paper since 1982.

This year our use of recycled paper will result in the saving of more than 15,300 trees. We will lower air pollution effluents by 54,000 pounds, save 6,300,000 gallons of water, and reduce landfill by 2,700 cubic yards.

MASTERING EXCEL 4 FOR WINDOWS

MASTERING EXCEL 4 FOR WINDOWS™

Carl Townsend

SYBEX ®

San Francisco • Paris • Düsseldorf • Soest

Acquisitions Editor: Dianne King
Developmental Editor: Kenyon Brown
Editors: Stefan Grünwedel, Savitha Varadan
Technical Editor: Bruce Gendron
Word Processors: Ann Dunn, Susan Trybull
Production Artist: Lucie Živny
Screen Graphics: Aldo Bermudez, Cuong Le
Typesetter: Thomas L. Goudie
Production Editor: Carolina Montilla
Proofreader: Edith Rex
Indexer: Anne Leach
Cover Designer: Ingalls + Associates
Cover Photographer: Mark Johann

Screen reproductions produced with Collage Plus.
Collage Plus is a trademark of Inner Media Inc.

Rolodex is a registered trademark of Insilco Corporation.

SYBEX is a registered trademark of SYBEX Inc.
TRADEMARKS: SYBEX has attempted throughout this book to distinguish proprietary trademarks from descriptive terms by following the capitalization style used by the manufacturer.

SYBEX is not affiliated with any manufacturer.

Every effort has been made to supply complete and accurate information. However, SYBEX assumes no responsibility for its use, nor for any infringement of the intellectual property rights of third parties which would result from such use.

Library of Congress Card Number: 92-81036
ISBN: 0-7821-1088-6

Manufactured in the United States of America
10 9 8 7

To Sandy

*for successfully fighting and winning a battle
with leukemia and surviving her bone marrow
transplant. Thanks to all the doctors, nurses,
friends, and the Good Lord for making it all
possible.*

Acknowledgments

I would like to express my appreciation to many people who helped make this book possible. A special thanks to Christy Gersich at Microsoft for supplying Excel and support during the writing of the book. Thanks also to Jack Sullivan for his help and advice.

At SYBEX, thanks to Stefan Grünwedel for editing the book. Thanks also to Kenyon Brown for helping me develop the manuscript.

CONTENTS AT A GLANCE

PART I

An Overview of Excel

TABLE OF

CONTENTS

Chapter 3

PART II

Getting Right to Work with Excel

Chapter 4

Chapter 5

Chapter 6

Chapter 7

PART III

Effective Database Management

Chapter 10
Basic Database Techniques **233**

PART IV

Using Excel Productively

PART V

High-Impact Presentations with Charts

Chapter 18

Chapter 19

Chapter 20

PART VI

Practical Solutions with Excel

PART VII

Powering Up with Macros

APPENDICES

Introduction

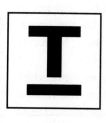here are corporate executives, wholesalers, retailers, and small-business owners who talk about their business lives in two time periods: before and after the electronic spreadsheet.

—Steven Levy

BACKGROUND

Before the invention of the personal-computer spreadsheet program, it was not unusual for a financial vice-president of a company to spend the night manually preparing the company's financial projections for an annual meeting, using nothing more than a hand calculator. If even a small error were made, it would ripple through all subsequent calculations on the entire spreadsheet. Spreadsheet programs did exist for large main-frame computers, but they were often cumbersome to use, and the computers were not very accessible to most employees.

The VisiCalc spreadsheet program, invented by Robert Frankston and Dan Bricklin in 1978 for the Apple II computer, suddenly changed all this. For the first time, a business manager could set up an entire financial model and analyze any number of scenarios quickly, accurately, and inexpensively.

The popularity and capabilities of personal-computer spreadsheet programs grew at a rapid rate. Sorcim's SuperCalc (1980), Microsoft's Multiplan (1982), and Lotus's 1-2-3 (1983) each added new features, capabilities, and integrated tools. These products represented important milestones in the evolution of the spreadsheet, but spreadsheet users wanted still more capabilities.

Users wanted more cells in their spreadsheets to build larger models, and they wanted to be able to link spreadsheets to form hierarchical relationships. They also wanted to be able to produce WYSIWYG (What You See Is What You Get) displays and make presentation-quality charts and worksheets. Users found macros to be the most powerful feature in spreadsheet programs, yet they were cumbersome to use in the products that included them, and they were not included at all in some spreadsheet programs marketed as late as 1985.

Excel changed all this. In 1985, Microsoft released Excel for the Macintosh, the first spreadsheet program designed specifically to address the needs of users who manage many types of data—those frustrated by the limitations of the numerical-analysis products currently available. In 1987, Microsoft introduced a version of Excel for the PC/AT, PS-2, and compatibles.

Excel has continued to mature as a product, and now is recognized by many as the most advanced spreadsheet product on the market. The newest release, Excel 4.0, incorporates a new sense of artificial intelligence and ease of use that will amaze the novice. Excel 4.0 offers drag-and-drop cell operations, automatic formatting, automatic filling of cells in a series, and automated chart generation. At the same time, Excel 4.0 has a new collection of features for even the most advanced user that includes analysis tools, Crosstab report generation, and automated trend analysis.

THE PHILOSOPHY OF EXCEL

Before you begin using Excel, it is important to understand some of the philosophy that went into the design of the product. Excel is an example of a *contextually integrated* product. That is, it combines the applications that are frequently used in the same context by users whose primary task is analyzing and processing numerical data. This contextual integration permits a user to move quickly from one application to another to see the results of an analysis.

Because Excel is designed specifically for users working with data in a large variety of numerical-analysis contexts, it supports the data-processing application more thoroughly than any other personal-computer software product. When used with Windows 3.1, Excel suports TrueType fonts, OLE, and multimedia extensions, and provides better execution stability and more printing control. Windows 3.1 also offers the capability of interfacing Excel data and objects seamlessly with word processors, communication programs, and presentation programs, such as Microsoft PowerPoint.

BOOK ORGANIZATION

This book is divided into seven sections. After a brief introduction (Part I), you learn the basic principles of working with Excel (Part II). Part III covers database management. Part IV describes special features of Excel. Part V covers charting and graphics.

Part VI includes five chapters on application design and the Excel utilities. Using specific applications, such as invoicing, financial management, and trend analysis, you will gain some understanding of how to use Excel to solve specific problems.

Finally, Part VII describes macros and how to use them. This section is primarily tutorial, but you will find a few examples to help you design your own macros.

Included in the appendices of this book are a glossary and an exhaustive list of macro language function commands. You will also find some tips to help you gain more speed from Excel and some notes on installing the software.

Throughout this book, you will be given many tutorial examples that show how Excel can meet a variety of needs. I encourage you to try these examples. Each of them will give you valuable insights into the special features of Excel.

VISUAL ELEMENTS OF THIS BOOK

Several features that will help you Master Excel are included in the text and margins of this book.

TEXT ELEMENTS

Fast Tracks at the beginning of each chapter give you quick access to key concepts, and direct you to pages in the chapter where you can find more detailed information.

Within the text, any data or keystrokes that you type appear in **boldface**. For example, you might read, "...and enter the formula **=C1+C3**."

Alternatively, words, data, or instructions that you read *directly* from the screen appear in *program font*. For example, you might read, "...either of the following displays **$123.00**."

MARGIN ELEMENTS

Features that are new to Excel 4.0 are highlighted for your information with an icon in the margin, shown here. Add-in utilities started from the Program Manager are also identified in the margin.

There are also three types of margin notes that appear in this book: Notes, Tips, and Cautions. Examples are shown in the margin here as well.

This is a note

This is a tip

This is a warning

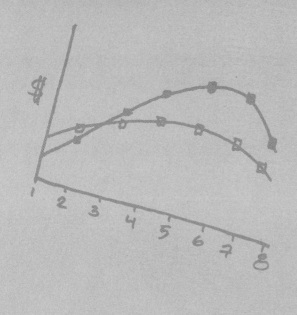

$$b = \frac{\Sigma xy - \bar{x} \Sigma y}{\Sigma x^2 - \bar{x} \Sigma x}$$

PART ONE

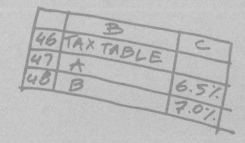

	B	C
46	TAX TABLE	
47	A	
48	B	6.5%
		7.0%

Part I: An Overview of Excel

Part I of this book is for those who would like to start using Excel quickly without learning many commands and instructions. You'll find out how to install Excel and explore Windows 3.1, and be guided through the creation of a simple worksheet and chart.

CHAPTER

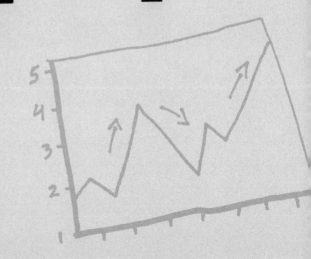

1

Introduction to Excel

Excel is an advanced worksheet (or spreadsheet) product for IBM AT or PS/2 compatibles that also supports database, graphic, and presentation features. A *worksheet program* is essentially a replacement for a ledger sheet, pencil, and calculator. The computer displays a two-dimensional worksheet, divided into rows and columns. Each intersection of a row and a column is called a *cell*.

An Excel worksheet may look very similar to a paper one, but it has several advantages:

◆ It can be much, much larger than its paper counterpart. In fact, one of Excel's outstanding features is the number of worksheet cells available—over 4 million cells in 256 columns of 16,384 rows.

◆ You can edit and change it quickly: changing one number affects immediately all calculations based on that number.

◆ The printed worksheet is presentation-quality and can be used for published reports or overhead projectors.

◆ The Excel worksheet is more accurate than the paper one, as it performs some level of self-checking.

FEATURES OF EXCEL

There are two types of features of Excel. *Analysis features* perform various calculations on data in the worksheet. *Presentation features* display information to the user.

ANALYSIS FEATURES

Excel offers several analysis features that many competing worksheets do not offer:

◆ Excel is easy to learn and use. The Windows interface includes windows, pull-down menus, dialog boxes for input, and mouse support.

◆ Excel can link worksheets and develop hierarchical relationships among them. For example, department managers can develop marketing and production worksheets independently, and then link their component worksheets to the larger corporate worksheet.

◆ Excel's problem-solving capabilities are extensive. Over 500 functions are provided with Excel—and you can create other functions of your own.

◆ Excel supports arrays and tables.

◆ Using "what-if" analysis, you can define an output value and then see what input values you need to reach this goal.

◆ When calculating, Excel includes only those cells that have changed since the last calculation. This provides quick worksheet updating.

◆ Users will find that repetitive tasks can be automated with Excel's easy-to-use macros and user-definable functions.

◆ Excel users can make extensive use of data already created with other worksheet software, even from other computers. Excel offers two-way file capability with Multiplan, dBASE IV, and Lotus 1-2-3, as well as any program using the Microsoft SYLK format.

◆ Excel includes integrated, full-featured graphing and charting capabilities.

◆ Excel supports on-screen databases with querying, extracting, and sorting functions.

◆ Excel provides extensive auditing control. You can give cells names, even name a range of cells with one name or give one cell several names. You also can add notes to cells or show the attributes (format, formula, value) of active cells.

◆ Excel permits you to add, edit, delete, and find database records.

◆ Macros can be used for two-way communication with other programs, and you can even use macros to add special commands to Excel by using programming languages.

PRESENTATION FEATURES

Excel produces presentation-quality worksheet printouts and offers you a wide selection of fonts and formats. Its presentation features include the following:

◆ Individual cells and chart text can be formatted to any font and font size supported by Windows.

◆ Variations in font style (normal, boldface, underline, strikeout, and italic) and alignment control (left, center, right, centered across columns, justify, and fill) can be determined at the cell level.

◆ There are seven border styles, as well as shading and shadow capability.

◆ Extensive pattern control is available for printing worksheets and charts with black-and-white printers.

◆ There are 27 predefined cell pictures.

◆ User-definable pictures are supported.

◆ There are 84 built-in chart formats, including 33 three-dimensional formats.

◆ You can add legends, text, arrows, patterns, scaling, and symbols to charts.

◆ Global zero suppression, which prevents the printing of zero values, is available.

◆ Worksheets can be printed horizontally (landscape) or vertically (portrait).

◆ Outline control is available for printing summary worksheets.

MICROSOFT WINDOWS AND EXCEL

Excel is a Microsoft Windows application program, which means it requires Windows 3.0 or later. Windows is a software shell that resides in memory with DOS. It provides windows, icons, pull-down menus, multitasking, and other features to application programs running under it (see below), while providing a common user interface with other Windows application programs.

FEATURES OF WINDOWS

Windows provides you with the following features:

◆   Excel can be combined with other programs, such as word processors or database managers that run under Windows.

◆   You can use the Clipboard to move data between Excel and other programs.

◆   The size of a spreadsheet is not limited by the conventional memory limit of 640K. Using Windows, Excel can take advantage of any extended memory installed. This means you can build much larger worksheets with Excel than you can with some competing programs.

◆   The graphical user interface is very easy to learn and is rapidly becoming the standard for many application programs.

◆   Access to peripheral devices from Excel is logical rather than physical; that is, Excel does not write to any specific type of printer or plotter. To install a new printer for all Windows application programs on the system, it is only necessary to add the new printer driver to Windows.

◆   The use of the mouse is integrated with both Windows and Excel. This makes it easier to move around in worksheets and to make selections than with nonmouse worksheet programs or programs in which the use of the mouse was designed after the fact.

◆   Windows includes support for the 8087, 80287, 80387, and 80486 math coprocessors.

◆   Networking is supported if the network is compatible with Microsoft Networks (Microsoft Corporation).

NEW FEATURES OF EXCEL 4

If you are already using Excel and upgrading to Version 4, you will find many new features that extend the analysis and presentation capabilities of Excel.

These are marked in this book with the icon to the left, but here is a quick summary of the new features.

New General Features

Excel supports several features of a general nature:

◆ Commands for a given cell or object are available by clicking the right button of the mouse. This gives you a shortcut menu for actions based on the location of the mouse pointer.

◆ Customizable toolbars simplify access to commands and procedures (such as building a chart).

◆ Object linking and embedding is supported.

◆ Excel supports pen input.

◆ Help buttons are now on dialog boxes for quick access to more help.

New Worksheet Features

Here are Excel's new worksheet features:

◆ You can drag or copy cells (or groups of cells) and their contents.

◆ You can extend a series or autofill a selection by dragging the corner of a cell.

◆ Autoformatting (applying a previously-defined format to a cell or cell range) is now supported.

◆ You can autoselect tables and named cell blocks.

◆ A new workgroup feature permits you to keep related documents in a single file.

◆ Worksheet printing is improved to include "reports." For example, you can create views with defined print settings and print by views. You can also define scenarios (a defined set of input values for one or two cells) and print by scenarios to get a sequence of worksheets.

◆ Header and footer control is expanded. You can also define a starting page number for printing and the direction for printing (down or across).

◆ You can use the new Crosstab ReportWizard to see different table views. Using this, Excel can quickly step you through the creation of tables from database data.

- ◆ You can now zoom in and zoom out on worksheet views.

- ◆ You can paste functions and format by category.

- ◆ More alignment options are available. You can center text over selected cells. You can also place text vertically in cells and control the orientation.

- ◆ The Goto command keeps a history.

New Charting Features

Below are Excel's new graphing or charting capabilities:

- ◆ The new ChartWizard feature enables Excel to walk you through the creation of a chart quickly.

- ◆ New chart types are featured, such as surface, wireframe, and radar charts, and 3-D charting has been improved.

- ◆ You can rotate 3-D charts with the mouse for the view you wish.

New Macro Features

Excel's new macro features are as follows:

- ◆ A new toolbar simplifies initiating actions.

- ◆ You can create global macro sheets.

- ◆ A new add-in Macro Manager is included.

- ◆ New event macros are included.

- ◆ CALL and REGISTER functions are expanded.

- ◆ A Record button is added to the Assign to Object dialog box.

- ◆ There is now a Pause Macro support.

- ◆ AUTO_ACTIVATE and AUTO_DEACTIVATE functions are added so you can run macros when a specified document is activated.

- ◆ Links are now updated automatically when the name or location of a macro sheet is changed.

New Presentation Features

Excel has several new presentation features:

◆ Excel supports multimedia extensions for adding sound to your worksheets.

◆ Create screen "slide shows" with your Excel documents.

◆ A spelling checker is included for checking those slides before that important meeting.

New Utilities

Finally, Excel 4 includes the following new utilities:

◆ A new Scenario Manager permits you to save what-if sets and create summary tables.

◆ The Solver is easier to use and faster.

◆ The Analysis Toolpak simplifies statistical, engineering, and scientific work.

WHAT CAN YOU DO WITH EXCEL?

Anyone who works with numerical data processing can take advantage of Excel's extensive worksheet capabilities. For administration and record-keeping purposes, you can use Excel to check registers, expense reports, annual reports, and five-year forecasts. Excel's financial applications include amortization schedules, cash-flow projections, general ledgers, accounts receivable, accounts payable, comparative investment analyses, personal net-worth statements, balance sheets, and tax planning. Some examples of sales and marketing applications are sales comparisons, marketing analyses, and product-line summaries, as well as sales-forecast and linear-regression analyses. For operations, you can use Excel for inventory-management systems, material-requirement planning, inventory-rate-of-turnover analyses, and last-in-first-out analyses.

Here are some examples of how users might apply their Excel systems:

◆ Donald, a building contractor involved in competitive bidding, puts all his cost factors into an Excel worksheet. Then he alters each factor to see how it affects his final proposed bid. In this way he can study and analyze each factor that controls his cost to produce a final bid that is as low as possible.

◆ Susan is trying to conserve energy in her home. She creates a model of her house on an Excel worksheet. This model includes factors that control heating and cooling costs, such as attic insulation, window caulking, and a high-efficiency furnace. She also can calculate the cost of installing each of these energy-saving features. By doing this, she can analyze the results to see how long it would take her to recover the costs of each energy-saving idea.

◆ Carol invests in stocks, commodities, and bonds. She uses Excel worksheets to create investment models and to perform what-if analyses to find the best investment opportunities.

◆ George is in charge of labor negotiations for his company. Every few years the union contracts are renegotiated. George has to be able to study proposals from the unions quickly and determine how they would affect the company's earnings on both short-term and long-term bases. Using a worksheet, he can create a financial model of the company and quickly see how the union proposals will affect profits.

◆ John likes to do a little real-estate business from his home. He manages several rental properties and needs to be aware of costs, such as up-keep, taxes, and depreciation. He also has to know when to buy and sell the properties that he manages. The Excel worksheet gives him instant information on his profits as these factors change.

◆ Widget Manufacturing creates an entire model of their financial operation on Excel, using a collection of interlinked worksheets. The first sheet is the source and application of funds worksheet. The last worksheets are the balance sheet and income statements. These are all interlinked, so if an update is made in the source and applications of funds, all subsequent worksheets change automatically.

All of these applications can be grouped into one of two broad classifications: reporting on what has happened (analysis) or forecasting what could happen (what-if analysis). In the first case, the user takes data that describe something that has happened in the past (such as the sales of a product in three areas of the country during the last three months) and puts them into a form that can be analyzed (such as a pie chart). From this, the user can make a decision (such as the marketing strategy for next month). In the second case, the user changes one or more variables and sees how these changes will affect a specific goal (for example, modifying various cost factors to see how each change would affect the bid on a project).

Now that you have some idea of what Excel is and what it can do, it's time to get started using Excel!

FAST TRACK CHAPTER 2

- Type **WIN EXCEL** (or **WIN** *FILENAME*.XLS) in DOS.
- Double-click the Excel (or file) icon in Windows.

Hold down the Alt key and press Tab until the name of
the application you wish to use appears on-screen. Then
release the Alt key.

- Use the Contents or Search command of the Help menu.
- Select a command or object and press F1 for context-sensitive
  help.
- Press Shift-F1 and click on a part of the worksheet or screen for
  help.
- Use the Help tool of the toolbar and select an object, tool, or
  command.
- Use the Help button on dialog boxes.

- Select File ➤ Exit.
- Double-click on the Control box of Excel.
- Click on the Control box, then choose Close.
- Press Alt-F, then X.

CHAPTER 2

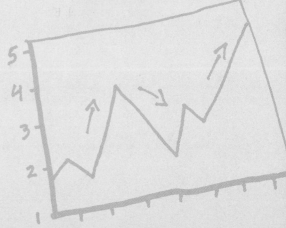

Getting Started

B eginning to use Excel is, without a doubt, an exciting adventure. Before starting, however, you should be sure that you have everything you need. You should also take certain initial precautions, as you would when beginning to use any new computer program.

This chapter provides step-by-step instructions on how to get started with Excel. It also includes a brief review of Microsoft Windows and how to get help if you need it.

WHAT DO YOU NEED?

As with any program, there is some specific hardware and software you need to run Excel. Excel 4 is available for DOS 3.1 or later and with the Windows 3.0 environment or later.

HARDWARE RESOURCES

The following is the minimum recommended hardware for using Excel 4.0 with Windows:

◆ An IBM AT, PS/2, or 286/386/486 computer that is DOS compatible. You also should have enough memory in your computer to run

Windows in either Standard or 386-Enhanced mode. This means at least 2MB of total memory (excluding any expanded memory). You can find out what mode Windows is running in and how much memory you have by selecting Help ➤ About Program Manager in Windows' Program Manager. Excel will not run in Windows 3.0's Real mode.

◆ A hard-disk drive with anywhere from 4.5MB (minimum installation) to 10MB (complete installation) of free space on it.

◆ A Windows-compatible printer.

◆ A VGA, EGA, Hercules, or other Windows-compatible monitor.

◆ A mouse.

Excel will run on slower PC compatibles, but for maximum efficiency you should run Excel in 386-Enhanced mode with a 386/486 processor and have four or more megabytes of extended memory, as well as a math coprocessor.

SOFTWARE RESOURCES

You need the Excel program disks, extra disks, and the documentation that came with Excel. You also will need a copy of DOS 3.1 and Windows 3.0. Later releases of either of these can also be used.

CREATING BACKUP COPIES

 Beginners should avoid the custom installation. Always install from a copy, as the installation will write to the disks.

Before installing Excel, you should create backup copies of the Excel disks. The Excel disks are not copy-protected, so you can copy them with any conventional copy program, such as the DOS COPY (or XCOPY) program. For example, you could place the first disk in Drive A and type

DISKCOPY A: A:

from the DOS prompt. The computer will prompt you when to change disks.

INSTALLING EXCEL

The installation program makes Excel easy to install:

1. Place the Excel Setup disk in drive A (or B).

2. Start Windows.

3. Select File ➤ Run.

4. In the dialog box type **A:SETUP** (or **B:SETUP**) and press Enter.

Follow the installation directions of the setup program. You will first need to enter your organization's name. Then you will be asked for the directory to which you wish to install Excel. A dialog box is then displayed from which you can choose your installation options.

STARTING EXCEL

Excel can be started from Windows or from the DOS prompt.

STARTING EXCEL FROM THE DOS PROMPT

Putting C:\EXCEL in your AUTOEXEC. BAT path statement allows you to load Excel from any directory.

To start Excel from the DOS prompt, first enter the directory you wish to use for your worksheets (the default is C:\EXCEL or wherever you've installed Excel). Then type

WIN EXCEL

and press Enter. This will start Excel and display an empty worksheet, as shown in Figure 2.1.

You can start Excel another way, if you know the file name of a worksheet you wish to edit. Again, first be sure you are in the directory containing the worksheet you wish to use (or the directory where you will create it). Then enter **WIN** and the worksheet name:

WIN *WORKSHEET.XLS*

Be sure to include the extension .XLS as a part of the file name. This will tell DOS to start Excel and load the worksheet.

STARTING EXCEL FROM WINDOWS

If Windows is already running, you can start Excel from it using any of the methods for starting Windows programs. The easiest method is to use the Program Manager and double-click on the Excel icon. This will start Excel with an empty worksheet.

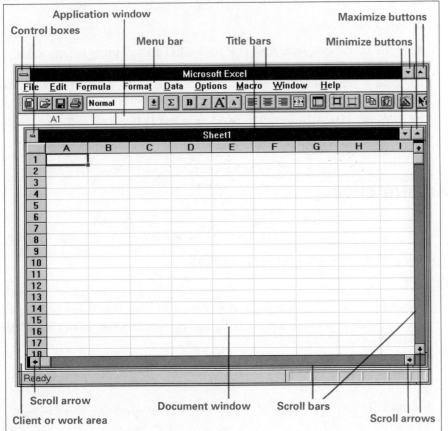

Application window
Control boxes
Menu bar
Title bars
Maximize buttons
Minimize buttons

Scroll arrow
Document window
Scroll bars
Client or work area
Scroll arrows

> **NOTE** *If you have trouble starting Excel with a worksheet name, there is probably no association for .XLS. Create an association in the File Manager.*

To start Excel with a specific worksheet, use the Windows File Manager and double-click on the worksheet name. A second method is to use the Run command on the Program Manager's File menu and enter the worksheet name, including its drive and path, in the Run dialog box (be sure to use the worksheet file-name extension .XLS). A third method is to put the data-file icon/program item in a Program Manager group and then double-click the data-file icon.

USING WINDOWS

Excel is much like any other Windows program. It has the same elements and user interface as any other Windows program.

THE MOUSE

If you move the mouse with your left hand, you can make the right button the mouse action button by double-clicking the Mouse icon in the Windows Control Panel and choosing Swap Left/Right buttons.

The cursor on the screen is controlled by the mouse. To move the pointer, simply move the mouse on any flat surface. If you run out of room, pick the mouse up and put it back down elsewhere on the surface. The pointer moves only when the mouse is moved across a surface. To click with the mouse, you usually press the left mouse button.

The primary mouse techniques are pointing, clicking, dragging, and double-clicking:

Pointing: Move the mouse until the cursor is at the desired cell or spot.

Clicking: Press and release the left mouse button.

Dragging: Position the pointer over an object and select it by holding the left mouse button down. Move the object (or highlighted area) to a new position and release the mouse button.

Double-clicking: Press the left mouse button twice in rapid succession.

You can also click on an object with the right mouse button to get an object-oriented short-cut menu.

THE WINDOW ELEMENTS

Let's look at the individual elements of the window on-screen. The Excel program has its own single *application window.* Within the work area of this window are any number of *document windows* for the application. In Figure 2.1 a single document window, called SHEET1, is displayed. Multiple applications can be opened at a time, each with its own application and document windows. These windows will overlay each other on the Desktop, but can be rearranged. Document windows must always remain inside the application window.

Although many application windows may be open at once, only a single application can be active (in use) at a time. Its title bar will have a different color or pattern than the other title bars on-screen. Several document windows also can be open at a time, but only one document window can be the *focus* of the keyboard, so that data typed at the keyboard will be placed in this window. The document window with the current focus is called the *active document window.*

Here is a summary of the basic application window elements:

Title bar shows the window title. Currently displays the name of the application program, **Microsoft Excel**.

Control box changes the size of the window, quits the program, and does other system-level operations. The box sits in the upper-left corner of the window and contains a horizontal bar.

Menu bar contains the names of the available command menus for the application program. The Excel menu bar options will vary depending on the mode in which Excel is running (e.g., the menu options for a worksheet are different from those for editing a chart).

Minimize button reduces a window to an icon at the bottom of the screen. It contains a downward-pointing arrowhead.

Maximize button zooms the window to full-screen size. It contains an upward-pointing arrowhead. When a window is maximized, the arrowhead changes to a double-headed arrow (the Restore button).

Client or work area displays the worksheets, charts, or macros in Excel.

Chapter 3 will describe document window features that are specific to Excel.

THE CONTROL BOX

The *Control box* is a small box containing a horizontal bar in the upper-left corner of the window. Notice that Figure 2.1 contains two Control boxes— one in the application window and another in the document window. Pressing Alt-Spacebar (application), Alt-Hyphen (document), or clicking the corresponding Control box will display the Control menu, which provides options for moving, sizing, minimizing, maximizing, restoring, and closing the application or document window. Notice that the two Control menus are slightly different. Close the menu by pressing Esc twice or clicking anywhere in the window outside the menu.

APPLICATION AND DOCUMENT WINDOWS

Let's explore how to activate, resize, move, enlarge, and close windows.

Making Windows Active

Although Windows permits you to load several programs into memory at once, only one of these can be *active* or available to the keyboard at a time. To make another application or document window active with the mouse, just click anywhere in it. You also can use the keyboard to change the active window. This is best used if the window you want to make active is not visible. Alt-Tab switches between application windows and Ctrl-F6 switches between document windows.

Alt-Tab is really a preview mode: it activates all the programs (including the inactive programs represented as icons) in the order in which they were loaded. Hold down the Alt key and press Tab until the desired program name appears. Release the Alt key. Alt-Shift-Tab rotates through the available windows in the order opposite to Alt-Tab. This works for all programs, whether they are Windows applications or not.

Another method is to use Ctrl-Esc to see the Task List and select the desired program to make active.

Resizing and Moving Windows

By resizing and moving windows you can place multiple windows side by side for comparing or doing related functions. You can resize and move windows with either the mouse or the keyboard.

 *You cannot resize or move a window if it is maximized.*

To resize windows using the mouse, move the mouse pointer to a border of the window until the pointer changes to a double-arrow. Click the (left) button. Drag the border to a new position, making the window either larger or smaller. As you drag the border, both the old and new window sizes are shown. When you release the mouse button, the window appears in its new size. If you wish to change two borders at once, select the lower-right corner of the window. The cursor will now become a two-headed arrow pointing diagonally. Drag the corner to create the new window size.

To move a window with the mouse, simply drag the title bar to the new location.

To change the size of a non-maximized application window from the keyboard, first press Alt-Spacebar to display the Control menu. Type **S** to select Size from the Control menu. (The mouse pointer will now look like a four-headed arrow in the window.) Select a new border location by hitting the → or ← keys. You also can press both keys to select the lower-right corner and change both borders simultaneously. The selected borders are now highlighted. Use the direction keys to move the borders to their desired location. Press Enter to lock the location or press Esc to abort the resizing. (Esc will not work after you've pressed Enter.)

To move a non-maximized application window from the keyboard, first make it active, then press Alt-Spacebar. Type **M** to select Move from the menu. Then use the direction keys to move the window to the new location. As you move a window, Windows shows you both the old and new locations. Press Enter. Press Esc before pressing Enter if you need to abort a move operation.

Maximizing Windows

Maximize Excel to get the maximum working area. Terminating Excel when it's maximized will ensure that Excel comes up maximized on starting.

Maximizing a window enlarges the window so that it occupies the entire screen. This reduces clutter by temporarily eliminating other windows and icons from the screen. It also gives you a larger display for viewing more of a worksheet.

To maximize a window with the mouse, click on the Maximize button (the upward-pointing arrowhead) in the upper-right corner of the window or double-click the title bar. The window will immediately fill the screen. To maximize a window with the keyboard, first make it active. Then press Alt-Spacebar if it is an application window or Alt-Hyphen if it is a document window, and type **X** for Maximize.

To restore a maximized window to its former size, make the window active and click the Restore button (double-arrow) in the upper-right corner or (for the application window only) double-click the title bar once again. Restore a window from the keyboard by making the window active and pressing Alt-Spacebar. Type **R** for Restore. To restore a document window, you can press Ctrl-F5.

Minimizing Windows

Minimizing an application window clears the program from the screen, but keeps it in memory only a few clicks or keystrokes away. To minimize an application, make the application active and select Minimize from the Control menu or click the Minimize button in the upper-right corner. This will close the application's window and place an icon, representing the window, at the bottom of the screen. Minimizing can help unclutter your screen. You can also minimize a document window.

Holding down the Alt key and pressing Tab brings you to your iconized application as well.

To restore the application window, double-click the icon. Or, from the keyboard, select the icon, press Alt-Spacebar, and choose Restore (or just press Ctrl-F10). The program will come back, looking just as it did before it was minimized. To restore a minimized document icon, double-click the icon or select the icon and press Ctrl-F10. Pressing Ctrl-F6 will cycle through the minimized icons.

Closing a Window

To close a window (application or document) with the mouse, double-click its Control box. This will remove the window from the Desktop or application workspace. To close an application window with the keyboard, make the window active and press Alt-F4-Spacebar. To close an active document window, press Ctrl-F4. (See "Keyboard Shortcuts" later for a faster way.)

If you wish to close an application window or document window that has had changes made to it, Windows will ask if you wish these saved.

MULTITASKING WITH WINDOWS

Windows permits you to keep several programs in memory at one time. They can be Windows application programs or non-Windows applications. This is important, as you may wish to run Excel while you run other programs.

To start another program, switch to the Program Manager and start the program from its program group, or use the Run command from the File menu and enter the program name with its path. The new program will start and its application window will overlay Excel's. As mentioned earlier, you can use Alt-Tab to switch among the programs currently in memory, or Ctrl-Esc to bring up the Task Manager.

SCROLL BARS

Excel worksheet and macro windows have scroll bars at the right or bottom that can be used to scroll the window over a larger area (see Figure 2.1). The scroll bar has arrows at the ends and a *scroll box* inside it, also called an *elevator*.

To scroll with the mouse, use the following techniques:

◆   Drag the scroll box in the bar to scroll the window to a desired place in the worksheet.

◆   Click either arrow at the top or bottom of the right scroll bar to scroll the window a row at a time.

◆   Click either arrow at the left or right of the bottom scroll bar to scroll the window a column at a time.

◆   Click anywhere between the arrows to scroll through a windowful of rows or columns at a time.

◆   Click on an arrow and hold the mouse button down to scroll continuously, until the rows or columns you wish to see are visible.

You also can scroll with the keyboard. Scroll in the desired direction by pressing any of the direction keys: ↑, ↓, ←, or →. Press PgUp and PgDn to move up and down a windowful of rows, respectively. From wherever you are in the workspace, press Ctrl-Home to move to column A or Home to go to the first cell in the workspace, A1. Press End and an arrow key to move to the last column that contains data in that direction (or Ctrl-End to go to the last column that contains data).

MENUS

Excel's commands are stored in the menus listed across the top of the screen. There are two ways to select a command with the mouse:

◆ Click on the menu name and drag the mouse down while *keeping the mouse button depressed*. When you highlight the command of interest, just release the button to select it.

◆ Click once on the menu name. The menu will remain open while you move the pointer to the command of interest. Click the mouse button again to select it.

Excel, like most Windows applications, provides keyboard access to commands as well by assigning each menu name and command a keyboard character, usually a letter in the name. These underlined letters are sometimes called *mnemonics*. To activate a command from the keyboard, press Alt and type the mnemonic for the desired menu name. Once the menu is open, type the mnemonic for the command. For example, to print a file, press Alt-F, P. (To cancel a command keystroke sequence while the menu is open, press Esc twice.)

If there is no character underlined in a menu option, you can still use the keyboard to access a command. Press Alt to highlight the first menu name on the left. Press → or ← until you've highlighted the menu you want to open. Press Enter or ↓ to open it. Press ↓ or ↑ to highlight the menu option and press Enter.

Menu commands be any one of three types: *direct command, state setter*, or *extended*. A direct command initiates an action immediately, such as the Save command of the File menu. State setters are toggles, and the command name in the menu is preceded by a check mark (✓) if the toggle is on. State setters permit the user to select from a list. An example would be selecting the chart type on Excel's Gallery menu when creating a chart. Finally, extended commands are always followed by an ellipsis (…): they bring up a dialog box. An example would be the Page Setup command under the File menu.

Menu items may be enabled or disabled. Items that are enabled can be selected and are shown in black. Disabled menu items can't be selected in the program's current state and are shown in gray ("grayed out" or "dimmed") lettering.

KEYBOARD SHORTCUTS

Menu commands may have *shortcuts* or *shortcut keys,* sometimes called *accelerator keys.* Shortcut keys permit you to initiate the command quickly from the keyboard without using the mouse. If a shortcut key exists for a command, it is generally faster to use it than handle the mouse or normal keyboard commands.

There are also keyboard shortcuts in the Control menus. The application window's Control menu contains only two: Alt-F4 closes the application and Ctrl-Esc starts Task Manager. All the document window shortcuts start with the Ctrl key. Pressing Ctrl-F4, for example, closes the current document window. Table 2.1 shows the full set of document window shortcuts.

OPERATION	SHORTCUT
Close document window	Ctrl-F4
Maximize document window	Ctrl-F10
Minimize document window	Ctrl-F9
Move document window	Ctrl-F7
Resize document window	Ctrl-F8
Restore maximized window	Ctrl-F5
Switch to next document window	Ctrl-F6

TABLE 2.1:

Document Window Shortcuts

DIALOG BOXES

Excel uses *dialog boxes* to request information from you and to output information that is not a part of the normal data display. If a menu item has an ellipsis (...) after a command, that means it will display a dialog box when you select it.

Dialog boxes contain one or more special features, or *controls.* Dialog boxes can support any of five types of controls. Figure 2.2 shows an example of some of them.

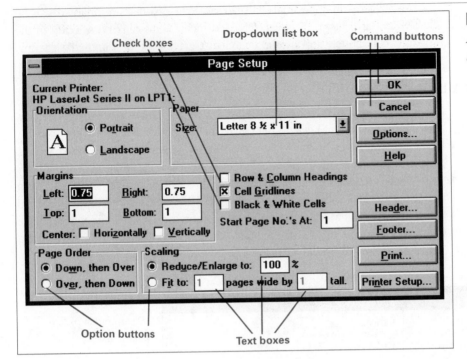

Command button: A command button looks like a labeled button. Examples include the OK and Cancel buttons. If the label ends with an ellipsis, clicking the button will activate another dialog box. If the button contains an underlined letter, it can be activated from the keyboard using the combination Alt-*Letter*.

Option button: A round button (or "radio button") that permits you to select only one item from a group. The button is displayed as a small circle. You can select the desired button with a mouse or use the direction keys and the spacebar.

Check box: A toggle that turns a feature or state either on or off. The toggle is displayed as a small square with an × in it. It can be toggled by clicking the mouse or pressing the spacebar.

List box: A box showing multiple choices, such as the file list with the Open command. With a list box, use the mouse or direction keys to highlight your selection. You also can press any letter to move the highlight to the first selection starting with that letter. For long lists, the control has a vertical scroll bar at the right that simplifies movement to the item. If the list allows multiple selections, you can use the spacebar to select other items after the first. In small dialog boxes with long lists, a *drop-down list box* is used to conserve space. The list is opened from a single-line list box with an arrow in a square box at the right (Figure 2.2). Click the arrow to open the list box. Then select an option with the mouse. From the keyboard, press Alt-↓ to open the box. Then select the option with the direction keys and press Alt-↓ again.

Text box: A box for entering text data. When it is selected, an insertion point appears in the box. You can enter or edit the text as you please.

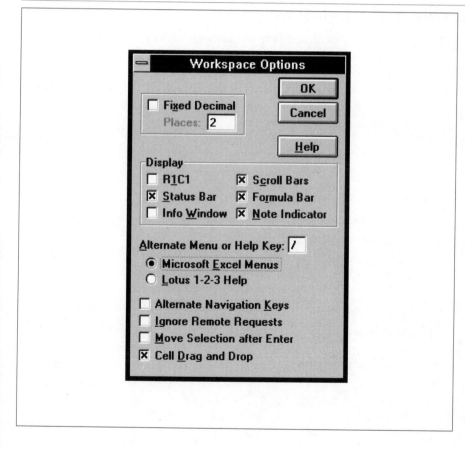

FIGURE 2.3:

The Workspace dialog box. Choose options to determine how the workspace should look on-screen.

You can use either the mouse or keyboard to move about in a dialog box and choose controls. The dialog box displays defaults settings. To select a control with a mouse, click it. To select a control with the keyboard, use Tab or Shift-Tab to move to the desired control. After the control is selected, use the list above as a guide for setting it. Close the box by clicking on OK (pressing Enter) or Cancel (pressing Esc).

Most Excel dialog boxes can be moved, but not resized. For example, look at the Define Name dialog box under the Formula menu. This box has a title bar and can be moved like any other window by dragging its title bar around. It also has a Control menu that permits some normal control options such as closing and moving. The controls work the same as with any other dialog box.

SETTING THE DEFAULTS

The first time you use Excel you will want to set some default values if they are not already set:

1. Select Options from the menu bar and choose Workspace. When the Workspace dialog box shown in Figure 2.3 is displayed, be sure the following options are selected:

   Status Bar

   Scroll Bars

   Formula Bar

   Note Indicator

   Microsoft Excel Menus

   Alternate Navigation Keys

   Cell Drag and Drop

   If any are not marked, click them to mark them. Then click OK.

2. If the standard toolbar is not displayed (see Figure 3.1), choose Toolbars from the Options menu. Select Standard and choose Show.

3. Set the printer type. Choose Page Setup from the File menu. In the Page Setup dialog box (Figure 2.4), choose Printer Setup. Select the printer type you are using in the list box shown below. Then select OK to return to the Page Setup dialog box and choose OK.

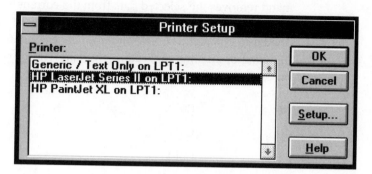

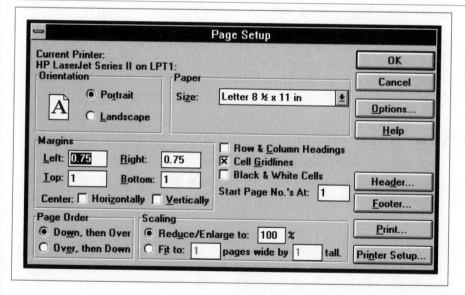

FIGURE 2.4:

The Page Setup dialog box. Choose options to determine how the worksheet will look when you print it.

USING THE CLIPBOARD

Microsoft Windows contains a Clipboard. You can use it as a common area of memory for all programs. The Clipboard permits you to move and copy data within Excel, between Excel and other programs, or even to or from some non-Windows applications.

The Clipboard is accessed through the Edit menu of Excel or other Windows applications. For non-Windows applications, use the Control menu and be sure the application is windowed. The Edit menu on most Windows applications usually shows the Copy, Cut, and Paste commands. The Cut command removes the selected data from the current location and places it in the Clipboard. The Copy command creates a copy of the data in the Clipboard. The Paste command copies data from the Clipboard to a specified location in the same or another application program. These commands have the following keyboard shortcuts:

Cut	Ctrl-X
Copy	Ctrl-C
Paste	Ctrl-V

The Clipboard can only store a single item at a time. Putting something in the Clipboard will delete whatever was already there. You can do multiple pastes from the Clipboard, however, as pasting does not clear the Clipboard. Once you close Windows, the contents of the Clipboard are lost.

You can look at the contents of the Clipboard at any time using the Clipboard Viewer. To start the viewer, choose Run from Excel's Control menu. Choose Clipboard and click on OK. Minimize or close the viewer after viewing its contents.

GETTING HELP

Excel provides five methods of getting help: the Help menu, the F1 key, the mouse, the help buttons of the various dialog boxes, and the question-mark tool on the toolbar.

USING THE HELP MENU

Excel, as with many Windows applications, has a help system only a few keystrokes away. To see how it works, click Help on the menu bar or press Alt-H. This will display the Help menu.

The Help menu has six options on it:

Contents displays a list or index of topics from which you can choose to get information.

Search gets information about a topic of interest.

Product Support helps you get information from Microsoft.

Introducing Microsoft Excel helps you see the new features of Excel and is a quick start for the more experienced user.

Learning Microsoft Excel is a basic tutorial for new users of Excel.

Lotus 1-2-3 helps you find the Excel equivalents of Lotus 1-2-3 commands. Use this if you have been using Lotus 1-2-3 and need help learning Excel.

Multiplan Help helps you find the Excel equivalents of Multiplan commands. Use this if you have been using Multiplan and need help learning Excel.

About gives you an information screen containing the current memory allocation. Use this when working on large worksheets to see the status of your memory resources.

The first three options of the Help menu start a separate Windows application program called WinHelp. This program displays a window with a menu bar and buttons (Figure 2.5). This application, like most Windows applications, has a menu bar. You can use the Print option from its File menu to print the entire help file for the item in Excel you sought help on. To close the Help window, double-click its Control box or press Alt-F4 with the Help window active.

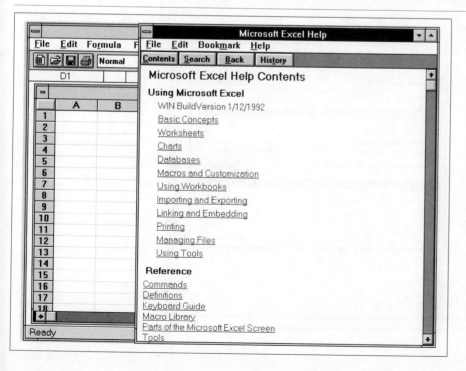

FIGURE 2.5:

The help index

Using the Help Index

If Excel is in Ready mode (**Ready** displayed in the lower left), you can use F1 or the Contents option under the Help menu to display the help index in a window. Once this window is displayed you can choose your topic by clicking the topic or by using the Tab, ↑, and ↓ keys to highlight the topic of interest and pressing Enter. The window has buttons for returning to the index, moving back, and searching.

The program is a type of hypertext tool. Click on a highlighted word and the help program will move to the selection for that word.

If you need help frequently for an application, keep the help window open and switch to it as necessary. An alternative is to minimize it: this will keep the window out of the way while keeping it in memory.

Searching for a Topic

Another way to get help is to use the Search command in the Help menu to find the topic of interest. Choosing this command opens a dialog box with a list of topics. Select a topic or enter your own in the text box and choose Show Topics. The topic will be transferred to the second list box (Figure 2.6). Choose Goto to jump to the topic of interest. The WinHelp program will open and display the help information. You can get to the same dialog box by clicking on the Search button on the help toolbar.

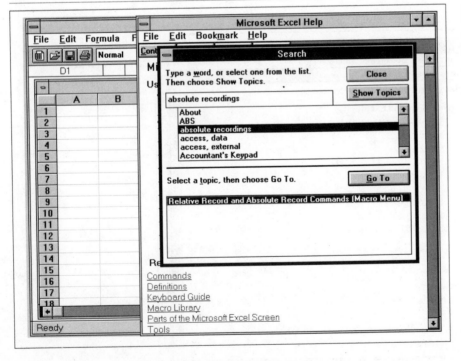

PRESSING F1 FOR HELP

You also can use the WinHelp system for finding context-sensitive help by pressing F1. For example, highlight Copy under the Edit menu and press F1. The help window will open to show a help screen on the Copy command.

USING THE MOUSE TO GET HELP

If you press Shift-F1, the mouse pointer becomes a question mark. Move the question mark to an element of the screen that you need help on (such as the toolbar icons), click, and the help system will open with a window that can help you.

GETTING HELP USING THE TOOLBAR

At the far right of the toolbar is a button with a question mark. Clicking this tool turns the mouse pointer into a question mark, as with Shift-F1. Now move the tool over a tool on the toolbar, a command, or an object of interest (as a cell) and click. Again, WinHelp opens with the help topic.

GETTING HELP FROM DIALOG BOXES

You can also get help directly from dialog boxes. Many of them contain a Help button (see Figure 2.2). To get help, click the button and the WinHelp program will open with help on the selected topic.

EXITING EXCEL

To quit Excel at any time, you can use one of these methods:

◆ Double-click the Control box of Excel (not the document).

◆ Click the Control box open, then choose Close.

◆ Click the File menu open, then choose Exit.

◆ Press Alt-F (to get to the File menu) and then type **X** (for Exit).

FAST TRACK CHAPTER 3

1. Enter the labels.
2. Enter the data.
3. Enter any formulas.
4. Format the worksheet.

Select File ➤ Save As command (F12), File ➤ Save As (Shift-F12), or the File Save tool on the toolbar.

Use the File ➤ Print command, Ctrl-Shift-F12, or the Print tool on the toolbar.

Select the data to chart, the ChartWizard tool, and then the worksheet area where the chart is to be placed.

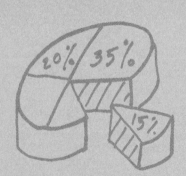

CHAPTER

A Quick Tour of Excel

Although Excel can solve very complicated problems, it is actually quite easy to use. You'll discover this for yourself right now if you follow along with the exercises in this chapter.

Here you will use Excel to do the following:

◆ Create a worksheet, complete with formulas

◆ Format the worksheet

◆ Save the worksheet

◆ Print the worksheet

◆ Create a chart using the worksheet

These exercises will give you a feel for Excel and let you learn what it can do. Don't worry too much about how or why you do things—you'll learn the details in later chapters.

WORKSHEET WINDOW FEATURES

Start the Excel program (see Chapter 2). It should display an empty worksheet window, as shown in Figure 3.1.

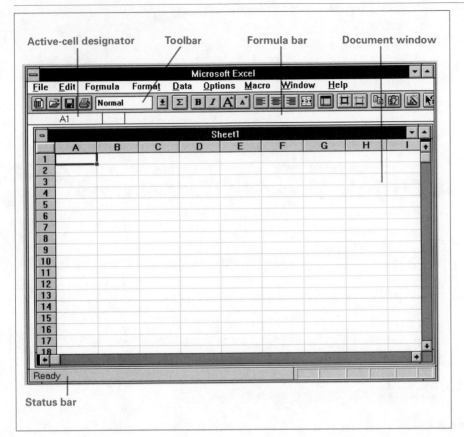

FIGURE 3.1:

*The main elements of
the Excel worksheet
window*

Notice the elements of the Excel application window:

◆ The common application window elements: title, Control box, menu
bar, Minimize button, and Maximize button.

◆ The *status bar* at the bottom of the screen for displaying messages. At
the present time it shows that Excel is in Ready mode. The right side
of the status bar shows the status of various keyboard toggles, such
as Cap Lock, Num Lock, Scroll Lock, End key, and extended selection (e.g., Shift-F8).

◆ The *toolbar* below the menu bar for doing some basic operations with
the mouse.

◆ The *active-cell designator* below the toolbar and to the left. This
indicates the location of the currently active cell. When you drag

the scroll box in either scroll bar, however, it shows the current row or column that will appear at the top or left of the screen, respectively, when you release the mouse.

◆ The *formula bar* to the right that displays the contents of the active cell. It is empty now.

◆ A single *document window,* a worksheet called SHEET1.

The document window also has certain distinct features (Figure 3.2):

◆ A title: **Sheet1**. The title is the name of the file to which the worksheet will be saved.

◆ A partial view of the underlying worksheet. The window can be scrolled over the worksheet.

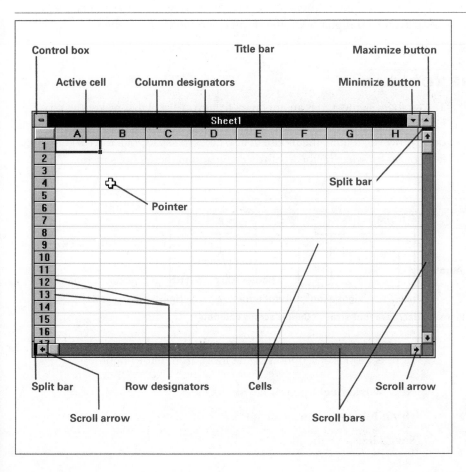

FIGURE 3.2:

An Excel document window for a worksheet

♦ The common document window elements: title bar, Control box, Maximize button, Minimize button, and scroll bars.

♦ Columns indicated by letters, rows by numbers. Each cell is shown as a box. Cells are designated by the column letter and row number. For example, cell B4 refers to the intersection of the second column and the fourth row.

♦ The first cell, A1, highlighted with bold lines. This is the *active cell*. The cell name is also in the active-cell designator box.

♦ The scroll bars. To the upper right and lower left of the scroll bars are some split bars for creating panes (see Chapter 7).

♦ The mouse pointer is in the shape of a cross when it is on the worksheet cell area. Look for it on your screen.

Move the mouse about and you will see the mouse cursor move around the worksheet on-screen. The highlighted cell does not change and neither does the active-cell designator on the display line under the menu bar.

THE TOOLBAR

The toolbar (Figure 3.3) is an important feature of Excel that makes the program easy to use. It permits you to do some operations with the click of a mouse. It does, however, require the mouse. It also takes the space of a row. You can turn it off or on by selecting the Toolbars command in the Options menu.

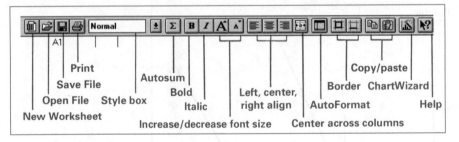

FIGURE 3.3:
The toolbar contains many useful features that you can access quickly with a mouse

Here is a brief description of the tools, from left to right:

New Worksheet opens a new worksheet.

Open File opens an existing file.

Save File saves the file.

Print prints the worksheet.

Style box applies a style sheet to a selected range.

Autosum button enters a sum formula in the active cell of a contiguous range of cells.

Bold and italics buttons format the selected cells to bold or italic.

Font size increases or decreases the font size.

Alignment buttons align selected cells to left, center, right, or over selected columns.

AutoFormat automatically formats the selected range.

Border control borders the selected cells with an outline or bottom border.

Clipboard tools (copy and paste): the first copies the selection to the Clipboard, while the second pastes the format from the Clipboard to the selected cells.

ChartWizard creates a chart on the worksheet from a selected range.

Help gets help on a tool, object, or command.

ENTERING ITEMS TO A SAMPLE WORKSHEET

The basic procedure for entering items to the worksheet is as follows:

1. Move and click the mouse pointer or press the arrow keys to select the cell or range of cells in which you wish to enter data. The active cell for the keyboard entry is highlighted.

2. Enter the data, text, or formula.

3. Press Enter or click the ✓ in the formula bar. This locks the data or formula into that cell.

Your general worksheet strategy usually is to create the labels first, then enter the numbers, followed by any formulas. Finally, format the worksheet.

ENTERING TITLES

Let's use the procedure outlined above to enter data to the worksheet. Move the cursor to cell C1 and click on it. Cell C1 is now highlighted, and the active-cell designator on the display line reads **C1**. Use the keyboard to type the title for your worksheet as **INCOME ANALYSIS**.

Notice that, as you enter your data, two new boxes appear to the left of the formula bar: the Enter box with a check mark (✓) and a Cancel box with an ×, as shown in Figure 3.4. The entire title appears in the formula bar, whereas only a portion of it appears in cell C1. After you type in the title, press the Enter key or click the Enter box to complete the entry. You will now see the entire title on the worksheet. The entire title is displayed only if the cell to the right (D1) is empty, as here. Excel always remembers the entire title, however, whether or not D1 is empty.

Enter the titles for the rows next:

1. Click on cell A5 and drag to cell A12 (Figure 3.5).

2. Type **Sales** and press Enter.

3. Type **Cost of Goods Sold** and press Enter twice (to skip one row).

4. Type **Gross Margin** and press Enter twice.

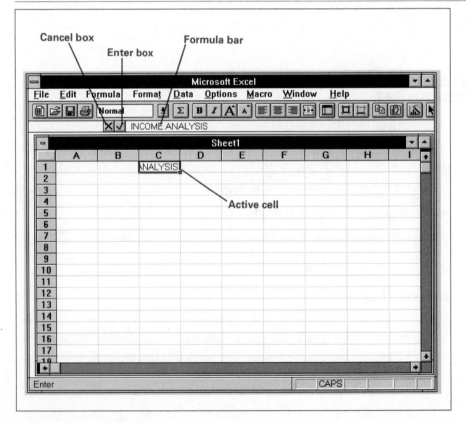

FIGURE 3.4:

Entering the title into cell C1. Because the title is longer than column C is wide, only part of it appears in the cell. The entire text appears above in the formula bar, however

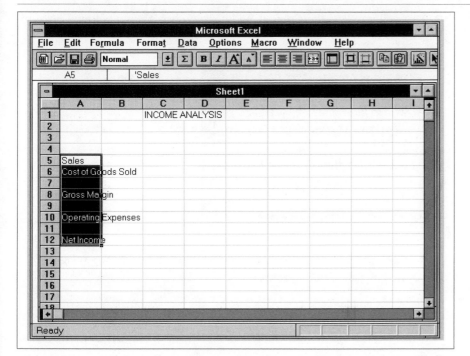

FIGURE 3.5:

*Entering the row
headings. Highlighting
the cell range first
ensures that the titles
entered stay in that
range*

5. Type **Operating Expenses** and press Enter twice.

6. Type **Net Income** and press Enter. (The active cell is A5 again.)

If you make a mistake in typing any title before you press Enter, you can use
the Backspace key to erase the error. If you notice a mistake after you've
pressed Enter, go ahead and finish entering the row titles, then click on the
cell to be corrected and reenter the title—or keep pressing Enter to cycle
through the cell range.

After you have entered the row headings, you will notice that column A
is not wide enough for all of the row titles. To widen the column:

1. Click once on the column header for A with the right mouse button.

2. Choose Column Width from the pop-up menu. (You could also use the
left mouse button and choose Column Width from the Format menu.)

3. You will now see the Column Width dialog box shown below. Click on the Best Fit button.

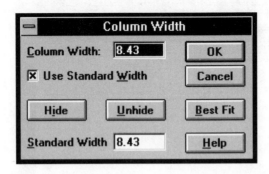

You will see column A widen to accommodate your titles, as shown in Figure 3.6. Now enter the column titles:

1. Click on cell B4 and drag to cell D4.

2. Type **1990** and press Enter.

3. Type **1991** and press Enter.

4. Type **1992** and press Enter.

ENTERING DATA

Now click on cell B5 and enter the numbers shown in Figure 3.7 into rows 5, 6, and 10. (Do not enter data into rows 8 or 12.) You can include commas in the numbers if you wish, but formatting later will add them automatically.

ENTERING FORMULAS

We now need formulas to subtract the correct numbers automatically. Enter the first formula by clicking on cell B8 and typing **=B5–B6**. Remember to type the equal sign first. This tells Excel that you're entering a formula—"subtract the amount in B6 from the amount in B5"—rather than text. After you type in the formula, press Enter. The gross margin, **240000**, will appear in cell B8. If you make a mistake, select cell B8 and enter the formula again.

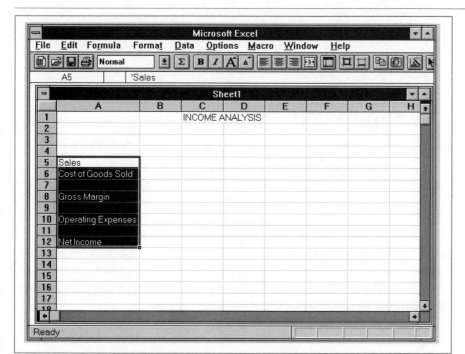

Here the column width has been adjusted to accommodate the length of the row titles

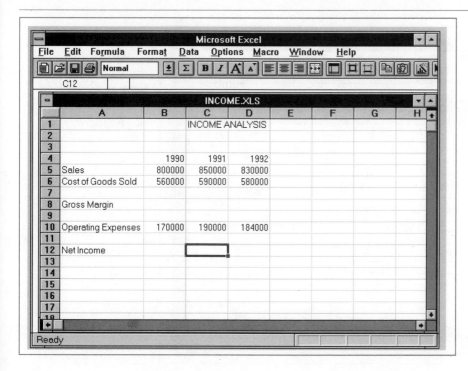

Here's how your worksheet should look after you've entered the data

Try a slightly different approach for entering a formula into cell B12, one that subtracts the amount in cell B10 from the amount in cell B8:

1. Click on cell B12 and enter an equal sign (=).

2. Click on cell B8 and enter a minus sign (–).

3. Click on cell B10 and press Enter.

The net income, **70000**, will appear in cell B12.

To enter the formulas in the rest of the cells in rows 8 and 12, you can use a faster method. Click on cell B8 and move the cursor over the lower-right corner of the cell. The cursor changes from a cross to a crosshair. Drag to cell D8. The correct totals will appear in row 8.

Click the lower-right corner of B12 and drag to D12 to copy the formulas in this row. In both cases, as the formula is copied from cell to cell, the cells referenced above it are automatically changed to reflect its new place in each column. Select cell C8 and examine the formula in the formula bar. Compare this with the formula shown when you select cell B8.

After you've entered all the formulas, your worksheet should look like Figure 3.8.

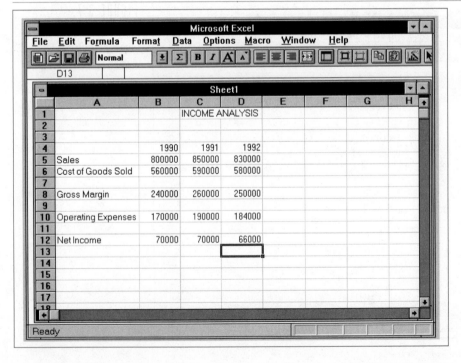

FIGURE 3.8:

This is how your worksheet should look after all the formulas are entered into their respective cells

FORMATTING THE WORKSHEET

Now you can format the worksheet. Excel remembers three things for each cell in the worksheet: the value (constant or formula), information on how the value is to be displayed, and any attached notes. Data are now displayed with text left-justified and numbers right-justified. This is the default "picture" and alignment. Place the cursor on cell B5 and drag diagonally to cell D12. Open the Format menu and choose Number. The Format Number dialog box shown below will appear. Choose the currency category, then the first currency format code (the one highlighted in the figure), and select OK. The screen now shows all numeric values in the selected range with a dollar sign and a comma every third digit.

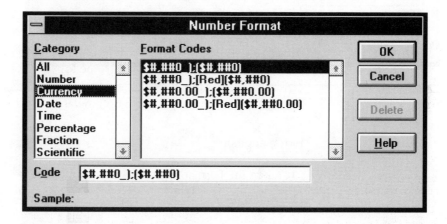

You can do a few more things to make the worksheet more readable. First, put the title in bold print:

1. Select cell C1.

2. Open the Format menu and choose Font.

3. The Font dialog box shown in Figure 3.9 appears. If you have Windows 3.1, choose the Arial TrueType font, Bold, and a point size of 12. Choose OK. (If using Windows 3.0, choose Helvetica, Bold, and 12.)

Next, center the column titles. Here's one way:

1. Select cell B4 and drag to cell D4.

2. Click the alignment tool for centering in the toolbar.

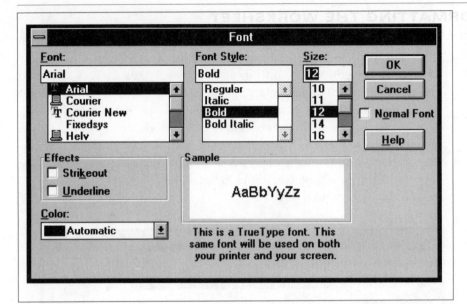

Formatting the title. In this dialog box you can choose the font, font style, point size, and color of entries in any cells you select

Here's another:

1. Open the Format menu and choose Alignment.

2. The Alignment dialog box appears. Choose Center, then click OK.

Finally, add some lines to separate the totals from the other numbers:

1. Select cell B7 and type one hyphen. Press Enter.

2. Open the Format menu and choose Alignment.

3. When the dialog box is displayed, choose Fill, then click OK.

4. Click on B7, select the lower-right corner of the cell, and drag to cell D7 to copy the filled hyphens to the other cells in the range.

5. Select B7 (the first cell with the filled hyphens).

6. Hold down the Ctrl key and drag the cell to B11 to copy the contents.

7. Drag the lower-right corner of B11 to D11 to fill the cells to the right with hyphens.

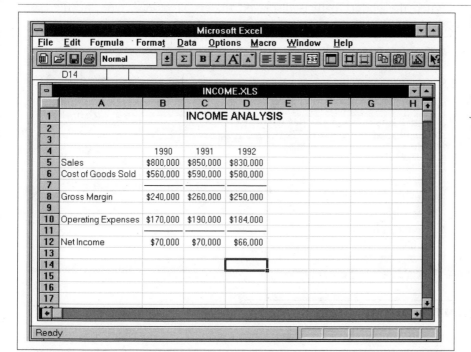

FIGURE 3.10:

*The final worksheet,
with columns of
numbers correctly
subtracted, titles
formatted, and lines
inserted*

Your final worksheet should look like the one shown in Figure 3.10. You can now experiment by changing the values in rows 5, 6, and 10. You'll see that the numbers in rows 8 and 12 automatically change to reflect the new values.

SAVING THE WORKSHEET

Before quitting Excel, you should save the worksheet. You must save the worksheet under a new name.

First, always check the worksheet over before saving. Be sure that the data in rows 5, 6, and 10 are correct. Then either click on the Save File tool on the toolbar, press F12, or open the File menu and choose Save As. The current path is displayed to the right of the File Name text box in the Save As dialog box, shown (**f:\ex4xls** here). Use the list box to change the path as necessary, selecting a new disk drive or directory. (Click a directory to open it.)

When the correct path is displayed under Directories, type the file name shown in the File Name text box and click on OK.

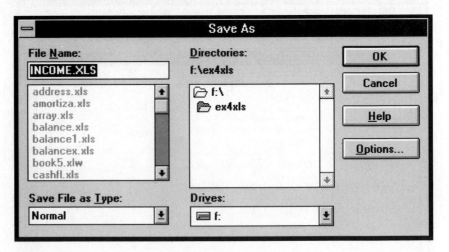

PRINTING THE WORKSHEET

Always save the worksheet before printing to prevent the loss of the spreadsheet, should there be an inadvertent lockup of the computer during printing. You should, however, do a page setup before saving, so that all relevant parameters are saved with the worksheet.

Before printing the worksheet, you should turn off the gridlines and row and column designators. This will make the output look nicer. To do this, open the File menu and choose Page Setup. The dialog box shown in Figure 3.11 appears. If either the Row & Column Headings or the Cell Gridlines option is marked, click on it to turn it off, then choose OK. Row and column designators and gridlines will still be displayed on the screen, but they will not print. Verify the remaining settings.

Now print the worksheet. Press Ctrl-Shift-F12 or open the File menu and choose Print. Be sure that the printer is on and ready. When the Print dialog box is displayed, choose OK. You can also print by clicking on the Print button in the toolbar or the Print button in the Page Setup dialog box. The final output is shown in Figure 3.12.

CREATING A GRAPH

Suppose you want to create a graph (or chart) from the sales figures on your Income worksheet. You will find that this takes only a few seconds with the new ChartWizard tool.

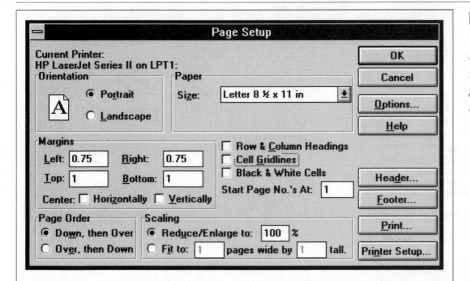

FIGURE 3.11:

You need to get to the Page Setup dialog box in order to turn off the gridlines and designators

Follow these steps:

1. Highlight cells A4 to D5 to indicate the data and headings to use for the graph, as shown in Figure 3.13.

2. Click the ChartWizard tool (second from the right).

3. The pointer changes to a cross hair. Drag it to define the location of the chart from A14 to E28.

4. The next dialog box verifies the cells to chart. Click Next.

5. Click the 3-D Column icon in the next dialog box, then Next (Figure 3.14).

6. Leave the default format selected in the next dialog box and click Next.

7. The next dialog box shows a sample of the final chart, as well as details how the data selected in the worksheet make up the chart. (Figure 3.15). Click Next.

8. In this dialog box of Figure 3.16, select for no legend. Enter the title as **Sales Analysis**, the category axis title as **Year**, and the Value axis title as **Sales**. Press Enter or click OK and the graph will be displayed on the worksheet (Figure 3.17).

FIGURE 3.12:
*The final printout. This
replicates the worksheet
on-screen*

INCOME ANALYSIS

	1990	1991	1992
Sales	$800,000	$850,000	$830,000
Cost of Goods Sold	$560,000	$590,000	$580,000
Gross Margin	$240,000	$260,000	$250,000
Operating Expenses	$170,000	$190,000	$184,000
Net Income	$70,000	$70,000	$66,000

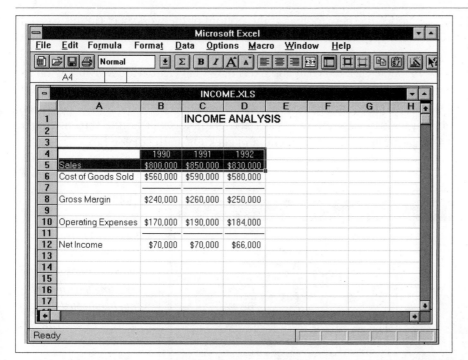

Selecting the data and headings in this way tells ChartWizard which data to chart

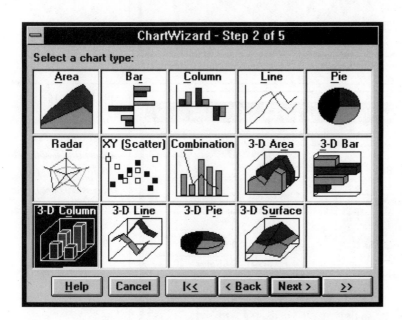

FIGURE 3.14:

Here you have 14 types of chart types to choose from. In this case, you want to select the 3-D Column type

Notice the new toolbar at the bottom of the worksheet (in this case). It is active whenever the chart is selected. Click outside the chart and it goes away; click the chart and it returns.

Double-click the chart and Excel draws the chart in a new window on the screen (Figure 3.18). The window with the chart now overlays the worksheet with *its* chart. Notice that there's now a different menu bar at the top of the screen. If you wish to view the worksheet and graph together on the screen, choose Arrange from the Window menu and click OK in the dialog box.

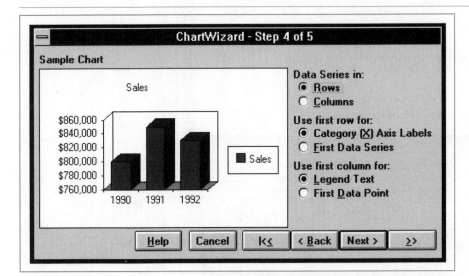

FIGURE 3.15:

The sample chart is displayed. On the right you can see how ChartWizard is interpreting the range of data highlighted in Figure 3.13 to create the final chart here

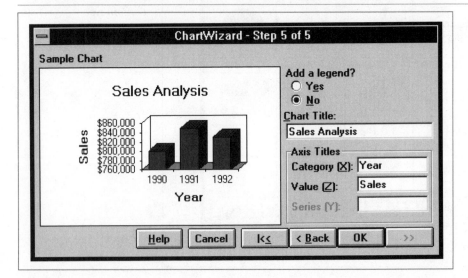

FIGURE 3.16:

In this dialog box you enter chart titles, determine whether to show a legend (not necessary here), and enter axis titles

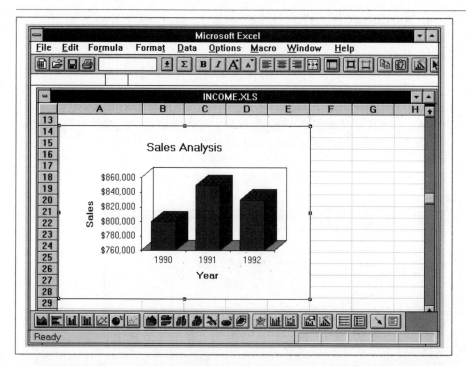

FIGURE 3.17:
The final chart, now part of the worksheet. Notice the new toolbar that appears on the bottom whenever the chart is selected

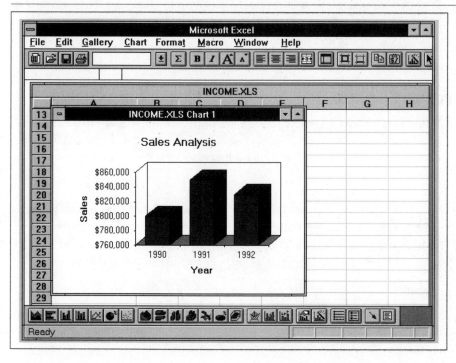

FIGURE 3.18:
The chart in a window. There's also a new menu bar at the top of the screen for modifying the chart

You can print this chart by following the steps that you used to print the worksheet: With the chart window active, open the File menu and choose Print, click the Print button on the toolbar, or press Ctrl-Shift-F12. Since the chart is a graphic, it will take longer to print than the plain worksheet did.

When you are finished with the chart, double-click the Control menu in the upper-left corner of the chart window or press Ctrl-F4. The window closes and the worksheet is displayed with the chart. Now close the worksheet by double-clicking its Control menu in the upper-left corner or by pressing Ctrl-F4. You will see the dialog box below, querying whether to save the updated worksheet with the chart. Choose No to indicate that you do not want to save the chart.

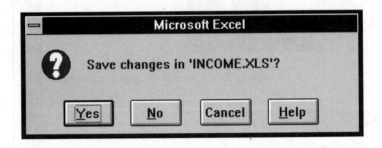

Notice that there was no query to save the chart as a chart document (.XLC extension). If you had saved the chart, it would have been an embedded chart in the worksheet document.

QUITTING EXCEL

NOTE *If you forget to save your document before quitting, Excel will catch this and prompt you with a message box, giving you another chance. Your best insurance, however, is always to save your document before quitting Excel.*

When you wish to leave Excel, there are only two simple steps to follow: save your work and exit. After using Save or Save As to save the document, double-click the Control box in the upper-left corner of the application window or press Alt-F4.

You have now created a simple worksheet of data and formulas, and a chart using some of the data. You also learned how to do some formatting, how to print the worksheet, and how to save it to disk. In the next chapter, you will learn how to design a worksheet and use additional features.

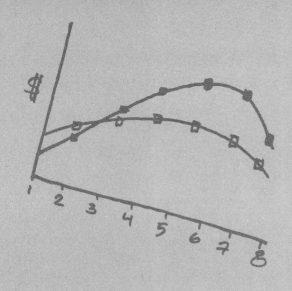

$$b = \frac{\Sigma xy - x\Sigma y}{\Sigma x^2 - x\Sigma x}$$

PART TWO

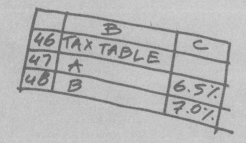

Part II: Getting Right to Work with Excel

The process of making a worksheet is divided into four steps: creating, editing, formatting, and printing. For each of these steps, there are several rules and procedures that you must be aware of and follow to work with any type of worksheet. Part II introduces you to the basic rules by teaching you how to create, edit, format, and print a simple balance sheet. Even if you have created worksheets before, take the time to work through these exercises. You will be surprised at how much easier it is to do them with Excel than with any other spreadsheet program you have used.

After you've created and printed the basic worksheet, we go on to introduce you to a few other basic features: window control, formulas and functions, and naming cells.

FAST TRACK CHAPTER 4

Type it in directly, using a minus sign for negative numbers, decimal notation for fractions, or the scientific notation format.

Type it in directly, starting it with a single quote (') if Excel could confuse it for a number, formula, date, time, etc.

Begin with an =. Enter the function. To include a cell address, type the cell address directly or click on the cell itself. Press Enter when finished.

- Highlight the source cell range. Select Edit ➤ Cut to move or Edit ➤ Copy to copy. Highlight the destination cell range, or upper-left cell of the range. Select Edit ➤ Paste.
- Highlight the source cell range. Move the cursor at the range border until it changes to an arrow pointer. To move, drag the cell to the destination. To copy, hold down the Ctrl key and drag.

- Select any cell in the column or the designator, Format ➤ Column Width, enter the new width in the dialog box, and press Enter.
- Point the mouse at the line between the column-heading designators. When the cursor changes shape, click and drag it to the right or left.

CHAPTER 4

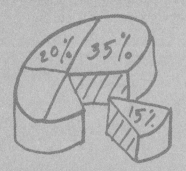

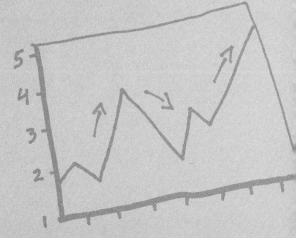

Creating the Worksheet

This chapter will show you how to create a worksheet. Do not be too concerned about any errors that you make when entering data. In the next chapter, you will learn how to correct those errors. First, let's review the basic parts of a worksheet and the techniques used to create one.

WORKSHEET DESIGN STRATEGIES

When creating a worksheet, you should have a specific goal in mind. It may be to show that a company's sales are better in a specific region, to show that the profit this year is better than in previous years, or perhaps to show the relationship between literacy and infant mortality in a given area. Whatever it is, the conclusion should stand out so that a busy reader can see it quickly.

Often a chart is the best method for presenting the result: it catches the reader's attention quickly and can convey information better than words. In other cases, the detailed numbers of a worksheet themselves may be more important. In either case, you are telling a story.

The basic rule of worksheets is that form follows function: what the worksheet or chart is supposed to convey should determine how it looks. Shadow boxes, arrows, and three-dimensional charts are great, but only if they help the reader see the conclusion.

The following are some general guidelines for creating useful worksheets:

◆ **Work out the general worksheet idea on paper before using Excel.** What is the objective of the spreadsheet? Who will use it? What type of input is required?

◆ **Partition large worksheets into blocks.** There should be four blocks on most worksheets: assumptions, input, calculations, and conclusions. Label the blocks. Data are entered to the input block, which is then used by the calculation block. The assumption block defines parameters that may vary in the future (interest rates, principal, etc.). This permits you to do what-if simulations by simply changing the assumptions. The results are in the conclusion block. If you have many input parameters, you should use several input blocks (which could even be on separate worksheets). Then feed the results into a master calculation block.

◆ **Use multiple worksheets instead of one large worksheet.** Consider using several worksheets and linking them together, such as putting the assumptions in a separate worksheet. This permits data to be shared by other worksheets, reduces worksheet loading time, and makes each worksheet easier to manage.

◆ **Enter labels first.** The general worksheet strategy is to enter labels first to define the framework, then the numbers, and then any formulas. Finally, format the worksheet.

◆ **Identify assumptions.** Be sure any assumptions are well documented. Specify the sources using notes, text boxes, or footnote text on the worksheet.

◆ **Use a header and add date and time stamps.** To help when tracking different versions of the worksheet, add the worksheet version number.

◆ **Explain the purpose.** Use a subhead, the title, or some beginning comments to explain the purpose of the worksheet.

◆ **Add notes to cells.** Use notes to explain complex formulas.

◆ **Give instructions.** Somewhere on the worksheet you should include instructions for how to use it. They should be in a language that the intended user can understand.

◆ **Use more formulas to link cells and avoid using absolute values unless necessary.** For example, the worksheet may have a price that affects several cells and periodically changes. Put the price in a separate block on the page and use a formula to reference it in other cells in the worksheet. This will enable you to update all references from a single cell, improving the accuracy of the overall worksheet.

◆ **Keep formulas short.** Break formulas over several cells, if necessary, to make them easier to read and use.

◆ **Use blank rows, columns, and cells liberally to improve worksheet readability.** White space and borders, when used properly, make the worksheet easier to read. If possible, use report formats with which the user is familiar. For example, on a large table of numbers leave every fifth or sixth row blank.

◆ **Use cell names.** With Excel, you can label cells or cell ranges. Naming them enables you to go quickly to a specific area of the worksheet. For example, naming an assumption area enables you to move quickly to this area by name to check or edit it. Names also improve the readability of the worksheet and, as a result, its accuracy.

◆ **Check the worksheet over carefully before printing it.** People have used electronic worksheets to make major decisions based on incorrect data. If the input data are wrong or if a formula is wrong, the results will be wrong. The computer can only do what you tell it to do. Don't assume it is correct just because there are no error messages.

◆ **Test the worksheet.** Try some example data you have already used and be sure the conclusions are what you expect.

BASIC WORKSHEET TECHNIQUES

To enter data to a cell, you must do three things:

1. Make the cell active.

2. Enter the data with the keyboard.

3. Lock the data into the cell.

In its simplest form, this procedure involves making the cell active by clicking on the desired cell, entering the data from the keyboard, and locking the data into the cell by pressing the Enter key.

With Excel, however, you have plenty of flexibility in entering data. The basic techniques for entering data into a worksheet are described in the next three sections. You will then use these techniques to begin creating a more complex worksheet than the simple one you set up in Chapter 3.

MAKING THE CELL ACTIVE

The *active cell* is the cell in which data are entered when you start typing on the keyboard. You may select one or more cells (such as a cell range), but only one cell can be active at a time. The name of the active cell always appears in the active-cell designator.

When you want to enter data or do an operation on a cell or cell range, you must first select that cell or range. Each time you do so, the previous selection will be canceled. You can tell which cell(s) are selected at any given time because they are highlighted. You can select a single cell, a row of cells, or a column—indeed, any rectangular block of cells. You also can select discontinuous ranges.

Selecting a range of cells does not change the contents of the cells. The cell contents will be changed only if you enter data from the keyboard or choose some operation (such as Clear or Cut from the Edit menu) after the cell is selected.

There are several ways to select a cell or cells in Excel:

◆ **Select a single cell** by placing the cursor on it and clicking the left mouse button once. From the keyboard, you can select a single cell by using the direction keys to highlight it. A border will appear around the cell and the cell's address will appear in the active-cell designator.

◆ **Select a cell range** by placing the cursor on the first cell in the range and dragging it to the last cell in the range. If the range occupies several rows or columns, start the selection in the upper left and drag to the lower right. If the final cell of the desired range is beyond the window border, keep on dragging: the window will automatically scroll as you drag the cursor beyond the border. To select a range from the keyboard, use the direction keys to select the first cell of the range and extend the range with the direction keys while holding down the Shift key. When you select a range of cells, the first cell from which you define the range becomes the active cell. The range is shown in inverse video, while the active cell is indicated by a heavy border. While defining a range, the active-cell designator displays the size of the range. When the mouse button is released, the designator displays only the active cell. (If you select an entire row or column with the mouse, the left or uppermost cell visible will be the active cell.)

◆ **Select an entire row** by placing the cursor on the row designator at the left of the window and clicking once (or pressing Shift-Spacebar from any cell in the row).

◆ **Select an entire column** by placing the cursor on the column designator and clicking once (or pressing Ctrl-Spacebar from any cell in the row).

◆ **Select the entire worksheet** by clicking the small box to the left of the column headings and above the row headings (or pressing Ctrl-Shift-Spacebar).

◆ **Select a range of rows** by clicking a row designator and dragging to another row. In the same way, you can select a range of columns by selecting a column designator and dragging to another column.

◆ **Select a block of cells** by clicking on the first cell and pressing F8. The status bar activates the **EXT** indicator. This shows that you are in *extended mode*. Now click the cell at the opposite end of the block. Press F8 again to get out of extended mode (and turn the status indicator off). Another way to select a range is to click the upper-left cell, hold down the Shift key, and click the lower-right cell of the range.

◆ **Select a large block of cells that extends beyond the window's border** by first making the upper-left cell of the range active, then pressing F8 to extend the range. The **EXT** designator should appear at the lower right. Now choose Goto from the Formula menu or press F5. In the Goto dialog box, enter the address of the cell at the lower right of the range, press Enter, and then press F8 to release you from the extended mode. (If you press Shift-Enter in the dialog box instead, you'll get out of extended mode automatically.)

◆ **Make multiple range selections** by defining the first range and pressing Shift-F8. **ADD** appears in the status bar to indicate *add mode*. Then select additional cells or cell ranges. Press Shift-F8 again to turn the indicator off. You can do this with a mouse by selecting the first range and holding down the Ctrl key while you select additional ranges. Multiple ranges selected in this way are called *discontinuous ranges*.

Before continuing, you should practice making each type of selection listed above.

To move the active cell around the worksheet, use the direction keys—or else Tab to move it one cell to the right and Shift-Tab to move it one cell to the left. If a range is already selected, these keys will still work, but the active cell will move only within the range. You can also press the Enter key to move the active cell downwards within a range.

Table 4.1 summarizes the mouse selection methods. Table 4.2 is a complete list of the keyboard selection commands. To move the active cell within a selected range with the mouse, hold down the Ctrl key and click the cell you wish to make active. (If you don't press Ctrl, you'll end up deselecting the range.) Table 4.3 summarizes how to move the active cell in a range with the keyboard.

ENTERING DATA

When entering data in a range of cells, highlight the entire range and enter the data for each cell. Use the Enter or Tab key, as appropriate, to lock the data and move to the next cell in the range. (The Enter key moves down a column and the Tab key moves across a row.)

Once an active cell is selected, the next step is entering data in the cell. You can enter either a constant value or a formula. There are four basic types of constant values that can be entered: text, numbers, dates or times, and logical values.

As soon as you start entering data in a cell, a flashing vertical bar appears in the formula bar. It acts as a cursor and is called the *insertion point*. Later you will learn how to move it for editing purposes.

When the insertion point appears, the Enter-box (✓) and Cancel-box (×) icons appear in the formula bar. The Enter box can be used, like the Enter key, to lock the data to the cell after you've typed them in. The Cancel box can be clicked, if you wish, to clear the typed-in data without locking the data to the cell. The Cancel box doesn't work (and even disappears) after pressing Enter or clicking the Enter box.

ACTION	MOUSE
Select single cell	Click cell
Select range	Drag over range
Select row	Click row designator
Select column	Click column designator
Select range of rows	Drag over row designators
Select range of columns	Drag over column designators
Select entire worksheet	Single-click rectangle at top of row designators
Select multiple ranges	Select the first range and hold down the Ctrl key while selecting others

TABLE 4.1:

Selecting Cells with the Mouse

ACTION	KEYSTROKES
Select cell	Use appropriate direction key to move active cell
Extend range by one adjacent cell	Use Shift with appropriate direction key
Move active cell to start of row	Home
Extend selection to start of row	Shift-Home
Move active cell to end of row	End, →
Extend selection to end of row	End, Shift-→
Select entire current row	Shift-Spacebar
Extend row selection to other rows	Shift-↑ or Shift-↓
Select entire current column	Ctrl-Spacebar
Extend column selection to other columns	Shift-← or Shift-→
Select cell at upper left of worksheet	Ctrl-Home
Extend selection to A1	Ctrl-Shift-Home
Select cell at lower right of worksheet	Ctrl-End
Extend selection to cell at lower right of worksheet	Ctrl-Shift-End
Select entire worksheet	Ctrl-Shift-Spacebar
Collapse selection to single cell	Shift-Backspace

TABLE 4.2:

Selecting Cells with the Keyboard

ACTION	KEYSTROKES
Move down one cell in range	Enter
Move up one cell in range	Shift-Enter
Move right one cell in range	Tab
Move left one cell in range	Shift-Tab
Move to next corner of range	Ctrl-.
Move to next range	Ctrl-Tab
Move to previous range	Ctrl-Shift-Tab

TABLE 4.3:

Moving within a Selection

Entering Numbers

You can enter numbers in one of three formats:

FORMAT	EXAMPLES
Integer	1, 45, −45, (45), $45,000
Decimal fraction	43.5, −56.75, (73.2), $98.60, 6.5%
Scientific notation	25E+23, 25e23, 4E−3, 4**−3

Unless you select otherwise, numbers are right-justified in a cell. If a number has too many characters to fit in a column, Excel will display a row of pound signs (######) in that cell to signify an overflow, or else use scientific notation. Regardless of how numbers are displayed, they are always stored to 15 digits of accuracy.

Enter fractions as decimal numbers, then use the Numbers command under the Format menu to select either of the fraction formats, # ?/? or # ??/??. Entering a fraction in fractional form (such as **1/4**) will confuse Excel; it will be formatted as though it were a date. If you want to enter a fraction that does not have a finite decimal value (such as ⅓ or 2⅔), enter a leading zero and a space, as in **0 1/3** or **2 2/3**.

Entering Dates or Times

Excel stores both dates and times as serial numbers. The serial number for a date represents the number of days since January 1, 1900, which has the serial date 1. Thus Excel can calculate the number of days between two dates by subtracting the earlier date from the later one. The serial number for a time represents the number of seconds elapsed since midnight. A date or time is converted into a serial number as soon as it is entered.

You can enter dates in the *mm/dd/yy* format using slashes or hyphens, as in **7/10/93**. Alternatively, you can use the general date-entry format, as in **September 1, 1994**. You also can enter dates in any of three other formats: *dd/mm/yy* (25/May/93), *dd/mm* (25/May), or *mm/yy* (May/93). If you enter a date in any other format, Excel will not display an error message; it will simply store it as text rather than as a serial number.

You can enter time values in either standard (3:30:30 PM) or military (13:15:45) format. Seconds are optional, and you can use *A* or *P* (or *a* or *p*)

NOTE NOTE *This is different from the Excel for the Macintosh, in which dates are measured from January 1, 1904. You can convert serial numbers from one format to another with the Options ➤ Calculation command.*

instead of *AM* or *PM*. You can enter both a date and a time into a single cell. Be sure to use a space between the time and its AM/PM indicator.

To enter a date or time into a formula, enter the date or time as text enclosed in double quotation marks. Excel will convert the date or time to a serial number value and evaluate the formula using that value.

If you need to enter a date as text, precede it with a single quotation mark (').

As a shortcut for entering dates, use Ctrl-; to paste in the current date and Ctrl-: to paste in the current time. *These are fixed values and do not change,* so this is a good way of date-stamping a worksheet. The next time the worksheet is changed, however, you must repeat the stamping to get the new time or date.

Entering Logical Values

You can enter logical values as either TRUE or FALSE. The use of logical values is discussed in Chapter 8. The logical value TRUE or FALSE can be entered in upper- or lowercase letters, but is always stored and displayed as uppercase in Excel.

Entering Text

Any characters that Excel cannot interpret as a number, date, time, logical value, or formula are considered text. Unless you select otherwise, text data are always left-justified in a cell. You can enter up to 255 characters in a cell.

If any part of a formula string is nonnumeric, Excel will assume that the entire string is text. For example, *234 Fox Drive* is assumed to be a text string, even though it begins with a number. You can enter text in text string formulas by enclosing the text in quotation marks.

For long text strings, you may wish to word-wrap them. To do so, choose Alignment under the Format menu and select Wrap Text. This will automatically increase the row height as necessary for the wrapped text.

Entering Formulas

The real power of Excel lies in its ability to calculate the value of a cell based on values in other cells. This is accomplished by *formulas,* which tell Excel exactly how to calculate a cell value from data in other cells, even from formulas in other cells. A worksheet, then, can become a very complex system of interwoven formulas and values. Changing one value on the worksheet can initiate a complex chain of calculations that will change cells in the entire worksheet.

Creating Formulas To create a formula, first select the cell or cell range that you want to contain the value calculated by the formula. You can enter the formula into the cell in one of three ways:

◆ Type the formula from the keyboard. First type an equal sign, then the formula. Complete the entry by pressing the Enter key.

◆ Click the cells that are referenced by the formula. For example, to enter "cell B5 minus cell B7," type an equal sign, place the cursor on cell B5 and click, type a minus sign, and then place the cursor on cell B7 and click. To complete the formula, click the Enter box or press the Enter key. You can use this method only with relative cell referencing (see Chapter 8).

◆ Type or paste the name that you assigned to a cell or range of cells. Once you've defined names for cells (see Chapter 9), you can use the Paste Name command on the Formula menu to enter the formula (Excel will automatically begin the formula with an equal sign). Alternately, you can type an equal sign and then type in the formula using the names. Again, press the Enter key to complete the formula.

If you make a mistake while you're typing in a formula, click the Cancel box on the formula bar or backspace through the error. After entering data, you can usually correct it with the Undo command (see Chapter 14). Methods for building and using formulas are discussed in detail in Chapters 8 and 9.

Formula Operators In creating a formula, you use *mathematical operators* to show how Excel is to do the calculation. These operators are as follows:

OPERATOR	FUNCTION
+	Addition
−	Subtraction
*	Multiplication
/	Division
∧	Exponentiation

You also can use an ampersand (&) as an operator to join two text values to create a new text value. For example =**"Mr. "&"Smith"** becomes *Mr. Smith*. You also can concatenate text to data or the contents of a cell in the same way, such as in =**"The total is: "&D5.**

You also can use a formula to compare cell values. The result of using *comparison operators* is always a logical value—TRUE or FALSE. The following comparison operators are available:

OPERATOR	FUNCTION
=	Equal to
<	Less than
<=	Less than or equal to
>	Greater than
>=	Greater than or equal to
<>	Not equal to

Reference operators are used to refer to two or more cells in formulas and function arguments. There are three reference operators available:

OPERATOR	NAME AND FUNCTION
:	Range—references all cells in the given range
,	Union—includes two references
space	Intersection—includes cells common to two references

For example, to show the range from cell A1 to cell A10 in the SUM function, you would type **=SUM(A1:A10)**. You also can use these operators with the names that you assigned to a cell or range of cells (see Chapter 9).

The union operator can be used for discontinuous sums, such as **=SUM(A1:A3, A6:A10).** The intersection operator is used with named cells. For example, if a row is named February and a column is named Receipts, **=SUM(February Receipts)** would return the value of the intersection.

Excel includes a large number of functions to simplify using formulas. For more information on using functions, see Chapter 8.

LOCKING THE ENTRY

Plan your data entry so that the cursor moves to the next cell in the range.

Once data are typed to a cell, you must lock the data in it. There are three basic ways to lock data:

◆ Press the Enter key. If only a single cell was selected, the active cell will remain highlighted. If a range was selected, the active cell will move down one cell.

◆ Press any key that moves the active cell: Tab, Shift-Tab, or an arrow key. Each of these will lock the data in the cell and highlight the adjacent cell.

◆ Click the Enter box. If only a single cell was selected, the active cell will remain highlighted. If a range was selected, the active cell will move down one cell.

THE DISPLAY OF CELL DATA

The true cell value and the displayed value may be two different things. Excel always remembers whatever you typed into a cell, exactly as you typed it (except for numbers, which are remembered to 15 digits). This is the true cell value. If you type a 50-character text string into a cell eight characters wide, Excel will show the entire text string, provided the cells to the right are blank. If they are not, the cell with the long text string will display only some of the characters of the text. However, the formula bar will show the 50-character string.

An Excel cell can hold up to 255 characters. However, you will probably never enter so many in one cell. (The default cell width is 8.43 characters.)

If you enter a large number into a cell that is not large enough to display all the characters, Excel will try to display the number in exponential notation. If the cell is not even wide enough for this, Excel will display pound signs (#). The number is always stored to 15 digits of accuracy, regardless of how it is displayed. You also can use the Format ➤ Number command to alter what is shown, as you will learn later. For example, if you enter the number 14.3245, you can format the cell to display **14.32**. The entire number, though, is still stored as the true cell value and will be used in calculations.

The displayed calculation on a cell range may not appear to be the right answer, since the displayed values are not necessarily the true cell values. If you wish to ensure that totals reflect the displayed cell values instead of the true cell values, choose Calculation from the Options menu and select Precision as Displayed. For example, enter **3.7** in A1 in a worksheet and the same value in A2. In A3, enter **=A1+A2**. The total is 7.4, which is what you would expect. Now select all three cells, select Number from the Format menu, and set the picture to the fourth picture in the list box (#,##0). A1 and A2 now show **4**, and A3 shows **7**—which is not what you would expect. Select Calculation from the Options menu and choose Precision as Displayed. A3 changes to **8**, but is now less precise. Be sure to set Precision as Displayed off before continuing. A3 won't change back, and A1 and A2 will keep their rounded values, too.

SPECIAL WORKSHEET TECHNIQUES

When creating a worksheet, there are several special worksheet techniques that are important to learn. These include clearing the worksheet, filling a range of cells, moving and copying, and changing column widths.

CLEARING THE WORKSHEET

To clear a specific range, select it and choose Edit ➤ Clear. For even faster clearing, press Ctrl-Del after selecting the range.

If you have some practice entries in your worksheet and you want to start over with a clean worksheet, you can clear it by following these steps:

1. Select the entire worksheet (see "Basic Worksheet Techniques" towards the beginning of this chapter).

2. Open the Edit menu and choose Clear. Select All and OK.

FILLING A RANGE OF CELLS

You can enter the same value into all the cells in a horizontal or vertical range by using the Fill commands:

1. Select the range, starting with the cell that already contains the value and moving down or right.

2. Open the Edit menu and choose Fill Right or Fill Down, as appropriate.

Excel will copy the value into each selected cell and adjust formulas that contain relative addresses automatically. (More on that in Chapter 8.)

You also can fill upwards or towards the left. To use one of these *reverse fills,* select the range, hold down the Shift key, and open the Edit menu. The menu will now show Fill Up and Fill Left as options. Select the desired fill.

For fast fills, highlight the cell containing the contents for filling and move the mouse pointer to the lower-right corner of the cell. The pointer changes to a crosshair. Drag the pointer over the cells to fill. For filling discontinuous ranges, copy the data to the first cell of the next range (see the next section), then drag to fill that range.

MOVING AND COPYING DATA

Save time by desig-nating the destination range by a single cell—the upper-left corner of the destina-tion range. The entire range will still be moved or copied.

When you copy, you take a value or a formula in one cell and copy it into a cell or range of cells. Moving is similar, except that the original cells are cleared. (When you use a Fill command, you are copying.)

To move data, select the source cell range, open the Edit menu, and choose Cut (Ctrl-X). This moves a copy of the current range data to the Clipboard. Select the entire destination range. The source range will remain marked with a moving dotted line. Open the Edit menu and choose Paste (Ctrl-V). The source cells will clear and the destination cells will then contain the data. Source and destination ranges can overlap if necessary.

To copy data, select the source range. Open the Edit menu and choose Copy (Ctrl-C). This creates a copy of the source range data in the Clipboard. Select the destination range. Again, the source range remains marked. Open the Edit menu and choose Paste (Shift-Ins). The destination range will then contain the same data as the source range. The data are still in the Clipboard. You can do more pastes with the same source range without reusing the Copy command.

When copying, you can specify a destination range that is an integer multiple of the source cells to create multiple copies. The destination range should be a single cell or an integer multiple in height and/or width of the source range. For example, if the source range is two cells, the destination range should contain two, four, six, or another even number of cells. Be sure not to overlap copy ranges.

For fast moves, place the mouse pointer on a border of the cell or range to move with the cell or range selected. The cursor changes to an arrow point-ing up and to the left. Then drag to the new location. For fast copies, use the same method but hold down the Ctrl key while dragging.

When formulas are copied into other cells, the formula references change to reflect their new position. This default method is called *relative ad-dressing*. It is possible to prevent this adjustment with *absolute addressing*. You will learn more about relative and absolute addressing in Chapter 8.

CHANGING COLUMN WIDTHS

In creating a worksheet, you will often need to change the width of a column to display the entire cell contents or to improve the appearance of the worksheet. You can change column widths either by using the Column Width command under the Format menu or by dragging the column separator with the mouse.

Changing the Column Width with a Command

You can use both methods to enter fractional column widths (for example, 20.5 characters). The mouse method, however, is more intuitive.

To change the width with a command, open the Format menu and choose Column Width. When the Column Width dialog box appears, type in the new width and click OK. The column width will change to reflect the value entered. The contents of the cells in that column will not be changed. You can have Excel automatically define a new width by clicking the Best Fit button, as long as the active cell or range contains the longest number, text string, or formula of that column.

Another way to change the column width is to use the shortcut menu. Click the right mouse button on the column designator to see the shortcut menu. Select Column Width and enter the new width as described above.

Changing the Column Width with the Mouse

To change the width with the mouse, move the cursor to the line between the column-heading designators. The shape of the cursor will change to a vertical line with two oppositely pointing arrows ($\leftarrow | \rightarrow$). Click and drag the column separator to the right or left. The width of the column on the left will follow the cursor. Release the mouse button at the desired width.

THE BALANCE WORKSHEET

In this and the next two chapters, you will create the worksheet shown in Figure 4.1. In this chapter you will use the techniques described so far to enter the worksheet data and formulas. At the end of this chapter the worksheet should look like Figure 4.2. In comparing the two figures, notice the difference in the quality of presentation that is achieved by formatting. Formatting is described in Chapter 6.

ACME MANUFACTURING COMPANY

Balance Sheet for 1992
(Figures in Thousands of Dollars)

	Qtr 1	Qtr 2	Qtr 3	Qtr 4
Current Assets				
Cash	$28,653	$42,894	$64,882	$91,053
Accounts Receivable	$35,700	$44,150	$48,450	$55,230
Inventory	$11,400	$12,930	$14,500	$16,490
Total Current Assets	$75,753	$99,974	$127,832	$162,773
Fixed Assets				
P,P, and E				
Furniture, Fixtures	$12,100	$12,100	$12,100	$12,100
Equipment	$6,500	$16,600	$21,100	$42,300
Office Equipment	$4,100	$4,100	$4,100	$4,100
Gross P, P, and E	$22,700	$32,800	$37,300	$58,500
Accumulated Depreciation	$6,600	$8,700	$11,400	$13,400
Total Fixed Assets	$16,100	$24,100	$25,900	$45,100
Total Assets	**$91,853**	**$124,074**	**$153,732**	**$207,873**
Current Liabilities				
Accounts Payable	$17,340	$41,000	$42,300	$75,200
Income Taxes Payable	$4,043	$6,132	$7,301	$9,245
Total Current Liabilities	$21,383	$47,132	$49,601	$84,445
Non-current Liabilities				
Long-term debt	$22,000	$20,000	$18,000	$16,000
Total Liabilities	$43,383	$67,132	$67,601	$100,445
Capital				
Acme Capital	$48,470	$56,942	$86,131	$107,428
Total Liabilities & Equity	**$91,853**	**$124,074**	**$153,732**	**$207,873**

FIGURE 4.1:

The final balance worksheet, neatly typeset with a title, boxes, dotted lines, and shading

	A	B	C	D	E
1		ACME MANUFACTURING COMPANY			
2					
3		Balance Sheet for 1992			
4		(Figures in Thousands of Dollars)			
5					
6		Qtr 1	Qtr 2	Qtr 3	Qtr 4
7					
8	Current Assets				
9	Cash	28653	42894	64882	91053
10	Accounts Receivable	35700	44150	48450	55230
11	Inventory	11400	12930	14500	16490
12		---------------	---------------	---------------	---------------
13	Total Current Assets	75753	99974	127832	162773
14					
15	Fixed Assets				
16	P,P, and E				
17	Furniture, Fixtures	12100	12100	12100	12100
18	Equipment	6500	16600	21100	42300
19	Office Equipment	4100	4100	4100	4100
20		---------------	---------------	---------------	---------------
21	Gross P, P, and E	22700	32800	37300	58500
22	Accumulated Depreciation	6600	8700	11400	13400
23		---------------	---------------	---------------	---------------
24	Total Fixed Assets	16100	24100	25900	45100
25					
26	Total Assets	91853	124074	153732	207873
27					
28	Current Liabilities				
29	Accounts Payable	17340	41000	42300	75200
30	Income Taxes Payable	4043	6132	7301	9245
31		---------------	---------------	---------------	---------------
32	Total Current Liabilities	21383	47132	49601	84445
33					
34	Non-current Liabilities				
35	Long-term debt	22000	20000	18000	16000
36		---------------	---------------	---------------	---------------
37	Total Liabilities	43383	67132	67601	100445
38					
39	Capital				
40	Acme Capital	48470	56942	86131	107428
41		---------------	---------------	---------------	---------------
42	Total Liabilities & Equity	91853	124074	153732	207873

FIGURE 4.2:

The balance worksheet before formatting: this is the basic information that becomes Figure 4.1 after a little creative formatting

CREATING THE WORKSHEET

To begin work on this worksheet, follow these steps:

1. Select cells A8 through A42 by selecting A8, pressing F5, and typing **A42**.

2. Hold down the Shift key and press Enter to highlight the column.

3. Enter the row titles shown in Figure 4.2. Press the Enter key after you've typed each title. Press the Enter key twice to skip a line. At the end, you can return to A8 by pressing Ctrl-.

4. Expand the width of column A by opening the Format menu and choosing Column Width. The dialog box shown below appears. Enter **25** and click OK.

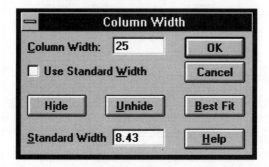

5. Drag the cursor from cell B6 to cell E6 and enter the column headings shown in Figure 4.2. Press Enter after each entry.

6. Add a title to the worksheet by selecting cell B1 and entering **ACME MANUFACTURING COMPANY** from the keyboard. Select cell B3 and enter **Balance Sheet for 1992**. Select cell B4 and enter **(Figures in Thousands of Dollars)**.

7. To enter the horizontal separators, first place one hyphen in the leftmost column (as in B12). Then open the Format menu and select Alignment. Click on Fill, then OK. Drag B12 from its lower-right corner to E12, and this will fill the hyphens right. (You can also fill right by selecting B12 to E12 and choosing Fill Right from the Edit menu.)

8. Select cells B12 to E12, place the cursor on a border of the selected range (it changes to a pointer), hold down the Ctrl Key and then drag the range to the corresponding position in rows 20, 23, 36, and 41 in turn. This will create the other rows of hyphens. (If you don't have a mouse, copy B12 to E12 to the Clipboard and paste to B20, B23, B36, and B41.)

9. Enter the numbers shown in Figure 4.2 into the worksheet. Enter the data for rows 9-11, 17-19, 22, 29-30, 35, and 40. Do not enter the values for rows 13, 21, 24, 26, 32, 37, and 42. You'll use formulas to fill these in, as described next.

10. Enter the following formulas into column B:

INTO CELL	ENTER THE FORMULA
B13	= B9 + B10 + B11
B21	= B17 + B18 + B19
B24	= B21 − B22
B26	= B13 + B24
B32	= B29 + B30
B37	= B32 + B35
B42	= B37 − B40

11. Fill the cells with the formulas. Click cell B13 and drag the lower-right corner to cell E13. Alternately, you could choose B13 to E13, open the Edit menu, and choose Fill Right. Repeat this procedure for all the rows that contain a formula.

In Figure 4.3, columns B through E show the values that should appear on your worksheet after you've entered the formulas for row 13.

SAVING THE WORKSHEET

After you have created the worksheet, you will need to save it on your disk. Although the worksheet is displayed on-screen, it is stored only in the computer's memory. If you were to turn the computer off or reboot without saving the worksheet, the worksheet would be lost.

The File menu contains two commands you can use to save your worksheet: Save and Save As. The Save command saves the worksheet under the name currently displayed in the worksheet title bar. This default name is Sheet1. The Save As command lets you save the worksheet under any name. The first time you save the new worksheet, either command brings up the Save As dialog box so you can specify the name for the worksheet. The title bar will then change to reflect this new name. On all subsequent saves, you can just use Save.

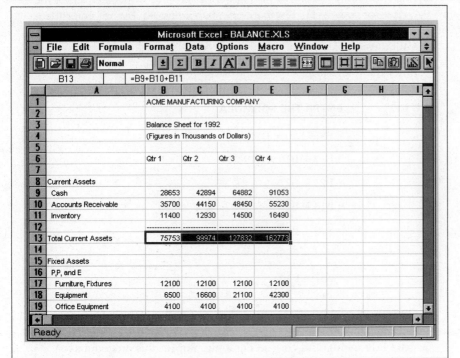

The worksheet after entering the formulas in cells B13 through E13. Each of these formulas sums the numbers above it

Try this now with your worksheet. Choose Save As under the File menu. A dialog box will appear (Figure 4.4). Use the Drives drop-down list box to select the drive to save to. In the Directories list box, choose the subdirectory in which to save the file by double-clicking the desired folder. Under File Name, enter the worksheet name **BALANCE** (do not include a period). You can use upper- or lowercase letters. Choose OK and it will be saved under the file name you specify, with an .XLS extension added. (Saving is described in more detail in Chapter 7.)

As a shortcut for using Save As, you can press F12 to get the Save As dialog box. If you wish to use the mouse and toolbar to save, click the File Save tool. The same dialog box will appear if this is the first time you're saving the file.

While you're creating a worksheet you should save it approximately every 20 minutes, depending on how much work you do in a given time period and how much you can afford to lose if the computer crashes. This will protect your work against power failures, hardware failures, or inadvertent user mistakes.

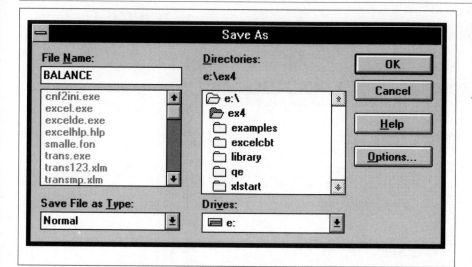

FIGURE 4.4:

*Saving a worksheet.
Here you enter the
name of the file and
place to save it*

EXPERIMENTING WITH THE WORKSHEET

Now you can try some different techniques. First, try copying a formula. Instead of entering the formulas for cells C13, D13, and E13 with the Fill Right command, copy the formula from cell B13 into the rest of the row (this will copy over what's already there):

1. Make cell B13 active.

2. Open the Edit menu and choose Copy (Ctrl-C). Notice that the highlighting on cell B13 changes.

3. Select cell C13 and drag to cell E13. Although cells C13, D13, and E13 are now selected, cell B13 is still marked to show the cell range for the copy.

4. Open the Edit menu again and choose Paste (Ctrl-V). The correct totals will immediately show in the rest of the row.

Notice that the totals in cells C13, D13, and E13 are correct. The formula in cell C13 was automatically adjusted for the new columns when it was copied. To check this, select cell C13 and look at the formula in the formula bar (Figure 4.5).

Now try a move. Just for practice, move row 42 to row 43:

1. Select A42 to E42.

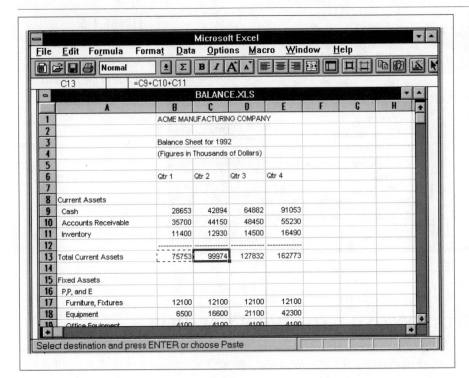

FIGURE 4.5:

*Examining the formula
created by the Copy
command: it adds
the cells immediately
above it*

2. Open the Edit menu and choose Cut (Ctrl-X). Notice that the entire range is marked.

3. Place the cursor on A43.

4. Open the Edit menu again and choose Paste (Shift-Ins). Row 42 will move to row 43 (and row 42 will be cleared). Notice that the formulas are automatically adjusted.

5. Recover the former worksheet immediately by selecting the Edit menu and choosing Undo Paste (or press Ctrl-Z). The worksheet should be restored. If something goes wrong here, remember that you have already saved the worksheet. You can use the Open command under the File menu to reload it. (Click OK in the dialog box that asks if you want to revert to the old version.)

*Avoid
copying or
moving en-
tire rows or
columns, unless neces-
sary. It uses a lot of
Clipboard memory
and is slow.*

Use the Clipboard for both cutting and copying. You can watch the Clipboard change during a cut-and-paste operation. First, click the application Control box. Choose Run, then select Clipboard, as below. The Clipboard window will open and become the active window, as shown in Figure 4.6. It displays the size of the last cut or copy (as long as the cut or copied text is still outlined).

In the next two chapters, you will be changing the worksheet you created in this chapter. When you leave Excel, you may see a message box, indicating that the document has been changed and asking whether you wish to save the new document. If you wish to save the altered document, choose Yes. If not, choose No.

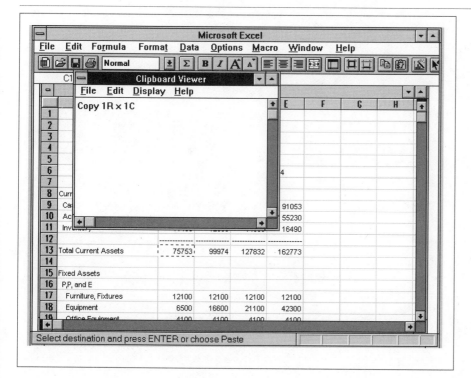

FIGURE 4.6:

The Clipboard Viewer

FAST TRACK CHAPTER 5

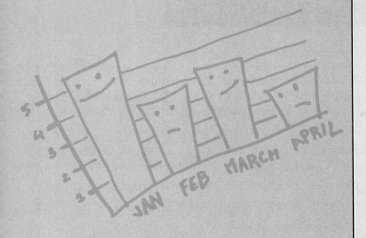

CHAPTER 5

Editing the Worksheet

Excel has many editing features that can make your work easier. You can clear a cell or cell range, recover from an accidental deletion, and insert or delete rows and columns. You also can use standard Windows editing techniques (cut, move, and paste) to edit any data in the formula bar.

In this chapter, you will learn the basic editing skills and techniques to use with Excel worksheets. These will enable you to correct any mistakes that you might have made in the exercises of the last chapter. Even if your worksheet does not have any mistakes, take the time to learn some of the editing techniques described here. More advanced editing techniques are discussed in Chapter 14.

EDITING TECHNIQUES

Excel offers you a variety of worksheet editing techniques, which make it easy for you to keep your worksheets up to date and accurate, as well as use one basic worksheet structure for many purposes.

Let's examine how you can edit a worksheet. The techniques discussed in this section include:

◆ Clearing cells

◆ Undoing various operations

◆ Repeating a command

◆ Editing cells

◆ Editing formulas

◆ Inserting and deleting rows and columns

LOADING THE WORKSHEET

To begin editing, start Excel and load the BALANCE.XLS worksheet, if you have not already done so. To open the worksheet, use any of these methods to get to the Open dialog box:

◆ Choose Open from the File menu.

◆ Press Ctrl-F12.

◆ Click the Open File button on the toolbar.

In the dialog box displayed (Figure 5.1), choose the drive containing the worksheet from the drop-down list box under Drives. Switch to the directory containing the worksheet by double-clicking the directory in the Directories list box. Choose the file name BALANCE.XLS (double-click it or use the direction keys to highlight it and press Enter). (See Chapter 7 for more help on opening worksheets.)

Here are a few tips for loading and saving worksheets:

NOTE
NOTE
As a document loads, the format and percentage loaded is displayed in the upper left of the window.

◆ Excel remembers the last four worksheets loaded. If the worksheet you wish to load is on the File menu, choose the name from the File menu instead of using the Open command.

◆ You can open Lotus 1-2-3 spreadsheets, dBASE files, and SYLKS documents from the Open dialog box shown in Figure 5.1. Use the List Files of Type drop-down list box to choose the file type to load. Excel is smart enough to figure out most spreadsheet formats and loads them automatically.

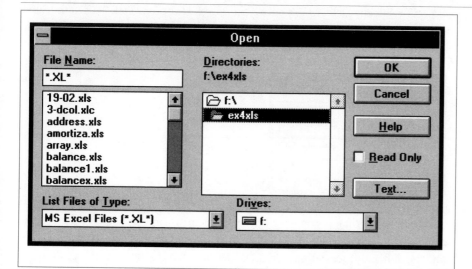

When saving, you can specify the format in the Save File as Type drop-down list box in the Save As dialog box. Try to use the normal Excel format as much as possible, since it makes saving and loading faster—and saves more information about your spreadsheet. When exchanging worksheets with nonlisted environments (such as Multiplan), try to use the SYLK format. This will save as much of the formulas and formats as possible. You'll generally save the most information if you use a direct translation—if you have that option.

CLEARING A CELL OR CELL RANGE

You can clear or delete any cell or cell range. *Clearing* removes the contents, format, and notes of a cell or cell range without removing the cell itself. This is done with the Clear command on the Edit menu or by pressing the Del key. *Deleting* physically removes the cell or cell range from the worksheet. Rows and columns are adjusted as necessary to recover the space. Deleting is done only with the Delete command on the Edit menu.

The simplest way to clear a cell or cell range is to select the cells and press Ctrl-Del. This will clear the cells (data and formulas) without so much as a query.

NOTE NOTE *For information on replacing a cell value instead of clearing it, see "Editing a Cell Value" later in this chapter.*

For selective clearing, choose the range and press Del. This is the same as choosing Clear from the Edit menu. The Clear dialog box shown below appears.

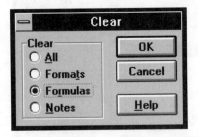

The Clear dialog box has options for clearing only formulas, formats, and notes Clearing a format puts the cell(s) in the default *General* picture (text aligned left, numbers aligned right). Clearing formulas clears the data in the cell(s), but not the format. Clearing notes clears any notes associated with the cell(s) (see "Adding a Note to a Cell" in Chapter 9). Choosing All clears the format, data, and notes. Click OK and the cell or cell range will be cleared.

You can try this now with your Balance worksheet. Select cells C13 to E13. Open the Edit menu and choose Clear. Click OK. The cells will clear. You also will notice that two totals in row 26 change, as you have just deleted data that were used to compute these totals. Before going on to anything else, open the Edit menu and choose Undo Clear (undoing is discussed next).

To clear an entire worksheet, select the entire worksheet by clicking the box above the row designators and pressing Ctrl-Del. This won't clear formats and notes, however. Use Edit ➤ Clear to clear these.

UNDOING AN EDIT

If you make a mistake while you're changing a worksheet, you can recover the previous version with the Undo command. The Undo command applies to most types of operations: inserting, deleting, moving, copying, pasting, formatting, etc. However, only the last operation can be undone—once you have gone on to something else, the undo capability is lost. Each time you open the Edit menu the Undo command will be shown highlighted, if available, and the function that you can undo will be the second word (such as **Undo Delete** or **Undo Paste**). You can press Ctrl-Z as a shortcut.

You saw how this worked just above, where you undid the clearing of cells C13 to E13. Now move row 13 to row 14 and undo the operation:

1. Select A13 to E13.

2. Open the Edit menu and choose Cut.

3. Select A14.

4. Open the Edit menu and choose Paste. Row 13 has now moved to row 14.

5. Open the Edit menu and choose Undo Paste (or press Ctrl-Z). Row 14 is now moved back to row 13.

You can undo the Undo command as well, restoring what you had inserted, deleted, moved, copied, pasted, formatted, etc. In that case, the Edit menu shows **Redo Delete**, **Redo Paste**, etc.

REPEATING A COMMAND

Sometimes you may wish to repeat a command that you have used. Rather than reselect the command and make perhaps several selections in a dialog box again, simply choose Repeat from the Edit menu or press Alt-Enter. For example, you may be formatting multiple ranges to the same format. Select the first range and format it. Then select each additional range and press Alt-Enter.

EDITING A CELL VALUE

To edit a cell, first select it (make it active). The current value will appear in the formula bar. You can edit cell values that appear there in three ways: by reentering the entire value, editing the current contents, or copying something into the value from another cell.

If the entry is long, your best approach is generally to edit the current value. For shorter entries, you may save time by simply retyping the entire value.

To reenter an entire value, simply type the new data into the formula bar and press Enter or click the Enter box. The new data will replace the old. Try this now with cell B10 of your BALANCE worksheet. Select the cell. The current value (**35700**) is displayed in the formula bar. Reenter the same value. After you type the first number, the formula bar clears and you will see a **3**.

To edit the current contents, move the cursor into the formula bar and click at any point on the value. (Notice that the cursor changes to an I-beam.) As you type characters from the keyboard they will be inserted at the insertion point's position. You also can press the Backspace key to remove characters before the insertion point and press Delete to remove characters to the right.

Another way to delete characters is to click anywhere in the formula bar and drag the cursor over the characters you wish to delete. Then open the Edit menu and choose Cut. The Cut, Copy, and Paste commands work with characters in the formula bar in the same way that they work in any word processor. You also can drag the mouse over a few characters and then reenter new characters over them.

To enter a value from another cell, select the source cells and choose Edit ➤ Copy. Then select the destination cell and choose Edit ➤ Paste. An even quicker way is to make the source cell active, hold down the Ctrl key, and drag the value.

EDITING A FORMULA

You can edit a formula that appears in the formula bar in the same way that you edit cell values; that is, by reentering the entire formula or editing the current formula. Copying and pasting from a cell that contains the correct entry is another way to edit a cell. If a formula is wrong, for example, it is often easier to copy the correct formula to the cell from another cell where it is already correct than to edit the formula bar or reenter the entire formula from scratch. The addressing mode is important here (relative or absolute). See Chapter 8.

Whenever the formula bar is active, you can click the cell you want to include in a formula instead of typing its address from the keyboard. To use this technique, first click the cursor in the formula bar where you want the reference to be inserted, then click on the cell in the worksheet. Add operators from the keyboard.

INSERTING AND DELETING ROWS AND COLUMNS

When you are creating a worksheet, you may find that you need to add or delete rows and columns. With Excel, this is as easy as two clicks. For example, you can add a blank row between rows 12 and 13. Since new rows are always inserted *above* the selected row, you need to select row 13. Select any cell in that row, open the Edit menu, and choose Insert. In the Insert dialog box, choose Entire Row to insert a row. Choose OK. Excel will create a new row 13 and move the old row 13 and all rows below it down one row, as shown in Figure 5.2. Formulas throughout the worksheet are adjusted for the moved data.

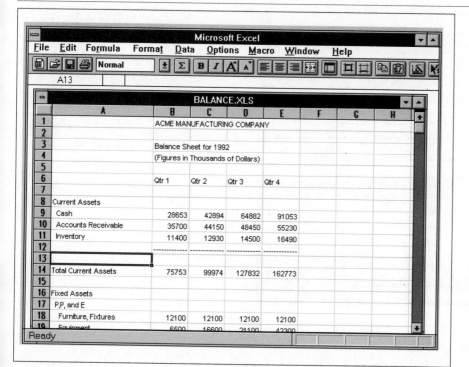

FIGURE 5.2:

The worksheet with an inserted row 13. The old row 13 and all rows below it have been moved down one row.

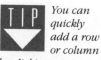

You can quickly add a row or column by clicking any row or column designator and choosing Insert from the Edit menu.

You can use the same procedure to add a column by choosing Entire Column in the Insert dialog box. The column is then inserted to the left of the selected column.

To delete a row, use the Delete command on the Edit menu. Delete the row you just added. Select any cell in row 13, open the Edit menu, and choose Delete. Choose Entire Row in the dialog box and click OK. The rows will move up and the worksheet will be as it was before. You also can select the row designator and choose Delete from the Edit menu to delete a row without going through the dialog box. This works for columns as well.

You also can insert or delete portions of columns or rows. To do this, select a cell or cell range. Then choose Insert or Delete on the Edit menu. The dialog box will ask whether other cells or rows should be shifted right or down to adjust for the insertion, or left and up for the deletion (see Figure 5.3). Choose the appropriate response and click OK.

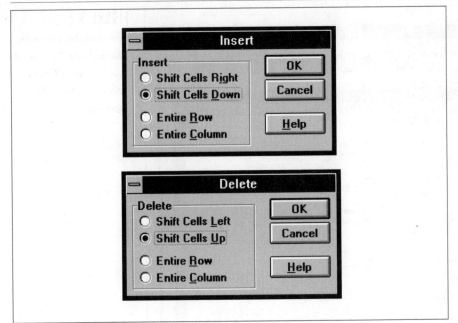

Depending on whether you insert or delete portions of columns or rows, you'll be asked to have Excel shift cells up, down, left, or right to adjust for the change

Try this with your Balance worksheet:

1. Select cells A17 through E19.

2. Open the Edit menu and choose Delete.

3. When the dialog box appears, choose Shift Cells Up (if it's not already selected) and click OK.

4. The cells will be shifted and several error messages (#REF!) will appear on your worksheet. (Can you guess why?)

5. To recover the deleted cells, open the Edit menu and choose Undo Delete. The deleted cells will reappear and error messages will disappear.

If you delete a cell or range of cells on which the values of other cells depend (because they are based on a formula that uses the deleted cell), the dependent cells will display #REF!. This shows that the cell's formula references a cell that has been deleted. You will then need to correct the formula. You can see how this works by deleting row 21 from the Balance worksheet. Because the values in what will be rows 23 and 25 after the deletion depend on the values that were in row 21, you will see #REF! in rows 23 and 25, as shown in Figure 5.4. Now restore row 21 by opening the Edit menu and choosing Undo Delete.

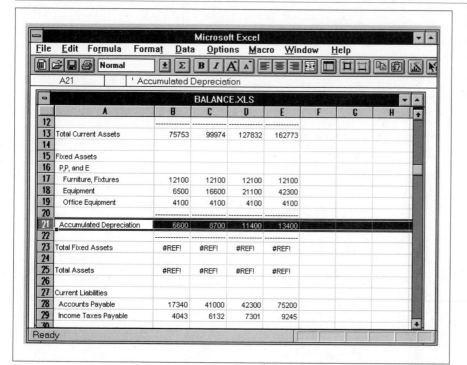

FIGURE 5.4:

Deleting cells on which other cells depend causes the dependent cells to display "#REF!"

Now try one more experiment. Add a new column before the first column. Notice that the new column is in the standard width. The former column A becomes B and remains wide. Now delete the column A that you added.

If you like, experiment some more with some of the techniques you've learned in this chapter, before reading on. Try inserting and deleting more rows and columns, and editing cell entries (formulas and values). When you are through, however, either save the worksheet under a different name (using the Save As command under the File menu) or close the document window without saving the changes you've made since you loaded it earlier (using the Close command under the File menu, or by double-clicking the document window's Control box). It's important that the BALANCE worksheet be preserved as it was at the end of Chapter 4 for working on it Chapter 6.

FAST TRACK CHAPTER 6

CHAPTER 6

Creating High-Impact Worksheets

The appearance of a worksheet is very important in communicating its conclusions effectively. In this chapter, you will learn how to control the appearance of your worksheets.

There are three things that Excel knows about each cell in a worksheet: its value (whether a constant or variable formula), its formatting information, and any assigned notes. The formatting information, which determines the appearance of a cell's display, includes the following:

◆ how numbers are to be displayed (the cell's picture)

◆ the alignment of the cell's display (left, center, or right)

◆ the font used in the cell's display; this includes the font family (Arial, Times Roman, Courier, and so on) as well as style (regular, boldface, underline, strikeout, or italics) and size

◆ the borders, patterns, and colors used for the cells

You can also add objects to a worksheet: lines, arrows, rectangles, text boxes, and more. In addition, you can check the spelling, add sound, control the display of the worksheet's grid lines, and turn the row and column designators off or on.

Formatting is important for three reasons:

◆ It makes a presentation-quality document.

◆ It makes the worksheet easier to read and understand.

◆ It emphasizes the conclusions you wish to portray so they stand out from the rest of the worksheet.

Excel offers you extensive formatting control, so you can exercise your creativity in setting up your worksheets.

FORMATTING YOUR WORKSHEET

Formatting defines the appearance of a cell or range. As you would expect, you will find most of the formatting commands on the Format menu. The other commands are either in the Display or Page Setup dialog boxes. The rule is simple: aspects of formatting that apply to a cell or cell range are on the Format menu, those that apply to the entire display of the worksheet are in the Display dialog box (select Options ➤ Display), and those that apply to the entire printed worksheet are in the Page Setup dialog box (select File ➤ Page Setup). There is an exception to this: if you use the Display command to change the worksheet to display *formulas* instead of formula *results* or zero values, you will print these when you select File ➤ Print.

Let's first look at formatting cells or cell ranges. Here is the general procedure: select the cell or cell range to format, open the Format menu, and choose the desired command. The three basic format controls are the *picture* (number), *alignment*, and *font* (font family, size, and style).

You can define the format before or after a cell entry. If you define a format before making a cell entry, there will be no visible indication, of course, until a cell value or formula is entered. Once you format a cell, the format remains the same even if you change the value or formula in the cell. The format will change only if you select a new format.

To clear a format (i.e., return it to its default setting) without erasing the cell value, open the Edit menu and select Clear. Choose Formats in the dialog box and click OK. To erase the values from a cell or cell range without changing the format, however, choose Formulas in the dialog box instead. To clear both content and format, choose All.

The format of a cell is copied with its value when you copy, fill, or use the Series command. Take advantage of this fact by formatting the source cell before you copy it.

UNDERSTANDING AND DEFINING CELL PICTURES

Pictures are the format codes you have for displaying numbers, dates, or times in your worksheet. For example, the picture **0.00** indicates that the value is to be displayed with two places to the right of the decimal. If necessary, the number is rounded off for the display. This does not affect the way the number is stored in the computer's memory, however.

Excel includes 27 predefined pictures for cell display: the general format (default), 12 for numeric and currency displays, and 10 for dates and times, and 5 other for fractions and scientific work. In addition, you can define custom pictures. Custom pictures are useful for worksheets that involve special values, such as foreign currency, social security numbers, or telephone numbers.

Plan your worksheet ahead and format before data entry as much as possible. Format by range to save formatting time. Because numeric pictures do not affect text cells, you can often apply a single numeric picture for a whole worksheet.

You can change the default format by creating a template with the formats you wish to use. You also can use the Style box on the toolbar to select quick formats for a range of cells.

Predefined Pictures

Excel's predefined pictures give you the following choices:

◆ how many digits appear to the right of the decimal

◆ whether commas are used in numbers

◆ whether a dollar sign appears

◆ whether a percent sign is used

◆ whether dates and times appear with hyphens, dashes, or colons

In the default mode (when you first start Excel), Excel displays all cells using the *General picture*. The General picture shows all numbers as precisely as possible. In other words, if you enter **123,** the cell will display 123; if you enter **123.23,** the cell will display 123.23. If a number with a General picture is too large for the current column width, Excel will display the number in exponential notation. For example, the default cell width is 8.5 characters. If you enter **100000000,** a nine-digit number, the cell will display 1E+08.

Now let's format a worksheet. Open the BALANCE worksheet you created in Chapter 4 (and played with, but didn't permanently alter, in Chapter 5). Choose a predefined picture for a cell or range of cells:

1. Select B9, press F5, and type **E42**. Hold down the Shift key and press Enter. This selects the range B9 to E42.

2. Open the Format menu and choose Number, or click the range with the right mouse button and select Number on the shortcut menu.

3. The Number Format dialog box appears. The highlight will be on General, as that is the default format. Select Currency from Category. Choose the first currency format (Figure 6.1). If need be, you can click the scroll arrows, drag the scroll box, or use the direction keys to see the picture code you need.

4. Click OK and the cell or cell range will be formatted according to the picture that you selected.

Now try a little experiment. Although B14 has no data in it, the cell has been formatted. Enter some data and press Enter. The number is displayed in the new format. Clear the cell before continuing.

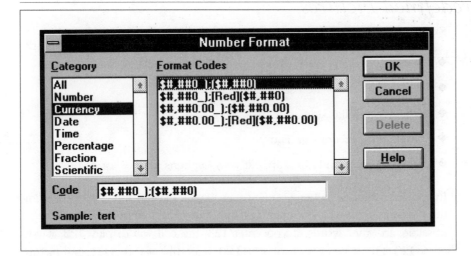

FIGURE 6.1:

Here you select a picture for a range of cells, in this case one that is for currency values

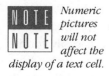 *Numeric pictures will not affect the display of a text cell.*

Here are some examples of how the predefined pictures can be used to format a particular display:

ENTRY	PICTURE	DISPLAY
123	0.00	123.00
123.67	0	124
123	$#,##0.00	$123.00
.1534	0.00%	15.34%

Most of the pictures are self-explanatory. The only confusing one is perhaps the percentage picture, which multiplies the entered value by 100; that is, if you enter **.1534** for a picture of **0.00%**, it will be displayed as **15.34%**.

Excel also contains two pictures for displaying fractions: **# ?/?** and **# ??/??**. The first allows only single-digit numerators and denominators; the second allows double-digit ones as well. For example, if you were to enter **0.53** in a cell that was formatted as **# ?/?**, the cell would read ¹/₂; but if it were formatted as **# ??/??**, it would read ⁴⁴/₈₃, a more accurate approximation of 0.53.

Defining a New Picture

Instead of using a predefined picture, you can create your own. For example, if you need to enter social security numbers, you can define a picture that automatically puts in the dashes. Other uses for custom pictures include telephone numbers and foreign currencies. You can even create a picture that uses text (such as **lbs**).

As an example, you can set up a picture that puts **No.** in front of any number entered into a cell. Follow these steps:

1. Select a blank cell or cell range on the screen, such as C14.

2. Open the Format menu and choose Number. Clear the text box at the bottom of the dialog box.

3. In the text box, enter **"No."** **####** (include the quotation marks). Then choose OK.

Enter a few numbers to the cell and see what happens. Remember that only the cell that you selected has been formatted.

Now that you have defined this new picture for the BALANCE worksheet, it will appear as one of your choices in the Number Format dialog box that is displayed when this worksheet is active. You can easily format other cells using the new picture by simply selecting it from the dialog box. However, the new picture that you define for *this* particular worksheet will not be available for another worksheet unless you either enter it into the Number Format dialog box when you're formatting that worksheet or make it part of a template.

You can use an asterisk in a picture to define a repeating character, following it with a character that you want to be repeated as often as necessary to fill the blank space in the cell. For example, the picture ##,##0.00*@ would display $123.23 as 123.23@@, with the @ symbol filling the rest of the cell. This is useful for printing a check in which the entire check-amount box must be filled.

Table 6.1 lists the symbols that you can use for creating your own pictures. You also can create new pictures from existing ones. When the dialog box is displayed, the current picture is shown in the code text box. You can click in it and edit the format as you wish. When you choose OK, the cell or range will be formatted to the new picture. The new picture will be added to the end of the picture list as well, for use later on. For example, you could add a new fraction format by highlighting # ??/?? and editing it to show # ???/???. (In that case, 0.53 would be formatted in the cell as 53/100.)

To delete a custom picture, highlight it and click Delete in the Number Format dialog box. You cannot delete a predefined picture.

If you examine the pictures in the Format Codes list box, you will see that some of them consist of multiple pictures that are separated by a semicolon, such as:

$#,##0.00~US);($#,##0.00)

These are *conditional pictures:* the first picture ($#,##0.00_)) is used for positive numbers and the second for negative numbers (see Table 6.1). You also can create conditional custom pictures. The first _) forces Excel to skip the width of a parenthesis so that positive numbers align with negative numbers.

SYMBOL	MEANING
0	Picture for a single digit. If the entry has fewer digits on either side of the decimal point than the picture does, Excel displays the extra zeros. If the entry has more digits to the right of the decimal than the picture does, Excel rounds the entry to the number of places in the picture. If the entry has more digits to the left of the decimal than the picture does, the extra digits are displayed. **Example:** Picture: 0.0; Entry: *.8*; Displayed: **0.8**
#	Picture for a single digit. Follows the rules for 0 above, except extra zeros are not displayed to the right and left of the decimal. **Example:** Picture #.#; Entry: *.8*; Displayed: **.8**
.	Decimal point. Use in conjunction with either the 0 or # symbol
%	Multiply by 100 and add a percent sign
,	Thousands separator. Thousands are separated by commas if this is included in the picture surrounded by #s or 0s. A comma following a # or 0 scales the number by a thousand; two commas by a million
E−, E+, e−, e+	Scientific format notation
?	Same rules as for 0, except that spaces are inserted for insignificant zeros so that decimals align
:, $, −, +, (,), /, *space*	Display the character. To display a character not shown here, precede it with a backslash (\)
@	Text placeholder. Text entered in the cell is placed in the format wherever the @ appears. Example: Picture: @+@; Entry: *text*; Displayed: **text+text**
_ (underline)	Skip width of next character; used with a parenthesis: for example, to skip the width of a parenthesis to force decimal alignment when negative numbers are in parentheses
*	Repeat next character to fill column width
m, mm, mmm, mmmm	Display the month in the following formats: m = numeric, no leading zeros; mm = numeric with leading zeros; mmm = 3-letter abbreviated name; mmmm = full month name

SYMBOL	MEANING
d, dd, ddd, dddd	Display the day in the following formats: d = numeric, no leading zeros; dd = numeric with leading zeros; ddd = abbreviated day of week; dddd = day of week
yy, yyyy	Display the year with two or four digits
h, hh	Display the hour without leading zeros
m, mm	Display minutes without leading zeros (must be after hours)
s, ss	Display seconds without leading zeros (must be after minutes)
AM/PM, A/P	Display hour using 12-hour clock with AM or PM
"*text*"	Displays *text*
[*color*]	Displays all contents in *color* (black, blue, cyan, etc.)

TABLE 6.1:

Symbols Used For Creating Pictures (continued)

NOTES:

1. Two pictures can be entered for a cell separated by a semicolon(s). With one semicolon, the first applies to positive numbers and the second to negative. If you use two semicolons, the third picture will be applied to numbers equal to zero.

2. If you do not want negative numbers displayed, enter the format for positive numbers followed by a semicolon without a second format following. If you do not want nonpositive numbers displayed, use two semicolons without a second or third format following. If you don't want any zeros displayed, use two semicolons with two formats following.

Another way to format cells is to use a shortcut command. Here are the keys for the common formats:

PICTURE	KEYSTROKE
General	Ctrl-Shift-'
#,##0.00	Ctrl-Shift-1
h:mm AM/PM	Ctrl-Shift-2
d–mmm–yy	Ctrl-Shift-3

PICTURE	KEYSTROKE
$#,##0.00_); ($#,##0.00)	Ctrl-Shift-4
0%	Ctrl-Shift-5
0.00E+00	Ctrl-Shift-6

Select the cell or cell range and enter the keystroke to format it instantly.

You can also put special symbols in your worksheet by holding down the Alt key in numeric mode (pressing the Num Lock key) and typing the ANSI code for the symbol to enter. For example, use Alt-0163 for the British pound (£), Alt-0174 for a registered trademark symbol (®), and Alt-0169 for a copyright symbol (©). You can even use these symbols in custom number formats.

DEFINING THE ALIGNMENT IN A CELL

Alignment refers to the position of the value in a cell. Excel offers you a choice of seven alignments:

General left-justifies text and right-justifies numbers.

Left left-justifies all entries (numbers, dates, and text).

Right right-justifies all entries.

Center centers each entry.

Fill repeats the entry until the cell is filled.

Justify justifies wrapped text.

Center across Selection centers the text over the selected columns.

When you first start Excel, all cells are set to General alignment. To change the alignment of text or numbers, first select the cell or cell range that you want to realign, open the Format menu and choose Alignment. The dialog box shown in Figure 6.2 appears. Choose the alignment that you want and click OK.

In the default mode, if a long text string doesn't fit in the cell's width, the cell will show only a small portion of the text if the cells to the right (when the text is left-justified) or left (when right-justified) are in use. If you select Wrap Text in the Alignment dialog box, however, the entire text string

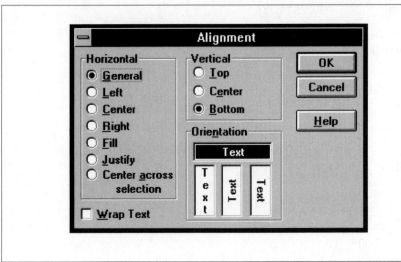

FIGURE 6.2:

*In this dialog box
you can choose the
alignment of cell
entries, both
horizontally and
vertically*

will be displayed: it will be wrapped over adjacent lines to fit in the cell. If the row height is not enough for the additional lines, double-click the line below the row heading to adjust the row height automatically for the new text.

The Justify option is available only for wrapped text. It doesn't work with numeric cell values. Extend the row height as necessary to accommodate the new text.

You can also use the Justify command on the Format menu to combine text from several cells to fit evenly within a range of cells. If the text is larger than the specified range, Excel will ask whether it should extend the range and overlap any cells containing data.

*To center
text quickly,
select the
range and
click the Center Align
tool on the toolbar.*

To enter a line break in a cell with several wrapped lines, press Alt-Enter. To insert a tab, press Ctrl-Tab.

Now center the information at the top of your BALANCE worksheet:

1. Select cells A1 through E6 by dragging.

2. Open the Format menu and choose Alignment (or click the range with the right mouse button and select Alignment from the pop-up menu).

3. Choose Center and click OK.

All the text in the selected cell range is now centered.

To align row headings (text) with the data below them (numbers), keep the numbers right-aligned and realign the text. If necessary, insert spaces for column alignment.

When you choose Center across Selection as an alignment, the text is centered over all the selected columns except the first, which is normally used for row headings. If you need to edit this later, you will find it a little tricky, as the text "owns" all the cells it is centered over. You must first select Edit ➤ Clear to clear cells that are no longer part of the range. For example, selecting B1 to B6 centers the text in the range B2:B6. To center the text over B1 to B3, you must first select Edit ➤ Clear B4:B6.

CHOOSING FONTS

The term *font* refers to four aspects of the cell display: family, size, style, and color. The first is the actual design of the characters. Typical family names include Helvetica, Times Roman, Prestige, and Courier. The second aspect, size, is the actual height of the characters measured in points. An inch is 72 points. Courier is often printed in 12 points and Prestige in 10 points. The third aspect is the style, which determines whether the character is displayed as normal, **boldfaced**, or in *italics*. Color is obviously the color of the text.

Fonts for Printing and Displaying

Which families, sizes, and styles are available depends on what fonts you have installed. Windows supports raster, vector, and scalable fonts. The fonts that are available depend on Windows, not Excel.

Raster fonts are bit-mapped fonts of a fixed size. Both printer and screen fonts must be installed for a given size in order for the font to work properly. For example, if you have a cartridge font for a laser printer (raster), you should install a software version of the same font to Windows as a display font. If you have printer software fonts installed for a laser printer, these will be stored on the computer and downloaded as necessary. The Fonts utility in the Windows Control Panel is used to install these soft fonts, but you must install them for both the printer and monitor. Windows 3.1 includes a few raster fonts, MS Serif and MS Sans Serif.

Vector fonts are stored as lines, polygons, and other mathematical entities. They can be resized as necessary. Windows includes a few vector fonts, such as Modern.

Scalable fonts are stored as outlines, and the computer creates the display and printer versions for a specific size as needed. Because of the quality of these fonts and the small disk space needed to store them, you should try to do all of your worksheets using scalable fonts.

If using Windows 3.0, you can use PostScript Type 1 scalable fonts with a PostScript printer. Optionally, you can purchase the Adobe Type Manager

Try to use high-quality scalable fonts for all of your work, such as the TrueType fonts. Avoid the Windows raster fonts (such as MS Sans Serif) and vector fonts.

(ATM) and use PostScript Type 1 fonts with a laser printer. ATM converts the PostScript font to a raster font at print time. Other companies also make font managers and fonts, but they are not compatible with each other. Most of these will also work with Windows 3.1.

If using Windows 3.1, you can use the existing commercial font managers or the Windows internal TrueType scalable font manager. Windows includes some sample TrueType fonts with it, and you can use the Fonts utility in the Control Panel to install others.

Changing the Font

Cells or cell ranges can be displayed in any installed font if it is available to your printer. To change the font, select the cell or cell range that you want to display in the different font. Open the Format menu and choose Font. The Font dialog box shown in Figure 6.3 appears. Choose the desired font, style, size, and color. An example of the highlighted font appears in the Sample box. Clicking the Normal Font check box sets the range to the default font. To change the default font, see "Using Styles" later in the chapter. When you've made your selection, click OK.

Choose Repeat Font under the Edit menu (Alt-Enter) to repeat a font setting in another cell or range, or select Undo Font under the Edit menu (or Ctrl-Z) to reverse a font selection. Save font settings as styles and select them from the toolbar or the Style option under the Format menu (see "Using Styles").

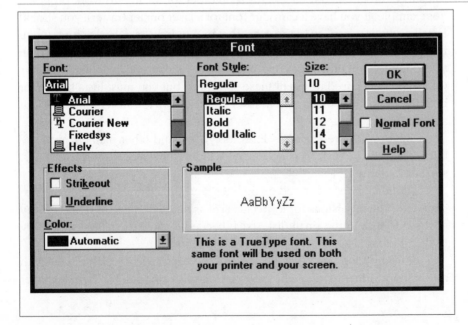

FIGURE 6.3:

You use this dialog box to determine the font, font style, size, effects, and color

Changing a Font on Your Worksheet

Now you can change the fonts on part of your BALANCE worksheet. The title should be in boldface, as well as the Total Assets and Total Liabilities & Equity rows. Follow these steps:

1. Select cell A1 to E42.

2. Open the Format menu and choose Font.

3. Select Arial (or Helv) and size 8. Then click OK.

4. Select B1 and click the Increase font tool on the toolbar four times to increase the size to 12 points. Click the Bold tool once.

5. Select B3 and B4.

6. Click the Increase font tool twice to increase the size to 10 points.

7. Select A26 to E26. Press Shift-F8 to select multiple ranges. (The Add indicator appears in the status area.) Click A42 to E42. Press Shift-F8 again to turn off the indicator. Both rows are now highlighted.

8. Click the Bold tool in the toolbar.

 When formatting, remember that the format information requires memory space. Instead of formatting an entire row, from column A to IV, format only the cells in use.

After the formatting, the totals in row 42 may overflow (depending on your monitor). If they do, change the column width to 10 by selecting columns B to E, opening the Format menu, choosing Column Width, and entering **10**. Choose OK.

The Total Assets line on your BALANCE worksheet now stand out from the rest of the entries, as shown in Figure 6.4.

DEFINING THE ROW HEIGHT

Excel defaults to an automatic row height that is slightly more than the height of the largest font used on the line. You can change the row height by selecting the row and using the Row Height command on the Format menu.

When the standard height is selected in the Row Height dialog box, changing the size of your text will automatically change the row height to accommodate the new font size. For example, if you type a worksheet title in a 16-point font, the cell height will increase accordingly to accommodate it. Row heights are not adjusted automatically for cells containing wrapped text, however.

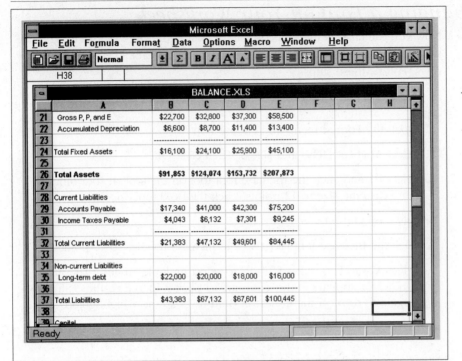

FIGURE 6.4:
The line showing total assets is now boldfaced to make it stand out from the rest of the numbers

Set the row heights to give the worksheet a good appearance. For example, adjusting the row height is useful for adding white space between rows when improving the image of the worksheet. Try this on the Balance worksheet:

1. Select row 5.

2. Choose Row Height from the Format dialog box, shown below.

3. Type in **16** as the new height (16 points) and click OK.

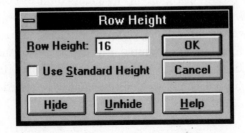

You can also adjust the row height by dragging the row separators under the row designators. When dragging, you can see the new row height in the active-cell designator. You can also reset the row height directly by double-clicking the line under the row designator. You can set multiple rows at a time by selecting a group of rows and then selecting Format ➤ Row Height.

Now use the Edit ➤ Undo command to restore the normal row height, as later we will put some graphics in this area.

ADDING BORDERS

Borders are useful for dividing your worksheet into areas to draw attention to specific cell ranges. You also can use them to create tables, calendars, and forms. To add a border, first turn off the grid lines using the Display command on the Options menu, as described in "Displaying Grid Lines" later in the chapter. (If the grid lines are not turned off, you may have a hard time seeing the borders on the display.) Next, select the cell or range of cells that you want to border. Open the Format menu and choose Border. When the Border dialog box shown below appears, select one or more options, then click OK.

Notice that you can select which edges of the range to border, the style, and the color. You also can choose to shade the cell range.

Excel offers these choices for borders:

Outline outlines the entire range with a border.

Left draws a vertical line at the left of each cell.

Right draws a vertical line at the right of each cell.

Top draws a horizontal line at the top of each cell.

Bottom draws a horizontal line at the bottom of each cell.

Shade shades every cell in the range.

Style sets the style for the border line.

Color sets the color of the border.

You can choose one or more of these border options for the selected cells. The added borders appear on both the screen display and the printed worksheet. By using a combination of styles and borders, you can emphasize any value on your worksheet. Figure 4.1 in Chapter 4 shows how bordering can be used effectively.

Now you can put the borders shown in Figure 4.1 on your BALANCE worksheet (be sure that the grid lines are turned off, or you may not be able to see them):

1. Select cell A8.

2. Open the Formula menu and choose Goto (or press F5). Enter **E42** into the Reference text box. Hold down the Shift key and choose OK. You have selected cells A8 through E42.

3. Open the Format menu and choose Border. In the dialog box, choose Outline. Notice you can also select the style of the border. For now, leave the default style selected. Click OK.

4. Select cells A26 to E26 and put a border around them using Outline and Shade. (Some checkboxes in the Border dialog box will be shaded now before you check them. This indicates that some cells in the range already have some type of border.)

5. In the same way, put a border around cells A42 to E42 using Outline and Shade using Edit ➤ Repeat Border.

6. Select the range B8 to E42 and put a border around it using Left (but no Shade).

Your worksheet should now show borders and shading. To create a double underline under a row, select the double-underline style from the Border dialog box. If you use the Color option on the Border dialog box you can define an outline color for presentations or color printers. Use one of the Style options to define the pattern or style of the border.

USING COLOR AND PATTERNS

You can add patterns to a worksheet to emphasize certain points or to improve its appearance. If the worksheet is for an on-screen presentation, or if you have a color printer, you should also set the background and foreground colors of ranges. The pattern and color of a range is set using the Patterns command in the Format menu.

With the Border command, you can shade a bordered range. With the Patterns command, however, you can set the fill pattern and colors or any selected range.

For tabular data, use the Patterns command to simulate the effect of green-bar computer paper. Use a light gray background for every other row to make the printout easier to read.

Try some patterns now with your worksheet. First, save the worksheet to preserve the state it's currently in. Then select a range on the worksheet and choose Patterns from the Format menu. Set the background and foreground colors, as well as the pattern to any desired values, in the dialog box shown below. Click OK. Later choose Undo or Clear from the Edit menu to restore the worksheet.

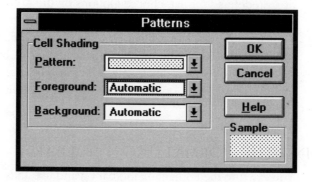

AUTOFORMATTING

You can speed your formatting work up by using the autoformatting feature of Excel or by using the toolbar.

To use the autoformatting command from the menu, select the range to format and choose AutoFormat on the Format menu. This will display the dialog box shown below, from which you can choose to apply a predefined format.

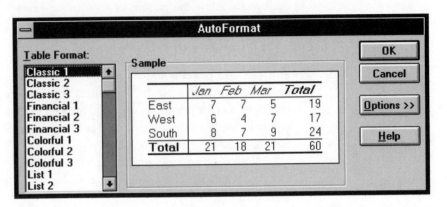

Choose the desired format. If you wish, you can select a range on the worksheet and try a few of these. Be sure to save the worksheet first, then choose Edit ➤ Undo AutoFormat to clear the format after each experiment.

You can selectively choose to apply the picture, borders, font, pattern, alignment, column width, or row height of a predefined format. To apply part of a predefined format, choose Options on the AutoFormat dialog box. Select the categories for which you wish to apply the format and click OK.

If an outline exists when you apply autoformatting, Excel will use that outline to determine the header information (see Chapter 9).

The toolbar is a quick way of autoformatting. Clicking the AutoFormat tool on the standard toolbar applies the first predefined format to the selected range.

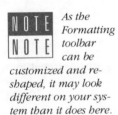

You can-not auto-format a single cell or nonadjacent selections.

Using the Formatting Toolbar

As the Formatting toolbar can be customized and re-shaped, it may look different on your system than it does here.

You can turn the Formatting toolbar on and use it instead of the Format menu. To turn the Formatting toolbar on, select Toolbars from the Options menu, select Formatting in the list box, and click on Show. The Formatting toolbar will then be displayed in a small window (Figure 6.5). You can move the tool-bar by dragging its title bar. You can resize the window to a certain degree by dragging the sides. You can close or hide it by clicking its Control box or by selecting Options ➤ Toolbars again, selecting Formatting in the list box, and clicking on Hide. (Notice that there is no Control menu.)

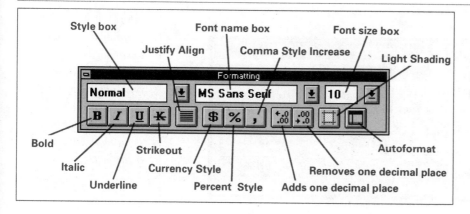

FIGURE 6.5:

The Formatting toolbar consists of many tools to help you format a document

To use the toolbar, select the range to format and apply the command by clicking the correct button in the toolbar.

USING STYLES

Excel provides another option for quickly setting the *styles,* a collection of attributes with a defined name. Each style has six attributes: picture, font, border, pattern, alignment, and protection. Once you have defined a style, it's easy to use: simply click it from the Style box in the toolbar or choose Style from the Format menu. All six attributes of the style are then applied to any cell or range selected. Excel has six default styles.

Styles are attached to worksheets. You can, however, save styles in templates or copy them from one worksheet to another.

DEFINING A STYLE

You can create additional styles, if you wish, by any of three methods: by example from an existing cell, by defining it with the Style command, or by copying it from another worksheet.

To define a style by example, first make active the cell that contains the style attributes you wish to use. If you have a mouse and are using the toolbar, move the cursor to the Style box and enter the name you wish to assign to the style. An alternative after selecting the cell is to choose Style from the Format menu and enter the name to assign to the style (see Figure 6.6). It will now appear on the drop-down list box for use with other cells.

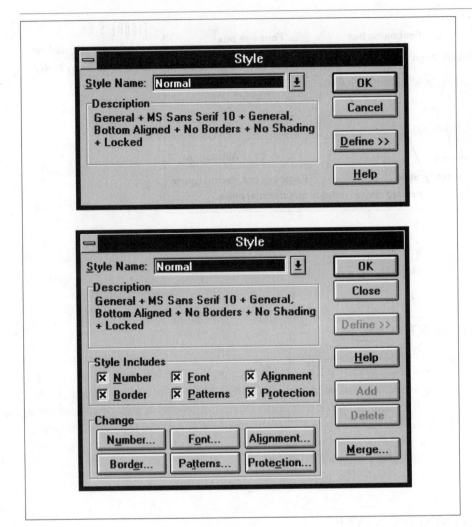

FIGURE 6.6:

*Defining a style: the
top dialog box is for
naming a style that
currently exists in the
active cell. The bottom
dialog box is for further
defining the style in the
active cell.*

To create a style by definition, select the cell to format and choose Style
from the Format menu. Then click the Define button in the dialog box. In the
expanded Style dialog box (see Figure 6.6), enter the name for the style. You
also will see six buttons at the bottom, one for each attribute: number (picture), font, alignment, border, patterns, and protection (cell protection is
covered in Chapter 14). Choose from any of these buttons to open the appropriate dialog box to define that attribute. Define each attribute as you wish
and click OK to close the dialog box. If you are adding several styles, keep
the dialog box open by clicking Add after defining each one.

To copy a style from one document to another, first open both documents and make the destination document active. Choose Style under the Format menu. Click on Define in the first dialog box and then click on Merge in the next. From the displayed list box, select the source document name. Choose OK, then Close.

EDITING A STYLE

You can edit a style by example or by definition. To edit by example, select the cell with the new format and reapply the style name at the toolbar by clicking the arrow next to the Style box and choosing the style to edit. In the prompt box, answer Yes. To edit by definition, select the Style command, choose Define in the dialog box, and edit the appropriate attribute. Choose OK.

DISPLAYING WORKSHEET FEATURES

The Display command under the Options menu is used to display gridlines, column and row designators, formulas, zero values, outline symbols, page breaks, and objects.

DISPLAYING GRIDLINES

On the worksheet, cells are separated by vertical and horizontal gridlines. However, you may want to turn these off to see how a worksheet looks without them. If the gridlines are already off, you can use this method to turn them back on.

To toggle the gridlines display:

1. Open the Options menu and choose Display. The Display Options dialog box shown in Figure 6.7 appears.

2. Select Cell Gridlines to remove the × in the box next to it, then click OK. Placing an × in the box will turn them on.

The Gridlines option is a toggle that switches the gridline display on and off. (If there is an × next to it, the option is on; if not, it is off.) However, even if you toggle the Gridlines option off, the gridlines will still be printed. This dialog box controls only the *screen display* of the gridlines, not the printed display.

To print a worksheet without gridlines, you have to use the Page Setup command on the File menu. Follow these steps:

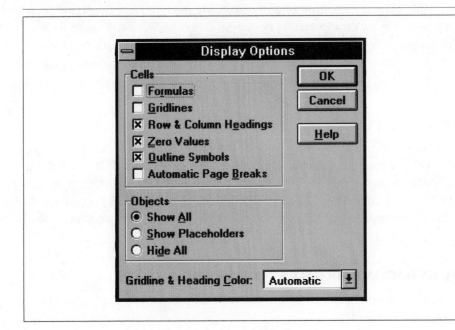

FIGURE 6.7:

The Display Options dialog box allows you to select the elements of the worksheet you want (or do not want) to display on-screen

1. Open the File menu and choose Page Setup.

2. The Page Setup dialog box shown in Figure 6.8 appears. Click on Cell Gridlines in the middle of the dialog box to remove the × in the checkbox next to that option, if it is there (it isn't by default).

3. Click OK.

Gridlines may still appear on the screen while you work with the worksheet (depending on whether you turned them on as detailed above), but they will not show on the printed copy.

DISPLAYING DESIGNATORS

At the top of each column of the worksheet is a column designator—A, B, C, and so on to IV. At the left edge are the row designators, numbered from 1 to 16,384. As with the gridlines, you can turn these off so that they don't appear on the worksheet on-screen. To do so:

1. Open the Options menu and choose Display.

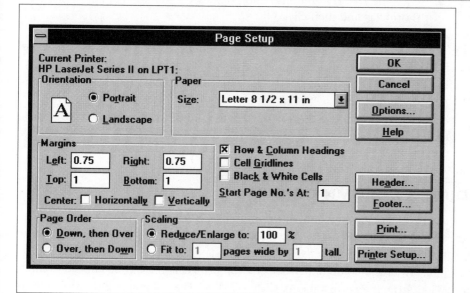

Here the Page Setup dialog box allows you to not show cell gridlines on the printed version of the worksheet

2. When the Display Options dialog box appears (see Figure 6.7), choose Row & Column Headings (another toggle) and click OK.

This removes the × in the box next to that option. Remember, the Display Options dialog box options control only the screen display, not the printed output.

To eliminate the designators from the printed worksheet, you must use the Page Setup command on the File menu. Follow these steps:

1. Open the File menu and choose Page Setup.

2. When the Page Setup dialog box appears (see Figure 6.8), choose Row & Column Headings. This removes the × in the box next to that option. Click OK.

Row and column headings may still be displayed on the screen, but you won't see them on the printed worksheet.

DISPLAYING FORMULAS

To toggle the formula display, press Ctrl-'.

There may be times when you need to see the formulas associated with a particular worksheet. To display formulas:

1. Open the Options menu and choose Display.

2. When the Display Options dialog box (see Figure 6.7) appears, choose Formulas and then click OK.

The screen display will then show the formulas. Each column will now be twice as wide as it was in your normal display to permit room for the formulas. You can switch the display off by repeating this operation. If the formulas appear on-screen, they will print out as well.

You can also use this dialog box to control the display of zero values, outline symbols, automatic page breaks, and objects.

HIDING A COLUMN OR ROW

There may be times when you want to hide a column or row on a worksheet so that it is not displayed or printed. This reduces visual clutter and can hide temporary work-area cells.

To hide a column, first select it (or just a cell in it). Then choose Column Width from the Format menu. Click on Hide. The column will disappear from the worksheet. To recover a column, position the cursor in the column header near the hidden column so that you get the column-width cursor (two vertical lines). Drag the hidden column out, then use Format ➤ Column Width if you wish to set the column to a specific width.

To hide a row, follow the same procedure as above, but choose the Row Height command under the Format menu. Click the Hide button. To recover a row, position the cursor in the row header near the hidden row so that you get the row-width cursor (two horizontal lines). Drag the hidden row out, then use Format ➤ Row Height if you wish to set the row to a specific height.

WORKING WITH GRAPHIC OBJECTS

If you have a mouse, you can add graphic objects to a worksheet or macro sheet to improve its appearance, and create graphic documents such as calendars, forms, and organization charts. Use the underlying cells as a grid for your work.

CREATING OBJECTS

The basic strategy for creating graphic objects is to define the object to be created using the Drawing toolbar, draw it on the worksheet, edit it, and format it. Let's add a text box for the title of the BALANCE worksheet and put it in a shadow box.

First, display the Drawing toolbar by selecting Toolbars from the Options menu. Click on Drawing in the list box and click the Show button. Figure 6.9 shows the resulting toolbar. Drag the toolbar (by its title bar) away from the title area. As it can be resized, reshaped, and customized, yours may look somewhat different from the one shown here. You can resize the window by dragging the edges. Clicking the Control box will close or hide the window. You can also hide it by selecting Options ➤ Toolbars again. For now, leave it displayed.

1. Delete the current title by clearing B1 to B4. Be sure the gridlines are on. Insert two lines at the beginning of the worksheet, putting the column headers in row 8.

2. Create a text box by clicking the Textbox tool in the toolbar. Then click the cursor near the upper-left corner of cell B1 and drag it to the lower-right corner of cell E6 to draw the text box.

3. Move the box to center it over columns A to E. Be sure the box is selected. To select an object, move the tip of the arrow pointer over the object and click it. When an object is selected it has *handles* on it, which are small black rectangles attached to a frame. The object identifier is also displayed in the active-cell designator.

4. Click the border (not a handle) and drag the box so the left edge is halfway into column A (see Figure 6.10).

5. Create the title text by placing the cursor near the upper left of the box. Press Enter (to make a space at the top) and type the first title line (see Figure 6.11). Press Enter twice, then enter the next two title lines.

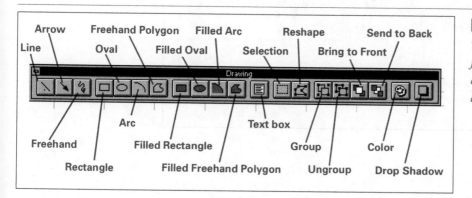

FIGURE 6.9:

The Drawing toolbar features many tools for drawing objects in documents

6. Click and drag the cursor to highlight all three lines, then select the Center Alignment button from the standard toolbar. Highlight the first line and select the Bold button from the main toolbar.

7. Select and format the text box in turn using the Format Font menu or toolbar. Set the title to Arial (Sans Serif or Helv), 12 point, bold. It will wrap to two lines. Set the other text to Arial and 10 point.

8. Add the shadow: select the box and click the Shadow tool or choose Patterns from the Format menu and then choose Shadow.

9. Delete the hyphens in B43 to E43.

You now have the title in a text box (Figure 6.12).

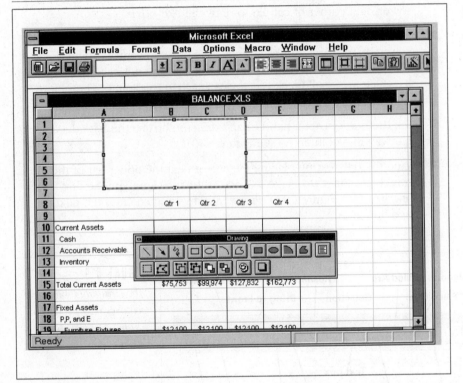

FIGURE 6.10:

Positioning the text box

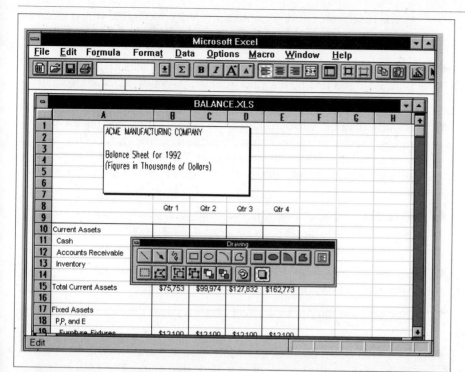

FIGURE 6.11:

The title box before formatting

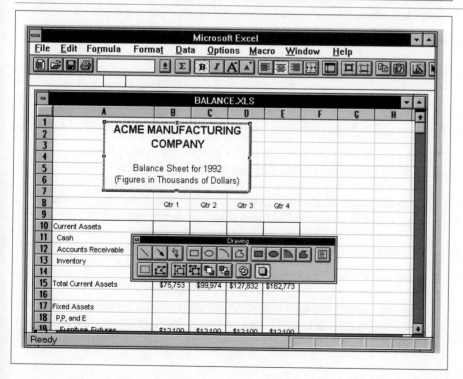

FIGURE 6.12:

The final title box

As you have seen, creating graphics involves selecting the Object tool from the toolbar and creating the object on the worksheet. Here are the basic rules:

◆ Select the tool. You can choose from lines, rectangles, ovals, arcs, polygons, and text boxes. Choose the tool you wish to use from the Drawing toolbar and move the cursor to the worksheet.

◆ Click and drag the cursor to create the object. When you release the mouse button, the graphic is marked with handles for moving and sizing, and the mouse pointer changes. The toolbar icon returns to normal. At the end of Chapter 18, you will find an example using an ellipse.

◆ To create multiple objects with the same tool, double-click the tool to select it. To cancel, click the tool again, click another tool, press Esc, or click another part of the worksheet without dragging.

◆ To align a graphic object with the gridlines, hold down the Alt key as you draw, move, or resize an object.

◆ When you use the Arc tool, Excel draws a curve that is a quarter of an oval.

◆ If you hold down the Shift key while drawing, lines will be restricted to being vertical, horizontal, or at a 45-degree angle. The Oval button will make circles and the Rectangle button will make squares.

◆ You can create complex objects by combining simple ones. Select the set of objects by holding down the Shift key as you select. Then choose Group from the Format menu. You can resize or move the objects as a group. To release a group, highlight it and choose Ungroup from the Format menu.

◆ You can hide the Drawing toolbar again by clicking its Control box.

◆ You can import graphic objects for pasting using the Clipboard. Copy an object to the Clipboard from another program and paste it into the worksheet. You can use the Paste Special or Paste Link commands, found in the Edit menu, to paste objects. With these commands, the object remains linked to the supporting document and changes when editing it (see Chapter 16). You can also use the Paste Special command to embed objects. For more information on this see Chapter 21.

◆ You can cancel a task at any time by pressing Esc.

The Reshape tools permits you to change the shape of a polygon. If a polygon is selected, you can click on this tool and then drag any handle of the polygon to reshape it.

EDITING OBJECTS

To edit an object, first select it. To select multiple objects, hold down the Shift key and select the objects. Another way to select multiple objects is to use the Selection tool. Click the tool, then draw a rectangle that completely encloses all the objects you wish to select. To select all objects in the worksheet, choose Select Special from the Formula menu, choose Objects, and click OK.

The following menu commands can be used after selecting an object:

◆ To change the order of objects so that you can work with covered objects, use the Bring to Front or Send to Back commands on the Format menu.

◆ To group objects into one super-object, select each object by holding down the Ctrl key and clicking each object, and use the Group command in the Format menu. To release all the objects in a group, select the group and choose Ungroup from the Format menu.

◆ To deselect an object from a collection of selected objects, hold down the Ctrl key and click the object.

◆ To move an object (or group), place the pointer on the object so that it is an arrow. Then drag the object to the new position. To move it horizontally or vertically, hold down the Shift key while dragging.

◆ To copy an object (or group), hold down the Ctrl key and drag the object. To copy horizontally or vertically, hold down the Ctrl and Shift keys as you drag. To align an object to a grid as you copy, hold down the Alt and Ctrl keys while dragging.

◆ To resize an object (or group), drag a handle. The cursor must be a pointer. To keep the object proportional, hold down the Shift key while dragging. To align with a grid, hold down the Alt key while dragging.

◆ Use the Edit menu to cut or copy a graphic, even to most other programs, especially other Windows programs.

◆ You can change the pattern of a selected object with the Patterns command on the Format menu. You can also format the object (including fill and foreground colors). You can also add arrowheads to lines or shadows to boxes.

◆ You can lock an object with the Object Protection command so that it cannot be selected, moved, resized, or formatted. To complete the protection, you must choose Options ➤ Protect Document, select Objects, and then enter a password.

◆ You can speed up your worksheet work by hiding objects or only
showing placeholders. To hide an object, use the Display command
in the Options menu and select Hide All, or use Ctrl-6 as a shortcut.
Ctrl-6 toggles among Show Objects, Show Placeholders, and Hide All.

DELETING OBJECTS

To delete an object, select the object and use the Cut command in the Edit
menu (Ctrl-X), which places it on the Clipboard. Another method is to use
the Del key.

CHECKING THE SPELLING

Before printing the worksheet or using it in a presentation, it's a good idea to
check the spelling. Excel will check the entire worksheet, including text
boxes, embedded charts, and buttons.

To check the spelling of the entire worksheet, select any single cell. Then
choose Spelling from the Options menu. Excel initiates a spell check, stopping on the first word that is not in its dictionary and offering an alternative
(Figure 6.13). You can then:

◆ Click Change to accept the new spelling in the Change To box and
continue.

◆ Choose the correct word in the list and click Change to accept another
suggested word.

◆ Click Ignore to ignore the word and make no changes.

◆ Type the correct spelling in the Change To box and choose Change.

Excel continues, and if the selected cell was not the first in the worksheet, Excel
will query at the end of the document if you wish to continue from the first cell.

To check the spelling of a range, select the range and choose Spelling
from the Options menu. To check the spelling of a single word, it must be in
the formula bar, a text box, or a button assigned to a macro. Select the word
and choose Options ➤ Spelling. Click on Change to accept the new spelling.

Choosing Change All in the dialog box changes all occurrences of the
selected word in the worksheet to the new spelling.

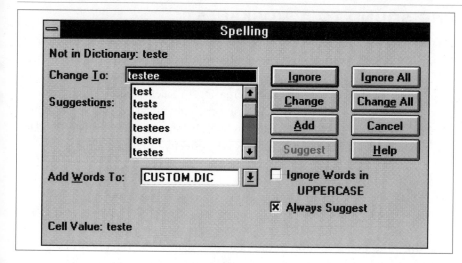

You can also create custom dictionaries with Excel. To add a word to a custom dictionary, enter the dictionary name in the Add Words To box and then choose Add.

If you need to spell-check frequently, customize a toolbar and add the Spelling tool to it. In the default installation, the tool will be on the Utility toolbar.

THE FINAL BALANCE WORKSHEET

If you followed along with the examples in this chapter, you have done the following with your BALANCE worksheet:

◆ Put the first lines of the title in a shadowed text box

◆ Centered all column headings

◆ Put rows 28 and 44 in boldface

◆ Turned off the gridlines and row and column designators in the printout

◆ Added borders, shading cells in rows 28 and 44

Complete each of these if necessary. Your final printout should look like Figure 4.2.

ADDING SOUND TO A WORKSHEET

If you have an audio card that supports the Windows multimedia extensions (MPC-specified), you can use the multimedia extensions in Windows 3.1 to add sound to a cell. For example, you might have a worksheet which shows that your company's widgets are increasing in sales while the competitors widgets are not doing so well. Clicking on a cell containing your data could create the sound of hand clapping, while clicking on the competitor's data creates an "Uh-Oh." This can create a very effective presentation.

To add a soundbite to a cell, follow these steps:

1. Select the cell to which you wish to attach the sound note.

2. Choose Note from the Formula menu.

3. Click the Import button in the Cell Note dialog box (Figure 6.14).

4. Select a sound file from the list.

5. Click on OK, then click on OK again.

The cell is marked to indicated it has a sound. Double-clicking the cell should play the sound.

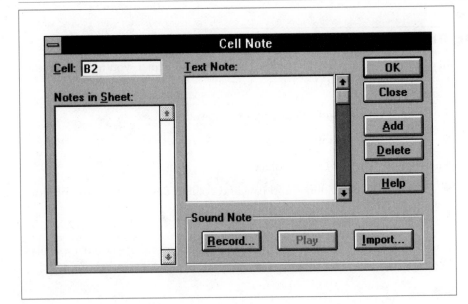

FIGURE 6.14:

Adding sound to a worksheet

You can also record your own sounds, such as a comment:

1. Select the cell for which you wish to record the note.

2. Choose Note from the Formula menu.

3. Click on Record. The dialog box shown below is displayed.

4. Click on Record. Click Pause to pause and Stop to end the recording.

5. To play the sound, click Play.

6. Click on OK.

You can copy a sound using the Copy and Paste commands in the Edit menu. You can erase a sound note by selecting Formula ➤ Note ➤ Erase. You can also add comments to a cell in several ways (see Chapter 9).

TIPS FOR CREATING A WORKSHEET

Chapter 4 contained some basic concepts for creating worksheets to improve their accuracy and improve your productivity. In this section let's look at some basic concepts for improving the impact and readability of a worksheet:

◆ Keep the worksheet as simple as possible. Eliminate or put on a separate linked worksheet data that are not essential to the conclusion.

◆ Use scalable fonts, such as TrueType.

◆ Remember how the worksheet will be used. Presentation worksheets are generally very simple with large font sizes. Color and perhaps sound can be used. If printed, the worksheet can be more complex, but you are generally limited to black and white. Patterns and font style variations can be used to draw attention to conclusions.

◆ Spell check the document before printing or presenting it!

◆ Use white space liberally to improve the worksheet's appearance.

◆ Be sure the worksheet is properly titled and dated.

◆ Use graphics—logos, arrows, clipart, and other graphic features—to make the worksheet more interesting.

FAST TRACK CHAPTER 7

Load the worksheets you want to group and make the data-input worksheet active. Select Options ➤ Group Edit and click OK. Select Window ➤ Arrange, then enable Documents of Active Group to see all the worksheets in the group.

Choose File ➤ New, select Workbook, and click OK. Use the Add button to add documents to the workbook. Use the Remove button the remove them. Drag documents to or from the workbook or move them with the Cut and Copy commands. To save a workbook, select File ➤ Save Workbook. Close the workbook from the workbook's Control menu.

- Click on the small black bar at the left end of the horizontal scroll bar and drag to the right to split the window vertically in two.
- Click on the small black bar at the top of the vertical scroll bar and drag downward to split the window horizontally in two.
- To automatically split cells, click in the cell that will be the upper-left cell of the split window. This is normally the cell under the first column heading and to the right of the first row heading. Then choose Window ➤ Split.

Choose Window ➤ Remove Split.

CHAPTER 7

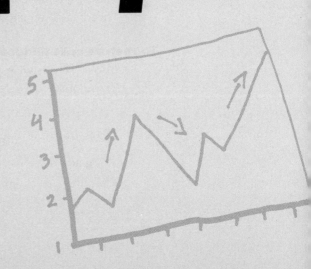

Managing Documents and Windows

Worksheet documents are always displayed in a window. With Excel, you can have several windows displayed simultaneously. Because you create and edit all documents in their respective windows, learning how to control windows is an important part of managing your worksheets.

In this chapter, you will learn some special Excel file and window-management techniques. You will learn more about:

◆ opening, closing, renaming, and deleting document files

◆ setting up groups

◆ setting up workspaces

◆ using automatic startup files

◆ protecting document files

◆ switching between windows

◆ opening additional windows in the same document

◆ creating panes in a window for entering data into large worksheets

♦ tiling windows

♦ hiding windows

♦ customizing window colors

♦ creating custom views

Besides worksheets, windows display almost any type of Excel data: charts, databases, templates—even macros. The basic window-management commands apply to any type of Excel document. You can scroll a window using the scroll bars, move a window by dragging its title bar, and resize a window by dragging the edges or corners of the window. Experiment with some existing worksheets for the next few sections.

MANAGING DOCUMENTS

While you are working with Excel, you will need to open, close, and delete documents. Worksheets, templates, charts, and macro sheets are saved as document files.

OPENING DOCUMENT FILES

To create a new document, click the New Worksheet tool in the toolbar or open the File menu and choose New. If you use the menu, the New dialog box shown below will appear.

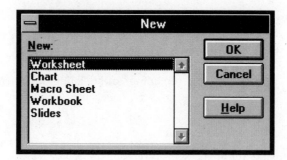

As this figure shows, Worksheet is already selected as the type of document. To create a new worksheet, choose OK. If you use the toolbar, there will be no dialog box and a new worksheet will be immediately opened.

Excel displays a blank worksheet titled "Sheet1." (If this title has been used since starting Excel, the new document will be called "Sheet2," "Sheet3," etc.)

The following keyboard shortcuts can be used when creating a new document:

DOCUMENT TYPE	SHORTCUT
Worksheet	Shift-F11
Chart	F11
Macro sheet	Ctrl-F11

To open a document that you have already created and stored on disk, use any one of these methods:

◆ Choose Open from the File menu.

◆ Press Ctrl-F12.

◆ Click the Open File button on the toolbar.

The dialog box shown in Figure 7.1 will appear. The left list box shows the names of the documents currently on the directory. If you highlight one of these, its name will be shown in the text box under **File Name**. You can use the scroll bar to list additional documents in the same directory. The name of the current disk and directory is just to the right of the text box.

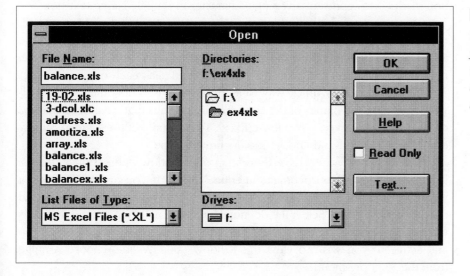

FIGURE 7.1:

This dialog box allows you to open an existing worksheet in any directory or disk drive, and in many formats

If the desired document name is displayed, you can complete the command either by double-clicking the document name or by highlighting the name in the File Name list box and clicking OK. This list box always displays the files in the directory selected at right that match the wildcard specification in the List Files of Type drop-down list box.

If the document name is not in the current directory, you must switch to the correct disk drive and directory:

◆ To change the drive, choose the corresponding drive letter in the Drives drop-down list box.

◆ To change the directory, double-click the corresponding subdirectory name in the Directories list box. You can move up or down the tree by double-clicking in this list box. For example, double-clicking the open file folder for the root directory of F will show all the subdirectories under it.

Notice that you can use the List Files of Type drop-down list box or wildcard file names in the File Name text box to control the file list display. The default text box contains *.XL*, which limits the display to Excel document files (worksheets, charts, macro sheets, templates, and workbooks). To load a foreign file (Lotus 1-2-3, dBASE IV, etc.), simply change the type so that the foreign file can be listed. Then select it above and click OK. Excel will load that file and convert it to its own native format (see Chapter 21). For wildcard selections, use an asterisk (*) to represent any group of characters and a question mark (?) to represent any single character in the File Name text box.

You can open multiple files at a time by selecting all the files you wish to open. To select consecutively listed files, highlight the first, hold down the Shift key, and highlight the last. (All files in between will be selected.) To select nonconsecutive files, hold down the Ctrl key and click each one separately.

There is another quick way to load recently-used documents. Excel always maintains the names of the latest four documents that have been opened on the File menu, even if you leave Excel. To open any of these again, simply open the File menu and choose the document name.

Excel allows you to have more than one window open at once; that is, it supports a multiple document interface (MDI). If you are working on a worksheet and need to open another document, open the File menu and choose New or Open. Select the document and you will then see the windows for both documents on the screen. The latest window loaded will be on top and active. If you wish to view the windows side-by-side, choose Arrange from the Window menu.

SAVING AND CLOSING DOCUMENT FILES

Saving a document means saving it on disk. *Closing* a document refers to removing it from the computer screen and memory. When you are finished working with an Excel document, you should close it. Before closing it, however, you may wish to save it so you can use it again. Whenever you close a document that has been changed, Excel will ask whether you wish to save the changes.

Saving Documents

To save a document under the displayed name at the top of the document without exiting Excel:

◆ Open the File menu and choose Save. The window will remain active. This method is useful for saving the worksheet periodically as you work on it.

◆ Press Alt-Shift-F2 (or Shift-F12). This is the same as using Save.

◆ Click the Save File tool in the toolbar.

You can close Excel from the Control box or by pressing Alt-F4. In either case, if any document's edits have not been saved, you will be prompted for saving those documents.

Use any of these methods if you wish to save the document under a *new* name:

◆ Open the File menu and choose Save As. You will see a dialog box with the current worksheet name, as shown in Figure 7.2. Enter the name you wish to assign to the document. Be sure that the directory assignment shown below the name area is correct. Change disks or directory if necessary. Then click OK. When you create a document, this is the dialog box that appears when you save it for the first time.

◆ Press Alt-F2 (or just F12). Enter the name you wish to assign to the document. Be sure that the directory assignment is correct. Then click OK.

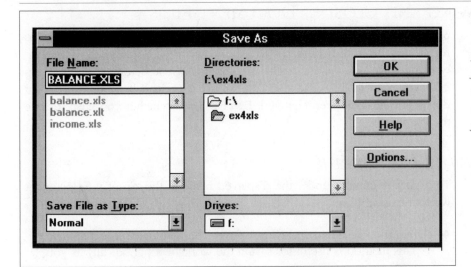

FIGURE 7.2:

The dialog box allows you to save a document file under any name, in any directory or disk drive, and in many formats

Closing Documents

To close a document and remain in Excel, use any of these methods:

◆ Double-click the *document's* Control box (not the Control box of Excel).

◆ Press Ctrl-F4.

◆ Open the Control box of the document and choose Close.

If the document has been changed in any way since you opened it, Excel will ask whether you wish to save the changes.

You can have several documents open at a time, closing them when you are through. When you close the last document you do not automatically exit Excel. After closing the last window, a short menu bar is displayed with only the File and Help options available. You can use the commands on the File menu to open or create another document. This method is useful if you have finished working with one document (or a batch of documents) and you wish to work on another.

Saving All Documents and Exiting

To save all documents under their current names and exit Excel, use any of these methods:

◆ Double-click the Excel Control box.

◆ Press Alt-F4.

◆ Open the Excel Control box and choose Close.

◆ Open the File menu and choose Exit.

Before Excel closes, you will be asked to save any files that have been modified since they were last saved.

Saving in Other Formats

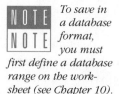

To save in a database format, you must first define a database range on the work-sheet (see Chapter 10).

You also can save a document under other formats for use with other spread-sheet and database managements programs (see Chapter 21 for more details on this). To save in another format, use the Save File as Type drop-down list box in the Save As dialog box (Figure 7.2). Select the desired format, and the File Name box will change to show the correct extension. Click OK to save the document.

RENAMING DOCUMENT FILES

Unfortunately, there is no way in Excel to directly change the name of a document that you have already saved. To rename a document, you must first close it. Then either exit Excel or minimize Excel to an icon. Then use the Windows File Manager to rename the document.

If you ac-cidentally delete the wrong file, use a Windows-based unerase utility to recover the file. If you exit Windows to recover the file in DOS, Windows may write over the file with its own files upon exiting.

If you inadvertently save a document under a wrong or misspelled name, there is another way to rename it that is quicker than going to the File Manager. Use the Save As command under the File menu to save the document under the correct name. Then use the Delete command on the File menu to delete the old document with the incorrect name (see below).

DELETING DOCUMENT FILES

To delete a document from the disk, open the File menu and choose Delete. You will then see the Delete Document dialog box shown in Figure 7.3. Select the document that you wish to delete, and click OK. A confirmation dialog box will appear, asking if you are sure you want to delete the file. Proceed

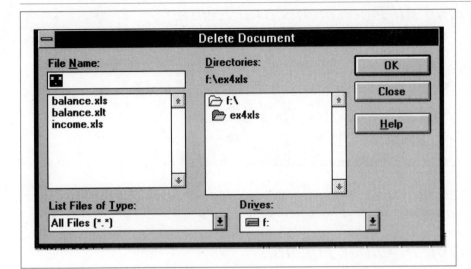

with caution, because you can't undo it once you confirm the deletion. In the default mode (no file name selected), it deletes all files on the current directory (*.*). It's a pretty dangerous command if used without paying attention.

USING GROUPS

There may be occasions when you wish to enter the same data or perform the same operation on a set of worksheets. Excel permits you to define the worksheets as a *group* and then use them as if they were a single worksheet.

For example, you might be setting up a group of year-end worksheets and using the same titles and headings for each. But you plan to format them differently and some details of each will differ. You could then create a group out of the worksheets, enter the common data, then release them as individual worksheets for more detailed entry.

To define a group, first load all the worksheets you plan to group. Make the worksheet active into which you wish to enter the data. Choose Group Edit from the Options menu. In the Group Edit dialog box, all worksheets currently loaded are selected (Figure 7.4). To add or delete a selection from the group, hold down the Ctrl key and click the name to toggle the highlight on and off. By default, all open worksheets are automatically selected. Click OK or press Enter.

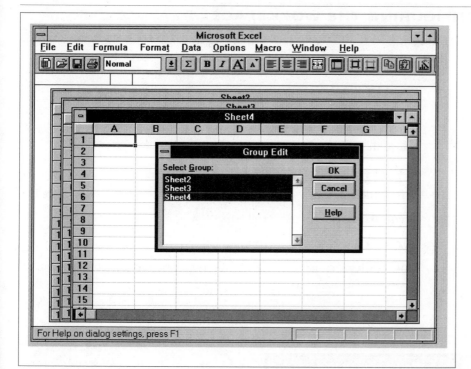

FIGURE 7.4:

Here you can see that Sheet2, Sheet3, and Sheet4 are loaded; they will be made into a group when OK is clicked

To see all worksheets in a group, choose Arrange from the Window menu, then check Documents of Active Group. Click OK. Only the group is displayed. The title bars indicate the group status of the workgroup.

You may want to leave a "deleted" file on-screen so you can group it later.

To add or delete a worksheet from a group, repeat the procedure with the Group Edit command again. You can select or deselect any file in the group. Whenever you delete or add another file to the group, you have to choose Window ➤ Arrange and check Documents of Active Group either to get rid of or make room for the image on-screen.

Now enter data to the active worksheet. The same data will be added *at the same place* to each worksheet in the group. If you perform any operation (such as formatting a range), it will be repeated on each worksheet in the group.

To cancel the group, select any worksheet other than the original by clicking it or from the Window menu.

CONFIGURING THE WORKSPACE

The workspace can be configured by choosing Workspace from the Options menu. This displays a dialog box (Figure 7.5), which has several available options:

Fixed Decimal determines the number of displayed decimal places in numbers that you enter.

R1C1 changes the way that rows and columns are labeled and cells are addressed (so **A1** becomes **R1C1**).

Status Bar displays the status bar.

Info Window displays a window with information on the selected cell.

Scroll Bars displays the scroll bars.

Formula Bar displays the formula bar.

Note Indicator displays a dot in the upper-right corner of cells that have notes attached to them.

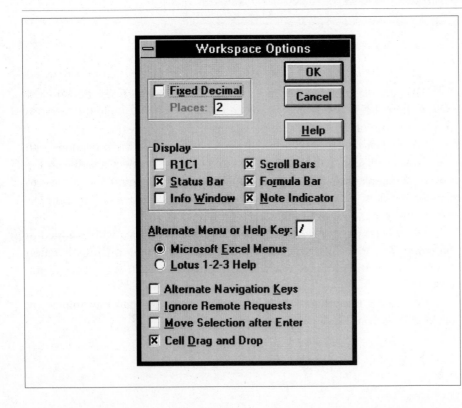

FIGURE 7.5:

This dialog box allows you to configure the workspace in several ways

Alternate Menu or Help Key specifies the key you have to type to activate the Excel menu bar or the Lotus 1-2-3 help system.

Alternate Navigation Keys provides an alternate set of keystrokes for navigating the spreadsheet.

Ignore Remote Requests controls the response to direct data exchange (DDE) requests (see Chapter 21).

Move Selection after Enter determines whether the cursor moves to the next cell down after you use the Enter key to enter a value in a cell.

Cell Drag and Drop enables you to toggle on or off the ability to move and copy a cell's contents by dragging.

When the desired options are set, click OK. The workspace settings are saved with Excel when you exit.

SETTING UP WORKBOOKS

Workbooks permit you to save a set of documents and options under a specified name. You can either store the workbook as *bound* (all worksheets and documents in a single file) or *unbound* (worksheets and other documents in separate files, with only a list in the workbook).

If you are working on several documents at a time, using a workbook is a good way to save the group as a unit and reload the entire set of documents. A workbook differs from a group in that all documents in the workbook are edited independently. You can define certain options (such as whether to have the toolbar or status bar on or off) and they will be saved with the workbook and restored to that setting when you restart it. You also can hide certain worksheets of the group, which will remain hidden when you load the workbook.

Here are some ways to use workbooks:

◆ When you are working with a set of documents (worksheets, charts, macro sheets) that support a given application and you wish to define them as a unit.

◆ For linking worksheets (see Chapter 16) so that you don't have to remember the linkages.

◆ When you wish to stop working temporarily on an application with several documents.

◆ As a startup document to set the starting worksheets and options for your particular configuration (windows, toolbars, display mode, calculation mode, etc.).

◆ To enable someone with no Excel experience to start Excel quickly and use it with a particular application. (This also could require some macros.)

◆ To improve security and file management by grouping like documents in a single "book" to transmit and secure.

To create a new workbook, choose New from the File menu. In the dialog box below, select Workbook. A new window is displayed, showing an empty workbook (Figure 7.6).

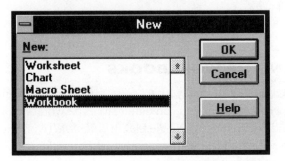

A document must be open to add it to the workbook. To add an open document to a workbook, click the Add button in the workbook window. In the Add to Workbook dialog box shown below, select the document (or documents) to add.

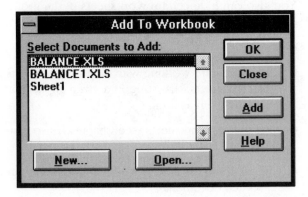

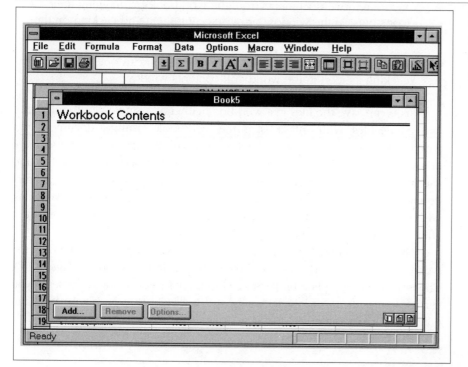

FIGURE 7.6:

*The workbook window
comes up when you
create a new workbook*

You can also add documents by dragging the selection square above the
row designators (and to the left of the column designators) of the worksheet
to the workbook window. To add a chart, select the chart and drag one of the
selection squares to the workbook window.

Here's what you can do with workbooks:

◆   Once a workbook is created, you can page between documents using
the paging buttons in the lower-right corner of the workbook window. These buttons remain as you switch between the various documents. Using the leftmost Contents button, you can return to the
workbook contents window.

◆   You can reorder documents in the workbook window by dragging
the icons around or by using the Cut and Paste commands from the
Edit menu.

◆   You can use multiple workbooks at the same time, dragging icons
between workbooks as necessary.

◆ You can remove documents from the workbook by dragging their icons outside the window or by selecting them and clicking on the Remove button in the window.

◆ If a document in the workbook is not open, you can open it by double-clicking its icon in the workbook contents window.

You can save the files in a workbook either as a single workbook file or as separate files, with only a list in the workbook. Listing a document in a workbook permits you to share it with other workbooks. Storing a document in a workbook, or *binding* it, permits you to keep related files together and use longer document names, and provides greater security. You can mix bound and unbound files in a single workbook, too. For example, you may wish to keep a macro sheet (described in Chapter 28) unbound and share it with other workbooks, while keeping other files bound.

To set a workbook file as bound or unbound, select the document in the workbook window and click the Options button in that window (Figure 7.7). Choose the desired option under Store Document In. For bound documents, you can use long names (i.e., longer than the standard eight-character DOS name) and enter them in the Document text box. Then click OK.

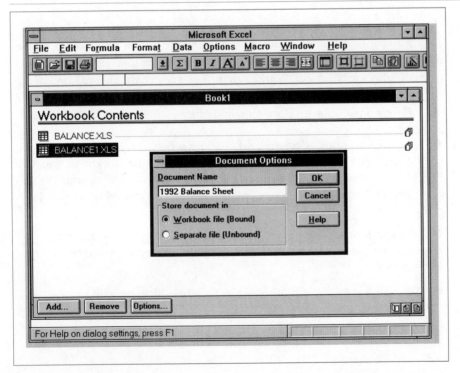

FIGURE 7.7:

Here you can define a document as bound or unbound, as well as give it a longer file name

To save a workbook, choose Save Workbook from the File menu. Enter the workbook name the first time you save it, choose the disk and directory, and click OK. Workbooks can be protected with passwords, as with other documents.

To restore a workbook, choose Open under the File menu. Choose the file name on the file list (with its .XLW extension) and click OK. All documents that were a part of the workbook will be opened.

You can set up workbooks to open automatically with Excel (see below) or use a macro to start a workbook.

USING TEMPLATES

A basic worksheet structure that has many uses is called a *template*. For example, you might have a worksheet form that you use each quarter for a report. It might contain titles, row headings, some formatted cells, and other common features that are used for each report. Figure 7.8 shows a template you could use for creating a balance sheet.

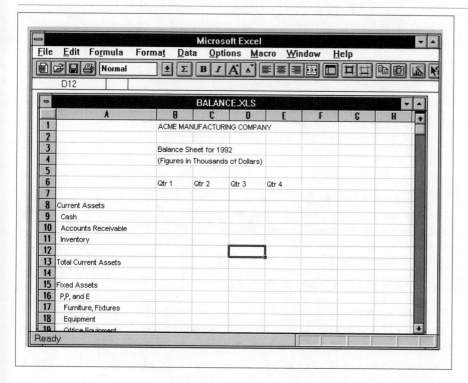

FIGURE 7.8:

A sample template, used to build multiple worksheets

A template offers several advantages:

◆ **It saves time.** You don't have to reenter text, data, and formats that are common to several worksheets.

◆ **It improves consistency.** By defining a set of templates for your company, you can ensure that your organization's worksheets have a consistent appearance.

◆ **It improves accuracy.** By reducing data entry, you improve accuracy. By using templates and macros to input new data to the basic worksheet, you enable users with a minimum of Excel experience to do productive work.

You might think that a template is a master worksheet that contains the starting formats and data, which is used each time as the beginning form and then saved under a different name thereafter. However, true templates give you an added degree of control and protection that simple "starting sheets" don't provide.

To create a template, you begin as if you were creating a worksheet:

1. Enter the basic data and formats, then choose Save As from the File menu.

2. In the Save File as Type drop-down list box, choose Template.

3. Determine the file name and destination directory and drive, if necessary.

4. Click OK. This saves the worksheet form as a template with an .XLT extension.

If you wish to edit the template, get to the Open dialog box, select the file, and hold down the Shift key while you choose OK. if you don't press the Shift key, the template will open as a normal worksheet.

To change a template into a standard worksheet, use Save As and change the selection in the Save File as Type drop-down list box to Normal.

USING STARTUP DOCUMENTS

Excel always opens with Sheet1. This can be modified to start with any document, set of documents, macro, template, or workbook. For example, a bank could write a very complex set of linked documents that are started automatically with Excel. A clerk at a branch office could then use the workbook with very little training, since it would start automatically with Excel and run itself from a macro, prompting as necessary when data needed to be entered.

Place startup documents in the startup directory called XLSTART (by default), a subdirectory of the Excel directory. For example, if you want the BALANCE worksheet to open automatically upon starting Excel, place BALANCE.XLS in the startup directory by copying it there with the File Manager.

You can create additional startup directories using the following procedure:

1. Choose Open from the File menu.

2. Open ALTSTART.XLA in the LIBRARY directory of the directory containing EXCEL.EXE.

3. Enter the additional startup directory you wish, without any file-name extension.

4. Click OK.

To delete a startup setup, move the documents from the startup directory or delete them altogether.

PROTECTING DOCUMENTS

Excel provides several alternatives for protecting documents from unauthorized access or editing. This prevents someone from using proprietary macros and formulas or editing important worksheets.

PREVENTING UNAUTHORIZED OPENING OR SAVING

Remember the password. If you forget it, you will never be able to open the document again!

To protect a document from unauthorized opening, save the document with a password:

1. Make the document active.

2. Choose Save As from the File menu.

3. Click the Options button in the dialog box.

4. In the Protection Password text box, enter a password. It will show up as asterisks:

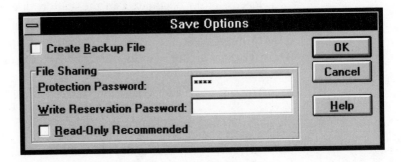

5. Click OK.

6. In the next dialog box, reenter the password to confirm it.

7. Click OK.

The document is now saved in protected form and can be opened only with the password. If a user tries to open the document, he or she will be prompted for the password.

If you later wish to remove this protection, use the Save As command again and click the Options button. Delete the asterisks from the Protection Password dialog box and click OK, then click OK again to close the first dialog box.

This security is not sufficient for many users, however. For maximum security, keep the document on a disk and remove it to a secure location when the documents are not in use. Don't save the documents to the hard disk. If the document has ever been saved to the hard disk, use a utility that "wipes" the hard disk upon file deletion, such as Norton Desktop for Windows.

PREVENTING UNAUTHORIZED EDITING

There may be times when you wish to make a document available to users without the need for a password, but you wish to protect against unauthorized editing of or changes to the document.

To protect against this situation:

1. Make the document active.

2. Choose Save As from the File menu.

3. Click the Options button to open the Options dialog box.

4. In the Write Reservation Password text box, enter a password (capitalization counts).

5. Click OK.

6. In the next dialog box, reenter the password to confirm it.

7. Click OK.

8. Click OK one more time to save.

To open the document, select it like any other from the Open dialog box. You will be prompted to enter a password or to open the file as read-only. Without the correct password, the user will not be able to open the file unless Read Only is checked.

You can cancel this protection by using the Save As command and deleting the asterisks from the Write Reservation Password text box in the Save Options dialog box.

There is another read-only mode that is sometimes useful on a network. It recommends to the user who has entered the password that the file should be opened on a read-only basis, unless changes need to be saved. To set this mode, click the Read-Only Recommended box in the Options dialog box described above.

If the backup option is toggled on, the original file will be kept as is, with the extension .BAK.

OTHER PROTECTION METHODS

You also can lock or hide individual cell or cell ranges, and protect graphic objects. This is discussed in Chapter 14.

MANAGING DOCUMENT WINDOWS

There may be times when you need to open more than one document window on your screen. Excel's multiple-window feature permits you to view two or more documents at once and to move data from one document to another. The other windows may show other documents or the *same* document, as described later in this section. (Linking worksheets in different windows is discussed in Chapter 16.)

The Clipboard commands under the Edit menu are still available when you have more than one window open, so you can easily move data and formulas between windows. Use the Copy and Paste or Cut and Paste commands, just as if you were working with a single window.

OPENING WINDOWS OF OTHER DOCUMENTS

Any time you are using one window and want to open a second document window, choose File ➤ Open, just as you did to open the first document. Select a document and choose OK. The new document will appear in a new active window. Only one window can be active at a time. You can change from one window to another simply by clicking anywhere on the window that you wish to make active. Another way to switch between windows is to open the Window menu and choose the name of the window that you want to make active. The Window menu always lists all open documents.

OPENING WINDOWS OF THE SAME DOCUMENT

There may be times when you need to open a second window of the same worksheet. Multiple windows are primarily useful with large worksheets in which one part of the worksheet is dependent on another. By looking at both parts at once, you can edit or change values in one part of the worksheet and immediately see the effect in the other window. This reduces the need to scroll through the worksheet excessively. Each window can be controlled independently by using the scroll bars on that window.

Try this now with your BALANCE worksheet:

 *The New Window command opens an additional window of the **same** worksheet. No new worksheet is created. Any change made in it affects the entire underlying worksheet.*

1. Open the BALANCE worksheet.

2. Make the window smaller (see Figure 7.9) by dragging the right edge of the window.

3. Open the Window menu and choose New Window.

4. When the new window opens, make it smaller, too, as shown in Figure 7.10.

Notice that the new window is titled BALANCE.XLS:2 and your original window has become BALANCE.XLS:1. You now have two windows of the same worksheet. If you scroll one window, the other remains stationary.

If you have more than one document open on-screen and you choose New Window, Excel will create a new window of the worksheet that is currently active.

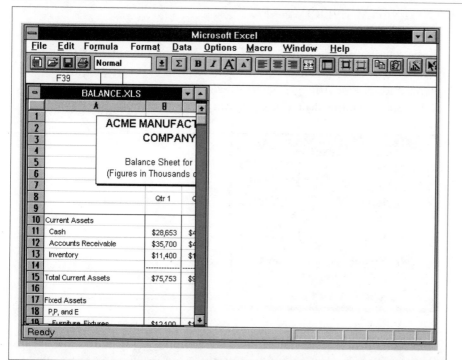

First Make the BALANCE window smaller

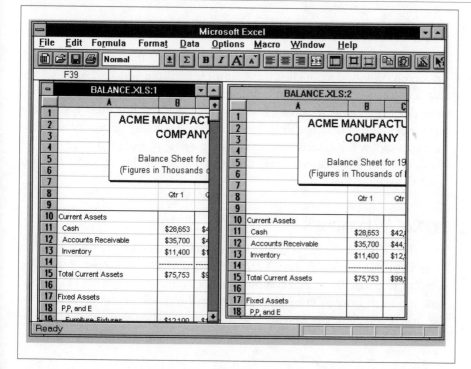

Next, open another window of the same document and size it next to the first

ARRANGING WINDOWS

Multiple windows are viewed like sheets of paper on a desk, with the most recent window on top. Often you may prefer to *tile* the windows, that is, put the windows side-by-side on the screen. To tile windows, open the Window menu and choose Arrange. Select Tiled in the Arrange box and click OK. Notice that from this dialog box you can choose other arrangements:

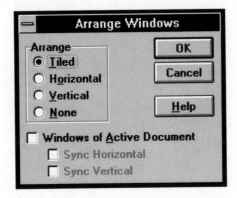

As an exercise, tile the two BALANCE worksheet windows that are displayed. Notice that only the active window has scroll bars.

CLOSING WINDOWS

To close a window when more than one window of the same document is on-screen, simply double-click the Control box of the window. This deletes that window and renumbers the remaining windows. Closing an extra window does not cause the loss of any worksheet data, nor does it save the worksheet. The underlying worksheet remains in memory. If you try to delete the last window for a document, Excel will assume you wish to close the file; if you've made any changes, it will display a dialog box that asks whether you want to save the file.

SPLITTING WINDOWS

In the next two sections, you will learn some strategies for working with a large worksheet. For instance, look at the BALANCE worksheet. Resize the window horizontally so that column E is not visible (see Figure 7.11). Notice how hard it is now to enter data and check formulas. Entering the data for the first few columns is easy, but what happens when you try to enter the data in the last columns? As Figure 7.12 shows, you no longer see the row numbers. What happens when you enter the last part of the data for any particular column? You will not be able to see the column headings. If the worksheet is very large with many rows and columns, you can quickly become lost in the worksheet.

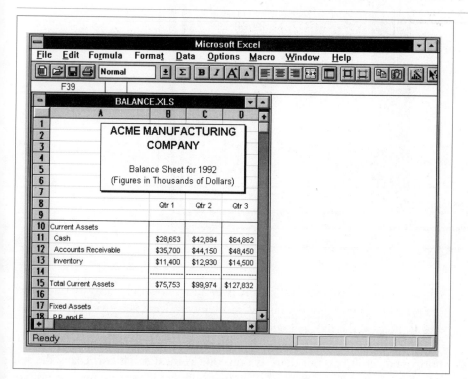

The BALANCE worksheet in a small window

With Excel, you can solve this problem by splitting the window into different *panes*. Panes let you view multiple parts of the same worksheet and scroll them together.

Creating Panes

Let's see how this works with your BALANCE worksheet. First, be sure cell A8 is in the upper-left corner of the window. Place the cursor on the small black bar at the left end of the horizontal scroll bar. The cursor will change

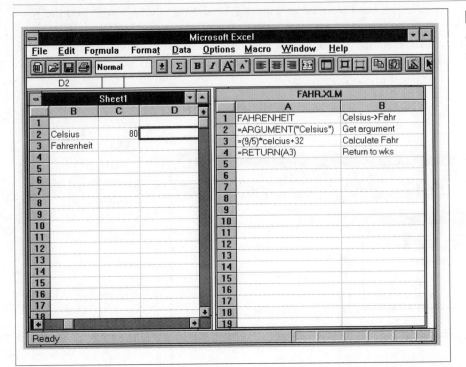

TIP *When
using
panes, start
with the*
*column-heading
row at the top and
the row headings at
the far left.*

into the shape of two vertical bars between two horizontal arrows. Click and drag the bar to the right until the vertical line above it is between columns A and B. Release the mouse button.

You now have two panes in a single window. Each pane has its own horizontal scroll bar, but there is only one vertical scroll bar. Leave the left pane as it is. Scroll the right pane so that only the three columns are visible, as shown in Figure 7.13.

Now you can create four panes. Be sure the column headings (Qtr 1, Qtr 2, and Qtr 3) are at the top of the window. Split the window again by placing the cursor on the small black bar at the top of the vertical scroll bar. Click and drag the mouse down so that the split bar is just under the top row that displays the column headings (row 8). Release the mouse button. Scroll the lower-right pane down one row so that the column headings are shown only once, as shown in Figure 7.14.

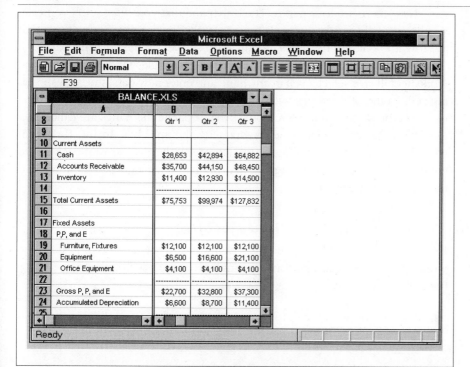

FIGURE 7.13:
The BALANCE worksheet with two panes

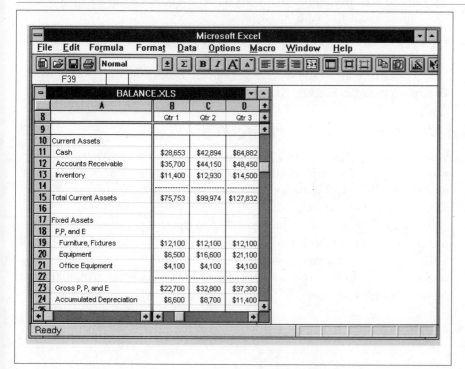

FIGURE 7.14:
The BALANCE worksheet with four panes

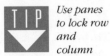

Use panes to lock row and column headings in view when working with a large worksheet.

Now there are four panes. The only pane that you *must* scroll vertically and horizontally for data entry is the one at the lower right. You will see that the row and column headings are always displayed in the adjacent panes.

Remember that you are looking at only a single window of the same worksheet. If you select a cell in any pane and enter new data, the corresponding cells in the other panes will also show the new data.

The black bars in the scroll boxes that separate the panes are called *split bars*. You can close any pane by dragging the split bar. In the BALANCE worksheet, for example, dragging the lower split bar all the way back to the left closes both left panes; dragging the split bar in the right scroll bar back to the top closes the top panes.

Automatic Splitting and Freezing

Excel can automatically split panes and freeze the row and column titles for working with the panes. Restore to a single worksheet window and try setting the panes automatically:

1. Make the upper-left cell for the new pane active. Normally this is the cell under the first column heading and to the right of the first row heading.

2. Choose Split from the Window menu. The window splits to the left and above the active cell.

3. To freeze the headings, choose Freeze Panes from the Window menu.

To unfreeze the headings, choose Unfreeze Panes from the Window menu. To remove the splits quickly, choose Remove Split from the Window menu.

Handling a Large Worksheet

With the BALANCE worksheet, panes would have helped some, but on a full window you really only need to split the column headings. With other worksheets, however, full panes can save you much time and improve the accuracy of the worksheet.

Look at the worksheet in Figure 7.15. This example illustrates how the use of panes can help you work with a large worksheet. Don't try to enter it (unless you like challenges), just examine the figures. By using panes, you could lock column and row headings, permitting you to scroll around the rest of the worksheet while the headings remained displayed.

FIGURE 7.15:

A huge cash-flow analysis worksheet

WIDGET MANUFACTURING
CASH FLOW ANALYSIS - 1992

	Assump:		
Interest Rate			9%
Cost of Goods/Sale o			0.55
Advertising/Sales			0.1

	Jan-92	Feb-92	Mar-92	Apr-92	May-92	Jun-92	Jul-92	Aug-92	Sep-92	Oct-92	Nov-92	Dec-92
CASH ON HAND	$43,000	$34,236	$63,507	$80,761	$162,282	$176,211	$179,147	$179,754	$224,074	$255,279	$271,356	$286,063
INCOME												
Sale of Goods	$83,394	$110,237	$114,563	$117,239	$123,291	$108,345	$98,234	$132,874	$143,819	$132,764	$123,127	$131,872
Sale of Services	$6,432	$10,234	$11,784	$76,123	$10,523	$11,239	$9,272	$11,555	$10,234	$12,812	$13,916	$14,123
Total Sales	$89,826	$120,471	$126,347	$193,362	$133,814	$119,584	$107,506	$144,429	$154,053	$145,576	$137,043	$145,995
Interest Income	$323	$323	$257	$476	$606	$1,217	$1,322	$1,344	$1,348	$1,681	$1,915	$2,035
Total Income	$90,149	$120,794	$126,604	$193,838	$134,420	$120,801	$108,828	$145,773	$155,401	$147,257	$138,958	$148,030
EXPENSES												
Cost of Goods	$45,867	$45,867	$60,630	$63,010	$64,481	$67,810	$59,590	$54,029	$73,081	$79,100	$73,020	$67,720
Rent	$11,543	$8,923	$8,923	$8,923	$8,923	$8,923	$8,923	$8,923	$8,923	$8,923	$8,923	$8,923
Salaries	$19,894	$15,234	$15,234	$15,234	$15,234	$15,234	$15,234	$15,234	$15,234	$15,234	$15,234	$15,234
Taxes	$1,204	$1,094	$1,094	$1,094	$1,094	$1,094	$1,094	$1,094	$1,094	$1,094	$1,094	$1,094
Supplies	$2,050	$2,050	$2,050	$2,050	$2,050	$2,050	$2,050	$2,050	$2,050	$2,050	$2,050	$2,050
Repairs	$2,873	$2,873	$2,873	$2,873	$2,873	$2,873	$2,873	$2,873	$2,873	$2,873	$2,873	$2,873
Advertising	$8,983	$8,983	$12,047	$12,635	$19,336	$13,381	$11,958	$10,751	$14,443	$15,405	$14,558	$13,704
Insurance	$734	$734	$734	$734	$734	$734	$734	$734	$734	$734	$734	$734
Utilities	$2,345	$2,345	$2,345	$2,345	$2,345	$2,345	$2,345	$2,345	$2,345	$2,345	$2,345	$2,345
Emp. Benefits	$1,234	$1,234	$1,234	$1,234	$1,234	$1,234	$1,234	$1,234	$1,234	$1,234	$1,234	$1,234
Dues, Subscriptio	$254	$254	$254	$254	$254	$254	$254	$254	$254	$254	$254	$254
Travel	$1,432	$1,432	$1,432	$1,432	$1,432	$1,432	$1,432	$1,432	$1,432	$1,432	$1,432	$1,432
Miscellaneous	$500	$500	$500	$500	$500	$500	$500	$500	$500	$500	$500	$500
Total Expenses	$98,912	$91,522	$109,350	$112,317	$120,491	$117,864	$108,221	$101,452	$124,197	$131,179	$124,251	$118,097
Net Income	($8,764)	$29,271	$17,253	$81,521	$13,929	$2,937	$606	$44,320	$31,205	$16,078	$14,707	$29,933
Net Cash on Hand	$34,236	$63,507	$80,761	$162,282	$176,211	$179,147	$179,754	$224,074	$255,279	$271,356	$286,063	$315,996

HIDING WINDOWS

There may be times when you wish to hide a window or document, yet leave it open. Hiding a window reduces clutter on the screen and helps prevent accidental edits. It does not, however, protect against viewing or unauthorized access. Macros and cell links are still active. For example, if you have a macro sheet with a library of common macros that you use, you can open it in a workbook and hide the macro sheet. You can then still use all the macros on the sheet by unhiding it as needed.

To hide a window, make the window active and choose Hide on the Window menu. To make it visible again, open the Window menu and choose the Unhide command. Then choose the window from the list that you wish to unhide and click OK.

CUSTOMIZING COLORS

An Excel document can display up to 16 colors at a time from a specified palette that you can customize. Customized palettes can be copied between documents.

To customize a palette for a worksheet, choose Color Palette from the Options menu. To customize a palette for a chart, choose Color Palette from the Chart menu. In the Color Palette dialog box, choose the color you wish to change. Click the Edit button. Select the new color you wish to use. Press F1 if you need help in using the palette. Edit other colors as you wish, then click OK on the first dialog box to save your changes in the Color Palette dialog box.

To copy a palette to another document, make the windows with the destination document active and choose Color Palette from the Options menu (for a worksheet) or Color Palette from the Chart menu (for a chart). In the Copy Colors From box, select the name of the document with the palette you wish to import. Click OK.

SETTING UP VIEWS

You can create different views of a worksheet and save each, enabling you to switch between views quickly. A given view contains the display settings, page setup settings, row heights, column widths, active cell designation, window size and position on the worksheet, panes, and frozen titles.

To create a view:

1. Set up the worksheet for the view you wish to save.

2. Choose View from the Window menu.

3. Select Add in the Views dialog box.

4. Enter the name of the view in the Add View dialog box shown below.

5. Select the settings you wish to save as part of the view.

6. Choose OK.

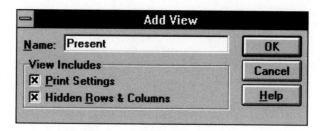

To return to this view later, choose View from the Window menu, select the desired view, and click on Show. To delete a view, choose View from the Window menu and select the view. Then choose Delete and Close.

FAST TRACK CHAPTER 8

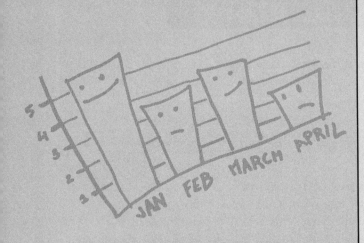

CHAPTER 8

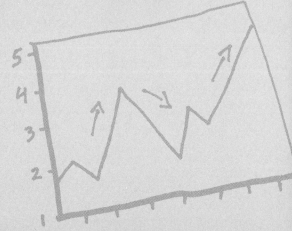

Calculating with Worksheet Formulas and Functions

Functions are abbreviations of formulas that enable you to perform a task quickly that would take much longer (or could not be done at all) using other operations. Excel provides a large assortment of functions for simplifying your work. In most worksheets, you will want to use one or more of these to calculate cell values.

In this chapter, you will use some of Excel's functions to create a very useful amortization schedule. *Amortizing* something means, literally, to put it to death. That is what you do when you pay off a car loan or house mortgage. In amortizing a loan, you make a series of equal payments for a fixed period of time. During this time, however, the proportion that you pay for the principal increases while the proportion that you pay for the interest decreases. If you are purchasing anything on credit, you may need to evaluate your loan consistently to calculate your taxes or to plan for refinancing. In this chapter, you will learn how Excel can help you to perform this evaluation.

However, before you can use this example and Excel's functions, you need to understand some basics of cell addressing and how functions work. The first part of this chapter provides that information. Later you will find an overview of Excel's functions and a summary of how to use each one.

CELL ADDRESSING

With formulas and functions, you can use either *relative, absolute,* or *mixed* cell addressing.

RELATIVE CELL ADDRESSING

The Income worksheet that you created in Chapter 3 and the BALANCE worksheet that you created in Chapters 4–6 both used relative cell addressing. In Chapter 3, you created the following formula for cell B8:

= B5 – B6

What you really stored in cell B8 was a formula that said, "Subtract the value in the cell two cells up from the value in the cell three cells up." This is why you could copy the formula to other cells, without having to retype it. *Relative cell addresses* refer to other cells by their position in relation to the current cell's location.

You can enter a relative cell address into a formula by typing it at the keyboard or by clicking the appropriate cell on the worksheet.

ABSOLUTE CELL ADDRESSING

There may be times when you want to make a permanent reference to a cell that will not change with a copy or fill operation. In other words, if you used B5 in a formula somewhere and then copied it into another cell, you might still want it to reference B5. The concept of making a specific cell reference is called *absolute cell addressing*.

To indicate this kind of addressing, you must insert a dollar sign before both the row and the column designators of the referenced cell, as in

= $B$5 – $B$6

If you copied or moved this formula, cells B5 and B6 would still be referenced in the new cell. Absolute cell references are generally entered from the keyboard. (Chapter 14 describes an alternative method.)

The cash-flow analysis worksheet in Chapter 7, shown in Figure 7.15, uses absolute cell addressing. Near the title, in column L, is a list of assumed parameters that were used in computing the project interest, cost of goods, and advertising costs. The formulas in column C used these assumptions. When these formulas were copied into the other columns, it was important that the referenced cells in column L were still referenced after the fill or copy operations. Thus, these formulas used absolute cell referencing. For example, advertising costs in column C were $L$5*B14—the advertising/sales ratio (a fixed number) times the total sales of the previous month (a variable).

MIXED CELL ADDRESSING

There may be times when you need to use a combination of absolute and relative cell addressing in a single cell. Excel allows you to make either the row or the column relative and the other absolute. For example, B$5 refers to a relative column B and an absolute row 5, and $B5 refers to an absolute column B and a relative row 5. This is called *mixed cell addressing*. Mixed cell references are generally entered from the keyboard.

WHAT IS A FUNCTION?

A *function* is an abbreviation of a formula. It provides a quick way to calculate the value of a cell that would often require a long expression. For example, in a worksheet you might use the following formula to find the sum of many cells:

= B5 + B6 + B7 + B8 + B9

You can imagine that it would be tedious to type it all into a cell. Instead, you could use the SUM function and specify a range of cells as its input:

=SUM(B5:B9)

See how much shorter the entry has become?

A *function statement* is a function whose arguments (see below) are in parentheses. An *expression* is an entire equation entered in a cell. For example,

=SUM(B5:B9)+ABS(B5)

is an expression: it contains two function statements, SUM and ABS. (SUM adds the values in cells B5–B9 together and ABS returns the absolute value of the number in cell B5.)

Functions also allow you to perform calculations that would be impossible with a formula, such as the square-root function SQRT( ).

FUNCTION ARGUMENTS

Arguments are the data that a function uses in its calculation. With the SUM function, for example, you can have as many as 30 cells or cell ranges as arguments. The number of arguments used by a particular function depends on the function. Some functions do not use any arguments.

Every function expects each of its arguments to be of a certain type. For example, the SUM function expects all its arguments to be numeric. There are ten argument types that can be used by Excel functions. These are listed in Table 8.1.

ARGUMENT	DEFINITION
Number	Anything that produces a number: numeric value, numeric formula, or a reference to a cell with a numeric value
Numbers	Anything that produces more than one number
Text	Anything that produces text: text, a text formula, or a reference to a cell containing text
Logical	Anything that produces a logical value
Logicals	Anything that produces more than one logical value
Ref	Anything that produces a reference
Value	Anything that produces a value
Values	Anything that produces more than one value
Array	Anything that produces an array
Vector	Anything that produces a one-dimensional array

Note: Text arguments must be enclosed in quotation marks.

TABLE 8.1:

Types of Excel Arguments

The arguments of an Excel function must be in a certain order, which is determined by the function. This ordering of arguments is detailed in the library of functions listed later in this chapter. Be sure to check the appropriate order, because Excel's argument order may be different from that of other worksheet programs, such as Lotus 1-2-3. Some functions may use one or more optional arguments as well.

ENTERING FUNCTIONS INTO CELLS

The following general rules apply for entering functions in your worksheet:

◆ Always begin an expression entry with an equal sign. This informs Excel that you are entering a function, not a text string.

◆ Function names are not case-specific.

◆ Referenced cells can contain other functions, making it possible to create hierarchies of calculations.

◆ Separate arguments with commas.

◆ A function can have up to 30 arguments.

◆ An expression can contain a maximum of 255 characters (the cell limit).

◆ You can use any of the three reference operators (:, , , *space*) to define the input for a function. For example,

=SUM(A3:A5,B6)

calculates A3+A4+A5+B6.

◆ Arguments can be constants. For example,

B8=SUM(100+B5)

stores the value of 100 plus the contents of cell B5 in cell B8.

◆ Arguments can be functions. For example,

=SUM(ROUND(A3,1),ROUND(C1,1))

sums the values in A3 and C1, each rounded to one decimal place.

If you enter the function by typing the name manually, use lowercase to check spelling. If a valid function name is spelled correctly, Excel will capitalize it automatically on entry.

There are two ways to enter a function into a cell. One is to type the function as a part of your formula. The second way is to paste the function name into the formula and then enter the arguments from the keyboard or by clicking:

◆ To enter a function manually, simply type the name. For example, find a blank cell on a worksheet and enter

=ROUND(2.34,1)

Notice that the cell displays **2.3**, the first argument rounded to one decimal place.

♦ To paste a function name into a formula, use the Paste Function command. Try the previous example this way. Select a blank cell and choose Formula ➤ Paste Function. Select the Math + Trig function category. Scroll to the ROUND function name, double-click the function, and enter the arguments from the keyboard. (Notice that it was not necessary to enter the equal sign.)

If you know the name of the function you want to paste, you don't have to scroll through all the functions. When the list box is displayed, just press the first letter of the function you want. For example, press **R** to get to the first function name beginning with *R*. Then find the function by scrolling and double-click on ROUND.

To enter a Tab space in the formula bar, press Ctrl-Tab. To enter a carriage return, press Alt-Enter.

AUTOMATIC PARENTHESIS COMPLETION

Excel can automatically complete the parenthesis when you enter a simple formula. For example, if you enter **=SUM(A1:A3** and press Enter, Excel will complete the entry with an additional parenthesis. This will not work for nested parentheses or for entering simple references, such as typing **=(B1+B2** and pressing Enter.

USING THE SUM TOOL

The Sum tool on the toolbar is useful for adding the sum function to a cell. Simply click on an empty cell at the end of a column or row of numbers and then click on the Σ tool. Excel will mark the cells it thinks you are trying to sum with dotted lines. If this is correct, press Enter. If not, select a new range to sum with the mouse and press Enter or edit the entry in the formula bar.

CREATING A WORKSHEET WITH FUNCTIONS

Figure 8.1 shows a part of a worksheet that you can use to experiment with functions. In this example, $8,000.00 is borrowed at 12 percent interest, and Excel is used to calculate the monthly payments, the total amount paid, and the amortization schedule. This example makes extensive use of both the PMT (periodic payment) and PV (present value) functions, which are used frequently for financial analyses. Once you create the worksheet, you can change the amount borrowed, the interest, and the term to see how it affects the schedule. This makes the example much more than a simple tutorial—you can save it and use it to calculate the schedule whenever you purchase something on credit. (You will find more information on the PMT and PV functions in Chapter 23.)

Note that the data-entry area for the user, marked in the upper left of the worksheet, has only three cells: B6, B7, and B8. Normally, you would want the rest of the worksheet protected, so that a user could change only those three cells (protecting cells is described in Chapter 14).

Begin the amortization worksheet by entering the titles in cells C1 and C2. Create the data-entry area in cells A5 through B8 and enter the input values shown in Figure 8.2 into this area. Remember to enter a percent sign each time you insert a value for cell B7; this identifies the cell value as a percent.

NOTE
NOTE
If you have been using Lotus 1-2-3, you will notice that the order of the arguments in Excel is slightly different from the Lotus convention. Excel's financial functions follow the HP-12C Financial Calculator's conventions.

Enter **Payment:** into cell A10 and **Total Paid** into cell A11. Enter the following function and formula according to the list below:

CELL	ENTRY
B10	= PMT($B$7/12,$B$8,–$B$6)
B11	= ($B$8 * $B$10)

Enter the column headings into cells A13 through G14. Then enter the month numbers sequentially into column A. (There are 48 payments.)

Enter these formulas for the values for the first row:

CELL	ENTRY
B15	=$B$6
C15	=–PV($B$7/12,($B$8–A15),$B$10)
D15	=$B$10
E15	=D15
F15	=B15–C15
G15	=E15–F15

	A	B	C	D	E	F	G
1			**AMORTIZATION SCHEDULE**				
2			*Amortization Payment Schedule by Month*				
3							
4	***************	************************	**********************	**			
5	Data Entry Area			*			
6	Principal	$8,000.00		*			
7	Interest	12.00%		*			
8	Term	48	Months	*			
9	***************	************************	**********************	**			
10	Payment:	$210.67					
11	Total Paid	$10,112.19					
12							
13	Month	Beginning	Ending	Payment	Total Paid	Tot. Princ.	Tot. Interest
14		Balance	Balance			Paid	Paid
15	1	$8,000.00	$7,869.33	$210.67	$210.67	$130.67	$80.00
16	2	$7,869.33	$7,737.35	$210.67	$421.34	$262.65	$158.69
17	3	$7,737.35	$7,604.05	$210.67	$632.01	$395.95	$236.07
18	4	$7,604.05	$7,469.42	$210.67	$842.68	$530.58	$312.11
19	5	$7,469.42	$7,333.45	$210.67	$1,053.35	$666.55	$386.80
20	6	$7,333.45	$7,196.11	$210.67	$1,264.02	$803.89	$460.14
21	7	$7,196.11	$7,057.40	$210.67	$1,474.69	$942.60	$532.10
22	8	$7,057.40	$6,917.31	$210.67	$1,685.37	$1,082.69	$602.67
23	9	$6,917.31	$6,775.81	$210.67	$1,896.04	$1,224.19	$671.84
24	10	$6,775.81	$6,632.90	$210.67	$2,106.71	$1,367.10	$739.60
25	11	$6,632.90	$6,488.55	$210.67	$2,317.38	$1,511.45	$805.93
26	12	$6,488.55	$6,342.77	$210.67	$2,528.05	$1,657.23	$870.82
27	13	$6,342.77	$6,195.53	$210.67	$2,738.72	$1,804.47	$934.24
28	14	$6,195.53	$6,046.81	$210.67	$2,949.39	$1,953.19	$996.20
29	15	$6,046.81	$5,896.61	$210.67	$3,160.06	$2,103.39	$1,056.67
30	16	$5,896.61	$5,744.90	$210.67	$3,370.73	$2,255.10	$1,115.63
31	17	$5,744.90	$5,591.68	$210.67	$3,581.40	$2,408.32	$1,173.08
32	18	$5,591.68	$5,436.93	$210.67	$3,792.07	$2,563.07	$1,229.00
33	19	$5,436.93	$5,280.63	$210.67	$4,002.74	$2,719.37	$1,283.37
34	20	$5,280.63	$5,122.76	$210.67	$4,213.41	$2,877.24	$1,336.18
35	21	$5,122.76	$4,963.32	$210.67	$4,424.08	$3,036.68	$1,387.40
36	22	$4,963.32	$4,802.28	$210.67	$4,634.76	$3,197.72	$1,437.04
37	23	$4,802.28	$4,639.63	$210.67	$4,845.43	$3,360.37	$1,485.06
38	24	$4,639.63	$4,475.36	$210.67	$5,056.10	$3,524.64	$1,531.46
39	25	$4,475.36	$4,309.44	$210.67	$5,266.77	$3,690.56	$1,576.21
40	26	$4,309.44	$4,141.87	$210.67	$5,477.44	$3,858.13	$1,619.30
41	27	$4,141.87	$3,972.61	$210.67	$5,688.11	$4,027.39	$1,660.72
42	28	$3,972.61	$3,801.67	$210.67	$5,898.78	$4,198.33	$1,700.45
43	29	$3,801.67	$3,629.01	$210.67	$6,109.45	$4,370.99	$1,738.46
44	30	$3,629.01	$3,454.63	$210.67	$6,320.12	$4,545.37	$1,774.75
45	31	$3,454.63	$3,278.51	$210.67	$6,530.79	$4,721.49	$1,809.30
46	32	$3,278.51	$3,100.62	$210.67	$6,741.46	$4,899.38	$1,842.09

FIGURE 8.1:

The first page of the amortization worksheet

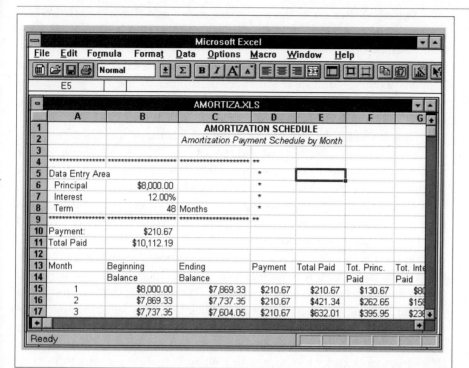

FIGURE 8.2:

Creating the
amortization worksheet

Copy cell C15 to C16 and enter the following into the row for Month 2:

CELL	ENTRY
B16	=C15
E16	=E15+D16
F16	=F15+B16−C16

Now you can have Excel calculate the remainder of the amortization schedule by using the Fill Down command under the Edit menu for each column, except the first. For columns B, C, E, and F, you will need to fill from the second row down. On the remaining rows, fill from the first row down. The resulting values should be the same as those shown in Figure 8.1.

Format the worksheet, set up the alignments, and set the styles for the titles, as shown in Figure 8.1. Refer to Chapter 6 if you need help. Format B7 as a percent.

Once you have set up the worksheet, save it using the name *AMORTIZA.* Then prepare a copy for printing by opening the File menu and choosing Page Setup. Set the options you wish and click OK. Now print the worksheet.

You can try changing any of the values in the data-entry area to see what happens to the amortization schedule. Remember to use the percent sign when you enter a different interest rate. Notice how fast Excel calculates the entire schedule.

 This worksheet, as others in this book, is intended as an example only. The author and publisher assume no liability for its accuracy or suitability for its intended purpose.

This is a valuable worksheet. Save it for calculating the schedule whenever you purchase something on credit—a house, automobile, computer, or whatever. It calculates the proper interest for income-tax purposes, also giving you the status of the principal in case you wish to refinance a loan.

If you are the adventurous type, you can try to create a pie chart from your amortization worksheet, showing the relative percentages of principal and interest paid on a 48-month loan. Select only cells F62 and G62, which contain the final totals. Open the File menu, choose New, and double-click Chart in the dialog box. A column graph appears. Open the Gallery menu and choose Pie to change the column chart that was automatically created into a pie chart. Choose pie chart style #6 and click OK. Now select Arrange from the Window menu, then select Tiled and click OK to show both the chart and worksheet. Change the interest on the worksheet and watch the chart change. (If you get stuck, refer to Chapter 18.) When you are done, close the chart window.

CHANGING FORMULAS TO VALUES

When you paste an expression into a cell, the cell value becomes dependent upon values in other cells, other variables (such as the date or time), or even values in other worksheets. There may be occasions, however, when you wish to lock the results of an expression into a cell; that is, you wish the current results of the expression to be a *value,* no longer dependent on other cells.

As an example, you might use the function =NOW( ) as an expression in a worksheet to enter the current date in a cell, thus date-stamping the cell. Enter this function in F4 of the amortization schedule worksheet. Set the date format using Number on the Format menu. The next time you open the worksheet, however, the cell date (or time) will read the new date (or time). That's not exactly what you wish. To convert the result of an expression to a fixed value, follow this procedure:

1. Select the cell or cell range you wish to convert to values. Select F4 in this case.

2. Open the Edit menu and choose Copy. The cell or cell range is marked.

3. Leave cell F4 selected.

4. Open the Edit menu and choose Paste Special.

5. In the Paste Special dialog box, choose Values, as shown below.

6. Click OK.

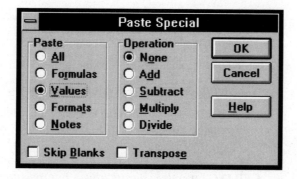

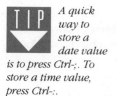

A quick way to store a date value is to press Ctrl-;. To store a time value, press Ctrl-:.

You can also convert a formula to a value in the formula bar using this method:

1. Select the cell and highlight all the characters in the formula bar.

2. Press F9.

Both methods convert the date to a value, and the value (not the equation) is stored in the worksheet.

TYPES OF FUNCTIONS

There is a large assortment of functions available to the Excel user. These can be classified into nine types: Mathematical (and trigonometric), statistical, database, logical, text, financial, date (and time), look up/reference, and information. Each function is described by type in the remainder of this chapter.

MATHEMATICAL AND TRIGONOMETRIC FUNCTIONS

The following are Excel's mathematical and trigonometric functions:

ABS(*number***):** returns the absolute value of *number*

ACOS(*number***):** returns the arccosine of *number*

ACOSH(*number***):** returns inverse hyperbolic cosine of *number*

ASIN(*number***):** returns the arcsine of *number*

ASINH(*number***):** returns inverse hyperbolic sine of *number*

ATAN(*number***):** returns the arctangent of *number*

ATAN2(*x number, y number***):** returns the arctangent of *x number* and *y number* (*x* and *y* coordinate)

ATANH(*number***):** returns inverse hyperbolic tangent of *number*

CEILING (*number, significance***):** returns *number* rounded up to nearest multiple of *significance*

COMBIN(*number, number chosen***):** returns the number of ways that *number chosen* objects can be selected from *number* objects, without regard for order

COS(*number***):** returns the cosine of *number*

COSH(*number***):** returns hyperbolic cosine of *number*

EVEN(*number***):** returns *number* rounded up to the nearest even integer.

EXP (*number***):** returns *e* raised to the power of *number*; EXP is the reverse of the LN (natural logarithm) function; to calculate the power to other bases, use the exponentiation operator: i.e., =2^3 returns 8

FACT(*number***):** returns the factorial of *number*

FLOOR(*number, significance***):** returns *number* rounded down to the nearest multiple of significance

INT(*number***):** returns the largest integer less than or equal to *number*; for example: INT(7.6) is 7

LN(*number***):** returns the natural logarithm of *number,* which must be positive. LN is the inverse of EXP

LOG(*number, base***):** returns the logarithm of *number* to *base*

LOG10(*number***):** returns the base 10 logarithm of *number*

MDETERM(_array_**):** returns determinant of _array_

MINVERSE(_array_**):** returns inverse of _array_

MMULT(_array 1, array 2_**):** returns product of two arrays

MOD(_number, divisor number_**):** returns the remainder after _number_ is divided by _divisor number_

ODD(_number_**):** returns _number_ rounded up to the nearest odd integer.

PI( ): returns the value of π; there is no argument

PRODUCT(_number 1, number 2, ..., number n_**):** returns product of _numbers_ (up to 30 arguments)

RAND( ): returns a random number between 0 and 0.999...; the value changes each time the worksheet is recalculated; there is no argument

ROUND(_number, number of decimal places_**):** returns _number_ rounded to _number of decimal places_

SIGN(_number_**):** returns 1 if _number_ is positive, 0 if it is 0, and −1 if it is negative

SIN(_number_**):** returns the sine of _number_

SINH(_number_**):** returns hyperbolic sine of _number_

SQRT(_number_**):** returns the positive square root of _number_, which must be positive

SUM(_number 1, number 2, ..., number n_**):** returns the sum of the numbers in a list of up to 30 arguments

SUMPRODUCT(_array 1, array 2_**):** multiplies corresponding components of the specified arrays and returns sum of those products (up to 30 arguments)

SUMSQ (_number 1, number 2, ..., number n_**):** returns the sum of the squares of the numbers in a list of up to 30 arguments

SUMX2MY2(_array 1, array 2_**):** returns the sum of the differences of the squares of corresponding values in two arrays

SUMX2PY2(_array 1, array 2_**):** returns the sum of the sum of the squares of corresponding values in two arrays

SUMXMY2(_array 1, array 2_**):** returns the sum of the squares of differences of corresponding values in two arrays

TAN(_number_**):** returns the tangent of _number_

TANH(*number*): returns hyperbolic tangent of *number*

TRUNC (*number, number of digits*): returns integer part of *number*

The RAND function is useful for creating random data when testing worksheets. The value changes with each recalculation, so sometimes you may wish to convert the expression result to a value to save time in iterative calculations.

Excel measures angles in radians rather than degrees. To convert both ways, use either of the following equations:

Angle in degrees = Angle in radians * (180/PI( ))

Angle in radian = Angle in degrees * (PI( )/180)

STATISTICAL FUNCTIONS

Excel has the following statistical functions:

AVEDEV(*number 1, number 2, ..., number n*): returns the average of the absolute deviations of data points from their mean (a measure of the variability of a data set)

AVERAGE(*number 1, number 2, ..., number n*): returns the average of the numeric arguments

BETADIST(*x, alpha, beta, a, b*): returns the cumulative beta probability density function

BETAINV (*probability, alpha, beta, a, b*): returns the inverse of the cumulative beta probability density function

BINOMDIST(*number s, trials, probability s, cumulative*): returns the individual term binomial distribution probability

CHIDIST(*x, degrees freedom*): returns the one-tailed probability of the chi-squared distribution; use this to compare observed and expected values

CHIINV(*probability, degrees freedom*): returns the inverse of the chi-squared distribution

CHITEST(*actual range, expected range*): returns the test for independence

CONFIDENCE(*alpha, standard dev, size*): returns the confidence interval for a population mean

CORREL(*array 1, array 2*)**:** returns the correlation coefficient of the *array 1* and *array 2* ranges; used to determine the relationship between two properties

COUNT(*number 1, number 2, ..., number n*)**:** returns the number of values in a list of arguments. For example, COUNT(A1:A5,A8) returns 6.

COUNTA(*number 1, number 2, ..., number n*)**:** returns the number of nonblank values in a list of arguments

COVAR(*array 1, array 2*)**:** returns covariance, the average of the products of deviations for each data point pair; use covariance to determine the relationship of two data sets

CRITBINOM(*trials, probability s, alpha*)**:** returns the smallest integer k for which the cumulative binomial distribution function is less than or equal to the criterion value *alpha*; used for quality assurance applications

DEVSQ (*number 1, number 2, ..., number n*)**:** returns the sum of squares of deviations of data points from their sample mean

EXPONDIST(*x, lambda, cumulative*)**:** returns the exponential distribution function; used to model the time between events

FDIST(*x, degrees freedom 1, degrees freedom 2*)**:** returns the F probability distribution

FINV (*probability, degrees freedom 1, degrees freedom 2*)**:** returns the inverse of the F probability distribution

FISHER(*x*)**:** returns the Fisher transformation at x; used to perform hypothesis testing on the correlation coefficient

FISHERINV(*y*)**:** returns inverse of the Fisher transformation at y

FORECAST(*x, known y's, known x's*)**:** returns a predicted value for x based on a linear regression of known x and y arrays.

FREQUENCY(*data, bins*)**:** returns a frequency distribution as a vertical array (both arguments are arrays)

FTEST(*array 1, array 2*)**:** returns the results of an F-test. Used to determine if two samples have different variances

GAMMADIST(*x, alpha, beta, cumulative*)**:** returns the gamma distribution function; used to study variables with a skewed distribution

GAMMAINV(*probability, alpha, beta*)**:** returns the inverse of the gamma cumulative distribution function

GAMMALN(*x***):** returns the natural logarithm of the gamma distribution function

GEOMEAN(*number 1, number 2, ..., number n***):** returns the geometric mean of an array or range of positive data; use to calculate average growth rate given compound interest with variable rates

GROWTH(*Y array, X array, new x's, const***):** returns an array with the y values as the exponential curve of regression $y=b*m^x$ for two variables represented by *X array* and *Y array; new x's* are the x values for which you want y values

HARMEAN(*number 1, number 2, ..., number n***):** returns the harmonic mean of a data set

HYPGEOMDIST(*sample s, number sample, population s, number population***):** returns the hypergeometric distribution; used for problems of finite population, where each observation is either a success or failure, and where each subset of a given size is chosen with equal likelihood

INTERCEPT(*known y's, known x's***):** returns the intercept of a linear regression line through data points in *known x's* and *known y's*. Y axis intercept

KURT(*number 1, number 2, ..., number n***):** returns the kurtosis of a data set. Kurtosis characterizes the amount of peakedness or flatness of a distribution

LARGE(*array, k***):** returns the kth largest value in *array*

LINEST(*Y array, X array, const, stats***):** returns the horizontal array of two elements, the slope and y intercept of the line of regression for $y=mx+b$ for two variables, X and Y, represented by *X array* and *Y array*. The slope may contain multiple numbers. If stats is TRUE, the function returns additional regression statistics

LOGEST(*Y array, X array, const, stats***):** returns a horizontal array of two elements, the parameters of m and b in the exponential curve of regression $y=b*m^x$, for two variables represented by *X array* and *Y array*

LOGINV(*probability, mean, standard dev***):** returns the inverse of the lognormal cumulative distribution function of x, where ln(x) is normally distributed with *mean* and *standard dev*. Use to analyze logarithmically transformed data

LOGNORMDIST(*x, mean, standard dev***):** returns the log normal cumulative distribution function of x

MAX(*number 1, number 2, ..., number n***):** returns the largest number in a list of arguments

MEDIAN(*number 1, number 2, ..., number n***):** returns the median of a list of arguments

MIN(*number 1, number 2, ..., number n***):** returns the minimum number in a list of arguments

MODE(*number 1, number 2, ..., number n***):** returns the most frequently occurring value in a range of data

NEGBINOMIST(*number f, number s, probability s***):** returns the negative binomial distribution.

NORMDIST(*x, mean, standard dev, cumulative***):** returns the normal cumulative distribution function

NORMINV(*probability, mean, standard dev***):** returns the inverse of the normal cumulative distribution for the specified *mean* and *standard dev*

NORMSDIST(*z***):** returns the standard normal cumulative distribution function

NORMSINV(*probability***):** returns the inverse of the standard normal cumulative distribution function

PEARSON(*array 1, array 2***):** returns the Pearson product moment correlation coefficient. Reflects the extent of a linear relationship between to data sets defined by the arrays

PERCENTILE(*array, k***):** returns the value from *array* at the *k*th percentile

PERMUT(*number, number chosen***):** returns the number of permutations of groups of *number chosen* objects that can be selected from *number* objects.

POISSON(*x, mean, cumulative***):** returns the Poisson probability distribution. Use to predict the number of events over a specific time

PROB(*x range, prob range, lower limit, upper limit***):** returns the probability that values in *x range* are between *lower limit* and *upper limit*

QUARTILE(*array, quart***):** returns a quartile from the data points in *array;* used in sales and survey data to divide populations into groups

RANK(*number, ref, order***):** returns the rank of a number in a list of numbers; in a sorted list, the rank would be the position in the list

RSQ(*known y's known x's***):** returns the r-squared value of the linear regression line through data points in *known y's* and *known x's*

SKEW(*number 1, number 2, ..., number n***):** returns the skewness of a distribution

SLOPE(*known y's, known x's***):** returns the slope of a linear regression line through the data points in *known y's* and *known x's*

SMALL(*array, k***):** returns the *k*th smallest value in a data set defined by array

STANDARDIZE(*x, mean, standard dev***):** returns a normalized value from a distribution characterized by *mean* and *standard dev*

STDEV(*number 1, number 2, ..., number n***):** returns an estimate of the standard deviation of the numbers in a list of arguments representing a sample from a population; used to determine how widely values are dispersed from the average, or mean, value

STDEVP (*number 1, number 2, ..., number n***):** returns the standard deviation of the numbers in a list of arguments given the entire population as arguments

STEYX(*known y's, known x's***):** returns the standard error of regression, or an estimate of the amount of error in the prediction of *y* from a value of *x*

TDIST(*x, degrees freedom, tails***):** returns the Student's *t* distribution; used in the hypothesis testing of small sample data sets

TINV(*probability, degrees freedom***):** returns the inverse of the Students *t* distribution for the specified *degrees freedom*

TREND (*knowny's, knownx's, newx's, const***):** returns an array, the *y* values on the line of regression $y = mx + b$ for the two variables *X* and *Y*, represented by *knownx's* and *knowny's*. This is like GROWTH, except it's linear rather than exponential

TRIMMEAN(*array, percent***):** returns the mean taken by excluding a percentage of data points from the top and bottom tails of a data set defined by *array*

TTEST(*array 1, array 2, tails, type***):** returns the probability associated with a Student's *t*-test. Use to determine if two samples are likely to have come from the same two populations with the same mean

VAR(*number 1, number 2, ..., number n*)**:** returns an estimate of variance of a population based on a sample from that population

VARP (*number 1, number 2, ..., number n*)**:** returns the variance of the population; VARP assumes you have the entire population in the data set; VAR assumes you have only a sample from that population; VAR will return a larger variance than VARP; the same holds true for other related functions here

WEIBULL(*x, alpha, beta, cumulative*)**:** returns the Weibull distribution. Use in reliability analysis

ZTEST(*array, x*)**:** returns the two-tailed P-value of a z-test. Use to assess that the probability of a particular observation is from a particular population

The SUM and AVERAGE functions ignore cells with blanks, logical values, or text. COUNT returns the number of cells with numbers. COUNTA, in contrast, tells how many cells include text, logical values, numbers, and error values. Both also do not count blank cells.

To enter the SUM function quickly from the tool bar for simple applications, click the sum tool in the tool bar. This will enter an expression that sums the cells above or to the left of the active cell into the selected cell.

For more information on using the statistical functions, see Chapters 16 and 23.

DATABASE FUNCTIONS

The following are Excel's database functions:

DAVERAGE(*database, field name, criteria*)**:** returns the average of the numbers in a particular field of a database that meet the specified criteria

DCOUNT(*database, field name, criteria*)**:** returns the count of the numbers in a particular field of a database that meet the specified criteria

DCOUNTA(*database, field name, criteria*)**:** returns the count of the nonempty cells in a particular field of a database that meet the specified criteria

DGET(*database, field name, criteria*)**:** extracts single field value matching criteria

DMAX(*database, field name, criteria*)**:** returns the maximum of the numbers in a particular field of a database that meet the specified criteria

DMIN(*database, field name, criteria***):** returns the minimum of the numbers in a particular field of a database that meet the specified criteria

DPRODUCT(*database, field name, criteria***):** returns the product of the numbers in a particular field of a database that meet the specified criteria

DSTDEV(*database, field name, criteria***):** returns an estimate of the standard deviation based on a sample of a population, using field values of a database that meet the specified criteria

DSTDEVP (*database, field name, criteria***):** returns the standard deviation of a population based on the entire population, using field values of a database that meet the specified criteria

DSUM(*database, field name, criteria***):** returns the sum of the numbers in a particular field of a database that meet the specified criteria

DVAR(*database, field name, criteria***):** returns an estimate of the variance, based on a sample of a population using values from a particular field of a database that meet the specified criteria

DVARP (*database, field name, criteria***):** returns the variance of a population using numbers in a particular field of a database that meet the specified criteria

For more information on using the database functions, see Part III of this book.

LOGICAL FUNCTIONS

The following are Excel's logical functions:

AND(*logical 1, logical 2, ..., logical n***):** returns TRUE if all logical values in the list of arguments are true. If any of the values are FALSE, the function will return a value of FALSE

FALSE( ) returns the value of FALSE.

IF(*logical, value if true, value if false***):** returns *value if true* if *logical* is true, otherwise returns *value if false*

NOT(*logical* **):** returns FALSE if *logical* is TRUE, TRUE if *logical* is FALSE

OR(*logical 1, logical 2, ..., logical n***):** returns TRUE if any of the logical values in the list of arguments is TRUE. If all logical values in the list are FALSE, it returns FALSE

TRUE( ) returns a logical value of TRUE. There is no argument

Logical expressions return a value of TRUE or FALSE. For example, look at the following expressions:

=(5*4)*7>480/4

=C4>D10

=D5="No"

Each of these is really a question. The answer, either TRUE or FALSE, is placed in the cell containing the expression. The first reads "Is (5*4)*7 greater than 480/4?" The answer is yes, or TRUE. The available operators are listed in Chapter 4.

TEXT FUNCTIONS

Text strings must be enclosed in double quotes.

The following are Excel's text functions:

CHAR(*number* **):** returns ANSI character of *number*

CLEAN(*text* **):** removes control characters from *text*

CODE(*text* **):** returns ANSI code of first character in *text*

DOLLAR(*number, decimal places* **):** rounds *number* to number of *decimal places*, formats it to currency format, and returns a text result

EXACT(*text 1, text 2* **):** returns TRUE if *text 1=text 2*, FALSE otherwise

FIND(*find text, within text, start* **):** returns location of *find text* in *within text*, starting at *start*

FIXED(*number, decimal places, no commas* **):** rounds *number* to number of *decimal places*, formats to a decimal format with periods and commas, and returns a text result; if *no commas* is TRUE, no commas will be included in returned text

LEFT(*text, number of characters* **):** returns left-most *number of characters* in *text*

LEN(*text* **):** returns a number equal to the length of *text*

LOWER(*text* **):** converts *text* to lowercase

MID (*text, start position, number of characters* **):** extracts *number of characters* from *text*, starting with *start position*

PROPER(*text* **):** returns *text* with first letters of each word in capitals

REPLACE(*old text, start, number, new text***):** replaces *number* of characters of *old text* with *new text* starting at *start* position

REPT(*text, number of times***):** repeats *text* for *number of times*

RIGHT(*text, number of characters***):** returns right-most *number of characters* of *text*

SEARCH (*find text, within text, start***):** returns location of *find text* within *within text* from *start*; you can use wildcard characters

SUBSTITUTE(*text, old text, new text, num***):** replaces *old text* with *new text* in *text*. *Num* indicates which occurrence of *old text* to replace

T(*value***):** returns text representation of *value*, or empty text if value does not refer to text

TEXT(*number, format text***):** formats *number* to *format text* and returns it as text

TRIM(*text***):** removes spaces from *text*, except single spaces between words

UPPER(*text***):** converts *text* to uppercase

VALUE(*text***):** converts *text* to a number (not necessary to use in a formula, as Excel converts it automatically if necessary)

The TEXT function is useful for displaying numeric text in a special format or alignment. For example,

=TEXT(C1,"##0.00")

would display 123.3 in cell C1 as **123.30**. Unlike a right-aligned number, however, the value would be left-aligned. Text always has a default left alignment. You can use most of the formatting symbols (see Chapter 6), but you cannot use the asterisk in the format to force a repeating symbol to fill a cell. For example,

=TEXT(230,"""Please remit: ""$#,##0.00")

would display

Please remit: $230.00

Because the second argument contains a text string within a text string, two sets of double quotation marks enclose the internal string. This is analogous to the convention in English of using single quotation marks to enclose a quotation within a quotation.

The DOLLAR and FIXED functions are often better alternatives in displaying currency values. For example, either of the following displays $123.00:

=DOLLAR(123,2)

=TEXT(123,"$#,##0.00")

But which is easier to enter? Both DOLLAR and FIXED automatically round the displayed value.

You should remember that the ampersand (&) is available for text operations. You can combine text, text with data, or text with the contents of a cell (see Chapter 4).

FINANCIAL FUNCTIONS

The following are Excel's financial functions:

DB (*cost, salvage, life, period, month*): returns the real depreciation of an asset for a specific period using the fixed-declining balance method

DDB (*cost, salvage, life, period, factor*): returns depreciation of asset using double-declining balance method

FV(*rate, nper, pmt, pv, type*): returns the future value of an investment, where *pv* is the present value (see PV for a description of the other arguments)

IPMT(*rate, per, nper, pv, fv, type*): returns interest payment for an investment

IRR(*values, guess*): returns internal rate of return of a series of cash flows, represented by *values*; *guess* is an optional argument, specifying the starting point for the iteration; if *guess* is omitted, it is assumed to be 0.1 or 10%; *values* should be an array or reference that contains numbers (at least one positive and one negative)

MIRR(*values, safe, risk*): returns a modified internal rate of return on a series of case flows, represented by the numbers in *values*, given *safe* and *risk*; *safe* is the rate returned by the investment that will finance the negative cash flows or the finance rate you pay; *risk* is the rate at which the positive cash flows can be reinvested

NPER(*rate, pmt, pv, fv, type*): returns the number of periods of an investment involving constant cash flows and constant interest rate

NPV(*rate, value 1, value 2, ..., value n***):** returns net present value of a series of periodic future cash flows, represented by the numbers in the list of values, discounted at a constant interest rate specified by *rate*

PMT(*rate, nper, pv, fv, type***):** returns the periodic payment on an investment involving constant cash flows and constant interest rate

PPMT(*rate, per, nper, pv, fv, type***):** returns payment on the principal for an investment with periodic payments and constant interest rate

PV(*rate, nper, pmt, fv, type***):** returns the present value. The arguments are as follows:

rate: interest rate per period (constant)

nper: number of periods

pmt: periodic payment

fv: future value

type: indicates whether payments occur at the beginning or end of the period. If *type* = 0, first payment is due after the first period. If *type* = 1, payment is at beginning. If argument is omitted, it is assumed to be 0

RATE(*nper, pmt, pv, fv, type, guess***):** returns the interest rate per period of an investment involving constant cash flows; *guess* is an optional argument that specifies the starting value for the iteration; if omitted, it is assumed to be 0.1 or 10 percent

SLN(*cost, salvage, life***):** straight-line depreciation of an asset

SYD(*cost, salvage, life, per***):** sum of years' digits depreciation for an asset

VDB(*cost, salvage, life, start period, end period, factor, no switch***):** returns depreciation of an asset for a specified or partial period using a declining balance method

The functions PV, FV, NPER, PMT, and RATE are all interrelated; you can calculate one given the values of the others. For more information on the financial functions, see Chapter 23.

DATE AND TIME FUNCTIONS

The following are Excel's date functions:

DATE(*year, month, day***):** returns the serial number of the specified day: if *day* is 0, it returns last day of previous month; if *month* is 0, it returns last month of previous year

DATEVALUE(*date text***):** returns the serial number of *date text*; use this to import dates form other worksheets if they are labels

DAY(*serial number***):** converts *serial number* to the day of the month

DAYS360 (*start date, end date***):** returns the number of days between two dates based on a 360-day year

HOUR(*serial number***):** converts *serial number* to the hour of the day

MINUTE(*serial number***):** converts *serial number* to the minute

MONTH(*serial number***):** converts *serial number* to the month of the year

NOW( ): returns the serial number of the current date and time (there is no argument)

SECOND (*serial number***):** converts *serial number* to the second

TIME(*hour, minute, second***):** returns the serial number for the specified time

TIMEVALUE(*time text***):** returns serial number of *time text*

TODAY( ): returns serial number of today's date (there is no argument)

WEEKDAY(*serial number***):** converts *serial number* to the day of the week (Sunday = 1)

YEAR(*serial number***):** converts *serial number* to the year

You can enter a date in a cell using the DATE function. For example, =DATE(92,04,15) stores the equivalent serial number for April 15, 1992, in the cell. If you enter an illegal date, Excel will try to calculate a serial date based on the number. For example, if you enter a day of 32 for a month with 31 days, the serial number returned will be for the first day of the next month. You will get no error message.

Once a date is entered, use the Number command under the Format menu to format the serial number to the desired date form.

You also can enter a date by clicking the cell and typing the date in the desired format. The cell will be formatted automatically. You can use custom date pictures by entering them with the Number command.

For dates in the 21st century, use a three-digit year number; e.g., =DATE(101,4,1) is April 1, 2001. You can use any year up to 2078 with this method.

You can write formulas to calculate the number of days between any two dates. (The calculations will be performed on the serial date numbers.) The result will be the true difference in days; to get the difference in weeks, divide by seven.

If the number of seconds is not important, you can omit the third argument. Be sure to keep the comma, though. Example: =TIME(7,15,)

The TIME function works in a similar way. For example, =TIME(3,15,10) becomes **3:15 a.m.** You can enter a time and then format it. You also can enter a time in any valid time format and it will be formatted automatically. The time is stored as a fractional number and represents the fraction of the day that has elapsed. For example, 8:00 a.m. is stored as 0.33333.

You also can take the difference of two times. The difference, when multiplied by 24, will give you the true difference in hours. (Remember that the fraction represents the fractional part of 24 hours that has elapsed.) To convert a fractional hour to minutes, multiply by 60. Use the INT function to subtract the fractional part of a date or to get the fractional part of an hour.

The NOW( ) function is useful for time-stamping your worksheets. Use the special format that includes both the date and time: *m/d/yy* h:*mm*. This will be wider than a standard cell width, so put it in a wide cell. The date and time will be updated each time you calculate the worksheet (see "Changing Formulas to Values" earlier in this chapter).

Using the techniques of Chapter 6, you can create custom date and time formats.

LOOKUP AND REFERENCE FUNCTIONS

Excel's lookup and reference functions are the following:

ADDRESS(*row, column, abs, ref style, worksheet***):** returns reference as text to a single cell

AREAS(*ref***):** returns the number of areas in *ref*; *ref* can refer to multiple areas; example: AREAS((A1:A5,B1)) equals 2

CHOOSE(*index, value 1, value 2, …, value n***):** returns the value from the list of arguments based on the value of *index*; if *index* is 1, *value 1* is returned

COLUMN(*ref***):** returns the column number of *ref*; if *ref* is omitted, it returns the column number of the current cell; *ref* cannot refer to multiple areas

COLUMNS(*array***):** returns the number of columns in *array*

HLOOKUP(*lookup value, compare array, index number***):** searches the first row of *compare array* for the largest value that is less than or equal to *lookup value*; the function moves down the column by the amount specified by *index number* and returns the value found there

INDEX(*ref, row, column, area***):** returns the cell that is defined in *ref* by *row* and *column;* if *ref* refers to multiple areas, *area* defines the areas from which the cell is to be obtained

INDEX(*array, row, column***):** returns the value of a single element within *array,* selected by *row* and *column*

INDIRECT(*ref, type of ref***):** returns the reference specified by *ref*

LOOKUP(*lookup value, compare vector, result vector***):** searches *compare vector* for largest value less than or equal to *lookup value;* the function returns the corresponding value of *result vector*; the values in *compare vector* can be text, numbers, or logical, but they must be in ascending order; Microsoft recommends using this version of LOOKUP rather than the next one

LOOKUP(*lookup value, compare array***):** searches first row or column of *compare array* for largest value that is less than or equal to *lookup value;* the function returns the corresponding value in the last row or column of *compare array;* whether the first row or column is searched depends on the size of the array; if it is square or has more rows than columns, LOOKUP searches the first column and gives a value from the corresponding last column; if it is square or has more columns than rows, the first row is searched and LOOKUP gives the value of the corresponding cell in the last row; the values in the array can be text, numbers, or logical, but they must be in ascending order

MATCH(*lookup value, compare vector, type***):** returns the corresponding number of the comparison value in *compare vector* that matches *lookup value;* example: If the lookup value matches the second comparison value, MATCH returns a **2**

OFFSET(*reference, rows, cols, height, width***):** returns a *reference* of specified *height* and *width* offset from another reference by a specified number of *rows* and *columns*

ROW(*ref***):** returns the row number of *ref* if *ref* references a single cell; if *ref* refers to a range of cells, a vertical array is returned; if the argument is omitted, the row of the cell containing the ROW function is returned; ROW cannot refer to multiple areas

ROWS(*array***):** returns the number of rows in *array*

TRANSPOSE(*array***):** returns an array that is the transpose of *array;* that is, the rows become columns and the columns rows

VLOOKUP (*lookup value, compare array, index number*)**:** identical to HLOOKUP, except that it searches the first column of *compare array*, moving right in that row the amount specified by *index number*

For more information on the lookup functions, refer to Chapter 13.

INFORMATION FUNCTIONS

The following functions are useful for obtaining information:

CELL(*type of info, reference*)**:** returns information on cell; use this when writing macros to get information on a cell

ERROR.TYPE(*error value*)**:** returns a number corresponding to one of Excel's error values; use this in a macro to determine the error type and the type of error handling routine to use

INFO(*type number*)**:** returns information on the current operating environment

ISBLANK(*value*)**:** returns TRUE if *value* refers to a blank cell

ISERR(*value*)**:** returns TRUE if *value* refers to any error except #N/A

ISERROR(*value*)**:** returns TRUE if *value* refers to any Excel error value

ISLOGICAL(*value*)**:** returns TRUE if *value* refers to a logical value

ISNA(*value*)**:** returns TRUE if *value* refers to a cell with #N/A (number not available)

ISNONTEXT(*value*)**:** returns TRUE if *value* does not refer to text

ISNUMBER(*value*)**:** returns TRUE if *value* refers to a number

ISREF(*value*)**:** returns TRUE if *value* refers to a reference or reference formula

ISTEXT(*value*)**:** returns TRUE if *value* refers to text

N(*value*)**:** returns numeric value of *value*

NA( ): returns the error value of #N/A (value not available); there is no argument

TYPE(*value*)**:** returns a code defining the type of *value:* 1 for number, 2 for text, 4 for logical, 16 for error, and 64 for an array; this is useful in user-defined functions to determine the type or argument passed to it

Use the ISERROR and ISNA functions to trap errors in your worksheet. This is especially useful in macros (see Part VII), since error conditions will terminate a macro execution. Using these functions, you can test for an error condition and, if you get one, branch for appropriate action.

SOLVING FOR X

Excel permits you to define a goal and work backward to find data values that will give you this goal. This is called "solving for x, the variable." There are two ways of doing this: using the Goal Seek command on the Formula menu and using the Solver utility provided with Excel. The utility is described in Chapter 25.

For now, let's see how to use the simple Goal Seek command. Use the amortization schedule worksheet and assume you are purchasing a car and can only afford $175 a month on the payments. How much of a loan can you assume if the interest remains constant?

With the amortization schedule loaded, make the cell active that contains the payment value. Choose Formula ➤ Goal Seek. Figure 8.3 shows the dialog box, which you can move by dragging the title bar if you need to see certain

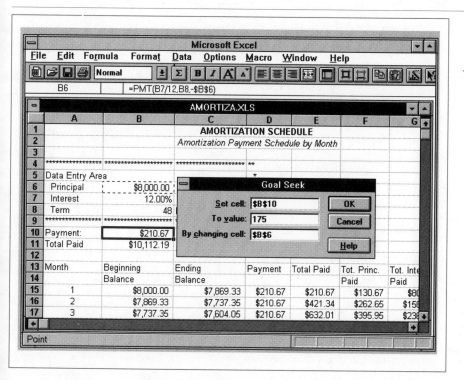

FIGURE 8.3:

Defining the parameters for Goal Seek to use

worksheet cells. The Set Cell text box contains the goal cell, or B10 here (absolute reference). This defines the cell for the payment. The To Value text box contains the goal value, or $175 here. The By Changing Cell text box contains the cell that can be changed to meet the goal. Enter **$B$6**, the cell containing the principal. Click OK.

Excel performs iterative calculations to find the correct value and then displays the worksheet with the new principal ($6645.44) for this payment. Click OK to keep the new principal and payment in the cells or Cancel to return to the unaltered worksheet.

For more complex simulations involving several cells, use the Solver (Chapter 25).

FAST TRACK CHAPTER 9

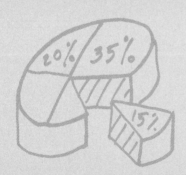

CHAPTER

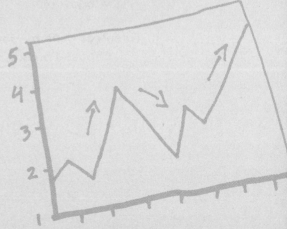

Organizing and Documenting Worksheets

How you organize and document your worksheets is important, as this makes the worksheet easier to read and improves its accuracy. In this chapter you will learn how to:

- ◆ name cells and cell ranges
- ◆ use the outline feature of Excel
- ◆ add comments to a cell
- ◆ audit your worksheets
- ◆ troubleshoot worksheets

While working with this chapter, you will be working with both the INCOME and BALANCE worksheets you have already created. You will be changing these, but avoid saving either of these worksheets with the changes. We also will be referring to some data in the cash-flow worksheet of Chapter 7. You do not need to create this worksheet; simply refer to Figure 7.15.

NAMING CELLS

When you are creating a worksheet, you may often find it advantageous to identify a cell or cell range. Here are a few reasons for using names:

◆   Names make worksheets and formulas easier to work with and read.

◆   Names reduce the likelihood of writing an incorrect formula, because you reference a cell's name, not its address.

◆   You can name areas of a worksheet to make it easy to go quickly to that area, such as an assumption area, for editing.

◆   You can name a constant, such as an interest rate. This makes it easier to understand what the constant represents.

◆   Using names ensures that links will remain consistent with worksheet editing.

Once you have defined a name, you can use it in functions and formulas, just as you would use a cell or cell-range reference. For example, you could name a cell range and use the range name in a SUM function. Some functions, such as the database functions, *require* the use of names. You also can use names with the Goto command to simplify moving to a cell or cell range.

You can use names for absolute, relative, or mixed cell references, although names are generally used for absolute references. For example, the cash-flow analysis worksheet shown in Chapter 7 used a series of constants in column L (near the top of the page). These were part of the worksheet calculations for each month (see Figure 7.15). The three cells in column L could be named *Interest, Cost_of_Goods_Ratio,* and *Advertising_Ratio,* respectively. The formula for cell C26, the advertising cost for February, would then be

=Advertising_Ratio*B14

where B14 is January's total sales. You also could give cell B14 a name. You would, however, have to use relative cell addressing in defining that name if you wanted to use a Copy or Fill command to copy the formula into other cells.

Defining Names

There are two ways that you can name a cell or cell range:

◆   Use the Create Names command on the Formula menu (or Ctrl-Shift-F3) to designate row or column titles as names.

◆ Use the Define Name command on the Formula menu (or Ctrl-F3) to create a name for any cell, cell range, or constant.

Using an Existing Name

NOTE *You do not assign a name with the Create Names command. The name is taken simply from the first cell in the row or column. Spaces are converted to underlines. If you wish to assign your own name, see the next section.*

The easiest way to define a name for a row or column is to use the row or column title:

1. Enter a name/title in the row/column you want to name, if it's not already there.

2. Select the entire row or column.

3. Open the Formula menu and choose Create Names (or press Ctrl-Shift-F3). The Create Names dialog box shown in Figure 9.1 appears.

4. Select Top Row if you wish to use column titles as names; select Left Column if you wish to use row titles as names. Notice that you also can name upward from a bottom row or to the left of a right column. You can use both row and column titles by choosing both Top Row and Left Column.

5. Click OK.

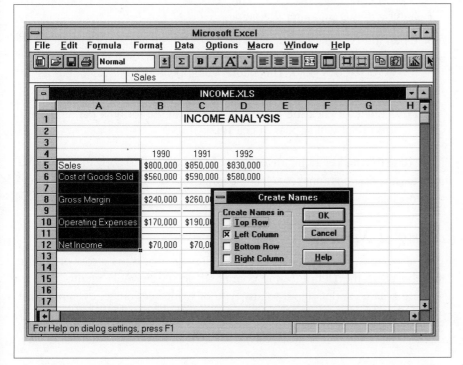

FIGURE 9.1:

The Create Names dialog box allows you to define a name for a row or column using the row's or column's existing title

As an example, let's use the simple INCOME worksheet that you created in Chapter 3 and see how names simplify your work and improve reliability. Now try the following exercise:

1. Select rows 5–12 by selecting the range A5 to D12.

2. Open the Formula menu and choose Create Names (or just press Ctrl-Shift-F3).

3. When the Create Names dialog box shown in Figure 9.1 is displayed, select Left Column, then click OK.

4. Select cell B8. The cell's current formula is displayed in the formula bar. This cell will now be named.

5. Open the Formula menu again and choose Paste Name (or just press F3). The Paste Name dialog box shown in Figure 9.2 appears. It lists the names that are currently available. These names are the row titles that you selected in Step 1. Notice that Excel converted all the spaces that were in the names into underlines automatically. This is because you cannot use spaces in names.

6. Double-click on Sales. The dialog box clears and an equal sign as well as the name **Sales** are entered in the cell (and formula bar), as shown in Figure 9.3.

7. Enter a minus sign after the name.

8. Open the Formula menu again and select Paste Name (or just press F3). When the Paste Name dialog box appears, double-click on Cost_of_Goods_Sold. This name will appear in the formula bar as part of the expression, as shown in Figure 9.4.

9. Press Enter, or click the Enter box (the ✓) in the formula bar, and the correct total will appear in cell B8.

Now drag the marker at the lower right of cell B8 to D8 to copy the new equation to the other columns (or select the range and use Edit ➤ Fill Right). Check the formulas in the cells after filling.

Creating a Name

You also can assign a name to a cell or cell range that is not a row or column title by using the Define Name command on the Formula menu. You can choose a name and assign it to any type of worksheet range, even a discontinuous range.

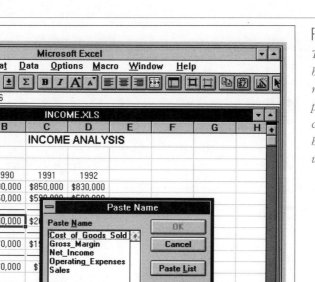

The Paste Name dialog box shows a list of names available for pasting, which correspond to the row headings on the worksheet

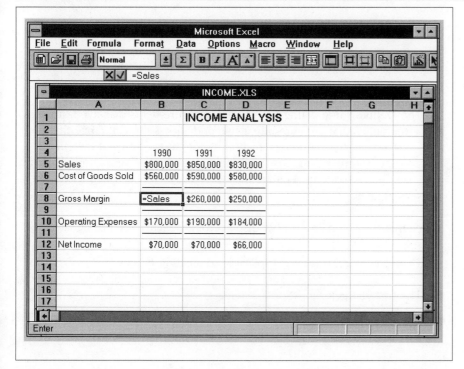

Cell B8, and the formula in it, is tentatively named "Sales"

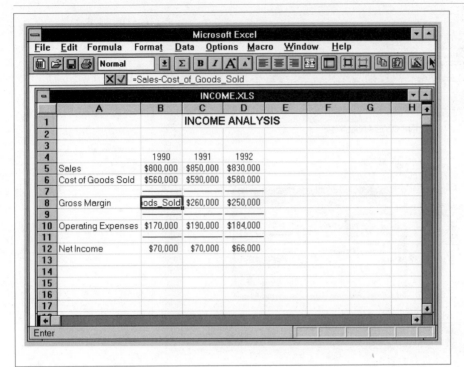

FIGURE 9.4:
*Cell B8, and the
formula in it, is now
fully, descriptively
named "Sales-Cost_
of_Good_Sold"*

Try creating a name for row 8 of your INCOME worksheet:

1. Select the cell range you want to name by selecting A8 to D8.

2. Open the Formula menu and choose Define Name (or press Ctrl-F3).

3. The Define Name dialog box shown in Figure 9.5 is displayed. It lists the names that are currently active and shows the cell range that you just selected in the Refers To box. Enter **Gross_Sales** at the cursor location in the Name text box, then press Enter. Use an underline instead of a space to separate the two words. Notice which letters are in capitals.

Notice that the cell name is now displayed in the active-cell designator.

The following rules are applicable to creating names:

◆ The first character must be a letter.

◆ Spaces are not allowed.

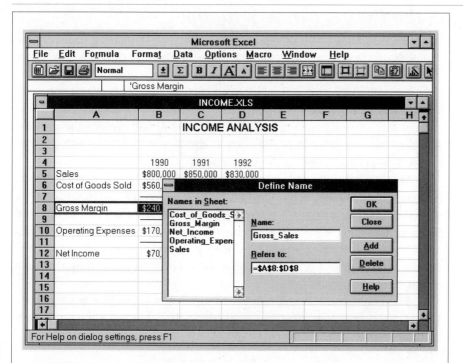

◆ Except for the first character, letters, digits, periods, and underlines can be used.

◆ Names can be up to 255 characters long.

◆ Uppercase and lowercase letters are not distinguished from each other.

◆ The name cannot look like an absolute, relative, or mixed cell reference, such as *$B$2.*

◆ Text and dates can be used to define a name.

◆ You can use discontinuous ranges to define a name, such as *H1:H3,H7:H12.*

If you try to use a name that breaks any of these rules, Excel will display an illegal-name message.

Using the Define Name Window

You can define more than one name at a time by clicking the Add button in the dialog box after each entry.

Instead of selecting a cell or cell range, you can use the Refers To box in the Define Name dialog box to define the range to which a name refers. You can even enter formulas or other names as part of the reference.

Any cell(s) that you select before you invoke the Define Name command will appear in the Refers To box when the window is displayed. You can change that entry and your new cell or cell range will replace the previous selection. You can also clear the entry in the Refers To box by selecting the entire contents and pressing the Backspace key.

You can enter the cell or cell range in the Refers To box either by typing it from the keyboard or by clicking the cell you want to reference in the worksheet before choosing Define Name. If you click a cell, its address will be entered as an absolute cell reference. (The opposite is true when you click a cell to enter it to the formula bar—then it is a relative cell reference.) You can, of course, enter a cell address from the keyboard as an absolute, relative, or mixed cell reference.

The commands on the Edit menu are not available for editing in the Define Name window. You can, however, edit using the shortcut keys of the Edit menu.

WORKING WITH NAMES

Once you have named a cell or cell range, you can use that name in many ways. You can perform move, copy, and fill operations in the same way that you did with other types of cell referencing. You can enter names into formulas, which you did earlier in this chapter, and you can use names with the Goto command.

Using Names and the Goto Command

Using names with the Goto command moves you directly to any specific cell or cell range. Try this with your INCOME worksheet. Open the Formula menu and choose Goto (or just press F5). When the Goto dialog box shown below is displayed, double-click on Net_Income. The cursor will move to this row on the screen right away. The active-cell designator will also show the name of the cell range.

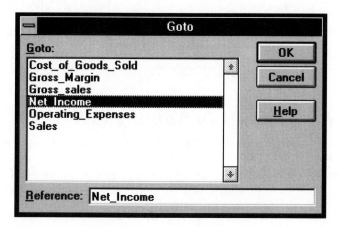

Editing and Deleting Names

To edit a name that you have already defined, open the Formula menu and choose Define Name (or press Ctrl-F3). The Define Name dialog box will be displayed. Scroll through the Names in Sheet listbox until the name that you want to edit is visible, then select it. The current name will be displayed in the Name text box and the current reference will be in the Refers To text box. The contents of either box can be edited. Click OK when you have completed your editing.

Use caution when renaming a range. If a range is already named and you select the same range and Formula ➤ Define Name again to rename it, the Define Name dialog box will prompt you for a new name and show the old name in the Name text box. If you edit the name displayed and click OK, both names will be with the worksheet and define the same range. For this reason, delete the old name after renaming a range.

If you want to delete a name that you previously defined, first edit any cell references in the worksheet that use the name so that they no longer use it. If you don't do this, all cells referencing that name will display an error message.

Invoke the Find command in the Formula menu to locate all references to the name. When the dialog box is displayed, type the name you will delete in the Find What text box. Check Formulas and Part in the Find dialog box and select either option in the Look By group. (Choose Part if the name might be part of a whole name—such as *SALES* in 92SALES and 93SALES; otherwise choose Whole.) When you click OK, the first occurrence will be displayed. Press F7 to find successive occurrences. As an exercise, delete the Gross_Sales name that you defined earlier:

1. Open the Formula menu and choose Define Name (or press Ctrl-F3).

2. When the Define Name dialog box is displayed, choose Gross_Sales.

3. Select Delete.

4. Click OK.

Precautions in Naming Cells

Keep the following precautions, notes, and tips in mind when naming cells:

◆   Deleting a cell name that is used in worksheet formulas will invoke error messages. Edit the cells first so that they no longer use the name.

◆   When you insert a row or column anywhere within a named range, the definition will change accordingly.

◆   If you cut and paste an entire named range, the definition will be changed accordingly.

◆   Avoid using relative references when naming cell ranges. The result will depend on the active cell when the name is defined. The referenced cells will also change if you copy the cell in which the name is used. Excel defaults to absolute references.

Applying Names to Existing Formulas

Composing a formula out of cell names, rather than normal cell references, makes the formula easier to read. As you can see, the formula

=Total_Sales*Tax_Rate

calculates the tax on a sale more intuitively than

=B4*A7

does. To create a formula that uses cell names, you first have to give the relevant cells names, then you have to apply the names to the formula. Naming a cell that a formula references will not automatically rewrite that formula. For instance, in the example above, giving cell B4 the name

Total_Sales and cell A7 the name *Tax_Rate* will not automatically change the formula =B4*A7 to =Total_Sales*Tax_Rate. But once those cells *are* named, it will be easy to rewrite the formula.

Try this:

1. Select cell B4.

2. Use Formula ➤ Define Name and name the cell **Total_Sales**. Click OK.

3. Select cell A7.

4. Use Formula ➤ Define Name and name the cell **Tax_Rate**. Click OK.

5. Select the cell containing the formula.

6. Open the Formula menu and choose Apply Names. The list box will show the active names in the worksheet (see the top dialog box in Figure 9.6).

7. Select the names you wish to substitute for references in the existing formula. You can select a block of names by holding down the Shift key and clicking with the mouse (or several separate names by holding down the Ctrl key and clicking with the mouse).

8. Make other selections as necessary (see below) and click OK.

At the bottom of the dialog box are two options: one determines whether to ignore relative/absolute references; the second whether to use row and column names. When the first option is checked, Excel ignores relative/absolute references; when it's unchecked, it replaces absolute references with absolute names and relative references with relative names. Leave this option turned on, unless you plan to copy cells to a new location and need to preserve the reference styles of the formulas. The second option, when selected, permits the Apply Names command to rename cells based on their row and column headings.

When the Use Row and Column Names check box is on, Excel uses the names of the ranges containing the cells referenced by the formula if a name for the specific cells can't be found. Excel will replace references with the column containing the cell referenced in the formula, the row containing the cell referenced in the formula, or both—depending on how the Omit boxes below are checked. When a cell referenced can be replaced by both a row-oriented range and a column-oriented range, Name Order determines which is used first.

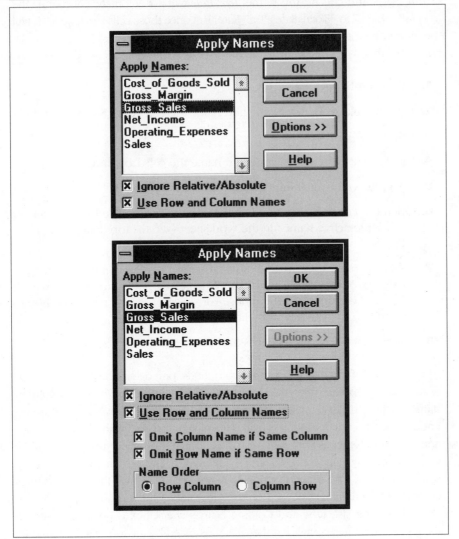

The Apply Names dialog boxes. The top one is the default box that allows you to apply names to a formula. The bottom one allows you to fine-tune the way you apply names.

Making a Name List

It's a good idea to make a list of named cells and their corresponding addresses on the worksheet, so that you have a handy record of the names. It takes up two columns and can be as long as necessary to list all the names.

This table will over-write any data in the columns it fills. If you overwrite worksheet data by mistake, select Undo from the Edit menu immediately.

Find a worksheet area that this will not erase and select the top two cells for the list. Open the Formula menu and choose Paste Name (or press F3). When the dialog box is displayed, click the Paste List button. This will paste the current names and their references in the two selected columns of the worksheet (see Figure 9.7).

This list is static: if you edit the names later you must repaste the list to update it.

You have now defined and pasted names using a simple worksheet. The same techniques can be applied to any type of document. You probably will use names quite often to clarify your worksheet formulas and function arguments.

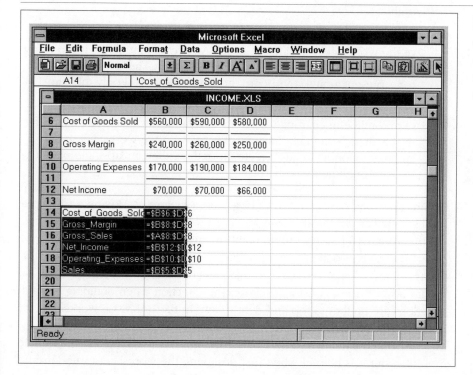

FIGURE 9.7:

Pasting a name list to a worksheet is a good way of keeping track of the names.

OUTLINING WORKSHEETS

Outlining is an important feature of Excel. Here are some useful applications for this feature:

◆ When working with a large worksheet, it is often hard to get the over-all picture due to the details at the row or column level. To view the results better, create an outline and collapse the worksheet so that only the summary rows and columns are visible.

◆ When using the Autoformatting command on the Format menu, first create an outline. Then the Autoformatting command can apply different styles to the various levels based on the outline.

◆ Using the outline feature, you can quickly create different views of the worksheet for different users. An accountant may wish to study the worksheet with all the detail levels shown. The same worksheet for a presentation to the Board, however, may need only the summary levels.

◆ Use an outline in charting to eliminate detail levels that aren't used in the chart. You might have weekly totals in the worksheet with summary monthly totals. Create an outline, then collapse the outline to chart only the monthly totals.

Excel can outline rows or columns. To simplify things we will limit the discussion to outlining rows.

Outlining involves grouping rows based on a hierarchy. Moving a row up a level is called *promoting* that row. Moving a row down a level is called *demoting* that row. Excel accepts up to eight outline levels.

Excel does its outlining automatically, using the direction in which the formulas reference other cells to determine level breakings. For this reason, you should always use a consistent referencing direction when outlining. Default directions are bottom to top and right to left. In the BALANCE worksheet, for instance, references always refer to rows above the current row.

You can manually promote or demote rows (or columns) in the outline from this, but it is helpful when first designing the worksheet to understand how the outlining works. Design your worksheet to support, as much as possible, Excel's automatic outlining feature.

Outlining can be done from the Utility toolbar or the menu bar. You can turn this toolbar on using the Options ➤ Toolbars command, choosing Utility in the list, and then clicking on Show. Figure 9.8 shows the buttons on the Utility toolbar that are used in outlining.

Promote button raises selected rows or columns to a higher level.

Demote button moves selected rows or columns to a lower level.

Show Outline Symbols button toggles the display of the outline symbols or, if no outline exists, creates an outline.

Select Visible Cells button selects only visible cells in an outline. Useful for charting or copying.

CREATING THE OUTLINE

To see how outlining works, let's create an outline from the BALANCE sheet. Open the BALANCE worksheet and follow these steps:

1. Select the range to outline: A10 to E44.

2. Choose Formula ➤ Outline.

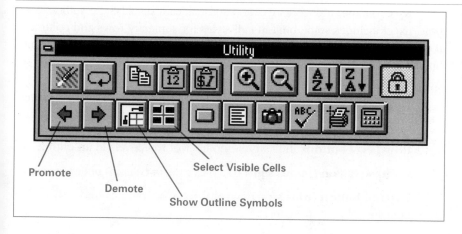

FIGURE 9.8:

The Utility toolbar buttons help you to outline a worksheet

Promote

Demote

Select Visible Cells

Show Outline Symbols

3. In the dialog box below, specify whether summary columns are to be included. Check the Summary Rows Below Detail check box and be sure Summary Columns To Right of Detail is not checked.

4. Click the Create button.

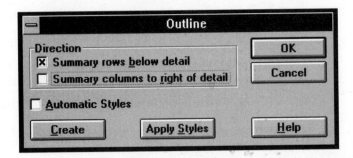

With Excel's outliner the summary information can appear below, above, or to the right or left of subordinate levels. In the default mode, the summary information is assumed to be below and to the right of the subordinate information. You can uncheck the Summary Rows Below Detail and Summary Columns To Right of Detail options in the Outline dialog box to switch this.

Another way to create an outline is to select the range and click the Show Outline Symbols button on the Utility toolbar. Then click OK in the Warning dialog box.

Excel outlines the worksheet and automatically displays the outline symbols. Excel includes some built-in cell styles for summary rows and columns. If you wish to apply these automatically, be sure Automatic Styles in the Outline dialog box is turned on. The summary row here is already formatted, so Automatic Styles is not selected.

Figure 9.9 shows the outlined worksheet. Notice the following features in the worksheet window (columns are not outlined in this example):

Row Level buttons indicate the number of row levels in an outline.

Collapse Button (minus sign) collapses rows or columns under this item.

Expand button (plus sign) expands rows or columns under this item (not shown in figure).

Row Level bars indicate the span of each level.

If you wish to hide the outline buttons, open the Options menu and select Display, toggle the Outline Symbols option off, and click OK. Toggling the check box on will display them again. Another way to toggle the outline symbols display is to click the Show Outline Symbols button on the toolbar.

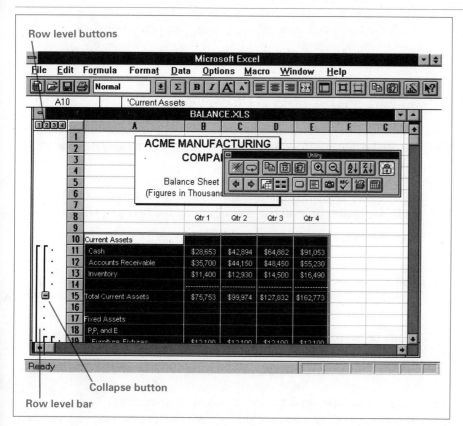

If you make a mistake in creating an outline and wish to start over, the easiest method may be to clear the outline from the worksheet. Clearing an outline does not affect the worksheet data. To clear an outline, first select the outlined area. Then repeatedly click the Promote button to promote all rows and columns to level one. The symbols will disappear.

EDITING THE OUTLINE

If you fail to select an entire row or column, Excel will ask you to specify whether you are promoting or demoting an entire row or column.

You can edit the outline so that rows (or columns) are correctly aligned by level. Do this by promoting and demoting the rows:

◆ To demote a row (i.e., move it to a lower level), select the *entire* row by clicking on the row numbers (as opposed to the row of the outlined block) and click the Demote button on the toolbar, or press Alt-Shift-→.

◆ To promote a row (move it to a higher level), select the entire row and click the Promote button on the toolbar, or press Alt-Shift-←.

Columns are demoted and promoted in the same way.

CONTROLLING THE LEVELS DISPLAYED

You can control the levels displayed by expanding or collapsing them. For example, you could create a summary worksheet by collapsing the worksheet around the summary totals:

◆ To collapse a level, find the row (or column) to collapse and click the collapse button or level bar encompassing the data you wish to hide.

◆ To expand a level, find the row (or column) and click the expand button for the data you wish to show.

◆ To display a specific level of the outline, click the corresponding row or column-level button. (This only works when collapsing; otherwise the button is hidden.)

◆ To quickly select all rows or columns grouped within a detail level, hold down the Shift key and click the collapse or expand button of the row or column. This is a fast way to select ranges for charting

Figure 9.10 shows the same worksheet after collapsing many rows.

Before continuing, clear the outline by selecting the outlined area and clicking the Promote tool until the outline is cleared.

ADDING COMMENTS TO A WORKSHEET

Excel provides three methods for adding comments to a worksheet:

◆ Placing the note (or label) as text directly into a cell on the worksheet. You can refer to it with asterisks or other special symbols from other cells in the worksheet.

◆ Adding it as a note attached to a cell. This type of comment is not directly visible, but is attached to the cell and can be viewed or printed using menu commands.

◆ Placing it in a text box and using arrows to point to the cell(s) to which it refers.

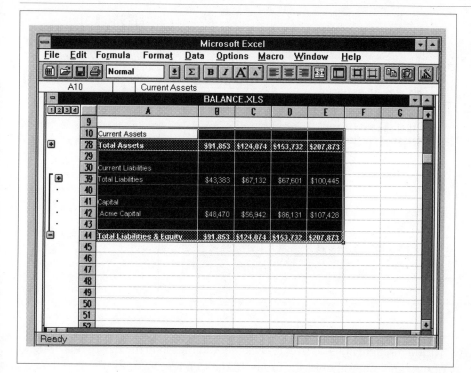

FIGURE 9.10:

The worksheet after collapsing several rows

The first method is straightforward. Let's look at the other two.

ADDING A NOTE TO A CELL

NOTE
NOTE

You can attach notes, sounds, or both to a cell. Soundbites attached to cells are useful for presentations, as described in Chapter 6.

Sometimes you may wish to add a comment about a cell that will be useful to someone entering data into the worksheet. You do not, however, want the comment to show on the worksheet at all times. Here is a way to add such a comment with Excel. Try this with the BALANCE worksheet:

1. Select the cell to which you wish to add the note, in this case cell B13.

2. Open the Formula menu and choose Note.

3. Type the note within the Text Note text box, as shown in Figure 9.11. Word-wrapping is automatically activated—do not use the Enter key at the end of a line.

4. When you have typed the complete note, press Enter or click OK. The Cell Note dialog box will disappear and you will be back at the worksheet. The cell will be marked to show that it contains a note.

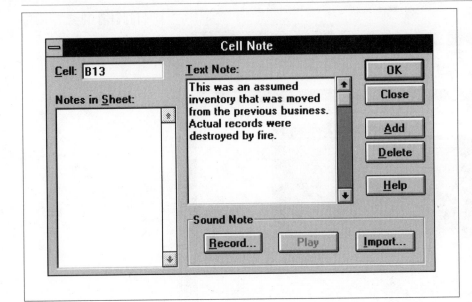

The Cell Note dialog box allows you to attach a note to a specific cell in the worksheet

To add multiple notes at a time, click the Add button in the dialog box, instead of OK, and enter a new cell addres in the Cell text box.

To view the note:

1. Select the cell to which the note is attached.

2. Open the Formula menu and choose Note. The note will appear in the Cell Note dialog box.

The Notes in Sheet list box contains available notes on the current worksheet. You can choose any of these to see the corresponding note to the right in the Text Note text box.

To view all notes in the worksheet, choose Workspace from the Options menu and toggle the Info Window option on. Click OK. This opens an information window. Choose Arrange from the Window menu, choose Tiled, and click OK to display the Info window tiled with the worksheet. Activate the worksheet and choose Select Special from the Formula menu. Select the Notes option and click OK (see Figure 9.12). You can now move from highlighted cell to highlighted cell on the worksheet with the Tab and Enter keys and see each note.

To copy notes, select the cell and choose the Edit ➤ Copy to place the cell contents in the Clipboard. Then choose Edit ➤ Paste Special and select Notes to paste just the note.

To print all notes in the worksheet, choose Show Info from the Window menu (make this window active), then choose Print from its File menu. Another method with the worksheet active is to select File ➤ Print and then select the Notes option at the bottom of the dialog box.

To delete notes, select the cell or cell range from which you wish to clear notes. Choose Clear from the Edit menu and select the Notes option. Another method is to select the cell that has the note, choose Note from the Formula menu, and select Delete. Perhaps an easier way still is to select Formula ➤ Note, select the note(s) to delete in the Cell Note dialog box, and click on the Delete button.

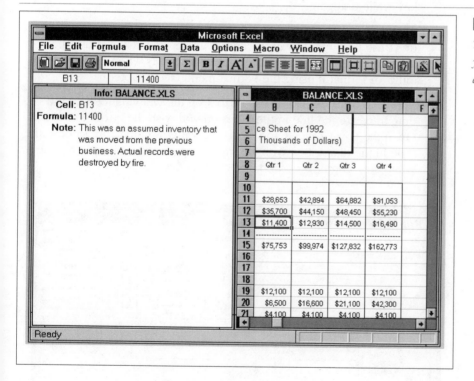

FIGURE 9.12:

The Info window allows you to view any note attached to a cell

ADDING A NOTE IN A BOX

Using the Drawing toolbar is a handy way to put a note in a box. Select Toolbars from the Options menu and then select Drawing. Click on Show. Refer to Chapter 6 for the buttons on this toolbar and more information on using text boxes.

To add a note in a box of the BALANCE sheet:

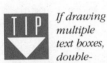

TIP *If drawing multiple text boxes, double-click the Text Box tool when starting, and click it again or another tool when finished.*

1. Open the BALANCE worksheet and Drawing toolbar.

2. Click the Text Box tool in the Drawing toolbar.

3. Click the mouse pointer at the upper-left corner of where you wish the box to sit (G10).

4. Drag the mouse to create a box of the size you wish to I12. If you wish the box to be anchored to the underlying grid, hold down the Ctrl key while dragging.

5. Type the desired comment into the box. Word-wrapping is active, so don't use the Enter key at the end of a line. You also can use the Edit menu to edit the text or copy to the text box, as when copying a formula, or format it using the Format menu (see Chapter 6).

6. To draw an arrow, click the Arrow tool on the Drawing toolbar and drag to create the line in the direction you wish the arrow to point. Open the Format menu and select the Patterns command. Choose the style in the dialog box with an arrowhead, as shown below. Set the width and length as desired and click on OK.

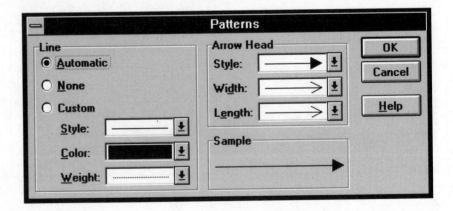

Figure 9.13 shows the worksheet with a text box. To delete a text-box note, select the box and the arrow. Then choose Clear on the Edit menu or press Del.

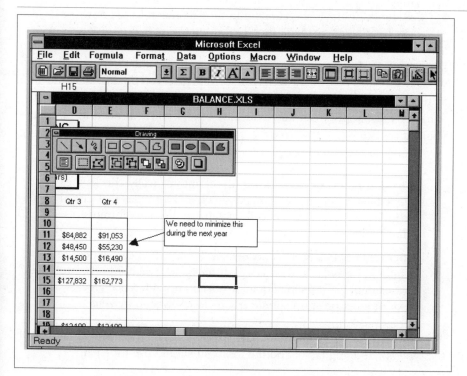

FIGURE 9.13:

Now the worksheet features a boxed note on-screen

AUDITING AND TROUBLESHOOTING WORKSHEETS

Once a worksheet is created, you should take the time to check, or *audit*, the worksheet. There are several techniques you can use in creating a worksheet to minimize errors and related problems:

◆ Plan the worksheet before starting. Where will the different types of data (assumptions, input, etc.) be placed?

◆ Use names for cells and cell ranges, and use the names in any expression. Put the name list on the worksheet.

◆ Add comments and use cell notes liberally.

◆ Avoid complex expressions. When writing an expression, break it down over several cells so that the expression in each cell is not too complex.

◆ Test the worksheet with data for which you know the results.

◆ Use the Print Preview command in the File menu to see how the resulting worksheet will look before you print it.

In spite of all these precautions, however, you will still need to audit each worksheet. Excel provides a variety of tools to help you do this. Take the time to use them to ensure that the worksheet is accurate and works correctly. Some of these tools work automatically: others you will need to discipline yourself to use.

There are two automatic tools:

Circular reference checking: Excel automatically checks the worksheet for circular references—i.e., cell formulas that directly or indirectly reference the cell containing the same formulas (see Chapter 14).

Formula checking: Excel checks to be sure that data types are consistent in formulas and issues error messages when it finds problems. For example, a numeric equation should not reference a cell with text, or an expression should not include division by zero.

There are also a few manual tools available for auditing. Here are a few of the types of auditing tasks, and the tool you should use for each:

Finding cells with error values: Use Select Special (and click on Formulas and Errors) or Find in the Formula menu and search for cells starting with #. Optionally, use the AUDIT.XLA macro provided with Excel.

Finding cells that are "different": Use Select Special and choose Row Differences or Column Differences. Use this to find cells that don't fit a pattern horizontally or vertically.

Review changes using the COMPARE.XLA macro provided with Excel.

GETTING CELL INFORMATION

To get specific information on a cell, select the cell and then choose Options ➤ Workspace. Toggle Info Window on and click OK. Once you have toggled this option on, a new Info window is displayed. You can resize or move the window on the screen; you also can use Arrange in the Window menu to tile it on the screen with the worksheet.

As you click the mouse over the worksheet, the Info window displays the information about the active cell (see Figure 9.14). With the Show Info window active, you can use File ➤ Print to print this information. You can preview the printout with the Preview command, just as with a worksheet.

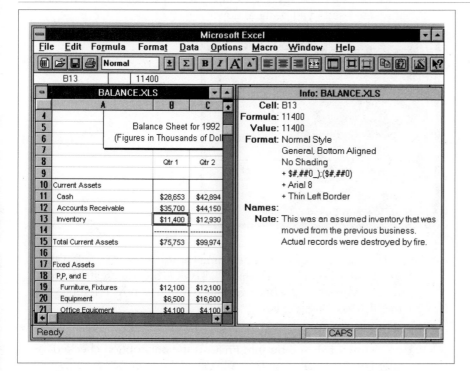

FIGURE 9.14:

The Info window allows you to audit your worksheet easily

You can control what type of information is displayed by opening the Info menu on the Info window. You can check to show cell addresses, values, formulas, formats, protection status, names, precedents, dependents, and notes. When you are through, you close the Info window by double-clicking its Control box.

SELECTING CELLS BY CONTENT

Another way to check cells is to select cells by their content. This type of auditing is done by using the Select Special command in the Formula menu. For example, let's try this with our BALANCE worksheet:

1. Select cells A10 to E44.

2. Create names from the row headings using Formula ➤ Create Names (or pressing Ctrl-Shift-F3).

3. With the same range selected, apply the names to the entire worksheet using Formula ➤ Apply Names. All names are selected by default, as shown below. Click OK. Check a few formulas, and you will see that names are used in all of them now.

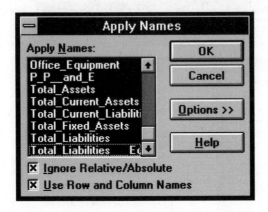

4. Now delete a name using Define Name (or press Ctrl-F3). Select the name Cash. Choose Delete, then click OK. This will create several error messages in the worksheet, since formulas now reference a name that no longer exists.

5. Choose Formula ➤ Select Special. Select Formulas in the dialog box (see Figure 9.15), and be sure Errors is the only option checked under Formulas. Click on OK. All cells with the error messages will be highlighted.

You can use the Select Special method to find cells with certain formulas, cells with notes, cells with constants, cells with no data, row differences, and column differences. For example, you might expect a certain cell to contain a formula and discover that it contains a constant value. This typically happens when formulas are converted to values for one reason or another. For example, if you paste a table value (see Chapter 13) to a cell, it is pasted as a value. It won't change as the table value changes (unless linked, as described in Chapter 16).

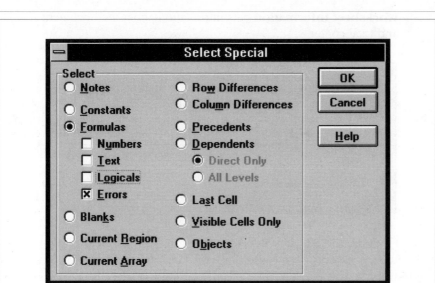

FIGURE 9.15:

The Select Special dialog box allows you to search for cells with error values

CREATING WORKSHEET EVALUATION REPORTS

Excel permits you to create a variety of reports to help you audit and evaluate the worksheet. You can use the Worksheet Auditor to create these. The Worksheet Auditor is an add-in macro that supports error checking, mapping, checking of cell dependencies, and interactive tracing.

To use the Worksheet Auditor, make the worksheet to check active. Then select File ➤ Open and open AUDIT.XLA in the Library subdirectory. From the Worksheet Auditor dialog box, shown below, choose the desired action and click OK:

Generate Audit Report creates a new worksheet with the error and problem reference listings in the active worksheet.

Map Worksheet creates a map of the worksheet that shows the type of contents in each cell.

Interactive Trace checks cell dependencies with an interactive trace.

Worksheet Information gets information about the document status and total contents.

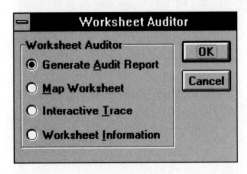

From the same Library directory, you can open COMPARE.XLA to compare two worksheets. This is useful for tracking changes and revisions. Open SUMMARY.XLA to get summary information on the worksheet. From any of these, you can select File ➤ Print to print the audit worksheet. If you use these add-in macros frequently, select Options ➤ Add-ins to open the auditor or other macro when you start Excel.

SPECIFYING A STARTUP DIRECTORY

With Excel, you can specify a startup directory. Any documents placed in this directory will automatically be opened at startup. Worksheets, templates, charts, macro sheets, workbooks, and add-ins can be placed in this directory. Here are a few applications for this directory:

◆ It's a useful place for putting macro sheets with functions and routines that you use frequently. The macro sheet can be hidden with everything available to the user. It is opened automatically upon starting.

◆ It's also a useful place for keeping templates that you use. Upon loading Excel, all available templates in the startup directory will be listed in the New dialog box. For example, you could create a template worksheet called SHEET1. You could then save it as SHEET1.XLT in a template format in the startup directory. It will now be the new default SHEET1 when starting Excel.

Excel defaults to using XLSTART (from the directory containing EXCEL.EXE) as the startup directory. A worksheet placed in this directory, for example, will open automatically upon startup. You can specify one additional startup directory if you wish, and documents in it will be opened after those in XLSTART. This allows you to create personal startup directories on a network.

To specify an additional startup directory:

1. Choose File ➤ Open.

2. Choose ALTSTART.XLA in the Library directory.

3. Click on OK.

4. Enter the new startup directory in the dialog box.

5. Click on OK.

To remove a startup directory, delete the directory from the disk.

The BALANCE worksheet has been modified in this chapter with various experiments. Don't save the BALANCE worksheet at this point (or else save it under a different name). In the next chapter you will start building a new worksheet to illustrate database management, tables, and charting.

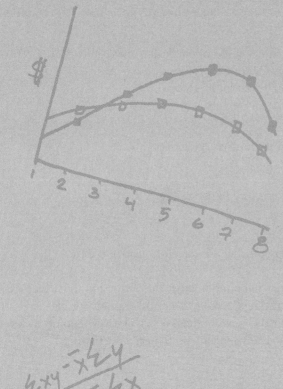

$$b = \frac{\Sigma xy - x \Sigma y}{\Sigma x^2 - x \Sigma x}$$

PART THREE

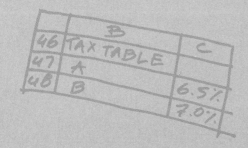

Part III: Effective Database Management

One of Excel's most useful features is its capacity for database management. You can use databases for any sort of application that requires management of groups of items with numerous components, such as the management of mailing lists, prospect lists, census data, a video tape library, or an organization's membership roster. In the case of a mailing list, for example, each database record is an address that includes the name, street address, city, state, zip code, and telephone number.

Excel's on-screen database-management capability allows you to create a database as part of a worksheet and use it to calculate cell values in other parts of the worksheet.

Part III consists of three chapters. Chapter 10 discusses the fundamentals of database management. You will create a database and learn how to add, edit, and delete records in it. In later chapters, this same database will be used to create complex reports and charts. Chapter 11 discusses how to find records in the database that meet a specific criteria. Chapter 12 discusses the techniques of sorting and ordering your database.

FAST TRACK CHAPTER 10

- Add the record manually to the range using Edit ➤ Insert to add any necessary rows. Then redefine the database.
- Use the Data ➤ Form command, choose New, and enter the new record. Choose Close and the record will be placed at the end of the database. The database range is updated automatically.

Add the field as a new column where you wish it, then redefine the database to include all the columns.

- Choose the row containing the record and select Edit ➤ Delete.
- Use the Data ➤ Form command, select (display) the record to delete, and choose Delete. Select Close.

- Edit the record on the worksheet.
- Choose Data ➤ Form. Scroll to the record, tab to the field, and edit the data. Choose Close.

CHAPTER 10

Basic Database
Techniques

You can regard the Excel on-screen database management system much as you would an electronic filing system. A *database* is a structured collection of data. The data may be about people, products, events—in short, anything about which you would like to store information. The primary use of a database is to manage the collection of data for reporting and making decisions.

DATABASE APPLICATIONS

You probably use one or more databases every day, although they are perhaps not electronic. Your address book, the telephone book, the recipe box, and the dictionary are all examples of commonly used databases. Each is a collection of data. In each case, the database is ordered so you can find the information you want quickly. Because none of these are electronic, however, they are relatively cumbersome to update.

Excel, however, permits you to create electronic databases that are easy to use and update. Here are some typical applications for an Excel database:

◆ Financial: general ledgers, accounts-receivable, payroll and accounts-payable systems

◆ Sales and marketing: contract management, sales projections, expense accounts, and prospect lists

◆ Business: personnel registers, telephone-extension directories, inventory listings, low-inventory reports, and material-requirement planning

◆ Home: cataloging of books and audio recordings, nutrition analyses, and recording of addresses

For example, Widget Manufacturing has a staff of sales representatives in each of four areas of the country. Each representative has a sales target, and the sum of the targets for the representatives in each area represents the sales target for that particular area. Widget also tracks sales performance by representative during each three-month cycle. These data are recorded in a database and used for a variety of reports. Management uses these reports to track the sales performance of each representative and the performance of each sales area.

THE DATABASE COMPONENTS

Figure 10.1 shows a sample Excel database. Notice that it is really nothing more than a rectangular range of worksheet cells. In Excel, a database is two or more rows of cells that span at least one column.

Each row represents a single item, or *record*. In Figure 10.1 there are 7 records visible in the database. Each column is called a *field*. In this sample database, the fields are LASTNAME, FIRSTNAME, ADDRESS, CITY, STATE, and ZIP. The first row of the database is used to define the field names. In the worksheet analogy, the records are rows and the fields are columns. Notice that the records do not have titles, but each field, including the first, has a name. You can put as many as 16,383 records in an Excel database (the top row must contain the field names).

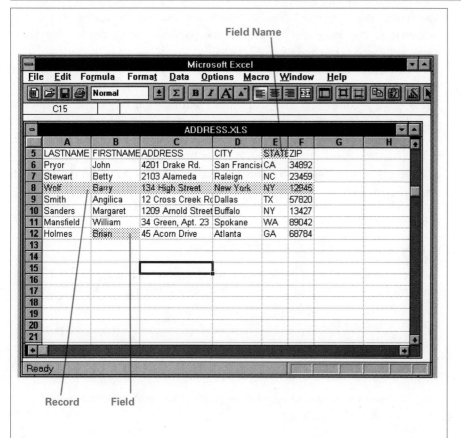

WORKING WITH DATABASES

The fact that an on-screen database looks very much like a worksheet makes the Excel database so easy to use. There are only two primary differences between the database and the worksheet: in a database, the rows no longer have a title and each column (including the first) has a name (a field name).

The features and commands that are available for working with worksheets are the same as those available for databases. The menu bar at the top of the screen also remains the same. You can define any part of a worksheet for a database and use the remainder for worksheet functions, or you can define the entire worksheet as a database. You can add, edit, and delete records and fields in a database in the same way that you work with cells in a worksheet. You can move data from a database to somewhere else on the worksheet (or from somewhere else on the worksheet to the database) using the familiar Copy, Cut, and Paste commands.

An Excel database can be sorted so that the records are in any desired order. For example, the database in Figure 10.1 could be sorted by name, address, or zip code. You also can extract information based on a particular criterion; for example, from this database you could extract the names of people living in New York. In this chapter, you will learn the basics of creating a database. In later chapters you'll learn how you can extract information (Chapter 11), sort the database in any order (Chapter 12), and create charts from databases (Chapter 19).

CREATING AN EXCEL DATABASE

Let's create the SALES database shown (as a printout) in Figure 10.2. There are four steps involved in creating and using a database:

1. Defining the fields.

2. Entering the data.

3. Formatting any data as necessary.

4. Defining the database range (that part of the worksheet that will be used as the database).

DEFINING THE FIELDS

You start creating a database exactly as you would begin a worksheet. Open a new worksheet for the database: open the File menu and choose New. You will see the New dialog box, shown below:

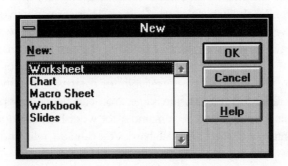

	A	B	C	D
13	LAST	FIRST	TARGET	REGION
14	Adams	Chuck	$118,000	South
15	Allen	Ellen	$90,000	East
16	Atkins	Lee	$113,000	East
17	Conners	Paul	$142,000	West
18	Ford	Carl	$191,000	Midwest
19	Glenn	John	$80,000	South
20	Harris	Ken	$176,000	West
21	Ellis	Nancy	$122,000	East
22	Jackson	Robert	$112,000	East
23	Keller	Janet	$105,000	West
24	Kennedy	Sandra	$135,000	East
25	Linn	Vera	$80,000	Midwest
26	Parker	Greg	$196,000	South
27	Peterson	Tom	$98,000	Midwest
28	Stevens	Carle	$110,000	East

Leave Worksheet selected (because a database is a part of a worksheet) and click OK. Excel displays an empty worksheet.

Enter the field names shown in Figure 10.2. Start in row 13, because you will need some working space at the top later. You may use any text (to a maximum of 255 characters) for field names, but it is a good idea to keep the names short to simplify searches. Field names must be text constants. If the field names contain numbers, they must be formatted as text. You also can use functions that produce text to create field names (such as =UPPER(B2)); however, you cannot use numbers or functions that produce numbers as field names.

You should plan your database before entering the fields. Usually you will want separate fields for first and last names. This permits you to treat each part of the name as a separate component. You could then use the FIRST field in a form letter (for example, *Dear Vera*). Any piece of data you might use for a search or sorting criterion should be put in a separate field.

You can use text, numeric values, or logical values for field values. You also can use calculated fields if you wish. For example, for an inventory database you might have a QOH field (Quantity-on-Hand) and a COST field. You could then define an extended cost field as QOH*COST (see Chapter 22 for an example).

ENTERING THE DATA

When entering formulas in calculated fields, use absolute references or names to refer to cells outside the database range and relative references to refer to cells inside the range.

Now enter the worksheet data shown in Figure 10.2. The best way to enter a large amount of data like this is record by record, because it follows the way we read: left to right and line by line. Select the entire entry area, then use the Tab key after each entry to move to the next cell. After all the data are entered, save the worksheet as SALES.

FORMATTING THE DATA

You can format any data in a database, just as you would any other cell or cell range in a worksheet. Set the picture by selecting Format ➤ Number. For any field width change, use Format ➤ Column Width. For any alignment changes, select Format ➤ Alignment. Fonts and font styles are set with Format ➤ Font.

To save time, format databases column by column, as all cells in a column are formatted the same. The column width should normally be equal to or greater than the longest cell entry in that field.

DEFINING THE DATABASE RANGE

The database range includes the field names.

Now you must define the area of the worksheet that will serve as your database:

1. Select cell A13.

2. Hold down the Shift key and click cell D28. You have now selected the entire database area (Figure 10.3).

3. Select Data ➤ Set Database. This assigns the name *Database* to the worksheet area that you have defined. You can now use this name in commands and formulas.

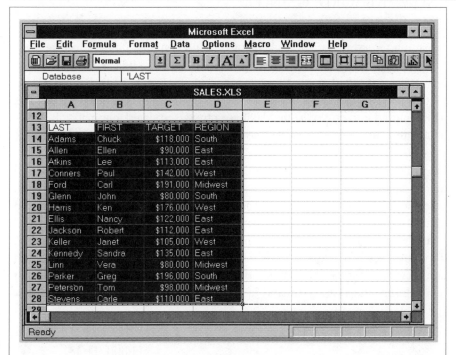

FIGURE 10.3:

Selecting the database range

There is really nothing special about what you have just done. You simply defined a range and then named that range Database. You also could have done it with the Define Name command, but the Set Database command is easier. If you choose Formula ➤ Paste Name, you will see **Database** listed as an available name. This name is used by the commands on the Database menu and the database functions to determine which area of the worksheet to operate on.

EDITING A DATABASE

Editing a database involves adding, deleting, editing, and moving records and fields. These operations are described in the following pages. Excel provides two methods of editing the records of a database: using menu commands or using a data form. You can use either method at any time. Choose the one that is the easiest for you.

ADDING A RECORD USING A MENU COMMAND

To add a record to the database using a menu command, first select the row designator where you wish to enter the record. Choose Edit ➤ Insert. A blank row will be inserted above the selected row (see Figure 10.4). Enter the data in the new record. It is not necessary to reset the database range or to format data entered into any cells: the database range is updated automatically to include the new record and the new record is formatted to match existing records.

There is one exception to the above rule. If you add a record to the end of the database, the database range must be reset (using Data ➤ Set Database), and the new record must be formatted. To eliminate the need to update the database range and format new data, put a dummy record as the last record that always stays at the end after any sort. The dummy record also should be formatted correctly. Any records inserted before the dummy end-record will automatically extend the range and be formatted. Name this last row so that you can use the Goto command to get to this row quickly.

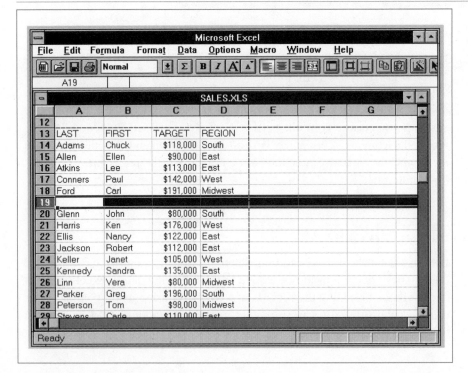

FIGURE 10.4:

Adding a record with a menu command

ADDING A RECORD USING A DATA FORM

To add a record using a data form, open the Data menu and choose Form. A dialog box will be displayed with the fields to the left of a scroll bar and push-button selections to the right of the scroll bar, as shown in Figure 10.5. Click the New button. The scroll box moves to the bottom of the scroll bar and an empty record is displayed. Enter the values for the cells in that record. Press the Tab key to move between fields. (Don't press Enter, as it moves to the next record.) When the record entry is completed, click Close or press Enter and the new record will be entered at the end of the database. You can also close the dialog box by double-clicking its Control box or by pressing Alt-F4. The database will be extended automatically and the new fields formatted.

To eliminate the necessity of updating the database range, add new fields within the current database range, instead of beyond it. Create a dummy field as the last field, which you always keep empty.

ADDING A FIELD

You can add a field to the database using menu commands, just as when you add records. (You cannot add a field using a data form.) To add a field to the right of the current fields, type the field name at the top of the column and enter the data for each record (see Figure 10.6). You will then have to redefine the database range to include the new field, as well as format the new field.

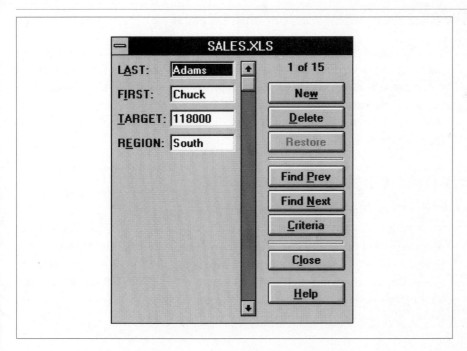

Adding a record using a data form

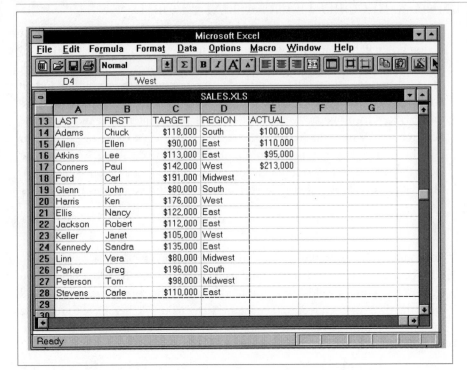

Adding a new field

You also can insert a field by adding a blank column with the Insert command in the Edit menu. Enter the field name at the top of the new blank column, then enter the data for each record. If you insert a field between other fields, the database range definition is updated automatically, but you probably still have to format the new field column. Fields often have different formats from adjacent fields.

You won't see a warning message or a dialog box when you delete a record using menu commands. If necessary, you can recover the deletion by selecting Edit ➤ Undo immediately afterwards.

DELETING A RECORD USING A MENU COMMAND

To delete a record from a database using a menu command, select the row designator for the record you wish to delete. Choose Edit ➤ Delete. The record will be deleted and the records below will move up to recover the space. Be sure there are no data on the row to the right or left of the database area before deletion, or they will be deleted as well. If there *are* other data on the row, only delete the database cells in that row.

To delete a field, follow the same procedure. Select the column designator for the field to delete. Then open the Edit menu and choose Delete. When either records or fields are deleted, the range definition is adjusted automatically and the database size decreased. Remember that any other data in the column outside the database area will also be deleted. If other data are in the column, select only the database portion of the column for deletion.

DELETING A RECORD USING A DATA FORM

When you delete a record using the data form, the record is permanently deleted and cannot be recovered with Undo. So be sure you have selected the correct record before deleting.

To delete a record with a data form, open the Data menu and choose Form. When the data form appears, scroll until the record you wish to delete is displayed. Click Delete. A message will be displayed verifying the deletion. Click OK, then choose Close.

At this point, delete any additional records you have added to the database that are not in Figure 10.2.

EDITING RECORDS

You can edit existing records either by editing the cells directly or by using a data form. To use a data form, open the Data menu and choose Form. Select the desired record by scrolling, then tab to or click on the desired cell and edit it. Click Close. You can click the Restore button to restore a field to its original value, just as you click the Cancel box in the formula bar to restore a cell.

MOVING RECORDS

To rearrange the order of records and fields in your database, follow the rules for moving cell ranges. Select the cells to move. Open the Edit menu and choose Cut. Select the new location, then choose Paste.

MULTIPLE DATABASES

You can create more than one database on a worksheet. Only one database, however, can be active as a database at a time. To use multiple databases:

1. Create each database and assign it a name using Formula ➤ Define Name.

    2. To use the database, use Formula ➤ Goto to go to the database and then Data ➤ Set Database to set it as the active database.

SAVING THE DATABASE

Before leaving this example, be sure the database is saved again. Open the File menu, choose Save, then click OK.

    You've now learned the basics of managing a database. The database is really nothing more than a named area of the worksheet, and as a result, is accessible to the options on the Data menu and the database functions.

EXCEL VERSUS OTHER DATABASE PRODUCTS

Excel is an excellent program for managing databases, but is not designed to replace any single-application database system you may be using, such as dBASE IV, FoxPro, or R:BASE. Single-application database management systems are designed to support database management only, and do it well. The data are stored on and listed or extracted from the disk. The amount of data that can be stored in the database is limited only by the size of the disk storage area. As a result, you can create very large databases and perform very complex operations on them. These systems also support programming, linked files (relational databases), report generation, and more.

    When you are working with a database in Excel, *all* the database data are stored in the computer memory at the same time. As a result, the size of the database that you can create is limited by the amount of computer memory available. (When the database is not in use, data are stored in a file on the disk, just as in a single-application system.) Because of this storage system, the entire database is in memory at once and database operations are much faster than in comparable single-application products. This limits the size of the database, but with Excel and extended memory you can still work with large databases. You also can use the database information in calculations in other areas of the worksheet directly, without having to import it.

    If you have a database that is very large and requires complex reporting and processing, you might consider using an external database-management system to store the data as well as using Excel to manage a portion of the database. For example, suppose that you are managing a pension fund for a company. You could keep the annual data for each employee in an Excel database and use an Excel worksheet to calculate the earnings for the year for each employee. After you've done this, you could transfer the results to an external database (using the procedure described in Chapter 21), which would store all the historical information and produce summary reports.

If you are running Excel with Windows in the 386-Enhanced mode, you have virtual memory; that is, Excel will use the disk as an extension of memory. If the database is very large, part of it will be kept on disk as you use it. Although this permits Excel to work with very large databases, you should still use a database manager for managing such databases (adding, editing, sorting, reporting, and deleting records) and use Excel for analysis and summary reporting.

Another option is to use the Q+E utility with Excel to manage external databases (see Chapter 25).

Here is a specification comparison of an Excel database with a dBASE IV database:

SPECIFICATION	EXCEL	dBASE IV
Maximum number of records	16,383	1 billion
Maximum number of fields per record	256	255
Maximum field size (characters)	255	254

FAST TRACK CHAPTER 11

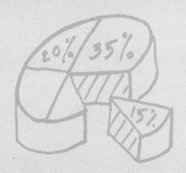

CHAPTER 11

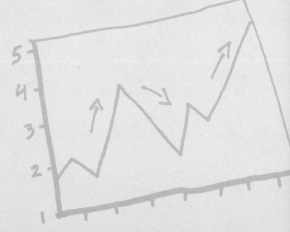

Using Databases Effectively

S o far you've learned how to create databases and edit them, but database management is far more than this. In this chapter you will learn how to use your Excel database to find records that meet specific criteria and how to use the Excel statistical functions to calculate statistics for the records that match the criteria you have defined.

USING CRITERIA

Criteria are rules or tests by which records are judged. If a record meets the rule (or passes the test), it is accepted, or said to *match*. Here are some typical applications that use criteria:

- Finding all the addresses with a specified zip-code range in a database of addresses

- Finding all the members with a membership expiration date equal to or earlier than a specified date in an organizational membership list

- Finding all the salespeople with sales exceeding a specified value in a sales database

◆   Finding all prospects that match a specified callback date ("tickle date") in a prospect list, indicating when they should be contacted again

Notice the single word used in each of these applications: *specified*. You are defining a specification, and you wish to find all records in the database that match it. The specification is called the *criterion*.

You also can create complex test relationships. For example, a record can be accepted if it passes Criterion A *or* Criterion B, Criterion A *and* Criterion B, or Criterion A *and not* Criterion B.

FINDING RECORDS BASED ON CRITERIA

As with adding or editing records, you can use either of two methods to find records based on criteria: a data form or menu command.

USING A DATA FORM TO FIND RECORDS

Often the easiest method to find a desired record is to use a data form. Try this now with the SALES database. Open the database you used in the last chapter, then open the Data menu and choose Form. A form will be displayed. Click the Criteria button. The Criteria button changes to a Form button and the Delete button changes to a Clear button, as shown in Figure 11.1.

Enter the desired criteria into the fields of the form. In this example, the form specifies to find all records with a sales target of less than $100,000. Click on the Find Next button. The first record with a sales target of less than $100,000 will appear on the data form.

To find additional records that match the criterion, choose Find Next again. To search backwards, choose Find Previous. When you are finished, select Close.

You use a data form only with limited criteria specifications. You cannot use computed criteria (see the section titled "Computed Criteria" later in this chapter) and you can use only exact text comparisons, though you can use wildcard specifications (* and ?). All text strings have an implicit asterisk appended, so **Rob** will match on *Robert* and *Roberta*.

For more complex criteria specifications, use the method described below.

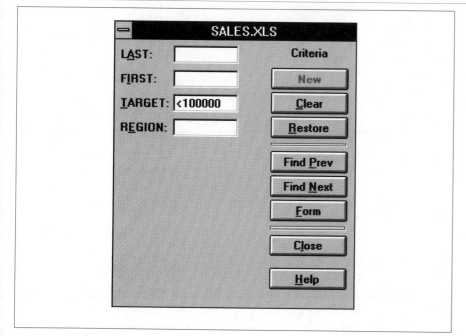

Finding records is easy, using a data form like this one

USING MENU COMMANDS TO FIND RECORDS

Finding records using menu commands is a three step process:

1. Define the criteria range.

2. Enter the specification.

3. Initiate the action.

It's more time consuming than simply using a form, but allows for more complex operations.

 You can enter the field names to the criteria area from the keyboard, but copying them to create the criteria range eliminates the possibility of misspelling the field names.

Defining a Criteria Range

Before you can define your criteria, you must create a range on the worksheet that can be used to specify the criteria. This is called the *criteria range*. You can create this range by copying the field names of interest as headers to this new range.

Create this range for the worksheet you used in the last chapter:

1. With the SALES.XLS worksheet open, copy all the field names you will use for the criteria. Click on A13 and drag to cell D13.

2. Copy this range to A3:D3. To copy by dragging, touch the border of the range until the cursor turns to a pointer. Hold down the Crtl key and drag the range to A3. The field names are now copied to a new area of the worksheet.

3. Select the criteria range. Select cell A3 and drag to cell D4. Notice that you have selected a range that includes *two* rows, as shown in Figure 11.2. You will enter criteria for searches in the second row.

4. Name this range. To do this, open the Data menu and choose Set Criteria. This assigns the name *Criteria* to the worksheet area that you just defined. You can use this name later in formulas and commands.

The criteria range must always include at least two rows. The first row contains the field names and the following row is used to enter values (or value ranges) for the fields. However, in some cases you may need three or

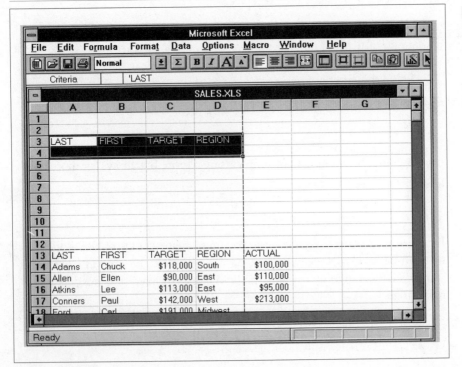

FIGURE 11.2:

The highlighted area has been set up as the criteria range, in which database searches will be defined

even more rows. Allow as many as necessary. Later in this chapter, you will see an example using more rows.

In defining the criteria range, it is not necessary to copy all the field names. Copy only those you will need for your searches. Field names must be identical with those in the database, but case is ignored—you can use upper- or lowercase letters in specifying the field names.

You also can redefine the criteria range at any time. Simply select the new range and issue a new Set Criteria command.

Entering the Specification

The next step is to enter the desired specification for the criteria. Enter **West** in cell D4 under the word REGION in cell D3, as shown in Figure 11.3.

When entering criteria, keep the following rules in mind:

NOTE NOTE *Select Edit ➤ Clear or press Ctrl-Del to clear a criteria cell.*

◆ The criteria you enter are not case sensitive. You can enter *WEST* or *West*.

◆ You can use wildcard characters, using an asterisk (*) to represent any group of characters and a question mark (?) to represent a single character. For example, W* would find all those in the West region in this example. (Asterisks need to come at the end of a string.)

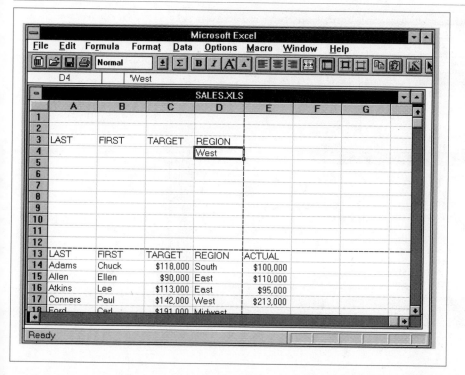

FIGURE 11.3:

Specifying this criterion will find records in the database that match the western region

◆ You can use numbers, labels, or formulas to define the criteria. The criteria must always be positioned directly below the field name to which they correspond.

◆ Be sure there are no rows left entirely blank in the criteria range. A blank row is like an asterisk wildcard and will match any database record; therefore it will cause the search to stop on the first record. As long as at least one cell in the row contains a criterion, the search will work, since cells in the same row will combine their criteria specifications.

Initiating the Action—The Find Command

Once the criteria are specified, you can use them to initiate any of three actions: find, delete, or extract. As an illustration, try the example below.

To find the first record that meets our REGION = West specification, select Data ➤ Find. Excel will highlight the first record in the database that meets the specified criterion, as shown in Figure 11.4. Notice several changes. The location of the field value in the database is displayed in the upper left

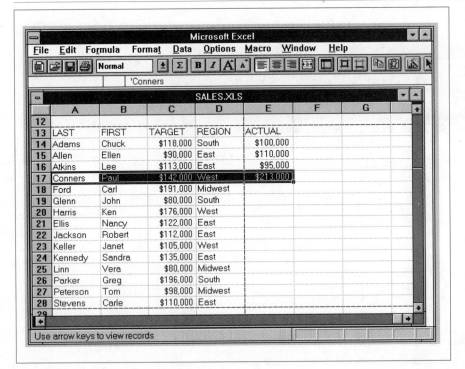

FIGURE 11.4:

As a result of the criterion specified in Figure 11.3, Excel searches the database and finds the first record that matches the criterion.

where the active-cell designator normally is. The Data menu has changed and no longer contains the Find option; it contains an Exit Find option instead.

To find the next match, click either scroll arrow or press ↓ or ↑. They permit you to move through the database to the next or previous record that meets the specified criterion. While in this search mode, the Edit commands (Copy, Cut, and so on) are still active. This allows you to edit the records once you find them. You also can use Delete in the Data menu to delete all records matching the criterion.

To exit the search, choose Data ➤ Exit Find or press Esc. You also could exit by clicking any cell in the worksheet outside the database range. You can now specify another criterion and search the database again.

When the Find command is activated, it starts from the beginning of the database if no cell in the database is active. If any database cell is active, the search starts after that cell's record.

COMBINING SEARCH CRITERIA

Now try to combine two search conditions. Enter **176000** in cell C4 under TARGET (leaving West in cell D4) and repeat the find operation. Notice that the two conditions are combined; Excel looks for the first record where the region is West *and* the target is $176,000. It is not necessary to click Set Criteria again. As long as the cell range used for criteria entry is not changed, you can continue to repeat searches using other criteria within that range. When you have more than one entry in a row, Excel will find only records that fit *all* the specified criteria. This is called an AND condition.

 To clear a criteria cell, always use Edit ➤ Clear. If you try to clear a cell by entering a space, all you will do is enter a space as a part of the search criteria.

Now clear cell C4 (press Ctrl-Del), leave West in D4, and enter **East** in D5. Expand the criteria range to A3 through D5 (using Data ➤ Set Criteria). Initiate a find, and Excel will stop on the first record in which the region is West *or* East. As you can see, more than one entry in a criterion column tells Excel to find records containing any one of the criteria. This is called an OR condition. If you are using both AND and OR conditions together, you can create complex Boolean operations. The next section describes methods of creating special criteria specifications.

Remember, if you use multiple rows for criteria, you must include them all in your criteria range. Issue a new Set Criteria command if necessary. If you clear some criteria rows, reset the criteria to exclude those rows; otherwise, Excel will search for either a blank record or the existing criteria, and the search will stop on the first record in the database.

Notice that you now have two areas on the worksheet: the database area and the criteria area. You can use the remainder of the worksheet for normal worksheet applications: formulas, text, or whatever you wish.

USING COMPLEX CRITERIA SPECIFICATIONS

 If you have a large database or criteria range, use two windows and tile them to simplify access: one for the database, another for the criteria range.

Excel criteria specifications can be divided into three broad categories: simple, comparison, and computed. In any given single search, you can mix these as necessary. You have already seen an example of simple criteria, where a single value is entered in the criteria range. Now let's look at comparison and computed criteria.

NUMERIC COMPARISON CRITERIA

You can use any of the relational operators listed in Chapter 4 to specify a numeric comparison criterion. For example, enter **>150000** in cell C4 under TARGET, clear D5, and be sure D4 still contains West. Reset the criteria range to A3 through D4. Initiate a find, and Excel will stop on the first salesperson in the western region whose target is greater than $150,000.

You can tell Excel to search for records with field values within a range by setting up two columns in the criteria-range row that have the same field name. Put one limit under one and the second limit under the other. For example, let's set up a criterion to find records within a target range of $100,000 to $150,000:

1. Enter the word **TARGET** in E3 and set the criteria range as A3 to E4 (Figure 11.5). Be sure D4 is clear.

2. Enter **>100000** in C4 to define the lower limit of the range.

3. Enter **<150000** in E4 to define the upper limit of the range.

4. Select Data ➤ Find. Excel will stop on the first record with a target value within this range (row 14 in this case).

TEXT COMPARISON CRITERIA

You can use the comparison operators (<, >, =, etc.) to compare text fields as well. In this system, *A* is "less than" *B* and *F* is "less than" *m*. Upper- and lower-case letters are considered equivalent (i.e., *D* "equals" *d*).

You also can use a question mark (?) to match a single character or an asterisk (*) to match a group of characters. For example, **J?dy** will match *Judy* and *Jody,* and **rob*** will match *Robert Jackson* and *Robin Leach.*

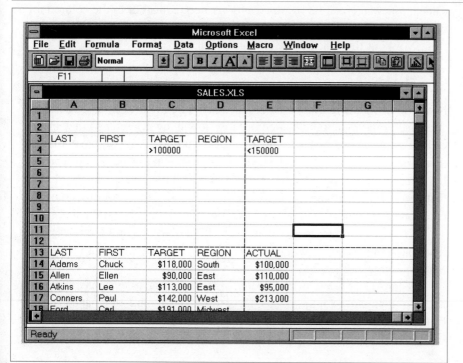

FIGURE 11.5:

This criterion will find records within the specified target range

In finding exact text matches, use extra care with Excel. Both **Rob** and ="**Rob**" in B4 would match *Robert Jackson*. In both cases, B4 would show only Rob. If you wanted to find only people with the first name Rob and not Robert, you would have to use an equal sign with the text inside a quotation:

="=Rob"

This would put =Rob in B4 and would match only the first name *Rob*.

COMPUTED CRITERIA

You also can use formulas to create criteria. There are, however, some precautions you must be aware of. Suppose you use the formula >E4 in C4 and put a value of 120,000 in E4. You might think this would match any record with a target greater than $120,000. But actually Excel would look for a text entry that matched >E4 in a cell. Entering =E4 also wouldn't work; you would get an error message.

To make this comparison work, you must first expand the criteria range to A3 through E4. Always remember to extend the criteria range to contain the calculation. Make cell E3 blank (you don't need a header in the column for a calculated criterion in the criteria range). Clear C4 and E4 (also B4).

Now put the following equation in cell E4:

=C14>$E$7

Note the absolute reference to cell E7. Any reference to a cell outside the database range must be absolute because it will always refer to that specific cell. Now put the value for comparison, **120000**, in E7. If you have followed this correctly, you should see **FALSE** in E4, as shown in Figure 11.6. You now have created a computed criterion in E4 in which the target value (C14 in the first record) is compared with the value in E7. The result of any computed criterion (a condition) is either true or false. Initiate the find, and Excel should stop on the first target greater than $120,000. Press ↓ to find the next targets that match the criterion. When you've reached the end, press ↑ to review the matched target values.

Figure 11.7 shows another example. A few actual sales figures have been added to compare with the targets. Enter these in column E. Format this column by copying the format from column C: copy a cell from column C to the clipboard,

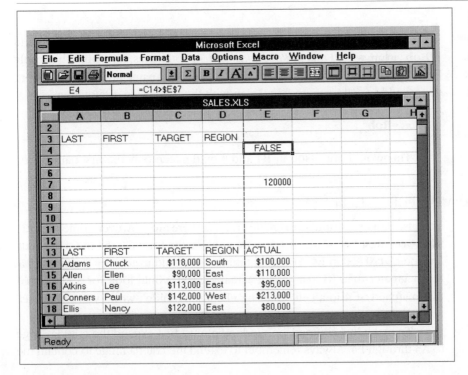

FIGURE 11.6:

As a result of specifying a computed criterion in cell E4, the first cell referenced, C14, causes the criterion to show "FALSE".

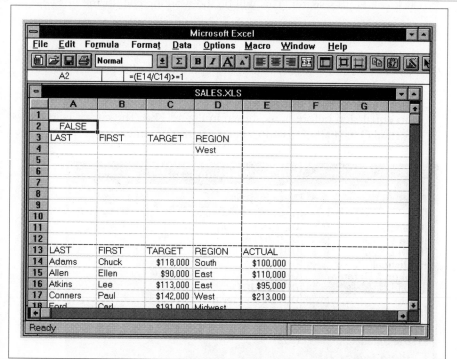

select the data in column E, and select Edit ➤ Paste Special to paste the format
only to column E. Be sure the database area is redefined to include this new field.
Be sure the database includes column E. Enter the formula **=(E14/C14)>=1**
in A2. Be sure the equal sign is included. Set the criteria range as A1 to A2.
This is requesting a match if the actual sales equal or exceed the target value.

You also can use functions in computed criteria. For example, you could
compare the square root of a list of fields to a fixed value with:

=SQRT(C14)>$E$7

DATABASE STATISTICAL FUNCTIONS

You use database functions in the same way that you use worksheet functions. Let's experiment with your original SALES database. As a goal, we wish
to find the sum of the eastern sales targets:

1. Set the criteria range from A3 to D4. Enter **East** into cell D4 (the
   criterion). Be sure that cells A4, B4, and C4 are clear.

2. Click cell E6 to select it. This will be the working cell for the answer.

3. Choose Formula ➤ Paste Function (or press Shift-F3).

4. The Paste Function dialog box shown below appears. Select Database as the function category. Scroll through the right list box until **DSUM** is displayed. Be sure Paste Arguments is checked off. Double-click DSUM. The function name is now entered into the formula bar with an equal sign before it, as shown in Figure 11.8. The cursor is in the formula bar ready for you to enter the first argument.

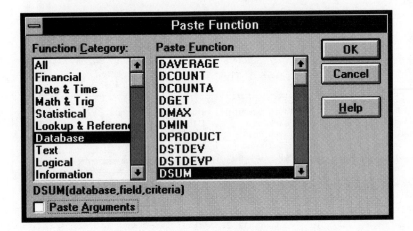

5. Choose Formula ➤ Paste Name (or just press F3). When the Paste Name dialog box shown below appears, double-click Database (the name of your database). It is now entered into the formula bar.

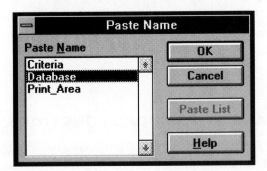

6. Type a comma and enter **"Target"** (with quotation marks) in the formula bar.

7. Type another comma and choose Formula ➤ Paste Name.

8. Double-click on Criteria, and what you've typed will be entered into the formula bar.

9. Click the Enter box (✓) or press Enter to complete the entry.

You now have a complete function:

=DSUM(Database,"Target",Criteria)

This matches the general form for this function: DSUM(*database, field name, criteria*). The sum of the eastern sales targets is now displayed in cell E6: **$682,000.** Enter **West** into cell D4, and the sum changes to **$423,000,** the sum of the western sales targets. You can specify any region and cell E6 will automatically change to reflect those target totals.

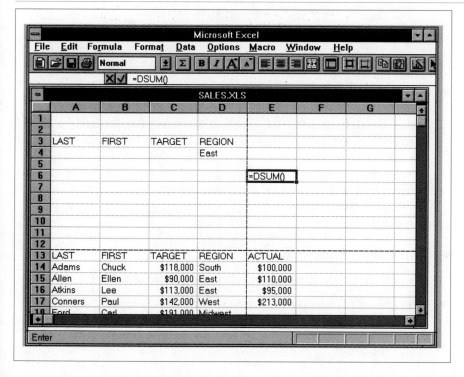

FIGURE 11.8:
Starting the formula entry. You can now enter the arguments to the function.

Although you created this formula by pasting the function and name, you could have entered the entire formula from the keyboard. If you need to review the database functions, see Chapter 8.

At this point, you should save the database again, as you will need it in the current form for the next chapter. Clear A1 to A2. Be sure the criterion is A3 to D4, and select File ➤ Save.

SOME DATABASE MANAGEMENT TIPS

Database functions are a valuable asset in building your worksheets. Here are a few tips:

◆ Use the CHOOSE and MATCH functions with your databases. For example, in the database of this chapter you had to enter the full region name for each region. To simplify entry and to eliminate misspellings, you could create a new field in column F called REGION CODE. Then you could put the equation

=CHOOSE(F14,"South","East","Midwest","West")

in D14 and copy it down the column. Entering a region code for each REGION CODE field (1, 2, 3 or 4) would then enter the corresponding region into the REGION field automatically.

◆ You can use the database functions on any continuous range of cells in the worksheet. Enter the continuous range as the database in the function and a range for the criteria. It is not necessary to define any database or criteria. For example, if you have a set of grades and wish to do some statistical calculations, you can use the statistical database functions, entering the database range for the database argument in the function. You still need a criteria range, but you don't have to define it with Set Criteria; just enter the cell addresses in the database function. For example

=DSUM(A13:E28,"Target",D3:D4)

works in the example with no database or criteria defined.

◆ You can set up multiple criteria on the worksheet. Although only one can be active at a time, you can have several criteria set up ready to use. Just use Set Criteria to select the one you wish to use, leaving the others still on the worksheet.

◆ You can use the field index number instead of the field name in the database function's second argument. The field index number is the order of the field in the record. For example, in the DSUM example of the previous section you could have used the number *3* (to refer to the third field), instead of the word *Target* as the second argument. You also can use a reference in the database to the field header. Just click on the field name to enter it into the database function.

◆ Don't confuse the Find command in the Data menu with the search capabilities of the Find and Replace commands on the Formula menu. The Find and Replace commands work on the entire worksheet, including the database. Data ➤ Find works only within the current database and searches are based on a criterion. If a QOH (Quantity-on-Hand) is 15 and needs to be changed to 19 in a database, using the Formula menu could change other 5s or 15s that shouldn't be changed. Using the Data menu gives you more control.

OTHER OPERATIONS THAT USE CRITERIA

You have seen how you can find records based on specified criteria. You also can extract or delete records based on criteria.

EXTRACTING RECORDS USING CRITERIA

You can extract the part of your database that matches specified criteria and place it in another area of the worksheet or in another worksheet. As an example here, extract all the western salespeople from the database.

Extraction is a three-step process: defining the criteria, defining the extraction destination range, and initiating the extraction.

Defining the Criteria

You define criteria for extraction just as you would define them for a search. Define A3 to D4 as the criteria range and enter **West** in D4 (See Figure 11.3).

Defining the Extraction Range

To define the extraction area, copy the cells that contain the field names into a new area of the worksheet or into another worksheet (the Actual field is not copied), as shown in Figure 11.9. Copy by dragging: select the range, then hold down the Ctrl key and drag the range to the new location. The extracted database will be placed below these field names. Be sure there is sufficient room for the extracted database. You may delete any field names that are not needed in the extracted database.

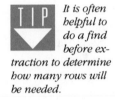

It is often helpful to do a find before extraction to determine how many rows will be needed.

Next, select the field names in the destination area to which you want to copy the extracted records. If you want to copy all the fields of the matching records, select all the field names of the destination range. If you want only a partial extraction (as here), select the field names and one or more additional rows of the destination range. Only those rows will be filled. This is useful if you don't know how many records will match the criteria and you are afraid the extraction might destroy (write over) other data.

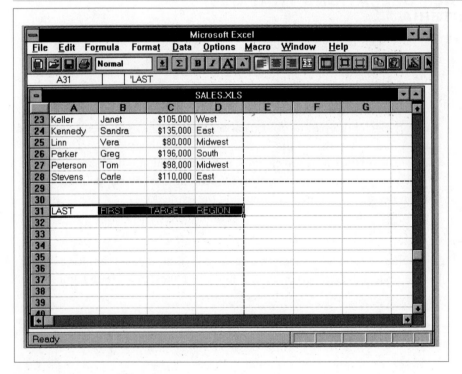

FIGURE 11.9:

To define the extraction range, copy the field names from the database

Initiating the Extraction

Use the Find command to preview records to be deleted before deletion.

Select A31 to D31. Choose Data ➤ Extract. You will then see the Extract dialog box shown below. Click on Unique Records Only, because you don't want the extracted file to contain any duplicates. Click OK. The extracted records will be copied into the new worksheet area, as shown in Figure 11.10.

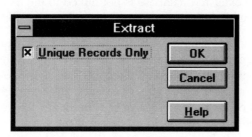

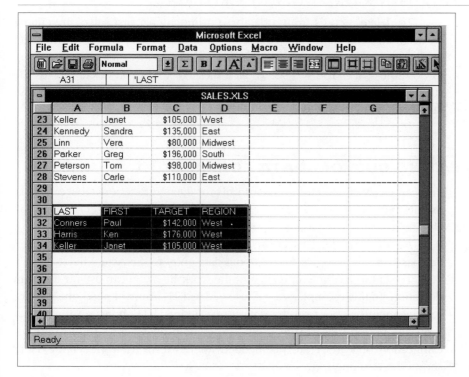

FIGURE 11.10:

The extracted records are now copied into a new worksheet area

An alternative is to select A31 to D31 (the destination field headings), choose Data ➤ Set Extract, and then choose Extract.

You should understand the following characteristics of extractions:

◆ The extracted database will contain only values. Formulas are extracted as values, not formulas.

◆ The extracted database is not linked to the master. If the master is updated, the extracted database will not be updated.

◆ If the destination range is defined by selecting one or more fields, all records in the original database that match the desired criteria will be transferred. Transferred records can overwrite existing cell data without Excel giving you a precautionary message. Select a cell range for the destination range or be sure that many cells under the destination field headers are cleared of data.

DELETING RECORDS USING CRITERIA

To delete records from a database using criteria, first select the criteria for deletion. Next, open the Data menu and choose Delete, then click OK. Excel automatically deletes the selected records and moves the remaining records up to close the space. You will see an alert message when you delete records. Be sure that the database is saved before you delete any part of it, because a database deletion cannot be undone.

CREATING CUSTOM DATA FORMS

You can easily create custom data forms for data entry to a database. This is useful if you wish the user to enter data to only a limited subset of the available fields of the database.

As an example, let's create a custom data entry form for the SALES database. In this case, we wish to omit data entry to the Actual field.

To start, select an empty area of the worksheet you can use for the form definition. In this example we will use F12 to L21. You will need one row for each element or object on the data form. Figure 11.11 shows a sample data form description that can be used. The column titles across the top are for clarification only; they are not needed for the form to work. Figure 11.12 shows the resulting form.

The first row of the data form range must be clear. The title row shown in the example is not necessary.

NOTE
NOTE

Let's examine the form and see what it does. The data form is really a dialog box. Each row of the description in Figure 11.11 defines a control on the data form in Figure 11.12. A *control* is simply an element of a dialog box.

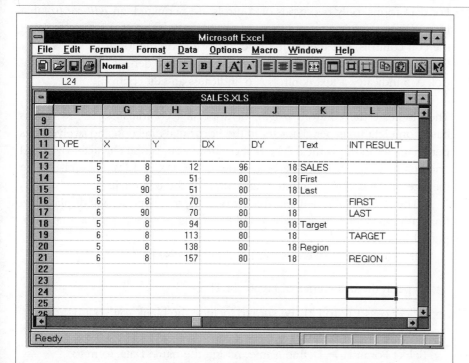

The entries needed to create a custom data entry form

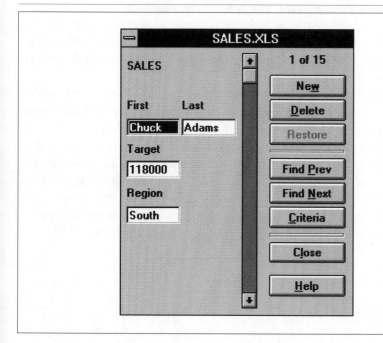

The extraction dialog box

For data forms, only two types of controls are permitted: an *edit control* that is used to receive input from the user, and a *text control* that is used to label the edit controls, title the form, or put other text on the form.

Each row defines one control. The first column defines the type of control. A *5* indicates a text control. A *6* indicates an edit control.

The next two columns define the position of the control in the window. They indicate the control's *origin,* or upper-left coordinates. The system is based on eight units per character in the horizontal direction and twelve units per character in the vertical. The first control, then, is one character over and one character down from the box's origin. The DX and DY columns define the size of the control, using the same units as the coordinates.

The next column defines which words the text controls will display. The final column defines the database field that will receive the value that is inputted in an edit control.

If you wish to make this form, follow these steps:

1. Type in the cell entries of Figure 11.11.

2. Select cells F12 to L21. Be sure to include the blank row, but not the title.

3. Select Formula ➤ Define Name. Assign the name Data_form to the area.

4. Now choose Data ➤ Form. You will see the new form.

When you use the Data ➤ Form command, Excel looks for a description named Data_form. If it doesn't find such a range, it uses its default description and includes all fields.

For the moment, we'll leave the subject of data forms until you've learned some things about Excel macros. The custom data form feature is very limited. It's primarily useful for limiting the fields available to the user for data entry. For anything more sophisticated, you need to customize some dialog boxes. The use of macros and dialog boxes permits you to design some very interesting forms for data entry. For example, you could display the regions from this example in a list box or as check boxes on a form, permitting a user to select from one of the four regions without the chance of an inadvertent typing error. For more information on this topic, see Chapter 28.

FAST TRACK CHAPTER 12

Select the range to sort and choose Data ➤ Sort. Choose the type of sort under Sort By. Identify the first key by clicking a cell in the row or column of the key. Click OK.

Select the range to sort and choose Data ➤ Sort. Choose the type of sort under Sort By. Identify the most important key as the first key by clicking a cell in the row or column of the key. Identify the second and third keys by clicking in their control groups on the worksheet, with the least important key as the third. Click OK.

Use the same sort method as with three or fewer keys, using multiple keys on multiple sorts. Start with the least important groups of keys, with the most important of these three keys first. Continue, sorting on the most important keys last.

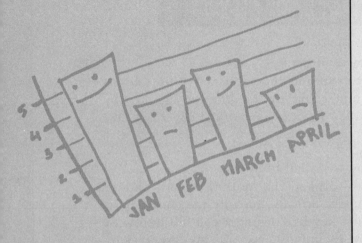

CHAPTER 12

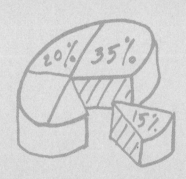

Sorting Data

With Excel, you can sort your database quickly in any desired sequence. Sorting is useful for many types of databases: you can sort a mailing list in either name or zip-code order, an inventory file in part-number order, or a prospect list in name or date order.

Usually when you enter records into a database, you do so in a random order (as most records come to you). When you finish entering the data, you can sort the records in whatever order you want. If you enter new records at a later time, you can either add them in their correct position (using Edit ➤ Insert) or add them to the end of the database and resort the database.

You can sort a database's rows or columns, with any number of fields, called *keys,* controlling the sort. Each field can be sorted in ascending or descending order. Usually you want to sort rows; a columnar sort rearranges the field order.

It is also important to understand that you can sort any data. They don't have to comprise a database. In fact, the Sort command, although on the Data menu, has no relationship to the database commands. Any area of the worksheet can be sorted at any time.

SORTING BY A SINGLE FIELD

Let's try sorting the SALES database by the region field:

1. Open the SALES worksheet. Select the range of cells to sort, A14 to D28. (Notice that you do not include the row containing the field names, since this is not a database command.)

2. Choose Data ➤ Sort. The Sort dialog box shown below appears.

3. Click any cell in column D (to sort by region) and this cell reference will be entered into the Sort dialog box as the first key. Click OK. The items are now sorted alphabetically by region, as shown in Figure 12.1.

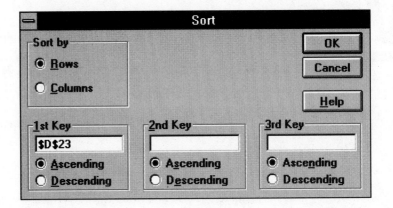

Here are some tips on sorting:

◆ After selecting the sort range and choosing Sort, select the key by clicking on a cell in the sort column. (Note that you can click any cell in the column to define the sort key, including the field name.)

◆ You can undo a sort by immediately selecting Edit ➤ Undo Sort. (After any other command is initiated, you cannot undo it.) If you think you might need to recover the original order, add a new field (column) that contains the database's record (row) numbers before you sort the database. Use the Series command to assign a sequential number to each record (see Chapter 14). After you've sorted the database, you can recover the previous order easily by sorting the database with the record-number field as the key.

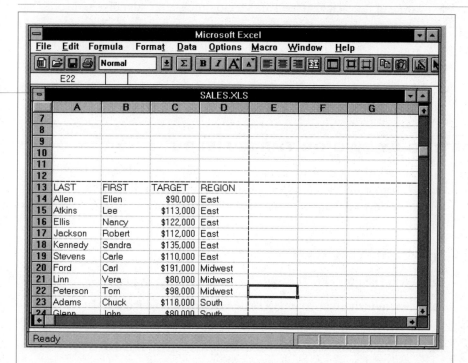

FIGURE 12.1:

The database sorted alphabetically by region

◆ When defining the sort range, be sure all fields of all records are selected—i.e., the entire database range *excluding* the field names. You cannot use the Goto command with the database name to select the database range for sorting, because it will include the field names.

◆ If you plan to sort the database often, name the sort range using Formula ➤ Define Name. Then you can use the Goto command to select this range.

◆ You can use range names or formulas to define the sort keys. For example, if you name C13 as *Target,* you can sort on target values by entering **Target** as the first key.

◆ If you use calculated fields, be sure to use absolute references for cells outside the database and relative references for cells inside the database. Otherwise, a sort will scramble the formulas.

◆ Numeric characters are sorted before alphabetic characters.

◆ Sorting a database will of course lose the order of entry. Include a field that shows a date (and perhaps time) of entry if you want to keep track of when each record was entered.

◆ You can use macros (see Part VII) to time stamp, identify, and sort entries.

◆ You can sort by any type of range. It does not need to be defined as a database.

◆ As an added precaution, save before sorting.

SORTING BY TWO OR THREE FIELDS

You can sort by two or three fields easily. Suppose, using the previous example, you want the database sorted by region, by last name within the region, and by first name if the last name is the same (there are no duplicate last names here, but we will assume that this could happen):

1. Select the range to sort.

2. Select Data ➤ Sort. The Sort dialog box will be displayed.

3. Click anywhere in column D, the first field by which the database will be sorted. *Do not press Enter or click OK yet.*

4. Click in the 2nd Key text box, then anywhere in column A, the column for the last name, for the second key.

5. Click in the 3rd Key text box, then anywhere in column B, the column for the first name, for the third key.

6. Click OK or press Enter.

The database will be sorted by region and by name within the region.

Keep in mind that sorting with multiple keys in this way is not the same as doing multiple sorts. If you try multiple sorts, each sort will rearrange the order of the previous sort. For example, if you sort the above database by region and then again by last name, the database will end up in last-name order only. Using multiple keys ensures that the second sort does not invalidate the first sort; that is, the database remains sorted by region after the sort on the last name is completed. Last names are then sorted only within the same region.

SORTING BY MORE THAN THREE FIELDS

Sometimes you may wish to sort by more than three keys. This can be done easily if you use the following procedure. Sorting makes an assumption that the most important keys are unique. For example, in a database of addresses you could sort by last name and first name, then by zip code and last name to get a database in zip-code, last-name, and first-name order. Assume the database is to be sorted by six fields, with key 1 as the most important and key 6 as the least:

1. Initiate one sort using the three least important keys; that is, key 4 (first key), 5 (second key), and 6 (third key).

2. Initiate another sort using the three most important keys: key 1 (first key), 2 (second key), and 3 (third key).

This method will work with any number of keys. Start with the least important keys, using the most important of these as the first key in the Sort dialog box. If the number of fields is not divisible by three, use a two- or one-key sort the first time with the two least or single least important key(s).

FINDING SALES TOTALS BY REGION

You can use these sorting techniques to find the sales totals for each region in the SALES database. Sort the database by region and add a small worksheet area under the criteria area. In cell B6, enter the sum of the eastern regions as **=SUM(C14:C19)**. Continue with the other sums:

Region	Cell	Formula
East	B6	**=SUM(C14:C19)**
Midwest	B7	**=SUM(C20:C22)**
South	B8	**=SUM(C23:C25)**
West	B9	**=SUM(C26:C28)**

Add the row titles **East**, **Midwest**, **South**, and **West** in cells A6 through A9, as shown in Figure 12.2. In Chapter 15, you will learn a better way to create this worksheet. For now, save the SALES worksheet for exercises in other chapters.

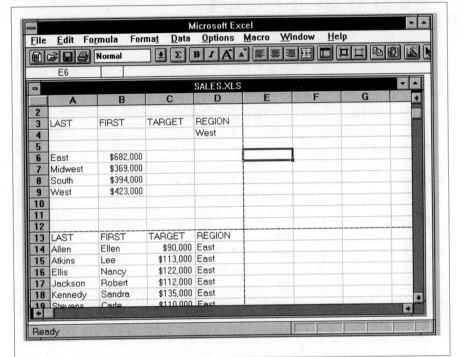

FIGURE 12.2:

Once the database is sorted by region, it's easy to define a worksheet area that shows the regional sums

SORTING WITHOUT A DATABASE

The Sort command does not require any defined database or criteria. It can be used on any worksheet range. For example, Figure 12.3 shows a worksheet (not a database) that indicates the sales of various salespeople for a four-year period. The sales are shown here in descending year order. Assume that for presentation purposes you need to rearrange this in ascending year order.

To do this, use a columnar sort instead of a row sort. Select C3 to F7 as the range to sort. Open the Data menu and choose Sort. Select Sort by Columns, and for the first key click anywhere in row 3. Figure 12.4 shows the resulting worksheet, sorted in increasing year order.

A columnar sort is seldom used for databases. Sorting by columns is generally not useful even for rearranging the field order because the Sort command can sort the columns with the field names only in ascending or descending order. To rearrange fields, use the edit commands instead, inserting a blank column and then moving the desired field column to the new position.

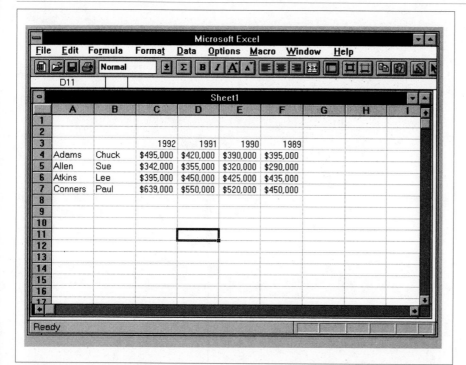

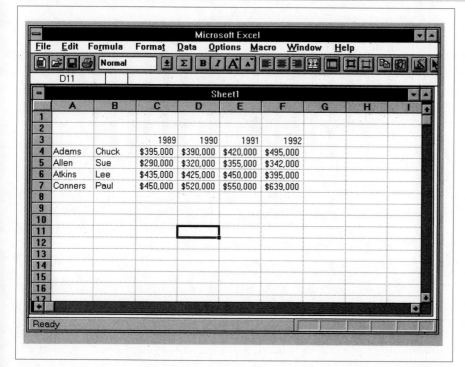

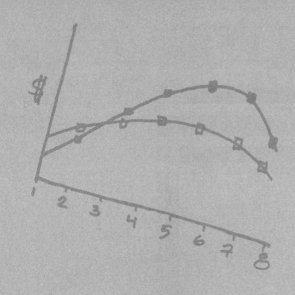

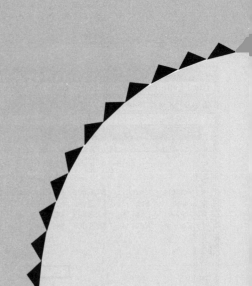

$$b = \frac{\Sigma xy - \bar{x}\Sigma y}{\Sigma x^2 - \bar{x}\Sigma x}$$

PART FOUR

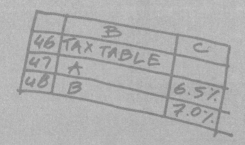

Part IV: Using Excel Productively

Excel provides many special techniques that are often not supported in competing products. Part IV introduces you to many of these techniques with application examples you can use in your own work. You will learn how to use arrays and tables, how to link and embed documents, and how to use the special printing features of Excel.

1. Place the formula that will be used for the table in the first row (or column) of the table. This is the single input cell for the value you wish to change.
2. Be sure the criteria and database are defined.
3. The first column (or row) should define the values that will be applied successively to the input cell.
4. Successive columns (or rows) are defined for the resulting values.
5. Select the range and then choose the Data ➤ Table command.

follow the same procedure, except that you define both a row input and column input cell. The row input cell is the header for a row of values to be applied successively, and the column input cell is the header for a column of values to be applied successively.

to find the number of days in the month, a tax rate, or a category. The lookup functions include CHOOSE(), MATCH(), INDEX(), LOOKUP(), HLOOKUP(), and VLOOKUP().

to create tabular tables from database data. To create a crosstab table, choose Data ➤ Crosstab.

CHAPTER 13

Producing Tables

There may be times when you want to change certain values on a worksheet to see how it affects the rest of the worksheet. For example, in Chapters 10–12, you created a database of sales targets. You then searched this database using various criteria. You could use only one criterion at a time, which is somewhat cumbersome if you want to use a series of criteria and then create a table or chart showing the results of each analysis. You *did* create a short worksheet portion showing the totals for each region, which were calculated using the SUM function. However, the calculations were only correct if the database was sorted by region. Entering the equation for each region was laborious and you were required to adjust the equations as you added or deleted records in the database.

In this chapter, you will learn how to use the Table command to avoid these problems. You will take the same example (the SALES database and worksheet) and use the Table command to search the database based on a series of criteria. You will see that tables are useful for what-if analyses with worksheets, because they allow you to perform multiple analyses with a series of input values.

You also will learn how to use look-up tables. These types of tables work with the LOOKUP, VLOOKUP, and HLOOKUP functions. They provide a quick way to find certain values in your worksheet.

USING THE TABLE COMMAND

If you wish to do a what-if analysis by applying several input values to a formula, you may wish to create a *data table*. Data tables permit you to apply a set of input values to one or two variables of a formula and see the resulting output values as a column, row, or table. If a single input variable is changed, the resulting output is a one-input table in a row or column. If two input variables are changed, the output is a two-input table in a tabular form on the worksheet.

In our first example, we will apply the four regions of the sales worksheet as a set of input values to create a single-input table.

ONE-INPUT TABLES

You use a one-input table to see how changes in one cell affect the values calculated by one or more formulas. To design a one-input table, you need three things:

◆ A single input cell containing the value that you wish to change.

◆ A column or row containing the values that will be applied successively to the input cell.

◆ One or more columns or rows to contain the resulting values, with formulas used as headings for each column or row. You can use formulas that refer directly to the input cell or to other cells on the worksheet. The formulas do not show on the worksheet.

Creating a One-Input Table

So that you can understand the basics of how a one-input table is used, let's experiment with the SALES database that you created in Chapters 10–12.

You'll set up a one-input table to search the database using a series of criteria.

Open the SALES database and worksheet, as shown in Figure 13.1. If necessary, restore the equation in E6 as =DSUM(Database,"Target",Criteria). For now, clear the few actual sales of column E. Be sure the criteria are defined correctly (A3:D4).

Our particular area of interest is the worksheet portion, rows 6–9, which contain the sales totals by region. These totals were obtained previously with the SUM function, which required the database to be sorted by region. Editing the database or sorting it can cause these totals to change and be incorrect.

To see this, sort the database (refer to Chapter 12 if you need help) so that the database is alphabetized by name:

1. Select the database range without the field names.

2. Use the Data ➤ Sort command, then for the first key click anywhere in column A. Then click OK.

The totals in the worksheet cells B6 through B9 will also change, becoming incorrect, as shown in Figure 13.2. This is because the formulas in these cells do not change with the sort.

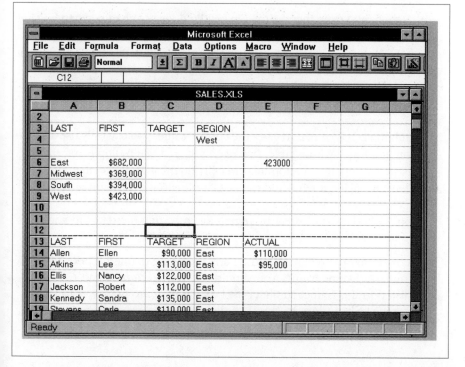

FIGURE 13.1:

The sales projections database and worksheet

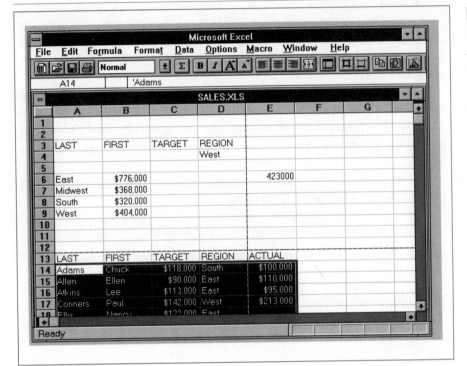

FIGURE 13.2:

The database after sorting, with incorrect worksheet totals in rows 6–9, compared to Figure 13.1

Notice, however, that the total in cell E6 does not change when you sort the database. This is because it is calculated using the DSUM function and a criterion—target sales in the West. Examine the formula for this cell and you will see that the total is based on the formula

=DSUM(Database,"Target",Criteria)

Although the DSUM function gives the correct value, you can only use a single criterion at a time. With a table, however, you can use multiple criteria.

Now let's change the formulas in cells B6 through B9, so that the values are calculated using a table and the DSUM function. Follow these steps:

1. Sort the SALES worksheet by region again so that the data are correct, and clear cell D4.

2. Be sure that the database and criteria range are defined. Choose Formula ➤ Define Name. You should see both *Database* and *Criteria* listed in the Names in Sheet list box. (If they are not, refer to Chapter 10.) Click Close to close the dialog box.

3. Create a heading cell containing the formula that will be used for the table by copying cell E6 into cell B5. (Select cell E6, touch its border to get a pointer cursor, hold down the Ctrl key, and drag to B5.) The formula must be in the first row of the table. Cell B5 is the heading cell for the column that will contain the results of the formula in B5.

4. Select the table area with the formula in the first row by clicking cell A5 and dragging to cell B9.

5. Choose Data ➤ Table. The Table dialog box below will be displayed. Move the dialog box (by dragging the title bar) so that cell D4 is visible, if necessary.

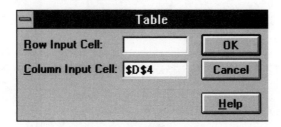

6. Click Column Input Cell on the dialog box, because the criteria will be from the Region column.

7. Click on cell D4. This is the single input cell that will contain each input value from the table. This indicates that the selected values in column A (cells A6 through A9) will be applied sequentially as a value in cell D4. The value *$D$4* is now displayed in the Table dialog box.

8. Click OK.

9. Save the worksheet.

The totals for cells B6 through B9 remain the same, but the formula for each cell is now different. Show the formulas by choosing Options ➤ Display ➤ Formulas (Ctrl-')—see Figure 13.3. What has happened? Each title in cells A6 through A9 was applied successively to cell D4, the *Criteria* used in cell B5. The formula in cell B5, the first row of column B in the selected range, was then used to evaluate the cell in column B across from the cell in column A. Figure 13.4 shows the results. Compare these numbers with Figure 13.1 and the erroneous Figure 13.2. As the result of cell B5 changing with each successive value in cells A6 through A9, the new results were recorded in cells B6 through B9.

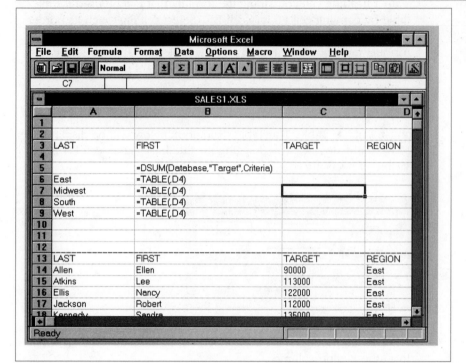

Now sort your database again by name:

1. Select A14 to D28, but be careful not to select row 13, which contains the database field names.

2. Choose Data ➤ Sort.

3. The Sort dialog box appears. With column A (the last name) defining the 1st Key field, click OK.

This time, the totals did not change. You can edit, resort, or otherwise modify the database, and the worksheet totals will always remain accurate.

Now look again at the three areas that we said earlier must be defined:

◆ The single input cell for all values that are to be changed is D4.

◆ The column or row that contains the values that will be supplied successively to the input cell is A6 to A9 (this is the criterion).

◆ The column that will contain the output values (with the formula as the heading) is B5 to B9. The formula is the heading for this column.

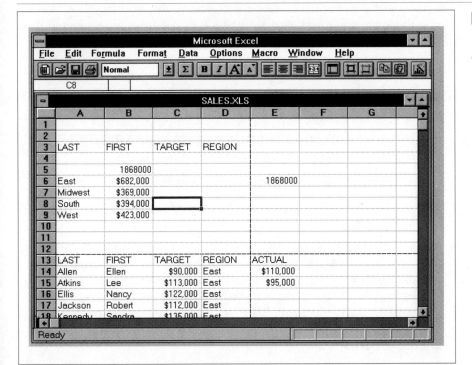

FIGURE 13.4:

*The worksheet values
calculated with the
Table command*

If you add or insert rows within the database range, your entries will be formatted correctly and the database totals will be updated to reflect the changes. The table definition has not changed. If you add data to the *end* of the database, however, you will need to redefine the database area in order for the totals to be correct. You also will need to format the new entries at the end of the database (by choosing Format ➤ Number).

Calculating Two Columns

Using the Table command, you can use multiple columns or rows to calculate the values for more than one formula.

Let's try an example with a two-formula table. Assume that you now have a few actual sales figures and you want to create a separate field for them in your database. Then you want to recalculate the worksheet total values using the Table command. First sort the SALES database by region and save it. Then follow these steps:

1. Add a new field to your database titled **ACTUAL**, as shown in Figure 13.5.

2. Enter the values shown in the figure into this field and format them.

3. Redefine your database area by selecting the range with the field names (A13 to E28) and choosing Data ➤ Set Database.

4. Add the new field name to your criteria area in E3.

5. Redefine your criteria area by selecting the range (A3 to E4) and choosing Data ➤ Set Criteria.

6. Copy the formula in cell B5 into cell C5 by selecting both cells and choosing Edit ➤ Fill Right or by selecting cell B5 and holding down the Ctrl key and dragging the small box at the lower-right corner of the cell. Then change the word TARGET to ACTUAL in C5.

7. Select cells A5 through C9.

8. Choose Data ➤ Table.

9. Click the Column Input Cell box in the Table dialog box and click cell D4, just as you did before. Then click OK.

Now both columns will be calculated and the results will be displayed. Format the results, as shown in Figure 13.6. Figure 13.7 shows the formulas. Save this version of the worksheet for use in Chapter 14.

Hide the numbers in B5 and C5 by defining a custom picture as ;;. Select B5:C5 and choose Format ➤ Number. In the Code box, delete the entry and enter ;;. Click OK.

TWO-INPUT TABLES

In a one-input table, a single input cell is used to calculate the values for one or more columns or rows. In a two-input table, as its name implies, Excel uses two input cells to calculate the formula's result for every combination of the input values to these cells. The results are displayed in a two-dimensional table.

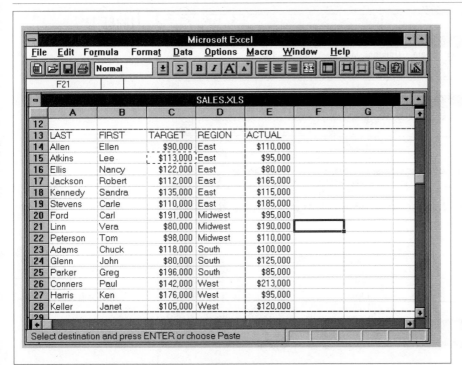

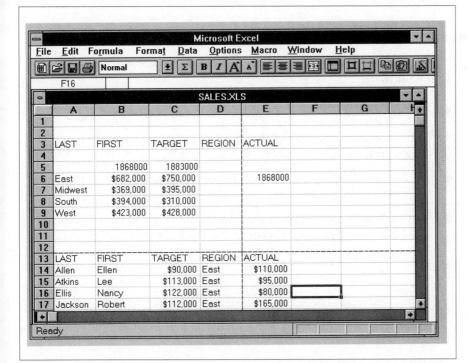

FIGURE 13.6:

*The worksheet showing
actual-sales results by
region*

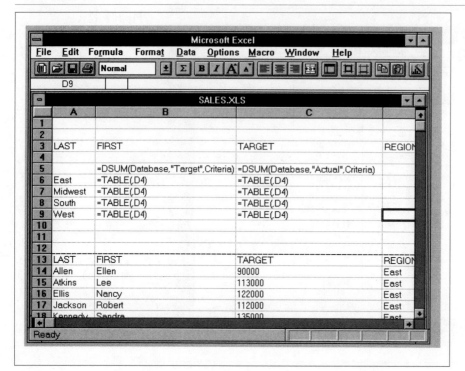

Designing a Two-Input Table

To design a two-input table, you need to define the following four areas on your worksheet:

◆ two input cells to contain the values that you wish to change

◆ a row containing the values that will be applied successively to one input cell

◆ a column containing the values that will be applied successively to the other input cell

◆ one or more columns or rows to contain the resulting values; you can use formulas that refer directly to the input cell or to other cells on the worksheet

Creating a Two-Input Table

You create a two-input table by following the same procedure that you used to create a one-input table, except that you will have both a row input cell and a column input cell.

Let's try an example. Open a new worksheet. Figure 13.8 shows a method of using a two-input table to calculate monthly payments for a variety of interest rates and time periods on an $8000 loan. Place the interest rates in column B and the period values (in months) in row 6. Two input cells must be defined: one for the interest values (B3) and one for the periods (C3). Place the following formula at the intersection of the input row and column (B6):

=PMT(B3/12,C3,–8000)

Don't worry about the **#DIV/0!** in B6; it's there because the two input cells are empty. Select B6 to F12. Choose Data ➤ Table to open the Table dialog box and click cell C3 for the row input cell. For the column input cell, click B3. Format the table and enter the headings; it should look like Figure 13.8. Notice that no database or criteria are defined; they are not needed to create a table. Using a table improves the reliability of the worksheet (less entry), makes it simpler to do additional what-if simulations, and saves time.

To improve the table's appearance, hide cell B6 by following the instructions in Chapter 14, or by creating and using the custom picture ;; (see "Calculating Two Columns" above).

This worksheet will not be used again, but you can save it if you wish.

EDITING TABLES

NOTE NOTE

A table must always be edited as a unit. You can't edit an output cell in a table.

You can edit the values used for input cells or the formulas of a table by using the commands on the Edit menu. The table will be updated automatically after you make any changes. However, you *cannot* edit the output columns or rows of a table (such as cells B6 through B9 in the SALES database and worksheet example).

For example, reload the SALES worksheet and try changing *Midwest* to *Europe* on the worksheet: select cell A7 and enter **Europe**. Because there are no records that match this criterion, the value in cells B7 and C7 become zero. You can't edit the individual cells B6 through C9 or even clear them. You also cannot clear a portion of the output range; you must clear the entire range.

If you copy a value from an output row or column into another cell of the worksheet, the new cell will contain only the value, not the formula.

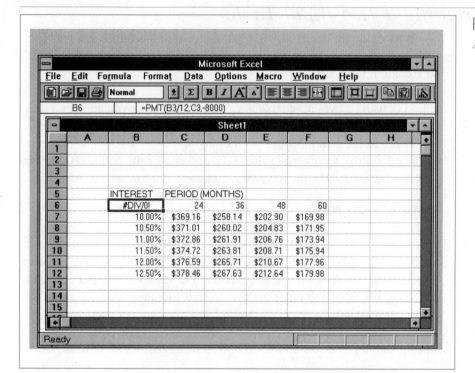

When you select cells in the output columns or rows, the formula bar will display the table reference. For example, for cells B6, B7, B8, and B9, the formula bar shows:

{=TABLE(,D4)}

(D4 is the input cell for the table.) The braces indicate that the formula is part of a table.

To delete a table or redefine it, select the entire table and select Edit ➤ Clear.

NOTES FOR USING THE TABLE COMMAND

The following notes apply to using the Table command:

◆ You enter the formula for the output into the first cell of each column or row that will contain the output values.

◆ Once you have defined a range as a table, the output range must be cleared or edited as a unit—tables cannot be partially cleared.

◆ There is no limit to how many tables you can have active at one time.

USING TABLES FOR LOOKUP ACCESS

Tables can substitute for formulas to produce an output value from an input value. Here you are using table functions, not the Table command. You can create such tables, called *lookup tables,* anywhere on a worksheet. Here are some typical applications for them:

◆ looking up the number of days in a month

◆ looking up a tax rate for a particular income

◆ looking up a category value for a product or employee

◆ looking up a price for a particular category value

In each of these cases there is no easy way to use a formula to get the desired value. A lookup table, however, provides a simple alternative.

The CHOOSE Function

The simplest and easiest type of lookup table to use employs the CHOOSE function. The CHOOSE function has the following syntax:

=CHOOSE(*index, value 1, value 2,…, value n*)

The table, is the linear list of arguments within the function call. The value of *index* determines which item of the list the CHOOSE function chooses and returns.

For example, the following command will return the current name of the day of the week:

```
=CHOOSE(WEKDAY(NOW(
)),"Sun","Mon","Tue","Wed","Thu","Fri","Sat")
```

THE MATCH FUNCTION

The MATCH function is used to return the position of the item in a list that most closely matches a lookup value. The general form is

=MATCH(*lookup value, lookup range, type*)

For example, assume the following cell values are in row 1: A1=22, B1=43, and C1=54. The function

=MATCH(43,A1:C1)

returns the value 2.

The general form of the function is:

=MATCH(*lookup value, compare vector,* [*type*])

The third argument is optional but, if used, defines the rules for the search. A value of 1 causes the function to return the largest value in the range equal to or less than *lookup value.* A value of 0 directs the function to accept only an exact match. If *type* is −1, the function returns the smallest value that is greater than or equal to *lookup value* in the range. If the argument is omitted, a default value of 1 is assumed. If nothing in the range matches the test condition, the error value #N/A is returned.

If you want to omit the type argument or specify it as 1, the table must be in ascending order. If you want the type to be −1, the table must be in descending order. If you want the type to be 0, the table may be in any order.

THE INDEX FUNCTION

The general form of the index function is as follows:

=INDEX(*index range, row, column,* [*area*])

This function returns the address of a cell. The cell containing the function displays the value from the specified cell in the table, as the following example illustrates.

To use the function, you must first create a table in a separate area of the worksheet. The table must be a rectangular range that includes at least four cells (i.e., a 2 × 2 array). The *index range* argument is used to define the range of the table. The next two arguments define the *row* and *column* for the retrieval. Each must be greater than zero. For example, if

A1 = INDEX(C1:E3,A5,A6)

A5 = 2

A6 = 3

returns the value of E2 to A1 (that is, row 2 and column 3 in the table defined by the first argument), A1 would display the contents of E2.

As an example, Figure 13.9 shows a worksheet for determining the percent a bank might charge for a loan, based on the credit risk. The risk categories are 1, 2, and 3 in column B. Row 5 shows the years of the loan. The formula in B11 to calculate the percent for the specified risk is

=INDEX(C6:F8,D1,D2)

The row and column headings are not used in the formula and are for labeling only. Cells D1 and D2 contain the actual table displacements.

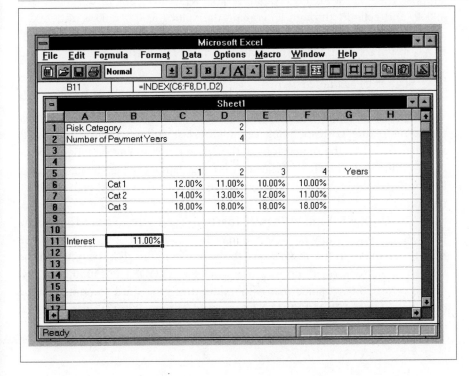

You also can use multiple areas, using the fourth argument to tell Excel which area to use:

=INDEX((C1:E3,F1:H3),2,3,2)

Here, the fourth argument value of 2 forces the use of the second table range, F1:H3.

The number of arguments is limited to 30, as with other functions. The expression width is limited to 255 characters.

THE LOOKUP FUNCTIONS

You also can access lookup tables in a separate area of the worksheet using the LOOKUP, VLOOKUP, and HLOOKUP functions (see Chapter 8). These functions permit you to locate a value in a table based on the value of a *test variable* (the first argument in a function). The second argument defines the lookup table as an array (see Chapter 15 on arrays).

The LOOKUP, VLOOKUP, and HLOOKUP functions search the first row or column of the table and returns the value of the cell that is equal to or less than the test value. The table values must be in ascending order. For example, suppose cells D1 through D3 contain a table with the values 10000, 20000, and 40000, and cells F1 through F3 contain the values 5.00%, 6.00%, and 7.00%, as shown in Figure 13.10. If you enter the function **=LOOKUP(25000,D1:F3)** in A1, it will return *6.00%*. The general form of LOOKUP is:

=LOOKUP(*value, array*)

The third argument is used the same way as in other spreadsheet programs, but has a different value than other programs. Remember that Excel counts the first column as column 1, while many other programs count it as column 0, and that table values must be in ascending order to work.

The function searches the first row or column of *array* for *value* and returns the value of the corresponding cell of the last column or row. LOOKUP searches based on the dimensions of the array. If it is square or wide, it looks for the value in the first row. If the array is taller than it is wide, the first column is searched. The LOOKUP function is identical to that of other worksheet programs.

The HLOOKUP and VLOOKUP functions each contain a third argument. HLOOKUP defines how far to move into the column and VLOOKUP defines how far to move in the row to find the value to return. For example, in the lookup table described above, the function **VLOOKUP(25000,D1:F3,3)** would return *6.00%*, since that is the value from the third column, and the function **VLOOKUP(25000,D1:F3,1)** would return *20000*, since the first column is 1 and the value is returned from that column.

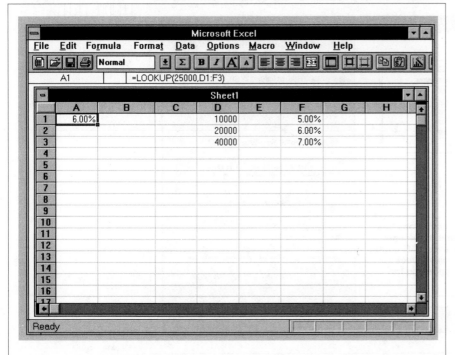

Lookup tables are useful for obtaining a value that cannot be calculated directly from other cells on the worksheet using a formula, such as a loan risk rating based on two specified variables.

You have now learned how to create two types of tables: what-if tables (using the Table command) and lookup tables (using the LOOKUP functions). What-if tables are used to apply a series of input values to one or more cells to create a series of output values. Lookup tables are used as substitutes for formulas for certain types of worksheet calculations.

USING CROSSTAB REPORTS

Excel contains a Crosstab ReportWizard feature that permits you to create reports automatically from a database. Let's try this now with the SALES database.

With the SALES database worksheet open, verify that the database range is defined correctly. Then choose Data ➤ Crosstab. A dialog box will open to initiate the creation of the Crosstab table (Figure 13.11). Notice the Explain

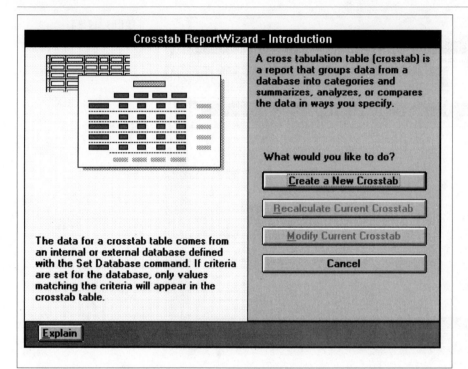

FIGURE 13.11:

*Starting to Create a
Crosstab Table*

button in the lower-left corner of the dialog box: you can use this for help at any time. Click the Create a New Crosstab button.

In the next dialog box (Figure 13.12), choose the fields to use as rows in the table. Choose REGION and click on Add. Click Next.

In the next dialog box (Figure 13.13), choose the field or fields to use as columns in the database. Choose TARGET and click on Add. Click Next.

In the next dialog box, choose the values to place in the table. Choose TARGET and click on Add. Then click on the Options button to define the type of value.

In the Value Field Builder dialog box, choose Sum as the Calculation Method, as we wish to see the sum for each value (Figure 13.14). Be sure the Values check box is checked. Click OK, then click on Next.

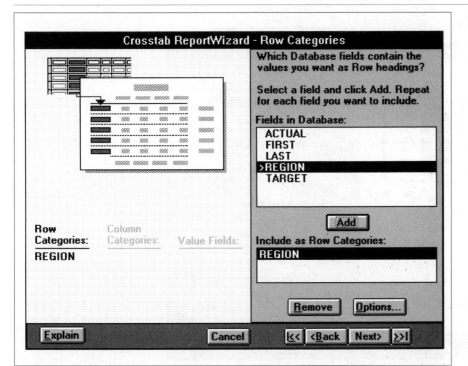

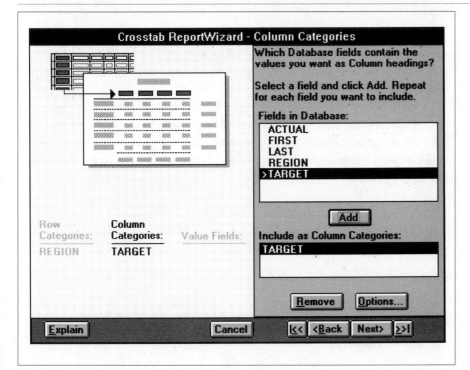

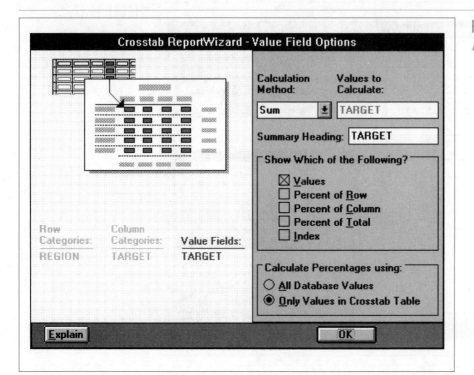

FIGURE 13.14:

Building the value field

In the final dialog box, click on Create It. A new worksheet will open and the Crosstab report will be built on it. Format it as desired and print it (Figure 13.15).

The final worksheet is displayed with an outline. You can collapse the outline and see the summary data, which is the same as the table created with the Data ➤ Table command of this chapter (Figure 13.16). Unlike the previous table, however, this report is static. If the database changes, you must create the report again.

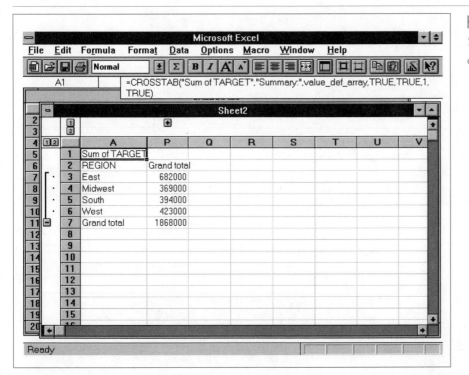

FIGURE 13.15:
*The Crosstab table,
collapsed*

FAST TRACK CHAPTER 14

CHAPTER 14

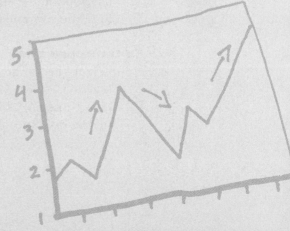

Using Special Features

Although you have created several worksheets, you have used the standard features only: moving, copying, formatting, and using functions.

In this chapter, you will be introduced to some of Excel's special features that make it even easier for you to create worksheets. These include copying and clearing only specific information, entering a series of values, controlling when calculations are done, protecting cells, and performing iterative calculations. You will try these various operations on worksheets you have already created. (Note that you shouldn't bother saving these changes for future operations.)

EDITING SELECTIVE PARTS OF CELLS

Excel stores three types of data about each cell: its value or formula, its format, and its notes. Excel's Clear and Paste Special commands allow you to work selectively with the values, formulas, notes, or formats of the selected cells.

SELECTIVE CLEARING

The Clear command on the Edit menu can be used to selectively delete the formulas, formats, or notes of specified cells as well as of an entire worksheet. Excel's default selection in the Clear dialog box is Formulas, which clears the formulas and values in the selected cells but retains the format and notes. If you select Formats in the dialog box, the selected cells will revert to the General template format but no data or formulas will be cleared. If you choose Notes, any notes assigned to that range will be cleared. If you choose All, the values, formulas, formats, and notes of the selected cells will be cleared.

Here are a few tips on clearing cells:

◆ Clearing formulas from a cell puts the cell value at zero. Formulas in the rest of the worksheet referring to that cell will assume that the cell has a zero value. By contrast, when you are deleting a cell (Edit ➤ Delete), the cell is removed from memory. Formulas referring to the cell will return the error value **#REF**.

◆ For a fast method of clearing formulas from a cell or cell range, select the range and press Ctrl-Del.

◆ Clearing a cell or cell range does not alter the column width or row height.

As an example, open your SALES worksheet and select a few target values in column C of the database. Select Edit ➤ Clear. Then select Formats and click OK. The format of the cells that you cleared returns to the General template format—the dollar signs and commas disappear. Reformat the cells to their previous format before you continue.

SELECTIVE COPYING

The Paste Special command on the Edit menu lets you control what you copy into another cell. You can copy just the values, formulas, formats, or notes of a cell instead of copying all the data from one cell or cell range to another. Excel's default selection in the Paste Special dialog box is All.

The Transpose option switches the rows and columns of the pasted data (see "Transposing Lists" at the end of this chapter). The Skip Blanks option blocks the pasting of blank cells.

The Operation group in the dialog box permits you to perform operations between cells as part of the copy process. This is particularly useful for combining data from several worksheets into a single summary worksheet. For example, a sales manager may receive worksheets from several sales areas. She could use the Add option in the Operation group in the Paste Special dialog box to combine the totals when she copies them into a summary worksheet.

Let's see how the Paste Special command works. First, add a name to the end of your SALES database. Notice that the value in the TARGET field is not formatted correctly. You could use the Format command to reformat the entry, but an easier method would be to use the Paste Special command to copy only the format:

1. Enter the values for the new salesperson in row 29, as shown in Figure 14.1.

2. Select cell C28, as it contains the cell format to copy.

3. Choose Edit ➤ Copy.

4. Select cell C29 and E29 as the destination cells. (Select C29, then hold down Ctrl and select E29.)

5. Select Edit ➤ Paste Special.

6. When the Paste Special dialog box appears, choose Formats, as shown below, then click OK.

The new entries in cells C29 and E29 are now formatted correctly, as shown in Figure 14.2.

To see how an Operation option works, select C28 and then choose Edit ➤ Copy. Select C29 and choose Edit ➤ Paste Special. When the Paste Special dialog box appears, leave All selected and choose Add in the Operation group. The contents of cell C28 will be added to the contents of cell C29 in the copy process, and C29 will read $210,000.

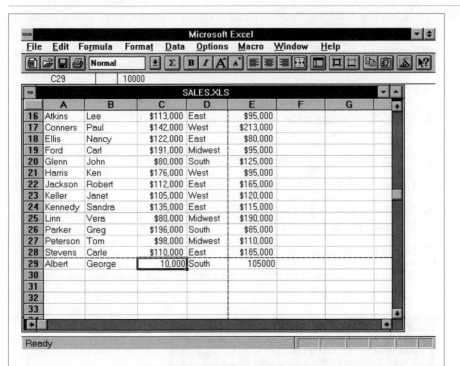

FIGURE 14.1:

*Adding a new
salesperson to the
SALES worksheet*

FIGURE 14.2:

*The result of using the
Paste Special command
on the new salesperson
entry in Figure 14.1*

Here are a few copying tips:

◆ As described in Chapter 5, use the Clipboard and the Edit menu to do your copying and moving. Invoke the Copy and Paste commands whenever possible to enter data into new columns and rows in a worksheet. This saves entry time and helps prevent mistakes.

◆ For quick copies, make the source range active. Then move the mouse to the border of the active cell until it changes to a small arrow. Hold down the Ctrl key and drag the range to the new location.

◆ Use the Paste Special command when you need to copy only the formulas, values, format, or notes of a cell.

◆ You also can move or copy cells or cell ranges using the Cut, Copy, and Insert commands. If you cut or copy a cell or cell range, **Insert** on the Edit menu changes to **Insert Paste**. You can then paste the cells in the Clipboard without writing over the destination cells.

◆ When copying cells, the column width or row height is not copied.

◆ You can use Edit ➤ Repeat to repeat a Paste, Paste Special, or Clear command.

◆ You can do multiple pastes from a single copy.

◆ You can use Ctrl-' to copy the value from the cell above to the current cell.

◆ You can copy or cut entire rows or columns by selecting the row or column designator, but this will require a lot of Clipboard space. For example, you can clear a record from a database by selecting an entire row and then deleting the row. The safer (in case there are data to the right of the database) and faster method is to select the record cells and then delete these. You can simplify the selection of cells by using a relative name reference that includes the entire record and select Edit ➤ Goto (or press F5) to get the entire record.

SPECIAL EDITING TECHNIQUES

Here are two helpful editing techniques to keep in mind:

◆ You can use the Edit menu to edit a formula in the formula bar as well as to move or copy cell contents. The Cut and Copy commands enable you to move a portion of a formula or copy a portion to another part of the formula.

◆   Use caution with the Paste Special command. If the Add option is selected, new values will replace the old ones in the range selected. You have no audit trail or track of what was there before. You can, however, undo the command (see next section). It would be better to create a new range, keeping the values in the new range that is added. The Paste Special command is very useful, however, for adding a constant in one cell to a range of cells.

THE UNDO COMMANDS

If you make a mistake in editing, you can recover the original worksheet quickly by using the Undo command on the Edit menu. For example, suppose you clear a range of cells accidentally. To recover the range, simply select Edit ➤ Undo Clear (or press Ctrl-Z). If you're typing data into a cell and have not pressed Enter yet, you can restore the cell to its previous value by clicking the × at the left of the formula bar.

You can undo a command only if no other command has been issued; that is, you can undo only the last command issued. Some commands do not support any Undo. Once the Undo command is initiated, the Edit menu changes to show a Redo command. Redo restores whatever was undone.

If you are working with a very large worksheet and try to move or copy a range of cells, you may get a message saying that the selection is too large and that you may continue without Undo. When this box appears, always select Cancel. Then select a smaller range to move or copy. This protects you in case an undo is later necessary.

DELETING AND INSERTING PARTIAL ROWS AND COLUMNS

Excel permits you to delete a partial row or column. Select the range to delete and choose Edit ➤ Delete (or press Ctrl--). A dialog box will then ask you how you want the space to be filled: by shifting cells left or up. Select the desired option and click OK.

Before deleting an entire row or column, check the rest of the row or column to be sure that no important data will be deleted, or that you will delete data on which a formula depends. Even in deleting partial rows and columns, check to the right or below (depending upon the direction of adjustment) before deletion.

You can use the Edit ➤ Insert command in the same way to insert partial rows and columns. Excel displays the same type of dialog box, which asks which way to shift the cells to move them out of the way.

Close the sales worksheet now without saving it.

CREATING A SERIES OF VALUES

Excel gives you two quick and easy ways to enter sequential numbers into columns or rows. These would have been useful when you created the amortization worksheet in Chapter 8. Column A of that worksheet contains a series of numbers. When you created the worksheet, you had to enter each number into column A sequentially—a laborious job because there were 48 payments in the example.

USING THE SERIES COMMAND

To use the Series command, you simply enter the starting value into the first cell of the row or column, select the cell range for the series (a row or column, including the starting cell), and choose Data ➤ Series. When you see the Series dialog box, choose whether you want the series in a row or column and choose the series type (as explained below). Then, enter a step value for each increment of the series (the default value is 1). After you've made your selections, click OK and Excel will enter the series values automatically.

You have a choice of three types of series:

◆ A **linear series**, in which each entry is increased by adding a constant amount. For example, a linear (or arithmetic) series with a starting value of 1 and a step value of 2 would increase 1, 3, 5, and so on.

◆ A **growth series**, in which each entry is multiplied by the step value. For example, a growth (or geometric) series with a starting value of 1 and a step value of 2 would increase 1, 2, 4, 8, 16, and so on. The growth series is useful for calculating compounded interest or growth rates.

◆ A **date series**, in which a date is increased by a unit (day, weekday, month, or year) that you select in the Date Unit group. For example, to create columnar headings for the months of the year, enter the first month, select the row for the column titles, select Data ➤ Series, choose Date, select Month, and click OK.

You also can choose a stop value for a series. For example, if you did not know how many rows or columns your series would require, you could select a larger range than you need and enter a specific stop value in the Series dialog box. The series would then terminate at that specified value.

You can use the series command to enter the data into column A of your amortization worksheet easily. Open this worksheet now. After you clear column A from row 15 down, follow these steps:

1. Enter the starting value of 1 into cell A15.

2. Select cell A15 and select Formula ➤ Goto.

3. Enter A62 into the Reference text box, then hold down the Shift key and click OK.

4. Choose Data ➤ Series.

5. When the Series dialog box appears, leave the default Columns and Linear options and step value selected and click OK.

With just a few clicks, the series is entered into column A.

CREATING A SERIES WITH AUTOFILLING

You can also create a series with a technique called *autofilling*. To create a series in this way, follow these steps:

1. Select a range of cells in the series and enter the first two values of the series. Leave the two cells selected.

2. Drag the fill handle at the lower-right corner of the active cell in the direction you wish to extend the series. You will see the current cell values in the formula bar as you drag.

3. Release the mouse button.

Autofilling cannot create an exponential forecast, nor can it alter the original data. If you want an exponential forecast or a linear regression that alters the original data, you must use the appropriate functions (see Chapter 24).

You can extend a series down, up, left, or right. You can use numeric values or dates. You can also drag the fill handle backward into a series to clear values that you no longer want.

You can use this same dragging technique to create a linear forecast. If you have a series of values, you can select the entire range and then use the fill handle to extend the range based on a linear forecast. This is the same as using the Data ➤ Series command and selecting a linear series.

CHANGING REFERENCE STYLES

Some Excel formulas require the use of the R1C1 style (such as ABSREF and RELREF).

Some worksheet programs designate rows and columns in a different style than Excel's. They reference a cell's location in R1C1 style—an *R* followed by the row number and a *C* followed by the column number—rather than Excel's column letter and row number (A1) style. For example, below is a formula for cell C15 of the amortization worksheet in Excel's reference style:

=–PV($B$7/12,(B$8–A15),$B$10)

And here is the same formula in R1C1 style:

=–PV(R7C2/12,(R8C[–1]–RC[–2],R10C2)

Notice the difference in both absolute and relative addressing. The absolute $B$7 reference in A1 style becomes R7C2—row 7, column 2. The mixed reference B$8 becomes row 8 and one column left (–1) of the current column, or R8C [–1].

If you are more familiar with the R1C1 style and would rather have Excel use it, you can change to that style by using the Workspace command on the Options menu. In the Workspace dialog box, click the R1C1 check box, then click OK. The worksheet's column letters will change into numbers so that both the rows and columns are referenced by numbers. (Change the worksheet back to Excel's normal referencing style for use in this book.)

MOVING TO AND FINDING CELLS

The Formula menu lists several commands that let you move quickly to particular cells and find cells that contain specific data.

MOVING TO SPECIFIC CELLS

If you are using a large worksheet, you will occasionally need to move quickly to a particular cell on it. The Goto command on the Formula menu allows you to jump to any specified cell. When you use this command, or press F5, you will see the Goto dialog box. Simply enter the reference to the cell that you want to make active in the Reference box and click OK.

There is an even easier way to move to a particular cell. If there is a cell or cell range on your worksheet that you use often, assign it a name using Formula ➤ Define Name (see Chapter 9). Then when you choose Goto or press F5, you will see that name in the dialog box's list of active names. Double-click the name and you'll move to that cell or cell range immediately.

TIP

If there is a cell range that you use often, select the entire range and assign a name to it. You can then use the Goto command to select that range quickly.

The Goto command actually has more uses than just getting you to a particular cell quickly: you can use it for range selection, formula entry, or viewing, as well. Let's try a few simple experiments so that you can see for yourself.

First, open your amortization worksheet and define a name for cell C18:

1. Select cell C18.

2. Choose Formula ➤ Define Name.

3. Type **Test** into the Define Name text box and click OK.

Now use the Goto command to select a range:

1. Select cell C15.

2. Choose Formula ➤ Goto or press F5.

3. Hold down the Shift key and double-click **Test** in the Goto dialog box.

You have now selected the entire cell range from C15 to C18. The result is shown in Figure 14.3.

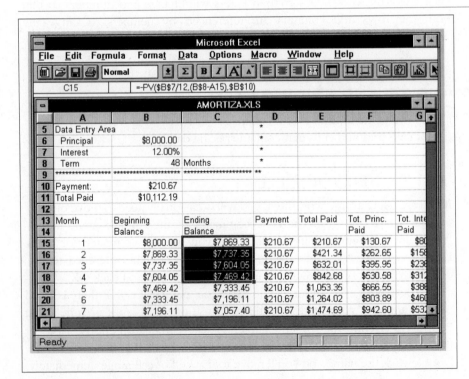

FIGURE 14.3:

Selecting a range with the Goto command

When using the Goto command, Excel keeps a history of the commands issued. The most recent Goto destinations are listed in the top of the list box when the command is initiated. It is somewhat awkward to use, however, as the cells are listed as absolute references instead of using any assigned names.

FINDING SPECIFIC CELLS

There may be times when you need to find the specific cell that contains a particular value or formula. You can do this by using Formula ➤ Find (or pressing Shift-F5). When you select the Find command, you'll see the Find dialog box. Once you've entered what you want to find in the Find What text box, you can have Excel look in formulas or in values, look for the entry as a whole or as part of other entries, and look by columns or by rows.

Here are other features of the Find command:

When you've finished editing a worksheet, use the Find command to locate all unresolved references by searching for #REF, using the default options.

◆ If you have a single cell selected when you use the Find command, the entire worksheet will be searched. If you have a range selected, only the range will be searched.

◆ The search will stop when Excel finds the first occurrence of the contents in the Find What text box.

◆ When entering the search string into the Find What text box, you can use the wildcard characters ? and *, where ? represents a single character and * represents a group of characters. You also can use any of the relational operators to specify the search string (see Chapter 4).

◆ The Look By group is used to specify the direction of the search—either by rows or columns. If you know the approximate location of the cell on a large worksheet, specifying the correct direction here can speed up the search.

◆ Press F7 to find the next occurrence or Shift-F7 to find the previous one. (These don't work when the Find dialog box is open.)

As an example, you can use the Find command to locate the cell on your amortization worksheet that contains the final payment. Follow these steps:

1. Choose Formula ➤ Find.

2. When the Find dialog box is displayed, enter **48**.

3. Choose Values to indicate that you wish to search in values instead of in formulas (otherwise it would stop on cell C48).

4. Choose Whole to indicate that you want to skip cells in which the value is a part of a cell's value (otherwise it would stop on cell C25).

5. Click OK.

The cursor should jump to cell A62, the month cell in the last payment row.

DISPLAYING THE ACTIVE CELL

You can use Formula ➤ Show Active Cell to find the current active cell. This is particularly useful when you select a cell or cell range, scroll away to view something else in the worksheet, and want to get back to where you were.

REPLACING CELL VALUES

The Replace command on the Formula menu can be used to replace characters in the worksheet or a cell range. Select the range to search and replace or, if you wish the command to apply to the entire worksheet, a single cell. When you search a range, the first cell in the range should be active. Select Formula ➤ Replace. The dialog box below will be displayed:

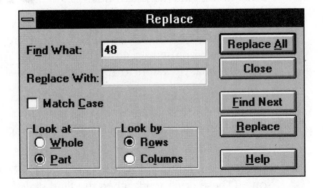

Enter the current value in the Find What text box and what it is to be replaced with in the Replace With text box. Choose Whole to match the contents of the Find What text box with the entire contents of a cell or Part to check for a match with any part of a cell's contents. You may use * and ? wildcards. The Look by Rows and Look by Columns options define which direction to search.

For global replacement, click the Replace All button. For selective replacement, first click on Find Next to find the next occurrence, then click on Replace to replace the single occurrence and look for the next occurrence of the characters you searching for. Click Find Next to skip the current selection and locate the next occurrence. Replace only applies to the currently active cell. To reverse to a previous occurrence, hold down the Shift key and click on Find Next. To exit, click on Close. To undo, select Edit ➤ Undo Replace.

SELECTING THE LAST CELL

Sometimes you may need to find the last cell of a worksheet. This command is useful if you simply want to move quickly to the last cell, but can't remember its location. To find the last cell, choose Formula ➤ Select Special. Then choose Last Cell (Figure 14.4) and click on OK.

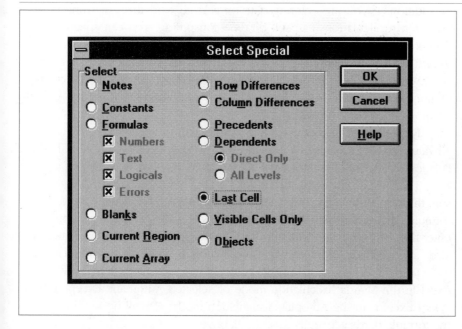

FIGURE 14.4:

This dialog box allows you to find the last cell in the worksheet

The last cell is defined as the last cell with any note for formatting information in it, so it could be empty. To minimize the size of worksheet files and to enable this command to function properly, format only the cells you use.

CALCULATION OPTIONS

The Calculation command on the Options menu allows you to tell Excel when to recalculate values and when to use iterations.

CONTROLLING RECALCULATIONS

Normally, whenever you change a value, formula, or name, Excel automatically recalculates all cells that are dependent upon the changed cells. The time required for Excel to recalculate a worksheet depends on the size of the worksheet, the number of dependent cells, and the number of open documents. Excel only calculates the cells that are changed as a result of an edit or addition. If you are entering data on a large worksheet or using tables, however, recalculations can still be time-consuming. You can speed up the data-entry process by using the Calculation command on the Options menu to turn off the calculations until you've entered all the data.

When you use the Calculation command, you will see the Calculation Options dialog box. Choose Manual in the Calculation group to turn off calculations, then click on OK.

For some worksheets, you may want Excel to recalculate automatically all values except the tables automatically. If you select this option in the Calculation dialog box, the tables will be recalculated only when you edit a table.

To calculate the worksheet after you have entered all the data, first be sure that the formula bar is not selected, then press F9 (Calculate Now). If the formula bar is active when you press F9, Excel will evaluate the formula and enter the result (not the formula) into the active cell if you press Enter. You also can select part of a formula and use press F9 to evaluate only that part.

Remember, you need use F9 (Calculate Now) only when you have set Excel in the Manual calculation mode or selected Automatic Except Tables. When Excel is in the Automatic calculation mode, F9 will do nothing unless the formula bar is active, as described above.

USING ITERATIONS

There may be times when your calculations require you to use formulas that depend upon each other in a circular manner. Excel allows you to perform the worksheet calculations repetitively, or use *iterations*. Let's try an example so that you can get an idea of how this works. Close the amortization worksheet without saving and open an empty worksheet.

Acme Manufacturing had a good year, and the Board of Directors decided to pay the employees a bonus. The amount allocated for the bonus payments was five percent of the net profit after the bonuses were subtracted from the gross profit. Let's create a worksheet to help Acme calculate the bonus (before starting, be sure that Automatic Calculation is enabled and Iteration is disabled in the Calculation Options dialog box):

1. Enter the row titles **Gross Profit**, **Bonus**, and **Net Profit** in cells A3, A4, and A6, respectively, and enter **23,500** as the value for Gross Profit in cell B3 (Figure 14.5).

2. Create the names in cells B3 through B6 by selecting A3 to B6 and then choosing Formula ➤ Create Names. In the dialog box, choose Left Column, then click OK.

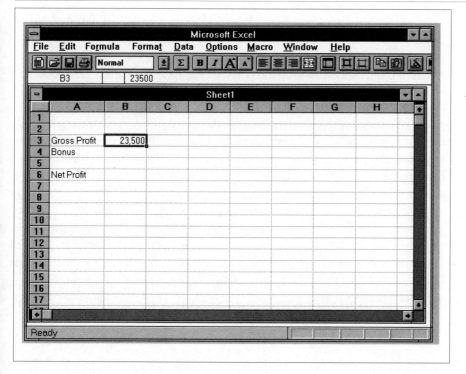

FIGURE 14.5:

The Acme Manufacturing worksheet. Entering formulas that create circular references causes an error message to appear.

3. Enter the formula for Net Profit as **=Gross_Profit–Bonus** in B6.

4. Enter the value of Bonus as **=Net_Profit*5%** in B4.

What happens? You will quickly get the error message shown below:

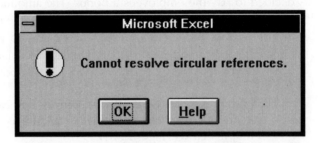

This message indicates that you have created formulas that depend upon each other. Here net profit is the gross profit minus the bonus, but you need to know the net profit before the bonus can be calculated. Solution: use iterations to make your calculation.

Continue with the worksheet:

5. Choose OK to cancel the message box, then choose Options ➤ Calculation.

6. When the Calculation Options dialog box appears (Figure 14.6), check Iteration, then click on OK.

Excel will repeat the calculations until the net profit and bonus change by 0.001 or less, or until a maximum of 100 iterations have occurred. As shown in Figure 14.6, these limits are set in the Calculation dialog box. The final iteration worksheet, after some numerical formatting, is shown in Figure 14.7.

Here the resulting values change less and less with each iteration. The iterations are said to "*converge* to a solution." In some examples, the resulting values may change more and more with each iteration. In this case, the iterations *diverge* and no real solution is possible. Both the design of the model and the starting values determine whether the solution converges or diverges.

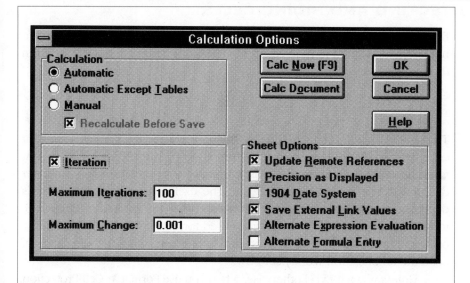

The Calculation Options dialog box with iterations turned on

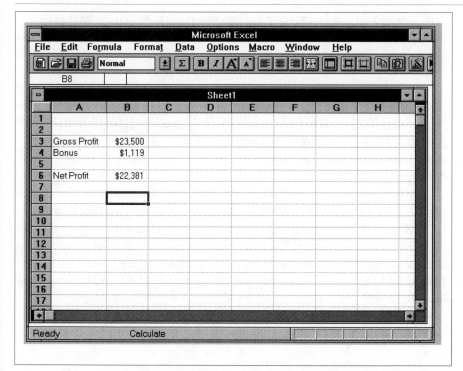

The final Acme Manufacturing iteration worksheet. Here Excel used iterations to calculate the formulas with circular references.

PROTECTING AND HIDING CELLS

Excel allows you to protect cells on your worksheet so that their contents cannot be changed, and to hide cells so that their formulas are not displayed in the formula bar.

PROTECTING CELLS

Protect as many cells as possible in your document, leaving only the cells that depend upon input data unprotected. This prevents someone from accidentally changing a formula or constant value that may be the basis of important decisions in a worksheet.

The Cell Protection command on the Format menu and the Protect Document command on the Options menu together allow you to protect cells on your worksheets. When you protect cells, you *lock* them so that no one can enter data into them or alter their contents. The usefulness of cell protection is demonstrated by the amortization worksheet that you created in Chapter 8, in which only three cells were actually used for data entry. All the remaining cells in the worksheet could be protected to prevent them from being altered. Load the amortization worksheet now.

Unless you tell Excel otherwise, when you use Format ➤ Cell Protection, *all* the cells of the document are locked after the document is protected. So the general procedure for protecting cells on a worksheet is first to select the cells that should *not* be protected. Then use Format ➤ Cell Protection to unlock these cells by toggling Locked off in the Cell Protection dialog box and clicking OK. Protect the rest of the worksheet by selecting Options ➤ Protect Document.

Excel prompts you to reenter your password for confirmation.

When you use the Protect Document command, you must enter a password. If you forget this password, you will never be able to unlock the protected cells. For this reason *always check the password that you enter before you click OK to be sure that it is what you intended.* Keep a record of your passwords, too. The exact same word must be entered to unprotect the document.

When you need to unlock a protected cell, the procedure is just the reverse. Select Options ➤ Unprotect Document and enter your password.

When a document is protected, many commands are no longer available for use with that worksheet. The menus change to reflect this—the unavailable commands are dimmed on the menus. For example, all the commands on the Format and Data menus, except Find, Form, Consolidate, and Crosstab, are inactive.

To see how cell protection works, try locking all but the data-entry cells on your amortization worksheet. Follow these steps with that worksheet:

1. Select cells B6 through B8 (the data-entry cells).

2. Choose Format ➤ Cell Protection.

3. When the Cell Protection dialog box appears, toggle Locked to unlock the cells that you selected. (Remove the × in the Locked check box to unlock the cells.) Then click on OK.

4. Select Options ➤ Protect Document.

5. When the Protect Document dialog box appears, enter the password **Secret** (capitalization is important). Notice that only asterisks are displayed as you type in the password. Press Enter or choose OK. Type the password again in the Confirm Password dialog box and press Enter. Notice that you can protect cells, windows, and objects.

Your amortization worksheet is now protected. You can enter a new interest rate, principal, or term, but you cannot alter the contents of any other cell. Try to edit the other cells just to see what happens. You will get an alert box with the message: **Locked cells cannot be changed.**

If it is ever necessary to alter the formulas or otherwise change the protected areas of your amortization worksheet, follow the reverse procedure:

1. Select Options ➤ Unprotect Document.

2. Enter **Secret** as the password in the Unprotect Document dialog box, then click OK.

If you forget which cells are protected, use the Display command on the Options menu to turn off the gridlines. The unprotected cells will be underlined if Document Protection is turned on, as shown in Figure 14.8.

HIDING CELLS

You may wish to prevent a user from seeing the formula used in a particular calculation. You can do this by hiding a cell, using a procedure similar to the one that you use to protect cells. First, select the cell or cell range that you want to hide. Then choose Format ➤ Cell Protection. When the Cell Protection dialog box appears, click the Hidden button. Then click on OK. Next select Options ➤ Protect Document. When the Protect Document dialog box appears, enter your password and choose OK. Reenter the password in the Confirm Password dialog box and click OK again. Now when the hidden cell is selected, its formula will not appear in the formula bar.

To recover the formulas in hidden cells, use Options ➤ Unprotect Document. Enter your password in the Document Password dialog box. As with protected cells, you must remember your password or you will never be able to view the formulas again.

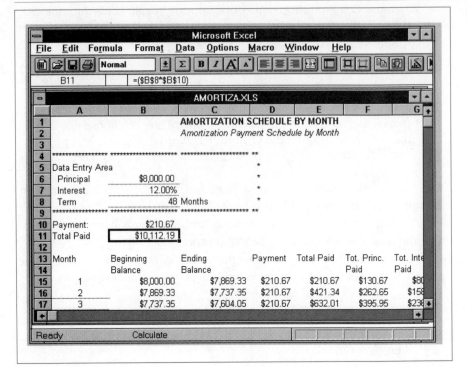

FIGURE 14.8:

Unprotected cells appear underlined after they were once protected

Here are a few tips about using hidden cells:

◆ Hiding a cell doesn't hide the cell value, only the formula used to obtain the value. To hide a cell value, select the cell and format it to a custom picture of ;; .

◆ Hide cells to protect proprietary formulas or hide entire macro sheets from unauthorized viewing.

◆ You *can* omit the password, but if you do so any user will be able to quickly unhide protected cells.

CONTROLLING THE NUMERIC PRECISION OF EXCEL CALCULATIONS

Excel stores all numbers that you enter into your worksheets with 15-digit precision. (*Precision* refers to the number of digits to which a value is calculated, stored, or displayed.) Excel performs all calculations and stores all values with this precision, without regard to how the number is displayed.

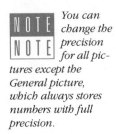

You can change the precision for all pictures except the General picture, which always stores numbers with full precision.

Sometimes you may wish to change this so that Excel stores numbers and performs calculations only with the precision displayed. For example, you may want to change the precision when the results of formulas do not seem to match the numbers used to calculate them.

To switch from full precision to the displayed precision, select Options ➤ Calculation (see Figure 14.6), check Precision as Displayed in the dialog box, and click on OK. A message explaining that data will permanently lose accuracy is displayed. Once this is option turned on, data are rounded off to the displayed picture. You cannot recover the former precision. To switch back, select Options ➤ Calculation, turn off Precision as Displayed, and click on OK.

TRANSPOSING LISTS

Excel also supports transposition, which can be useful for rearranging columns and lists. The top of Figure 14.9 shows a worksheet with long names for the column titles. In this form, the column titles are not very readable. If the columns were increased in width, the numbers would be lost on the page in the too-wide columns.

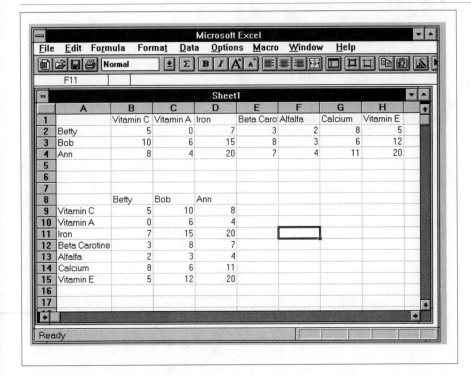

FIGURE 14.9:

The top worksheet needs transposing because column titles are long and the entries are narrow. The transposed worksheet below is more readable than the worksheet above.

To solve this problem, transpose the list so that the column titles are row titles and the row titles become column titles. Select A1 to H4, then choose Edit ➤ Copy to copy this range to the Clipboard. Select A8 (an empty cell away from the data) and choose Edit ➤ Paste Special. In the dialog box, click on Transpose. Then click OK. Adjust the column width of A slightly. The rows and columns are switched and the worksheet becomes more readable (see bottom of Figure 14.9). The numbers aren't lost on the page.

Formula integrity is maintained and formulas are adjusted. You also can choose Values when transposing and paste values instead of formulas.

CONTROLLING MAGNIFICATION OF A WORKSHEET

With Excel, you can control the magnification with which the worksheet is displayed. To change the magnification, choose Windows ➤ Zoom. Select the desired magnification in the Zoom dialog box shown below and click on OK:

FAST TRACK CHAPTER 15

CHAPTER 15

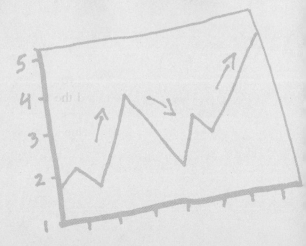

Calculating with Arrays

or some applications, you may want to use multiple values as an argument for a function, or you may want a function to produce multiple values. Such a list of multiple values is called an *array*.

In all the examples in the previous chapters, you have used only simple functions. In a simple function, each argument refers to a single value—a single cell or a single cell range. For example, the result of the formula =SUM(A1:A11) is the sum of the values from cells A1 through A11—a single cell range. In this chapter, you will learn about Excel's capability of using multiple-value arguments. The basic idea of using an array will be illustrated with a simple example. Then you will work through a more complex example that shows clearly how an array can make your worksheet calculations much easier.

ENTERING AN ARRAY

Suppose that you have an inventory worksheet that lists four products, the cost of each, and the quantities-on-hand, as shown in Figure 15.1. The extended cost of each product equals the quantity-on-hand multiplied by the cost. The total inventory value, then, is the sum of the extended costs of the product.

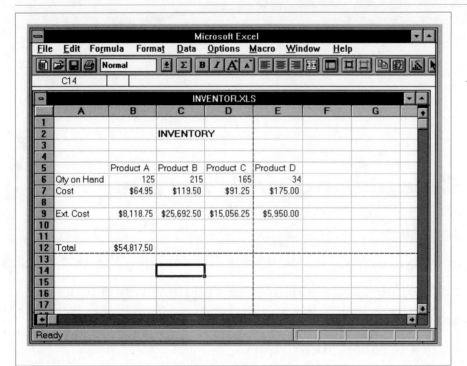

Create this worksheet. Enter the labels for column A and row 5, the title, and the data for rows 6 and 7. Select cells A6 to E9 and choose Formula ➤ Create Names. Choose Left Column and click OK. Enter the formulas to row 9 as shown in Figure 15.2. Calculate the total in cell B12.

Notice that you entered the same formula four times in the Ext. Cost row. It would be easier to calculate the total value of the inventory using an array. To do so, type in the following formula for the total in cell B14, *but do not press Enter:*

=SUM(B6:E6*B7:E7)

After you have typed in the formula from the keyboard, *hold down the Control and Shift keys while you press Enter.* This will force Excel to accept the arguments as an array. Clear A9 to E9. As shown in Figure 15.3, the displayed total in cell B14 is still the same as it was in B12 before (in Figure 15.1), but the formula used to calculate that total is different than the formula in B12. Before doing anything else, undo the clear using Undo Clear.

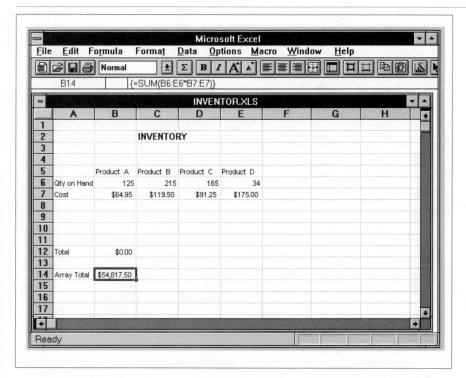

These are the inventory worksheet formulas that you should enter to get the worksheet shown in Figure 15.1

	INVENTORY			
	Product A	Product B	Product C	Product D
Qty on Hand	125	215	165	34
Cost	64.95	119.5	91.25	175
Ext. Cost	=Qty_on_Hand*Cost	=Qty_on_Hand*Cost	=Qty_on_Hand*Cost	=Qty_on_Hand*Cost
Total	=SUM(B9:E9)			

FIGURE 15.3:

Here the worksheet uses an array to calculate the total cost of the products in inventory

Examine the formula in B14. Notice that it is exactly as you entered it, except that by using the Shift and Control keys you enclosed it in braces:

{=SUM(B6:E6*B7:E7)}

The values for cell ranges B6 through E6 and B7 through E7 are treated as arrays, or lists of values. The SUM function multiplies the corresponding values in each list and then sums the products to get the final total. The formula is identical to

B14 = B6*B7+C6*C7+D6*D7+E6*E7

Change any value in row 6 or 7 and the total will change to reflect the new quantity-on-hand or cost.

In this case, arrays were used to speed up data entry: they eliminated the necessity of naming the rows, entering the first formula, and then filling right. (You named the rows for the equations in row 9, not for the array in B14.) Only the final total formula was entered, and no names were used with the formula.

You also can use range names in an array formula. In the inventory worksheet, you could enter the formula in B14 as

{=SUM(Qty_on_Hand*Cost)}

The keyboard entry of the braces doesn't work here because the equal sign is not the first character; use Ctrl-Shift-Enter instead.

Many functions listed in Chapter 8 *require* array arguments. With these functions, it is not necessary to use the Shift and Control keys, because Excel assumes the argument is an array. Later in the chapter, you will use one of these functions.

Save your worksheet as INVENTOR, as you will need it in the next chapter.

CALCULATING MULTIPLE OUTPUT VALUES

In the previous example, multiple input values were used to obtain a single output value. At imes you may need multiple output values; that is, the output of the function should be an array as well. To understand how you can use multiple outputs, let's look at the following linear regression example.

Linear regression is often used to project a future trend from known data about the past. For instance, this technique is used by manufacturing operations to project data on future productivity based on changes in the number of employees, working conditions, and other factors. It also can be used by a sales department to plan warehousing, marketing, and sales representation.

Suppose, for example, that your company discovered there was a relationship between the disposable income per person in various areas and the sale of its product. You have information about the disposable income in future years and you wish to project your sales for these years. This would enable you to plan how much warehouse space is needed, the number of sales representatives to employ, your marketing costs, and other factors. You'll use linear regression to make this projection. In the following example, you'll first do the linear regression using conventional worksheet techniques. Then you'll do the same linear regression using the more convenient arrays.

LINEAR REGRESSION WITHOUT ARRAYS

Figure 15.4 shows a good example of why linear regression should be done with arrays. Without arrays, *six* columns are needed to perform the calculation. As we shall soon see, arrays can reduce this to *two* columns. Figure 15.5 shows the formulas used, and the values are plotted in Figure 15.6 (the *x* axis is the disposable income and the *y* axis is the sales). As the graph shows, there seems to be a correlation that could be used to plan future sales.

The data for the disposable income and sales are used to calculate the constants for the linear regression. This calculation is done in cells C29 and C30 using the following formulas:

$$a = y - bx$$

$$b = \frac{\Sigma xy - x\Sigma y}{\Sigma x^2 - x\Sigma x}$$

$$y_n = a + bx_n$$

Here x is the range A11 to A20, y is the range B11 to B20, and x represents the average of x (B27).

If you wish to try this, enter the data for the entire worksheet shown in Figure 15.5. You can use the Edit➤Fill Down command or dragging to enter much of the data, but you will probably still find it cumbersome to use this approach to obtain your projections. Whether you enter the data or not, look over the example.

LINEAR REGRESSION WITH ARRAYS

Now try the same thing using two arrays:

1. Enter the years as column A, as in the previous example. Place the first year in A11 and use Data ➤ Data Series to create the column.

LINEAR REGRESSION EXAMPLE

Year	Disposable Income ($K)	Projected Disp. Income ($K)	Sales	Disp. Income X Sales	Disp. Income Squared	Projected Sales ($K)
1983	200		2350	470000	40000	
1984	260		2500	650000	67600	
1985	270		2400	648000	72900	
1986	190		2390	454100	36100	
1987	119		2360	280840	14161	
1988	115		2260	259900	13225	
1989	325		2575	836875	105625	
1990	350		2550	892500	122500	
1991	302		2503	755906	91204	
1992	212		2475	524700	44944	
1993		250				2,453.40
1994		275				2,480.62
1995		325				2,535.07
Sum	2343		24363	5772821	608259	
Average	234.3		2436.3	577282.1	60825.9	

Value of b= 1.08898019

Value of a= 2181.15194

2. Place the disposable income in column B for each year. (If you tried the previous example, copy from columns B and C of that worksheet to column B of the new worksheet to create a single column B.

3. Create the Sales column in column C (D in previous example) and enter (or move) the values for each year. Again, you can also do this by dragging.

	A	B	C	D	E	F	G
1		LINEAR REGRESSI					
2							
3							
4							
5							
6							
7	Year	Disposable	Projected		Sales	Disp. Income	Disp. Income	Projected
8		Income	Disp. Income		($K)	X Sales	Squared	Sales
9		($K)	($K)					($K)
10								
11	1983	200		2350	=B11*D11	=B11*B11	
12	1984	260		2500	=B12*D12	=B12*B12	
13	1985	270		2400	=B13*D13	=B13*B13	
14	1986	190		2390	=B14*D14	=B14*B14	
15	1987	119		2360	=B15*D15	=B15*B15	
16	1988	115		2260	=B16*D16	=B16*B16	
17	1989	325		2575	=B17*D17	=B17*B17	
18	1990	350		2550	=B18*D18	=B18*B18	
19	1991	302		2503	=B19*D19	=B19*B19	
20	1992	212		2475	=B20*D20	=B20*B20	
21	1993		250				=$C$30+($C$29*C21)
22	1994		275				=$C$30+($C$29*C22)
23	1995		325				=$C$30+($C$29*C23)
24							
25	Sum	=SUM(B11:B20)		=SUM(D11:D20)	=SUM(E11:E20)	=SUM(F11:F20)	
26							
27	Average	=B25/10		=D25/10	=E25/10	=F25/10	
28							
29		Value of b=	=((E25-(B27*D25))/(F25-(B27*B25)))				
30		Value of a=	=(D27-(C29*B27))				

FIGURE 15.5:

The formulas for the linear regression example done the hard way

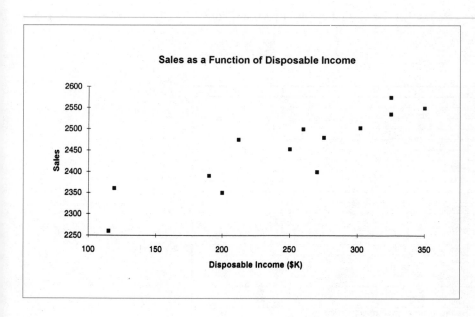

FIGURE 15.6:

The chart of the linear regression

4. Delete the rest of the worksheet data if you tried the earlier example.

5. Label the columns as shown in Figure 15.8. Add the worksheet title, **LINEAR REGRESSION EXAMPLE**. Disposable Income will be the input array. Sales will be the output array.

6. Enter the first array formula. You will need to use two functions, SUM and LINEST. The LINEST function has two arrays for an input and one array for an output (see Chapter 8). Enter the following formula into cell C21:

=SUM(LINEST($C$11:$C$20,$B$11:$B$20)*{250,1})

Manually enter the braces for the array (it works here because the equal sign is the first character).

7. Copy the formula in cell C21 into cells C22 and C23 using the Fill Down command (or hold down Ctrl and drag the cell by its lower-right corner), then edit the SUM functions in cells C22 and C23 so that the **250** in the next-to-last argument reads **275** and **325**, respectively—the proper disposable incomes. Your final formulas should look like those shown in Figure 15.7.

8. Format the worksheet as shown in Figure 15.8, then print it.

FIGURE 15.7:

The linear regression example using arrays

	A	B	C	D
1		LINEAR REGRESSI		
2		Using Arrays		
3				
4				
5				
6				
7	Year	Disposable	Sales	
8		Income	($K)	
9		($K)		
10				
11	1983	200	2350	
12	1984	260	2500	
13	1985	270	2400	
14	1986	190	2390	
15	1987	119	2360	
16	1988	115	2260	
17	1989	325	2575	
18	1990	350	2550	
19	1991	302	2503	
20	1992	212	2475	
21	1993	250	=SUM(LINEST($C$11:$C$20,$B$11:$B$20)*{250,1})	*
22	1994	275	=SUM(LINEST($C$11:$C$20,$B$11:$B$20)*{275,1})	*
23	1995	325	=SUM(LINEST($C$11:$C$20,$B$11:$B$20)*{325,1})	*
24				
25		* Projected Sales		

LINEAR REGRESSION EXAMPLE

Using Arrays

Year	Disposable Income ($K)	Sales ($K)
1983	200	2350
1984	260	2500
1985	270	2400
1986	190	2390
1987	119	2360
1988	115	2260
1989	325	2575
1990	350	2550
1991	302	2503
1992	212	2475
1993	250	2453 *
1994	275	2481 *
1995	325	2535 *

* Projected Sales

FIGURE 15.8:

The final printout of the regression using arrays

The final projected values are the same as those that were obtained the hard way in Figure 15.4, but here they are generated with much less work.

Let's review the array formula that you just used. The LINEST function returns an array of two values: the slope (b) and the intercept (a) of the line of regression, represented by $y = a + bx$. These are the same constants that you calculated earlier using multiple columns, squares, sums, and averages. Excel does it all with a single function.

The general form of the LINEST function is

LINEST(*y array, x array*)

The *y* array is the known and projected sales (C11:C23). The *x* array is the known and projected disposable income. The LINEST function returns an array of two values: the slope of a regression line that fits the points and the *y* intercept of the line. This returned array is then used with the SUM function (as in the previous example) to calculate the *x* value for a known *y* value. The formula multiplies the first argument of the LINEST function (the slope) by an *x* value (250) and adds the second part of the LINEST function (the *y* intercept) multiplied by 1:

$$y \text{ value} = (x \text{ value}) * \text{slope} + (y \text{ intercept}) * 1$$

The 1 is really a dummy constant and is necessary only to keep both arrays the same size.

You also could try an exponential regression using the LOGEST function. The other functions that require arrays are GROWTH, TREND, COLUMNS, ROWS, and TRANSPOSE. The LOOKUP functions and others (such as MIRR) can also use arrays. Even functions that normally use single-value arguments, such as SUM, can work with array arguments (as you have seen).

Chapter 24 will introduce you to more examples of linear regression and explain how to do more complex regressions.

CREATING A REGRESSION CHART

The creation of charts is described later in Part V, but you can take the time now to make the regression graph of Figure 15.6 if you wish. Start with the worksheet of Figure 15.7:

1. Select B11 to C23. Choose Edit ➤ Copy. This puts the series data in the Clipboard.

2. Select File ➤ New. Choose Chart in the dialog box. An empty chart will be displayed.

3. On the chart menu bar, select Edit ➤ Paste Special. In this dialog box choose Categories (X Labels) in First Column. This will map the first column to the category axis and the second column to the value axis. Click on OK.

4. Choose Gallery ➤ XY (Scatter). Double-click the first option for the scatter chart.

5. To make the *x* axis start at 100, click the axis and select Format ➤ Font. Click the Scale button. Specify under Auto, Minimum: 100. Click on OK. Select Chart ➤ Attach Text to add axis labels and a chart title. Add any axis labels or titles desired.

ARRAY CONSTANTS

In Chapter 7 you created the cash-flow analysis worksheet that had a parameter file with several constants. These constants served as inputs for formulas used elsewhere in the worksheet. In the same way, you can store an array as a single constant and use it in a formula.

To enter an array constant into an array formula, type the values into the formulas and enclose them in braces ({ }). Separate values in the same row with commas and separate rows with semicolons. For example, {1,2,3;4,5,6} is an array of two rows and three columns.

RULES FOR USING ARRAYS

Here are some general rules for using arrays:

◆ The values of an array must be constant values and not formulas. An array can contain numeric, text, logical, or error values (such as #VALUE!). Text values must be enclosed in quotation marks.

◆ You can use an array with most functions.

◆ When an array is used with a function, the type of values must be consistent with what is required by the function.

◆ When an array formula is entered into a range of cells, the formulas should produce an array that is the same size as the selected cell range. For example, in Chapter 24 the LINEST function is entered to a range of two cells, since the function returns an array of two variables, the slope and intercept.

◆ Relative cell addresses in an array are considered relative to the cell in the upper-left corner of the range. If you copy an array, the relative references will be adjusted.

◆ You cannot type an array that has a mixed number of columns in the rows. For example, {4,9,1;3,4} is illegal.

◆ If an array is used as an argument in a function, all other arguments in the same function should be arrays of the same size.

◆ You cannot edit the individual cells of a constant array.

◆ Excel permits a maximum of 6,500 elements in an array.

EDITING AN ARRAY FORMULA

As you know, you can enter an array formula into a range of cells in the same way that you enter any formula into a range of cells, except you hold down the Shift and Control keys while you press Enter. There is a difference, however, when you are editing a formula that has been entered into a range of cells. After an array formula is entered into a range, you cannot edit or clear an individual cell or delete rows or columns within that range. The entire cell range must be treated as a unit. You can only select, edit, or clear the entire range.

You can edit an array formula by using the commands on the Edit menu. If you click the cursor on any point in the formula bar, whatever you type will be entered at the cursor location. You also can drag the cursor in the formula bar to mark a range of characters, then use the Cut command to delete the marked characters. Once you have finished editing the formula, pressing Enter will complete the entry. (Remember, If you enter a constant array to a range of cells, the individual cells of the array cannot be edited.) You will find several examples of entering and editing array formulas in Chapter 24. You will also see how the array brackets can be entered to a formula from the keyboard.

FAST TRACK CHAPTER 16

> 1. Open the worksheets to be consolidated and an output worksheet.
> 2. Select the output range on the output worksheet for the consolidated data.
> 3. Choose Data ➤ Consolidate.
> 4. Select input ranges, one at a time (with labels), and choose Add on the Consolidate dialog box.
> 5. When all input data are selected, select OK. Consolidated worksheets can be static or linked, with the option chosen on the Consolidate dialog box.

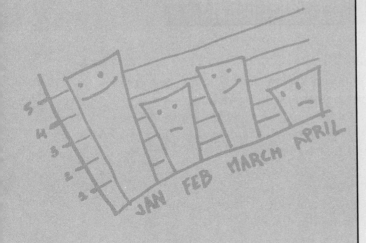

CHAPTER 16

Working with Multiple Documents

Excel provides extensive support for working with multiple documents simultaneously. This chapter shows you how to link documents and consolidate documents to create summary worksheets.

LINKING DOCUMENTS

One of Excel's most valuable features is its ability to *link* documents together. Why is this important? A major corporation could create a complex system of interlinked worksheets that simulates the company's financial flow, then use the model to see what happens as they change various parameters. One financial vice-president told me that the ability to link documents was one of the most important features of the spreadsheet that he uses. His entire company's financial picture could be modeled with a collection of linked worksheets.

When linking Excel documents, you create a relationship in which a change in one document will automatically affect the other. In Chapter 3, for example, you created a chart that was linked to a worksheet. When you made any changes in the worksheet, they were immediately reflected in the chart.

You can link cells or cell ranges in two or more documents. This allows you to set up a hierarchical structure of worksheets that will always reflect your most current data.

Linked documents are useful for:

◆ consolidating data from many source worksheets into a single summary worksheet

◆ creating different views of the same data

◆ creating a large model from several smaller models

In this section, you will learn some basic concepts of linking documents. You will be guided through a simple example, then you will use it to study the more complex aspects of linking documents.

When you link cells in different worksheets, the values in one will change whenever you change the values in the other. This is an easy way to be sure that your associated worksheets are up-to-date without having to enter new data into each one. You can link individual cells of worksheets or whole cell ranges.

LINKING SINGLE CELLS

Let's link two worksheets together to see how linking works. In the following example, you'll link one cell in the sales worksheet that you created in Chapters 10–13 to a cell in a new cash-flow analysis worksheet.

Assume that your sales worksheet was prepared by the sales department manager of a company. She needs to copy the sales totals for all the regions into a new worksheet that will be used by another department in the company for a cash-flow analysis. The projected sales total will change as the year progresses, and the company's managers want to have the cash-flow analysis worksheet updated automatically to reflect each change.

After you open your sales worksheet, which you used in Chapter 13, follow the steps below to create two linked documents:

1. Sort the sales worksheet in name order if necessary. Add the hyphens in cell B10 (add one hyphen and use Format ➤ Alignment to set the type to Fill). Make B11 the sum of B6 through B9. Add the word **Total** in cell A11 and then save this worksheet.

2. Select File ➤ New (or press Shift-F11) to open a new worksheet. Select Window ➤ Arrange and choose Tiled, then click OK to see both worksheets.

Using linked worksheets is easier than creating large worksheets that are cumbersome to scroll and update.

N O T E
N O T E

In this and the more complex examples in the next few chapters, I'll assume that you know the basic procedures. Although you'll be told what to do, I won't include all the steps. If you need help, refer to the chapters in the first part of the book.

3. Enter the title **Acme Manufacturing** in cell B2 on the second worksheet and **Sales** and **Cost of Goods** in cells A6 and A7, respectively, as the first two row headings (see Figure 16.1). Widen column A for the row titles.

4. Click cell B11 in SALES and select Edit ➤ Copy (or press Ctrl-C) to place the contents in the Clipboard.

5. Click cell B6 on the new worksheet twice to indicate that the sales total will be placed in this cell.

6. Select Edit ➤ Paste Link.

7. Widen column B to accommodate the total.

8. The sales total from cell B6 of the sales worksheet is now in cell B6 of the new worksheet, as shown in Figure 16.2.

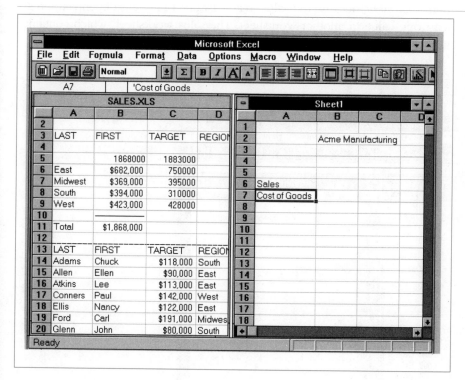

FIGURE 16.1:

Adding labels to the second worksheet

Instead of using the Paste Link command, you could have held down the Shift key when you opened the Edit menu and selected Paste Picture Link to paste the total as a linked text box in the destination worksheet.

Take a few minutes to examine your worksheets. Look at the formula for cell B6 in the formula bar (see Figure 16.2). It contains the linked worksheet's name, an exclamation point, and an absolute reference to cell B11 of the linked worksheet. You could have entered the same formula directly from the keyboard.

Now experiment with the linked worksheets to see what happens when you make changes. Change one of the Target figures in cells C14 through C28 in the sales database. You will see the totals change in cell B11 of the sales database *and* cell B6 of the new worksheet.

DEPENDENT AND SUPPORTING DOCUMENTS

Whenever the values of targets in the sales worksheet change, the values in the new worksheet also will change. The new worksheet is called the *dependent document,* because the value in at least one of its cells depends upon at least one value in another worksheet. The sales worksheet, which contains the value for the dependent worksheet, is called the *supporting document.*

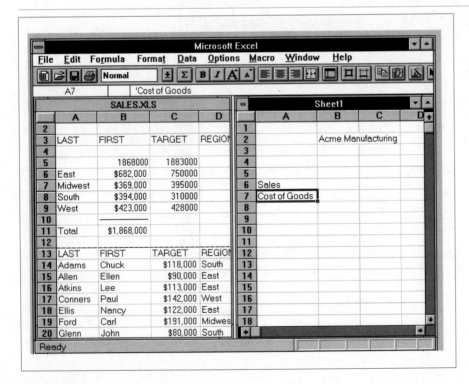

FIGURE 16.2:

The sales total on the second worksheet, linked to the total on the first

To quickly load a group of worksheets that are linked, assign them to a workbook. When you load the workbook (Chapter 7), all documents will be opened. (For information on linking charts, refer to Chapter 19.)

The dependent worksheet contains an *external reference formula*—a formula that refers to a cell or cell range on the supporting document.

You can create complex and interlinked hierarchical documents that depend upon each other at several levels. You also can link several supporting documents to a single dependent document. For example, our theoretical company could have sales worksheets for several regions and use them as supporting documents for a single company-wide sales worksheet, which would, in turn, support another dependent document.

Before leaving this section, continue to experiment with the link that you created. What happens, for example, if you save and close the dependent worksheet, change the values for a target in the supporting worksheet, and then open the dependent worksheet again? Have the values in the dependent worksheet been updated to reflect your change?

LINKING CELL RANGES

In the previous example, you linked a single cell in one worksheet to a single cell in another worksheet. You also can link a range of cells in one worksheet to a range of cells in another worksheet by using the same basic procedure.

To link cell ranges, select the range of cells on the dependent worksheet that you want to contain the formulas. Type in or copy the formula, referencing the appropriate cell range on the supporting worksheet. Then hold down the Shift and Ctrl keys and press Enter. You can also do this by selecting the range, choosing Edit ➤ Copy, then selecting the destination range and choosing Edit ➤ Paste Link.

You can try this with the new worksheet if you wish. Find an empty cell in Sheet 1 and paste the SUM function to that cell (Formula ➤ Paste Function). Now select cells B6 to B9 in the SALES worksheet to enter that range as the formula argument. Edit the display in the formula bar as necessary (you'll probably have to erase **number 2,** ...) and press Enter.

MOVING SUPPORTING CELLS

Use names for linking worksheets. This gives you more reliability with cutting and pasting, particularly with older versions of Excel.

If you create linked worksheets and then use the Cut command to move cells in the supporting worksheet, the relative cell addresses in the formulas will be adjusted properly.

Let's try an example: with your linked SALES and new worksheet open, select cell B11 on your sales worksheet. Click on cell B11 and move the pointer over the lower-right corner of the cell border so that you get a thinner pointer, and drag to C11 to move the cell there.

You'll see that the total on the dependent worksheet is still correct. In other words, the dependent worksheet has been adjusted to refer to the new location of the sales total cell in the supporting worksheet.

Before saving the worksheet, move C11 back to B11.

SAVING LINKED DOCUMENTS

Saving linked documents is as easy as saving documents that are not linked. Use the Save (Shift-F12) or Save As (F12) commands on the File menu to save each open document. Save any supporting document(s) (in this case, SALES.XLS) before saving any dependent document(s). This ensures that names are not changed in the supporting document. Save the dependent document as SALEST.XLS. Close all documents by double-clicking their document Control boxes. When you open a dependent document without the supporting document, you are asked if you want to update it. If you select yes, regular links are updated but not picture links.

Try keeping all dependent and supporting documents in the same directory. That way they all don't have to be open to be linked. If one document *is* in a different directory, you won't have to open it yourself, but you will have to find it for Excel.

VIEWING AND OPENING LINKED WORKSHEETS

To open a linked document:

1. Open the dependent worksheet first (SALEST). You will get a message box asking if you wish to update from supporting worksheets. Choose Yes.

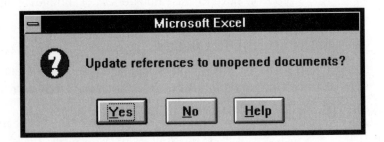

2. Once the dependent worksheet is opened, select File ➤ Links. This will display a dialog box showing the name of each supporting document (see Figure 16.3). If all you need is a view, or list, of the supporting documents you can choose Close. If you wish to open one or more supporting documents, go to Step 3.

3. Be sure **Excel Links** is displayed in the Link Type drop-down list box.

4. In the Links list box, select the documents to open and update. To open multiple documents, hold down the Shift or Ctrl key as you click on the names. Highlight the one document and click on Open.

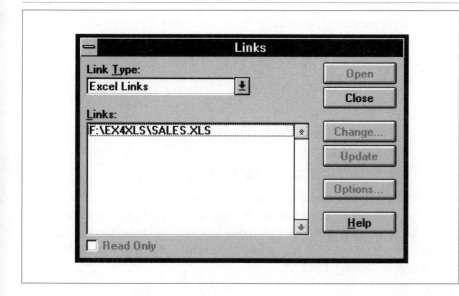

FIGURE 16.3:

Create the link in this dialog box

REMOVING DOCUMENT LINKS

To remove the links in a dependent worksheet, you need only remove the references to the supporting document. If you wish to scan a document and be sure that all the links are removed, select Formula ➤ Find (or press Shift-F5). Don't use Data ➤ Find. Then search the formulas for the name of the supporting worksheet, or search for an exclamation point.

An alternative is to convert the formula or part of the formula referencing the supporting worksheet to a value; for instance, changing the contents in cell B6 from =SALES.XLS!$B$11 to 1,868,000.

REDIRECTING LINKS

At times, you may wish to redirect a link to another supporting worksheet. You should do this if the supporting document is moved to another directory or changes its name.

To redirect a link:

1. Open the dependent document and choose File ➤ Links.

2. In the Link Type drop-down list box, choose Excel Links.

3. In the Links list box, select the names of the supporting worksheets whose links you need to redirect.

4. Click on the Change button.

5. On the Change Links dialog box, select the supporting document name and directory, or enter the name with the path in the File Name text box.

6. Click OK.

7. Repeat steps 3–6 for each link you want to change.

LINKING WORKSHEETS WITH ARRAYS

A worksheet that uses array formulas and references can be linked to another worksheet by using external references, just as if it used any other linked formula. To see how this works, link a cell in a new worksheet to the cell that contains the total value in the inventory worksheet that you created at the beginning of Chapter 15:

1. Open the inventory worksheet and be sure the row titles on it are defined as names (see Chapter 9).

2. Open up a new worksheet window and display both windows on the screen.

3. Enter the title **Inventory Summary** in cell B1 of the new worksheet.

4. Select cell B3 in the new worksheet as the cell for the total and choose Formula ➤ Paste Function (or press Shift-F3). You'll see the Paste Function dialog box. Select the Math & Trig category. Be sure Paste Arguments is off. Scroll to the SUM function and double-click it.

5. Click anywhere in the inventory worksheet and select Formula ➤ Paste Name (or press F3). You'll see the Paste Name dialog box. Double-click Qty_on_Hand.

6. Type an *.

7. Press F3 or select Formula ➤ Paste Name. Double-click Cost in the Paste Name dialog box.

8. Hold down the Shift and Ctrl keys and press Enter.

The correct total is now in cell B3 of the new worksheet and the formula is in the formula bar, as shown in Figure 16.4.

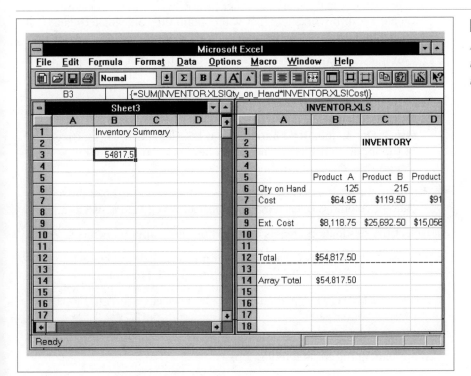

FIGURE 16.4:

Linking an array. The total at left is linked to the array total at right

USING GROUPS

Groups are useful for permitting you to enter the same data to multiple worksheets at the same time. Using a group reduces keystrokes and the possibility of errors, and saves you time as well. You can only use worksheets and macro sheets in the workgroup (no charts). See Chapter 7 for details on how to create one.

CONSOLIDATING WORKSHEETS

Consolidation is a useful method for summarizing large amounts of data in a single summary worksheet. For instance, monthly or quarterly reports can be easily summarized in yearly reports.

Langer Products manufactures a variety of products. They wish to consolidate data for a few years so they can determine how much their sales vary quarterly. Let's look at this example and see how consolidating worksheets can help them.

1. Create each of the three annual Langer worksheets shown in Figure 16.5. Create a fourth worksheet that will contain the consolidated data. Call it OUTPUT.

2. Use Window ➤ Arrange, choose Tiled, and then click OK to tile all windows.

3. Use Options ➤ Group Edit to link LANG1990, LANG1991, and LANG1992. (Do not link OUTPUT.) Enter the row headings **Qtr 1**, **Qtr 2**, **Qtr 3**, and **Qtr 4** into cells B4, B5, B6, and B7, respectively, of the input worksheets. The object here is to consolidate by categories—each quarter, in this case.

4. Ungroup the worksheets by clicking in another window. Enter the input data for column C of each input worksheet, using Figure 16.5 as a guide.

5. Select the destination area as B4 to C7 on the output worksheet.

6. Choose Data ➤ Consolidate. The dialog box shown in Figure 16.6 appears. Reposition the box so that LANG1990 is visible.

7. Click on LANG1990 to make it active, then select cells B4 to C7 as the first source range.

8. Click on the Add button in the dialog box. The range you selected appears in the All References box.

9. Continue by selecting the similar ranges in LANG1991 and LANG1992, clicking Add each time.

10. Click Use Labels in Left Column in the dialog box, as the labels are in the left column.

11. Select the desired function in the Function list box. SUM is the default function and the one we wish to use here.

12. Click on OK.

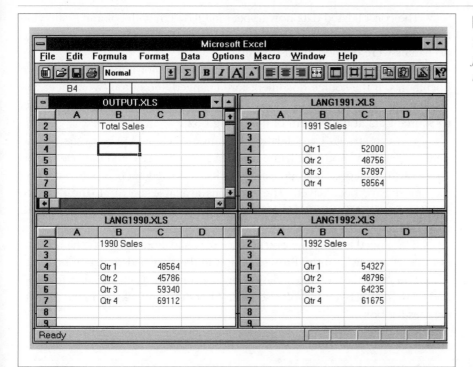

The Langer worksheets for 1990–1992, tiled on the workspace

FIGURE 16.6:

The Consolidate dialog box allows you to apply a function to references in several open worksheets and display the result in another worksheet

The consolidated data now appear in OUTPUT, with column C showing the total sales for each quarter, summed by year (see Figure 16.7). Notice that no names were defined in this example.

At the moment, the destination worksheet is not linked to the source documents. If the source documents are changed, the output worksheet will not change. To link them, select Data ➤ Consolidate and click on Create Links to Source Data at the bottom of the dialog box.

You can specify consolidation by range (such as A1:C3) or, as we did here, by category. You can define up to 255 source areas, and they can be on different worksheets. The source area worksheets need not be open, but if not, they must have been saved. The functions available are SUM (the default), AVERAGE, COUNT, COUNTA, MAX, MIN, PRODUCT, STDEV, STDEVP, VAR, and VARP.

If you need to open a worksheet for consolidation and you can't remember the name, click on the Browse button in the Consolidate dialog box.

You can edit the consolidation by selecting the Consolidate command and editing the reference. You also can add or delete references in the All References list box.

> **TIP** *Consolidate by category (that is, by using cell names) whenever possible, as this ensures greater reliability. This also makes the worksheet expressions less likely to change with editing.*

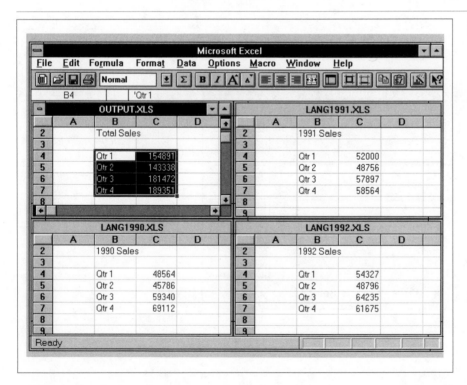

FIGURE 16.7:

The consolidated Langer output worksheet

In the Reference text box you can use wildcards to reference a group of worksheets; LANG19??.XLS!$B$3:$C$7 could be used in the previous example to include all three worksheets. You also can use names in references.

Only values are consolidated. Text, formats, and formulas cannot be consolidated.

FAST TRACK CHAPTER 17

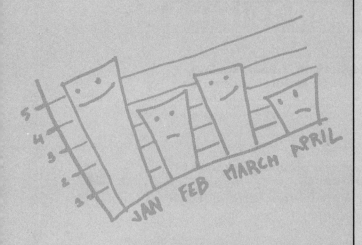

CHAPTER

17

Printing Worksheets

Excel includes many features that make it easy to create presentation-quality reports from your worksheet. You can add headers and footers, define page breaks, print specific worksheet ranges, print a report with landscape orientation, control the margins, and turn gridlines on and off. This chapter will provide an overview of these and other printing features.

Printing is controlled from three commands on the File menu and four on the Options menu. The File menu commands include Print, Page Setup, Print Preview, and Print Report. Those on the Options menu are Set Print Area, Set Print Titles, Set Page Break, and Display.

Excel uses the Windows environment for printing. The software that controls the printer is called a *printer driver* and is a part of Windows. If you change printers or add a new one, you install the new printer driver to Windows using the Windows Control Panel utility. Once installed, the printer is available for all Windows application programs, including Excel. This means that if you have a problem with printing, it is normally a Windows problem, not an Excel problem.

BASIC FONT MANAGEMENT

The typefaces and fonts that are available for printing in Excel are determined by what you have installed in Windows. A *typeface* is a type design or family, such as Helvetica or Times Roman. The same type family is generally available in various styles (regular, bold, italic) and sizes. Each is a separate *font*. The font size is a measure of the height of the letters and is measured in points. There are 72 points in an inch, so a 12-point font is (roughly) one-sixth of an inch high. Windows and Excel use three types of fonts: *raster, vector,* and *scaled*.

RASTER FONTS

Raster fonts are bit-mapped fonts that must be stored for each size and style for each typeface. In addition, you must use a separate font set for the printer and display. You can resize a raster font, but should only resize it as an integer multiple. Raster fonts can reside on a printer cartridge or as soft fonts on the disk, downloaded to the printer and displayed as needed. Windows includes some raster fonts such as MS Serif and MS Sans serif. If you have a raster font cartridge for a laser printer (such as Microsoft Z), you won't get an accurate display unless you can get a matching display soft font. Soft fonts, another type of raster font, are installed from the Windows Control Panel using the Printer option, and are therefore printer-dependent.

VECTOR FONTS

Vector fonts are those in which the characters are stored as mathematical entities or objects. These can be resized easily, but lack body and quality. Windows includes a few, such as Modern. You might find these useful at small sizes for fitting a large spreadsheet on a single page. Your best alternative, however, is to use the scalable fonts.

SCALABLE FONTS

These fonts are stored on the disk as outlines, with the characters made on-the-fly to the desired size. This minimizes disk storage and permits high-quality fonts. The disadvantage is the slower printing speed.

If you have a PostScript printer, the font-scaling system is internal to the printer and you can purchase additional Adobe Type 1 fonts.

If you have a non-PostScript laser printer, you can use scaling software to simulate the same effect. There are several scaling systems available for

Excel and Windows. Whichever system you use will work with all your Windows applications, as the font-management system is internal to Windows, not the application.

Windows 3.1 supports its own internal TrueType system, with several fonts, such as Arial, included with Windows. You can purchase additional TrueType fonts. You can also purchase the Adobe Type Manager (ATM) and use it with Windows, which permits using any of the Adobe Type 1 fonts. You can use both TrueType and ATM with Windows at the same time. Other font-scaling systems are also available, but each uses a proprietary outline system and is not compatible with the other.

THE FILE MENU PRINTING COMMANDS

The commands on the File menu control most aspects of the final printout:

Page Setup sets up the page image. This command controls headers, footers, margins, orientation, printer selection and options, positioning on the page, sizing, scaling, and starting page number. In addition, for worksheets and macros you can control the printing of row and column headings, gridlines, and page order. This only affects the current document being printed.

Print Preview gives you a display image of what the printout will look like. You also can control the margins in this mode.

Print controls print quality, the page range to print, and the number of copies. You also can choose to print the sheet, notes, or both.

Print Report prints documents based on views and scenarios, permitting the printing of more complex reports.

You can also move between some of the options directly without using the menu, such as printing from the Print button in the Page Setup dialog box.

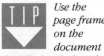

Use the page frame on the document (marked with dotted lines) to see the current paging. Adjust margins, fonts, and column widths as necessary to define the page frame for printing.

EXAMINING THE PAGE SETUP DIALOG BOX

To control headers, footers, margins, row and column headings, orientation, and gridline printing, printer setup, scaling, paging order, and starting page number, use the Page Setup command of the File Menu (Figure 17.1). If you use Options ➤ Display to turn on automatic page breaks, the page frame for the current page settings is shown on the worksheet with dotted lines. As you

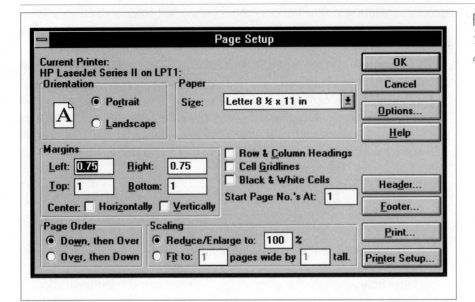

change orientation or margins, the frame will change. Using this frame, you can check which columns and rows will print without having to preview or print the document. All the page-setup settings are saved with the document.

Setting the Margins

NOTE *Laser printers normally require approximately a half-inch margin at the top, bottom, left, and right.*

The Margins options in the Page Setup dialog box permit you to control the amount of space between the edge of the paper and the printed area. The margins at the top, bottom, left, and right of the page can be set independently. The margin settings do not affect headers or footers, so margins should be large enough to prevent printing the worksheet over the header or footer. Clicking on Center Horizontally or Center Vertically controls where the print image is placed on the page.

Setting the Orientation

Set the desired orientation with the Page Setup command: select Page Setup ➤ Printer Setup ➤ Setup from Excel's File menu. Portrait is the normal orientation (like the way this book is printed); Landscape is for a sideways printout. All Page Setup settings are saved with the worksheet. There is a second way to set orientation: double-click the Printers icon in the Windows Control Panel and click the Setup button. You should avoid setting the orientation this second way, however, as doing so sets it for all documents in all applications. Setting it from File ➤ Page Setup applies it to the single document only—and with File ➤ Save, saves that information in the one document file.

The raster fonts (typefaces, style, and size) available for printing the worksheet will change with the orientation, since Portrait and Landscape printing use a different set of raster fonts. You can use Format ➤ Font to check the fonts available in the current orientation.

Defining Headers and Footers

A *header* is a line of text that prints at the top of every page. A *footer* is a line of text that prints at the bottom of every page. To set a header or footer, choose File ➤ Page Setup. When the Page Setup dialog box (see Figure 17.1) appears, click Header to enter a header or Footer to enter a footer. Enter the header or footer desired (see Figure 17.2), click OK, then OK again in the Page Setup dialog box.

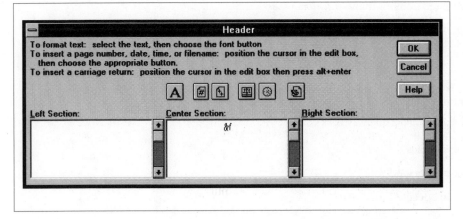

FIGURE 17.2:

The Header dialog box allows you to enter text in three sections of the header. Here the placement of the &f code prints the name of the document in the center of the header.

In either the Header or Footer dialog box, you can enter header or footer information to three areas of the page: left-aligned, centered, or right-aligned. Six buttons permit you (from left to right) to control the font, as well as enter the page number, the total number of pages, date, time, and file name to any area.

Excel defaults to printing the worksheet file name as a centered header and the page number as a centered footer. To clear these selections, select Header or Footer (dragging if necessary to select the box contents) and press Delete.

You can manually enter control codes for the header or footer, including a date, time, and page number. You also can control the style of headers and footers. The control codes that you can use in creating headers and footers are listed in Table 17.1.

SYMBOL	FUNCTION
&L	Left-justify following characters
&C	Center following characters
&R	Right-justify following characters
&P	Print page number
&P+*number*	Print page number plus *number*
&P−*number*	Print page number minus *number*
&N	Print total number of pages in document (see text)
&D	Print current date
&T	Print current time
&F	Print the name of the document
&B	Print in boldface
&I	Print in italics
&"*font*"	Print in specified *font*
&*size*	Print in specified font *size*
&S	Print in strikethrough
&U	Print in underline
&&	Print an ampersand

Note: You can combine two or more of these in a header or footer.

TABLE 17.1:

Header and Footer Control Codes

Use &N to designate the total number of pages. For example, to print *Page 4 of 12* enter:

Page &P of &N

in the Footer box.

You can combine the control codes for any desired header line. For example,

&L&"Helv"&10Acme Manufacturing&C&P&R&D

prints *Acme Manufacturing* at the left margin in 10-point Helvetica, centers the page number, and prints the current date at the right margin. You can break these appropriately for each area of the line.

Try turning off the default headers and footers on your Balance worksheet. Load the worksheet, then choose File ➤ Page Setup. When the Page Setup dialog box appears, click Header and highlight the current header entry (&F). Press the Delete key and the box will clear. Click OK, Footer, and drag the cursor over the current footer until it is selected. Then press the Delete key again to clear the current footer entry. Click OK and print your worksheet using the Print button.

Other Page Setup Options

The Row & Column Headings and Cell Gridlines options with a worksheet or macro sheet indicate whether these will print. Scaling permits you to control the size of the printed worksheet on the page. Page Order defines the printed order for a large worksheet and Start Page No.'s At defines the page number to use on the first page. Black & White Cells, when selected, prints cells and text boxes in black-and-white.

Avoid using this to set the print orientation for an individual document. Printer Setup controls the default orientation, which most users keep at Portrait. Use Page Setup to set the orientation for a particular worksheet.

Setting Up the Printer

If you need to choose the printer or to change the setup for a printer, choose Printer Setup from the Page Setup dialog box. When the Printer Setup dialog box is displayed, as shown below for Windows 3.1, select the printer you are using and click OK. The dialog box lists all printers installed to Windows that are available. (The dialog box will vary with the version of Windows that you are using.)

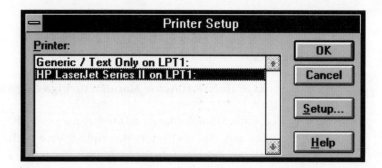

To change the options for a given printer, use the Printer Setup button on the Page Setup dialog box. Highlight the printer and select Setup on the Printer Setup dialog box. Changing the setup options affects the options for all Windows applications. This second dialog box (Figure 17.3) is dependent on your printer and Windows version; that is, it is a part of the printer driver. It's identical with the one you would see if setting up the printer from the Windows Control Panel. For the Hewlett-Packard LaserJet Series II printer shown here, you can control the print orientation for all Windows applications, the graphics resolution, the type of paper used, the paper source, and the memory and cartridges used with a laser printer.

Select the desired options. Click on OK to return to the first Printer Setup dialog box shown above, then click OK again to return to the worksheet.

PREVIEWING THE PRINTOUT

The Print Preview option is particularly useful for seeing how the finished page will look. To turn on the preview mode, select File ➤ Print Preview. A reduced copy of the first page of the final printout is displayed on-screen (see Figure 17.4). The scroll bars permit you to scroll between document pages. To see an area in more detail, display the page and click on the Zoom button (or press **Z**) or move the mouse cursor (which is now a magnifying glass) and click the area of the worksheet to which you wish to zoom. Scroll bars now permit you to scroll within the zoomed window. Press **Z** again or click anywhere on the screen to restore the reduced-size view. The Zoom button (and clicking the mouse anywhere on the worksheet, except the margin lines)

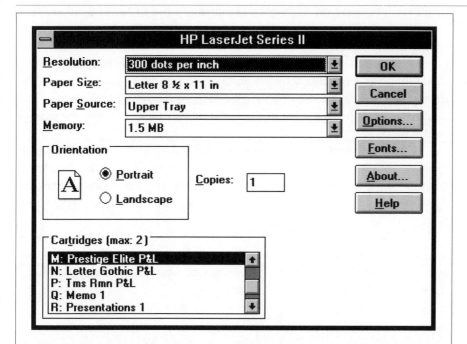

The second Printer Setup dialog box, this for an HP LaserJet Series II printer

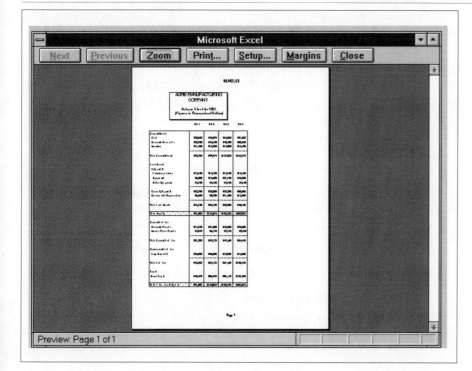

A print preview, showing how the printed copy will look

toggles you between normal view and full-page view. Click the Next and Previous buttons to move to the next or previous page. Click the Close button (or press Esc) to exit the preview mode.

Many page and page-setup commands are available while in the preview mode, making it possible to adjust the page image. For example, to change the margins, display them by clicking the Margins button. Drag the margin line while watching the status bar at the bottom of the screen to see the margin setting.

You also can change the column widths in the preview mode. With Margins selected, column handles are displayed at the top of the page over each column. Move the mouse over a column handle or column border line and the status bar displays the column width. Drag the column handle or column border line to change the width.

To control more features on the page setup, click the Setup button in the preview mode. You will see the Page Setup dialog box, and you can adjust any setup parameters you wish. Choosing OK returns you to the previewed document with the new parameters active.

PRINTING THE WORKSHEET

You initiate printing with the File ➤ Print command or by pressing Ctrl-Shift-F12). The Print dialog box (see Figure 17.5) appears. It controls which pages will be printed, the number of copies to print, and gives you some control over the print quality. Modify the desired options and click OK. As a shortcut, you can click the Print tool to print, which skips the dialog box.

Excel remembers your selections and applies them to the next print cycle unless they are changed. If you print ten copies and later want only one, you will need to reset this to 1 before you print again.

The following options are available in the Print dialog box:

Print Quality defines the print resolution.

From/To selects which pages to print. Use this option if you make minor changes to a worksheet and need only a part printed. Put the same number in both boxes to print only that page.

Copies determines how many copies of the worksheet are printed.

Print chooses whether to print document, notes, or both.

Preview displays a preview image.

Fast, but no graphics prints the text only.

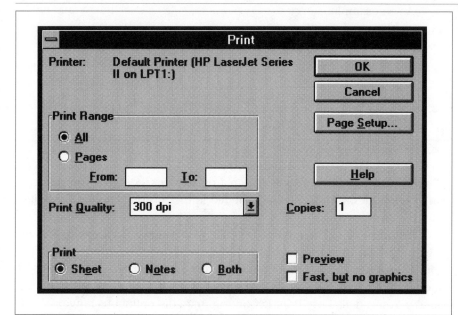

THE OPTIONS MENU PRINTING COMMANDS

The Options menu controls the printing of ranges, titles, break settings, and whether formulas or values are printed.

PRINTING A RANGE

You can, if you like, print just part of a worksheet. This is particularly useful when you're working with only a portion of a very large worksheet. To print part of a worksheet, first select the range to be printed. Open the Options menu and choose Set Print Area or use the Set Print Area tool on the Utility toolbar. Excel names the area that you selected as *Print_Area*. You can refer to this area in other commands by using this name with the Define Name and Paste Names commands. To print just this area, choose File ➤ Print and then choose OK.

Subsequent printings will again print this range. To turn off the printing of a range and again print the entire worksheet, use Formula ➤ Define Name (or press Ctrl-F3) and delete the *Print_Area* name.

If you have a problem getting the printer to print only part of a worksheet, it probably has a print area defined. Use Define Name to delete this name, then print the worksheet again.

As an example:

1. Select the cell range that you wish to print.

2. Choose Options ➤ Set Print Area or click the Set Print Area tool on the Utility toolbar.

3. Select File ➤ Print or press Ctrl-Shift-F12—or click the Print tool and skip Step 4.

4. When the Print dialog box appears, choose OK.

Your printout will contain only the area of the worksheet that you selected. An example of this procedure is included in the section "Printing Formulas" later in this chapter.

You can print a discontinuous range by selecting it and defining it as the print area. Select the first part of the range and press the Control key while you select other areas. (From the keyboard, select one range, press Shift-F8, and select the other range(s) by pressing Shift-F8 after selecting all but the last range.) You can also use Print Report to print a discontinuous range.

If you constantly need to print various range settings from the same worksheet, assign each a different name. Find an empty cell and name it *Print_Area*. Then to print a range named PrintX, use Formula ➤ Define Name. Select *Print_Area* as the name and enter **=PrintX** in the Refers To box. This sets the print area to PrintX. You can also do it by defining each as a view and printing by view using File ➤ Print Report.

SETTING A PAGE BREAK

You also can force a page break at any point in the worksheet. To do so, select any cell in the row *before* which you want the page break to come. Then choose Options ➤ Set Page Break. The row with the selected cell will be the first row of the next page. For a worksheet that is two pages wide, setting a page break will create four pages.

To remove a page break, first select a cell in the row below or to the right of the page break. Choose Options ➤ Remove Page Break.

The Options ➤ Display command determines whether the automatic page breaks are displayed on the worksheet. When turned on, automatic page breaks are marked with a dotted line on the worksheet. Manual page breaks are always displayed this way.

PRINTING ROW AND COLUMN TITLES

If you print a worksheet that has a few columns but many rows, the column titles will only appear on the first page; subsequent pages of the printout will only contain the data under them. To keep the columns aligned with their respective titles, you would need to paste the pages end to end into one long sheet. Since this is seldom practical, Excel provides a way to repeat the titles on every page of the printout.

Select the entire row of the worksheet that contains the titles and choose Options ➤ Set Print Titles. Edit or enter the titles in the dialog box shown below and click OK.

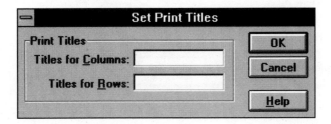

Similarly, to repeat row titles on the pages of a large worksheet that extends over many columns, select the entire column that contains the titles (typically column A) and choose Options ➤ Set Print Titles. Enter the titles and click OK.

Excel names the title area that you select as *Print_Titles*. You can refer to this area in other commands by using this name. (See Chapter 9 for information on using names.)

PRINTING FORMULAS

To quickly set the display so that it shows formulas, press Ctrl–'. Another Ctrl-' will toggle the formula display off.

You can print the formulas that are used in a worksheet. The basic procedure is simple: display the formulas and print the worksheet:

1. Open the Options menu and choose Display.

2. When the Display Options dialog box shown in Figure 17.6 appears, check Formulas, then click on OK. The formulas are now displayed in each cell. Notice that the columns are twice as wide as your regular column setting so that the formulas will fit.

3. Choose File ➤ Page Setup and be sure the Row & Column Headings and Cell Gridlines options are both selected (see Figure 17.1).

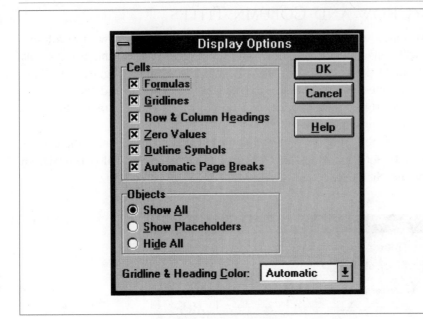

4. Be sure the orientation is set to Landscape and that the selected font can print in this orientation.

5. Adjust column widths in the worksheet as necessary. In particular, check totals and be sure they fit.

6. Select File ➤ Print. Click OK.

Chapters 8 and 13 contain some examples of printouts with formulas.

Do not use the Display command to turn off row and column headings or the gridlines for printing. These options refer only to the *display*. Use the Page Setup command to turn these features off while *printing*.

PRINTING REPORTS

A *report* is a set of documents that represent different views or input data (scenarios). Views are set with the Window ➤ View command; scenarios are set with the Scenario Manager.

Views define a set of display and print settings. Views are saved with the worksheet and include print settings (margins, orientation, headers, footers, row and column heading selection, cell gridlines selection, etc.), row heights, column widths, display options, selected cells, window size and position, panes, and frozen titles. Views are discussed in Chapter 7. A *scenario* is a group of input values for specified cells saved with a name. Scenarios are discussed in Chapter 25.

To print a report, make the worksheet active with the views and scenarios defined. Then choose File ➤ Print Report. If no report currently exists, you will get the Print Report dialog box. Click Add (Figure 17.7).

In the Add Report dialog box, assign a name to the report in the Report Name text box. Specify the view and/or scenario to use, then click on Add. If none is specified, the default value is the current view and scenario. Choose OK to exit to the Print Report dialog box, shown below:

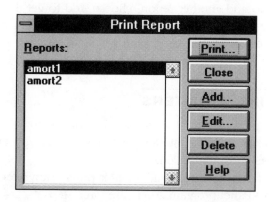

FIGURE 17.7:

Defining the report

Click on Print to print the report. Specify the number of copies and click OK:

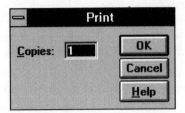

To add another report, choose Add to get the Add Report dialog box. On the Print Report dialog box, you can choose Edit to edit the selected report or Delete to remove it.

INSTALLING PRINTERS

At the time you install Excel, you can decide to install one or more printers. When you use the Printer Setup command, you choose from any of the printers already installed.

If you wish to install another printer at a later time, use the Windows Control Panel program. There are three steps:

1. Install the printer driver.

2. Configure the printer (i.e., set the connection).

3. Set up the printer.

To use the Control Panel program, select Control ➤ Run. When the Run dialog box is displayed, choose Control Panel and click OK:

When the Control Panel appears, double-click the Printers icon. Figure 17.8 shows the subsequent dialog box that is displayed (for Windows 3.1).

To install the driver, you will need the disks that came with Windows or from the printer manufacturer. Click Add in the dialog box. Figure 17.9 shows the next dialog box. Choose the printer to install from the List of Printers list box and click on Install. Follow the prompts and insert the proper printer-driver disk that came with Windows, if prompted for it.

The next step is to configure the printer. Click on Connect in the Printers dialog box and select the connection (see Figure 17.10). The first printer (if it is a parallel port printer) is normally assigned to LPT1. Click OK. You can assign multiple printers to the same port if your system is configured this way, using, for example, an external buffer box with multiple printers on a single port.

Finally, set up the printer. Select the printer in the Installed Printers list box and click the Setup button. The dialog box here is determined by the printer you are using. Figure 17.3 shows the dialog box for a Hewlett-Packard LaserJet Series II. Set the parameters in this box to match your printer. Here the most important parameters are the memory size, cartridges in use, default orientation, and graphics resolution. Then click OK.

Click Close to return to the Control Panel, then close the Control Panel from its Control box to return to Excel again.

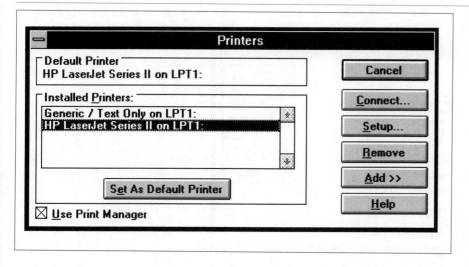

FIGURE 17.8:

Starting the printer installation

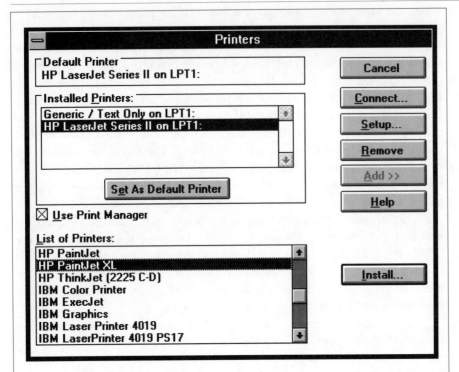

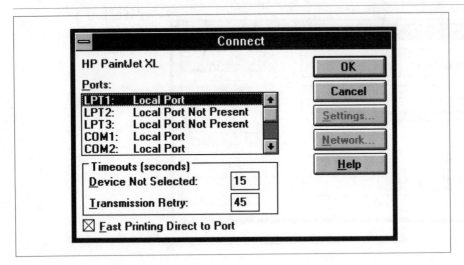

USING THE PRINT MANAGER

Print Manager is a utility program provided with Windows that permits you to continue working with a worksheet while another worksheet is printing, or to share the printer between several programs running under Windows. When using the Print Manager, you actually print to a disk file very quickly, so that Excel is ready to do more work.

Normally, Print Manager defaults to being in use. If it's not, start the Windows Control Panel as described in the previous section and double-click the Printers icon. At the bottom of the dialog box (see Figure 17.8), check Use Print Manager. Then click OK.

The Print Manager is loaded automatically when a print request is made and its icon appears at the bottom of the screen (only if Excel isn't maximized). Double-clicking it displays the Print Manager window (Figure 17.11). Using this window, you can view the print queue and control the printing status of several documents.

The Print Manager requires disk space for saving documents to print. In addition, it takes a little longer to print a document, as it must first be printed to the disk, then to the printer.

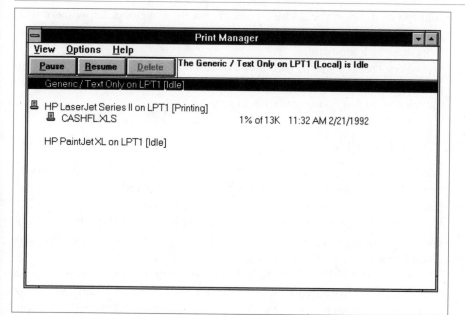

FIGURE 17.11:

The Print Manager window allows you to view the print queue and control the printing status of your documents

Many users also spool to a buffer box external to the printer. In this case, Print Manager is still advantageous to use because it allows the printer to be shared by several programs when they are in use at the same time.

SPECIAL PRINTING JOBS

Following are some guidelines for printing envelopes, labels, and forms.

PRINTING ENVELOPES

If you are using a dot-matrix printer, envelopes are generally purchased as pinfeed envelope stock and fed to the printer in portrait orientation. With laser printers, you feed normal envelope stock (including company stationery) manually to the printer. Some printers make an envelope tray available as an accessory, but these generally hold only a few envelopes. The envelopes are printed in landscape orientation.

In either case, the best method for printing addresses is to define an area on the worksheet that will be temporarily used to print each address. This is defined as Print_Area and the Page Setup command is used to define the frame for this area. The paper size is left at the normal letter size and the margins adjusted to position the address correctly on the envelope. Experiment with paper stock until you get it correct. Once you have this defined, save the worksheet as a template.

Now create a macro (see Part VII) to copy each address in turn to the print area and print it. With some worksheets, you may need to transpose the address to put columnar fields in rows.

PRINTING LABELS

Printing labels is much like printing envelopes, as far as the worksheet is concerned: define a print area, use the Page Setup command to define the page frame, and then use a macro to set up and print each label.

Dot-matrix printers can use pinfeed stock to print the labels as continuous labels. Be sure never to turn the platen backwards, as the labels will peel off and stick to the rollers. It's very hard to clean the rollers if this happens.

For laser printers, purchase laser printer labels as sheets. Avery makes a 5261 label sheet with two columns of labels. This is the best choice for most applications, although it is expensive. You can put these labels in the tray and print them with automatic feed, but be sure the laser printer can handle their thickness. If the printer has a tray that opens at the back to shorten the feed path, use it. Never use labels that are not designed for laser printers, as the heat inside the printer can cause them to stick to the laser printer rollers. This happened to me once. If it happens to you, you will need a repair person to get the rollers out, retrieve the label pieces, and clean the rollers.

PRINTING FORMS

Although you may not have realized it, Excel is a great tool for printing forms and other graphic images. The worksheet grid is ideal for helping you align objects and text. You can turn the grid off for printing or displaying to check the final copy. With the new graphic tools in the Drawing toolbar, you can add graphic objects, including text objects. You can draw calendars, organization charts, project charts, and more. They will be presentation-quality and easy to create, edit, and print.

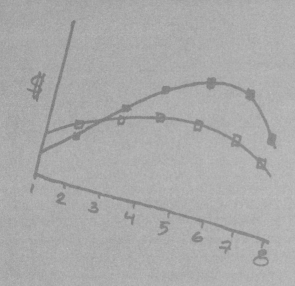

$$b = \frac{\Sigma xy - \frac{x \Sigma y}{\Sigma x^2 - \frac{x \Sigma x}{}}}{}$$

PART FIVE

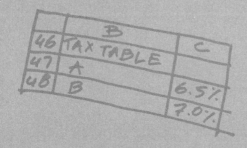

	B	C
46	TAX TABLE	
47	A	
48	B	6.5%
		7.0%

Part V: High-Impact Presentations with Charts

Excel's charting capabilities give you an easy and effective way to illustrate the results of your worksheet and database analyses. Charts convey in a concise and persuasive manner the full significance of what you are presenting. You can use them to show relationships, comparisons, and trends.

Part V shows you how to create a graphic representation of your data with only a few clicks of the mouse. The graphs are dynamically linked to your data—i.e., whenever the data change, your graphs change, too. There is a wide choice of formats and features from which to choose different types of graphs, including three-dimensional formats. You can add arrows, text boxes and other objects, legends, and comments to the chart to improve clarity, as well.

FAST TRACK CHAPTER 18

CHAPTER 18

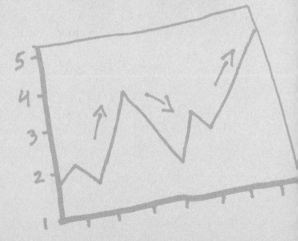

Creating Graphs and Charts

You will produce a simple graph in this chapter from a worksheet that you created earlier. While you're working with this graph, you will see the advantages of adding graphic presentations to your reports.

UNDERSTANDING GRAPHS AND CHARTS

Graphs and charts show visual relationships. They are especially useful for relaying information to busy people who don't have the time to pore over tables of numbers. Notice how much easier it is to reach conclusions about which regions have better sales and are meeting their targets from the chart in Figure 18.1 than it is to reach these same conclusions from the SALES worksheet in Figure 13.6.

Figure 18.1 shows the various components of a chart. These components are described below:

◆ **Axes** are the straight lines used on a graph for measurement and reference. A pie chart has no real axis; all other types have two: the x axis (the horizontal line) and the y axis (the vertical line). The x axis shows the data classification and the y axis shows the quantity or unit of measure.

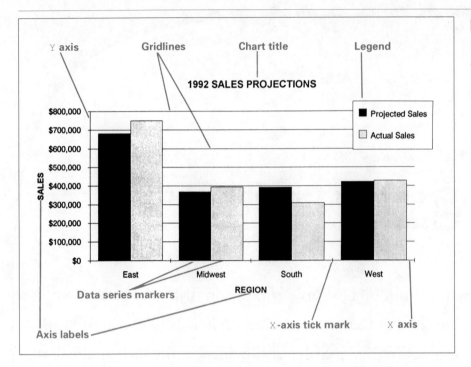

FIGURE 18.1:

The components of a chart

◆ **Markers** are the types of indicators used on a graph to represent the data. A column graph uses vertical bars filled with a pattern for markers. A line graph uses small symbols.

◆ **Tick marks** are the small lines that divide the axes. They are used to indicate categories (for example, quantities or regions) and scales (for example, dollars or another type of measurement).

◆ **Plot area** is the area bounded by the axes or, in the case of a pie chart, the area within the circle.

◆ **Scale** is the range of values covered by the *y* axis of the chart.

◆ **Legend** shows the symbols and labels used to identify the different types of data on the chart.

◆ *X*-axis label is the title for the *x* axis.

◆ *Y*-axis label is the title for the *y* axis.

◆ **Chart title** is the main title for the chart.

◆ **Gridlines** are the optional horizontal or vertical lines in the plot area that help the viewer determine the value of a marker.

Each marker on a graph represents a data point. A *data series* is a set of related markers. You can plot several data series on a single graph by using different types of markers. Figure 18.1 shows two data series. In a pie chart you can represent only a single data series.

CREATING A CHART

Now let's create a chart. Charts can be created on a worksheet or as separate documents. When created on a worksheet, the chart is saved with the worksheet and is said to be an *embedded document*. When created as a separate document, it is saved with the File ➤ Save As command with a file name and the extension .XLC. For this example, we will create a chart as a separate document. Later in this chapter you will see how to create charts on a worksheet.

Start Excel and open the SALES worksheet that you created in Chapter 13. To chart the regional sales as a column graph, follow these steps:

1. Identify the data series that you want to show on the graph by clicking cell A6 and dragging to cell B9.

2. Press Alt-F1 or F11, or choose File ➤ New. When the New dialog box appears, choose Chart, then click OK.

You should now see the chart shown in Figure 18.2. Excel creates the chart in a default format. This chart is a column type, using the first format of that type.

Notice that Excel scales the y axis automatically, creates the column categories, and labels the columns automatically. You also will see a different menu bar at the top of the screen. A new Chart toolbar is also displayed. Although shown here at the bottom of the screen, it can be moved and appear anywhere on the application window, can be resized, and can be customized. The toolbar here is at the bottom of the screen and "docked," that is, locked to the lower edge of the application window, with no title bar visible.

The chart still needs a title and axis labels. You can create these by following the steps below:

1. To add a title, choose Chart ➤ Attach Text. When the Attach Text dialog box is displayed, click the Chart Title option button, then click OK. Type the title **1992 SALES PROJECTIONS** in the formula bar for the title area now marked on the graph. Press Enter to complete the entry.

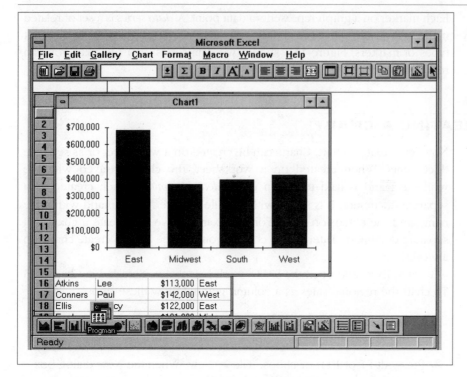

FIGURE 18.2:

The chart after the initial plot. The menu bar also changes and the Chart toolbar appears

2. Put the title in boldface and larger print. With the title area still selected, choose Format ➤ Font. When the Font dialog box is displayed, choose Arial (Swiss or Helvetica for Windows 3.0), 12 points for the size, and Bold in the Font Style list box. Then click OK. (You can also use the standard toolbar to boldface a font.)

3. To add a label for the *y* axis, select Chart ➤ Attach Text. When the dialog box appears, choose Value (Y) Axis, then click OK. Type **SALES**. Press Enter to complete the entry (see Figure 18.3). An even shorter way is to click the right mouse button on the axis, then choose Attach Text from the shortcut menu.

4. To format the *y*-axis label, be sure the label is still selected and choose Format ➤ Font. Choose Arial, 10 points, and Bold.

5. To add a label for the *x* axis, open the Chart menu and choose Attach Text (or click the axis with the right mouse button and choose it from the shortcut menu). Choose Category (X) Axis in the dialog box, then click OK. Type the title **REGION** and press Enter to complete the entry. Format the label as with the *y* axis.

When you've finished creating the chart, you can print it. Press Ctrl-Shift-F12, click the Print tool, or choose File ➤ Print. Then click OK in the dialog box. Figure 18.4 shows the final printout.

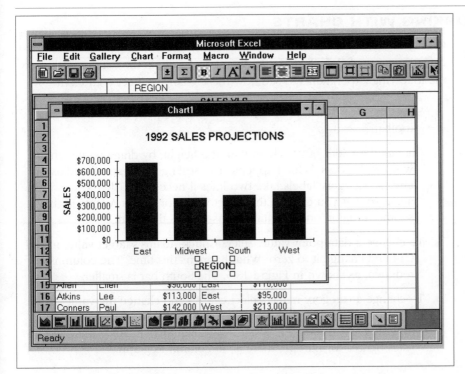

FIGURE 18.3:

Labeling the y axis

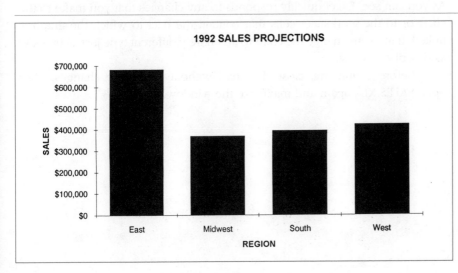

FIGURE 18.4:

The final chart printout

Save the chart: click the Save File tool, press Shift-F12, or choose Save As from the File menu. In the Save As dialog box, enter **SALES** and click OK. The chart is saved as SALES.XLC.

WORKING WITH CHARTS

Once you have created a chart, you can change its size, data-point values, and category names. Select Window ➤ Arrange to position the windows, then try the following experiments to see how these changes affect your chart:

1. Select the worksheet, then the chart. What happens to the menu and toolbars?

2. Change the width of the chart, then the height, by dragging the chart window borders. What happens? The scaling automatically adjusts and the category labels take two lines if necessary. Tile the windows again so that you can see the target value for Chuck Adams in the southern region on the database, as well as the chart.

3. To change a data-point value, select Chuck Adams's target value in cell C14 and change it to zero. What happens this time? The columns are redrawn, as shown in Figure 18.5. The South bar is smaller.

4. To change a category name, select cell A6 and change the value to "Europe." What happens to the chart? The category labels change, and the chart is redrawn, as shown in Figure 18.6. Since there are no sales figures for Europe, there is no column to graph.

As you can see, Excel quickly responds to any changes that you make to the chart or to the worksheet cells that contain the data to which the graph is linked. It also can change the chart to an entirely different type just as quickly, as described below.

Before continuing, close the chart without saving the changes. Then open SALES.XLC again and maximize the window.

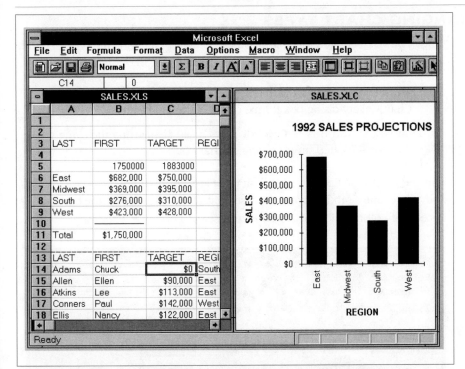

FIGURE 18.5:
Changing Chuck Adams's target value to zero causes the southern total in the chart to fall

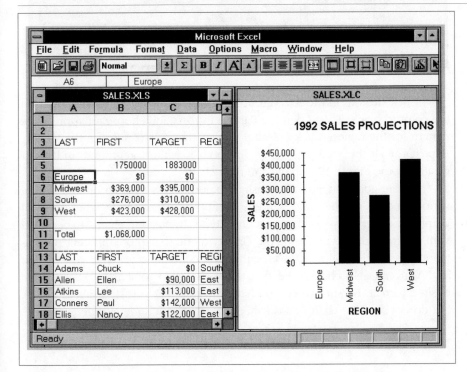

FIGURE 18.6:
Changing the "East" category name to "Europe" replaces the eastern total in the chart with the European total—which is zero in this case

CHANGING CHART TYPES

Once you've re-created the chart, you can practice changing the type, legend, and other features. This is how you would change it into a pie chart:

1. Select the chart window, then open the Gallery menu and choose Pie. The Chart Gallery dialog box for pie charts, shown in Figure 18.7, is displayed.

2. Double-click on Box 5. Excel displays a pie chart using the same data that were plotted on your original bar chart.

This pie chart won't print too well on most laser printers, as they print in black and white only. Modify your chart so that it shows patterns for the regions instead of colors. Click on a wedge and select Format ➤ Patterns:

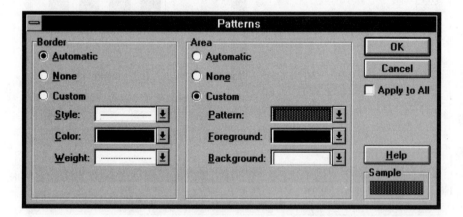

Click Custom in the Area group, open the Foreground list box, and set the color to black. Then open the Pattern list box and choose an appropriate pattern for the region. Click OK after you've chosen a pattern for the wedge. Repeat for all the wedges, giving one both a white foreground and background color. Figure 18.8 shows the final chart.

Before going on, you may wish to experiment with other options on the various menus on the chart window menu bar. Try creating other types of graphs. It is very easy to change a chart type. In creating charts, experiment with different chart types using the Gallery menu to explore different presentation possibilities. Choose the type that best communicates what you wish to say. You can also change the type from the chart toolbar by clicking the desired format. Be sure when you have finished that you close all windows, but do not save the chart or worksheet again, except under a different name.

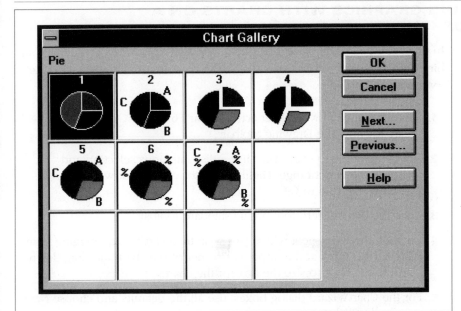

FIGURE 18.7:
*The Chart Gallery
dialog box for pie charts*

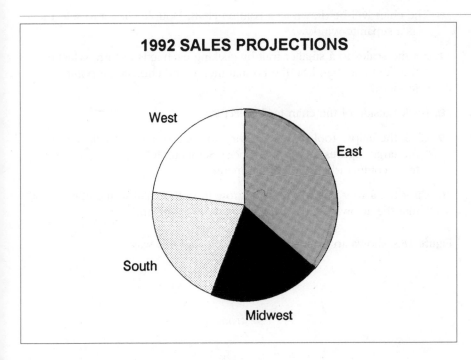

FIGURE 18.8:
*The pie chart with
patterned wedges for
better legibility when
printed on a laser
printer*

USING GRAPHICS WITH CHARTS ON A WORKSHEET

In Chapter 6 you created a text box on a worksheet. With Excel, you can combine graphic objects, charts, and worksheet data on a single worksheet. Let's try this now:

1. Make the original worksheet active. Clear E6. Select Options ➤ Toolbars to show the Drawing toolbar.

2. Select the range to chart. Let's use a discontinuous selection and choose the target range. Highlight A6 to A9. Hold down the Ctrl key and highlight C6 to C9.

3. Click the ChartWizard tool on the standard toolbar.

4. Click on the worksheet where you wish the chart to be, dragging from E6 to H11. Click at the upper-left corner of the chart and drag down and to the right to size the box for the chart.

5. For the ChartWizard dialog boxes, use all the defaults and choose Next on each. Click OK on the last.

6. The chart will be drawn as a column chart. Double-click it to select it as a separate window.

7. Set the scales to a smaller font by clicking each axis in turn, selecting the Font command on the Format menu, and choosing 8-point Modern.

8. Click outside of the chart to deselect it.

9. Click the ellipse tool on the Drawing toolbar to draw an ellipse around the target figures on the worksheet. Set its fill to None with the Patterns command on the Format menu.

10. Click the arrow tool to draw an arrow from the chart to the ellipse. Format the arrowhead by using the Patterns command.

Figure 18.9 shows an example of a chart created this way.

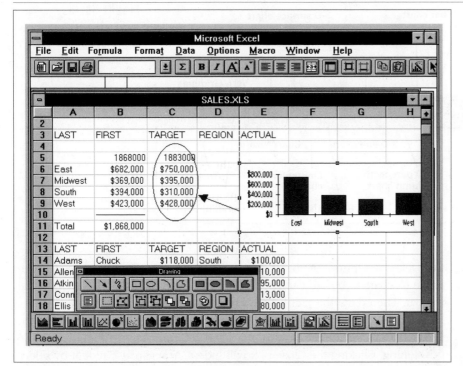

When an object is selected, it has selection *handles* for moving and resizing. When the selection handles are black, the object can be formatted (with the Format menu, toolbar, or right mouse button) and moved or sized (with the mouse). When they are white (such as a chart axis), the object cannot be sized or moved directly. You may, however, be able to format the object.

USING THE TOOLBARS TO SIMPLIFY YOUR WORK

You can simplify much of your charting work by using the toolbars. For example, create a chart on the worksheet using the charting toolbar (Figure 18.10). To clear the existing chart, use Chart ➤ Select Chart and press

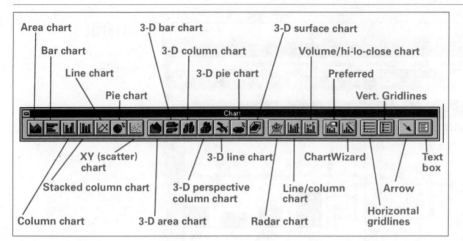

Ctrl-Del. Use Options ➤ Toolbars to turn the Charting toolbar on. Select the range to chart as before (A6:A9, C6:C9). Click the Column chart tool on the toolbar. Then draw the graph from E6 to H11 as before.

The Charting toolbar can be moved and resized. Try dragging it to the left of the screen. It may or may not have a Close box, depending upon its positioning. Clicking the Close box will hide it. You can also hide it by selecting Options ➤ Toolbars.

CHAPTER 19

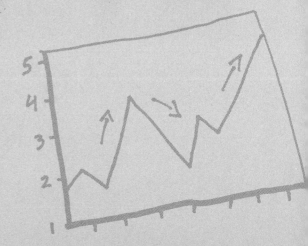

Advanced Charting Techniques

C hapter 18 introduced you to Excel's charting capabilities. This chapter discusses how Excel treats the data series that you chart and how it uses the SERIES function to control what is graphed.

CHART FILE MANAGEMENT

Chart file management is similar to that of worksheet file management. To create a new chart, you define the data range to be charted and then select File ➤ New ➤ Chart. Charts are saved with the Save or Save As command. Templates can be created, as with worksheets, to standardize chart making and reduce the time it takes to create a chart.

WHAT IS A DATA SERIES?

Charts are created from one or more *data series*, which is a collection of data points, each point related to the other by some aspect. *Markers* are used to represent the data points on the chart. In a column graph, the data marker is a column; in a line graph, it's a tiny symbol. The eastern sales total, for example, is a single data point in the SALES worksheet.

A data series also could be considered a series of values corresponding to a set of categories. In Figure 19.1, for example, the data series has four data points. The categories are the four regions, and the values for the categories are the sales projections.

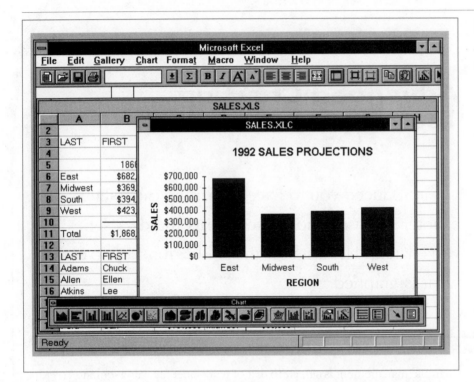

A data series with four data points

A data series is always made up of numeric values. Categories can be either text or numeric values. If you do not specify the categories, Excel will assume that they are sequential numbers (1, 2, 3,...).

Charting a data series is very easy:

1. Select the data series on the worksheet that you wish to chart.

2. Create the chart using either of these methods:

◆ Press F11.

◆ Select File ➤ New. Choose Chart in the New dialog box and click OK.

DATA-SERIES ASSUMPTIONS

Understanding how Excel defines a data series is very important. Figure 19.2 shows some examples of how the data series, names, and categories are defined. When you create a new chart or copy an existing one, Excel makes the following assumptions about the data series:

◆   If a data block has more rows than columns, the text in the left-most column is used to define the categories, and each column thereafter is assumed to be a data series. The column heading, if selected, is used as the data-series name.

◆   If the data block is a square or has more columns than rows, the column headings are used to define the categories, and each row of values is assumed to be a data series. The row heading, if selected, is used as the data-series name.

◆   If the category headings are numeric, Excel does not define any categories for the chart and each row of values is used as a data series.

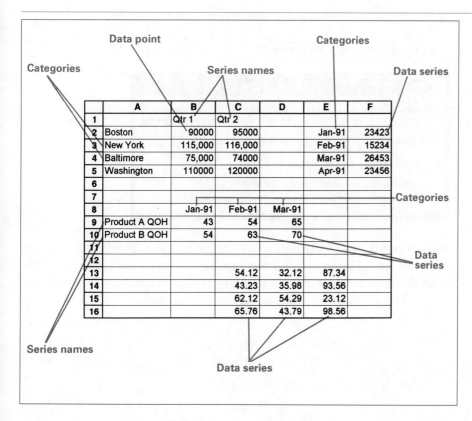

FIGURE 19.2:

Examples of data blocks, series names, and categories

If Excel has difficulty defining the series (such as no apparent category names in the selection), you will get the dialog box below, in which you specify what is in the first row. You can then define the series and choose OK.

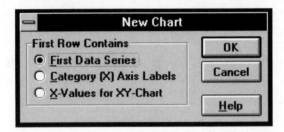

CHANGING DATA-SERIES DEFINITIONS

You can change the way Excel defines a data series by default by copying the series to the chart through the Clipboard:

1. Without a range selected, press F11 to create a blank chart document.

2. Select the range to plot and choose Edit ➤ Copy.

3. Make the blank chart active and choose Edit ➤ Paste Special.

The dialog box below will appear:

The options in this box permit you to define whether the values (y) are in the rows or columns and whether the series names and categories are defined in the selection. An example of changing the normal definitions was shown in Chapter 15 in a linear regression chart.

CHARTING DISCONTINUOUS SERIES

If you select A6 to C9 in the SALES worksheet and press F11, you will chart two continuous data series. You can, however, chart discontinuous series. To do so, select the range as you would any other discontinuous range: with the mouse select the first range, then hold down the Ctrl key and select each additional series. Be sure both ranges are the same size, including blank cells if necessary. To do it from the keyboard, define the first range and press Shift-F8. The *ADD* indicator appears in the status bar. Select additional cells or cell ranges. Press Shift-F8 after selecting all but the last range to stay in ADD mode. Once the ranges are selected, press F11 to create the chart.

You can use discontinuous ranges with ChartWizard when creating embedded charts as well as when creating charts on separate documents.

ADDING A DATA SERIES TO A CHART

After you've created a chart, you can easily add another data series to it. First, select the values for the new data series on the worksheet. Then choose Edit ➤ Copy. Click anywhere on the chart to select it. Then, use either the Paste or Paste Special command (as described above) on the chart Edit menu to paste the data series onto the chart.

As an example, let's first create a chart from a single data series, then add another data series to the existing chart. Open the SALES worksheet and create the chart from the first data series and its corresponding categories:

1. Select cells A6 through B9.

2. Press F11 or choose File ➤ New ➤ Chart. You will see the chart shown in Figure 19.3. If you wish, save this under a new name.

Now copy and paste the second data series onto this chart:

1. Select cells C6 through C9 on the sales worksheet.

2. Open the worksheet Edit menu and choose Copy.

3. Select the chart. Use the Windows menu if necessary or Ctrl-F6.

4. Choose Edit ➤ Paste.

The final chart is shown in Figure 19.4.

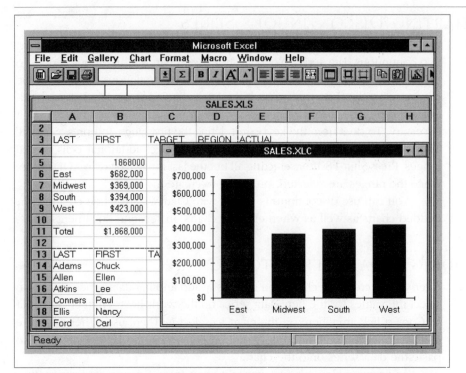

FIGURE 19.3:

Charting a single data series

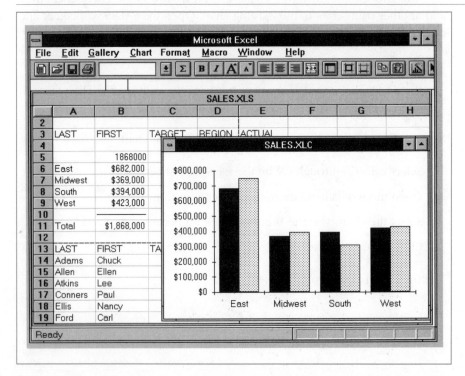

FIGURE 19.4:

The final chart with two data series

Using this method, you can continue to copy and paste additional data series onto the chart, either from the same or another worksheet.

THE SERIES FUNCTION

Excel uses the SERIES function to create graphs. This function has four arguments:

◆ the data-series title, if one exists, in quotation marks

◆ the category titles, which include the external reference to the supporting worksheet

◆ the data-series definition, which also includes a reference to the supporting worksheet

◆ the plot-order value

If you have several data series and include the row or column titles when you select the worksheet area to be graphed, Excel can use the titles for each of the series name arguments automatically, if they are selected. For a single data series, the column or row title is used for the chart title instead. The category titles and the data-series definition arguments are actually arrays and follow the rules for using arrays (see Chapter 15).

You can enter all the SERIES arguments by pointing and clicking, or by typing them in from the keyboard. The function can be edited in the formula bar, just like any other formula. For example, you can enter your data-series title and then point and click to enter the next two arguments.

You can see an example of the SERIES function by clicking any one of the columns on the graph that you just created. The formula bar will display the SERIES function used to create that graph, as shown in Figure 19.5. In this example, the first argument is missing because a data-series title did not exist. The second argument defines categories and the third argument defines the values for the data series. The fourth argument defines the plot order, which equals 1 because this data series is the first one plotted on the graph. The white dots indicate the selected series.

Now click any column of the second series and the formula bar will display the function with slightly different arguments. The first argument, the

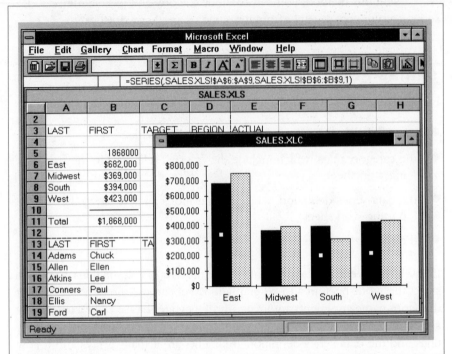

FIGURE 19.5:
*The SERIES function for
the first data series*

data-series title, is omitted as before. The second argument defines the same categories used for the first plot. The third argument defines the cells with the values for the second data series. The plot-order argument has a value of 2, indicating that this is the second plot on the graph.

CHARTS LINKED TO WORKSHEETS

Whenever you create a chart, it is automatically linked to a supporting worksheet. This way, if you change values in a supporting worksheet, the chart will be updated to reflect the new values. The procedure for linking charts follows the same rules for linking worksheets:

◆   When you copy and paste a chart, Excel creates the data-series formulas and external references automatically.

◆   You can block recalculation of a chart by selecting Options ➤ Calculation and choosing the Manual option in the Calculation dialog box.

◆ External references in a data-series formula should be absolute cell addresses or named references.

You can see how a chart and a supporting worksheet are linked by examining the sales worksheet. Select any column on the chart. You will see the data-series formula in the formula bar with the reference to the worksheet that created the chart. The formula uses a simple external reference. This means that you can open the chart without opening the worksheet and Excel will get the values it needs from the disk.

As the chart is linked to the worksheet, the chart remains unaffected if you shift an area of the worksheet by inserting a row or column. This is true even if the ranges are not named.

EDITING A SERIES

You can edit any series function from the formula bar. Another way to edit or add a series is to use the Edit Series command. Select the series to edit. Open the Chart menu and choose Edit Series. Notice that the *x*-label range and *y*-value ranges are displayed in the dialog box below.

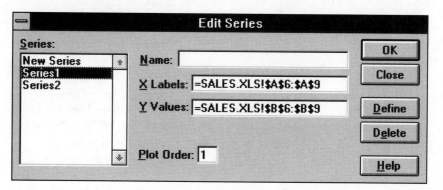

EDITING DATA-SERIES TITLES AND LEGENDS

Now let's add the data series titles and a legend. You will need the series titles for the legend. There are two ways to add the series titles: you can either edit them with the Edit Series command or use the formula bar directly.

To edit with the Edit Series command:

1. Select the first series of the chart (the dark bar here).

2. Choose Chart ➤ Edit Series.

3. Enter the series name in the Name text box as **Projected Sales** (see below) and click on the Define button (the equal sign and quotation marks are not needed—Excel will add them).

4. Select the second series from the Series list box and type in the name **Actual Sales**.

5. Click OK.

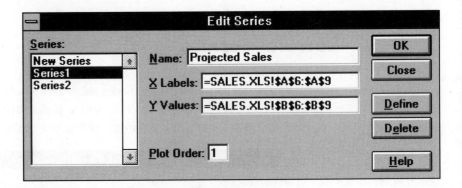

At this time, choose each series in turn and examine the formula bar. The series name has been added to the function (see Figure 19.6).

You also can add a series name from the formula bar by editing the series in the formula bar directly. To do this, select each series and add the name, with quotation marks, in the formula bar.

Now add a legend that uses the data series names:

1. Choose Chart ➤ Add Legend. A legend will appear to the right of the chart (Figure 19.7).

2. Select Format ➤ Legend. In the dialog box, choose Bottom and click OK.

The final chart should look like Figure 19.8. Save the chart under a new name (select the File menu and choose Save) —you will need it later.

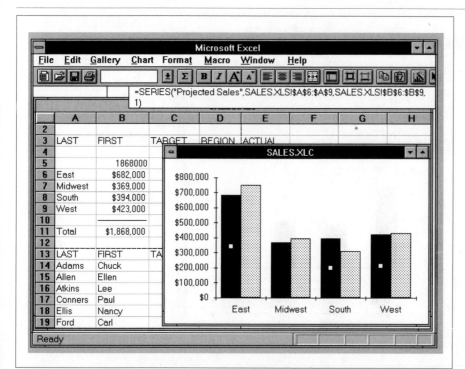

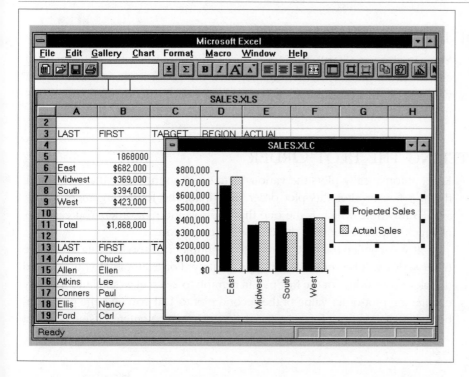

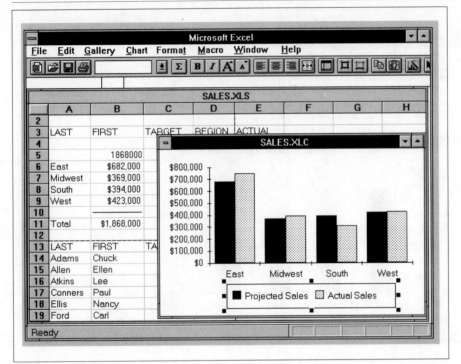

EDITING A SERIES WITH CHARTWIZARD

You can also use ChartWizard for adding or editing data series on embedded charts on a worksheet. For example, click the series in the worksheet you wish to edit, then click the ChartWizard tool. Follow the displayed directions from ChartWizard.

ALTERING THE PLOT ORDER

Excel automatically plots the various data series in the order that you select them. You can alter this plot order by editing the fourth argument in the SERIES function, which is the one that controls the plot order. You can also change the plot order with the Edit Series command.

If you change the plot number to the number of another data series, the other series will be renumbered appropriately. For example, if you changed the plot-order value for the first plot in a graph to 2, Excel would automatically change the plot-order value of the second plot to 1. If you omit the plot number when you enter a formula, the data series will be entered using the next available plot number. After you edit the function and press Enter, Excel will redraw the chart and change the legend.

Try changing the plot order on your example chart. Select the first data series and change the last argument of its formula to 2. Click the Enter box, and Excel will redraw the chart. Click the second data series (now the first) and notice it is now assigned a plot order of 1. Edit the formula for the first data series again so that it is the first series plotted.

If you wish, you can change the plot order with the Edit Series command. Notice the Plot Order text box in this dialog box. You can change this number in the same way to control the plot order.

DELETING A DATA SERIES

If you wish to remove a data series from a chart, use the following procedure:

1. Select the series you want to delete from the chart by clicking it.

2. Choose Edit Series from the Chart menu.

3. Click the Delete button, then click OK.

Here is another way to delete a series:

1. On the chart, click the data series that you want to delete. Its formula will appear in the formula bar.

2. Erase the formula with the Backspace key or by using Edit ➤ Cut.

3. Press the Enter key.

The chart will be redrawn without that data series. You can also delete a series by selecting the series, pressing Del, and choosing Series in the Clear dialog box. Then click OK.

You can clear all the data series in a chart by using the following procedure:

1. Choose Chart ➤ Select Chart. Markers will appear to show that the entire chart is selected.

2. Select Edit ➤ Clear.

3. When the Clear dialog box appears, choose Formulas, then click OK.

The entire chart will clear, but the formats (chart types) will remain. If you copy and paste other data series into the chart, they will be in the format of the previous graph.

COPYING A DATA SERIES

As with worksheets, you can easily copy data from one chart to another. To copy a data series and insert it in another chart, follow these steps:

1. Be sure that the source chart (the one with the data series that you are going to copy) is active.

2. Choose Chart ➤ Select Chart. The entire chart will be marked.

3. Select Edit ➤ Copy. The chart will be marked with moving dotted lines, as with any other copy operation.

4. Make the destination chart active by clicking it or select File ➤ New to create a new chart.

5. Select Edit ➤ Paste Special.

6. When the Paste Special dialog box appears, choose Formulas, then click OK.

The data series is copied to the second chart, but the format information (chart type) is not copied. This means that if you copy a data series that was displayed as a column graph into a line graph, the copied data series also will be plotted as a line graph.

CHOOSING THE CHART TYPE

When you change the chart type using either of these methods, all the data series plotted on the chart will change to the new type. If you want to change the type of only one data series on the chart, use the overlay method (described next).

The Gallery menu can be used to change quickly from one chart type to another. There are fourteen basic chart types on the menu: Area, Column, Bar, Line, Pie, XY (Scatter), Radar, Combination, 3-D Area, 3-D Bar, 3-D Column, 3-D Line, 3-D Pie, and 3-D Surface. Each menu selection, in turn, displays a dialog box from which you can select a subset of the basic type. For example, the dialog box for the Column chart type is shown in Figure 19.9.

To change the type of displayed chart, open the Gallery menu and choose the new chart type. When the dialog box for that type appears, choose the new format and click OK. Excel will redraw the chart in the new type. You can also change the type by clicking the desired type in the Chart toolbar. When you change the chart format in either of these ways, all custom formatting, such as the patterns of the series markers and gridline settings, is lost.

Another way to change the graph type is to choose Format ➤ Main Chart. This method permits you to change the type of chart without loosing previous format settings. When the dialog box shown in Figure 19.10 is displayed, choose the desired type of chart and click OK.

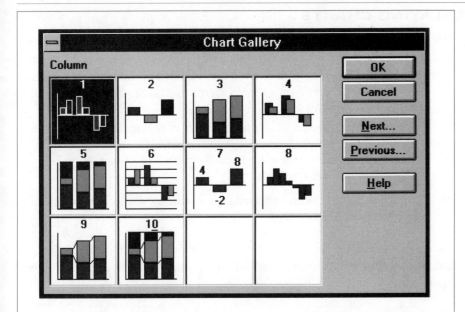

FIGURE 19.9:
Selecting the Column chart type

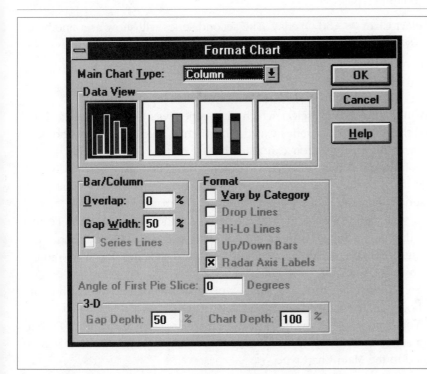

FIGURE 19.10:
The Format Chart dialog box for column charts

OVERLAYING CHARTS

An *overlay chart* is a second chart plotted as another layer on the main chart. You can plot two data series in different graph types by overlaying the charts. The overlays can even have different axes. The chart containing the overlay is called a *combination chart*. Overlay charts are useful for comparing different kinds of data or for showing correlations.

You can create overlay charts using either of two methods:

◆   If the chart is already customized and formatted, use Chart ➤ Add Overlay to add the overlay.

◆   If the chart has not been customized, you can use Gallery ➤ Combination to create the overlays.

As an example, let's use the SALES worksheet values and plot the projected sales as a column graph and the actual sales as an overlay line graph. Follow these steps:

1. Open the graph you saved earlier with both data series charted as column types.

2. Select Chart ➤ Add Overlay. The second series will show as a line type (see Figure 19.11).

3. If you wish to change the overlay chart type, choose Format ➤ Overlay. In the dialog box (see Figure 19.12), choose the overlay chart type.

Notice that you did not select which data series was the overlay. Excel assumed that the first data series was the main chart type and the second data series was the overlay. You can alter this by editing the plot order in the SERIES function. If there are more than two data series, they will be divided equally between the main and overlay types. If there is an odd number of data series, the extra series will be charted in the main chart type.

If you wish to define the starting series for the overlay, choose Format ➤ Overlay. In the Series Distribution group, select the First Overlay Series option button. Then enter the number for the first data series you want plotted in the overlay. Click OK.

Switch the chart back to a single-type chart by opening the Chart menu and choosing Delete Overlay.

You cannot add an overlay to a 3-D chart. If you try to create a 3-D chart from a series in an overlay, the overlay will be deleted and all charts will be returned to the Main Chart type.

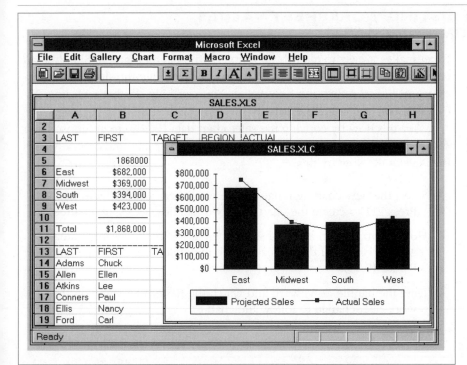

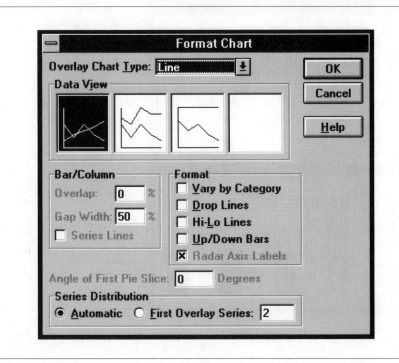

ADJUSTING WORKSHEET VALUES FROM THE CHART

Excel makes it easy to alter the positions of points on a graph. Simply click on and move a point on-screen and Excel will change the data in the necessary cell(s) to reflect the new value. You can only do this with line, XY (scatter), bar, and column charts.

Try this now by copying the sales chart data (B6:B9) to an unused area of the worksheet, such as E6:E9. Use Paste Special to paste, and choose Values, then click OK. Now try this:

1. Select the new charting range on the worksheet as B6:B9 and E6:E9. Press F11 to create the chart. The two identical series are charted.

2. Hold down the Ctrl key and select the bar for the E6 Eastern category. A small black handle appears at the middle of the top of the bar (see Figure 19.13).

3. Drag the handle downward and watch the Eastern E6 value on the worksheet change to follow the chart.

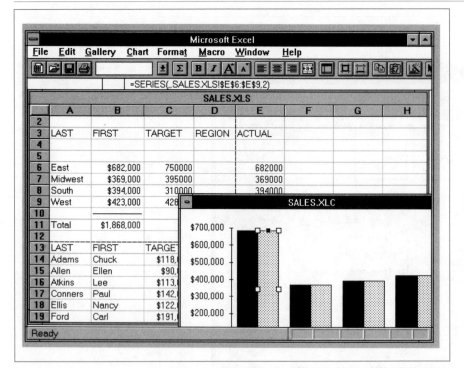

Now try the same thing with the Eastern A6 bar. What happens? The charted data are part of the table and Excel switches to Goal Seek mode and displays the Goal Seek dialog box, shown below. Enter a cell for the value to adjust, such as C15. Be sure to adjust a cell with an Eastern region value, or Excel will never be able to find a solution. The value adjusts to follow the handle.

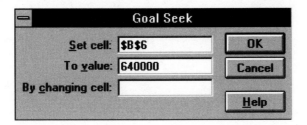

WORKING WITH EMBEDDED CHARTS

Charts embedded in a worksheet are created with the ChartWizard tool on the toolbar (see Chapter 18). You can activate the charting mode from within the worksheet by double-clicking the chart. The Excel menu will change to the Chart menu and the Chart commands will become active. This permits you to quickly change the chart type and other formatting aspects of the embedded chart.

If you have an embedded chart and wish to change it to saving it as a separate document, first double-click the chart to open it as a separate window. Then use File ➤ Save As to save it as a separate document. This will not remove it from the worksheet.

If you have a chart saved as a document and wish to embed it in a worksheet, first open both the chart document and the worksheet. Make the chart window active and select the chart. Choose Edit ➤ Copy. On the worksheet, select the upper left-hand corner for the chart and choose Paste from the Edit menu.

FAST TRACK CHAPTER 20

CHAPTER 20

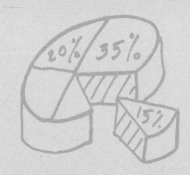

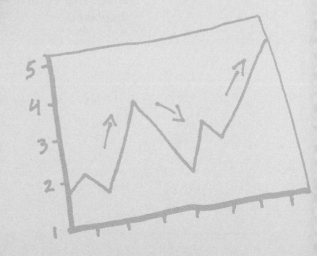

Creating High-Impact Charts

With Excel, you can design presentation-quality charts that communicate ideas quickly and effectively. Excel's charting features are extremely flexible.

This chapter describes some basic principles of effective charting. You will learn not only how to make charts convey the information and conclusions you wish to communicate, but also some basic design principles and pragmatic aspects of formatting a chart. You also will learn about the details of adding text, legends, and gridlines.

BASIC PRINCIPLES OF CHART DESIGN

Chart design serves two functions, to communicate a single conclusion to the viewer effectively and to be aesthetically pleasing. Communication, however, is ultimately more important than aesthetic design. Communication is also a tricky goal. If you are not careful, you may use your chart as a drunk man uses a lamppost: for support rather than illumination. Be sure your facts are correct, then design your chart to emphasize your conclusions.

Try, as much as possible, to keep a chart simple. Use a single data series if possible, using multiple graphs as necessary. If the conclusion depends on showing the relationship of two series, a scatter chart (see "Types of Charts" below) may be simpler than a chart with two series charted independently.

The amount of data on a chart often depends on how it is used. Overheads must be very simple, as the audience generally has little time to see the chart and absorb its message. People who view charts frequently can usually handle a complex one if it is designed properly and is in a printed form that can be digested at leisure.

By taking aesthetics into consideration, you can ensure that a chart catches the reader's attention. This is important for busy people who are information-overloaded and need to see your conclusion quickly.

Keep a chart balanced and use good contrast. Keep a consistent font (don't use one font for the y axis and another for the x axis) and don't use too many different fonts. Remember that contrast is often lost when you try to print a color chart on a black-and-white printer; in this case use patterns to help give the proper contrast.

TYPES OF CHARTS

Excel can create any of 14 basic types of charts—eight two-dimensional and six three-dimensional (3-D). Each basic type, in turn, supports a number of built-in formats. Your selection of type and format should depend upon what you are trying to communicate. Charts can be divided into fourteen general categories, and are depicted in Figure 20.1–20.14.

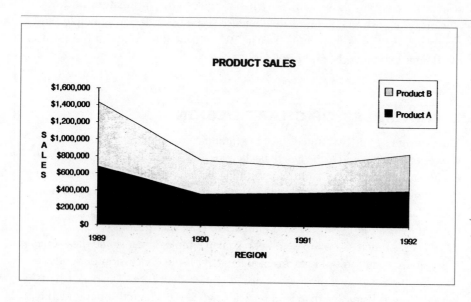

FIGURE 20.1:

Area charts are useful for showing the relative importance of different data over a period of time. The sum of the plotted values is emphasized, with the different data series as distinct rows. This figure shows an area graph that compares the sales of two products over time

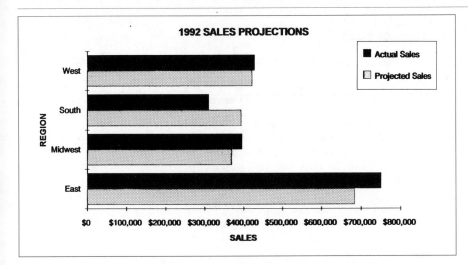

FIGURE 20.2:

Bar charts are the same as column graphs, except that they are rotated by 90 degrees. The categories are on the vertical axis and the values are on the horizontal axis. This figure shows a bar graph that is used to compare sales-forecast figures with actual sales.

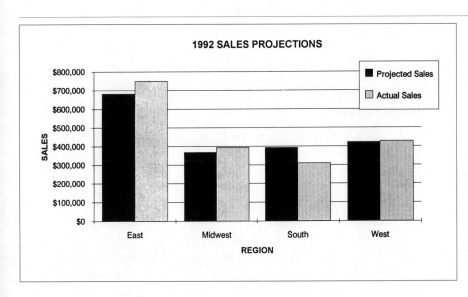

FIGURE 20.3:

Column charts are useful for representing quantitative information, particularly for making comparisons between groups of data. Stacked formats are useful for showing the relationship to the whole. This figure shows an example of a column graph

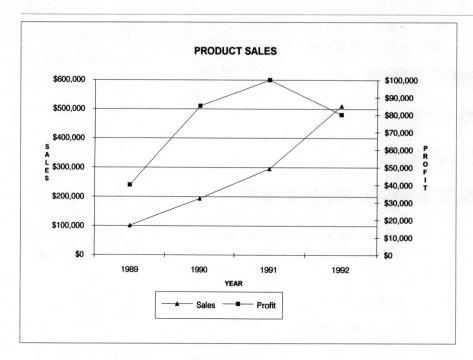

FIGURE 20.4:
Combination charts are useful for comparing different types of data. Axes can have different units

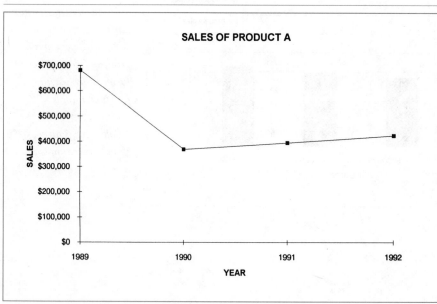

FIGURE 20.5:
Line charts are useful for describing and comparing numerical information, especially for showing trends or changes over time. This figure shows a line graph that indicates the growth in sales of a product over a period of time

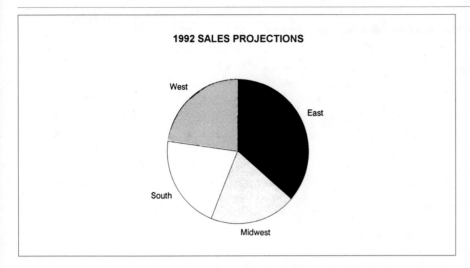

FIGURE 20.6:
*Pie charts help to show
the relationship of
quantitative data as
they relate to the whole.
This figure shows a pie
chart created from the
product A sales data*

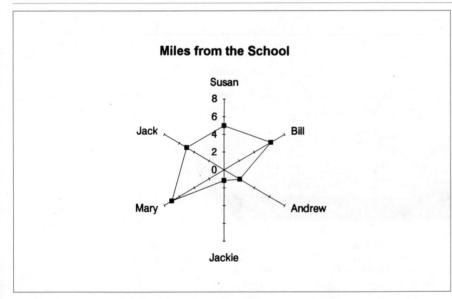

FIGURE 20.7:
*Radar charts show
changes or frequencies
of data relative to a
center point and to
each other. Use radar
charts for making
relative comparisons
between items. Each
category has a value
axis that radiates
from the center.
Lines connect all
data markers in the
same series*

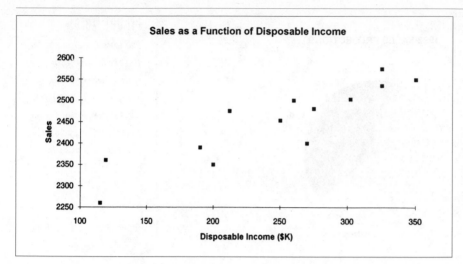

FIGURE 20.8:
*Scatter (or XY)
charts can show the
relationship between two
series. The individual
data points are marked
but the relationship
between these points is
left to the observer. This
figure shows a scatter
graph with points
showing how disposable
income affects sales*

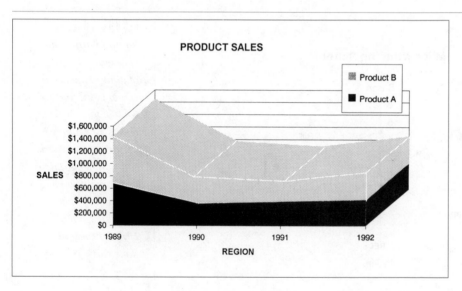

FIGURE 20.9:
*3-D Area charts show
the 3-D view of an area
chart, emphasizing the
sum of plotted values,
and separates the data
series into distinct rows
to show the differences*

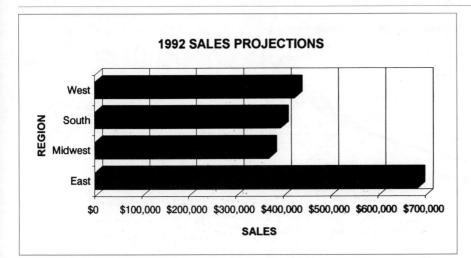

3-D Bar charts show a 3-D view of a bar chart, emphasizing the relative value of different items

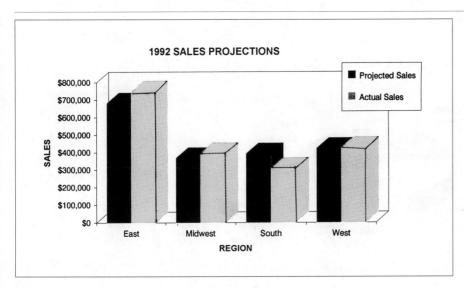

3-D Column charts show a 3-D view of a column chart, which—like the bar chart—shows the relative value of different items

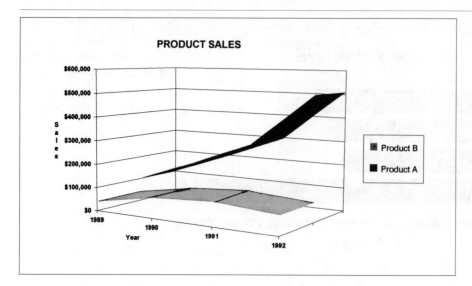

FIGURE 20.12:
3-D Line charts show the lines of a line chart as 3-D ribbons. This permits easier viewing of intersecting lines of the chart

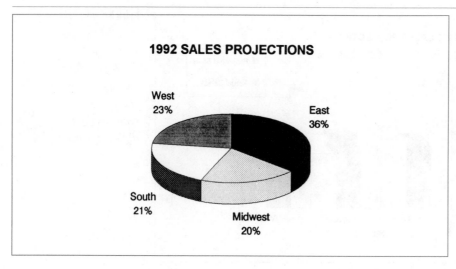

FIGURE 20.13:
3-D Pie charts show a 3-D view of a pie chart, emphasizing the data values as relative parts of the whole

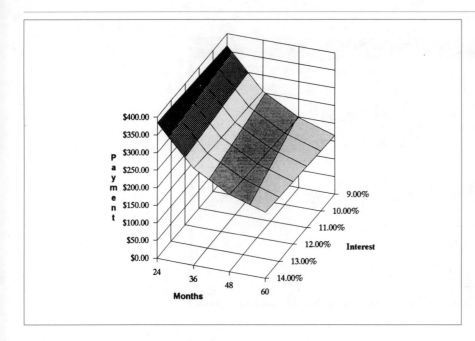

FIGURE 20.14:

3-D Surface charts are useful for finding the desired combination from two sets of data. Colors and patterns don't mark the series, but rather show areas of the same height. 3-D Surface charts are the best way to show tables of data, such as plotting several series of data with many values in each (z = f(x,y)

SETTING THE CHART TYPE

To select the type of chart, choose the general type from the Gallery menu, then choose the specific type from the Chart Gallery dialog box. You can also select chart types from the Chart toolbar.

CHOOSING THE SPECIFIC TYPE

Each selection on the Gallery menu has a dialog box containing a selection of subtypes of that graph. Figure 20.15 shows the ten subtypes for the default column graph:

1. Simple column type, one column for each data point in the series and each series a different color.

2. Simple column type, one column per data point, with each column a separate pattern or color

3. Stacked column

4. Overlapping columns

5. 100-percent stacked, each series shown as a percent of the total for the data point

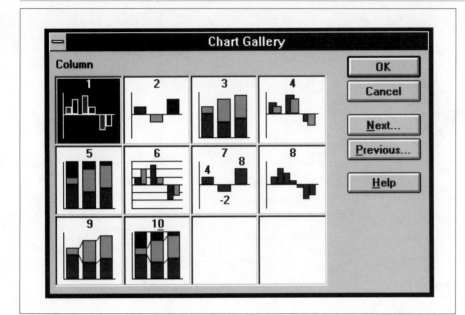

6. Simple column chart with horizontal gridlines

7. Simple column chart with labels

8. Step chart without spaces between columns

9. Stacked column chart with series lines

10. Stacked 100-percent column chart with series lines

The bar chart is similar to the column chart, except that only ten options are available and the gridline option shows vertical gridlines. The options are the same as for the column chart.

The line chart has the following variations:

1. Lines and markers

2. Lines only

3. Markers only

4. Lines and markers with horizontal gridlines

5. Lines and markers with horizontal and vertical gridlines

6. Lines and markers with logarithmic scale and gridlines (horizontal only)

7. Hi-lo chart with markers (requires two series)

8. Hi, low, close chart (requires three series)

9. Open, hi, low, close chart

The XY (Scatter) chart has the following variations:

1. Markers only

2. Markers and lines

3. Markers with horizontal and vertical gridlines

4. Markers with semi-logarithmic gridlines (one axis logarithmic, one axis arithmetic)

5. Markers with log-log gridlines

The area chart has the following options:

1. Simple area chart

2. Area chart showing series as percent of total

3. Area chart with vertical gridlines

4. Area chart with horizontal and vertical gridlines

5. Area chart with labels

The pie chart options are displayed in Figure 20.16 and are as follows:

1. Simple pie chart

2. All wedges have the same pattern and color, and are labeled by category

3. First wedge exploded

4. All wedges exploded

5. Simple pie with category labels

6. Simple pie with values labeled as a percent of the total

7. Simple pie with category labels and value labels expressed as percentages

The combination type permits you to mix two chart types in a chart, with the data series split between the two types.

You may create a chart and then decide that the type of graph you selected does not suit the chart's purpose. This is not a problem—you will find

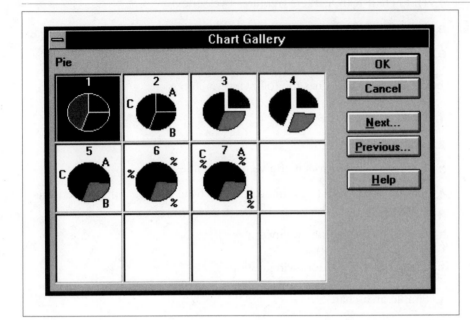

FIGURE 20.16:

The pie chart options

it very easy to convert one type of Excel graph to another with only a few clicks of the mouse. You should feel free to experiment with the different types until you've created a chart that communicates what you intended.

SETTING THE PREFERRED TYPE

If you wish, you can set a preferred chart type that will be used each time you create a chart. By default, Excel draws a column chart; in all examples in this book, the first graph is a column graph. To change the preferred type, first set the active chart to the desired preferred type. Then open the Gallery menu and choose Set Preferred. To use a preferred type with other worksheets, save the chart document as a template.

After you've selected a chart type as your preferred type, you can still select that type from the Gallery menu, just as you would any other type. You may find it useful to set a preferred type if you are going to alter your chart, but may want to switch back to the earlier type. Before you change the type, save the current one as the preferred type. Then if you need to switch back, select the preferred type from the Gallery menu (Gallery ➤ Preferred). This way, you won't have to remember which type was used for the original chart.

CHART PRESENTATION FEATURES

NOTE NOTE NOTE NOTE *To utilize most of the commands mentioned in this chapter, you need a mouse. For systems without a mouse, use the Move and Size commands on the Format menu to move and resize objects.*

Excel offers you many options that you can use to improve the appearance of your charts. You can add text at any point in the chart, control the font and size of the text and values, add arrows to emphasize parts of a chart, add titles to axes, change the legend position, and add gridlines. In this section, you'll practice using each of these features on the column chart that shows the projected and actual sales values from the Sales worksheet.

Start with a new chart: open the SALES worksheet, select A6 to C9 (see Figure 20.17), and press F11 (or choose File ➤ New ➤ Chart).

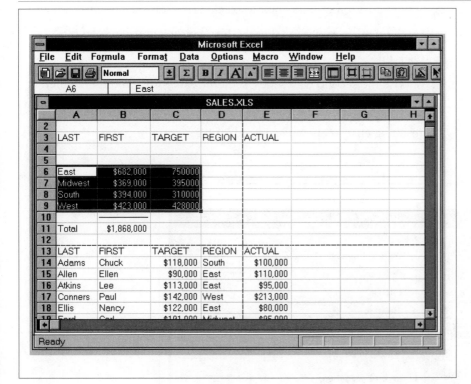

FIGURE 20.17:

Selecting the chart range

WORKING WITH COLOR

Excel makes it easy to change the colors of your charts. With the chart selected, choose Format ➤ Patterns. Set the foreground color by choosing it from the Foreground list box in the Area section. Set the background pattern from the Pattern list box. Select border styles from the controls in the Border group.

WORKING WITHOUT COLOR

If you have a color monitor, you know how dazzling a colorful chart can look. If you are in the likely situation of printing charts on a black-and-white printer, however, you need to design your chart with this in mind. This means carefully using patterns to differentiate data series and choosing symbols for data points.

For the column chart used so far, follow this procedure:

1. Click on a column for the first data series.

2. Open the Format menu and choose Patterns (see Figure 20.18).

3. Set the area foreground color to black. (This sets the color to Custom.)

4. Set the pattern as desired. For the first, you might use a solid fill.

5. Click OK.

6. Choose the second data series, set it the same way, and use a different pattern.

The resulting chart is shown as Figure 20.19.

Formatting for black and white printing

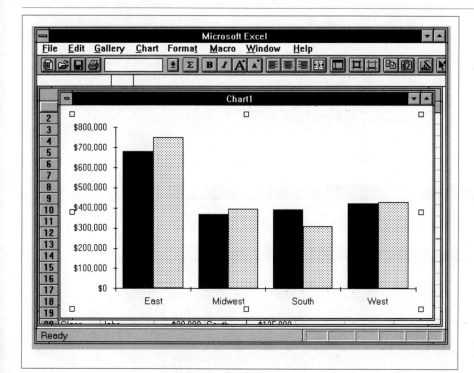

FIGURE 20.19:

The chart after adding patterns

WORKING WITH TEXT

You can add text to any part of a graph. If text is added to a predefined area (axis, data series, data point, or title), it is called *attached text* because it is connected to that specific area. Text that is not associated with any particular part of a graph is called *unattached text*.

Adding a Title

Add a title to your chart as attached text:

1. Choose Chart ➤ Attach Text.

2. When the Attach Text dialog box appears, select the area to which the text is to be attached. Because we will add a title first, choose Chart Title and click OK. There will now be a marker on the chart where the text is to be entered.

3. Enter the text from the keyboard. It will be entered into the formula bar and you can edit it just as you would edit any formula. Enter **1992 SALES PROJECTIONS**.

4. Use the Font command of the Format menu to format the title Arial, bold, and 12. If using Windows 3.0, use the Helvetica font.

5. Press the Enter key. The title will now be displayed on the chart, as shown in Figure 20.20.

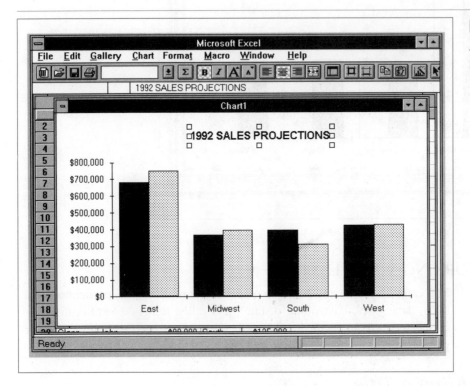

Another way to add a title to a chart of a single data series is to add it as a header to the data series in the worksheet. For the SALES worksheet, this would mean cell B5 if you were to chart only the Target sales data. We can't use that here, however, as it is used for the Table formula. Keep this idea in mind, however, as it is a good way to provide a title from the worksheet. When charting, be sure to select the cell with the title as a part of the charting range.

You can also use text from the worksheet for a title or other text on the chart by linking the chart text to the worksheet. For example, to reference worksheet text for a chart title use the Attach Text command from the Chart menu. When entering the text, enter an equal sign. Then click the worksheet cell with the text or enter the reference manually into the text box. Press Enter.

Adding Unattached Text

Add a subtitle to the chart as unattached text:

1. Click anywhere in the chart outside the title area. Type the subtitle **Target and Actual Sales by Region** on the keyboard. It appears in the formula bar and can be edited.

2. Press the Enter key. The text will be entered approximately in the center of the chart with handles around it.

3. Click the text and drag it to a place right below the title.

4. Use Format ➤ Font to format it as Arial, 10, bold italic. The chart should now look like Figure 20.21.

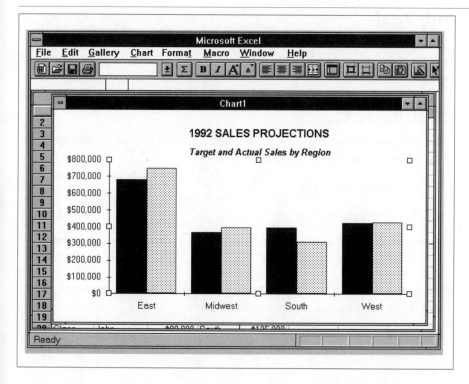

FIGURE 20.21:

Adding the subtitle to the chart

Unattached text is useful for adding text boxes with arrows. Using the Patterns option on the Format menu, you can add a box (border) around the text. You will see an example of this when we discuss adding arrows.

Adding Axis Titles

You can use the same basic procedure to add a title to either or both axes, as you did in Chapter 18. Figure 18.9 shows how axis titles appear on a graph. To add them, open the Chart menu and choose Attach Text. When the dialog box appears, select the axis that will be titled. Then type in the title from the keyboard and press Enter. Enter **SALES** as the y-axis label. Fornmat it using Format ➤ Font as Arial, 10 points, bold. Add **REGION** as the x-axis label and format it in the same way.

Adding Text to Data Points

You can add text to data points as easily as to other objects. This is a good way to label pie and area charts. To add the label, hold down the Ctrl key and click the data point. Then choose Attach Text from the Chart menu. Choose Series and Data Point and click OK. Type the text and press Enter.

Editing Text

You can easily edit attached or unattached text. Click the text and it will appear in the formula bar. Edit the text there and press Enter to place the edited version on the chart.

Positioning Text

You can position text as you wish, aligning it and setting the orientation. Let's change the orientation of the y-axis label:

1. Select the y-axis label.

2. Choose Format ➤ Text.

3. In the Text dialog box, choose the lower left Orientation option (see Figure 20.22) and click OK.

You can use this same command to set alignment of unattached text on the worksheet, such as in a text box with an arrow.

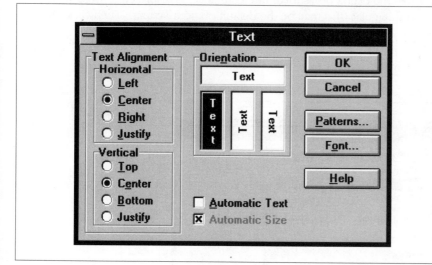

Setting Text Patterns

You can set the pattern of the text: its color, pattern, and border. This enables you, for example, to put a title in a shadow box. To set the pattern, select the text and choose Patterns on the Format menu. Choose the desired options in the Patterns dialog box (see Figure 20.18).

Removing Attached and Unattached Text

To remove attached or unattached text, select the text and press Backspace and Enter. For now, leave all text in place.

Formatting Text

Excel lets you change the font, size, and style of any text on your chart. To format both attached and unattached text, first select the text, then use the Font command on the Format menu. The title, unattached text, and axis labels are already formatted. Follow these steps to format the remaining text on each axis:

1. Click on the *x* axis, which contains the categories to be formatted.

2. Choose Format ➤ Font.

3. When the dialog box shown in Figure 20.23 is displayed, choose Arial, 10, and Regular (this may be the default on your system). Then click OK.

4. Select the *y* axis, then select Format ➤ Font again. Choose Arial, 10, and Regular. Click OK.

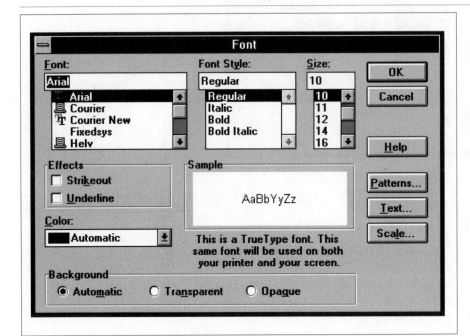

Your chart should now look like Figure 20.24.

Using this strategy, you can define the font for any object on the screen: title, unattached text, axis labels, or axis values. Just click to select it, then use Format ➤ Font.

You can also use any format tool on the standard toolbar to format the text, such as the Bold or Italic tool as well as the tools to change the font size. You can also choose Chart ➤ Select Chart, then Font to set the font for the entire chart.

ADDING AND MOVING LEGENDS

A legend is used to define the symbols and labels in the chart. On a pie chart, it defines the categories. On other charts, it defines the data series. Once you've added a legend to a chart, you can move it and reformat it.

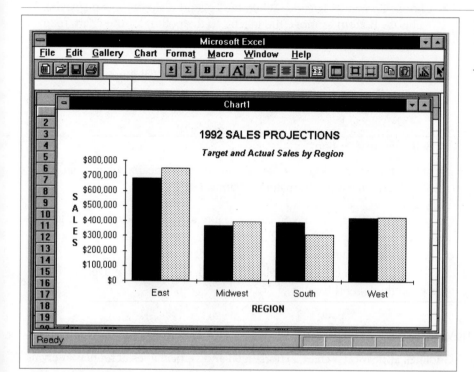

FIGURE 20.24:

The chart after formatting

Before adding a legend, be sure that each data series has a name, as the name is used in the legend. To name a series, click it and select Chart ➤ Edit Series. Type the name in the Name text box and click OK. In this case, name the first data series **Projected Sales** and the second **Actual Sales**. At this time, the names will not show on the chart.

To add the legend, simply select Chart ➤ Add Legend. Excel will place the legend at the right of the plot area and resize the graph to make room for the legend. The legend shows the markers and names for each data series.

You can readjust the legend box size if necessary by dragging the legend handles. To reposition the legend, use Format ➤ Legend or you can click on the legend and drag it to the desired position. The legend will change shape and the chart will adjust for better fit.

Now add a legend to the chart:

1. Choose Chart ➤ Add Legend.

2. Choose Format ➤ Legend. When the Legend dialog box is displayed, choose Bottom to move the legend to the bottom of the chart, then click OK.

The last thing you should do with your legend is format it:

1. Click the legend area on the chart to select the legend, if it is not already selected.

2. Select Format ➤ Font.

3. When the Font dialog box (see Figure 20.23) appears, select Arial, 10, and Italic from the formatting options. Click OK.

Once the legend is created, you can drag it to any chart location. The legend adjusts as necessary to fit the different border areas and can overlay portions of the chart if you wish.

If you want to delete a displayed legend, select Chart ➤ Delete Legend. (But keep the legend for now.)

FORMATTING GRIDLINES

Gridlines appear on a chart as horizontal and vertical lines at regular intervals in the plot area. They help you to determine the value of a data point. You can add major gridlines (at tick marks), minor gridlines (between tick marks), or both, and control their thickness.

To add gridlines to a chart, follow these steps:

1. Choose Chart ➤ Gridlines.

2. When the Gridlines dialog box is displayed, choose the type of gridlines you want, then click OK. For the sales chart, choose major y-axis gridlines.

To control the weight of the lines, follow these steps:

1. Click a horizontal or vertical gridline.

2. Choose Format ➤ Patterns.

3. Select the line weight, color, and style in the Patterns dialog box. Then click OK. For now, leave each at its default value.

The weight selection in the Patterns dialog box applies to the gridlines, axis, or arrow selected before you invoked the command. Figure 20.25 shows the chart at this point.

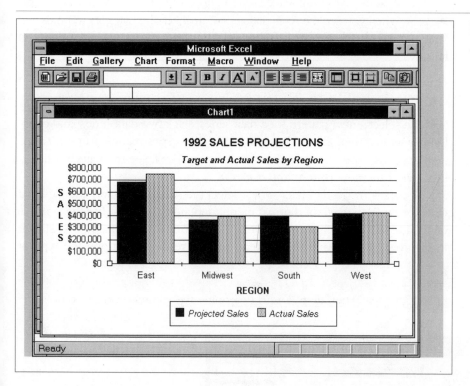

FORMATTING AXES

You can format either axis. The Scale command on the Format menu lets you control the tick marks, order of the categories, number of categories, scaling, and zero crossing of an axis. To do these things, select the axis and choose Format ➤ Scale. You will see a different Axis Scale dialog box, depending on whether you are formatting the y axis or the x axis. See Appendix C for an explanation of the options in these dialog boxes. (Earlier, Figure 20.5 showed a scatter chart with the axis beginning at $100, not the default 0. The Scale command was used to set this.)

You also can change the line weight of an axis. First click the axis, then open the Format menu and select Patterns. When the Patterns dialog box appears, select the line weight and style that you want.

To change the font, size, or style of the tick-mark or category labels on the axes, click any label on the axis and use Format ➤ Font. When the Font dialog box appears, select the desired format options, then click OK. To change the format of an axis label, click the label, then follow the same procedure.

To hide the axes (but leave the category and value headings) select Chart ➤ Axes. When you see the Axes dialog box, uncheck the Category (X) Axis and Value (Y) Axis check boxes to remove them from the chart. Leave them on for now.

FORMATTING A DATA SERIES

You can select a new pattern for a data series, stack two data series, and overlap bar and column charts. To change the data series marker pattern, select the data series and choose Format ➤ Patterns. You'll see the Patterns dialog box. Select the new pattern and click OK.

To stack or overlap data series, select the series to set and choose Main Chart or Overlay from the Format menu, depending on whether the series is defined as the main chart or an overlay. The Format Chart dialog box shown in Figure 20.26 appears. Which items are active depends upon the type of

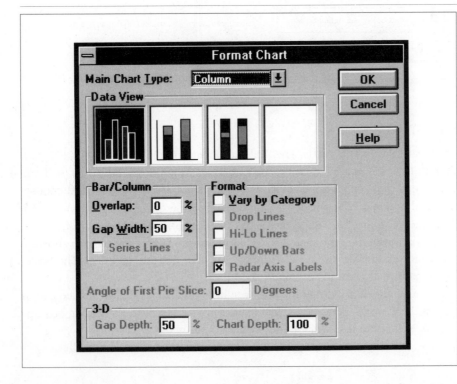

FIGURE 20.26:
Controlling data-series spacing and overlap

chart you are using. This figure shows the dialog box for a column chart. From this you can adjust the gap between the columns and how the series columns overlap each other. The three-dimensional options control the gap depth and chart depth.

ADDING ARROWS

Another one of Excel's presentation features is the ability to add arrows to emphasize any part of a chart. You can add an arrow to a chart using either of these methods:

◆   using Chart ➤ Add Arrow

◆   clicking the arrow tool on the Chart toolbar

You can then format the arrow using Format ➤ Patterns or by dragging and resizing it.

Add an arrow and text box to the sales chart as follows:

1. Select Chart ➤ Add Arrow. An arrow will appear on the chart, as shown in Figure 20.27.

2. Position the arrow as you want it (see Figure 20.20). You can resize the arrow by dragging the handle at either end. Move the arrow by clicking it in the middle and dragging it. Use Format ➤ Patterns to change the width of the arrow line and the type of arrowhead.

3. Type the text shown in Figure 20.28 as unattached text and position it by dragging. Click the chart, enter **Eastern sales reached $750K!**. Drag the text to the lower left of the window and resize the box by dragging the handles. Word-wrapping is automatic.

4. With the text selected, select Format ➤ Text to left-align it and Format ➤ Font to set the font (Arial, 10-point).

5. Add the border and shadow. Select Format ➤ Patterns. In the Border area, select Automatic and Shadow.

You can repeat this procedure and add as many arrows as you want to any chart.

To delete an arrow, click the arrow and select Chart ➤ Delete Arrow. You can also delete it by clicking the Arrow tool on the Chart toolbar. To delete text in a text box, select the box and backspace over the text. Use Patterns to turn the text box border off (be sure to turn off the Shadow option). For now, delete the text box and arrow, and save the chart under a new name. You will use it shortly to create a 3-D chart.

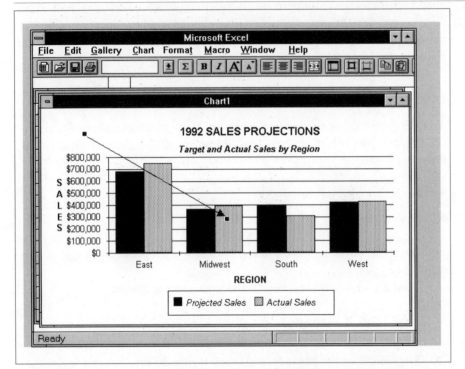

FIGURE 20.27:

Adding an arrow

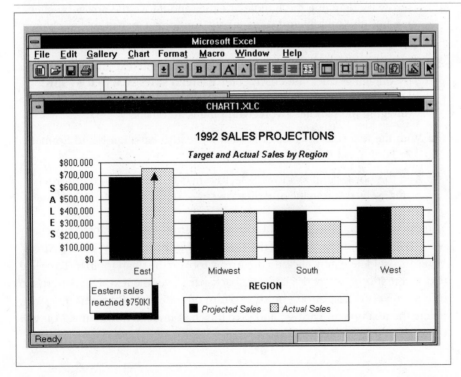

FIGURE 20.28:

Using an arrow and text box for emphasis

SPELL CHECKING

Before using a chart for a presentation, it's always a good idea to spell-check it, and Excel includes a spell checker. To check the spelling of all text in a chart, choose Spelling from the Chart menu. For more information on this, see Chapter 6.

WORKING WITH PIE CHARTS

A pie chart is different from other chart types since it graphs a single data series *only*. If you select more than one data series on a worksheet and try to create a pie chart, only the first series will be plotted. The legend lists categories instead of data-series titles.

When you *explode* a wedge in a pie chart, you separate it from the rest of the pie, as shown in Figure 20.29. To do this, simply select the wedge and drag it to the desired location.

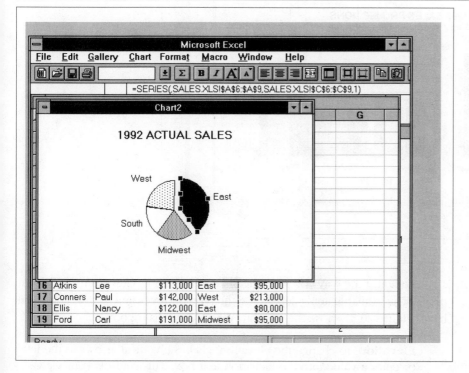

FIGURE 20.29:

A pie chart with an exploded wedge

EXPLORING THREE-DIMENSIONAL CHARTS

Excel supports three dimensional charting, which is useful for making charts that seem to leap right out of the page. Open the worksheet you saved after creating and deleting the textbox, and try a little three-dimensional experimenting with your chart to see how you like it.

To convert the chart to three dimensions, choose 3-D Column from the Gallery menu and click OK. Figure 20.30 shows the resulting chart (you may have to format the *y*-axis label or set the data series pattern again).

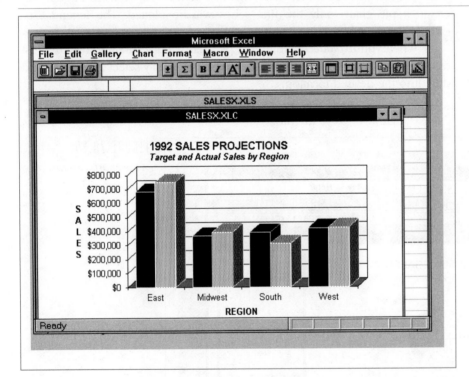

FIGURE 20.30:

The sales chart as a three-dimensional column chart

To adjust the way you view the chart, choose 3-D View from the Format menu. The available items depend on the type of three-dimensional chart you have. Figure 20.31 shows the displayed 3-D View dialog box.

Elevation: to change the elevation, click the vertical arrows at the left or enter a value into the Elevation text box. This controls your viewpoint of the graph. A value of 0 puts you at eye level.

Rotation: click the rotation arrows beneath the picture of the chart or enter a new value in the Rotation text box to rotate the view (0 is head-on, 90 is sideways).

Perspective controls the perspective. Larger values here make the data markers at the back of the chart smaller than those at the front, giving a sense of distance. Use larger values here if the chart contains a lot of data. The value defines the ratio of the front of the chart to the back of the chart. If a value of 0 is entered, there is no perspective. For 3-D bar and column charts, there is no perspective.

Right Angle Axes: click here to place the axes at right angles (giving you an oblique view). Click off to add perspective to the axes.

Height controls the height of the z axis relative to the x and y axes. It is measured as a percentage of the x-axis (base) length. Enter a value greater than 100 to make the chart taller, less than 100 to make it wider.

Auto-Scale scales the plot area so that the chart fills both the width and height of the chart window. If selected, you cannot define the height. If cleared, the plot area is drawn in a square shape.

You can also change the viewing angle of a 3-D chart by dragging. Click the chart to display the black handles, then drag any black handle to create the desired view.

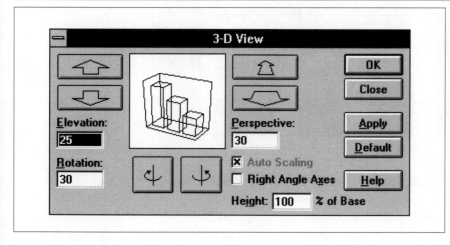

FIGURE 20.31:

The 3-D View dialog box

DESIGNING PICTURE CHARTS

Excel permits you to import graphics and use them as pictures in creating chart markers. The graphic image for the chart is imported through the Clipboard. For best results, import using the Windows metafile format. This means creating the graphic with software that can create such an image, such as Arts & Letters (Computer Support Corporation). To show how this works, we will use a simplified chart with a single data series (see Figure 20.32). Here is the general procedure:

1. Create the graph in Excel (shown here as a column chart).

2. Minimize Excel and start the graphics program.

3. Create the symbol and copy it to the Clipboard.

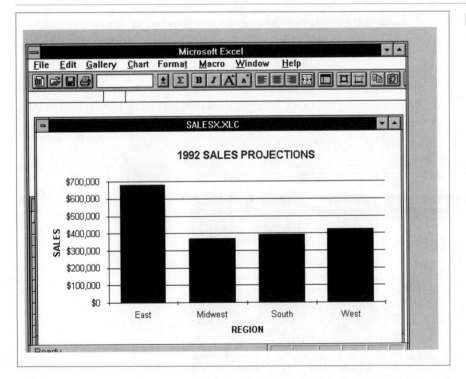

FIGURE 20.32:

The starting chart

4. Minimize the graphics program and restore Excel.

5. Select the data-series marker you wish to change.

6. Choose Edit ➤ Paste. The marker will change to the picture (see Figure 20.33).

7. To change to a stacked marker, use the Patterns command on the Format menu and choose Stack (see Figure 20.34).

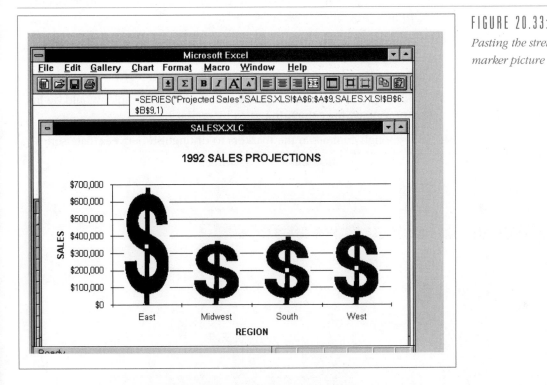

FIGURE 20.33:

Pasting the stretched marker picture

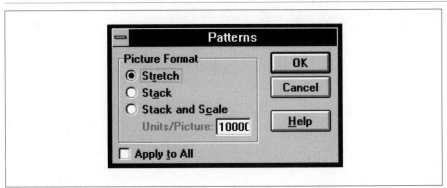

FIGURE 20.34:

Changing to a stacked marker pattern

TIPS FOR CHARTING

Here are some basic charting tips:

◆ Keep charts simple. Use as few data series as possible.

◆ If you have a problem fitting a chart on a page, reduce the font (6-point Modern is a good small font). An alternative is to use File ➤ Page Setup to change the margins or orientation.

◆ Use language that the viewer can understand (e.g., avoid abbreviations unless generally known).

◆ Remember how the chart will be used—i.e., as an overhead, with text in a document, on the worksheet, or as a stand-alone chart. (Overheads need larger fonts and thicker lines than other printed charts.)

◆ Choose the proper chart type. (A line chart, for example, would be inappropriate for comparing sales by region.)

◆ Set enough contrast in the markers to distinguish between data series.

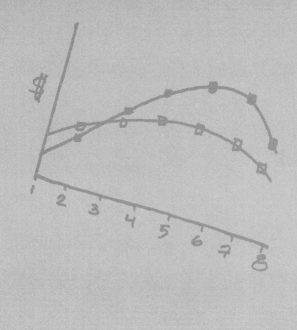

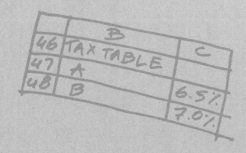

PART SIX

Part VI: Practical Solutions with Excel

Now that you've gained some basic experience with Excel's features, you are probably interested in using the program to solve problems. Although the application possibilities for Excel are far too numerous for this book, Part VI shows you six of the most common types of applications: data conversion between programs, sharing data with other programs, embedding objects in your documents, inventory control, financial management, and trend analysis. You will also be introduced to three of Excel's utilities: Q+E (which allows you to use Excel with external databases), plus the Solver and the Scenario Manager (for what-if simulations).

CHAPTER 21

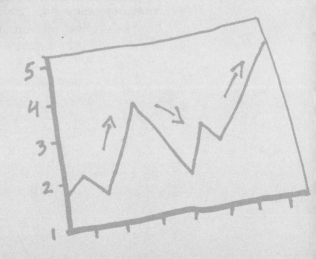

Using Excel with Other Software

Now that you've become familiar with Excel, you may want to use it with other software products, such as other spreadsheet programs, word processors, and database managers. You can transfer data from most of these programs to Excel, and vice versa. With some Windows applications, you also can create dynamic links or embedded objects.

Here are some typical reasons for using Excel with other software:

◆ You can insert an Excel worksheet or chart into a word-processed document created with Microsoft Word for Windows and *hot-link* the worksheet to the document, so that if it changes, the document will reflect those changes automatically.

◆ You can embed an object from Excel into another document or an object from another application into Excel. Embedded objects are intelligent in the sense that if you double-click the object, it's parent application opens with it for editing and formatting.

◆ If you have several Lotus 1-2-3 worksheets, you can print them with Excel's presentation features and have the printing macros in those worksheets converted automatically.

◆ If you have a communications program that runs under Windows and can support linking, you can link the incoming data to an Excel stock-analysis worksheet automatically.

◆ You can transfer an Excel worksheet you created at home on your Macintosh to an IBM PC you are using at work.

Excel also supports so many formats of other products that you can use it as a very good data conversion program. You might, for example, get a file of data in Lotus 1-2-3 format. You could read it into Excel, edit the headings, and then save it as a dBASE file.

The basic techniques for transferring data between programs include using the Clipboard, the File menu, dynamic data exchange (DDE), and object linking and embedding (OLE). This chapter will cover each of these, as well as describe a few related techniques, such as parsing data.

USING THE CLIPBOARD TO TRANSFER DATA

You've already used the Clipboard to copy data within Excel. Now you can use it to transfer Excel data to or from other Windows application programs running under Windows, such as Microsoft Word for Windows, PageMaker, and PowerPoint. You can transfer worksheet ranges, graphic objects, and charts. In addition, you can use the Clipboard to paste graphic objects, such as company logos, into your Excel documents.

Excel supports the following Clipboard formats:

ID	FORMAT
BIFF, BIFF3	Microsoft Excel file format
TEXT	Text, tab delimited
RTF	Rich Text Format for Windows or the Macintosh (from Excel only)
CSV	Comma-separated values

ID	FORMAT
SYLK	Symbolic link format
WK1	Lotus 1-2-3 Release 2.0
DIF	Data interchange format
NATIVE, OwnerLink, others	Embedded object
METAFILE	Metafile format
BITMAP	Bit-mapped format

Data transferred using the Clipboard is static; that is, if you paste some cells to a word-processor document, they won't change if the worksheet changes in the future. If the worksheet *does* change, you will have to paste the values in the word-processing document again.

COPYING DATA WITH THE CLIPBOARD

To copy a cell range on the worksheet to another application, first select the cell range, then use the Cut, Copy, or Copy Picture command on the Edit menu:

◆ **Cut** places a copy of the cell range in the Clipboard and removes it from the source location upon pasting.

◆ **Copy** copies the cell range from the worksheet to the Clipboard.

◆ **Copy Picture** copies a picture of the current cell range to the Clipboard.

Make the desired window in the destination application active and choose Edit ➤ Paste to copy from the Clipboard to the destination application.

Using these commands with a chart is similar, except that you first use Chart ➤ Select Chart to select the chart, then use the Edit menu's commands.

After a cut or copy, you can view the Clipboard by selecting the Run command on Excel's Control menu. The Clipboard will not show the data, but only a message about the size of the range in the Clipboard, such as *1R × 4C*. This would mean one row of four columns in the Clipboard (see Figure 21.1).

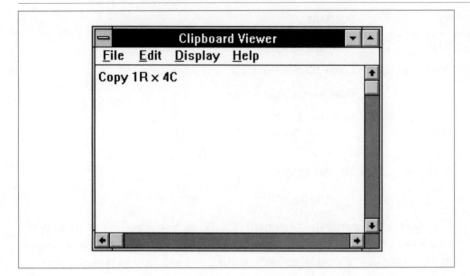

FIGURE 21.1:
*Viewing the Clipboard's
contents. Here one
row of four columns
has been copied to the
Clipboard*

To use the Copy Picture command, hold down the Shift key and open the Edit menu. Now you'll see the Copy Picture option. Select this command. A dialog box is then displayed (Figure 21.2—the top one for a worksheet, the bottom one for a chart). Select the desired option(s) and click OK. Copy Picture copies a picture of the selected range to the Clipboard. Viewing the Clipboard would *now* show a full image of the copied cells.

Copy Picture creates a Clipboard image in a metafile format, which has a higher resolution and quality than the Copy command creates. Some applications cannot receive this type of image, however. You can see the difference by pasting both types of images of a chart to a worksheet and printing the worksheet. If an application cannot receive a metafile image, the Paste command of the destination program will be grayed and unavailable, even though the Clipboard has data.

COPYING GRAPHICS

You can copy graphics from other Windows applications to Excel, and vice versa. To copy an Excel object to another program, select the object and use the Copy command. Switch to the destination program and select Paste.

To copy graphics to Excel (such as a company logo), use a graphics program to copy the desired graphic to the Clipboard. You can also use the Paintbrush program for limited conversion of graphic formats. To use Paintbrush, open the graphic in Paintbrush. Then select it and use Copy to place it in the Clipboard.

FIGURE 21.2:

The Copy Picture dialog boxes. The top one is for a worksheet, the bottom one for a chart

NOTE NOTE

If the Paste command is dimmed in Excel, the graphic image is not in a form recognized by Excel. Convert the graphic first to another format that Excel recognizes, such as PCX.

To put the graphic into Excel, switch to Excel, select the location for pasting, and use Paste. If the image is inverted, use the Paintbrush Pick menu to reorient the graphic before copying it to the Clipboard.

If you have other graphic programs, such as Arts & Letters (Computer Support Corp.) or CorelDRAW (Corel Systems Corp.), you have a lot of flexibility in creating graphics and converting graphics for your Excel documents. Converter programs, such as HiJaaK (Inset Systems, Inc.), permit you to convert graphic formats for Excel. Convert the format to PCX, then use Paintbrush to put the image in the Clipboard for Excel.

USING THE CLIPBOARD WITH DOS APPLICATIONS

You can also use the Clipboard with DOS applications when they are running under Windows. DOS applications run either in windowed or full-screen mode. If running in windowed mode, the familiar Control menu is available, which now also has an Edit option.

To copy to the Clipboard with the mouse, choose Edit ➤ Mark from the Control menu, click the start of the area to copy, then drag to select the entire area to copy. Then select Edit ➤ Copy from the Control menu to copy it to the Clipboard where it can be pasted.

If you are running in full-screen mode, first press Alt-Spacebar to switch to windowed mode. Open the Control menu, then follow the directions for the windowed mode.

TRANSFERRING DATA USING THE FILE MENU COMMANDS

The File menu has several commands that are useful for transferring Excel worksheet data to or from standard DOS programs, where the Clipboard is limited. *Exporting from Excel* means moving data from Excel to another program. *Importing to Excel* means moving data from another program to Excel.

Excel supports the following file formats:

FORMAT	DOCUMENT TYPE
CSV	Comma-separated values
DBF 2	dBASE II
DBF 3	dBASE III
DBF 4	dBASE IV
DIF	Data interchange format (VisiCalc)
Normal	Excel Version 3 format
SYLK	Symbolic link (Microsoft Multiplan, older Excel versions)
Text	ANSI text for Windows, ASCII for OS/2, text for Macintosh, ASCII for DOS
WK1	Lotus 1-2-3 Release 2
WKS	Lotus 1-2-3 Release 1, Lotus Symphony
WK3	Lotus 1-2-3 Release 3
Excel 2.X	Excel Version 2.X

Transferring Excel Data to Another Program

Use the following general procedure to transfer worksheet data to another program from Excel:

1. Open the File menu and choose Save As.

2. Enter the file name.

3. In the Save File as Type drop-down list box, select the desired transfer option in the list.

4. Verify that the proper file extension is now in the file name box.

5. Choose OK.

Copy a worksheet from Excel to a word processor by first saving the Excel worksheet data in text form. Use the File ➤ Save As command, and in the Save File as Type list box choose Text File. Then use the word processor to read this file. When the worksheet is saved in text form, each row becomes a line with the columns separated by tabs. Formatted data is converted to text as it appears on the screen.

When copying from Excel to a dBASE file, first select the database range on the worksheet, open the Data menu, and choose Set Database. Be sure to select the field names. Excel creates a dBASE range with the column titles as the field names. Any existing database file with that name will be overwritten. Be sure to use column titles of ten characters or fewer, as dBASE is limited to ten characters in a field name. You also must be aware of, and work within, any other dBASE constraints for the version you are using. Save the worksheet in the appropriate dBASE format using File ➤ Save As.

Transferring Data from a Program to Excel

To read a file of another program to Excel, follow this procedure:

1. Select the File menu and choose Open.

2. In the List Files of Type list box, select the correct type.

3. Choose the correct path.

4. Select the file name in the File list box and click OK.

The file will load into Excel, which automatically converts the data as necessary. (Excel is smart enough to recognize the various formats.) As the file loads, Excel displays in the active-cell designator, the format it is reading, and the percent of the file read so far.

Before you transfer data from a word processor to Excel, the word-processed file must be in the correct format: each line should end with a carriage return and columns should be separated by tabs. Save the word-processed data as text using the option in your word processor that saves the file in an ASCII or unformatted form. Numeric data in the word-processor file will automatically be in a formatted numeric form (for example, *$3.43* in the text file will be a numeric *$3.43* on the worksheet).

To load text data, choose File ➤ Open and select Text Files in the List Files of Type list box. Click the Text button and select the delimiting character. Choose the file origin, too, and click OK. Select or enter the name of the file to open and click OK.

USING DYNAMIC DATA EXCHANGE TO TRANSFER DATA

Another method of transferring data between Windows applications is to use the Windows Dynamic Data Exchange (DDE) facility. This creates *hot links* between the source document with the data and the destination document. For example, if you paste worksheet data into a word-processor document using DDE, any further edits in the worksheet will be reflected in the document. As another example, a communications program could download stock information while you are using an Excel worksheet to analyze it. With dynamic links, the stock prices are in a data area that is common to the communications program and Excel. There is only one copy of the data, and it is with the source program.

Excel provides two methods of supporting DDE. One is with the use of remote references, the second is with the use of macros.

To create a hot link, both documents must be Windows applications and both must support dynamic linking. If a document supports dynamic linking, use Paste Link or Paste Special on the Edit menu.

Creating dynamic links is much like creating links between worksheets or a chart and a worksheet (see Chapter 16).

USING MENUS TO CREATE LINKS

The easy way to create links (if the programs support it) is to use the Edit menu of both programs. As an example, let's link a worksheet range in Excel with a document in Microsoft Word for Windows:

NOTE
NOTE *The rules for setting up the link varies with the application, as there are no clear standards. On some programs for pasting you must choose Paste Link, then Auto Update.*

1. Make the Excel worksheet active and select the range in the worksheet to copy to the word-processing document.

2. Choose Edit ➤ Copy.

3. Make the word-processor document active.

4. Place the cursor where you wish the worksheet cells to be inserted.

5. Choose Edit ➤ Paste Special.

6. Choose Unformatted Text and then click on the Paste Link button.

7. Edit the document for column titles or other additions.

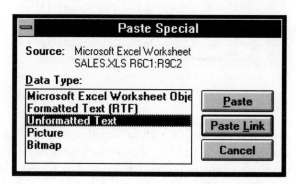

Figure 21.3 shows the regional sales figures from the SALES worksheet (right) linked to a memo (left). If you edit the worksheet, the memo will mimic the change.

As another example, suppose a communications program called Stock-Plus is the source and is open with its data linked to Excel. Excel contains a database Stock document with records representing the stock and price. Within Excel you could refer to the cell range for a stock that is coded ACM on the document as

=STOCKPLUS I STOCK!ACM

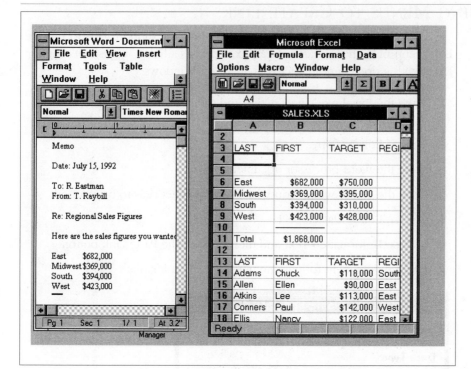

The reference begins with an equal sign, then has the application program name, a vertical bar, the source document name, an exclamation point, and the name of the cell, range, field, or data referenced.

This makes it possible to link documents in different application programs, just as you can link two documents in Excel. To create the link, you must first have both applications running under Windows 3.0 or higher. Assume, for example, that a cell in a worksheet is dependent upon a field in the StockPlus program:

NOTE *Documents being linked must support a data format compatible with DDE.*

1. Open the dependent worksheet (the Excel worksheet).

2. Click the supporting application document window (StockPlus).

3. Select the range to link and choose Edit ➤ Copy in the supporting document (STOCK).

4. Click the dependent worksheet and the upper-left cell of the destination cell range.

5. Open Edit and either choose Paste Link or type the remote reference. If typing the reference, hold down the Shift and Ctrl keys while pressing Enter. Remote references are entered as array formulas.

The cells are now linked.

OPENING DOCUMENTS WITH REMOTE REFERENCES

Opening and starting documents with remote references (provided that the supporting document is open) is no different than starting documents without remote references. The link is automatically reestablished and the dependent document is updated, if necessary.

If the supporting document is not open and the dependent document is opened, Excel queries whether you wish to reestablish the link. If you choose Yes, the supporting application will be loaded (if necessary) and the supporting document opened. If the link can't be established, an error message will appear in the appropriate cell.

SUSPENDING REMOTE REFERENCES

To suspend a link and use only the last values, open the Options menu and choose Workspace. Turn on the Ignore Remote Requests option and click OK. The dependent cell will then remain locked to its last value. To turn the link back on, click off Ignore Remote Requests again.

USING DDE WITH MACROS

Macros, which will be introduced in Part VII, are another method of transferring data between Windows application programs. With macros you can start another application, send data to it, get data from the application, and even execute commands in the other application.

USING OBJECT LINKING AND EMBEDDING TO TRANSFER DATA

Object Linking and Embedding (OLE) is a new and powerful concept in Excel, borrowing heavily on the object-oriented programming model.

WHAT IS OLE?

In object-oriented programming, objects contain within them the information needed to interpret their contents. With OLE, you are using these intelligent objects. An Excel chart, for example, can be embedded in a Word for Windows document. Double-clicking the chart in Word for Windows opens the chart in Excel.

Think of your documents as really being compound documents. Each document can contain many types of objects, all in different formats. You have already seen one example of this when you embedded a chart in a worksheet document. The chart is an intelligent object in the worksheet. It is linked to the data, and if the data change the chart changes, too. Double-clicking the chart in the worksheet changes you to Chart mode and permits editing of the chart. In another example, you might embed a worksheet range or chart in a presentation created with Microsoft Powerpoint. Selecting the object would open Excel with the object. In this chapter we see the concept extended further, with objects embedded and linked across applications.

The original object is called the *parent object*. Every copy of the object in any other document is called a *child object*. There is a single parent object. Each instance is really a set of instructions for locating, displaying, and processing the parent object. This is how OLE differs from DDE. Change any OLE-linked object, and all OLE-linked changes appear in all documents.

Some of the application may be packaged with the object, giving you some level of editing without opening the application that created it. Selecting a chart on an Excel worksheet, for example, gives you the charting toolbar and some level of editing.

OLE EXAMPLES

To try your hand at OLE: load one of the sales worksheets with any one of the charts. Also open Write, which is a Windows accessory that supports OLE:

1. Enter a bit of text for a memo to the word processor, then switch to the Excel chart.

2. Choose Chart ➤ Select Chart and the chart will be marked with some handles.

3. Choose Edit ➤ Copy to put a copy in the Clipboard.

4. Now switch to the word processor and choose Edit ➤ Paste Special. You will see a list box with Microsoft Excel Chart Object in the Data Type list box.

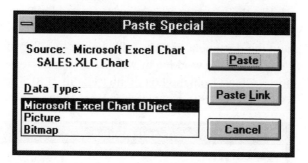

5. Choose this object type and click on Paste. The chart will appear in the word-processing document (Figure 21.4).

You now have an instance of a chart embedded in a word-processing document. You can double-click the chart in the word processor and Excel will open with

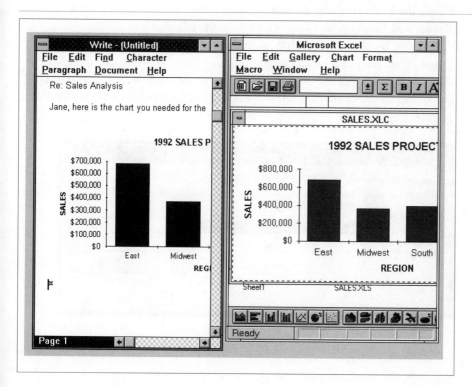

FIGURE 21.4:

The document embedded in the word-processed document. Because it is not linked, changes made to the chart at right will not appear in the letter at left

the object. In this case the chart is embedded, but not linked to the parent. If you edit the parent, the word-processed document will not change.

Now try the same steps as above, except in the last step click on Paste Link in the Paste Special dialog box instead of Paste. The chart is pasted again, but this time it's linked to the parent. Now, if you edit the worksheet, the chart and the document in Write will change to reflect the update.

If you are working in Write and wish to create a new worksheet, choose Insert Object from the Edit menu (Figure 21.8). Then choose the type of Excel object you wish to create: worksheet, chart, or macro sheet.

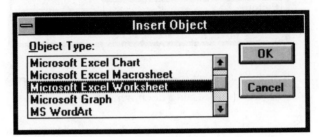

Click OK and Excel will load with the blank worksheet or chart for creation. Create the Excel worksheet, chart, or macro sheet in Excel. When finished, save the file and then choose Close or Exit from the File menu of Excel.

Now try the reverse; that is, embed an object in an Excel worksheet. Open Paintbrush and create an object. Save the object to a file using File ➤ Save As. Then select the object and choose Copy from the Edit menu to copy the object to the Clipboard. Now open an Excel worksheet and choose Paste Special from the Edit menu.

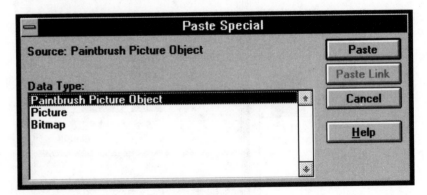

Choose the highlighted object from the list and click on Paste. The object appears in the worksheet. Clicking Paste Link button instead of Paste will link the embedded object to the parent.

If you wish to create a new object on a worksheet in Excel, you can choose Insert Object from the Edit menu. Then choose the type of object, such as Paintbrush Picture:

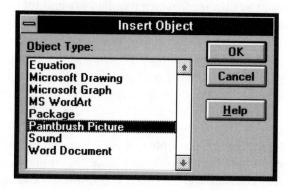

Click OK. The application (Paintbrush) will load and you can create the object in that program. When finished, save the file and choose Close or Exit from the File menu of that application.

Here are a few interesting experiments you can try to gain some understanding of embedding:

1. When embedding, open the Clipboard Viewer after choosing Edit ➤ Copy and look at the Clipboard. What is there?

2. Can you embed several instances from the Clipboard after copying to it or only a single instance?

3. Copy any one of the Sales charts to the Clipboard, then place the embedded and linked object in Write. Now make Excel active again and select Windows ➤ Arrange to arrange the windows, which will distort the chart some. What happens to the instance of the chart in Write?

USING EXCEL AND LOTUS 1-2-3

If you already have been using Lotus 1-2-3 or Symphony for your spreadsheets, you can import your Lotus worksheets into Excel, or vice versa. When you transfer in either direction, the cell properties of your worksheet, including values, formulas, format, protection, and any names that you assigned, are converted. However, window properties (such as panes) are not converted. Although the function arguments and their order in Excel are often different from those in Lotus 1-2-3, when you transfer files, Excel automatically converts them. For example, you can take the amortization worksheet that you created in Chapter 8, which has the PMT and PV functions, and transfer it to Lotus 1-2-3, whose functions use different arguments. The Lotus 1-2-3 worksheet will be calculated correctly using the proper formulas.

If the Excel worksheet has a feature that is not supported by Lotus 1-2-3, it will not be converted correctly. If you plan to do many transfers from Excel to Lotus 1-2-3, avoid using any of Excel's special functions.

You also can use Excel's Macro Translation Assistant to translate Lotus 1-2-3 macros to Excel macros. Simple macros will be converted directly. More complex macros probably will need some editing after conversion. To start a macro translation, choose Run from the application's Control menu. Select Macro Translator on the dialog box displayed and click OK. Press F1 in Excel to get help with the translator.

USING EXCEL AND OTHER MICROSOFT SPREADSHEETS

Excel also can be used with Microsoft Multiplan, Macintosh Excel, and other products that use the SYLK format. This is a standard format that can be used for transferring data to or from Excel. To save a worksheet in this format, select Save As from the File menu. In the Save File As Type box, choose SYLK. Enter the file name, and click OK. Worksheets already saved in the SYLK format can be read automatically by Excel when you open them.

If a worksheet won't load with a new version of Excel, save the old worksheet version in SYLK format. Then use your new Excel version to load the SYLK-formatted file.

When using the SYLK format, only formulas that can be interpreted by both application software products will be transferred correctly. Formulas specific to either will not be transferred. As with Lotus 1-2-3, data, formulas, formats, and names are transferred within this limitation, but window properties (such as panes) are not transferred. Multiplan does not support arrays and cannot support as large a numeric range as Excel. All Multiplan functions except DELTA and ITERCNT are supported by Excel. Many Excel functions, however, are not supported by Multiplan.

You also can read a Multiplan worksheet using the SYLK format. Just open the worksheet in Excel. Excel recognizes it and converts it. Multiplan will read an Excel worksheet only if it is in the SYLK format.

If you experience problems transferring files between Excel and any Microsoft program or another version of PC or Macintosh Excel, revert to the SYLK format. For example, save the Excel file as a SYLK file. The receiving program, if it is a Microsoft program, can generally detect the SYLK format and load the program correctly.

EXCEL AND dBASE VERSIONS

Save the worksheet in a normal Excel format as well as the dBASE format. A field name that is too long (and other problems) can prevent the saved database from loading to dBASE. If you save the original form, you can always reload the worksheet and try again.

Excel will export data to dBASE II, dBASE III, and dBASE IV, and can import data from any of these to a worksheet. The conversion is automatic and you do not have to use any special conversion routines or dBASE programs.

To import data and create a worksheet from a dBASE file, choose File ➤ Open (Figure 21.5). In the List Files of Type drop-down list box, choose dBASE Files (*.DBF). Choose the proper directory and file name (.DBF extension). Click OK. The file will be imported and a worksheet created from it. Each field will be in a separate column, and each record in a separate row.

To export data to a dBASE II, dBASE III, or dBASE IV file, first be sure the worksheet area is in a database form. The field names should be in the first row and follow the field naming rules of dBASE. Use the Set Database command to define the database area on the worksheet. Once it is defined, save the database with the Save As command. When the Save As dialog box

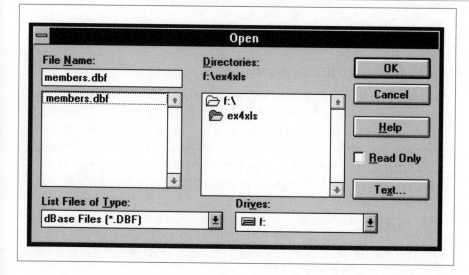

FIGURE 21.5:
Importing a dBASE file is easy: just check the right file type at the bottom and select the file name

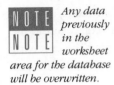

Any data previously in the worksheet area for the database will be overwritten.

is displayed, choose the format type in Save File as Type (Figure 21.6). Select the format desired (DBF 2, 3, or 4). Click OK. The database file is created from the worksheet with the .DBF extension. If any file with the same name currently exists, you will be prompted. If you elect to continue, the file will be overwritten.

When exporting data to dBASE II or dBASE III, some format information will be lost. For example, *$3.43* will be saved in the dBASE III file as *3.43*. Text fields that are too long may be truncated.

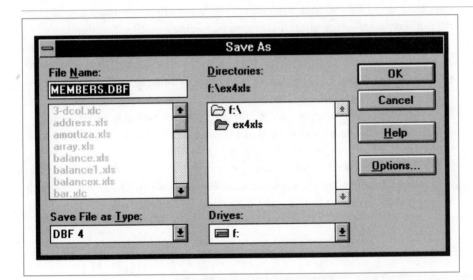

FIGURE 21.6:

Exporting an Excel file in a dBASE form

USING THE PARSE COMMAND

On occasion, you may wish to import columnar data and break them out to an Excel worksheet or database. Assume, for a moment, that you downloaded a list of addresses in text form using a communications program. The file is generally in a .DOC, .PRN, or .TXT form. There is a linefeed and carriage-return character at the end of each line. There are no tab separators for the columns (Figure 21.7). Use spaces to separate columns. If you display the list using the DOS command TYPE, you will see the data in columns.

To create a worksheet from this data, choose File ➤ Open and under List Files of Type choose Text Files (*.TXT;*.CSV). Choose the file and click OK. The data are read and placed in a spreadsheet (Figure 21.8). As there are no tab separators, however, all the data are in column A. It doesn't look aligned here, since Excel defaults to a proportional print. Select column A and set the font to Courier New or Courier using Format ➤ Font. This removes the proportional spacing. The data are now aligned by columns, but are still all in column A (see Figure 21.9). We wish to break it out so that the first and last name, address, city, state, and zip code are all in separate columns.

```
John Doe     Box 75        Portland  OR  97212
Mary Smith   1025 Park St. Portland  OR  97218
John Rogers  125 Fox Ave.  Portland  OR  97213
```

FIGURE 21.7:

The initial data in dBASE

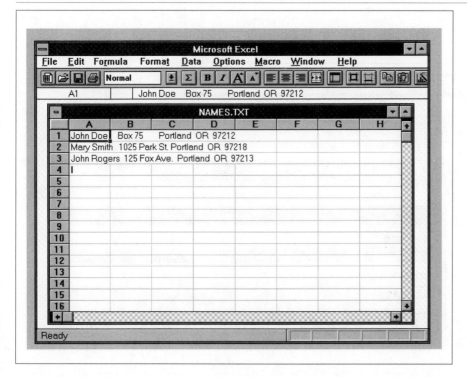

FIGURE 21.8:

Data as initially read: proportional font and all in column A

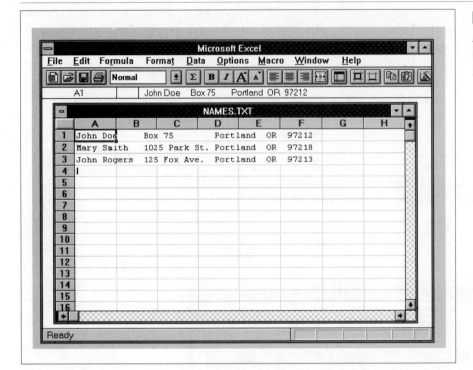

FIGURE 21.9:
*Data after some
monospace formatting,
but still all in column A*

To do this, select all the data in column A (A1:A3) and choose Data ➤ Parse. Excel displays the first line, as shown below:

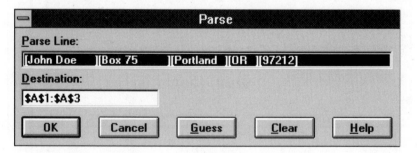

Verify that the line is parsed correctly, with each part defined as a separate field. If not, click on Guess and Excel will try to parse the record on its own. If necessary, finish the parsing by inserting additional brackets after the city and state. Click OK.

Excel will now break all selected records as per the parsed definition, with the first and last name, address, city, state, and zip code all in separate columns. Widen the columns as necessary (see Figure 21.10).

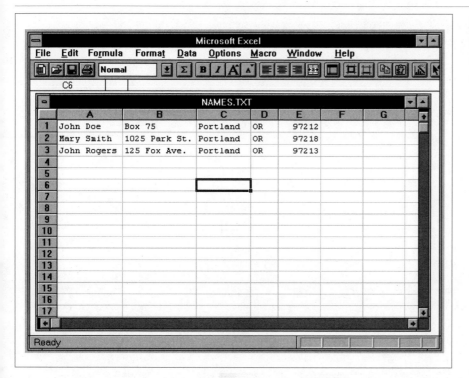

FIGURE 21.10:

The finished worksheet, with data in separate columns

This method is very useful for converting downloaded reports on a communications system to a dBASE format. Read the report to Excel, parse the records, define a database, and save it as a dBASE file.

FAST TRACK CHAPTER 22

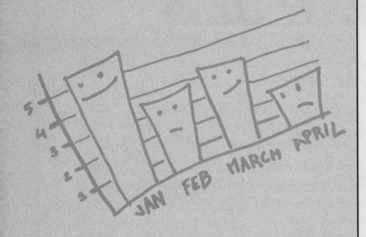

CHAPTER 22

Inventory Control and Invoicing

! f you have a business, you know that creating invoices is a time-consuming chore that is better delegated to a computer. This chapter illustrates the basic concepts of invoicing with Excel. It shows how to create an invoice using an inventory database with multiple price schedules and how to add a tax to the final price based on a tax-rate table.

CREATING THE INVENTORY DATABASE

One of your first objectives should be to create the inventory database. Fields should include the part or item number, the description, and a column for each price schedule. For inventory control, you may also wish to add fields for the cost, the current quantity-on-hand (QOH), and the extended cost (quantity-on-hand times the cost). This permits you to calculate quickly the current value of the inventory.

Create the sample database shown in Figure 22.1. The database starts on row 50 to leave room for the invoice worksheet above (it also could be on a separate worksheet and linked to an invoice worksheet). Each inventory item

	A	B	C	D	E	F
50	PARTNO	DESCRIPTION	RETAIL	WHOLESALE	QOH	EXT COS
51	10008	General Purpose Cleaner 1 qt.	$5.00	$4.10	3	$12.30
52	10010	Industrial Cleaner 1 qt.	$7.25	$5.25	3	$15.75
53	20014	Lecithin	$9.75	$7.05	5	$35.25
54	20031	Zinc	$5.20	$3.50	1	$3.50
55	20042	Alfalfa	$8.75	$6.25	7	$43.75
56	20049	Multi-vitamin	$12.50	$8.50	9	$76.50
57	20051	Iron+Vitamin C	$7.75	$5.10	3	$15.30
58	20061	Beta Carotene	$16.50	$10.75	1	$10.75
59	20081	Vitamin E/Selenium	$10.10	$7.20	3	$21.60
60	20082	Vitamin C (Chewable)	$6.25	$4.10	8	$32.80
61	20083	Vitamin C S/R 500	$6.40	$4.60	8	$36.80
62	20088	Fiber Wafer	$4.50	$3.25	4	$13.00
63	20143	Iron	$8.00	$5.10	4	$20.40
64	20250	Calcium Magnesium	$6.50	$4.50	5	$22.50
65	20310	B Complex	$10.80	$7.50	4	$30.00
66	20810	EPA	$17.50	$12.75	1	$12.75

is a record, entered as a separate row. The prices can either be entered as discrete values or as formula-based prices of another column. Sometimes you may wish to have separate price categories based on the quantity sold. In this example there are only two price categories, Retail and Wholesale. There should be no blanks in this (or any) inventory database, as they can cause incorrect data to be entered in the invoice later.

For the invoicing to work properly, the records need to be in order by part number. You may enter them in any order, but then use Data ➤ Sort to sort by part number. (Remember, do not include the field name when you define the sort range.)

Before leaving this section, you may wish to experiment with the database. You can set up a criteria range and find or extract records based on any criteria.

For the example in this chapter, the invoicing system will not really use this area as a database, but as a lookup table. You do not *need* to name it as a database for the invoicing system to work; however, from the user's perspective naming it as a database is helpful because it permits you to use the Goto command for updating quickly.

NOTE
NOTE
You can use the inventory database without sorting on the part number by creating macros using the Data.Find function of the macro language (see Part VII). This adds another degree of complexity, but the capability is there if you need it.

CREATING THE INVOICE

A sample output of the invoice system is shown in Figure 22.2. Begin creating the invoice, using Figure 22.3 as a guide. Fill in everything as shown. You can store a blank form of this invoice as a template on disk and use it for multiple invoices by filling in the areas that change between invoices. The item descriptions, prices, and the extended price columns will be filled in by Excel. For the line items, you enter only the item number and the quantity to ship. The totals will also be calculated automatically.

INVOICE

Remit to:
ABC Health Products
48 Midway Lane
Berkeley, CA 94702

Date:	6/25/92
Invoice #:	4023
Tax Code:	B
Terms:	A

Sold to: John Albert
34 Shady Lane
Berkeley, CA 94702

Ship to: John Albert
34 Shady Lane
Berkeley, CA 94702

Item #	Description	Price	Qty	Ext Price
20143	Iron	$5.10	1	$5.10
20083	Vitamin C S/R 500	$4.60	2	$9.20
20810	EPA	$12.75	1	$12.75
			Subtotal	$27.05
			Tax	$1.89
			Grand Total	$28.94

FIGURE 22.2:

A sample invoice printout

	A	B	C	D	E
1		**INVOICE**			
2					
3	**Remit to:**			Date:	6/25/92
4	ABC Health Products			Invoice #:	4023
5	48 Midway Lane			Tax Code:	B
6	Berkeley, CA 94702			Terms:	A
7					
8					
9	Sold to:	John Albert	Ship to:	John Albert	
10		34 Shady Lane		34 Shady Lane	
11		Berkeley, CA 94702		Berkeley, CA 94702	
12					
13					
14	Item #	Description	Price	Qty	Ext Price
15	20143			1	
16	20083			2	
17	20810			1	
18					
19					
20					
21					
22					
23					
24					
25					
26				Subtotal	
27				Tax	
28				Grand Total	
29					

FIGURE 22.3:

The invoice worksheet

Place the following function in cell B15:

=LOOKUP(A15,$A$51:$A$66,$B$51:$B$66)

This tells Excel to look up the value in A15 (the item number) in the range $A$51:$A$66 of the inventory database and return the corresponding value (the description) found in the range $B$51:$B$66. The LOOKUP command assumes that the range is sorted by increasing item numbers. Here the range is our inventory database. Now drag to fill or use Edit ➤ Fill Down to copy the function from cell B15 to cells B16 through B25. In doing so, the relative reference to cell A15 will change to reference cells A16, A17, etc. You should now see the item descriptions in column B.

You have one problem at this point. For each row with a blank item number, there appears an *#N/A* in column B:

	A	B
15	20143	Iron
16	20083	Vitamin C S/R 500
17	20810	EPA
18		#N/A
19		#N/A
20		#N/A
21		#N/A
22		#N/A
23		#N/A
24		#N/A
25		#N/A

They appear because there is no value from column A to plug into the LOOKUP function. To eliminate these, modify the function in B15 to include the IF function, using the ISNA function (see Appendix F) to test for the instances of N/A:

=IF(A15=0," ",LOOKUP(A15,$A$51:$A$66,$B$51:$B$66))

Now copy *this* formula from B15 to cells B16 to B25.

This may be somewhat confusing, so let's look at the basic form of the IF function:

=IF(*condition, value if true, value if false*)

The program uses A15 = 0 as a conditional test for a blank cell. If a value in A15 is not found, the first expression is used to evaluate the cell value, leaving cell B15 blank (since there is no second argument in this function). If a value *is* found, the second expression is used to find the cell value.

The next thing you have to do is fill the Price field with a function to find the prices. It is a bit more complicated, because the price depends not only on the item number, but also on the Terms code entered in E6. The term code tells Excel whether to use the retail price or the wholesale price. Enter the following function in C15 (without the line break):

=IF(A15<>0,IF($E$6="A",LOOKUP(A15,$A$51:$A$66,$D$51:$D$66),
IF($E$6="B",LOOKUP(A15,$A$51:$A$66,$C$51:$C$66)," "))," ")

If an item number is entered on a line, Excel evaluates the expression *$E$6="A"*. If this condition is TRUE, the next LOOKUP function is used to find the price from the table, using column D. If it is FALSE, the next IF function is evaluated. This tries another condition and, if it is TRUE, activates another LOOKUP function. This time, column C will be used for the prices. Now copy the function from C15 to cells C16 through C25 (drag to fill).

Before entering the function for the extended price in column E, name columns C and D "Price" and "Qty", respectively, using Formula ➤ Create Names. Now enter the extended price function in E15:

=IF(AND(A15<>0,Qty<>0),Price*Qty," ")

Copy this down through to cell E25 (or drag to fill).

Now add the following tax table in rows 46–48 of the worksheet:

	B	C
46	TAX TABLE	
47	A	6.50%
48	B	7.00%

Cell E5 determines which tax rate to use to calculate the tax in E27. The final formulas to enter are listed below:

CELL	FORMULA
E26	=SUM(E15:E25)
E27	=LOOKUP($E$5,$B$47:$B$48,$C$47:$C$48)*E26
E28	=E26+E27

Now set the alignment, style, and formats for the cells as desired. You should see the worksheet shown in Figure 22.4.

	A	B	C	D	E
1		INVOICE			
2					
3	Remit to:			Date:	6/25/92
4	ABC Health Products			Invoice #:	4023
5	48 Midway Lane			Tax Code:	B
6	Berkeley, CA 94702			Terms:	A
7					
8					
9	Sold to:	John Albert	Ship to:	John Albert	
10		34 Shady Lane		34 Shady Lane	
11		Berkeley, CA 94702		Berkeley, CA 94702	
12					
13					
14	Item #	Description	Price	Qty	Ext Price
15	20143	Iron	$5.10	1	$5.10
16	20083	Vitamin C S/R 500	$4.60	2	$9.20
17	20810	EPA	$12.75	1	$12.75
18					
19					
20					
21					
22					
23					
24					
25					
26				Subtotal	$27.05
27				Tax	$1.89
28				Grand Total	$28.94
29					
30					
31					
32					
33					
34					
35					
36					
37					
38					
39					
40					
41					
42					
43					
44					
45					

FIGURE 22.4:

The final invoice worksheet

Select Format ➤ Borders to set the borders. (You can see the borders more easily by using Options ➤ Display to turn off the gridlines.) Finally, use Page Setup to turn off the row and column headings as well as the gridlines on the printed invoice. Print the document. The resulting invoice should look like Figure 22.2.

IMPROVING YOUR INVOICING SYSTEM

This invoicing system is really just a starting point for designing any type of invoice system to meet your needs. A few possible enhancements are listed below:

◆ You could add a backorder system, checking the quantity ordered against the quantity in inventory.

◆ You could add features to modify the inventory on shipping, keeping the quantities in inventory updated automatically.

◆ You could use the database as a true database, using forms to fill in the invoice cells (see Part III) and eliminating the need to keep the database records sorted.

◆ You could enter the addresses from a database of customers.

◆ You could use the NOW function to automatically enter the date.

FAST TRACK CHAPTER 23

CHAPTER 23

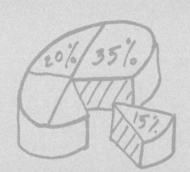

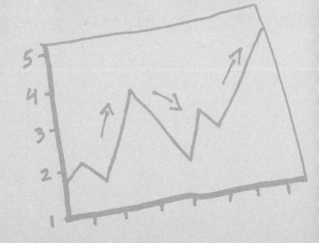

Performing Financial Management

One of the most important applications of any worksheet program is financial management. Using Excel, you can calculate loan payments, make decisions about purchasing or selling investments, and compare investment returns. This chapter will introduce you to Excel's seven basic financial functions: PV, NPV, FV, PMT, RATE, IRR, and MIRR. In almost any business environment today, the knowledge of how to use these types of financial calculations is essential for the success of the business.

THE PRESENT-VALUE FUNCTION

The present-value function, PV, is used to calculate the present value of the return over time, on an investment. This is useful for evaluating a potential investment.

As an example, suppose you have $5000 to invest. A friend offers you an investment plan for your $5000 that will pay $1500 a year, at the end of each year, for the next five years. Would you take it?

To figure out whether this is a worthwhile investment, you need to compute the present value of the return your friend will give you. The general formula in Excel for this calculation is

=PV(*rate, number_of_ periods, payment, future_value, type*)

(The future value and type are optional.) For the moment, let's ignore the last two arguments, because they are not needed for the example. We need to assume an interest rate for projecting the investment back to the present. Let's assume that nine percent is the current money-market rate at the bank. There are five periods, and the payments are $1500. So you need to set up the following equation (see also Figure 23.1):

=PV(9%,5,1500)

This returns −5834, or $5834, which is the present value of the annual payments. This means that if you were to put the $1500 payments in a bank that paid nine percent interest, you'd end up with the same amount ($8975) as that paid by a bank on a one-time deposit of $5834. Since you are only investing $5000, your friend is offering you a good deal (or at least a better deal

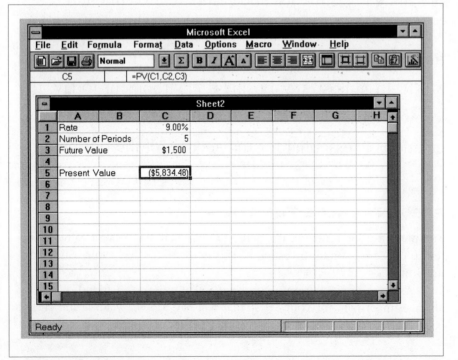

FIGURE 23.1:

The worksheet to calculate the present value

than the bank can offer you). The result of the PV function is negative because it represents money that you would *pay*.

NOTE
NOTE
Be sure the interest rate corresponds to the payment period. If you have x payments at semiannual intervals, make sure you use a semiannual interest rate.

The present value of an investment depends on three factors: the interest rate, the number of periods, and the amount of the payment. The number of periods and the payment values are normally fixed. The interest rate, however, is a variable you can assume. For practical purposes, you generally use the best rate that you could get at the bank. It is the hurdle over which the investment must leap before it becomes attractive, and so is often called the *hurdle rate*.

Now suppose your friend offers you a different plan. Instead of $1500 for each of five years, you could get $8500 at the end of the five years for the initial $5000 investment. Is it still a good deal? Is it better or worse than the last deal?

Now you don't have a payment, but you do have a future value. The interest and the number of periods is the same (note that an extra comma must be inserted to indicate a missing argument):

=PV(9%,5,,8500)

This time the result is −5524. This means that at a nine percent interest, you should be willing to invest $5524 now to get $8500 in five years. Since we only have to invest $5000, it is still a good deal. It is not as good as the last offer, but it is still acceptable.

The *type* argument in the PV function is a flag that indicates whether the payments are made at the beginning or end of the period. If *type* is 1, the payments occur at the beginning of the period. If *type* is 0, the payments are at the end of the period. If the argument is omitted, *type* assumes a default value of 0, and payments are assumed to be at the end of the period.

THE NET-PRESENT-VALUE FUNCTION

NOTE
NOTE
The NPV function assumes the payment is at the end of the period. You can't change this.

The net-present-value function, NPV, is similar to the present-value function, except that it permits the user to assume unequal payments. If the function returns a value of zero or greater, the investment is considered a good one.

The general form of the function is

=NPV(*rate, inflow 1, inflow 2,... inflow n*)

(The *inflow 2,... inflow* portion is optional.) Let's return to the original problem. The initial investment is an outflow, so it must be represented as a negative number. The returns in subsequent years would be inflows as shown below:

=NPV(9%,–5000,1500,1500,1500,1500,1500)

This returns a value of $766. In using this function, an investment is assumed acceptable if the result is greater than zero. Since this value is greater than zero, the investment is acceptable. Unfortunately, however, this is not the correct answer! The NPV function assumes that all payments are evenly distributed and made at the end of the period. The first cash flow—the initial investment—is assumed to occur one time period from today. Here, the initial inflow (the –$5000) is made at the beginning of the first period. To adjust for this, subtract the initial investment, as shown below, instead of including it as an inflow:

=NPV(9%,1500,1500,1500,1500,1500)–5000

This gives a result of $834, which is the correct value. This is the most common way to use the NPV function: using the payback values as the inflow values and subtracting the initial investment.

Now you can try it with unequal payments. Assume you still invest $5000, but the return is $1000 the first year, $1600 the next two years, $1700 the next year, and $1800 the last year. To solve this, create a new worksheet and store the return values in cells A1 through A5. You can then use the following calculation in A6:

=NPV(9%,A1:A5)–5000

This returns $873, which indicates that this is a better investment than the fixed payment schedule, as $873 > $834. The inflow arguments represent cash coming back, and, in this case, are positive. You can use positive or negative values for the outflow arguments. For example, if you pay out more cash later, you can use a negative outflow value for that period.

THE FUTURE-VALUE FUNCTION

The future-value function, FV, is used to calculate the future value of an investment. It is, therefore, the opposite of PV and NPV. For example, if you are making payments into an IRA or Keogh account, the FV function will tell you the future value of that account.

The general form of the FV function is

=FV(*rate, number_of_ periods, payment, present_value, type*)

where *rate* is the interest rate, *number_of_ periods* is the number of payments, and *payment* is how much you pay each time. The last two arguments are optional and will be explained later.

Now let's try an example. Assume you are 48 years old and begin an IRA in which you invest $4000 a year. How much will you have when you are 65? The number of payments is 65 − 48, or 17. Assume an interest rate of 11 percent. The equation becomes

=FV(11%,17,−4000)

which returns a value of $178,003.

Because there is no *type* argument in this example, the above calculation assumes a default value of zero, which means that the payments come at the end of the period. If the payments are at the beginning of the period (i.e., you're making your first today), you must set up the equation as follows:

=FV(11%,17,−4000,,1)

With this kind of payment schedule, you will have $197,584 if you take it out when you are 65.

You can use the fourth argument (*present_value*) to indicate a lump-sum investment when two payments are used. For example, if you were creating an IRA with a $5000 investment and you planned no further payments, you would use the following equation:

=FV(11%,17,,−5000,1)

This IRA account would return $29,475 when you reached 65.

You also can combine an initial fixed investment with later payments, as in the following equation

=FV(11%,17,−4000,−5000,0)

which returns $227,059. The $5000 is the lump-sum amount.

THE PAYMENT FUNCTION

Be sure that, if monthly periods are used, you convert the annual interest to monthly interest and convert the years for the payments to months.

The payment function, PMT, is useful for calculating the payments required to amortize a loan. This is useful when you are borrowing money for a car or house and you want to calculate the payments you can expect. The general form is as follows (with the last two arguments optional):

=PMT(*rate, number_of_ periods, present_value, future_value, type*)

For example, assume you are purchasing a $12,000 car at 11 percent interest. Payments are monthly for a five-year period. The resulting formula is

=PMT(11%/12,5*12,12000)

which results in a monthly payment of $261. There are 60 payments (5 × 12), and the monthly interest for each payment period is 11 percent divided by 12. You can find a more extensive example of this function in the amortization worksheet of Chapter 8.

Again, the *type* argument indicates whether the payments are at the beginning or end of the period.

CALCULATING THE RATE OF RETURN

Sometimes you want to do an inversion of the previous formulas; that is, you want to calculate the rate of return and then compare this rate with the rate of return of other investments. Excel provides three functions for calculating the rate of return.

THE RATE FUNCTION

Assume you are back to the initial problem of lending $5000 with a return of $1500 for the next five years. This time you wish to calculate the rate of return for this investment. This would be the percentage for which the NPV is equal to zero. You need to use the RATE function. The general form for this function is as follows (the last three arguments are optional):

=RATE(*number_of_ periods, payment, present_value, future_value, type, guess*)

For this example you have

=RATE(5,1500,–5000)

which returns a value of 15.24 percent—quite a good investment.

The *future_value* argument is used to indicate a lump-sum return. For example, if instead of yearly payments you would receive $8500 at the end of five years, the formula would become

=RATE(5,,–5000,8500)

yielding a 11.20 percent return. This is not as good as the previous plan.

Excel uses an iterative process to calculate the rate using a net present-value function. The *guess* argument is used to define a starting point for calculating the interest. Omit the value when starting. If you get a *#NUM!* returned from the function, try using a *guess* argument as a starting point for the calculations. (It should be a percent.)

THE IRR FUNCTION

The IRR function, like RATE, is used to calculate the rate of return on an investment. Use it to compare different investments and see which one may be the best. IRR is different from RATE in that it can be used with uneven payments (like NPV). The general form is as follows (*guess* is optional):

=IRR(*values, guess*)

Notice that there is only one argument for values. The trick is to put the values as a range on the worksheet. *Values* is an array or reference to cells that contain the numbers for which you wish to calculate the internal rate of return. *Guess* is a number that you guess is close to the IRR. The first value in the range is normally negative, indicating the initial payment or investment.

If A1 contains –5000 and each cell from A2 through A6 contains 1500, the formula becomes

=IRR(A1:A6)

and returns 15.24 percent, as before. You can now change any payment value, and see the resulting change in the rate of return. You can even make them all zero except the last one, setting the last payment to $8500. That will give you 11.20 percent, the same as in the previous example.

The internal rate of return calculated by RATE or IRR is a commonly used financial statistic. Like the net present value (NPV), you can use it to compare financial investments. In the section on the NPV, you learned that an attractive investment is one in which the net present value, discounted at a specified hurdle rate, gives an NPV of zero or greater. The IRR and RATE functions turn this around: in essence, the internal rate of return is that value for which the NPV is zero.

THE MIRR FUNCTION

The MIRR function gives a modified rate of return of a series of cash flows. The general form is

=MIRR(*values, safe, risky*)

For example, assume you invest $5000 to finance an investment that will return $1400 a year for the next five years. Use the IRR function by entering −5000 in cell A1 and $1400 in cells A2 through A6. Calculate the rate of return as follows:

=IRR(A1:A6)

This results in 12.38 percent. If the returned money is reinvested at a rate of 10 percent, use the MIRR function:

=MIRR(A1:A6,9%,10%)

which yields 11.32 percent. The first argument is the range of values, the second is the interest you pay for the borrowed money, and the third is the interest you will earn when you reinvest your inflows.

FAST TRACK CHAPTER 24

CHAPTER 24

Analyzing Trends and Relationships

E xcel can be very useful when you need to predict future data based on historical trends and when you want to explore the relationships between variables. Below are some examples:

◆ A company has tracked sales for several years and wishes to use these data to predict sales in future years.

◆ A city is planning for city roads and wishes to predict future automotive traffic on certain roads based on historical data (traffic records).

◆ An environmental agency has obtained some data on the local increase in certain types of cancer and the change in air quality in several areas. The agency wishes to calculate the degree of relatedness of cancer rates with the various air-quality variables.

◆ Educational leaders have tracked the number of local students for several years and wish to use their data to project education resource needs for the future.

Predicting future data from current data is called *regression analysis*. Analyzing the relationship of variables is *correlation analysis*. This chapter will look at how you can do both with Excel.

REGRESSION ANALYSIS

The basic goal for any type of regression analysis is to estimate one variable based on one or more related variables. Chapter 15 presented a simple regression analysis. Let's now look at more specific aspects of this type of analysis.

LINEAR REGRESSION

One variable is said to be *linearly related* to another if an increase or decrease in one causes a proportional increase or decrease in the other. As an example, let's assume we have accumulated 14 years of sales data for a company, shown in Table 24.1.

YEAR	SALES ($100K)	YEAR	SALES ($100K)
1	6.50	8	60.10
2	14.20	9	64.10
3	23.50	10	65.60
4	30.10	11	68.80
5	38.80	12	68.90
6	48.40	13	68.80
7	55.50	14	70.20

TABLE 24.1:

Fourteen Years of Sales Data for a Company

For this example the y variable is the sales total, and the x variable is the year. We wish to estimate the value of y corresponding to the x values 15, 16, 17, and 18 (i.e., the next four years). Once you have estimated these values, you can estimate budget values for employment levels, inventory, and the warehouse.

As a start, assume a linear relationship. If this is true, an equation can be found that approximately fits the data of the form:

$$y = a_0 + a_1 x$$

You now need to solve for the values of a_0 and a_1. The resulting curve is said to be the *regression curve* of y on x, as y is estimated from x; that is, can be graphed as a straight line function of x.

These constant values can be solved easily with Excel using the LINEST function. The function has two input arguments: the array of y values and the array of x values. It returns an array of two values: a_0 and a_1.

The worksheet for this example is shown in Figure 24.1. Enter the values for A8 to A25 and B8 to B21 as shown. The array function is entered into A31 and B31 as follows:

1. Select A31 and B31.

2. Enter the following equation in the formula bar:

=LINEST(B8:B21,A8:A21)

	A	B	C
2			
3		LINEAR REGRESSION	
4			
5			
6			
7	YEAR	ACTUAL	PREDICTED
8	1	$6.50	$16.05
9	2	$14.20	$21.09
10	3	$23.50	$26.13
11	4	$30.10	$31.18
12	5	$38.80	$36.22
13	6	$48.40	$41.26
14	7	$55.50	$46.30
15	8	$60.10	$51.34
16	9	$64.10	$56.38
17	10	$65.60	$61.43
18	11	$68.80	$66.47
19	12	$68.90	$71.51
20	13	$68.80	$76.55
21	14	$70.20	$81.59
22	15		$86.63
23	16		$91.67
24	17		$96.72
25	18		$101.76
26			
27			
28			
29			
30	SLOPE	INTERCEPT	
31	5.041538	11.0098901	

FIGURE 24.1:

The worksheet for the linear regression

3. Hold down the Ctrl and Shift keys while pressing Enter to enter the function as an array.

The slope of the line should now be in A31 and the y intercept in B31.

Now enter the formula for the first predicted value in C8 as follows:

=$B$31+$A$31*A8

Copy this formula to cells C9 to C25 (Fill Down). This should give you the array of predicted values in column C.

You now need to calculate the *r-squared value*. This is the number that indicates how well the line fits the data points. The general equation for this value is

$$r^2 = \frac{\Sigma(Y_{est} - Y_{avg})^2}{\Sigma(Y - Y_{avg})^2}$$

You can use the worksheet to calculate this by creating a column for each sum and entering the following equations in the first cell for each:

COLUMN	TITLE	EQUATION
D	(Y−Yavg)^2	=(B8−$B$28)^2
E	(Yest−Yavg)^2	=(C8−$B$28)^2

The columnar sums are stored in row 27 (cell B27 contains *=SUM(B8:B21)*). The average ($B$28) is calculated in column B as the total of that column divided by the number of points in the array (i.e., B27/14). The closer the *r*-squared value comes to 1, the better the fit of the data to the linear equation represented by the array function. The *r*-squared value in cell D31 is then E27/D27, or 0.89966, which represents a good fit (Figure 24.2).

There is another and simpler method of calculating this *r*-squared value. There should be a linear-regression line such that

$$x = b_0 + b_1 y$$

This is the regression curve of x on y. You can use the LINEST function to calculate b_0 and b_1 by simply reversing the arguments in the function used earlier. The *r*-squared value can then be calculated as follows:

1. Store LINEST(A8:A21,B8:B21) in A33:B33.

2. Store A31*A33 in A36.

A36 returns r^2 as .899663.

	A	B	C	D	E
1					
2					
3		LINEAR REGRESSION			
4					
5					
6					
7	YEAR	ACTUAL	PREDICTED	(Y-Yavg)^2	(Yest-Yavg)^
8	1	$6.50	$16.05	1791.10332	1073.8729
9	2	$14.20	$21.09	1198.64332	768.8675793
10	3	$23.50	$26.13	641.174745	514.6964787
11	4	$30.10	$31.18	350.491888	311.3595982
12	5	$38.80	$36.22	100.429031	158.8569379
13	6	$48.40	$41.26	0.17760204	57.18849763
14	7	$55.50	$46.30	44.6033163	6.354277515
15	8	$60.10	$51.34	127.206173	6.354277515
16	9	$64.10	$56.38	233.434745	57.18849763
17	10	$65.60	$61.43	281.520459	158.8569379
18	11	$68.80	$66.47	399.143316	311.3595982
19	12	$68.90	$71.51	403.149031	514.6964787
20	13	$68.80	$76.55	399.143316	768.8675793
21	14	$70.20	$81.59	457.043316	1073.8729
22	15		$86.63		
23	16		$91.67		
24	17		$96.72		
25	18		$101.76		
26					
27	SUM	683.50		6427.26	5782.39
28	AVERAGE	48.8214286			
29					
30	SLOPE	INTERCEPT		R squared	
31	5.0415385	11.0098901		0.89966632	
32					

FIGURE 24.2:

Calculating the r-squared value by averaging the values in columns D and E and determining their quotient

Now chart the two data series (actual and predicted) using the following technique:

1. Select B8 to B21 on the worksheet.

2. Create a new chart and use the Gallery menu to make it a line chart.

3. Select the first option on the Chart Gallery dialog box.

4. On the worksheet, select C8 to C25.

5. Copy the series to the Clipboard.

6. Select the chart and paste the series to the chart.

7. Add axis labels and a chart title as desired, using Chart ➤ Attach Text. Format the markers using Format ➤ Patterns.

You should see the graph shown in Figure 24.3. Notice that the points are very close to the line predicted by the linear regression equation, but the scattering of the actual points about the line is not random. Those in the middle are above the line and those at the end are below the line. The curve of the actual sales line indicates that sales predicted by this linear regression are higher than could realistically be expected from looking at the data for the last few years. This suggests a curved line probably would be a better fit. This alternative will be examined in the next section.

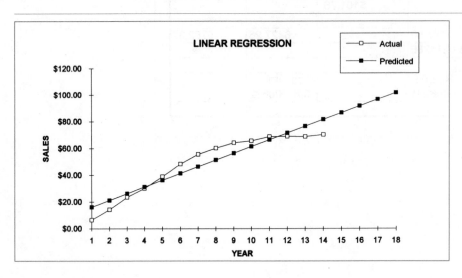

FIGURE 24.3:

The linear regression chart

The TREND function is similar to the LINEST function, except that it returns the actual array of values. For example, you could select C8:C21 as an array, then enter *=TREND(B8:B21,A8:A21)* as an array by holding down the Ctrl and Shift keys while pressing Enter. You will get the same predicted values.

EXPONENTIAL REGRESSION

The same worksheet can be modified easily for an *exponential regression*. The LINEST function in row 31 is changed to a LOGEST function. The arguments remain the same:

={LOGEST(B8:B21,A8:A21)}

The equation in C8 is changed to

=$B$31*$A$31^A8

This is then copied down column C. Our predicted sales values are now even higher (Figure 24.4), but are they realistic?

The chart shown in Figure 24.5 shows the new predictions. The predicted sales look good, but do not match up with what could be expected realistically. The actual sales are fairly steady over the last few years. The exponential curve predicts growth that clearly does not fit the data too well. Sometimes (as with population growth curves), however, an exponential regression can be quite realistic. The r^2 value is now .425. Use the full form of the function to get this value—not the former equation. Use:

LOGEST (B8:B21,A8:A21,TRUE,TRUE)

CURVILINEAR REGRESSION

In the real world, you can often accomplish a good fit by extending the linear regression to include additional terms as necessary:

$$y = a_0 + a_1x + a_2x^2 + a_3x^3 + a_ix^i + \ldots + a_nx^n$$

	A	B	C
1			
2			
3		**EXPONENTIAL REGRESSIO**	
4			
5			
6			
7	**YEAR**	**ACTUAL**	**PREDICTED**
8	1	$6.50	$15.72
9	2	$14.20	$18.22
10	3	$23.50	$21.13
11	4	$30.10	$24.50
12	5	$38.80	$28.40
13	6	$48.40	$32.93
14	7	$55.50	$38.18
15	8	$60.10	$44.27
16	9	$64.10	$51.32
17	10	$65.60	$59.50
18	11	$68.80	$68.99
19	12	$68.90	$79.99
20	13	$68.80	$92.74
21	14	$70.20	$107.53
22	15		$124.67
23	16		$144.55
24	17		$167.60
25	18		$194.32
26			
27	SUM	683.50	
28	AVERAGE	48.8214286	
29			
30	SLOPE	INTERCEPT	
31	1.1594303	13.555215	
32			

FIGURE 24.4:
Predicted sales using the LOGEST function, higher than they were for the LINEST function

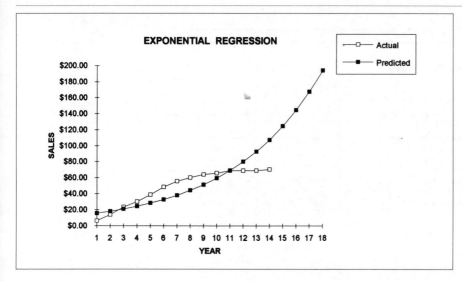

This is the general form for a *curvilinear regression,* or a regression in which a curved line that fits the data points is calculated. The calculations aren't for the faint of heart, but the rewards are often well worth including at least the a^2 term, giving a polynomial regression. There is no general function that creates the constants for the equation, so you must calculate them using the following equations:

$$\Sigma Y = a_0 n + a_1 \Sigma X + a_2 \Sigma X^2$$

$$\Sigma XY = a_0 \Sigma X + a_1 X^2 + a_2 \Sigma X^3$$

$$\Sigma X^2 Y = a_0 \Sigma X^2 + a_1 \Sigma X^3 + a_2 \Sigma X^4$$

The worksheet used to calculate the various coefficients and the resulting *r*-squared value is shown in Figure 24.6. This gives the following equations:

$$683.5 = 14a_0 + 105a_1 + 1015a_2$$

$$6273.2 = 105a_0 + 1015a_1 + 11025a_2$$

$$65419.6 = 1015a_0 + 11025a_1 + 127687a_2$$

	A	B	C	D	E	F	G	H	I	J
1										
2										
3		POLYNOMIAL REGRESSION								
4										
5	Degrees of freedom		14							
6										
7	YEAR	ACTUAL	PREDI	X^2	X^3	X^4	XY	X^2 * Y	(Y-Yavg	(Yest-Y
8	1	$6.50	$4.10	1	1	1	6.5	6.5	1791.1	1999.9
9	2	$14.20	$14.66	4	8	16	28.4	56.8	1198.6	1167.1
10	3	$23.50	$24.30	9	27	81	70.5	211.5	641.17	601.49
11	4	$30.10	$33.01	16	64	256	120.4	481.6	350.49	249.86
12	5	$38.80	$40.81	25	125	625	194	970	100.43	64.123
13	6	$48.40	$47.69	36	216	1296	290.4	1742.4	0.1776	1.2717
14	7	$55.50	$53.65	49	343	2401	388.5	2719.5	44.603	23.359
15	8	$60.10	$58.70	64	512	4096	480.8	3846.4	127.21	97.508
16	9	$64.10	$62.82	81	729	6561	576.9	5192.1	233.43	195.91
17	10	$65.60	$66.02	100	1000	10000	656	6560	281.52	295.84
18	11	$68.80	$68.31	121	1331	14641	756.8	8324.8	399.14	379.62
19	12	$68.90	$69.67	144	1728	20736	826.8	9921.6	403.15	434.66
20	13	$68.80	$70.12	169	2197	28561	894.4	11627	399.14	453.43
21	14	$70.20	$69.64	196	2744	38416	982.8	13759	457.04	433.47
22	15		$68.25							
23	16		$65.94							
24	17		$62.70							
25	18		$58.55							
26										
27	105	683.5	683.5	1015		11025	1E+05	6273.2	65420	6427.3	6397.5
28		$49								
29										
30	SLOPE	INTERCEPT		683.5 =		14	105	1015		
31	5.04153846	11.0098901		6273.2 =		105	1015	11025		
32				65420 =		1015	11025	127687		
33	0.17845075	-1.2122205								
34				a1=	11.93576923		Solve for a0			
35				a2=	-0.459615385		6607.2	135.33	1015	9811.7
36	0.89966632			a0=	-7.374725275		6273.2	105	1015	11025
37							----------	----------	----------	----------
38	R-SQUARED	0.99537567				#1	333.97	30.333		-1213
39										
40							68140	1140.5	11025	119754
41							65420	1015	11025	127687
42							----------	----------	----------	----------
43						#2	2720.3	125.52		-7933
44										
45						Mod of	2183.5	198.32		-7933
46							----------	----------	----------	----------
47							536.88	-72.8		
48										
49							Solve for a2			
50						Mod of	1381.9	125.52		-5021
51						#2	2720.3	125.52		-7933
52							----------	----------	----------	----------
53							-1338			2912

FIGURE 24.6:

The polynomial regression worksheet

These can be solved to get the following constants:

$$a_0 = -7.3747253$$
$$a_1 = 11.9357692$$
$$a_2 = -0.4596154$$

The following equation is then used in column C to find the predicted values:

$$y = a_0 + a_1 x + a_2 x^2$$

The r-squared value is solved the same way as it is with linear regression. Notice that the r-squared value is now close to 0.995, an extremely good fit.

Here are the column definitions that you should enter:

ROW	TITLE	FIRST CELL EQUATION
A	YEAR	
B	ACTUAL	(entered)
C	PREDICTED	=$E$36+$E$34*A8+$E$35*A8*A8
D	X^2	=A8*A8
E	X^3	=A8^3
F	X^4	=A8^4
G	XY	=A8*B8
H	X^2*Y	=A8*A8*B8
I	(Y–Yavg)^2	=(B8-$B$28)^2
J	(Yest–Yavg)^2	=(C8-$B$28)^2

The resulting constants are calculated and stored as follows:

CELL	CONSTANT
E34	a_1
E35	a_2
E36	a_0

Here are some of the formulas to enter in the worksheet. Some of the equations are shown in Figure 24.7. Row 27, as before, contains the following sums:

Curvilinear Equation Cell Values

CELL	FORMULA
D30	=B27
F30	=C5
G30	=A27
H30	=D27
D31	=G27
F31	=A27
G31	=D27
H31	=E27
D32	=H27
F32	=D27
G32	=E27
H32	=F27

Solving for the a_0 Constant

CELL	FORMULA
G35	=D30*G31/G30
H35	=F30*G31/G30
I35	=G30*G31/G30
J35	=H30*G31/G30
G36	=D31
H36	=F31
I36	=G31

A	B	C	D	E	F	G	H	I	J
=SUM(A8:A21)	=SUM(B8:B21)	=SUM(C8:C21)	=SUM(D8:D21)	=SUM(E8:E21)	=SUM(F8:F21)	=SUM(G8:G21)	=SUM(H8:H21)	=SUM(I8:I21)	=SUM(J8:J21)
	=B27/C5								
SLOPE	INTERCEPT			=	=C5	=A27	=D27		
=LINEST(B8:B21,A8:A21)	=LINEST(B8:B21,A8:A21)		=B27	=	=A27	=D27	=E27		
=LINEST(A8:A21,B8:B21)	=LINEST(A8:A21,B8:B21)		=G27	=	=D27	=E27	=F27		
			=H27			Solve for a0			
=A31*A33			a1=	=(D30-F30*E36-H30*E35)/G30		=D30*G31/G30	=F30*G31/G30	=G30*G31/G30	=H30*G31/G30
			a2=	=G53/J53		=D31	=F31	=G31	=H31
R-SQUARED=	=J27/I27		a0=	=G47/H47	#1	=G35-G36	=H35-H36		=J35-J36
						=D31*G32/G31	=F31*G32/G31	=G31*G32/G31	=H31*G32/G31
						=D32	=F32	=G32	=H32
					#2	=G40-G41	=H40-H41		=J40-J41
					Mod of #1	=G38*J43/J38	=H38*J43/J38		=J38*J43/J38
						=G43-G45	=H43-H45		
						Solve for a2			
					Mod of #1	=G38*H43/H38	=G38*H43/H38		=J38*H43/H38
					#2	=G43	=H43		=J43
						=G50-G51			=J50-J51

FIGURE 24.7:
The curvilinear regression equations in their cells

CELL	FORMULA
J36	=H31
G38	=G35–G36
H38	=H35–H36
J38	=J35–J36

The actual list is much longer than this, but there is nothing unusual in the calculations. You can use normal algebraic methods to solve for the matrix variables.

Figure 24.8 shows the chart of the polynomial regression. Notice that the curve is now a very good fit, but the sales projections are not as good. The projections actually show a dip in sales. This indicates management should begin to take some action to turn things around.

It is a good idea to use cell references instead of numbers when creating the formulas to solve the equations for the constants. This enables the worksheet to function as a template for other polynomial regressions. For example, the number of samples is stored in C5, permitting it to be used in B28 to calculate the average. This way, you don't have to remember to adjust C5 if rows are inserted or deleted.

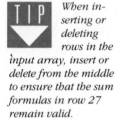

When inserting or deleting rows in the input array, insert or delete from the middle to ensure that the sum formulas in row 27 remain valid.

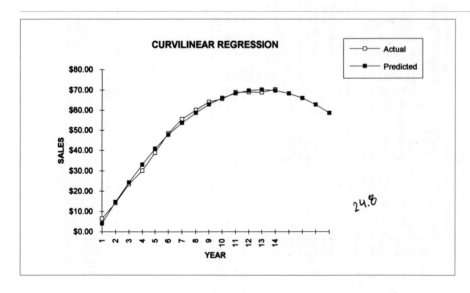

FIGURE 24.8:

The curvilinear regression chart. This time the actual and predicted sales match very well

You can simplify your work in solving for the constants by modifying the x array so that the sum is 0. For a 15-element array, you would start at −7. For example, instead of using the values 1 to 15 for the year, use −7 to 7. The second equation can then be solved directly for a_1. There are then only two unknowns, and the other two equations can be solved for the other two constants.

CORRELATION ANALYSIS

In *correlation analysis,* you try to discover how well an equation describes the relationship between two variables. The problem is closely related to regression analysis. In regression analysis, you try to find a curve that fits the data; in correlation analysis, you are measuring how well the curve fits the data. Indeed, you have already calculated the r-squared value for the examples of this chapter. In correlation analysis, this is called the *coefficient of determination.* The square root of this value is the *coefficient of correlation,* or the measure of the fit of the curve. The value can vary from 0 (no correlation) to 1 (perfect correlation). The general equation for r squared (the coefficient of determination) is the same as in the previous sections:

$$r^2 = \frac{\Sigma(Y_{est} - Y_{avg})^2}{\Sigma(Y - Y_{avg})^2}$$

As an example, assume you want to find how much correlation there is between the height of a father and the height of his oldest son. To simplify your work, assume a sample of 14 father-son pairs. Figure 24.9 shows this sample in a worksheet. The fathers are shown as the x array, the sons as the y array.

The basic worksheet is similar to the earlier examples. The A26:B26 cells contain the array *LINEST(B7:B20,A7:A20)*. The sums are in row 22. The r-squared value is calculated as E22/C22. The coefficient of correlation is the square root of this, or 0.7668.

You also can calculate an error of estimate with the following equation:

SQRT(SUM((Y−Yest)^2)/N)

In this case, the error of estimate is 1.4899 inches. If the sample is large enough, 68 percent of the sample will fall within 1.4899 inches of the regression line. You also will find 95 percent of the sample within twice this distance and 99.7 percent within three times this distance.

Before charting this, be sure the category column is in ascending order. Here the data were entered in order. If you must sort, select rows 7 to 20. Then

	A	B	C	D	E	F
1						
2		**CORRELATION ANALYSIS**				
3						
4	Degrees of freedom=		14			
5						
6	X	Y	(Y-Yavg)^2	PREDICTE	(Yest-Yavg)	(Y-Yest)^2
7	62	66	2.93877551	65.0803571	6.93757972	0.84574298
8	63	66	2.93877551	65.6071429	4.44005102	0.15433673
9	64	65	7.36734694	66.1339286	2.4975287	1.28579401
10	65	68	0.08163265	66.6607143	1.11001276	1.79368622
11	66	65	7.36734694	67.1875	0.27750319	4.78515625
12	66	66	2.93877551	67.1875	0.27750319	1.41015625
13	67	68	0.08163265	67.7142857	0	0.08163265
14	67	67	0.51020408	67.7142857	0	0.51020408
15	68	69	1.65306122	68.2410714	0.27750319	0.57597258
16	68	71	10.7959184	68.2410714	0.27750319	7.61168686
17	69	68	0.08163265	68.7678571	1.11001276	0.58960459
18	70	68	0.08163265	69.2946429	2.4975287	1.67610013
19	71	70	5.2244898	69.8214286	4.44005102	0.03188776
20	72	71	10.7959184	70.3482143	6.93757972	0.42482462
21						
22	938	948	52.8571429		31.0803571	
23		67.7142857				
24						
25	SLOPE	INTERCEPT		Err of Est	1.489975	
26	0.52678571	32.4196429		R SQUARE	0.58800676	
27				R	0.76681599	
28	0.52678571	32.4196429				

select Data ➤ Sort and click OK. The values in column A should now be in ascending order. All the rows should have been sorted.

To chart this, select A7:B20. Then select Edit ➤ Copy. Open a new chart. The chart area will be blank. Select Edit ➤ Paste Special. Choose Categories (X Labels) in First Column and click OK. This will create the first-level graph. Use the Gallery menu to change it to an XY scatter graph of the first type. Set each data series to start at 61 by selecting each axis in turn and using Format ➤ Scale and entering **61** in the Minimum text box.

Now add the second data series. Select D7:D20 on the worksheet and copy it to the Clipboard. This time use the Paste command to add it to the chart. Open the Chart menu and choose Add Overlay. Use Format ➤ Overlay, if necessary, to change the overlay to a line chart. This will give you a regression line that passes through the scattered points. Add labels and the resulting graph should look like Figure 24.10. The graph indicates a definite correlation between the height of a father and his oldest son.

The regression analysis only finds a mathematical equation that approximates the existing data. There is no guarantee that future points will fall on the line. The equation defines an observed relationship between two variables. Here are some issues to consider:

◆ There may really be no relationship between the variables. The observed relationship could be strictly by chance.

◆ The two variables may be two effects of a single cause. For instance, although there may appear to be a positive relationship between local smog and cancer rates, in reality, both factors may be the effects of a single cause—for example, a nearby corporation that produces a pollutant which causes both the smog and cancer.

◆ There may be other causes to consider. Historical data can be used to predict highway traffic in the future for an area. But if a new shopping center is built nearby, don't expect the same equations to work.

Excel can be used to analyze trends and perform both regression and correlation analysis. Although linear and exponential regression can be done with Excel's built-in functions, curvilinear regression and correlation analysis require the use of formulas.

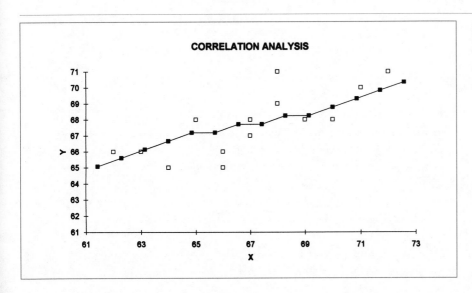

FIGURE 24.10:

Chart of the correlation analysis of father-son heights

FAST TRACK CHAPTER 25

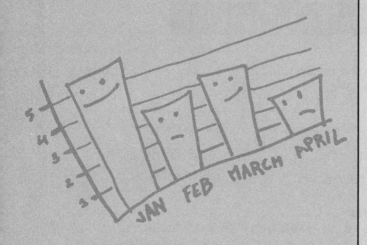

CHAPTER 25

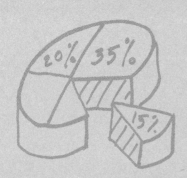

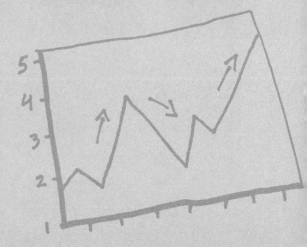

Data Analysis: Using the Q+E and Add-In Utilities

xcel provides a number of add-in utilities for data analysis. In this chapter we will look at the Q+E manager for external databases, what-if analysis using the Solver and Scenario Manager, and the Analysis Tool.

USING Q+E FOR WINDOWS

Q+E (for "Query and Edit") is a Windows application for managing databases. You can use it with dBASE (II, III, and IV), text files, SQL, Oracle, OS/2 Extended Edition, and Excel worksheet files with databases defined.

Excel performs some level of database management, but Q+E can simplify some tasks and do a few things that Excel can't. Use Q+E with Excel when you wish to:

◆ use an Excel worksheet with external databases

◆ query database files that are linked on common fields

◆ process mailing labels

◆ link databases with other documents

For the examples in this chapter, we will use Q+E with dBASE files. You won't need dBASE for the examples, however, since you can create dBASE files with Excel.

OPENING AN EXISTING DATABASE FILE

To explore Q+E, you can use an existing database file or a worksheet with a database. Create a dBASE file from your sales worksheet. Open SALES in Excel and define the database to include cells A13 through E28. (Use Data ➤ Set Database.) Save the file as SALES.DBF, first using Save File as Type in the File Save As dialog box to save it as a dBASE III (.DBF3) or IV (.DBF4) file. Now minimize Excel to get it out of the way for the moment.

Start Q+E by double-clicking the Q+E icon in the Excel 4 group window in the File Manager. Q+E will start and display the blank startup screen. There are two menu options, File and Help, at the extremes of the menu bar.

Choose File ➤ Open. In the Open dialog box, choose the database name to open. Be sure the source is a dBASE File. Select SALES.DBF and click the Options button. In the Options dialog box, be sure IBM PC is selected as the file character set. Click OK twice to back out of the dialog boxes. The database will open and be displayed (see Figure 25.1). If you wish, you can use Layout ➤ Font to change the font.

Notice that the database is displayed in a query window (Query1). The title bar indicates that this is a query and displays the query file name. The database name appears in brackets.

With Q+E, you are working with *two* kinds of files: database files and query files. The database file has the data for the queries. The query file defines the database(s) that is used and determines how the data are to be displayed. You can have several query files for a single database or several databases for a single query file. So far, you have opened a single database file. You are starting to create a query window, which eventually will be saved as a query file.

The menu has changed to show the various options:

File opens and closes the database, opens and saves query files, creates new database files, saves queries (and database structures when creating files), and prints query results.

Edit edits, moves, and copies data and adds and deletes fields and records.

Sort sorts records in a query.

Select chooses records from a database that meet a specific condition.

The Help menu is always available for online help. As in Excel, you also can get help by selecting a command and pressing F1.

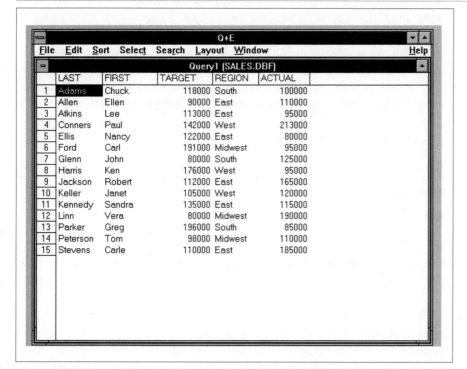

FIGURE 25.1:

*The sales database
imported into Q+E
from Excel*

Search looks through the database for records containing a specified text string, or takes you to a specific record number.

Layout moves, removes, edits, and adds columns; defines fonts and column widths; and calculates summary totals and fields.

Window changes windows or gets information about the current query.

Help provides information about using Q+E.

The database is displayed in columns, with the field names as the column titles. Each record is identified with a record number at the left.

Moving the Cursor and Selecting Data in a Query Window

You select data with the mouse in Q+E in much the same way you do with Excel. Begin by clicking a field value to select it. Drag through a range of field values to select them. To select multiple ranges, select the first range and hold down the Ctrl key while selecting other ranges. To select characters in a text field, drag through the characters. You also can scroll through a database. (There are no scroll bars in Figure 25.1 because the database does not extend beyond the window.)

To select with the keyboard, you must move the cursor to the starting point and then make the selection. Press these keys to move the cursor:

TO MOVE TO	PRESS
Next field	Tab
Previous field	Shift-Tab
First field	Home
Last field	End
First field of first record	Ctrl-Home
First field of last record	Ctrl-End
Next record	↓
Previous record	↑

As with Excel, you can press the Ctrl key to select discontinuous ranges. Press PgUp and PgDn to scroll vertically and Ctrl-PgUp and Ctrl-PgDn to scroll horizontally a screen at a time.

To select elements with the keyboard, press these keys:

TO SELECT	PRESS
Character to left	Shift-←
Character to right	Shift-→
Entire record	Shift-Spacebar
Entire column	Ctrl-Spacebar
Entire window	Ctrl-Shift-Spacebar

To select multiple fields values, select the first field value, press F8, and use the direction keys to select additional field values. Press F8 again.

To select from multiple records, select the first field values of the first record and press F8. Use the direction keys to select additional field values in this record. Press Shift-F8 to keep the selection and select additional records. Press F8 again to select multiple field values. When you are through, press F8 again.

PERFORMING BASIC QUERY OPERATIONS

You can edit any field value, find a record with a specific field value, go to a specific record, or zoom a field value.

Editing a Record

Field values can be edited from the Edit menu. Select the field value (or portion of a field value) to edit, then choose Edit ➤ Allow Editing. The familiar Cut, Copy, and Paste commands are on the Edit menu. Use them as you would in Excel: Cut removes the selected data to the Clipboard and Copy creates a copy in the Clipboard. Paste moves the data to the new location, even if it is in another Windows application.

Finding a Record

Sometimes you may need to find a record knowing only the value of a field it contains. To initiate this kind of search, use the Find command.

Assume, for example, we wish to find Vera Linn's record in the database.

1. Select any one cell in the first column to execute the query in that field.

2. Choose Search ➤ Find.

3. Enter the value for which you wish to search in the Find dialog box, in this case **Linn** (see below).

4. Click OK.

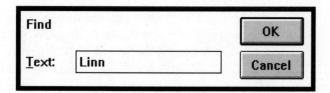

The cursor will be sent to the first location that contains the value. You can press F7 or use the Find Next command to find the next matching field value. (There is none here.) To find a previous match, use the Find Previous command.

Going to Specific Records

To scroll quickly to a specific record in a large database, use the Goto command. For example, to get to record 7:

1. Open the Search menu and choose Goto.

2. Enter the record number to which you wish to go in the dialog box (see below).

3. Click OK.

The cursor will move to record 7.

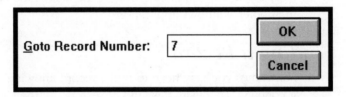

Zooming to Display an Entire Field

If a field value is too large for the current column width, it will not fit in the displayed column. To view such a field, choose Zoom Field from the Edit window. The entire field value will be displayed in a separate window. You can close the window from its Control box.

SORTING A DATABASE

The database query window defaults to displaying the records in the same order as they appear in the database. You can use the Sort command of the query window to display the records in a different order. Note that this does not change the record order in the database, only the *displayed* order.

The records are now displayed in ascending order based on the Last field. To reorder the display to show the records by Region in ascending order:

1. Select any field value in the Region column.

2. Choose Ascending from the Sort menu.

The records are now ordered by region in alphabetical order. Remember that the database record order is not changed, only the query display.

To reset the display to the normal database order, choose Reset Sort from the Sort menu.

You can sort by multiple columns, as well. Sort on the primary order first, then the secondary. For example, to sort in alphabetical order by Region and then backwards alphabetical order by Last, sort in "ascending" order by Region as you just did, then select any entry in the Last field and choose Sort ➤ Descending (see Figure 25.2). Select Show Info from the Window menu to see the current sort order (see Figure 25.3). Close the window from its Control box. Choose Reset Sort to restore the normal database order.

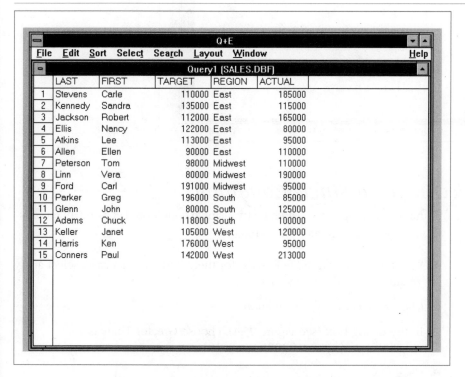

FIGURE 25.2:

An example of a multiple sort. Salespeople are sorted in backwards alphabetical order within their regions, which are sorted in alphabetical order

QUERYING A DATABASE

You can extract records from a database using Q+E by defining a criterion and searching with it. Let's try this now with our database.

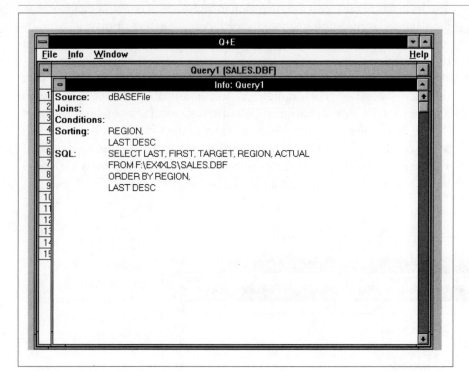

FIGURE 25.3:

*This window allows you
to examine the sort order*

Selecting by a Single Condition

As an initial example, try searching by a single condition. Let's find all records with a target value greater then $100,000:

1. Select any entry in the field used for the criteria. In this case, select any value in the Target column.

2. Choose Select ➤ Add Condition.

3. In the dialog box (see Figure 25.4), choose Greater Than as the operator and enter **100000** in the Value text box.

4. Click OK.

The query window will change and now show only those records with a target value greater than $100,000.

If you are searching through a text field, you can use wildcard characters to match text patterns. With text fields, the Like operator becomes available in the Add Condition dialog box. You can use the asterisk (*) to match any

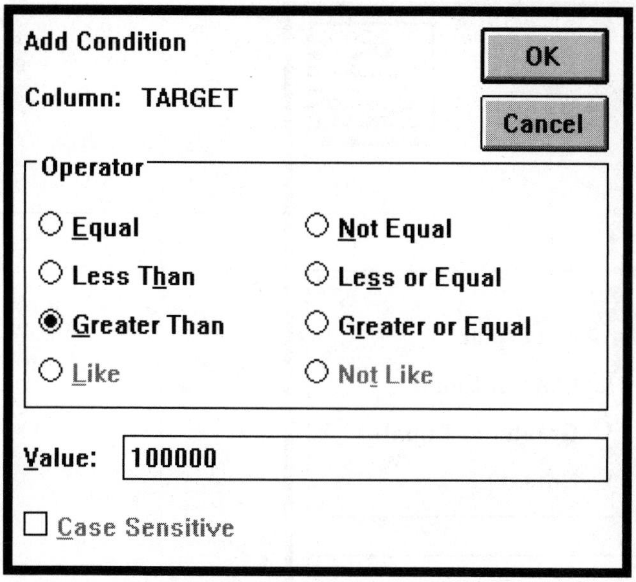

FIGURE 25.4:

This dialog box allows you to specify a single criterion

Add Condition

Column: TARGET

OK

Cancel

Operator

○ **E**qual ○ **N**ot Equal

○ **L**ess T**h**an ○ **Le**ss or Equal

◉ **G**reater Than ○ **Gr**eater or Equal

○ **L**ike ○ **N**ot Like

Value: | 100000

☐ **C**ase Sensitive

character(s) and a question mark (?) to match a single character. For example, **R*** will match any field that starts with an *R*, and ***T** will match any field that ends with a *T*. Specifying **R?B** will match on any three-character value that starts with *R* and ends with *B*.

Selecting by Multiple Conditions

To select on multiple conditions, first specify the first condition and click OK. The window will change to reflect the records that match that condition, as in the last example. With the cursor still in the Target field, choose Add Condition from the Select menu again. Notice that the dialog box has now changed (see Figure 25.5), permitting you to specify whether the new condition should be "ANDed" or "ORed" with the previous condition (see Chapter 11). Leave it at the default AND. Choose Less Than as the operator and enter **150000** in the Value text box. Click OK. The query window now shows only those records with target values greater than $100,000 *and* less than $150,000.

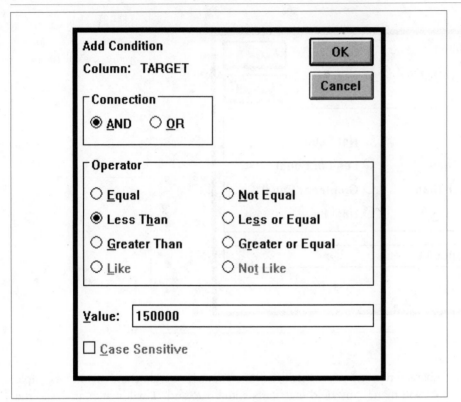

FIGURE 25.5:

Choosing Add Selection
from the Select menu
again allows you to
select by a second
condition

Viewing the Condition

To view the current criteria setting, choose Show Info from the Window menu. The Info window (see Figure 25.6) displays the current criteria. Close the Info window from its Control box.

Resetting the Database Display

To restore the default display of all records in the database, choose Reset Conditions from the Select menu. The entire database will again be displayed. Reset the conditions of your query to display the entire database.

Saving the Query

When using Q+E, you are working with two types of files: database and query files. The database file contains the data. The query file defines how you wish to look at the data. The database file is opened from a query file or, if no query

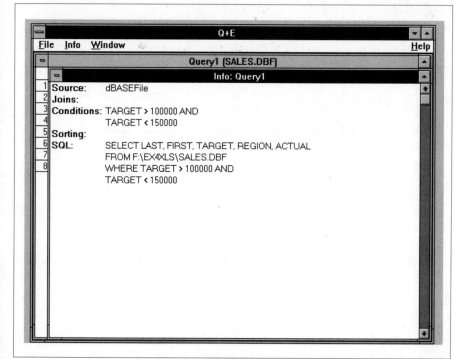

FIGURE 25.6:

Viewing the current criteria setting

file exists, with the Open command. As you edit the file, the database file is automatically updated.

To save the current query under a new name, choose File ➤ Save As. Enter the file name for saving (SALES) and click OK. Notice that you can't change the directory here. A query file is always saved in the same directory as the database. To save a query under the current query name displayed in the window title bar (QUERY1), choose File ➤ Save.

FORMATTING THE DATABASE

You use the Layout menu to format the database: i.e., change column widths, change headings, move columns, change the font, and set the formatting.

Changing the Column Width

To change a column's width, you can use the mouse or the Layout menu. With the mouse you can drag the column separator, as in Excel. From the Layout menu, choose Column Width. Enter the desired width and click OK.

Changing the Column Heading

To change a column heading, double-click the current heading. In the dialog box enter the new name in the Heading text box and click OK. The Expression text box is used to define the data to be displayed in the column.

Moving Columns

To move a column, first select a cell in the column to move. Then choose Move Column from the Layout menu. Point to the new location and click.

Removing Columns

To remove a column, select a cell the column to remove and choose Remove Column from the Layout menu. This does not delete the data from the database, but only removes the data from the query form.

To restore a column, select Define Column, choose the column to restore, and choose a location for the column.

Changing the Font

To change the character font, select a field and choose Font from the Layout menu. As in Excel, you can choose the font, size, and style you wish from the dialog box.

Setting the Picture

Q+E doesn't provide much formatting control over the picture, as does the Number command on Excel's Format menu. The picture defaults to that set by the Control Panel in Windows. To change this, use Control Panel to set the International settings.

You can specify whether the thousands separator is to be used. You also have some control over the date, time, and currency formats. Select Layout ➤ Options to turn the separator off or on.

If you need more picture control than this, you can link the results to a worksheet and use the formatting control of Excel to print your output.

PRINTING THE RESULTS

You can print the results of a query much as you can print a worksheet. Select File ➤ Page Setup to define the page. Then select File ➤ Print to print the worksheet.

CREATING NEW DATABASE FILES

You also can use Q+E to create a new database file using the Define command on the File menu. After the basic file structure is defined, it is saved as a database file using Save As. You can then open a query window to add records to the new file.

Some database systems, such as SQL systems (Structured Query Language), save the data in tables. In this chapter we will refer to a table as a database.

Creating a Database from an Existing Database

Now let's create a new database for the employees, transferring the names in the current database to a new file. We want to copy the Last and First fields from the SALES database to a new SALESID database, then add fields for the employee address: Address, City, State, Zip, and Phone. Follow this procedure:

1. Choose File ➤ Define. The Define dialog box will open.

2. Enter the old database name (Source is dBASEFile) as **SALES** and click OK.

3. A new database window is opened with the structure of the current SALES database (see Figure 25.7). Each row represents one field in the new database. The columns are as follows:

FIELD NAME	Name of the field
TYPE	Type of field (character, date, float, numeric, logical, memo)
WIDTH	Width of the field
DECIMAL	For dBASE numeric fields, the number of decimal places

4. Delete the Target, Region, and Actual fields by selecting rows 3–5 and choosing Edit ➤ Delete Fields (see Figure 25.8).

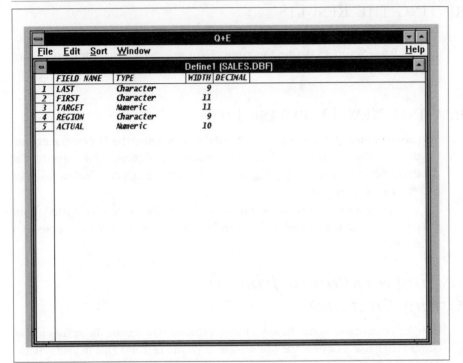

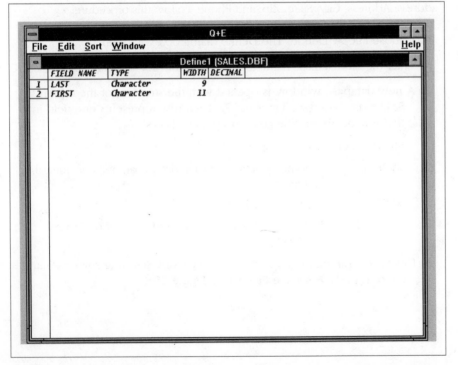

5. Enter the first new field by selecting a cell in row 1 and choosing Edit ➤ Add Before.

6. Enter **ID**.

7. Tab to the Type column. A pop-up menu defines available data types (see Figure 25.9). Choose Character.

8. Tab to the next column and enter **5** for the width.

9. Select the First field (i.e., row 3) and choose Edit ➤ Add After.

10. Enter the Address, City, State, Zip, and Phone fields as shown in Figure 25.10. Enter the correct type and width for each, too.

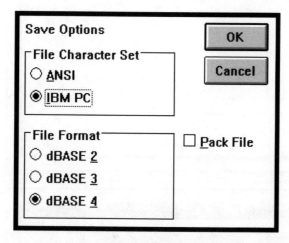

11. Save the database as SALESID. Select dBASEFile as the destination. The extension DBF is added automatically. Click the Options button to select the dBASE option, (see below). Choose OK twice.

The database structure is saved and now you can open a query window on the new structure (by selecting File ➤ Open).

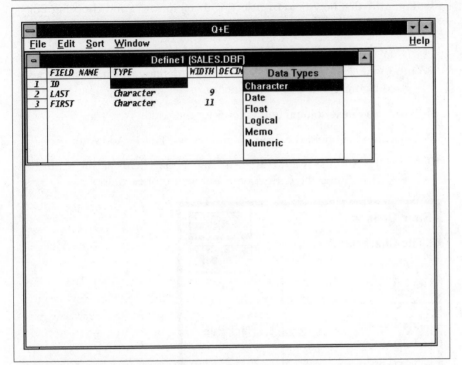

FIGURE 25.9:
*Choosing the data type
for a new field*

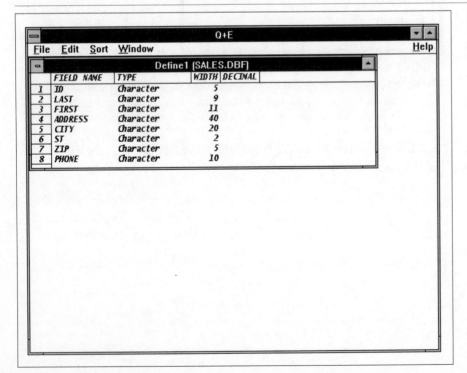

Creating a New Database

To create a new database with new fields, start as though you were using an existing database. Choose Define from the File menu, but then click the New button in the dialog box. Enter all the fields for the database. Finally, save the database. To add records, open a query form on the database.

EDITING RECORDS IN A DATABASE

You can edit existing records, add new records, and delete records in a database.

To edit records, first open the database. Choose the proper source (dBASEFile here) and select the file name (SALESID). The file will open with a default query form. Any data in the database will be displayed. In this case, the Last and First fields have already been copied from our SALES database. Choose Edit ➤ Allow Editing to permit editing.

It is not necessary to save the database after editing. You are entering the data directly to a database with the query form. In fact, you can't save an open database (you can only close it). You can, however, save the query form.

Editing Records Using the Menu

You can edit directly on the query form. Select each ID field and enter an ID number. Enter the remaining data, as shown in Figure 25.11. The first address is Box 75, Jackson, MS 39205. The second is 1602 S. Blount, Raleigh, NC 27610. You need a few addresses, but phone numbers are not needed for this exercise.

Editing Records with a Form

To edit records with a form, choose Edit ➤ Form or double-click the record number. Edit the entries in the form (see Figure 25.12). Notice that this is easier than directly editing records with many fields, since the entire record's entries are displayed. Use the scroll bar or arrow keys to move through the record. Press the Tab and Shift-Tab keys to move across the fields. Press ↑ and ↓ to move across records. Exit Form mode by clicking the Exit button.

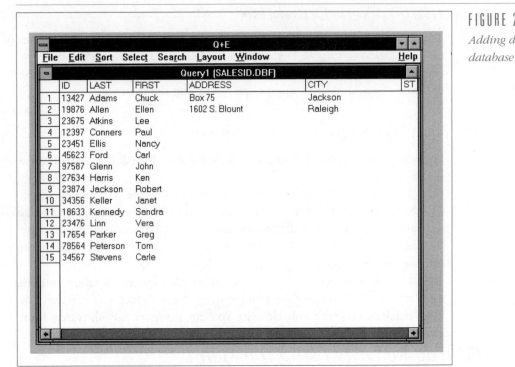

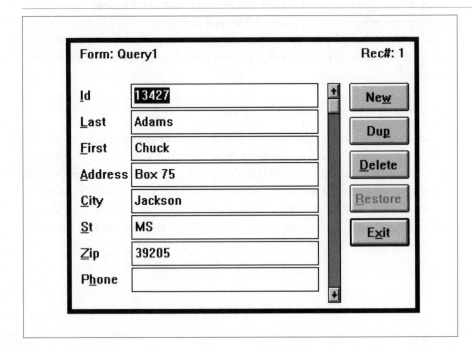

To edit a form, choose Form Setup from the Edit menu. Enter the number of columns for the form in this dialog box below, the fields per column, and the maximum width for a form field. Then click OK.

```
┌─────────────────────────────────────────────┐
│  Form Setup                    ┌──────────┐  │
│                                │    OK    │  │
│  ┌Maximum──────────────────┐   └──────────┘  │
│  │                         │   ┌──────────┐  │
│  │  Number of Columns:  [3]│   │  Cancel  │  │
│  │                         │   └──────────┘  │
│  │  Fields per Column:  [99]                 │
│  │                                           │
│  │  Field Width:        [25]                 │
│  └───────────────────────────────┘          │
└─────────────────────────────────────────────┘
```

Adding Records

To add a new record from the menu, select Add Record from the Edit menu. To use a form to add a record, select Form and click the New button. Then enter the data for the record.

To add records by copying records, select the record to copy by clicking the record number and choosing Edit ➤ Copy. Then select Edit ➤ Paste Append. The record is added at the end of the database.

You can duplicate existing records by choosing the record to duplicate, selecting Edit ➤ Form, and clicking the Dup button.

Deleting Records

To delete a record, select the record and choose Edit ➤ Delete Records. You can undo the deletion with the Undo Delete Records command. You also can delete a record with a query form by selecting Form, selecting the record, and clicking Delete. If you delete with a form, you cannot undo the deletion.

Updating the Query Window

As you edit a query form, records are not resorted or checked against the criteria again. To update the query window after editing, choose Query Now from the Select menu.

WORKING WITH MULTIPLE FILES

One advantage of Q+E over Excel, when working with databases, is that Q+E supports *relational database management;* that is, you can join multiple files on common fields.

To see how this works, open both the SALES and SALESID databases in Q+E. Next join them on the common Last field, making it possible to see the employee IDs in the Sales query. Here's the procedure:

1. Be sure both databases are open. Choose Arrange All from the Window menu so you can see both at once.

2. In the source window (SALESID), click the column designator for the field that has the common value (Last).

3. In the destination window (SALES), click the same column designator.

4. Be sure the destination window (SALES) is active, and choose Join from the Select menu.

The destination window now shows the fields of both databases. Clean up the display by deleting and moving columns:

1. Remove all but the ID, SALES.LAST, SALES.FIRST, REGION, TARGET, and ACTUAL columns by selecting the designators for the columns to delete and choosing Remove Column from the Layout menu. Delete SALESID.FIRST, ADDRESS, CITY, ST, ZIP, and PHONE.

2. Move the ID column to the first column position by selecting the column designator, choosing Layout ➤ Move Column, and then clicking in the first column in the query.

3. Using the same procedure, move the REGION column so that it comes after SALES.FIRST.

Figure 25.13 shows the query form at this point. Both database names are displayed in the query window's title bar and they are linked on the common Last field.

You can create complex joins with Q+E, with many databases and fields linked. Fields can be joined in a *one-to-one* or *one-to-many* relationship. The above example is a one-to-one join: one record in a database is joined to a single record in another. In a one-to-many join, one record in one database is joined to many records in another. To see an example of a one-to-many, assume that an inventory database of parts has notes in another database, with the database files linked by part number. There may be several notes for a part. You can link the files in the same way and the query will show all related notes.

The Join command shows the records of the destination database only if a matching record exists in the source database. If you wish to see all records of the destination database (even if there is no matching source record), select Outer Join. An example might be a destination customer database used for creating invoices (the source). Outer Join would display the entire customer database.

CREATING SUMMARY FIELDS

You can use Q+E to calculate column totals or other summary data. To calculate summary data, select the columns to use and choose Totals from the Layout menu. Choose the type of summary data desired and then click OK:

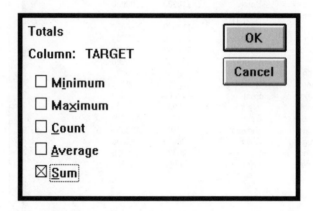

Figure 25.14 shows the query after Sum is selected. You can make multiple selections.

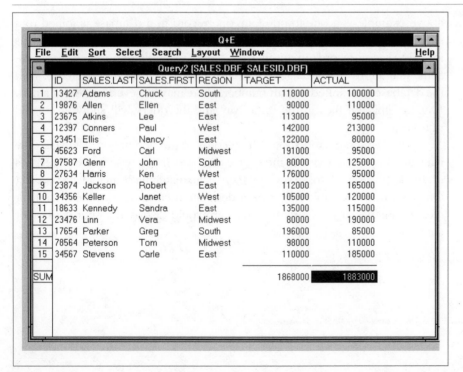

FIGURE 25.14:

The query after summing target and actual values

CREATING CALCULATED FIELDS

You also can create calculated fields in a query. Open the inventory database used in the invoice system example in Chapter 22. Open it as an Excel worksheet (Source is ExcelFile) within Q+E. Be sure the database is defined and save it in a dBASE III format. Load it to Q+E as in the last example. Q+E will select the database and display it. Delete the EXT COST column by selecting it and choosing Remove Column from the Layout menu. Now add the column from Q+E:

1. If you have a problem here, save the database from the Excel worksheet as a dBASE file and then load it to Q+E, as in the last example.

2. Choose Layout ➤ Define Column.

3. In the Define Column dialog box, enter the heading and expression for the column (see Figure 25.15). Click Add.

4. Click after the QOH column to place the new column.

5. The new Extcost column is added to the query form (see Figure 25.16).

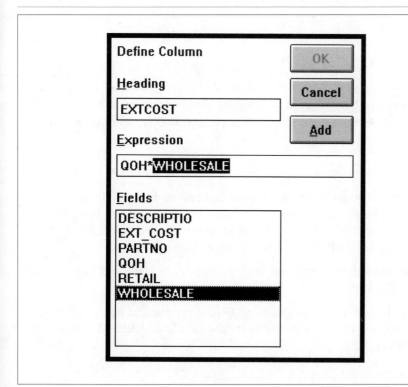

FIGURE 25.15:

This dialog box allows you to add a calculated field, in this case called Extcost, which multiplies the quantity-on-hand by the wholesale cost

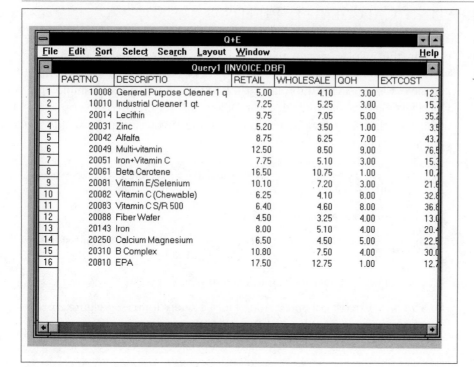

FIGURE 25.16:

*Part of the query after
adding the calculated
field*

MAKING MAILING LABELS

Excel is not too good at printing mailing labels, but Q+E makes it simple. The basic strategy is to define each field for the label by clicking each sequentially, then use File ➤ Save As to save it as a mailing label file. Let's try it with the SALESID file:

1. Open a query file on the SALESID database (using File ➤ Open).

2. Click the column designator for the first line of the label. In this case two fields are to be used in a single label line (First and Last). First, move the columns to the line order you will need; move First before Last in the query form. (Use Layout ➤ Move Column).

3. Hold down the Ctrl key and drag the cursor over First and Last. Release the Ctrl key.

4. Keep the first selection active and hold down the Ctrl key while dragging the cursor over the fields for the next line (Address). Release the Ctrl key.

5. Hold down the Ctrl key again and drag the cursor over City, State, and Zip for the third line. Release the Ctrl key.

6. Save the file as SALES. Choose MailingLabels from the Destination drop-down list box.

7. Click Options and see the dBASE expression for the label (see Figure 25.17). Edit as necessary.

8. Click OK twice.

The mailing label file is created. Use it as a mail-merge file with any word processor. (See the form-letter instructions in your word-processor documentation.)

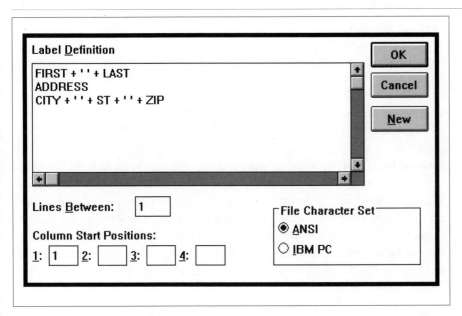

FIGURE 25.17:

Creating a label from parts of the database

USING Q+E WITH OTHER APPLICATIONS

Q+E supports the Clipboard and DDE (see Chapter 21), making it easy to link input data to other sources (spreadsheets, communication programs, etc.) and the results of a query to other programs (spreadsheets, presentation programs, word processors, etc.).

Using the Clipboard

To copy data through the Clipboard, select the data and use Cut or Copy to place them in the Clipboard. Then paste them in the destination application. In the same way, you can paste data through the Clipboard from another application to Q+E.

You also can use Copy Special in Q+E to copy data to the Clipboard for another program. When you choose this command, a dialog box appears, permitting you to choose what you wish to copy. Here you can choose to include column headings, record numbers, link formulas, SQL text for Excel 2.X (includes the SELECT statement in SQL), or to link data (see below). Click OK.

Linking Data

One valuable feature of Q+E is its ability to link field values to other programs. This means that as long as the database file is open, the field values in that file echo data input from another program. In the same way, an output document (word-processor letter or presentation slide) can always contain the latest data from the database. Data links can be created only with Windows application programs that support DDE. The linking techniques are identical to those described in Chapter 16 for worksheets and in Chapter 21 for DDE.

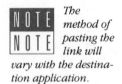

The method of pasting the link will vary with the destination application.

Linking from Q+E to Another Application Data in Q+E can be linked from Q+E to another application, such as a cell in Excel or a document in Microsoft Word for Windows. To create the link, select the information to link and choose Copy from Q+E's Edit menu. To select special options, use Edit ➤ Copy Special. Open the dependent document, select the destination, and choose Paste Link. Be sure to save both the query and destination document to preserve the link. Once this is done, the dependent document values will always follow those of Q+E.

Linking Other Applications to Q+E You can link Q+E to another document, making the Q+E query the dependent document. For example, to link a query file result to an Excel document:

1. Open the worksheet document and the Q+E query.

2. Select the records and fields to copy in the Q+E query window.

3. Select Copy (or Copy Special for special copying) from the Edit menu.

4. Choose the starting cell for the paste in the Excel worksheet.

5. Select Paste Link from the Edit menu.

Figure 25.18 shows the result of pasting the first four names of the database into the worksheet. Notice that the worksheet formula indicates that this is an array. If entered manually, you would need to press Ctrl-Shift-Enter.

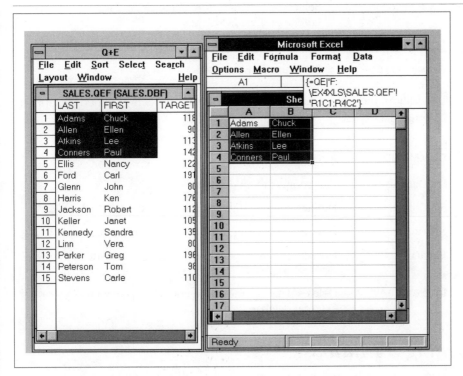

The pasted database names

USING EXCEL WITH EXTERNAL DATABASES

> **NOTE** *If you wish Excel to always start with database support, move the QE.XLA file to the \EXCEL\XLSTART directory.*

Q+E can be used with databases external to Excel. Modifying Excel for external database support involves nothing more than executing a single macro:

1. Start Microsoft Excel and open the SALES worksheet.

2. Open the File menu and choose Open.

3. Choose QE.XLA from the \EXCEL\QE directory.

Once the macro sheet is open, you will see three new commands on the Data menu:

COMMAND	FUNCTION
Paste Fieldnames	Selects field names from database files for criteria and extract ranges
SQL Query	Extracts results of an SQL SELECT statement
Activate Q+E	Starts the Q+E program

In addition, the other Data menu commands have been modified to support external databases:

COMMAND	FUNCTION
Set Database	Can connect to an external database
Set Criteria	Defines criteria range. Works with external database
Set Extract	Defines extract range. Works with external database
Extract	Extracts data that meet the criteria. Works with external database
Delete	Deletes data that meets the criteria. Works with external database

Opening a Database

Databases can be *internal* or *external*. An internal database is one on the worksheet, such as the invoice or sales database. An external database resides in an external file.

To open an external database:

1. Select Data ➤ Set Database. Click the External Database option button and then click OK.

2. In the next dialog box, (shown below), select the file type and name. In the Source drop-down list box, determine the type of database file by choosing dBASEFile. If the source is not displayed on the Source list, click the Sources button to log on to an external source:

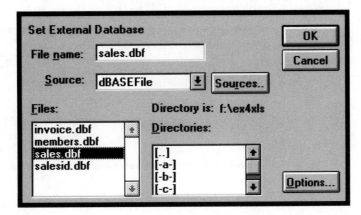

3. Choose the directory in which you stored SALES.DBF earlier in this chapter.

4. Choose SALES.DBF. Click Options for additional options, as in Q+E.

5. Click OK and you are returned to the Set Database dialog box. The Change and Add buttons are visible now. Click the Add button if you wish to join another database. Click OK to end.

To open an internal database on the worksheet, select the database and choose Set Database, just as you would with an external database. Choose Current Selection in the dialog box, then click OK.

To change the database selection, use Set Database, too. Click Change to change the current external database definition, or click Add to join another database.

Extracting from an Internal Database

To extract a criterion, you must open the database and paste the fields to the worksheet. Try this with the SALES.DBF database:

1. Select the cell for the first field name and choose Data ➤ Paste Fieldnames. For example, with the SALES database open and an internal database selected, choose G6 on the worksheet and select Data ➤Paste Fieldnames.

2. The Paste Fieldnames dialog box opens with the database fields. Select the field names from the Fields list box and click Paste. To paste all field names to the worksheet in the current order, click Paste All. To paste field names in a different order, click the Order Fields button:

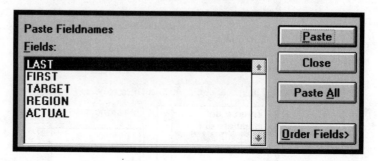

3. When pasting fields in a different order, the Paste Fieldnames dialog box expands (see Figure 25.19). To add a field, choose the field in the Available Fields list box and click Add. You also can insert a field name anywhere in the output list by choosing the field to add in the Available Fields list box, the field below the insertion point in the Selected Fields list box, and clicking Add. Clicking Remove removes a field from the output list, and Clear All clears the Selected Fields list box. Select All places all field names in the output list. Click Clear All, Select All, Add, and then Paste.

You can then define a criteria range or extraction range with the list (see Chapter 11).

Extracting from an External Database

Using criteria and performing extractions from an external database is identical to doing so from an internal database. You can use Data ➤ Paste Fieldnames as we just did or copy the field names you wish to use to the specified area. Then use Set Criteria or Set Extract. With extraction, you can use a joined file by opening both database files with Set Database. Once this is done, the extracted data will contain the fields of both databases. Here is the procedure summary for extractions:

1. Open the database (or databases) with Set Database.

2. Select all the field names with Paste Fieldnames.

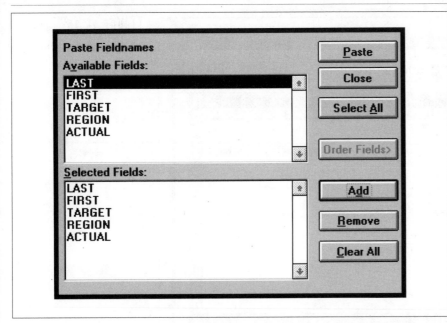

3. Define the criteria and extraction ranges with Set Criteria and Set Extract.

4. Enter the criteria.

5. Initiate the extraction with Data ➤ Extract.

Now try an extraction with the external SALES database.

1. Copy G6:K6 to G10 to get another range (see Figure 25.20).

2. Define the criteria range by selecting G6:K7 and selecting Data ➤ Set Criteria.

3. Define an extraction range by selecting G10:K23 and selecting Set Extract.

4. Enter a criteria by entering **West** into cell J7.

5. Select Data ➤ Extract.

6. In the Extract dialog box, click OK.

The extracted database is then entered to the worksheet (see Figure 25.21).

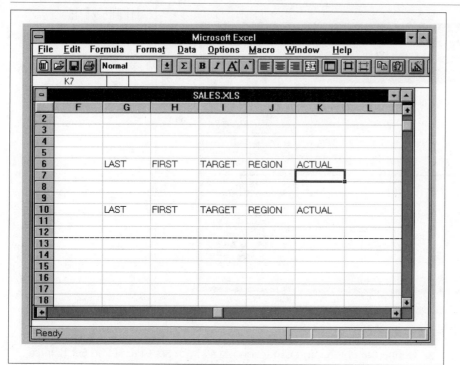

FIGURE 25.20:

The pasted field names

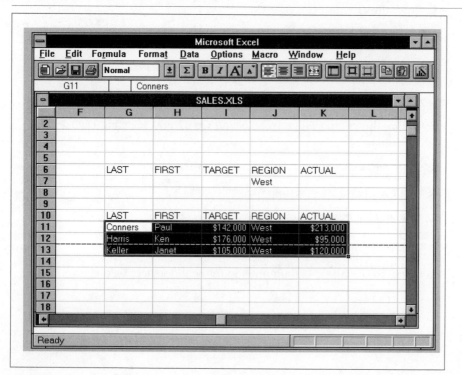

FIGURE 25.21:

The extracted database

DOING WHAT-IF ANALYSIS

Excel provides several tools for doing what-if analysis. With what-if analysis, you are trying to find a set of input values that will give a desired output. In this case you design a model, or a set of worksheets to solve a particular problem. The model is then tested with known data; that is, data for which you know the output for a given input. You can then use the model with unknown input to find the output, or with specified output to find what input values will produce that input.

You have already used two tools for doing what-if analysis: goal-seeking (Chapter 8) and tables (Chapter 13). Goal-seeking permits you to define an output value and then change a single input cell value to achieve the output value. Tables permit you to vary two input values to achieve a table of output values.

In this chapter we will look at two more tools Excel provides for more complex what-if analysis. This analysis is done with add-in utilities. One is the Solver, the other is the Scenario Manager. Use the Solver for complex input definitions and constraints. Scenario Manager is used when defining a set of worksheets with different input values. One or more cells can be used for the input values. You can then create a summary worksheet from the set.

DOING WHAT-IF ANALYSIS WITH THE SOLVER

Here are some examples of uses for the Solver:

◆ You have a cash-flow worksheet (as in Chapter 7) and you wish to plan how much to spend on marketing to maximize sales. This assumes that you know the relationship between sales and marketing costs. An example is shown in the Solver manual and the worksheet is included with the Solver.

◆ You have a series of simultaneous equations to solve (as in the trend analysis example of Chapter 24).

◆ You need to work backward from a goal to find input variables, given a number of constraints. A simplified example was shown in Chapter 8 with the amortization schedule.

Solver can solve complex interrelationships among variables, even when equations don't exist and you need to use lookup tables. To see how Solver works, let's first try a simple example. To really show its power, we will then show a more complex example.

The Amortization Schedule

Let's use Solver with the amortization schedule from Chapter 8, setting a goal for the size of the payment and trying to find how much principal you can afford at a given interest rate. (In Chapter 8 you did this using the Goal Seek command on the Formula menu.) To start, load the amortization worksheet. Then follow these steps:

1. Open the Formula menu and choose Solver. A dialog box is displayed. You can move the dialog box around the screen by dragging the title bar as necessary.

2. In this case, we simply want to solve for a payment of $150 in B10. We want to find the principal we can afford at this payment and the fixed 9-percent interest. Clear and click in the By Changing Cells text box in the Solver Parameters dialog box, then click B6 to enter the absolute reference in the box:

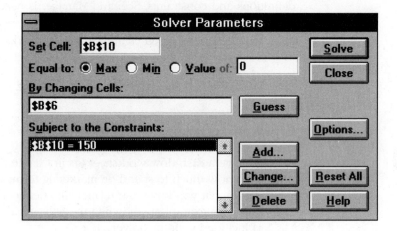

3. Click Add to enter a constraint.

4. In the Add Constraint dialog box, click B10 to enter that cell in the Cell Reference text box.

5. From the drop-down list in the middle of the dialog box, choose = as the operator.

6. Click or tab over to the Constraint text box, then enter **150** in the dialog box. Click OK.

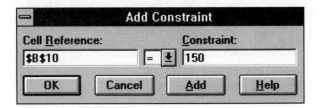

7. Click Solve.

Solver will initiate execution. Once the Solver has finished, it will display a dialog box saying that it has found a solution and that you can choose whether to accept the new values:

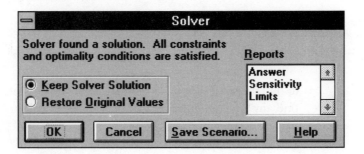

Choose OK. The final constant values will be displayed on the worksheet (see Figure 25.22).

Solving Polynomial Equations

In Chapter 24 you did a curvilinear regression (see Figure 24.6) by solving a series of simultaneous equations of the form

$$683.5 = 14a_0 + 105a_1 + 1015a_2$$

$$6273.2 = 105a_0 + 1015a_1 + 11025a_2$$

$$65419.6 = 1015a_0 + 11025a_1 + 127687a_2$$

	A	B	C	D	E	F	G
1			**AMORTIZATION SCHEDULE BY MONTH**				
2			*Amortization Payment Schedule by Month*				
3							
4	*******************	************************	**********************	**			
5	Data Entry Area			*			
6	Principal	$6,027.72		*			
7	Interest	9.00%		*			
8	Term	48	Months	*			
9	*******************	************************	**********************	**			
10	Payment:	$150.00					
11	Total Paid	$7,200.00					
12							
13	Month	Beginning	Ending	Payment	Total Paid	Tot. Princ.	Tot. Inte
14		Balance	Balance			Paid	Paid
15	1	$6,027.72	$5,922.93	$150.00	$150.00	$104.79	$45
16	2	$5,922.93	$5,817.35	$150.00	$300.00	$210.37	$89
17	3	$5,817.35	$5,710.98	$150.00	$450.00	$316.74	$133

to find the values for a_0, a_1, and a_2. Once these values were found, you could find any y value in the series by using the equation

$$y = a_0 + a_1 x + a_2 x^2$$

Unless you were very brave, however, you probably didn't try the entire worksheet. Solver makes this easier.

Let's see how. First, open a new worksheet and enter **a0**, **a1**, and **a2** in cells A1, A2, and A3, respectively. Cells B1 through B3 should hold the constants for which we wish to solve. For now, enter zero in these. Select Create Names on the Formula menu to name cell B1 as A0, B2 as A1_ and B3 as A2_. Because A1 and A2 are cell locations, Excel adds an underline after them when naming cells B2 and B3.

Set up the equations in B5 to C7 as shown in Figure 25.23. (Cells B1:B3 should be 0 at this time.) Now you are ready to start:

1. Select Solver from the Formula menu. Move the dialog box to the bottom of the screen so you can see the rest of the worksheet (click on the title bar and drag).

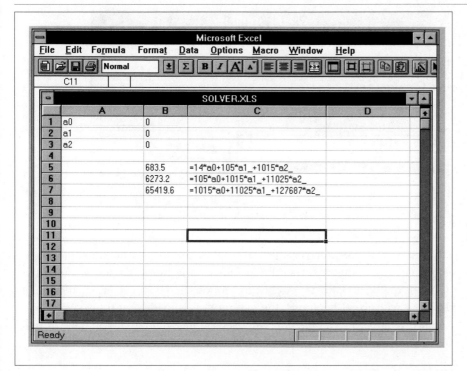

FIGURE 25.23:

Solving a polynomial equation

2. Click in the By Changing Cells text box, then select cells B1 through B3 on the worksheet. Excel enters $B$1:$B$3 automatically. The Set Cell text box should be blank.

3. Click the Add button to get the Add Constraint dialog box. (Move it to the bottom of the screen as well.) Select cell B5 as the cell reference and choose = as the operator. Click in the Constraint text box, then select cell C5. Notice that Excel automatically enters absolute addresses.

4. Click the Add button to add two more constraints: $B$6=$C$6 and $B$7=$C$7. After you enter the third constraint, click OK to get back to the Solver Parameters dialog box.

Below is the Solver Parameters dialog box after it is set up for this problem. Click Solve and the constraints will appear in B1:B3. The values should be:

$$a_0 = 10.01642$$

$$a_1 = 7.147701$$

$$a_2 = -0.18444$$

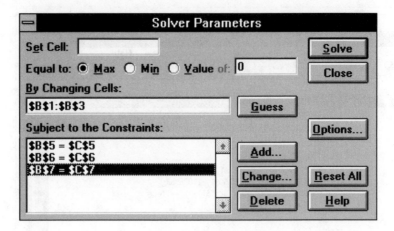

Solver uses iterative calculations to find a solution. The iteration process stops when a solution is found that satisfies the limits defined in the Solver Options dialog box. Find it by clicking Options in the Solver Parameters dialog box. As with Excel iterations, the assumption is made that the solution converges. There is also a time limit imposed on the solution. If you have trouble finding a solution:

◆ Be sure the definitions are correct.

◆ Try different starting values (zeroes were used in the previous example).

◆ Be sure the problem converges.

◆ Change the options. For example, checking Assume Linear Model may not be a valid assumption.

◆ Try checking Show Iteration Results in the Solver Options dialog box.

Using the Solver is similar to the goal-seeking example of Chapter 8, but notice you have more options here:

◆ You can choose to define the goal as setting a cell to a specific value or as maximizing or minimizing a cell.

◆ You can set multiple constraints and choose their operators.

◆ You can solve multiple problems on a worksheet.

When you save your worksheet, the last Solver solution is attached to the worksheet and saved with it. If you do multiple Solver solutions, however, only the last one is saved with the worksheet. If you used Solver to solve several problems on the worksheet, save the problem model on the worksheet. To do so, select an empty range on the worksheet and click Save Model in the Solver Options dialog box.

Solver can create three types of reports: the Answer Report, the Limits Report, and the Sensitivity Report. The Answer Report defines the set cell and adjustable cells, with original and final values. It also shows the constraints and how well the constraints are met. This is useful if the constraints have a range. The Limits Report lists the cell in the Set Cell text box, the adjustable cell, the limits and target results. This is useful if a range of input values meet the target results. The Sensitivity Report shows how sensitive the output values are to a change of input values.

DOING WHAT-IF ANALYSES WITH SCENARIO MANAGER

The Scenario Manager permits you to create a set of worksheets by varying one or two input cells. Now let's use Scenario Manager with the amortization schedule to find an interest or term that can give us a monthly payment that is feasible. The principal is held constant, so we can only vary two variables.

1. Load the Amortization worksheet, then choose Formula ➤ Scenario Manager.

2. As there are no currently-defined scenarios, a dialog box is displayed for adding a new scenario:

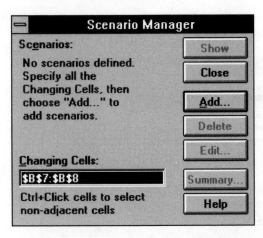

3. Enter the cells to change as $B$7:$B$8, the interest and term.

4. Click Add to add a scenario.

5. Enter the interest ($B$7) as 12 percent and the term ($B$8) as 36

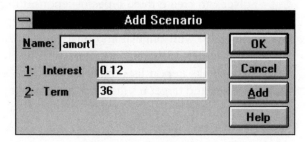

months in the Add Scenario dialog box. Name the scenario **AMORT1**:

6. Click Add and add three more scenarios in turn:

NAME	INTEREST	TERM
AMORT2	12 percent	48
AMORT3	12 percent	60
AMORT4	13 percent	36

7. Click OK after the last scenario. Click Close after defining the scenarios.

To show the data for any scenario, choose Scenario Manager from the Formula menu. You'll see the following dialog box:

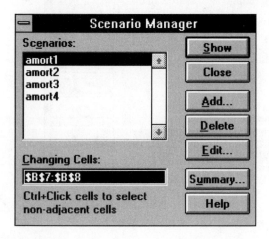

Choose the scenario you wish to use and click on Show. The worksheet will change to reflect the new input values.

To see a summary of the results of all the scenarios choose Scenario Manager from the Formula menu. Click the Summary button. In the Scenario Summary dialog box, enter the result cell or cells for the analysis:

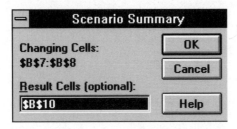

Click OK. A new worksheet will be created with the summary results (Figure 25.24).

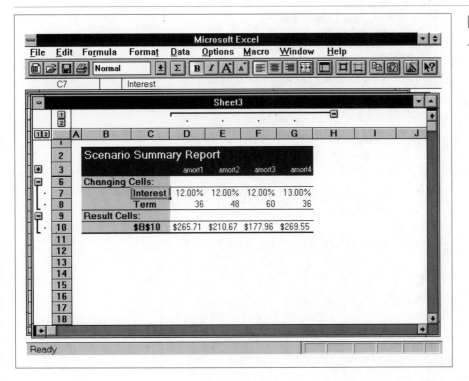

FIGURE 25.24:

A Scenario Summary

USING THE ANALYSIS TOOLS

If you do statistical analysis, you will find the new statistical tools in Excel will be a great asset. Before using a tool, the input data that you plan to use should be arranged in a column or row on the worksheet. The analysis tool will then create an output table of the results.

For example, let's use an analysis tool to do the linear regression of Chapter 24:

1. Open the linear regression and copy $A$8:$B21 to $B$6 of a new worksheet. We will use this new worksheet for the regression.

2. Choose Options ➤ Analysis Tools.

3. In the Analysis Tools dialog box, choose Regression:

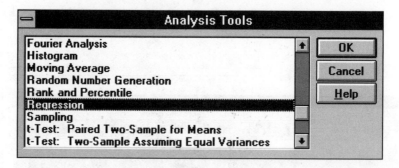

4. In the Regression dialog box, enter the input range for the x and y values and the starting location for the summary output range (Figure 25.25).

5. Click OK and the regression analysis will be placed on the worksheet (Figure 25.26).

The results are identical to those achieved in Chapter 24.

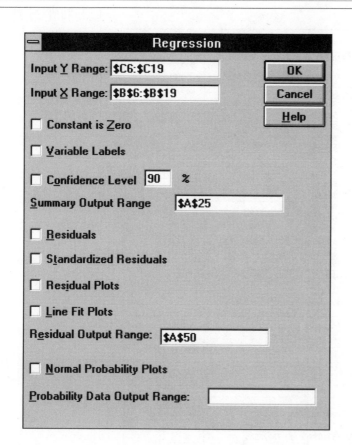

Defining the regression

	LINEAR REGRESSION USING ANALYSIS TOOLS					
	1	$6.50				
	2	$14.20				
	3	$23.50				
	4	$30.10				
	5	$38.80				
	6	$48.40				
	7	$55.50				
	8	$60.10				
	9	$64.10				
	10	$65.60				
	11	$68.80				
	12	$68.90				
	13	$68.80				
	14	$70.20				
	15	$86.63				
	16	$91.67				
	17	$96.72				
	18	$101.76				
Regression Statistics						
Multiple R	0.94850741					
R Square	0.89966632					
Adjusted R Square	0.89130518					
Standard Error	7.33070616					
Observations	14					
Analysis of Variance						
	df	Sum of Squares	Mean Square	F	Significance F	
Regression	1	5782.392538	5782.392538	107.6009	2.41E-07	
Residual	12	644.871033	53.73925275			
Total	13	6427.263571				
	Coefficients	Standard Error	Lower 95%	Upper 95%		
Intercept	11.0098901	4.138320424	1.993264631	20.02652		
X1	5.04153846	0.486021086	3.982589503	6.100487		

FIGURE 25.26:

The final Regression Report

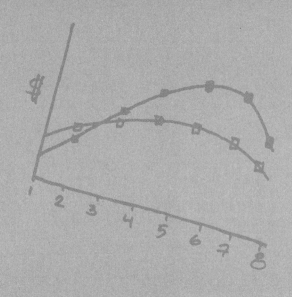

$$b = \frac{\Sigma xy - \bar{x}\Sigma y}{\Sigma x^2 - \bar{x}\Sigma x}$$

PART SEVEN

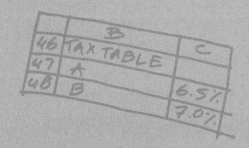

	B	C
46	TAX TABLE	
47	A	
48	B	6.5%
		7.0%

Part VII: Powering Up with Macros

 macro is a series of Excel commands that performs a specific action. In effect, macros permit you to write and name your own application programs using worksheet commands, as well as create your own functions. For this reason, macros are generally considered one of the most important features of any worksheet program.

Although macros are a part of many worksheet products, Excel's macros have three major distinctions: They are easy to use, they don't take up worksheet room (since they're saved on separate macro sheets), and they extend Excel's command language.

Excel provides the capability of creating two types of macros: command macros and function macros. In Chapter 26 you learn when to use command macros and how to create them. Chapter 27 introduces you to the use of function macros, and Chapter 28 provides some insights on more advanced macro techniques, such as debugging, creating custom menus, and designing your own dialog boxes. (The available Excel macro language functions are listed in Appendix F.)

FAST TRACK CHAPTER 26

To create a command macro, ... **578**

1. Open a macro sheet.
2. Set the range by selecting the column and Macro ➤ Set Recorder.
3. Start recording the program using Macro ➤ Start Recorder.
4. Record the commands.
5. Stop the Recorder using Macro ➤ Stop Recorder.
6. Name the macro using Formula ➤ Define Name.
7. Save the macro sheet using File ➤ Save As.

For quick recording, ... **585**

Use Macro ➤ Record. This will open a macro sheet if necessary, set a range, prompt for a name, and start recording.

CHAPTER 26

Introduction to Macros:
The Recorder

xcel allows you to create two types of macros: command macros and function macros. In this chapter, you will learn when to use command macros and how to create them. Excel's Recorder makes creating simple command macros very easy. Function macros will be discussed in Chapter 27.

COMMAND MACRO USES

A *command macro* is a series of commands that accomplishes a desired action. The commands are stored as a single program, which can be executed as often as necessary.

Command macros are used primarily when it is necessary to repeat a complex series of steps many times. Should you find yourself repeating certain Excel operations frequently, chances are that you should consider using a command macro. Here are some examples of applications you might use frequently:

◆ Putting headings in a worksheet.

◆ Creating schedules for financial calculations.

◆ Entering the labels of a frequently used worksheet.

◆ Simplifying a task (or tasks) for someone else with a minimum of Excel experience.

◆ Creating forms for data entry, custom dialog boxes, or a custom menu.

◆ Doing a complex series of calculations with proprietary equations.

◆ Creating a calendar for the month or a weekly schedule with the date and day of the week as headers.

◆ Doing mail-merge letters or envelopes from a database of addresses.

◆ Creating a new application-oriented menu for a user who doesn't know how to use the default Excel menus.

Command macros also can simplify and improve the accuracy and efficiency of a task that must be completed within a tight schedule. For example, suppose that a series of annual reports must be prepared from data that will not be available until a few days before the annual meeting. Weeks before the meeting, you could create macros to produce the final report from dummy data. Once the actual data are available, the same macros could be used by almost anyone to create the final reports in a very short time.

As another example, assume a bank sets up a very complex worksheet for making decisions on granting loans to businesses. The five-year history of the business is entered, and Excel uses this to make projections for the next five years, based on assumptions about several variables, such as interest rates. Two worksheets are created: the history worksheet and the projection worksheet. The worksheets are linked using Excel's linking abilities. Macros are used to set up the link and to prompt the user for input. These worksheets can then be used at various bank locations by people who have little experience with Excel. When Excel is started, a menu worksheet can be displayed automatically, guiding the user through the entire problem-solving process with macros.

You can do just about anything with a macro that you can do directly on the worksheet: open new worksheets, create charts, create and paste names, display dialog boxes for entry, or select and print worksheets. You also can do a few things with macros that you can't do with the normal Excel commands, such as create input dialog boxes and data-entry forms or custom menus.

Excel allows you to put a button on the worksheet (like a dialog box button) and attach your text and macro to it. For example, a button could say **Printer**. Clicking it would print the worksheet. You also can attach macros to any graphic object, even invisible objects. For example, you can attach a hidden object to a cell and then activate a macro (for example, to display help) by clicking the cell.

WHAT IS A MACRO?

Briefly examine the macro example in Figure 26.4, which you will create later. You should recognize many commands on the Macro1 sheet because they match the menu options you have already used. Don't worry about understanding them now; just keep the following ideas in mind:

◆ Although it is not obvious here, each macro has a name. The first cell in the macro is named by the user, and that becomes the name of the macro.

◆ The commands are listed in a vertical column. They are executed starting at the named cell and continue downwards until the macro function RETURN, HALT, or GOTO is reached. A RETURN or HALT terminates the macro execution. GOTO causes a branching to its argument. (Macro functions are described in Chapter 27.)

COMMAND MACROS VERSUS TEMPLATES

Templates, which you have already used, are useful for simplifying repetitive tasks. There is a big difference, however, between a template and a command macro. A template is a blank form that has only some formats already specified. You fill in the blank form to create a worksheet. Templates are useful for many applications and should be used whenever possible. Macros, however, permit automatic execution of Excel commands, with prompts for input. An example will clarify this.

Assume you run an advertising agency in which employees are working on jobs for several clients during the course of the day. For each period of the day, employees need to keep track of which client they were working for and the job category (since categories are billed at different rates).

You could create a blank time sheet and save it as a template; however, employees would still need to fill in information such as their names and the date. In addition, they might enter invalid categories accidentally or neglect to fill in certain time slots if, for instance, they couldn't remember the category or preferred not to say what they did during that time. Finally, with a template the user is still required to know how to use Excel.

Using a macro permits you to automate the entire process. The macro could prompt for the employee's code and the input information. The employee's name could then be obtained from a lookup table using the code. The macro could also look up categories, reject invalid entries, and calculate totals based on category rates. It could be designed to block the possibility of any time slot being left empty. Finally, it could print the time sheet automatically. The user wouldn't have to know anything about Excel except how to load the worksheet and answer the prompts.

CREATING A COMMAND MACRO

There are two ways to create a command macro with Excel, by using the Recorder or by entering the macro manually. The Recorder is the easiest method but is less flexible than manual entry. In this chapter, you will learn the Recorder method. The manual entry of command macros is discussed in Chapter 28.

There are four steps to follow when creating a command macro using the Recorder:

1. Open the macro sheet and set the range.

2. Record the program.

3. Name the macro.

4. Save the macro sheet.

Suppose that you are a manager at Acme Manufacturing. You have created many quarterly reports that all use the same heading, as shown in Figure 26.1. You've decided to take advantage of Excel's macro capabilities and create a macro that will add the heading to the quarterly report worksheet. The following sections describe how to create this command macro.

OPENING THE MACRO SHEET AND SETTING THE RANGE

The macro you create will be recorded on a separate macro sheet, which is much like any Excel worksheet. First, open a regular worksheet. Then follow these steps to open the macro sheet and set the range for the macro:

1. Press Ctrl-F11 or select File ➤ New. Choose Macro Sheet and click OK. A new document titled "Macro1" will open on the screen. (The menu bar has not changed. The row and column headings are the same,

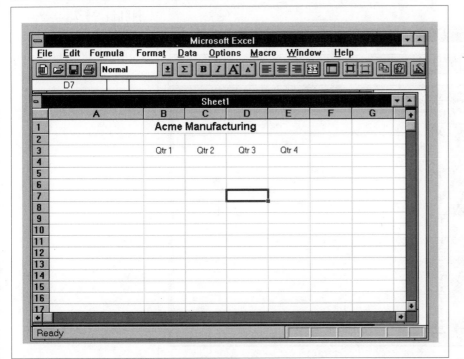

FIGURE 26.1:

*The standard heading
for your quarterly
reports*

too. Notice, however, that the columns are twice as wide as they are on a typical worksheet document. This permits you to see the formulas you enter in their entirety. The Options ➤ Display command is set to display formulas automatically, but you can switch this back to show data if necessary. Here, however, you are interested in the formula, not the result.)

2. Arrange the windows so you can see column A of the macro sheet and columns A to D of the worksheet (see Figure 26.2). You will only use A–E of the worksheet, but column A will be widened later. Use Window ➤ Arrange.

3. Set the macro range by clicking the column A designator on the macro sheet (Macro1). Choose Macro ➤ Set Recorder.

4. Open the Macro menu again. You will want to record absolute references. This means that the third-to-last menu item should read **Relative Record**. In this case, clicking the menu item would switch you to relative recording. If the last item reads **Absolute Record**, click it to record absolute references. (The menu item now reads **Relative Record**.)

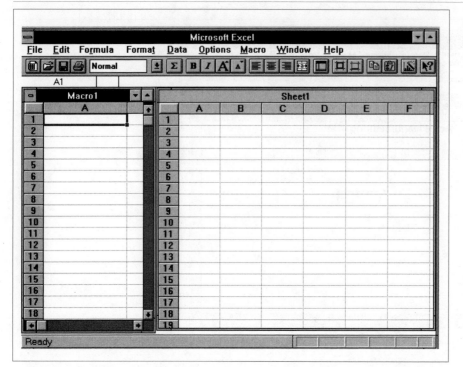

If you select a column designator or a single cell in a column when you choose Set Recorder, Excel assumes that the *entire* column is the Recorder range. If you select two or more cells as the range, Excel assumes that only the *selected* range is the Recorder range. If the macro recording attempts to exceed this range, a message will be displayed, as shown in Figure 26.3. Select a larger range and continue recording.

RECORDING THE PROGRAM

Now you must turn on the Recorder and then actually perform the task that you want the macro to accomplish. Click on the macro sheet to make it active. Choose Macro ➤ Start Recorder. A Recording message appears on the status bar. As you execute the steps to create the heading, you will see each step recorded in the macro sheet. Carry out the steps that you want the macro to execute:

1. Make the worksheet active, then select cell C1.

2. Enter the title **Acme Manufacturing**.

3. Widen column A on the worksheet by selecting column A, opening the Format menu, and choosing Column Width. When the dialog box appears, change the width of column A to 20 characters and click OK.

4. Enter the column titles by selecting cell B3 and dragging the cursor to cell E3. Enter the column titles shown in Figure 26.1.

5. Center the titles by selecting B1 to E3, choosing Format ➤ Alignment, and double-clicking Center.

6. Put the title in boldface print by selecting cell C1, and choosing Format ➤ Font. When the dialog box appears, click Arial (or Helv), twelve points, and Bold, and then click OK.

 After recording a macro, Excel automatically sets a new range as the next completely empty column on the macro sheet. Defined ranges are saved with the macro sheet. If an entire column is defined as a macro range, Excel will begin recording in the cell where the last =RETURN( ) is located (and will record over it).

Now stop the Recorder by choosing Macro ➤ Stop Recorder.

If you make a mistake during entry, correct it; your correction will be recorded in the macro automatically. You can also click the Cancel button on the formula bar to clear an entry before it is entered on the macro sheet.

Widen the first column of the macro sheet so that you can see the commands. Your macro sheet should now look like Figure 26.4. Notice that your commands have been stored in column A using a special language. Column A contains a series of formulas that look much like the formulas you have used before. They contain functions from the Excel macro language. Like any functions, these have arguments. The SELECT function selects the cell(s) specified in the argument, and the FORMULA function is used to enter data into a specified cell or cell range. Compare each function in the column with the steps you followed above to be sure the macro is correct.

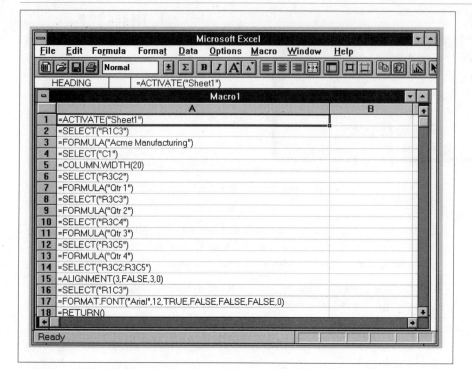

In any macro, the recorded statements may be of four types:

◆ Action statements that move the cursor, format, and do any menu
   activities.

◆ Assignment statements that assign a value to a variable.

◆ Control statements (such as those that use the IF function) that control
   which statements are executed based on a specified condition.

◆ I/O statements that receive keyboard information from the user based
   on a prompt or display message.

You may also have comments, the macro name, and other features in your
macro. In Chapter 28, you will learn more about how to use Excel's macro
language.

NAMING THE COMMAND MACRO

The macro has now been recorded, but it must be assigned a name before you can use it. You could assign it a keystroke sequence as well as a name so that you can start it with that keystroke.

Follow these steps to name your macro:

1. Select the macro sheet.

2. Select the first cell in the macro commands (i.e., cell A1).

3. Choose Formula ➤ Define Name. You will see the dialog box shown in Figure 26.5. Notice that the familiar box now has some new options that apply only to macros, and that the Refers To text box references $A$1, the first cell of the macro commands. The cursor is in the Name text box.

4. Enter the name **HEADING** in the Name box. Do not click OK yet.

5. In the Macro group, click the Command option button to indicate that you are creating a command macro.

6. Tab to the Key: Ctrl+ text box. Hold down the Shift key and enter **X**. (The Shift key is necessary only because an uppercase *X* is desired.) The key you enter here is the "hot key" to activate the macro. You can use any key from *A* to *Z* or *a* to *z*.

7. Click OK.

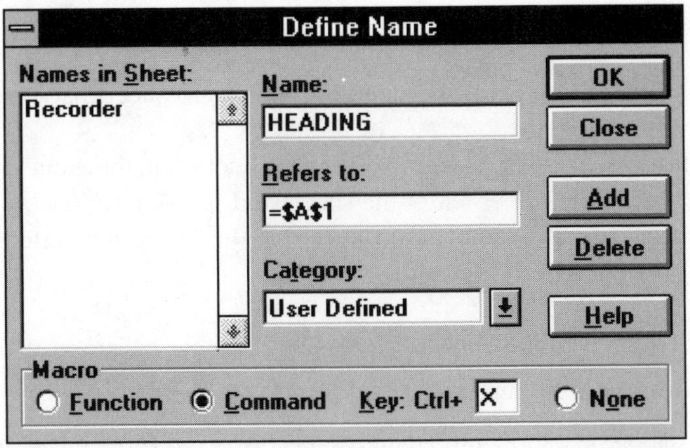

FIGURE 26.5:

The Define Name dialog box for command macros

You have now named your command macro and defined a keystroke sequence that you can use to execute it.

SAVING THE COMMAND MACRO

Name macros using the same rules for naming functions: Use underlines instead of spaces if the name has more than one word.

The macro that you created is not associated with any worksheet or chart document; it must be stored as a separate macro document. You must save the macro sheet after it is created if you want to use the macro later on or with other worksheets.

Follow these steps to save your command macro:

1. Select the macro sheet.

2. Choose File ➤ Save As.

3. When the dialog box appears, enter the name **HEADING**.

4. Click OK.

You can store any number of macros in a single macro document. That way, whenever you open that document, all the command macros stored with it will be available for your use.

EXECUTING YOUR COMMAND MACRO

You can use either of two methods to execute your HEADING macro:

◆   Execute it using Macro ➤ Run.

◆   Press the hot-key sequence from the keyboard.

However, before you use either method, the macro sheet that contains the macro must be open.

Before you start, clear your worksheet by selecting the entire worksheet (click the bar at the upper-left of the sheet) and pressing Ctrl-Del.

To execute your command macro using the Macro menu, follow these steps:

1. Be sure that the worksheet is clear and selected.

2. Choose Macro ➤ Run.

3. The dialog box shown in Figure 26.6 is displayed (note the short-cut key just before the name). Double-click the macro name HEADING.

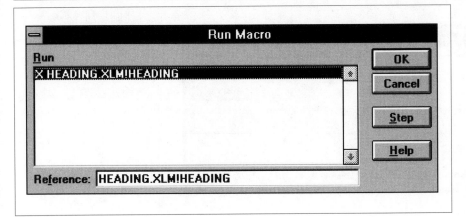

FIGURE 26.6:

The Run Macro dialog box

Excel will execute the macro and the heading will be entered onto the worksheet. Your worksheet should look like Figure 26.1.

To execute a command macro from the keyboard, first clear the worksheet area. Then hold down the Control key and press the key that you assigned to the macro (Shift-*X* for this example). The macro will be executed to create the worksheet heading shown in Figure 26.1.

QUICK RECORDING

A quick way of recording a macro is to choose Record ➤ Macro on the worksheet. If no macro sheet is opened, Excel opens a new sheet (such as Macro1), sets a range, and prompts for a name for the macro to be recorded (see Figure 26.7). Recording starts immediately.

If a macro sheet is already opened and a range set, Excel uses that sheet and range. If no range is set, recording starts in the next blank column. If you choose Set Recorder in a column that already has a macro, then choose *Record;* your new macro will be placed in the next empty column.

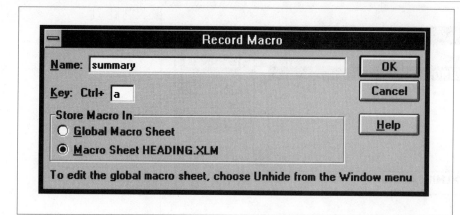

EDITING A MACRO

You edit the macro sheet just as you would any other Excel document: change arguments, delete or insert rows, etc. Experiment by making the following changes in your macro sheet:

1. Change the width of column A to 25 characters.

2. Put the title in italics instead of boldface by changing the style command to read:

=FORMAT.FONT("Arial",12,FALSE,TRUE,FALSE,FALSE,0)

Now, execute your new command macro.

Next, try editing the macro name. To change the name or keystroke sequence, follow these steps:

1. Select the macro sheet.

2. Select the first cell of the macro.

3. Choose Formula ➤ Define Name.

4. When the Define Name dialog box appears (see Figure 26.5), click the macro's name.

5. Edit the name in the Name text box or the keyboard code in the Macro group.

6. Click OK.

You can easily add new entries to the end of an existing macro. If you choose Start Recorder after selecting a range that already has entries, the previous entries will not be deleted. Instead, Excel temporarily removes the *=RETURN( )* at the end. The new entries are added, and the *=RETURN( )* is appended again at the end. If this is not what you want, redefine the Recorder range first or begin entries *after* the previous *=RETURN( )*.

Be careful when editing macros that you do not insert a blank cell in other macros on the same worksheet. For example, you might insert a row to add a new line to a macro; at the same time, however, this could open a new blank cell in other columns in every macro.

USING COMMAND MACROS

This chapter is intended only as a brief introduction to command macros. Here are some basic rules and tips for recording macros:

◆ Be sure that you think through what you are trying to accomplish before you enter the commands. You may wish to make a dummy run to test the sequence before you record it. In this way, you can avoid entering errors or unnecessary steps into the macro sheet.

◆ Generally, the first step after you start recording is to activate the worksheet and position your cursor at the desired point on the worksheet. Don't forget to start the Recorder, *then* activate the worksheet and position the cursor.

◆ Don't be afraid to use macros. Anytime you find yourself repeating a command sequence, save it as a command macro.

◆ Make the macros as readable as possible. The use of presentation features, such as style and border control without gridlines, can increase readability.

◆ Put the name of the macro in the first named cell of the macro (see Figure 27.3 in Chapter 27).

◆ Put many macros on one macro sheet, each with its own name. You can then use the macro sheet as a library, opening it when you first load Excel and using it with many worksheets during the day.

◆ Document your macros: Add comments to clarify what the macro is doing. The best place for comments is in the column immediately right of the macro column.

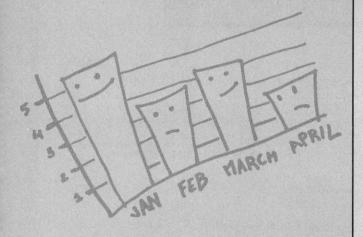

CHAPTER 27

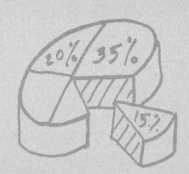

Utilizing Function Macros

**E**xcel's function-macro capability permits you to create your own functions, thereby extending the function library that is already a part of Excel. You can decide which arguments are needed in your functions and which results are to be returned in the worksheet cell. Once you create a function macro, it will be on the function list of the Paste Function dialog box and you can include it in worksheet formulas, just as you would use any other Excel function.

Excel's built-in functions can be used for most standard applications. Here are some examples of functions you may wish to create:

◆ Functions for numeric conversion, as from English to metric units.

◆ Special functions with lookup tables, such as a function to look up the UPS Zone and shipping cost based on a zip code.

◆ Special functions used in a scientific or engineering specialty.

In this chapter, you will learn how to create function macros. You'll find a complete list of the macro language functions in Appendix F.

FUNCTION MACRO USES

A *function macro* is essentially a user-defined function. It calculates a dependent output variable (or array) from one or more independent input variables (or arrays). As explained in Chapter 8, a function is an abbreviation for a formula. It contains one or more arguments that are used to calculate a result. When you create a function macro, you define the arguments and formulas to calculate the results.

You should create function macros whenever you need to use special formulas many times in several worksheets. If you use function macros, you don't have to remember the formulas to get your results. All you need to remember is the name of the function and the type and order of the arguments.

CREATING A FUNCTION MACRO

Create a simple function macro that converts a temperature from celsius to Fahrenheit. There are four steps to creating a function macro:

1. Defining the formulas and arguments.

2. Entering the function.

3. Naming the macro.

4. Saving the macro sheet.

DEFINING FORMULAS AND ARGUMENTS

The formula for the temperature-conversion function is

$$b = (9/5) \times a + 32$$

where b equals the temperature in degrees Fahrenheit and a equals the temperature in degrees celsius. The function will have the name "Fahrenheit" and contain one input argument for the temperature in metric units.

ENTERING THE FUNCTION MACRO

To create the function macro, first open a macro sheet by pressing Ctrl-F11 or selecting File ➤ New ➤ Macro Sheet, and clicking OK. This will open a blank macro sheet. Function macros must be entered manually—you cannot use the Recorder.

Now, follow these steps to enter the Fahrenheit function macro:

1. Enter the function macro title **FAHRENHEIT** into cell A1, as shown in Figure 27.1. Widen column A to 12 characters.

2. In cell A2, define the input argument for the function using the ARGU-MENT macro-language function. Enter **=ARGUMENT("celsius")**, including the quotation marks with the argument name.

3. In cell A3, define your formula: **=(9/5)*celsius+32**.

4. In cell A4, use the RETURN macro-language function and reference the cell on the macro sheet that contains the result by typing **=RETURN(A3)**. (This is A3 in the macrosheet, not the worksheet.)

5. Add the relevant comments in column B, as shown in Figure 27.1.

When entering a function macro, keep in mind the following rules:

◆ Excel's macro-language functions must be preceded by an equal sign, as with any other function.

Include comments in function macros. If the macro is entered to column A, use column B to comment on your macro. For instance, specify the arguments, results, and calculations.

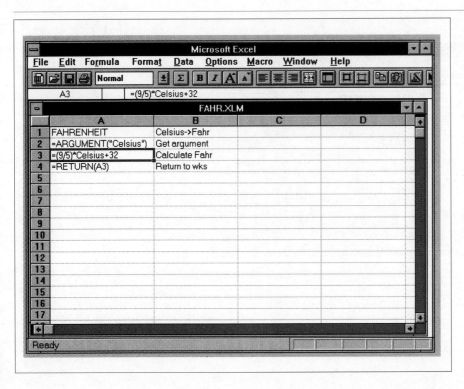

FIGURE 27.1:
Entering the function macro

◆ In the macro-language functions, the names of the values for the input arguments are enclosed in quotation marks (because they are text strings), using ARGUMENT statements. They must be listed in the same order as they are to be entered in the function.

◆ In the formulas, the names of the input arguments are not enclosed in quotation marks (because they are variable names).

NAMING THE FUNCTION MACRO

The next step is to assign a name to the function macro:

1. Be sure that the first cell of the macro sheet is selected.

2. Choose Formula ➤ Define Name from the macro sheet.

3. When the Define Name dialog box appears, the name **FAHRENHEIT** from the first cell is displayed in the Name text box, as shown in Figure 27.2.

4. Select Function in the Macro group and click OK.

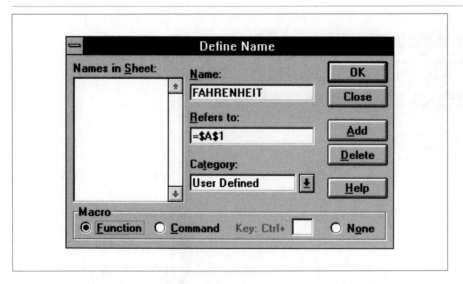

FIGURE 27.2:

The Define Name dialog box for function macros

SAVING THE FUNCTION MACRO

Before you use this function macro, save the macro sheet by following these steps:

1. Select the macro sheet.

2. Choose File ➤ Save As.

3. When the dialog box appears, enter the name **FAHR**.

USING FUNCTION MACROS

Once you've defined a function macro, you can use it in formulas on a worksheet, just as you would use any other function. Let's use the Fahrenheit macro to see how a function macro works:

1. Create the simple worksheet shown in the left of Figure 27.3. Enter the row titles **Celsius** and **Fahrenheit** in cells A2 and A3, respectively. Widen column A to 10 characters. Enter **80** in cell B2.

2. Now enter the formula:

    a. Select cell B3.

    b. Open the Formula menu and choose Paste Function.

    c. Choose the User-Defined category and click the name of your new function, as shown in Figure 27.4. Turn off Paste Arguments and click OK. The formula for cell B3 should now appear in the formula bar, as shown in Figure 27.5.

    d. If necessary, click to place the cursor between the parentheses in the formula bar, then click cell B2 on the worksheet. This will enter B2 as the argument to the function in B3, which means entering 80 in the FAHRENHEIT function.

    e. Click the Enter box or press Enter. The result *176* is displayed in cell B3, as shown in Figure 27.6.

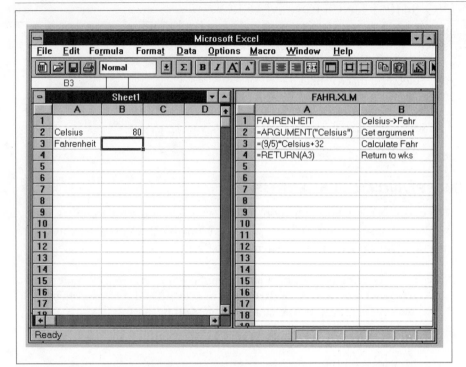

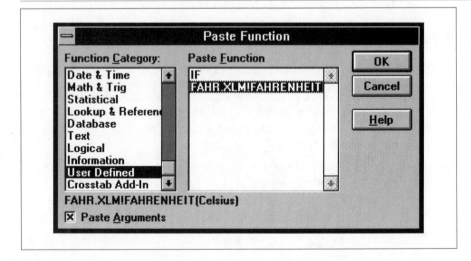

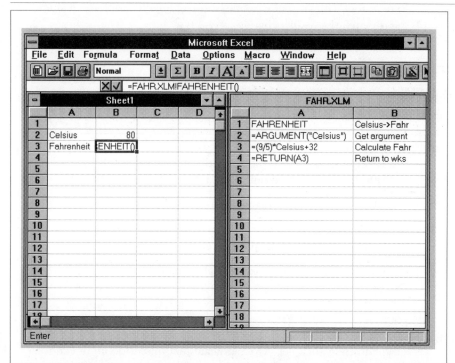

FIGURE 27.5:

Entering the formula

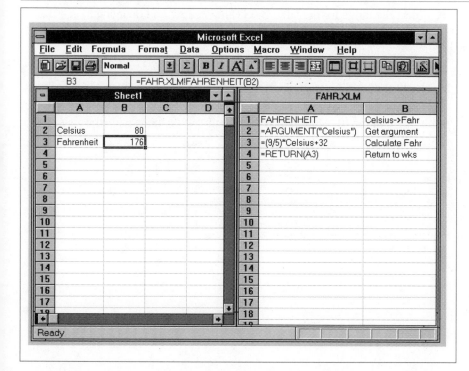

FIGURE 27.6:

Result of formula macro

Experiment with your new worksheet—enter a few different values into cell B2 and watch the results change in cell B3.

PUTTING A FUNCTION MACRO IN A TABLE

Here is the procedure for using your Fahrenheit macro in a table:

1. Create two columns, A and B, for the temperatures. In row 5, label the first column **Celsius** and the second column **Fahrenheit**, as shown in Figure 27.7. Widen column B to 10 spaces.

2. In cell A7, enter the first celsius temperature to be used: **0**.

3. Use Data ➤ Series with a Step Value of 5 and a Stop Value of 100 to fill in the rest of column A to 100 degrees.

4. Put the formula that references the Fahrenheit macro in cell B7. To do this, select cell B7, open the Formula menu, and click Paste Function. When the Paste Function dialog box (see Figure 27.4) appears, select your new FAHRENHEIT function, turn off Paste Arguments, and click OK. Next, click between the parentheses in the formula bar, if necessary, and then click cell A7 to indicate that this is the input cell for the argument. Finally, click the Enter box.

5. Select the range for the table by clicking cell A7 and dragging to cell B27.

6. To set up the table, choose Data ➤ Table. When the Table window appears, click Column Input Cell, select cell A7, and then click OK.

Excel will then apply each input celsius temperature to cell A7, will use this as an input to the FAHRENHEIT formula in cell B7, and will then put the results in column B. Figure 27.8 shows the worksheet with the calculated values.

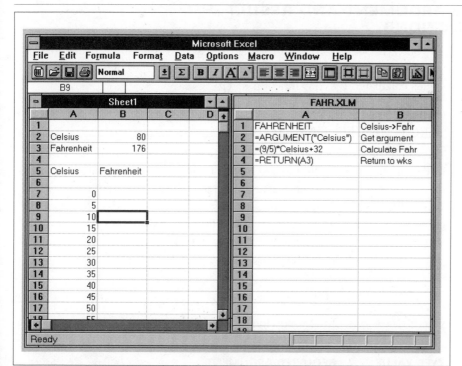

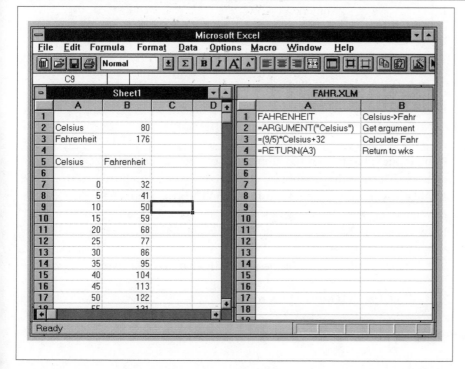

THE ARGUMENT AND RESULT FUNCTIONS

As you have seen in the example above, Excel's ARGUMENT and RESULT macro language functions can be used to control the types of input and output values calculated by your function macro.

THE ARGUMENT FUNCTION

The ARGUMENT function passes values from the worksheet to the function. In the previous example, the ARGUMENT function contained a single argument. You can use an additional argument to control the type of value passed. This optional second argument is primarily used to ensure that the proper argument type is always included in a function macro. Another purpose of the second argument is to permit the use of arrays as arguments.

The form of the function with the second argument is

=ARGUMENT(*name, type*)

where *type* is one of the following numbers:

TYPE VALUE	REQUIRED ARGUMENT
1	Numeric
2	Text
4	Logical
8	Reference
16	Error
64	Array

If the input value for the function is not of the proper type, Excel will try to convert it. If the value cannot be converted, Excel will return the error value **#VALUE!** without executing the function. The *type* argument values can be combined to permit the entry of several data types. If the argument is omitted, Excel uses 7 (1+2+4) as a default value, which permits the entry of numeric, text, or logical values.

There is a third form of the ARGUMENT function as well:

=ARGUMENT(*name, type, ref*)

Here, *ref* is used to refer to a specific cell on the macro sheet. You can then use formulas on the macro sheet to refer to the input value by a name or by a cell reference. For example, on your Fahrenheit macro sheet, you could change cell A2 to read

=ARGUMENT("celsius",1,A5)

and change the formula in cell A3 to read

=(9/5)*A5+32

The formula still works. The third argument, A5, refers to a cell on the macro sheet. Try this and you'll see that the celsius value from the worksheet is entered into cell A5 on the macro sheet, which is used as the input cell for the formula.

When you are defining a function, you can include several arguments. Each is specified in a separate cell of the macro worksheet, using the ARGU-MENT function. As an example, suppose we wish to create our own PMT function and call it PMTX. The built-in PMT function uses five arguments. For instance, to calculate the payments for borrowing $24,000 at 15 percent for three years, you would use:

=PMT(.15/12,36,24000,,0)

The last two arguments are not used (the fourth is omitted and the fifth is zero).

You could, however, write your own function using only three arguments and calculating the interest in the macro by using the macro shown in the Macro4 window of Figure 27.9. This uses three input values to calculate a single output value.

In a similar way, you can use arrays as inputs to a function or have a function return an array value.

It is also possible to create function macros that use no input arguments. An example might be a function that prompts for a value, then returns the value to the program.

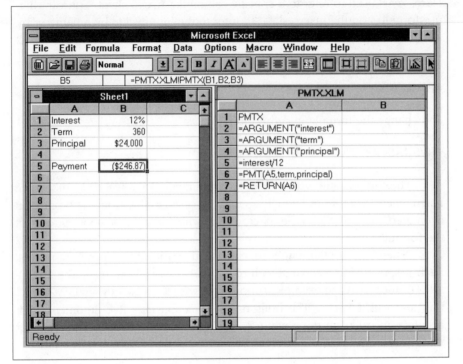

FIGURE 27.9:

*Defining a function
macro that uses
multiple input values*

THE RESULT FUNCTION

*The
RESULT
function is
not the
same as the RETURN
function. RESULT
should be used as the
first formula in your
function macro on
the macro sheet.*

You can use the RESULT function to indicate the type of returned value in the same way that you use the ARGUMENT function to control the input value. The function takes the form:

=RESULT(*ref, type*)

The numeric values for *type* are the same as those for the ARGUMENT function. If the result of the function is of a type different from the one defined, Excel will try to convert it. If Excel cannot do this, it will return the error value **#VALUE!**.

As with the ARGUMENT function, you can use the second argument of the RESULT function to pass an array as the output. Just be sure that you use the proper type value (64) for an array. You also can combine values so that your output can be several types of data. For example, a value of 71 (1+2+4+64) would permit numeric values, text, logical values, or arrays.

COMMAND MACROS VERSUS FUNCTION MACROS

You have now seen how to create two types of macros: the command macro and the function macro. When should you use one instead of the other?

Command macros are generally used to automate tasks that involve a sequence of commands. No arguments are passed to the function and no value is returned. They can be created with the Recorder or entered manually to a macro sheet.

Function macros are used much like other functions, and return a value to a cell based on a defined procedure. They cannot be created with the Recorder.

Command macros and function macros are compared in Table 27.1.

COMMAND MACROS	FUNCTION MACROS
Perform actions.	Are used as part of formulas to return values based on a defined procedure.
Do not have arguments.	Have arguments. You can pass values to a function.
Do not return a value.	Can return a value.
Can be recorded with the recorder.	Can't be recorded with the recorder.
Are initiated with the Macro Run command or with a defined keystroke.	Are part of formulas in cells.

TABLE 27.1:

Command Macros vs. Function Macros

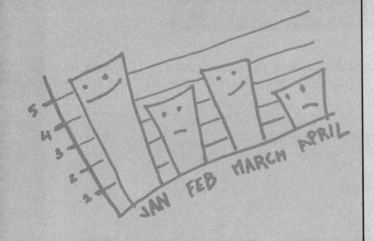

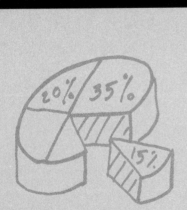

CHAPTER 28

Advanced Macro Techniques

Excel supports the most extensive macro library available in any spreadsheet product—as well as features never before available in this type of product, such as dynamic menus and dialog boxes. Learning to use macros gives you an important pathway to taking full advantage of the potential of Excel.

Let's look at some of Excel's advanced macro features. Someone with a minimum of experience with Excel can create command macros easily by using the Recorder. You cannot, however, create very complex macros this way. To create more advanced command macros, you must use Excel's macro language. If you are designing an application, you probably will need to use the Recorder and enter macros manually.

This chapter covers the following topics:

◆ Using both relative and absolute cell addressing in macro sheets.

◆ Writing interactive macros.

◆ Using control structures.

◆ Debugging the macros you create.

◆ Organizing your macro sheets.

◆ Deciding when to use the Recorder and when to enter macros manually.

◆ Creating macros that automatically start when a document is opened or when you start Excel.

◆ Creating macros that start in special situations (times, key-presses, and error conditions).

◆ Creating custom pull-down menus.

◆ Creating custom dialog boxes.

◆ Attaching macros you create to buttons on the worksheet or to other graphic objects, including invisible objects.

See Appendix F for a directory of the Excel macros.

Before beginning this chapter, be sure that you have used the Recorder to create a few command macros.

RECORDING CELL REFERENCES

You may want to include both relative and absolute cell references in your macros. Excel's Recorder can handle both types of cell addressing.

To switch the mode of cell addressing, open the Macro menu. If *Relative Record* is displayed, this means that Excel is set to record absolute addresses; selecting Relative Record will switch you to relative recording. If *Absolute Record* is on the menu, Excel is set to record relative addresses. You normally should record absolute addresses (so *Relative Record* is displayed).

*The recording **mode** can be set only after the recording **range** has been set.*

You can switch from relative to absolute cell addressing and back at any time while you are recording; the final macro can be a mixture of both types. However, once the macro is recorded, the references cannot be switched by using a command on the Macro menu; you have to edit the macro sheet instead.

WRITING MACRO PROGRAMS

When you create macros, it is often better to record a simple version of the macro first, then insert the extra steps without the Recorder.

You may need to create a command macro with some special features that cannot be added using the Recorder. Typical examples include interactive macros and macros that contain branches and loops. To create macros with these features, you will need to write your own macro sheet or alter an existing one. In this section, you will learn more about these programming techniques.

CREATING INTERACTIVE MACROS

There may be times when you want your command macro to stop during execution and obtain an input value from the user, then continue. This is called an *interactive macro*. Interactive macros can be used for very simple tasks as well as for complex programs, such as creating advanced macro sheets automatically. The user has to enter only the data needed at the proper steps. Remember, however, that the development of complex macros takes quite a bit of time.

There are three ways to make an Excel macro interactive:

◆ With the INPUT function.

◆ With the question-mark form of a command.

◆ With the ALERT function.

Let's take an example and try each of these methods.

In this example, you will create a simple interactive macro that inserts a worksheet heading containing the starting and ending months, which the user specifies. You record the basic macro, then modify it to make it interactive.

To start, you will create a macro that will generate the worksheet shown in Figure 28.1 by using the Recorder. Follow these steps (refer to Chapter 26 if you need help):

The first step when creating a macro that generates the initial labels is usually to select the worksheet. This ensures that if the cursor is on any other window, the macro output is directed to the worksheet.

1. Clear the worksheet you now have, if necessary (select it and press Ctrl-Del).

2. Open a macro sheet and set the Recorder (column A of the worksheet).

3. Check for Absolute addressing.

4. Start the Recorder and select the worksheet.

5. Select cell C1, enter the title, and put it in Arial (or Helv), 12 points, and boldface print.

6. Expand column A to 20 characters by using the Column Width command on the Format menu.

7. Enter **Jan-93** in cell B3.

8. Enter the remaining months by selecting columns B–M of row 3 and choosing Data ➤ Series. Then select Month in the Date Unit box of the Series dialog box (see Figure 28.2). Click OK. (Don't use the drag feature for this, as we want the Data Series function here.)

9. Center the data in the first three rows (A1:M3).

10. Stop the Recorder.

11. Name the macro by selecting cell A1 of the macro sheet, choosing Formula ➤ Define Name, and entering **Title**. Click Command in the Macro control group, then OK.

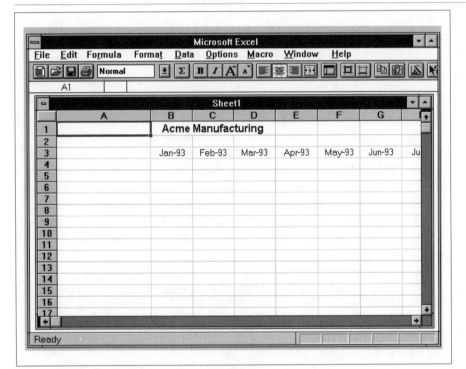

FIGURE 28.1:

The worksheet after executing the interactive command macro

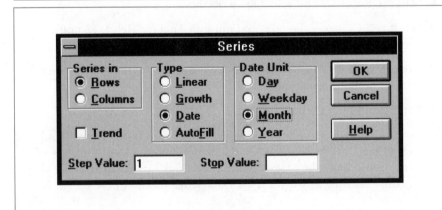

FIGURE 28.2:

The Series dialog box

The final macro sheet should look like Figure 28.3. Save and run the macro to be sure that it works.

You will now make the command macro interactive by modifying this macro sheet in the three different ways mentioned at the beginning of this section.

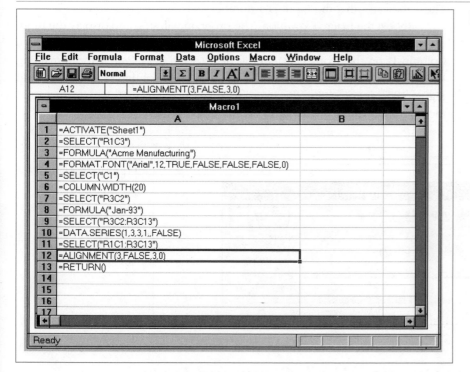

FIGURE 28.3:

The macro sheet

The INPUT Function

You can replace any of the macro sheet's existing function arguments with the INPUT function. Then, when the macro reaches that function, it will stop and ask for the input value. The form of the INPUT function is INPUT(*prompt, type, title*). Its arguments represent the following:

◆ *Prompt* is the message to be displayed to the user in the window.

◆ *Type* is an integer that represents the type(s) of input numbers that can be accepted (see Chapter 27).

◆ *Title* is the name of the window. If *title* is omitted, it is assumed to be "Input."

Now, edit cell A8 (or FORMULA("Jan-93") on the macro sheet) so that it reads

=FORMULA(INPUT("Enter the starting date",1))

The 1 indicates that the input is a number.

Repeat the macro execution. The program will stop and display the Input dialog box. Enter the starting date **nov-92** and click OK (see Figure 28.4). Column B on the worksheet is now headed by *Nov-92*, and the remaining headings are automatically generated as increments of that date, as shown in Figure 28.5. Try repeating this exercise, entering letters that don't form a valid month abbreviation, such as **Apl**. What happens then?

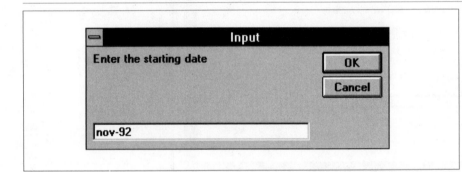

Entering the starting date

The Question-Mark Command Form

Another method for obtaining input is to use the *question-mark form* of the command. Most macro language commands that produce a dialog box use a question-mark form. When a macro gets to that command it stops and automatically displays the command's dialog box.

To specify the ending month in the heading that your macro creates and thereby control the number of columns printed when the macro is executed, you need to use the Series dialog box. Cell A10 on the macro sheet (see Figure 28.3) contains the DATA.SERIES command. Replace it with

=DATA.SERIES?( )

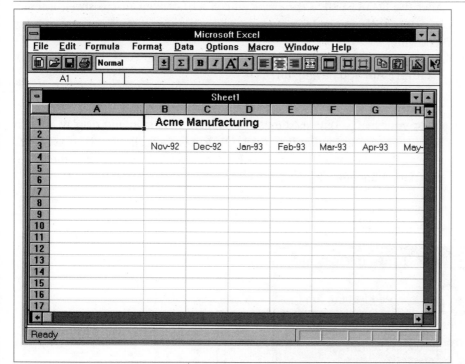

FIGURE 28.5:
*The worksheet after
entering a date in the
input dialog box*

Now clear the worksheet and execute your macro again with **Nov-92** in
the first cell. After you have filled in the Input dialog box and clicked OK, you
will see the Series dialog box. Click Month, enter a stop value of **Jan-93**, and
click OK. Your worksheet will be printed with only three columns.

The ALERT Function

A third way to obtain input during a macro execution is to create an alert box
using the ALERT function. The form of the ALERT function is =ALERT(*text, type*),
where *type* is a value for the type of icon and buttons to display and *text* is the
prompt to display in the box. The values available for *type* are listed below:

TYPE	ICON	BUTTONS
1	? (caution)	OK, Cancel
2	i (note)	OK
3	! (stop)	OK

After the DATA.SERIES? command in cell A10 of your macro sheet, insert a new line (select row 11 and choose Edit ➤ Insert). On this line, add the following:

=ALERT("Are you having fun?",1)

The last argument indicates that a question mark is to be used. Now execute your macro one last time. The program will stop and display an alert box, as shown in Figure 28.6. Click OK to continue the macro. If you click Cancel, the function will return a logical value of FALSE. In this case, the macro execution continues, because the return value is not tested.

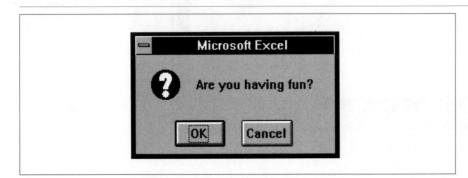

FIGURE 28.6:

Using an Alert box

MAKING DECISIONS WITH CONTROL STRUCTURES

There are two types of control structures you can add to your macro programs: conditional structures (branches) and iterative structures (loops).

Using Conditional Structures

Conditional structures are those in which a program can choose one of several groups of statements to execute, based on the value of a control expression (see Figure 28.7).

One of the simplest types of conditional structure is the IF statement, in which a group of statements is executed if a statement is true. For example, you could use the ROWS function in cell A1 of the macro sheet to return the number of rows in a range selection. It would have the following form:

=ROWS(SELECTION( ))

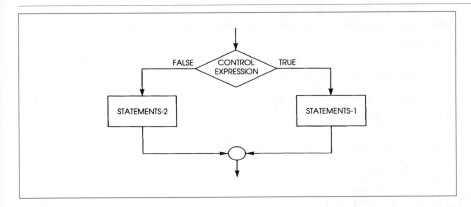

Later in the program, the macro could examine this value and make a decision based on the number of rows specified. For example, the command

=ALIGNMENT(IF(A1=1,3,2))

would adjust the alignment according to the number of rows. If there were one row, the ALIGNMENT function would use 3, and the display would be centered. If not, the ALIGNMENT function would use 2, and the display would be left-aligned. The first value applies if the IF function is true; the second, if the function is false.

You can combine the IF function with the GOTO function to control the order in which the commands in the program are executed. For example, the command

=IF(A2=1,GOTO(A13))

would cause the program to go to cell A13 if the value in cell A2 were 1.

You can also use Boolean operators (AND, OR, and so on) to combine conditions. For example, the command

=IF(AND(A2=1,A3=1),GOTO(A13))

would cause the program to go to cell A13 only if both cells A2 and A3 contained a value of 1.

The GOTO function can even be used to branch to another macro and, when that macro is completed, return to the calling macro to continue.

Be careful not to confuse IF and GOTO. IF is an Excel function, and returns a value based on a condition. GOTO is a macro function, and it defines the cell from which the next program statement will be read.

You also can create a block of functions, executing one part of the block if the control expression is true and another part if it is false. The general form with macros is

IF(*conditional expression*)

statements–1

ELSE( )

statements–2

END.IF( )

Iterative Structures

The iterative structure, or loop, permits the program to execute a group of control statements a specified number of times or for as long as a control expression is true (see Figure 28.8). The control expression is tested at the beginning of the loop.

You can create iterative structures using the IF function. To do so, you must first set a variable in a cell to an initial value using the SET.VALUE function. For example, the command

=SET.VALUE(A25,1)

in cell A2 would put the value of 1 in cell A25 on the macro sheet. Inside the loop, the following would be entered:

=SET.VALUE(A25,A25+1)

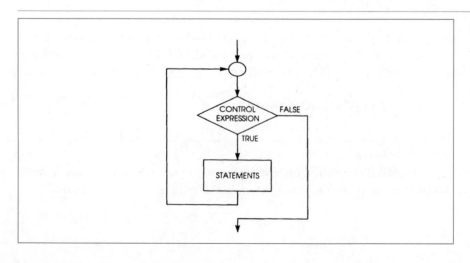

FIGURE 28.8:
A schematic of the iterative structure

This increases the value in A25 each time it is executed.

When the macro is invoked, the value of that cell will increase by 1 each time the above statement is encountered. You can then have the macro test the condition after the value in cell A25 is increased, and determine whether it should remain in the loop, by using the following command:

=IF(A25<=25,GOTO(A3))

Be sure that you loop back *after* the SET.VALUE function.

An example of a loop is the function that calculates the greatest common denominator (GCD) of two numbers, as shown in Figure 28.9. Notice that two columns are used for the macro. The Create Names command on the Formula menu is used to define the cells (select A5:B13 for naming, use Create Names, and mark the Create Names in Left Column check box). Define a macro name in B1 (function macro) by using GCD. The function expression in cell B3 of the worksheet is =(MACRO1!GCD(B1,B2)). Paste the function name to B3 to avoid entry errors.

TIP *Placing labels in the left column (A), macro statements in the middle column (B), and documentation in the right column (C) permits you to name the cells by using Formula ➤ Create Names.*

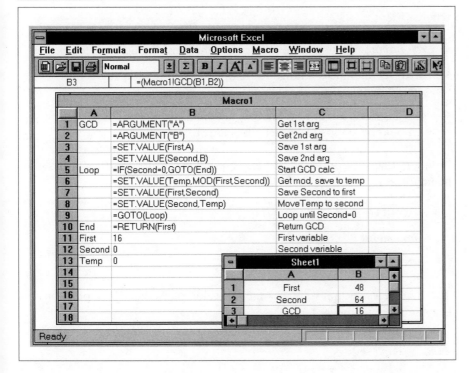

FIGURE 28.9:

A macro that calculates the GCD of two numbers

You also can use the FOR function in a FOR...NEXT form to create a loop. This function has the form

=FOR(*counter_text, start_num, end_num, step_num*)

where

◆ *counter_text* defines a counter variable that monitors the number of times the loop has been executed.

◆ *start_num* defines the starting value of *counter_text*.

◆ *end_num* defines the value for *counter_text* beyond which the loop stops.

◆ *step_num* defines the increment value of *counter_text* for each loop cycle.

For changing a cell range, the FOR.CELL...NEXT form is a better alternative:

=FOR.CELL(*ref_name, area_ref, skip_blanks*)

where

◆ *ref_name* is the text name of a cell in the range being operated on.

◆ *area_ref* references a range to be operated on (the default is the current range).

◆ *skip_blanks* is a logical value that determines whether blank cells should be skipped (the default is FALSE).

Another function supported by Excel permits WHILE loops and has the general form

=WHILE(*control expression*)

statements

=NEXT( )

The statements section must change the value of the control expression, or else the loop will never terminate.

Figure 28.10 shows the GCD function using a WHILE loop.

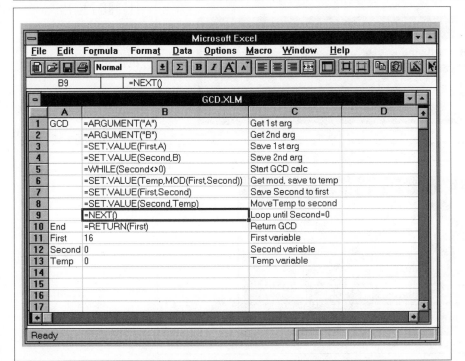

FIGURE 28.10:
*The GCD function with
a WHILE loop*

INTERRUPTING A MACRO EXECUTION

You can interrupt the execution of a macro, just as you would interrupt a printing, by pressing Escape. A macro execution can also interrupt itself if an error is found. The dialog box shown in Figure 28.11 is then displayed. This box shows the current cell to be calculated on the macro sheet and has five buttons: The Halt button terminates the macro execution, the Continue button continues the execution, and the Goto button takes you to the cell where the macro stopped. The Step button displays the Single Step dialog box shown in Figure 28.12. You can use this dialog box to check one step at a time a macro that doesn't work properly. If you need help, use the Help button.

USING MACRO SHEETS

With many other spreadsheet products, a macro is stored on the actual worksheet with which it is used and can be run only with that worksheet open, unless you copy the macro into another worksheet. Because macros

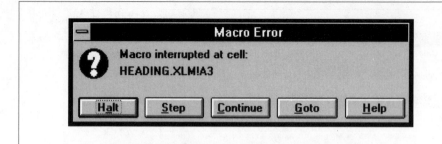

The dialog box displayed when you interrupt a macro

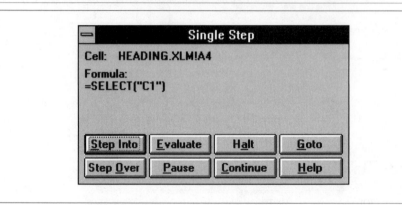

The Single Step dialog box

are entered into a remote area of the worksheet, the resulting worksheet is quite large and requires a lot of computer memory. Excel's macros, on the other hand, are stored in separate macro sheets and can be used with any worksheet open. You should, however, be careful when creating links or when using names as external references on macro sheets, because these features do need specific worksheets open in order to run.

Use the GET.FORMULA function to get the contents of a worksheet cell on a worksheet as it would appear in the formula bar. The general form is:

=GET.FORMULA(*reference*)

If the cell contains an expression, it is retrieved in text form.

To get a value from the active worksheet, place an exclamation point before the cell address. GET.FORMULAS(!A12), for example, gets the value from A12 of the active worksheet. This permits you to create generic macros that will work with many worksheets.

When designing a macro to work with a specific worksheet, be sure to use the worksheet name to prevent possible macro misuse (e.g., GET.FOR-MULA (SALES!$B$11)).

MACRO DESIGN TECHNIQUES

Here are some suggestions for designing your macros:

◆ Plan your macros first. Write out the procedure as a flow diagram. Break complex or long macros down into a hierarchical system of smaller macros. The main routine should be short, with a collection of subroutines. Each subroutine, in turn, can call others. Macros should be short and simple, calling other macros as necessary. Each macro should perform a single function.

◆ Use descriptive names for your macros that have a meaning within the context of the problem you are solving.

◆ Document your macros. Write comments for each step.

◆ For a command macro, record as much as possible by using the Recorder. Then insert steps as necessary to do whatever additional work needs to be done. This minimizes errors.

◆ Trap errors using ARGUMENT and RESULT functions to be sure that the correct data types are passed to and from a function. Check for FALSE returns from functions. Create an error subroutine that is called when an error is sensed, and pass an error code to the routine. Use the ERROR function to customize this.

◆ Generalize your macros by using the INPUT function to prompt the user for information.

◆ Test macros with parallel testing; that is, first use data for which you know the results.

◆ Anticipate the types of errors that may occur with user input and try to trap these: e.g., invalid dates, out-of-range data, no data entry.

◆ Check for FALSE and error codes upon return from functions. Use the ERROR macro function to customize this (see Appendix F for details).

◆ Always save your macro before testing it.

◆ To simplify your work, create libraries of macros that you commonly use. Put the command macros that you use frequently on a single macro sheet, assign it a name, and then use this with other programs as a library. This will save you development time. (What's more, you already know that they work!)

MACRO SPEED TIPS

Almost all macros can be improved. The Excel macro language is quite diverse, and there are generally several ways of accomplishing the same objective.

Here are a few techniques to keep macro execution fast:

◆ Use the echo function to turn off screen updating (use ECHO(FALSE)). This will speed up many macros by a factor of ten. Screen updating is automatically turned back on when the macro terminates.

◆ Turn off automatic calculations. Do the calculation just before printing.

◆ Hide the macro sheets you are using. You can do this with HIDE( ) or by saving the macro in a hidden state. To save a macro in a hidden state, select Hide from the Window menu.

◆ Use external references instead of ACTIVATE. For example, here is a slow version of a program:

```
=ACTIVATE("Sheet1")
=SELECT("R3C3")
=FORMULA("=2+3")
=ACTIVATE("Sheet2")
=RETURN( )
```

Here is the fast version:

```
=FORMULA("=2+3","Worksheet1!R3C3")
=RETURN( )
```

◆ Minimize the use of file operations (such as OPEN and SAVE commands).

◆ Keep dialog boxes simple. Complex dialog boxes take longer for Excel to create.

◆ Minimize the use of names. Use SET.VALUE in assignment operations (for example, SET.VALUE(X,4) instead of X=4). SET.VALUE is up to two times faster than SET.NAME on a macro sheet.

◆ When possible, use SET.VALUE instead of FORMULA to change the contents of a cell on the macro sheet; it's about three times faster.

◆ For loops, using a cell as a counter with SET.VALUE may be faster than using FOR…NEXT or WHILE…NEXT loops.

◆ Use SET.NAME instead of DEFINE.NAME; it's about twice as fast.

◆ Minimize loop operations.

◆ Minimize the use of text operations. Manipulate references as references rather than as text. When possible, use OFFSET, ROW, and COLUMN instead of TEXTREF and REFTEXT.

◆ CUT, COPY, and PASTE operations are relatively slow. Use them only with large ranges of cells. For smaller selections, use the FORMULA command in a loop with external references or use the SET.VALUE command.

In addition, you can make macros *seem* faster by distributing *waits* (periods of seeming inactivity) over several operations and through background processing. Dead screens (blank or no activity) make any wait seem longer. Keep the user informed of what is happening with dialog boxes.

Note that adding names does not slow down macro execution. Names improve macro reliability as well as minimize problems caused by rearranging the worksheet. Names are enclosed in quotation marks only when the name text, rather than the current value of the name, is important.

DEBUGGING MACROS

Here are a few tips to prevent bugs from entering your macros:

◆ Save macros frequently as you develop them.

◆ If you experience problems in creating a macro, try to simplify what you are doing and then build toward the complex. Use the Recorder to build the basic part of the macro, then add the decision controls and other enhancements manually. If you already have a complex macro that has problems, try to break out the troublesome part and test it separately.

◆ Put the STEP function in the macro where you wish to test a result.

◆ For debugging purposes, use Options ➤ Display to make the macro sheet temporarily display values instead of formulas.

◆ Use the Recorder to enter the basic components of a command macro, then add to it.

◆ The default ARGUMENT and RETURN modes do not pass arrays (see Chapter 27). Be sure to put the 64 type value in if you are passing an array.

◆ Keep ECHO on while debugging.

◆ Use comments liberally.

◆ Try to anticipate the types of errors you may encounter and build in traps for them.

◆ Use the Paste Function command to eliminate function name misspellings.

SPECIAL MACRO TECHNIQUES

Excel permits you to modify existing Excel menus, create special menus, run macros automatically upon opening documents, create dialog boxes, and carry out many other special operations with macros that cannot be performed with normal Excel commands. This section is an overview of some of these techniques.

CREATING MENUS

With Excel, you can modify the existing menu bars and drop-down menus, or even create your own menus. As an example, assume a company approaches a bank for loans periodically. The bank needs a spreadsheet system for analyzing these requests. You could create a system in which the data about the company is first entered into a historical worksheet that contains the last four years of the company's financial data. A projections worksheet is then opened and linked to both this historical worksheet and an assumption worksheet (with interest rates and other variables). From these, the projections worksheet calculates the next four years of financial data for the company. This worksheet system could be used at bank branches by users who have little or no experience with Excel. In addition, chances of mistakes could be minimized by automating as much of the process as possible.

Consider using a batch file to start Excel automatically. Macros could automatically load and start, displaying a menu. Only those options you wanted available to the user would be displayed. The macro sheet would be

*Such a system is **really** locked in.* As long as the macro sheet is open in this example, there is no File or Edit menu—or any other familiar Excel command. This protects the user from making mistakes, but once the macro is executed the user is locked into the new menu.

hidden; the user would be essentially locked into a closed system.

Excel contains nine menu bars: the main menu bar for the worksheet and macros, the Chart menu bar, a short form of each of these, a special menu bar for the application when a file is not open, and a menu bar for the info system. You can modify any one of these or create your own. In this example, we will create a completely new menu bar.

The macro worksheet for creating this menu is shown in Figure 28.13. The main macro is in cells A11:A14. The ADD.BAR( ) function creates a new menu bar, but does not display it. The function returns the next menu ID number that is available.

Excel has nine built-in menu bars with IDs. The IDs for the internal Excel menus are as follows:

ID	MENU
1	Worksheet and Macro menu, full
2	Chart menu, full
3	Null menu (no documents open)
4	Info window menu
5	Worksheet and Macro menu, short
6	Chart menu, short
7	Cell or workspace shortcut menu
8	Object shortcut menu
9	Chart shortcut menu

In this case, we are inserting a new menu bar with an ID of 10. The ADD.MENU( ) function creates an option on this menu bar. The function form is

ADD.MENU(*bar_ID,menu_ref,position*)

The *bar_ID* for the bar is the menu ID to which the function refers (10 in this case). The *menu_ref* argument references a cell range that defines the menu (here, C11:G13). The *position* argument is new with Excel 3, and optionally defines the menu position on the bar.

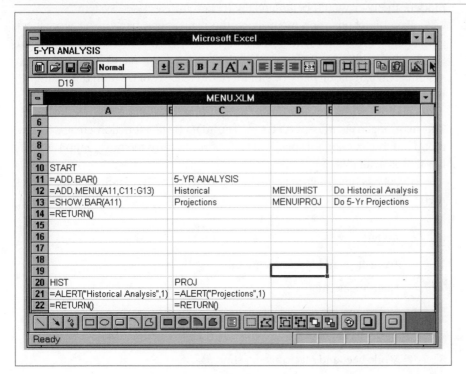

Cell C11 in Figure 28.13 contains the title of the pull-down menu. Below it are the various menu commands. Column D names a command macro that is initiated by each option. Column F defines a text line that will be displayed in the Status area when that command is selected. Column G contains pointers to the custom-help topics that are available. Use Formula ➤ Define Name to name A11, A21, and C21 by their contents. A21 and C21 define command macros.

The programs run by the menu are subroutines, one starting in A21 and the second in C21. At the moment they only display alert boxes, but in the final program they will activate their appropriate routines.

If you wished to use an existing menu and add a new command option to it, you would use the function

ADD.COMMAND(*bar_id, menu_pos, menu_ref,position*)

where *bar_id,* as before, references the menu to be modified. The *menu_pos* argument determines which menu bar selection is to be modified, starting from the left. You can use either the menu name, such as Edit, or the numeric position

(Edit is 2). The *menu_ref* argument, as before, defines the menu command. You can use a single hyphen in the first column to denote a separator bar.

Other functions that are useful for creating and displaying menus are the following:

FUNCTION	ACTION
DELETE.MENU (*bar_id, menu_pos*)	Deletes a menu bar.
DELETE.COMMAND (*bar_id, menu_pos, cmd_pos*)	Deletes a command on a menu.
RENAME.COMMAND (*bar_id, menu_pos, cmd_pos, name*)	Renames a menu command.
ENABLE.COMMAND (*bar_id, menu_pos, cmd_pos, state*)	Enables a command. If *state* is TRUE, the command is enabled; if it is FALSE, the command is not enabled.
CHECK.COMMAND (*bar_id, menu_pos, cmd_pos, state*)	Checks a command. If *state* is TRUE, the command is checked; if FALSE, it is not checked.
GET_BAR()	Returns ID of current menu bar (see Appendix F).

Executing Macros Automatically

You can use macro commands to run a macro whenever a worksheet is opened, whenever a particular command is executed, at a specific time you define, in response to a particular keystroke, whenever an error occurs, or on encountering a specified condition in another document.

In this example, we wish the menu macro to run automatically when a document is opened. In this case, we could make it possible for the bank to create a batch file that opened a blank worksheet. To select a macro for automatic execution when a worksheet is opened:

1. Make the document active. Select the first cell of the macro.

2. Choose Formula ➤ Define Names.

3. Enter the macro name as **AUTO_OPEN**. You can use any name that begins with AUTO_OPEN, such as AUTO_OPEN_ONE. Verify that the reference is correct, select Command Macro, and click OK.

Here are some notes and tips on using AUTO_OPEN macros:

◆ If you ever wish to open the document without running the macro, hold down the Shift key while clicking OK when opening the document.

◆ Be sure the macro is saved before testing. In this example, you won't be able to save the macro once it's been executed.

◆ Be sure the macro is tested before naming it AUTO_OPEN.

◆ If a document with an automatic macro is opened from within a macro, the automatic macro will not execute.

If you wish to create a macro that executes automatically when a document is closed, name it "AUTO_CLOSE." Holding down the Shift key while choosing Close will close the document without executing the macro.

Here are the Excel functions that support automatic macro execution under other conditions:

CONDITION	MACRO FUNCTION
At a particular time	ON.TIME
When a particular key is pressed	ON.KEY
Upon an error condition	ERROR
Upon a macro interruption	CANCEL.KEY
Upon a change in linked data	ON.DATA
When a window is activated	ON.WINDOW
When a document is recalculated	ON.RECALC
Upon a mouse double click	ON.DOUBLECLICK
Upon entering data to any cell	ON.ENTRY
Upon command	(Use customized menus, as in the last example)

Sometimes you may wish to load and execute a macro sheet when Excel is started. To do this, place the macro file in the EXCEL\XLSTART directory. Then, when you start Excel, it will open the document and execute any AUTO_OPEN macro.

CREATING DIALOG BOXES

You are already familiar with the dialog boxes that are a part of many commands. You can also create your own dialog boxes that can be called from macros. These can be used for almost any type of input and are much more versatile than the Input box or direct entry to a cell.

As an example, look again at the Sales worksheet used in Chapters 10–13. Let's create a dialog box to use with the worksheet for entering records. Figure 28.16 shows the final dialog box. Notice that you now have more control over data entered: The user can select from only one of the four regions.

To create the dialog box, start the Dialog Editor from the Program Manager's Excel group. An application window is displayed with three menu options (File, Edit, and Item) and an empty dialog box. We will use this editor to create the entry form.

Select Edit ➤ Info to see the current box dimensions. Turn off any auto options and enter the new values as:

X	150	Postion to start dialog box
Y	42	Position to start dialog box
Width	305	Width of dialog box
Height	237	Height of dialog box

Click OK. The new dialog box frame is displayed in its new size.

You can also enter the dialog box data directly to the worksheet if you wish and not use the Dialog Editor at all.

Enter each item (or control) for the dialog box, as follows: Choose the item from the Item menu, place it where you wish on the frame, and then select Edit ➤ Info to enter specific information about the item. You can use Edit ➤ Clear to remove any object you need to delete. Following these steps, add each of the objects shown in Figure 28.14.

Once the dialog box is created, select it (choose Edit ➤ Select Dialog) and choose Copy to copy the dialog box to the Clipboard. (Notice that there is no Save As or Save on the File menu; you place the dialog box on the worksheet through the Clipboard.) Minimize the Dialog Editor to get it out of the way, and load the Sales worksheet. Select cell F12 on the worksheet as the starting point for the dialog box description and choose Select Paste. Add the column titles in row 11, as shown in Figure 28.15. Enter the text in M13:M16 and define this range as REGION using Formula ➤ Define Names. The worksheet should look like Figure 28.15.

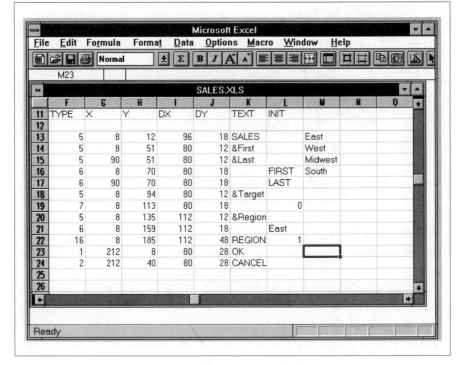

Object	Item (Control)	X	Y	Width	Height	Text	Init/Result
Title	Text	8	12	96	18	SALES	
FIRST label	Text	8	51	80	12	&First	
LAST label	Text	90	51	80	12	&Last	
FIRST entry	Edit box (Text)	8	70	80	18		FIRST
LAST entry	Edit box (Text).	90	70	80	18		LAST
TARGET label	Text	8	94	80	12	&Target	
TARGET entry	Edit box (Integer)	8	113	80	18		0
REGION label	Text	8	135	112	12	&Region	
REGION entry	Edit box (Text)	8	159	112	18		East
REGION list	List box (Standard)	8	185	112	48	REGION	1
OK button	OK button	212	8	72	28	OK	
CANCEL button	Cancel button	212	40	80	28	CANCEL	

FIGURE 28.14:

The dialog box particulars

FIGURE 28.15:

The dialog box description

The column heads used here are the same as those used to create a data form. They are as follows:

NOTE *You can use no more than 64 controls, 32 items that take or return arguments, 4 list boxes, and 1,024 text characters in each dialog box that you design.*

◆ TYPE is a code for the type of dialog-box element or *control* (see Table 28.1).

◆ X and Y are the coordinates for the upper-left corner of the control, as measured from the upper-left corner of the dialog box in points. The horizontal units are ⅛ the width of one character in the system font. The vertical units are 1/12 the height of one character.

◆ DX and DY are the size of the control. They are measured in the same units as X and Y.

◆ TEXT indicates how to display the text. An ampersand prefix indicates that the following letter should be underscored. (This is a "hot key": pressing Alt and the underlined letter accesses the control quickly.) For list-box controls, this column specifies the range M13:M16 for the list.

◆ INIT/RESULT is the column that contains the default value that is displayed for the control. After the dialog box function is executed, it contains the returned value. For a list box, it contains the number of the default item in the box and returns the number of the item selected.

TYPE	CONTROL	COLUMN	DESCRIPTIONS
1	Default OK button	TEXT	The text to appear on the button
2	CANCEL	TEXT	The text to appear on the button
3	OK button	TEXT	The text to appear on the button
4	Default CANCEL Button	TEXT	The text to appear on the button
5	Text	TEXT	The text to display
6	Text box	TEXT	(not used)
		INIT/RESULT	Initially, the default value for the box; after the box is displayed, the returned value
7	Integer box	TEXT	(not used)

TABLE 28.1:

Dialog Box Controls

TYPE	CONTROL	COLUMN	DESCRIPTIONS
		INIT/RESULT	Initial integer value, returns integer entered
8	Number box	TEXT	(not used)
		INIT/RESULT	Initially, the numeric value; returns the numeric value entered
9	Formula box	INIT/RESULT	The formula with the cell value and the result of the formula
10	Reference box	INIT/RESULT	The reference with the cell value and that of the reference cell
11	Option button group	INIT/RESULT	The number of the Option button selected in the subsequent group (see type 12)
12	Option button group	TEXT	The name of the button
13	Check box	INIT/RESULT	TRUE to turn on the check box, FALSE to turn it off
14	Group box	TEXT	The text to appear at the top of the group box
15	List box	TEXT	A reference for the items in the list box
		INIT/RESULT	The number of the initial item; returns the number of the item selected
16	Linked list box	TEXT	A reference for the items in the list box
		INIT/RESULT	The number of the initial item; returns the number of the item selected

TYPE	CONTROL	COLUMN	DESCRIPTIONS
17	Icon	TEXT	1 to display a question mark, 2 to display an "i", 3 to display an exclamation point
18	Linked file list box	TEXT	(ignored)
	List box	INIT/RESULT	(ignored)
19	Linked Drive and Directory list box		Permits altering the directory
		TEXT	(ignored)
		INIT/RESULT	(ignored)
20	Directory text	TEXT	(ignored)
21	Drop-down list box	TEXT	Reference to items in the list
		INIT/RESULT	Number of selected list item
22	Drop-down combination edit/list box		Reference to items in the list
		INIT/RESULT	Number of selected list item

TABLE 28.1:

Dialog Box Controls (continued)

To activate the new dialog box, open a macro sheet and create a new macro:

=DIALOG.BOX(SALES.XLS!$F$12:$L$24)

=RETURN( )

Use the correct name of your document in the DIALOG.BOX function as the first argument. Name the macro and execute it. You will then see a form displayed (see Figure 28.16) for data entry. Fill out the form and then click OK.

After you return from the form, the values you entered will be in cells L16, L17, L19, and L21. These values can be used by the rest of the macro. For example, for a macro to add a record, you would copy the values to the bottom of the database. For an edit macro, you would copy the values to edit to cells L16,

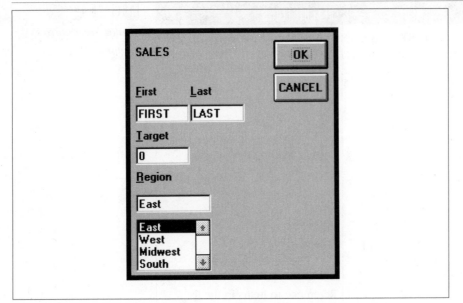

L17, L19, and L21 as the starting values, set L22, use the form, and then copy the new values back. For the list-box control, the selected item will be returned in the text control immediately before it. The number 1 in cell L22 indicates that the first list-box value will be highlighted when the box is displayed.

Dialog boxes can be activated with Data ➤ Form using this method:

1. Create the dialog box with the editor.

2. Copy it to the worksheet.

3. Select the dialog box area and name it DATA_FORM.

Now, if you select Data ➤ Form, you will see your new dialog box. There is one serious limitation, however: You can use only text, buttons, and edit box controls. You can't use list boxes, as in the example here.

ACTIVATING MACROS WITH BUTTONS

You can place pushbuttons (or other graphic objects) on a worksheet and attach macros to them. As an example, let's add a button to the Sales worksheet so that a user can print the worksheet by clicking this button.

Load the Sales worksheet and try this procedure to add the pushbutton:

1. First, create a toolbar with the button function. Show the drawing toolbar. With this toolbar displayed, choose Options ➤ Toolbars ➤ Customize ➤ Drawing, and find the button tool. Drag it to the end of the drawing toolbar to add it.

2. Open a macro sheet and enter the macro you wish to use. For the print macro, enter:

    PRINTER

    =PRINT(1,,,1,,,,,)

    =RETURN( )

    Name the macro PRINTER using Formula ➤ Define Name. Define it as a command macro.

3. Make the worksheet active. Click the button tool on the worksheet and drag from the upper-left corner of the area in which you wish to place the button. For a square button, hold down the Shift key as you drag. To align the button with the grid, hold down the Alt key as you drag. When you release, Excel places a button with a number at that location and prompts for a macro name using an Assign to Object dialog box.

4. Select the name for the macro in the dialog box (see Figure 28.17). Click OK.

5. Edit the text in the button by dragging over the existing text with the I-beam cursor and entering the desired text. Type **Printer** and click off of the button. You can format the text using the Format menu, if you wish (see Figure 28.18).

To print the worksheet, simply click the button!

If you wish to assign a macro to a graphic object that is not a button, click the object, then choose Macro ➤ Assign To Object. Choose the macro name and click off of the object.

If you wish to edit the macro assignment, hold down the Ctrl key and click the object. Choose Macro ➤ Assign to Object and edit the assignment in the dialog box.

To attach a macro to an invisible object, create the object and assign the macro to it. Then select the object and use Format ➤ Patterns to set the border to None and set the Fill as None. Use this method for attaching macros to specific cells—create the object at the cell location, attach the macro, and make the object invisible.

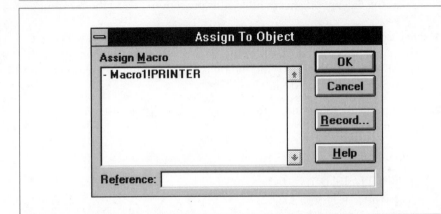

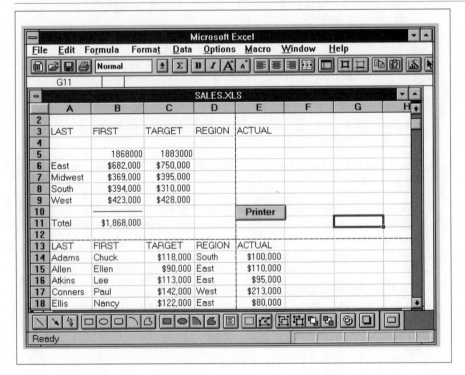

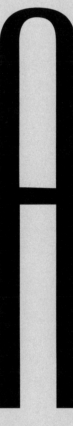

APPENDIX

Glossary

Throughout this book, you may encounter unfamiliar terms. Below is a glosssary of terms used in this book.

Absolute reference A reference to a specific cell or group of cells on a worksheet. An absolute cell reference does not change with moving or copying. In the A1 format, an absolute reference is designated by a dollar sign before both the row and the column, such as $A$5. In the R1C1 style, an absolute reference is just written out as R#C#; for example, R1C5 is an example of an absolute cell reference written in this style.

Active cell The selected cell in which any current keyboard entry would be stored. The active cell is always indicated with a heavy border. The formula bar always shows the contents of the active cell.

Active window The window that is currently selected.

Alignment The position of text or a value in a cell. Alignment can be left, right, centered, filled, justified, or centered across a selection. Alignment specifications can be for vertical or horizontal placement.

Argument The value used as input to a function or command macro to calculate an output value.

Array A two-dimensional set of values, normally arranged in rows and columns.

Attached text Text created with the Attach Text command on the chart menu and connected to a specific object on the chart: title, axis, legend, and so on.

Autofill A feature that enables the user to automatically fill cells or extend a series by dragging.

Autoformat A feature that enables automatic formatting of cell ranges based on a predefined outline.

Axes The straight lines used on the graph for measurement and reference. A pie chart has no real axis; other types have two or three.

Border The line around an area on a worksheet or chart.

Cancel box The small box with a × in the formula bar. Clicking this box discards any changes you have made to a cell using the formula bar.

Category A name associated with a numeric value in a data series. Each data point in a series has a category name and a value.

Cell The basic unit of the worksheet used for storing values, formulas, text, and notes; also the intersection of a row and a column.

Chart One or more graphs displayed in a single document.

Chart format The basic information that defines how a data series is plotted.

Chart object Any part of the chart: axes, markers, lines, legend, plot area, chart, arrows, unattached text, and so on.

Chart style The basic type of chart used. Excel has seven basic chart types: area, bar, column, line, pie, radar, and scatter.

ChartWizard A new tool in Excel 4 for quickly creating charts from specified data.

Circular references Two or more formulas that depend upon each other for results.

Client area (See *Work area.*)

Constant value Anything entered to a cell that is not a formula.

Control menu A menu activated by clicking the Control-menu box (see below). The application Control menu is used to close Excel, resize or move the application window, maximize or minimize Excel, and activate programs that run with Excel. Control menus on the documents can close, resize or move, and maximize the document.

Control-menu bar A small horizontal bar in the upper left of the Excel application window and on each document that opens the Control menu.

Criteria A test used to find, extract, or delete records in a database.

Crosstab ReportWizard An add-in utility that permits creating summary reports from a database.

Database An organized collection of data arranged in one or more records. Each record takes up a row in the database. Information about each record is recorded in fields or columns.

Database range That part of a worksheet that contains the database—including both records and field headers. It is defined with the Set Database command.

Data form A type of dialog box used for updating and searching an Excel database.

Data point A chart category with a corresponding numeric value.

Data series A collection of data points, each related to the other in some respect.

Dependent document Any document containing a reference to another worksheet (the *supporting document*).

Designators The indicators at the top and left of the display area that indicate the rows and columns. At the left of the worksheet are the row *descriptors,* and at the top are the column *descriptors.*

Dialog box A window or box that is used in Excel and other Windows application programs for user input. On a menu, the names of commands that activate dialog boxes end with an ellipsis. You can create your own dialog boxes for data input in a macro.

Document Any worksheet, chart, macro sheet, or slide, either active or saved to the disk.

Dynamic Data Exchange (DDE) A method of accessing a common data area in Windows that can be shared by several Windows application programs.

Embed To insert data (an object) created in one document into another document.

Embedded object Data created in one document that is inserted into another document. A chart on a worksheet is an embedded object.

Enter box The small box with a ✓ in the formula bar that is clicked to complete an entry or edit.

Excel macro language A special group of functions used for writing programs in Excel.

External reference A reference to a specific cell or group of cells, normally on another worksheet. The reference format consists of the worksheet name, an exclamation point, and the cell reference. You can also refer to the currently active worksheet as an external reference by including an exclamation point before the cell reference. This is useful in macros that must refer to cells in several worksheets generically.

Extract To copy from a database records that meet specific criteria.

Field Any column of data in a database, or the individual values in a Field column.

Font A specific design of text (Microsoft definition).

Format Information that controls how the contents of a cell will be displayed. It consists of a picture, style, alignment, font, font size, border patterns, protection, column height, and row width.

Formula A mathematical arrangement of one or more values, cell references, names, functions, and operators that produce a numeric value.

Formula bar An area below the menu bar that displays the contents of the active cell.

Function An abbreviation of a formula. A function produces an output value (or values) from a specified input. (Some functions require no input value.)

Graph A visual representation of one or more data series. It includes the plotted area, labels, legends, and comments.

Gridlines Optional horizontal or vertical lines on a chart to help you determine the value of a marker.

Input cell The cell that holds each of a series of input values.

Label In a chart, text used to identify that part of the chart.

Legend The symbols, with corresponding labels, that are used to identify the different series of data on the chart.

Link To create a reference in a destination document to an object in a source document. The linked object can be edited directly from within the destination document without changing the source document. When the object changes in the source document, the changes also appear in the destination document.

Lock To protect a cell so that its contents cannot be altered.

Macro A collection of functions that can be executed to produce some specified result.

Macro sheet A worksheet used to store macros.

Main chart The primary graph on a chart.

Marker A type of indicator used on a graph to make a data point. In a column chart, each column is a marker.

Mixed reference A reference that consists of both absolute and relative addresses.

Multimedia extensions An extension of the Windows API (Application Programming Interface) that supports sound, CD-ROM, and other features for Windows applications.

OLE Object linking and embedding. A reference to a method of sharing data between applications in which information for processing an object is stored with the object.

Outline A type of structure that permits you to control the level of the worksheet rows and columns that are displayed. Collapsing an outline, for example, permits you to hide detail rows on a worksheet temporarily.

Overlay chart A second graph that is plotted in the same chart window as the main chart.

Pane A subdivision of a worksheet window.

Picture One or more characters used to format a number, time, or date in a cell.

Plot area The area bounded by the axes or, in the case of the pie chart, the area within the circle.

Precision The number of digits to which a value is stored or used in calculations.

Print area That part of the worksheet that is printed when you invoke the Print command.

Protect To protect the contents of a cell, cell range, or worksheet from unauthorized or unnecessary access.

Q+E A utility provided with Excel for interfacing with external databases. It can query, edit, and extract from databases based on a criterion.

Range One or more cells on a worksheet.

Record Any row of data in a database range.

Relative reference A reference to a cell or group of cells located relative to others on a worksheet.

Scale The range of values covered by the *y* axis on the chart.

Scenario Manager An add-in utility that permits what-if simulation by applying a set of input values to one or two cells of the worksheet.

Shortcut Menu An object-oriented menu available by clicking an object with the right mouse button.

Solver An add-in utility provided with Excel for supporting what-if simulations.

Split bar The small black rectangle at the top of the vertical scroll bar and the left of the horizontal scroll bar, used to separate a window into panes.

Status bar An area at the bottom of an Excel window that displays the current status of the program.

Style The appearance of the font on the worksheet (bold, italic, etc.).

Supporting document Any document in which one or more cells are referenced by another worksheet (the *dependent document*).

Table A range of cells that contains the results of applying a series of values to an input cell.

Tickmarks Divisions of an axis used to indicate categories or scale.

Title bar A bar at the top of the application window that contains the program name (such as *Microsoft Excel*) and at the top of each open document displayed in the work area that contains the current file name.

Tool bar An optional bar displayed with a worksheet that can simplify some worksheet operations with a series of function/control/command buttons.

TrueType fonts Scalable fonts supported internally with Windows 3.1.

Unattached text Text on a chart that is not attached to any object and can be moved and resized with the mouse.

Wildcard Special characters used to stand for any character(s) in the text. The question mark (?) is used to represent any single character; the asterisk (*) represents any group of characters.

Work area The area in the Excel window that displays documents and other program-related features (such as the status bar, formula bar, and so on). It is also called the *client area*.

Workbook A defined collection of documents that can be managed as a unit.

Worksheet A grid of cells 256 columns wide and 16,384 cells high, in which you can enter formulas and values.

***X* axis** The horizontal (or category) chart axis.

***Y* axis** The vertical (or value) chart axis.

APPENDIX

B

Speed Tips

Excel runs fastest under Windows 3.1 in 386 Enhanced mode. The use of several megabytes of extended memory will minimize disk swapping (which slows down Excel), so if you are expanding your system and want speed to be a priority, buy more extended memory. You should also use an operating system (and memory managers if necessary) such as DOS 5 that can load DOS high and load drivers and TSRs to the UMB area.

Periodically, you should defragment each disk drive using a compression utility such as PC Tools Compress (Central Point Software) or Norton Utilities Speedisk (Symantec). This ensures that all the sectors of each file are physically adjacent on the disk and speeds up disk access.

To maximize the speed of Windows and Excel in 386 Enhanced mode, install a permanent *swap file*. This is a hidden file that is installed on the disk as an extension of memory. The 386 Enhanced mode is the only mode that supports a permanent swap file. The file is installed at a fixed location on the disk, and Windows can bypass DOS in accessing this file, which permits higher access speeds.

If you are using Windows 3.1 and a standard disk controller, you may be able to use the FastDisk feature of Windows 3.1 to gain even more speed by bypassing DOS for file I/O. If available, FastDisk will be an option when choosing 386 Enhanced from the Control Panel.

Another way to improve the speed of Excel is to install a *disk cache*. A disk cache is a buffer area in memory that manages the transfer of data to and from the disk. Database managers that do a lot of disk reading and writing need large caches. Excel isn't that demanding, but a good disk-caching program can help speed up things. Windows includes its own SMARTDRIVE disk cache, which can be installed by adding the following line to the CONFIG.SYS file:

DEVICE=SMARTDRV.EXE 512 256

Microsoft's SMARTDRIVE is for computers that have a hard disk and extended (512K) or expanded (256K) memory. The first number is the cache size (in kilobytes) assigned to the cache upon booting DOS. The second number defines the *minimum* size of the cache in kilobytes. You may wish to explore some commercial disk-cache programs. Many are faster than the Windows version and will work with Windows 3.1.

Windows is a multitasking system. You can speed execution by closing or suspending applications you are not using. Printing in the background will also slow down Excel.

Here are some speed tips specifically for Excel:

*With Windows 3.1, SMARTDrive 4.0 caches when reading and writing to the disk. Other products cache when reading **and** writing, such as PowerCache +1.25 (Intelligent Devices Corporation) and PC-Kwik 2.00 (MultiSoft Corporation). SMART-Drive is not installed when third-party disk drivers are used.*

◆   Turn off automatic calculations with Options ➤ Calculation. Do the calculation just before printing by pressing F9.

◆   For faster recalculation, calculate only the active worksheet by pressing Shift-F9.

◆   Hide the documents you are temporarily not using. Hiding a macro sheet, for example, keeps it available but makes the screen faster. You can do this with the HIDE( ) function, the Window ➤ Hide command or by saving the macro in a hidden state.

◆   Avoid performing operations (such as Cut or Copy) on an entire row or column. These take up more Clipboard space and require more time than operations performed only on the relevant cells.

◆   Use a macro sheet that automatically loads with frequently used macros. Then add an Auto_Open macro to it starting in cell A1 to block the loading of Sheet1 when you start Excel. Keep the macro in the EXCEL\XLSTART directory to automatically load and execute. Give the macro sheet any name you wish, but select Formula ➤

Define first to name $A$1 as Auto_Open. An example is the following:

```
Auto_Open
=HIDE( )
=OPEN?( )
=IF(A3=TRUE,GOTO(A6))
=NEW(1)
=RETURN( )
```

This hides the macro sheet and displays a dialog box to open a file. If you cancel, Sheet1 will be loaded.

- Select the document names from the bottom of the File menu to load recently used documents.

- Keep templates of frequently used worksheets. Keep custom pictures in the templates, as well as your custom styles.

- Explore creative font management to speed printing. For example, a Microsoft Z cartridge with Helvetica 10 is fast, but trying to download it as a soft font from the computer for landscape printing is slow. In this case, printing the document in portrait mode is definitely faster.

- Place tables on a separate worksheet to control their recalculation better.

APPENDIX C

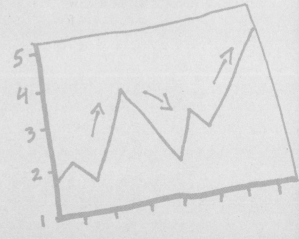

Installation Tips

 hen you install Excel, the installation procedure creates a new EXCEL4.INI file with the initialization parameters for Excel, and also modifies the Windows WIN.INI file to include Excel-specific parameters.

THE WIN.INI FILE

The WIN.INI file defines the system parameters for the Windows environment. This defines startup programs, associations (file extensions for starting programs from a data file), embedding definitions, and fonts.

You can edit the WIN.INI file at any time to customize your system, using the Windows Notepad, Windows Sysedit, or any editor. You should not, however, use a word processor to modify the file unless the word processor can save the new file in ASCII format. This means saving the file as text only, without any formatting codes.

 Before altering WIN.INI, always create a backup. This way, if you do make a mistake you can always get home again.

Now let's take a look at a typical WIN.INI file. We won't look at the entire file, but a few parts are relevant for Excel:

```
[windows]
load=
run=

[Extensions]
.

.

.
xls=F:\EX4\EXCEL.EXE ^.xls
xlc=F:\EX4\EXCEL.EXE ^.xlc
xlw=F:\EX4\EXCEL.EXE ^.xlw
xlm=F:\EX4\EXCEL.EXE ^.xlm
xlt=F:\EX4\EXCEL.EXE ^.xlt
xll=F:\EX4\EXCEL.EXE ^.xll
xla=F:\EX4\EXCEL.EXE ^.xla
xlb=F:\EX4\EXCEL.EXE ^.xlb

[Embedding]
.

.

.
ExcelMacrosheet=Microsoft Excel Macrosheet,Microsoft Excel Macro-
sheet,F:\EX4\EXCEL.EXE,picture
ExcelChart=Microsoft Excel Chart,Microsoft Excel
Chart,F:\EX4\EXCEL.EXE,picture
ExcelWorksheet=Microsoft Excel Worksheet,Microsoft Excel
Worksheet,F:\EX4\EXCEL.EXE,picture



.

.

.
```

You'll find that the file is divided into sections, each with some type of [*xxx*] heading that defines a section, and then a list of lines of the form:

parameter=value

Each line sets a certain parameter to a value or text string. You can edit parameter values, add new parameters, or delete parameters.

At the beginning of the list is a collection of parameters under *[windows]*. *Load* defines programs that are automatically loaded as minimized icons upon starting Windows. You can put Excel here if you wish Excel to be started in Windows as an icon. Be sure to add the full path name and file extension. Here is an example:

load=d:\excel\excel.exe

The *run* parameter defines any program automatically started with Windows. Putting Excel here will not only load it, but make it active as well. You can also force Excel to start with Windows by placing Excel in the Startup group of Program Manager. To do this, hold down the Ctrl key and drag the Excel icon to the Startup group.

Finally down under *[extensions]*, you will find a parameter list that defines which program is started when you select a data file. This list is automatically modified when you install Windows applications, and permits you to start Excel with a document by double-clicking that document from the Windows File Manager. You can also add entries to this from File Manager by using the File ➤ Associate command.

Finally, you will find a section for your printer. If you have installed any soft fonts for that printer, they will be listed here. You will note that soft fonts are printer and port specific.

THE EXCEL4.INI FILE

You should also find an EXCEL4.INI file in your windows directory. It contains basic startup information used by Excel, such as:

```
[Microsoft Excel]
Options3=6
StickyPtX=409
StickyPtY=306
Maximized=1
Comment=The open=/f lines load custom functions into the Paste
Function list.
Options=87
Basics=1
Open=F:\EX4\LIBRARY\CROSSTAB\CROSSTAB.XLL
Open1=/F F:\EX4\LIBRARY\REPORTS.XLA
Open2=/F F:\EX4\LIBRARY\SCENARIO.XLA
Open3=/F F:\EX4\LIBRARY\SLIDES\SLIDES.XLT
```

Open4=/F F:\EX4\LIBRARY\VIEWS.XLA
Open5=/F F:\EX4\LIBRARY\SOLVER\SOLVER.XLA
Open6=/F F:\EX4\LIBRARY\ANALYSIS\ANALYSF.XLA
Open7=/F F:\EX4\LIBRARY\ANALYSIS\ANALYSIS.XLA

[Recent File List]
File1=F:\EX4XLS\19-02.XLS
File2=F:\EX4XLS\TREND3.XLS
File3=F:\EX4XLS\CURVI.XLC
File4=D:\XLS\TREND4.XLS

[Init Commands]
Comment=This section adds commands to Excel menus.
Syntax=menu_bar_num,menu name,command name,macro,place before command,mac key,status text,help reference
addinmgr=1, Options, Add-&ins…,'F:\EX4\LIBRARY\ADDINMGR.XLA'!STUB,----,,Add or remove addins,EXCELHLP.HLP!1707
reports=1, File, Print R&eport…,'F:\EX4\LIBRARY\REPORTS.XLA'!STUB,---,,Create and print named reports,EXCELHLP.HLP!1731
scenario=1, Formula, Scena&rio Manager…,'F:\EX4\LIBRARY\SCENARIO.XLA'!STUB,,,Create and examine what-if scenarios,EXCELHLP.HLP!1733
views=1, Window, &View…,'F:\EX4\LIBRARY\VIEWS.XLA'!STUB,-,,Create and view named views of data,EXCELHLP.HLP!1730
solver=1, Formula, Sol&ver…,'F:\EX4\LIBRARY\SOLVER\SOLVER.XLA'!STUB,,,Find solution to worksheet model,EXCELHLP.HLP!1830
analysis=1,Options,Ana&lysis Tools…,'F:\EX4\LIBRARY\ANALYSIS\ANALYSIS.XLA'!STUB,,,Select an analytic procedure,EXCELHLP.HLP!1780

[Line Print]
Comment=This section controls Lotus macro line printing settings.
Options=2
LeftMarg=4
RightMarg=76
TopMarg=2
BotMarg=2
PgLen=66
Setup=

[WK? Settings]
Comment=This section controls Lotus file open and save settings.
WYSIWYG_Save=1

```
Load_Chart_Wnd=1
AFE=2
Monospace=1
Gridlines=0

[Spell Checker]
Speller=Spelling 1033,0
```

Notice that this file defines the last parameters used by Excel. It can be modified by an editor as well, but the same rule applies to EXCEL4.INI as to WIN.INI—save the current file first.

APPENDIX

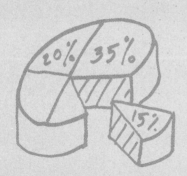

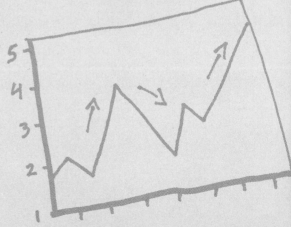

Displaying and Customizing Toolbars

Excel contains nine built-in toolbars: Standard, Formatting, Utility, Chart, Drawing, Microsoft Excel 3.0, Macro, Stop Recording, and Macro Paused. You can edit any of the toolbars as well as create your own toolbars using existing tools or custom tools. You can display more than one toolbar at a time. Excel "remembers" the displayed toolbars each time you exit and, when restarted, displays the same toolbars at the same location. You can change which toolbars are displayed by using the Options ► Toolbars command.

Toolbars can be displayed at the edge of the screen, locked to the left, right, top, or bottom edge; in this case, they are said to be "docked" and look as if they were a part of the application window, with no Close box. Toolbars can also be dragged away from the edge with the mouse and in this case are said to be "floating" toolbars. Floating toolbars look much like windows and have a small Close box in the upper left. Clicking the Close box hides the toolbar. You can quickly undock a toolbar by double-clicking it. You can redock a floating toolbar by double-clicking its title bar.

The width of an undocked toolbar can be changed by dragging one of its edges. This changes the aspect ratio (height/width) of the toolbar, wrapping the tools on the toolbar as necessary to display them all. Once you dock a toolbar, the toolbar assumes its full width. Moving the toolbar away from the dock restores the previous width.

You can display or hide any toolbar by using the toolbar shortcut menu (just click a toolbar with the right mouse button) and selecting a toolbar to hide or display. You can also show or hide a toolbar by using the Options ➤ Toolbars command. You can click the toolbar background with the right mouse button to display the Toolbars short menu.

To add a tool to an existing toolbar, choose Options ➤ Toolbars and Customize. In the Categories list box, choose the category of tools you wish to use. You can add a tool from any category. To find the tool you wish, click each tool and read its description in the dialog box. To add a tool, drag it from the dialog box to a toolbar.

To delete a tool from an existing toolbar, choose Options ➤ Toolbars and Customize. Drag the tool you wish to delete from the toolbar to anywhere off the toolbar (including to the dialog box). Any category can be selected, as the category of tools isn't used for customizing. The tool is removed from the toolbar, but is still available if you need it again later.

To copy or move a tool to somewhere else on the toolbar or to another toolbar, first choose Options ➤ Toolbars and Customize. To copy, hold down the Ctrl key and drag the tool to its new location. To move, simply drag the tool to its new location.

To create a new toolbar, choose Options ➤ Toolbars. Enter the name of the new toolbar in the Toolbar Name text box. Choose Add or Customize. A blank toolbar is displayed. Add the tools you wish to the new toolbar by dragging them from the dialog box, as when adding tools to an existing toolbar.

To delete a custom toolbar, choose Options ➤ Toolbars. Select the name of the toolbar to delete and then select Delete.

APPENDIX

Using Excel with Lotus 1-2-3

hen a file is transferred in either direction between Lotus 1-2-3 (Lotus Development Corporation) and Excel, the following items convert:

- Cell values, formulas, and formats
- Names

The following items do not convert:

- Window properties
- Macros
- Lotus charts to Excel graphs

Although many functions in Lotus have a different order of arguments, they will still convert, and the worksheet will operate properly when transferred in either direction. See Chapter 21 for information about how to convert files. Here are some additional notes:

- Some Lotus formulas cannot be converted; you will be alerted by a dialog box when these are encountered. Some Excel functions are not supported in Lotus.

◆ Lotus uses logical functions in a different way from Excel. For example, the Lotus expression

IF(A25>5#AND#A25<25,"","Entry not in 5–25 range")

becomes this in Excel:

IF(AND(A25>5,A25<25),"","Entry not in 5–25 range")

◆ Excel permits the use of text as constants in formulas; Lotus does not. Any Excel formula containing a text argument or operand will not convert.

DATA ENTRY DIFFERENCES

With Excel, you first select the cells, then choose the command. With Lotus, the opposite is true. Excel has the advantage of permitting you to do several operations on the same selection. You can also select multiple and discontinuous ranges.

Lotus uses the first typed character of a cell entry to determine whether the entry is a value or text. Excel looks at the *entire* cell contents before making a decision. For example, *1-2-3* is considered a numeric entry for Lotus and a text entry for Excel. This means that Excel can interpret an address entry that begins with a number as a text string; Lotus cannot.

When defining a range of cells, Excel uses a colon in the same way that Lotus uses a double period. Lotus functions start with an ampersand. Excel begins them with an equal sign. Thus, @SUM(A8..A14) in Lotus is =SUM(A8:A14) in Excel.

When reading a Lotus worksheet, Excel automatically takes care of these differences.

FUNCTIONS

Most Lotus and Excel functions are identical, but you will find some that differ in name or in how they are used. For financial functions, Excel considers anything you pay out to be a *negative* cash flow. For this reason, some financial functions return negative values. For Lotus, the same functions return *positive* values.

Lotus defines the LOOKUP functions slightly differently, too, with the offset beginning at 0 instead of 1.

Use caution as well with the order of the arguments. In some cases, Excel orders them differently from Lotus. This is particularly true of financial functions.

FORMATTING

When converting, the formatting information will be maintained as much as possible. When converting from Excel to Lotus, the existing alignment for text cells is maintained; all nontext cells will be right-aligned.

MISCELLANEOUS

Excel emphasizes presentation-quality reporting with both worksheets and charts. If you have been using a particular Lotus worksheet and want to add some graphic elements to it, set it up with Lotus and use Excel to create the final image; i.e., import the final worksheet to Excel and add the extras there.

APPENDIX

F

The Macro Language Function Directory

This appendix lists all of the macro functions available to the Excel for Windows user, with the exception of functions for pre-Excel 3.0 versions that are supported for compatibility only. The functions are in alphabetical order, with each listing giving the argument(s), purpose, one or more examples (where helpful), and menu equivalents. Macro function arguments fall under the same categories as those of other functions: text, numeric, logical, reference, error, and array.

For each function, typing a question mark after the command keyword displays the command's dialog box (if available), from which you can choose the desired options.

The typographical conventions used in this appendix are as follows: Required arguments appear in parentheses in lowercase; optional arguments appear within square brackets. Text arguments are indicated with the suffix *text*; when entered, they must be enclosed in quotes (" "). As they are throughout the book, menu options are separated by a ➤ symbol. Thus, "Formula ➤ Define Name" means "the Define Name command in the Formula menu."

A1.R1C1(logical)

Switches display mode to A1 if *logical* is TRUE. Switches display mode to R1C1 if *logical* is FALSE.

Example: =A1.R1C1(TRUE) switches display mode to A1.

Menu Equivalent: Options ➤ Workspace ➤ R1C1

ABSREF(ref_text, ref)

Returns an absolute reference defining cells that have a relative relationship to *ref*, as specified by *ref_text*. *Ref_text* must be an R1C1-style relative reference. (OFFSET is a preferred function for this.)

Example: =ABSREF("R[–1]C[–2]",C4) equals $A$3.

ACTIVATE([window_text, pane_no])

Activates the window defined by *window_text*, and *pane_no* is the pane.

Example: =WINDOW("Sheet1") activates Sheet1.

Menu Equivalent: Window ➤ *window_name*

ACTIVATE.NEXT( )

ACTIVATE.PREV( )

Activates the next/previous window.

Menu Equivalent: Ctrl-F6/Ctrl-Shift-F6.

ACTIVE.CELL( )

Returns reference to active cell in the selection.

Example: The function =SET.NAME("Cost",ACTIVE.CELL( )) assigns the name "Cost" to the currently active cell.

ADD.ARROW( )

Adds an arrow to the active chart.

Menu Equivalent: Chart ➤ Add Arrow

ADD.BAR([bar_number])

Creates a new and empty menu bar in the system. If *bar_number* is already used, restores the previous menu bar associated with *bar_number*.

Example: See Chapter 28.

ADD.COMMAND(bar_number, menu_pos, menu_ref, [position])

Adds a command bar defined in a range of macro sheet cells: *menu_ref* on the sheet to the menu at *menu_pos* in menu-bar number *bar_number* (see Chapter 28 for example).

BAR_NUMBER	MENU BAR
1	Worksheet and macro sheet menu bar (full menus)
2	Chart menu bar (full menus)
3	Null menu bar (the menu when no documents are open)
4	Info menu bar
5	Worksheet and macro sheet menu bar (short menus)
6	Chart menu bar (short menus)
7	Cell or workspace shortcut menu
8	Object shortcut menu
9	Charting shortcut menu

Position indicates the placement of the bar. Commands are added above the specified position. If not specified, the command is put at the bottom.

Example: See Chapter 28.

ADD.MENU(bar_number, menu_ref, [position])

Adds a menu defined in range *menu_ref* on the sheet to *bar_number*. The optional *position* argument specifies the placement on the bar. The new menu is placed at the left of the specified position. If omitted, the menu is placed at the end of the menu bar.

Example: See Chapter 28.

ADD.OVERLAY( )

Adds an overlay to the active chart.

Menu Equivalent: Chart ➤ Add Overlay

ADD.TOOL(bar_id, position, tool_ref)

Adds one or more tools to toolbar, where *bar_id* specifies toolbar:

BAR_ID	TOOLBAR
1	Standard toolbar
2	Formatting toolbar
3	Utility toolbar
4	Chart toolbar
5	Drawing toolbar
6	Excel 3.0 toolbar
7	Macro toolbar
8	Macro recording toolbar
9	Macro paused toolbar

Position specifies position, with 1 at the far left. *Tool_ref* defines the tool, and is either a number specifying a built-in tool or a reference to an area on the macro sheet that defines a custom tool.

Menu Equivalent: Options ➤ Toolbars ➤ Customize

ADD.TOOLBAR(bar_id, [tool_ref])

Creates toolbar with the specified tools (see ADD.TOOL).

ALERT([text, type])

Displays an alert box with the message *text*. The box can be one of the three following types:

The type 1 alert box can be used to give the user a choice between two options.

TYPE	ACTION
1	Caution alert with the ? icon and both the OK and Cancel buttons
2	Note alert with the "i" (information) icon and the OK button
3	Stop alert with the ! icon and the OK button

Example: =ALERT("Number must be less than 10",2) displays a note-alert box with **Number must be less than 10** in it.

ALIGNMENT(x_align, [wrap, y-align, orient_num])

Aligns the selected cells to the *x_align* format:

TYPE	FORMAT
1	General
2	Left
3	Center
4	Right
5	Fill
6	Justify
7	Center across selection

The *wrap* argument specifies whether text is to be wrapped in the cell. The value for **y-align** defines the vertical alignment: 1 = top, 2 = center, and 3 = bottom. *Orient_num* defines the orientation: 0 = horizontal, 1 = vertical, 2 = upward, 3 = downward. The default for all options is the current text setting.

Example: =ALIGNMENT(3) centers the selected cells.

Menu Equivalent: Format ➤ Alignment

APP.ACTIVATE([title_text, wait_log])

Activates *title_text*. If *wait_log* is TRUE, the application will not be activated until you switch to Excel; if it is FALSE or omitted, the named application activates immediately.

Menu Equivalent: (Application Control) Run

APP.MAXIMIZE( )

Maximizes the application window.

Menu Equivalent: (Application Control) Maximize

APP.MINIMIZE( )

Minimizes the application window.

Menu Equivalent: (Application Control) Minimize

APP.MOVE([x_number, y_number])

Moves the window to the specified location. The question-mark form of the command does not display a dialog box but permits moving with the mouse or keyboard.

Example: =APP.MOVE(100,150) moves the Excel window so that there are 100 points from the left edge of the screen to the left edge of the window and 150 points between the top edge of the screen and the top edge of the window (1 point equals $1/72$ of an inch).

Menu Equivalent: (Application Control) Move

APP.RESTORE( )

Restores the active window.

Menu Equivalent: (Application Control) Restore

APP.SIZE([x_number, y_number])

Resizes window to *x_number, y_number.* The question-mark form does not display a dialog box; it permits the window to be resized with the keyboard or mouse.

Example: =APP.SIZE(200,250) sizes the window to be 200 points wide and 250 points high (1 point equals $\frac{1}{72}$ of an inch).

Menu Equivalent: (Application Control) Size

APP.TITLE([text])

Changes title of application workspace to the title specified by *text.* If no argument is specified, the title will be "Microsoft Excel." Use this to customize Excel for your system.

APPLY.NAMES(name_array, [ignore, use_rowcol, omit_col, omit_row, name_order, append])

Searches for the definition(s) of a name or names in *name_array* through formulas and replaces the definition(s) with the name(s).

Menu Equivalent: Formula ➤ Apply Names

APPLY.STYLE(style_text)

Applies the specified style to the selected cell(s).

Menu Equivalent: Format ➤ Style

ARGUMENT(name_text, [type])

ARGUMENT([name_text, type,] ref)

Permits passing arguments to a macro. For each argument of a macro, there must be one ARGUMENT function in the macro. ARGUMENT functions must come before any other formulas in the macro except the RESULT function. If you use the form ARGUMENT(*name_text, type*), then *name_text* refers to the value passed in the macro. If you use the form ARGUMENT(*name_text, type, ref*), the value is passed to a cell on the macro sheet designated by *ref_text,* and *name* refers to the cell where the value is stored.

The value of *type* determines what types of values Excel will accept for the argument. If the value passed is not the correct type, Excel will attempt to convert it. If it cannot be converted, Excel will return the error value #VALUE!.

TYPE	ARGUMENT TYPE ACCEPTED
1	Number
2	Text
4	Logical
8	Reference
16	Error
64	Array

You can combine these for multiple types. For example, a value of 3 for *type* would permit a number or text to be accepted. If *type* is omitted, a default value of 7 will be assumed. This permits numbers, text, or logical values. *Type* must be specified to use arrays or references.

Example: See Chapter 27.

ARRANGE.ALL([arrange_num, active_doc, sync_horiz, sync_vert])

Rearranges displayed windows in work area. Arrange_num defines how to arrange the windows:

ARRANGE_NUM	RESULT
1	Tiled (default)
2	Horizontal
3	Vertical
4	None
5	Horizontally arranges and sizes
6	Vertically arranges and sizes

Active_doc, if TRUE, arranges windows only on the active document. If FALSE or omitted, all open windows are arranged. *Sync_horiz* and *sync_vert* define if the appropriate synchronization is applied on scrolling.

Menu Equivalent: Window ➤ Arrange

ASSIGN.TO.OBJECT([ref])

Assigns a macro to be run when the object is clicked. *Ref* defines the macro to be run when the object is clicked.

Example See Chapter 28.

Menu Equivalent: Macro ➤ Assign to Object

ASSIGN.TO.TOOL(bar_id, position, [macro_ref])

Assigns a macro to a tool (see ADD.TOOL for parameters).

Menu Equivalent: Macro ➤ Assign to Tool

ATTACH.TEXT(attach_to_number, [series_number, point_number])

Attaches text to title, axis, series, or data point. The value of attach_to_number defines what the text is attached to:

ATTACH_TO_NUM	ATTACHES TEXT TO
1	Title
2	Value (y) axis, or value (z) axis on 3-D charts
3	Category (x) axis, or series (y) axis on 3-D charts
4	Series or data point or category (x) axis on 3-D charts
5	Overlay value (y) axis, or series or data point on 3-D charts
6	Overlay category (x) axis (2-D charts only)

If a series and data point are specified, the *series_number* argument defines the series and the *point_number* argument defines the data point.

Menu Equivalent: Chart ➤ Attach Text

AXES([x_main, y_main, x_over, y_over])

AXES([x_main, y_main, z_main])

The arguments are logical values that turn the designated axis off or on.

Menu Equivalent: Chart ➤ Axes

BEEP([number])

Sounds the built-in tone, specified by *number,* from 1–4. Useful for alerting the user after a specified action is completed.

BORDER([outline, left, right, top, bottom, shade, outline_color, left_color, right_color, top_color, bottom_color])

Creates a border around the currently selected cells. The first five arguments are numbers specifying line types for the corresponding border (0 = no border, 1 = thin line, 2 = medium line, 3 = dashed line, 4 = dotted line, 5 = thick line, 6 = double line, and 7 = hairline). *Shade* corresponds to that option on the box. The color arguments are numbers specifying the color (corresponding to the colors in the Color drop-down list).

BORDER TYPE	DESCRIPTION
0	No border
1	Thin line
2	Medium line
3	Dashed line
4	Dotted line
5	Thick line
6	Double line
7	Hairline

Colors have a value of from 1 to 16, corresponding to the colors in the drop-down box. A value of 0 is no color.

Example: =BORDER(1,0,0,0,0) draws an outline around the currently selected cells.

Menu Equivalent: Format ➤ Border

BREAK( )

Interrupts the execution of a FOR...NEXT or WHILE...NEXT loop.

BRING.TO.FRONT( )

Puts the selected objects on top of others.

Menu Equivalent: Format ➤ Bring To Front

CALCULATE.DOCUMENT( )

Calculates the active document. (Does not work for charts.)

Menu Equivalent: Options ➤ Calculation ➤ Calc Document

CALCULATE.NOW( )

Initiates a calculation on all open documents.

Menu Equivalent: Options ➤ Calculation ➤ Calc Now

CALCULATION(type, [iteration, number_of, change, update, precision, date_1904, calc_save, save_values, alt_exp, alt_form])

Specifies the type of calculation to use as controlled by the Calculation dialog box. There are three types:

TYPE VALUE	CALCULATION TYPE
1	Automatic
2	Automatic except tables
3	Manual

The arguments are as follows:

◆ *Iteration* is a logical value where TRUE indicates checked and FALSE indicates not checked

◆ *Number_of* and *change* are numbers representing the maximum number of iterations and the maximum amount of change respectively

◆ *Update* represents the Update Remote References check box. *Precision* represents the Precision As Displayed check box. *Date_1904* represents the 1904 Date System check box

◆ *Calc_save* is the Recalculate Before Save check box

◆ *Save_values* represents the Save External Link Values check box

◆ *alt_exp* corresponds to the Alternate Expression Evaluation check box

◆ *Alt_form* represents the Alternate Formula Entry check box

Example: =CALCULATION(2,FALSE) sets the calculation type to automatic except for tables.

Menu Equivalent: Options ➤ Calculation

CALL(register_id, [argument1,..., argumentn])

CALL(module_text, [procedure, type_text], [argument1,..., argumentn])

Calls a procedure in a dynamic link library (DLL) or code resource. *Register_id* is the value returned by a previously executed REGISTER function. *Module_text* defines the name of the DLL or the name of the file with the code resource. *Procedure* is the name of the procedure or code resource. *Type_text* is quoted text specifying the data type of the function return value, the number of arguments, and the data types of the arguments. *Argumentx* defines arguments passed to the procedure.

CALLER( )

Gives the reference of the cell containing the function that called the current macro. If the function was part of an array formula in an array of cells, CALLER( ) gives the reference of the range. This is useful in a macro if the calculation depends on the location or size of the calling reference.

Example: =ROWS(CALLER( )) returns the number of rows in the calling cell or array.

CANCEL.COPY( )

Cancels marquee on a range after a cut or copy operation.

Menu Equivalent: Escape.

CANCEL.KEY([enable, macro_ref])

Disables macro interruption. *Macro_ref* references a macro that is run when *enable* is TRUE and Esc is pressed.

CELL.PROTECTION([locked, hidden])

Specifies cell protection or hiding on the selected range. *Locked* and *hidden* are logical values where TRUE is checked and FALSE is not checked.

Menu Equivalent: Format ➤ Cell Protection

CHANGE.LINK(old_link, new_link, [type_of_link])

Changes a link between worksheets. *Type_of_link* is either 1 (Excel link) or 2 (DDE link). *Old_link* is quoted text defining the old link to change. *New_link* defines the new link as quoted text.

Menu Equivalent: File ➤ Links ➤ Change

CHART.WIZARD([long,] [ref,] [gallery_num, type_num, plot_by, categories, ser_titles, legend, title, x_title, y_title, z_title])

Use the macro recorder to enter this function on the macro sheet.

Formats a chart of a type *type_num*:

TYPE_NUM	CHART
1	Area
2	Bar
3	Column
4	Line
5	Pie
6	XY (Scatter)

TYPE_NUM	CHART
7	3-D Area
8	3-D Column
9	3-D Line
10	3-D Pie
11	Radar
12	3-D Bar
13	3-D Surface
14	Combination

If *long* is TRUE or omitted, a five-step Chart Wizard equivalent is used; if FALSE, a two-step Chart Wizard is used. *Ref* references the source cells for the chart. *Gallery_num* identifies the format option (from the Gallery command dialog box). *Plot_by* is 1 to indicate the data series are in rows, and 2 to specify in columns. *Categories* is 1 to indicate the first row or column contains labels, and 2 to indicate data. *Ser_titles* is 1 to indicate the first row or column contains series titles, and 2 to indicate data. *Legend* is 1 to include the legend, and 2 or omitted to exclude a legend. *Title* is the chart title. *x_title* is the x-axis title, *y_title* the y axis title, and *z_title* the z axis title.

Menu Equivalent: Equivalent to choosing the Chart Wizard tool on the standard or chart toolbar.

CHECK.COMMAND(bar_number, menu_pos, command_pos, check)

Adds or removes a check mark from beside the command in position *command_pos* on the menu *menu_pos* in bar number *bar_number*.

CLEAR([parts])

Clears the specified cell range. There are four possible values for *parts*:

PARTS	CLEARS
1	All
2	Formats

PARTS	CLEARS
3	Formulas
4	Notes

Example: =CLEAR(1) clears everything from the cell range.

Menu Equivalent: Edit ➤ Clear

CLOSE([save_logical])

Closes currently active window. If *save_logical* is TRUE, the document is saved first if altered; if it is FALSE, the document is not saved; if the parameter or argument is omitted, the user is prompted.

Menu Equivalent: File ➤ Close

CLOSE.ALL( )

Closes all unprotected windows.

Menu Equivalent: File ➤ Close All

COLOR.PALETTE([file_text])

Copies color palette from open document to active document. *File_text* is the document to copy a color palette from. The document is specified by a quoted text string and must be open.

Menu Equivalent: Copy Colors From option in Options ➤ Color Palette dialog box.

COLUMN.WIDTH([width, ref, standard, type_number], [standard number])

Changes the width of currently selected columns. The new width will be *width*. If *ref* is specified, it changes the width of the columns containing *ref* to *width*. *Ref* should be an external reference to the current sheet or an R1C1 reference in a text style (in quotation marks). *Standard,* if TRUE, sets the column to standard width. *Type_number* specifies other options (1 = Hide, 2 = Unhide, 3 = Best Fit). *Standard number* specifies the standard width in characters.

Examples: =COLUMN.WIDTH(16) changes the currently selected column(s) to a width of 16.

=COLUMN.WIDTH(16,!$B:$C) changes the width of columns B and C to 16.

Menu Equivalent: Format ➤ Column Width

COMBINATION(type)

Selects the combination chart type from the menu. *Type* is a number corresponding to a format in the Chart Gallery dialog box.

Menu Equivalent: Gallery ➤ Combination

CONSOLIDATE([source_refs, function_number, top_row, left_col, create_links])

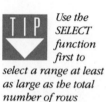

Use the SELECT function first to select a range at least as large as the total number of rows and columns to consolidate.

Consolidates data from multiple ranges on multiple worksheets to a range on a single worksheet. *Source_refs* are external references to areas to be consolidated. *Function_number* specifies the function to use where:

FUNCTION_NUMBER	FUNCTION
1	AVERAGE
2	COUNT
3	COUNTA
4	MAX
5	MIN
6	PRODUCT
7	STDEV
8	STDEVP
9	SUM
10	VAR
11	VARP

The remaining functions correspond to the check boxes in the Consolidate dialog box.

Menu Equivalent: Data ➤ Consolidate

CONSTRAIN.NUMERIC([numeric_logical]

Constrains handwriting recognition to numbers and punctuation only. Use to improve handwriting recognition with Windows for Pen.

Menu Equivalent: Constrain Numeric tool of the Formula toolbar

COPY( )

Copies the selected cells or objects to the Clipboard.

Menu Equivalent: Edit ➤ Copy

COPY.PICTURE(appearance, [size], [type_num])

Copies selection to the Clipboard as a picture. *Appearance* must be the number 1 or 2, with the following meanings:

1	copy as shown on the screen
2	copy as it will be printed

Size applies only to a chart and has the following meanings:

1	copy using the same size as the window displaying the chart
2	copy as it will be printed

type_num specifies the format of the picture: 1 = picture (default), 2 = bitmap).

Menu Equivalent: Edit ➤ Copy Picture (with Shift)

COPY.TOOL([bar_id, position])

Copies tool face to Clipboard (see ADD.TOOL).

Menu Equivalent: Equivalent to selecting a tool and Edit ➤ Copy ➤ Tool face

CREATE.DIRECTORY([path_text])

Creates a directory inside the current directory of name *path_text*.

CREATE.NAMES([top_row, left_column, bottom_row, right_column])

Creates names using row or column headings. Arguments must be logical values (corresponding to the check boxes in the Create Names dialog box), with TRUE indicating checked and FALSE indicating not checked.

Menu Equivalent: Formula ➤ Create Names

CREATE.OBJECT(object_type, ref_1, [x_offset1, y_offset1,] ref_2, [x_offset2, y_offset2, text, fill])

For lines, rectangles, ovals, arcs, pictures, text boxes, buttons.

CREATE.OBJECT(object_type, ref_1, [x_offset1, y_offset1,] ref_2, [x_offset2, y_offset2,]array[, fill])

For polygons.

CREATE.OBJECT(object_type, ref_1, [x_offset1, y_offset1, ref_2, x_offset2, y_offset2, xy_series],[fill, gallery_num, type_num])

For embedded charts.

Draws an object on the worksheet or macro sheet from *ref_1* to *ref_2* with the specified offset (in points, $1/72$ of an inch) defined by *x_offset1, y_offset1, x_offset2, y_offset2*. *X_offset1* and *y_offset1* are measured to the upper left corner of a bounding rectangle. *X_offset2* and *y_offset2* are measured to the lower right corner of a bounding rectangle. *Object_type* defines the object:

OBJECT_TYPE	OBJECT
1	Line
2	Rectangle
3	Oval
4	Arc
5	Embedded chart
6	Text box

OBJECT_TYPE	OBJECT
7	Button
8	Picture (using camera tool)
9	Closed polygon
10	Open polygon

Text boxes and buttons are labeled with *text*. The *xy_series* argument is used for embedded charts (as on a worksheet) and specifies how the series is arranged in the chart:

XY_SERIES	RESULT
0	Displays dialog box if selection is unclear
1	First row/column is the first data series (default)
2	First row/column contain the category (*x*) axis labels
3	First row/column are *x* values; created chart is an XY (scatter) chart

Fill, if TRUE, specifies the object as filled. *Array* is an $n \sim X\ 2$ array of values or reference to range that defines the position of each vertex of the polygon relative to the upper left corner of a bounding rectangle.

CROSSTAB([label,] expression)

CROSSTAB([label], "Columns:", columns_array)

CROSSTAB([label,]"Rows:, rows_array)

CROSSTAB([label], "Summary:", values_array)

Defines the structure and content of a cross-tabulation table. Use Crosstab Wizard to create table, then use Crosstab functions to modify it. *Label* is the text to be displayed in the cell containing the CROSSTAB formula. *Expression* is the name or formula used to compute the table. *Rows_array* is a two-dimensional array that specifies a set of fields that appears in each row of the table. *Columns_array* is a two-dimensional array that specifies a set of fields that appears in each column of the table. *Values_array* is a two-dimensional array that specifies each field that appears as a value field.

CROSSTAB.CREATE[(rows_array, columns_array, values_array, create_outline, create_names, multiple values, auto_drilldown, new_sheet])

Creates cross-tabulation table (see CROSSTAB). *Auto_drilldown,* if TRUE, places drilldown formulas in the result cells. *New_sheet,* if true, places the table on a new worksheet. *Create_outline,* if TRUE, creates an outline for the resulting table. *Multiple_values* is a numerical value that specifies how to handle multiple summaries (1 = inner columns, 2 = outer columns, 3 = inner rows, 4 = outer rows).

Menu Equivalent: Data ➤ Crosstab

CROSSTAB.DRILLDOWN()

Performs a database query to retrieve the records that are summarized in the cell.

Menu Equivalent: Equivalent to double-clicking a cell containing a summary value in a cross-tabulation table.

CUSTOM.RECALC([rebuild])

Recalulates existing cross-tabulation table. *Rebuild* is a logical value that specifies the type of recalculation. If TRUE, the table is recreated from row, column, and value definitions. If FALSE or omitted, the recalculation is made from the current layout and elements.

Menu Equivalent: Data ➤ Recalculate Existing Crosstab

CUSTOM.REPEAT([macro_text, repeat_text, record_text])

Creates a custom Edit ➤ Repeat command. *Macro_text* references a macro to run when Edit ➤ Repeat is chosen. It can be a name or macro-cell reference. Repeat_text defines the repeat command to use on the Edit menu. *Record_text* is the formula you want recorded. If *Record_text* is omitted, the macro recorder records normally.

CUSTOM.UNDO(macro_text, [undo_text])

Creates a custom Edit ➤ Undo command. *Macro_text* references (in R1C1 style) a macro to run when Edit ➤ Undo is chosen. It can be a name or macro-cell reference. *Undo_text* is the text you wish to use as the command in the Edit menu.

Displays Toolbars: Customize dialog box. (Dialog box syntax only.) *Category* defines the category of tools to display in the dialog box:

CATEGORY	CATEGORY OF TOOLS
1	File
2	Edit
3	Formula
4	Formatting (non-text)
5	Text formatting
6	Drawing
7	Macro
8	Charting
9	Utility
10	User-defined

Menu Equivalent: Options ➤ Toolbars ➤ Customize

CUT( )

Deletes the selected range from the sheet and copies it to the Clipboard.

Menu Equivalent: Edit ➤ Cut

DATA.DELETE( )

Deletes the records from the database that meet the specified criteria.

Menu Equivalent: Data ➤ Delete

DATA.FIND(logical)

The value of *logical* determines the action. If *logical* is TRUE, Excel attempts to find a record that meets the specified criteria. If *logical* is FALSE, Excel attempts an Exit Find.

Menu Equivalent: Data ➤ Find and Data ➤ Exit Find

DATA.FIND.NEXT( )

DATA.FIND.PREV( )

Finds the next or previous record in the database that matches the specified criteria.

Menu Equivalent: Equivalent to pressing ↓ or ↑ after the Data ➤ Find command has been chosen.

DATA.FORM( )

Displays a data form for modifying or searching a database.

Menu Equivalent: Data ➤ Form

DATA.SERIES([series_in, type, date_number, step, stop], [trend])

Creates a data series in the selected range. There are two choices for the *series_in* argument:

SERIES_IN	OPTION
1	Rows
2	Columns

The choices for the *type* argument are as follows:

TYPE	OPTION
1	Linear
2	Growth

TYPE	OPTION
3	Date
4	Autofill

The four choices for the *date_number* argument are below:

DATE_NUMBER	OPTION
1	Day
2	Weekday
3	Month
4	Year

Step and *stop* are numbers indicating the stepping value and stopping point for the series. *Trend* corresponds to the Trend check box. If *trend* is TRUE, Excel generates a linear or exponential trend.

Example: =DATA.SERIES(2,1,,1,) creates a linear series in the selected column.

Menu Equivalent: Data ➤ Series

DEFINE.NAME(name_text,[refers_to, type, key, hidden], [category])

Defines a name for a cell range. The arguments are defined as follows:

name_text	Text value for range name
refers_to	If an external reference, refers to cells named. If omitted, selected range is assumed. If a number, text, or logical value, assigns the name to the value
type	Defines the macro type: 1 is a function, 2 is a command, 3 is none (*name_text* does not refer to macro)
key	Defines the letter to activate the command. It must be in quotation marks, as in "Z" (macro sheet only)
hidden	A logical value that specifies whether the name is hidden

category   Defines the function category, as listed in the
Category drop-down list box in the Define Name
dialog box. (1 corresponds to the first category.)

Examples: =DEFINE.NAME("TEST","=R1C2") assigns the name "TEST" to cell B1.

=DEFINE.NAME("INCOME",) assigns the name "INCOME" to the currently selected range.

=DEFINE.NAME("QTY","=R1C2:R6:C2") assigns the name "QTY" to the range B1:B6.

Menu Equivalent: Formula ➤ Define Name

DEFINE.STYLE(style_text, [number, font, alignment, border, pattern, protection])

This macro is used to set a selected range to a defined style. This command has seven forms, depending on the aspect of the style being set and how the command is used. Consult Excel's function manual for more information. The above form is used to set a style by example. *Style_text* is the name of the style; the other arguments correspond to the options of the Style dialog box.

Menu Equivalent: Format ➤ Style Define

DELETE.ARROW( )

Deletes the selected arrow.

Menu Equivalent: Chart ➤ Delete Arrow

DELETE.BAR(bar_number)

Deletes the custom menu bar identified by *bar_number*.

DELETE.COMMAND(bar_number, menu, command_pos)

Deletes the command in position *command_pos* on the menu *menu* in menu *bar_number*.

Example: The expression =DELETE.COMMAND(Income,"Reports","Income Report") removes the Income Report command from the Reports menu on a custom menu bar created by the ADD.BAR function in a cell named "Income."

DELETE.DIRECTORY([path_text])

Deletes the empty directory specified by *path_text*.

DELETE.FORMAT(format_text)

Deletes custom *format_text* from the list of formats (or pictures) in the Format Number dialog box. You cannot use this to delete Excel's built-in pictures.

Example: =DELETE.FORMAT("#,##0.0") deletes the custom-designed number formatting scheme #,##0.0 from the list.

Menu Equivalent: Format ➤ Number (Delete)

DELETE.MENU(bar_number, menu_pos)

Deletes the menu *menu_pos* in bar number *bar_number*.

DELETE.NAME(name_text)

Deletes *name_text* from the name list.

Example: =DELETE.NAME("QTY") deletes the name "QTY" from the current list.

Menu Equivalent: Formula ➤ Define Name ➤ Delete

DELETE.OVERLAY( )

Deletes an overlay from a chart.

Menu Equivalent: Chart ➤ Delete Overlay

DELETE.STYLE(style_text)

Deletes the style *style_text* from a worksheet. You can delete styles only from the active document.

Menu Equivalent: Format ➤ Style ➤ Delete

DELETE.TOOL([bar_id, position])

Deletes the tool at *position* from the toolbar specified by *bar_id*. (See ADD.TOOL).

DELETE.TOOLBAR([bar_id])

Deletes the toolbar specified by *bar_id*. (See ADD.TOOLBAR and ADD.TOOL).

DEMOTE([rowcol])

Demotes the selected rows or columns in the outline. If *rowcol* is 1 or omitted, rows are demoted. If *rowcol* is 2, columns are demoted.

Menu Equivalent: Equivalent to clicking the demote button on the Utility toolbar.

DEREF(ref)

Returns the value of the cells in *ref*. If *ref* is a single cell, it gives the value in that cell. If *ref* is a range, an array of values is returned.

Note: In the SET.NAME function and others, references are not converted to values automatically. In such cases, the DEREF function must be used.

Example: =SET.NAME("QTY",DEREF(B2)). Here, DEREF converts the reference to cell B2 to its value. The SET.NAME function then names that value QTY.

DIALOG.BOX(dialog_ref)

Displays the dialog box described by *dialog_ref* on the macro or sheet (see Chapter 28).

DIRECTORIES([path_text])

Returns a horizontal array of all subdirectories in the specified path or the current path.

DIRECTORY([path_text])

Sets the current drive and directory to path *path_text* and returns the name of the new directory as text. Use with the Open and Save As functions to set the correct directory.

DISABLE.INPUT(logical)

Blocks all input from the keyboard (except for dialog boxes) and mouse if *logical* is TRUE. Used with DDE. Be sure to turn keyboard input back to FALSE before leaving the macro.

DISPLAY([formulas, gridlines, headings, zero, color, reserved, outline, page_breaks, object_number])

DISPLAY([cell, formula, value, format, protection, names, precedents, dependents, note])

First function: Changes the display form. The arguments refer to the check boxes in the dialog box, with TRUE indicating checked and FALSE indicating not checked. *Object_number* ranges from 1 to 3 (1 = Show all, 2 = Show placeholders, and 3 = Hide). *Color* defines the gridline and heading color and ranges from 0 to 16 (0 = automatic, other values correspond to those in the dialog box).

Second form: Logical values that correspond to commands with the same name on the Info menu. When TRUE, the command is turned on. Use the WORKSPACE macro to turn the Info window on.

Example: =DISPLAY(TRUE,TRUE,FALSE) turns on formulas and gridlines and turns off row and column headings.

Menu Equivalent: Options ➤ Display (first and second functions). Info menu (third function), displayed with the F1 key.

DOCUMENTS([type_number], [match_text])

Returns a horizontal text array of the currently opened documents in alphabetical order. Using the INDEX function, you can then select a document name from the array to use as an argument in another function. If *type_number* is 1 or omitted, the function returns all except add-in documents. If it is 2, add-in documents are returned only. If it is 3, all documents are returned. *Match_text* specifies the documents whose names you want returned, and can include wildcard characters. If omitted, the function returns the names of all open documents.

Example: =DOCUMENTS( ) might equal {"Sheet1","Sheet2"}.

DUPLICATE( )

Duplicates a selected object.

ECHO([logical])

Turns screen updating off (*logical* = FALSE) or on (*logical* = TRUE) during macro execution. Macros run faster when updating is off. If the argument is omitted, the function is a toggle.

EDIT.COLOR(color_number, [red_value, green_value, blue_value])

Defines a custom color to substitute for any one of the 16 in the Color Palette dialog box. *Color_number* must be from 1 to 16. Other arguments can be from 0 to 255, and specify the amount of each color added.

Example: =EDIT.COLOR(2,0,0,0) sets the second color in the Color Palette dialog box to black.

Menu Equivalent: Options ➤ Color Palette Edit

EDIT.DELETE([direction])

Removes the selected range from the sheet. *Direction* must be a number: 1=shifts cells left to adjust, 2=shifts cells up, 3=deletes an entire row, and 4=deletes an entire column. If the argument is omitted, the range is shifted up and left.

Example: =EDIT.DELETE(1) deletes the range and shifts cells left. The same command deletes the entire current row if the row heading is selected.

Menu Equivalent: Edit ➤ Delete

EDIT.OBJECT([verb_num])

Starts the application associated with the selected object and makes the object available for editing. *Verb_num* is a number specifying what verb to use with the object. As a general rule, 1 = edit and 2 = play. If omitted, *Verb_num* is assumed as 1.

Menu Equivalent: Edit Object command from object shortcut menu

EDIT.REPEAT( )

Repeats the last Edit command, if available.

Menu Equivalent: Edit ➤ Repeat

EDIT.SERIES([series_number, name_ref, x_ref, y_ref, z_ref, plot_order])

Creates or edits a data series on a chart. The arguments correspond to the options on the dialog box. To delete a series, use the SELECT and FORMULA macro functions (see the FORMULA function).

Menu Equivalent: Chart/Edit ➤ Series

ELSE( )

Use with IF...END.IF in control structures to support branching (see Chapter 28).

ELSE.IF(logical_test)

Use with IF...END.IF in control structures to support branching. Supports nested structures (see Chapter 28).

ENABLE.COMMAND(bar_number, menu_pos, command_pos, enable)

Enables or disables the command in position *command_pos* on the menu *menu_pos* in menu bar *bar_number* (see ADD.COMMAND and Chapter 28).

ENABLE.TOOL(bar_id, position, [enable])

Enables or disables the tool at *position* on the toolbar *bar_id* (see ADD.TOOL). If *enable* is TRUE or omitted, user can access the tool.

END.IF( )

Ends a control structure for conditional branching.

ENTER.DATA([logical])

Switches Excel to a data entry mode and permits the user to select and enter data to unlocked cells in the worksheet or current selection.

ERROR(logical, [ref])

Turns macro error checking on or off, and optionally defines a macro to run on an error condition. If *logical* is TRUE, error checking is turned on. If an error is encountered during the macro execution, the control branches to *ref.* If *ref* is omitted, a dialog box is displayed upon finding an error. If *logical* is FALSE or 0, errors in the macro are automatically ignored and execution continues. If TRUE or 1, normal checking is enabled and an optional macro can be specified to run on an error. If 2 and the second argument are omitted, error handling is normal except that the Cancel button in an alert message returns FALSE and the macro is not interrupted. If 2 and the second argument are included, the macro is run on an error message. A Cancel button in an alert message would return FALSE again and the macro would not be interrupted. *Ref* tells the macro to run if *logical* is TRUE.

EVALUATE(formula_text)

Evaluates the formula or expression *formula_text* that is in the form of text and returns the result.

EXEC(program_text,[window_number])

Starts the program *program_text* in a window type defined by *window_number* (1 = normal, 2 = minimized (default), and 3 = maximized). Be sure *program_text* includes a path if the program is not on the current path.

Example: =EXEC("NOTEPAD.EXE",3) loads the NOTEPAD program and displays it in a maximized window.

EXECUTE(channel_number, execute_text)

Carries out the command *execute_text* in the application defined by *channel_number* (see INITIATE).

EXTEND.POLYGON(array)

Adds vertices to a polygon. It must immediately follow a CREATE.OBJECT or another EXTEND.POLYGON function. *Array* is an array of values (or reference to a range of cells containing values) that indicate the position of vertices in the polygon.

EXTRACT([unique])

Extracts records from the database based on the specified criteria. If *unique* is TRUE, duplicate values are not extracted.

Menu Equivalent: Data ➤ Extract

FCLOSE(file_num)

Closes the file specified by *file_num*. *File_num* is the number returned by the FOPEN function that opened the file.

FILE.CLOSE([save_logical])

Closes the active document. *Save_logical,* if TRUE, saves the file on closing. If FALSE, the file is not saved. If omitted, a dialog box is displayed for the save query.

Menu Equivalent: File ➤ Close

FILE.DELETE(document_text)

Deletes *document_text* from the disk. If *document_text* is not on the current or specified directory, you will have to enter the name in a warning dialog box. In the question-mark form, you can use wildcard expressions when entering the name.

Menu Equivalent: File ➤ Delete

FILE.EXISTS(path_text)

Returns TRUE if the specified file exists in the specified path.

FILES([directory_text])

Returns a horizontal text array of file names in the directory specified by *directory_text*. Use the COLUMNS function to count the number of entries or the TRANSPOSE function to convert to a vertical column of names.

Example: The function =FILES("S*.*") returns the names of the files on the current directory starting with the letter *S*.

FILL.AUTO([destination_ref, copy_only])

Automatically fills the selected range from the first cell in the range. *Destination_ref* is the destination range. *Copy_only* is a logical value. If TRUE, a copy is done. If FALSE or omitted, a fill is done.

Example: FILL.AUTO("RC:R[4]C",FALSE)

Menu Equivalent: Equivalent to copying cells or automatically filling by dragging.

FILL.DOWN( )

FILL.LEFT( )

FILL.RIGHT( )

FILL.UP( )

Fills the selected range with the value in the first cell of the range. Multiple ranges can be selected.

Menu Equivalent: Edit ➤ Fill Down, Edit ➤ Fill Left, Edit ➤ Fill Right, and Edit ➤ Fill Up

FILL.GROUP(type_number)

Fills the contents of the active worksheet's selected area to the same area in all worksheets of the workgroup. Use this function to fill identical ranges of cells on all worksheets at once. *Type_number* defines what to fill (1 = All, 2 = Formulas, 3 = Formats).

Menu Equivalent: Edit ➤ Fill Group

FOPEN(file_text, [access_number])

Opens the file specified by *file_text*. *Access_number* specifies the manner in which it is opened: 1 = read/write (default), 2 = read only, and 3 = create *and* read/write. It returns the file number that is used with other functions. Closes with FCLOSE. Unlike with OPEN, the file is not loaded into memory. FOPEN establishes a channel with the file for exchanging information with it.

Menu Equivalent: (None—this is not File ➤ Open.)

FOR(counter_text, start_number, end_number, [step_number])

Starts a FOR...NEXT iterative structure (loop). See Chapter 28.

FOR.CELL(ref_name, [area_ref, skip_blanks])

Starts a FOR.CELL...NEXT iterative structure (loop). The instructions in the loop are repeated in/over a range of cells. There is no loop counter. *Ref_name* gives the one cell in the range currently being operated on. *Area_ref* is the range on which you wish the loop to operate. *Skip_blanks* is a logical value that specifies whether to skip blank cells.

FORMAT.AUTO([format_num, number, font, alignment, border, pattern, width])

Formats the selected range from a gallery of formats. *Format_num* is a number corresponding to the fonts listed in the dialog box. If omitted, it is assumed as 1. The other options are logical and correspond to the checkboxes in the dialog box..

Menu Equivalent: Format ➤ AutoFormat ➤ Options.

FORMAT.FONT([name_text, size_number, bold, italic, underline, strike, color, outline, shadow])

FORMAT.FONT([name_text, size_number, bold, italic, underline, strike, color, outline, shadow, object_id_text, start_number, char_number])

FORMAT.FONT([color, backgd, apply, name_text, size, bold, italic, underline, strike, outline, shadow])

Applies fonts to the current selection. The first form is for cells, the second is for text boxes and buttons, and the third is for charts. The arguments correspond to those in the dialog box. The *outline* and *shadow* options are not available for fonts with Excel for Windows; they are provided for Macintosh compatibility. To use shadow and outline fonts in Excel for Windows, a character set with those features must be installed as a separate font. *Object_id_text* identifies the text box to format. If omitted, the selected text box is assumed. *Start_number* specifies the first character to be formatted, and defaults to 1. *Char_number* specifies how many characters to format, and defaults to All. *Backgd* defines the type of background to apply to text (1 = automatic, 2 = transparent, 3 = opaque). *Apply* corresponds to the Apply to All check box.

Menu Equivalent: Format ➤ Font

FORMAT.LEGEND(position_number)

Sets the position and layout of the legend on a chart indicated by *position_number* and returns TRUE (1 = Bottom, 2 = Corner, 3 = Top, 4 = Right, 5 = Left).

Menu Equivalent: Format ➤ Legend

FORMAT.MAIN(type_number, [view, overlap, gap_width, vary, drop, hilo, angle, gap_depth, chart_depth], [up_down, series_line, labels])

Formats the main chart. The *type_number* argument corresponds to the type of chart:

TYPE_NUMBER	CHART TYPE
1	Area
2	Bar
3	Column
4	Line
5	Pie
6	XY (Scatter)
7	3-D Area
8	3-D Column
9	3-D Line

TYPE_NUMBER	CHART TYPE
10	3-D Pie
11	Radar
12	3-D Bar
13	3-D Surface

The *view* argument corresponds to one of the views in the Main Chart dialog box. The other arguments correspond to the options on the Format Chart dialog box. *Series_line* is available only for stacked bar and column charts, *up_down* for line charts, and *labels* for radar.

Menu Equivalent: Format ➤ Main Chart

FORMAT.MOVE(x_offset, y_offset, [reference])

FORMAT.MOVE(x_pos, y_pos)

For worksheet objects, moves the upper-left corner of the selected object to a position specified by *x offset* and *y offset,* measured in points (¹/₇₂ of an inch) from the upper-left corner of the *reference* cell (or A1 if omitted).

For chart items, moves the base of the selected item to a position specified by *x_ pos* and *y_ pos,* measured in points from the base of the object to the lower-left corner of the window.

Example: =FORMAT.MOVE(20,25,!$C$3) moves the object 20 points horizontally and 25 points vertically offset from cell C3.

Menu Equivalent: Format ➤ Move; equivalent to moving an object with the mouse.

FORMAT.NUMBER(format_text)

Sets the formatting scheme or picture of the selected cells to *format_text*. *Format_text* is a format string, such as "#,##0.00".

Menu Equivalent: Format ➤ Number

FORMAT.OVERLAY(type_number, [view, overlap, width, vary, drop, hilo, angle, series_dist, series_number, up_down, series_line, labels])

Formats the overlay chart. *Type_number* can be from 1 to 6, and corresponds to the first six types of the FORMAT.MAIN function. *View* is a number specifying one of the views in the Data View box of the Overlay dialog box. The other arguments correspond to those in the dialog box. *Series_dist* specifies automatic or manual series distribution (1 = automatic and default, 2 = manual). *Series_number* specifies the first series in the overlay chart.

Menu Equivalent: Format ➤ Overlay

FORMAT.SHAPE(vertex_num, insert, [reference, x_offest, y_offset])

Reshapes an existing polygon. *Vertex_num* is a number that defines the vertex to insert, move, or delete. *Insert* defines the action: TRUE=insert vertex before, FALSE=delete or move vertex. *Reference* defines the reference from which the vertex you are inserting or moving is measured. The offsets define the distance to move. If *insert* is FALSE and the remaining arguments are omitted, the vertex is deleted.

Menu Equivalent: Equivalent to clicking the reshape tool on the toolbar and editing a polygon.

FORMAT.SIZE([x_offset, y_offset,] reference)

FORMAT.SIZE([width, height])

The first function sizes the selected object (worksheet, relative), according to *x_offset* and *y_offset,* which specify the width and height, respectively, of the object. These are measured in points ($1/72$ of an inch) from the lower-right corner of the object to the upper-left corner of *reference.*

The second function sizes the selected object (worksheet object or chart item, absolute) as per *width* and *height,* both measured in points.

Menu Equivalent: Format ➤ Size (only for charts), or the same as sizing an object with the mouse.

FORMAT.TEXT([x_align, y_align, orient_number, auto_text, auto_size, show_key, show_value])

Formats the selected text as defined by argument check boxes. *X_align* is a number from 1 to 4 specifying the horizontal alignment (1 = Left, 2 = Center, 3 = Right, 4 = Justify). *Y_align* specifies the vertical alignment (1 = Top, 2 = Center, 3 = Bottom, 4 = Justify). *Orient_number* sets the orientation (0 = Horizontally, 1 = Vertically, 2 = Upward, 3 = Downward). *X-align, y_align,* and *orient_number* default to 1 when omitted. *Show_key* corresponds to the Show Key check box, and *show_value* to the Show Value check box. The other parameters correspond to the options in the Format ➤ Text dialog box.

Menu Equivalent: Format ➤ Text

FORMULA(formula_text, [ref])

FORMULA(formula_text)

Inserts *formula_text* in the active cell or in a reference. The second form enters a text label or SERIES formula to a chart.

Examples: =FORMULA(5) enters 5 to the active cell.

=FORMULA(INPUT("Enter: ",0),P20) prompts for a formula to enter into cell P20.

To delete a series:

```
=SELECT("S2")
=FORMULA(" ")
```

deletes the second series.

FORMULA.ARRAY(formula_text, [ref])

Inserts *formula_text* as an array to the active range or *ref*. It is equivalent to entering an array formula while pressing Control-Shift-Enter.

FORMULA.CONVERT(formula_text, from_a1, [to_a1, to_ref_type, rel_to_ref])

Changes the reference style and type of formula between A1 and R1C1 modes and between absolute and relative. *Formula_text* is the formula, entered as text. *From_a1* is a logical value that specifies whether *formula_text* is A1 or

R1C1 (TRUE = A1). *To_a1* is a logical value specifying the destination reference style (TRUE = A1). *To_ref_type* specifies the type of returned reference (1 = Absolute, 2 = Absolute row, relative column, 3 = Relative row, absolute column, 4 = Relative). *Rel_to_ref* is an absolute reference that specifies to which cell the relative references are relative.

Examples: =FORMULA.CONVERT("=B2+B6",TRUE,TRUE,1) converts =B2+B6 to =$B$2+$B$6.

=FORMULA.CONVERT("=B2+B6",TRUE,FALSE,1) converts =B2+B6 to =R2C2+R6C2.

FORMULA.FILL(formula_text, [ref])

Inserts *formula_text* in each cell of the currently selected range or the range *ref*. It is the equivalent of entering a formula while pressing the Ctrl key.

Example: If B1:B6 is selected, =FORMULA.FILL(4) enters **4** in each cell of the range.

FORMULA.FIND(find_text, look_in, look_at, look_by, [dir_number, match_case])

Searches for a formula, value, or note in the current sheet. The *find_text* argument is the text for which to search. The *look_in* argument has three choices:

LOOK_IN	TYPE OF SEARCH
1	Formulas
2	Values
3	Notes

The *look_at* argument has two choices, depending upon whether you are matching a whole cell or a part of a cell:

LOOK_AT	MATCH TYPE
1	Whole
2	Part

The *look_by* argument has the following choices:

LOOK_BY	SEARCHES BY
1	Rows
2	Columns

Dir_number specifies direction (1 = Forward (default), 2 = Backward or previous) and *match_case* is logical and specifies whether the case should be matched.

Example: =FORMULA.FIND("6",2,1,1) searches the sheet for the first cell with the value of 6 and makes the cell active if found.

Menu Equivalent: Formula ➤ Find or Shift-F5

FORMULA.FIND.NEXT( )

FORMULA.FIND.PREV( )

Finds the next or previous cells on the sheet that match the search criteria.

Menu Equivalent: Equivalent to F7 and Shift-F7, respectively.

FORMULA.GOTO([ref, corner])

Goes to the cell referenced as *ref*. *Ref* can be a name or external reference (using A1- or R1C1-style referencing). *Corner* is a logical value that specifies whether to scroll the window so that *ref* appears in the top-left cell of the active window.

Example: If A2 is "INCOME", the following are all equivalent:

    =FORMULA.GOTO(!$A$2)

    =FORMULA.GOTO("R2C1")

    =FORMULA.GOTO("INCOME")

    =FORMULA.GOTO(!INCOME)

Menu Equivalent: Formula ➤ Goto (or pressing F5)

FORMULA.REPLACE(find_text, replace_text, [look_at, look_by, active_cell, match_case])

Replaces *find_text* with *replace_text*. The options match those of the dialog box. *Active_cell* is a logical value specifying the cells for replacement. If TRUE, replacement is made for the active cell only. If FALSE, replacement is made for the entire selection or (if a single cell selected) the entire document.

Example: =FORMULA.REPLACE("TOO","TWO") replaces *TOO* with *TWO* in the entire document.

Menu Equivalent: Formula ➤ Replace

FPOS(file_number, [position_number])

Positions the document *file_number* at the position *position_number*. *File_number* is the file ID number returned by the FOPEN command. Position_number is the location in the file for the character to be read or written.

FREAD(file_number, number_chars)

Reads *number_chars* from the document *file_number*, starting at the current position, which can be set by FPOS. *File_number* is the file ID number returned by the FOPEN command.

FREADLN(file_number)

Reads the next line from the document *file_number*. *File_number* is the file ID number returned by the FOPEN command.

FREEZE.PANES([logical, col_split, row_split])

Splits the active window and freezes heading panes on the active worksheet. If *logical* is TRUE, this is equivalent to the Window ➤ Freeze Panes command. If FALSE, it is equivalent to Window~Unfreeze Panes. *Col_split* and *Row_split* defines where to split the window.

Menu Equivalent: Window ➤ Freeze Panes or Window ➤ Unfreeze Panes

FSIZE(file_number)

Returns the number of characters in the document *file_number*. *File_number* is the file ID number returned by FOPEN.

FULL(logical)

Controls the size of the displayed document window. If *logical* is TRUE, Excel makes the displayed window full-size. IF *logical* is FALSE, Excel returns the active window to its previously smaller size. If omitted, the display is toggled.

Menu Equivalent: Equivalent to maximizing the current document window or restoring it. Also equivalent to Ctrl-F10 (full size) and Ctrl- F5 (previous size) or double-clicking the title bar when the document isn't maximized.

FWRITE(file_number, text)

Writes *text* to the document *file_number,* starting at the current position. Position is set by FPOS.

FWRITELN(file_number, text)

Writes *text* with a carriage return and line feed to the document *file_number,* starting at the current position. Position is set by FPOS.

GALLERY.3D.AREA(type_number)

Converts the currently displayed chart to a 3-D Area form. *Type_number* is a number (1–7) that must correspond to a valid format in the gallery.

Menu Equivalent: Gallery ➤ 3-D Area

GALLERY.3D.BAR(type_number)

Converts the currently displayed chart to a 3-D Bar form. *Type_number* is a number (1–4) that must correspond to a valid format in the gallery.

Menu Equivalent: Gallery ➤ 3-D Bar

GALLERY.3D.COLUMN(type_number)

Converts the currently displayed chart to a 3-D Column form. *Type_number* is a number (1–7) that must correspond to a valid format in the gallery.

Menu Equivalent: Gallery ➤ 3-D Column

GALLERY.3D.LINE(type_number)

Converts the currently displayed chart to a 3-D Line form. *Type_number* is a number (1–4) that must correspond to a valid format in the gallery.

Menu Equivalent: Gallery ➤ 3-D Line

GALLERY.3D.PIE(type_number)

Converts the currently displayed chart to a 3-D Pie form. *Type_number* is a number (1–7) that must correspond to a valid format in the gallery.

Menu Equivalent: Gallery ➤ 3-D Pie

GALLERY.3D.SURFACE(type_number)

Converts the currently displayed chart to a 3-D Surface form. *Type_number* is a number (1–4) that must correspond to a valid format in the gallery.

Menu Equivalent: Gallery ➤ 3-D Surface

GALLERY.AREA(type_number, [delete_overlay])

Converts the currently displayed chart to an Area form. *Type_number* is a number (1–5) that must correspond to a valid format in the gallery. *Delete_overlay* is a logical argument that determines whether overlay charts are to be deleted.

Menu Equivalent: Gallery ➤ Area

GALLERY.BAR(type_number, [delete_overlay])

Converts the currently displayed chart to a Bar form. *Type_number* is a number (1–10) that must correspond to a valid format in the gallery. *Delete_overlay* is a logical argument that determines whether overlay charts are to be deleted.

Menu Equivalent: Gallery ➤ Bar

GALLERY.COLUMN(type_number, [delete_overlay])

Converts the currently displayed chart to a Column form. *Type_number* is a number (1–10) that must correspond to a valid format in the gallery. *Delete_overlay* is a logical argument that determines whether overlay charts are to be deleted.

Menu Equivalent: Gallery ➤ Column

GALLERY.LINE(type_number, [delete_overlay])

Converts the currently displayed chart to a Line form. *Type_number* is a number (1–9) hat must correspond to a valid format in the gallery. *Delete_overlay* is a logical argument that determines whether overlay charts are to be deleted.

Menu Equivalent: Gallery ➤ Line

GALLERY.PIE(type_number,[delete_overlay])

Converts the currently displayed chart to a Pie form. *Type_number* is a number (1–7) that must correspond to a valid format in the gallery. *Delete_overlay* is a logical argument that determines whether overlay charts are to be deleted.

Menu Equivalent: Gallery ➤ Pie

GALLERY.RADAR(type_number,[delete_overlay])

Converts the currently displayed chart to a Radar form. *Type_number* is a number (1–5) that must correspond to a valid format in the gallery. *Delete_overlay* is a logical argument that determines whether overlay charts are to be deleted.

Menu Equivalent: Gallery ➤ Radar

GALLERY.SCATTER(type_number, [delete_overlay])

Converts the currently displayed chart to an XY (Scatter) form. *Type_number* is a number (1–5) that must correspond to a valid format in the gallery. *Delete_overlay* is a logical argument that determines whether overlay charts are to be deleted.

Menu Equivalent: Gallery ➤ XY (Scatter)

GET.BAR( )

GET.BAR(bar_number, menu, command)

The first version returns the number of the active menu bar. The second version returns the name or position number of a specified command on a menu. Use the second with functions that add, delete, or alter menu commands. *Bar_number* is the number of the menu bar (see ADD.COMMAND). *Menu* is the menu where the command is (either the name in quotes or the number— menus are numbered from left to right, beginning with 1). *Command* is either the name or number of the command you want returned (the top command on a menu being 1). If *command* is the name, *get_bar* returns the position number. If position number, *get_bar* returns the name.

If you do not use *any* arguments, the function returns the number of the active menu bar. Use this form in macros when you need to know which menu bar is active, so that you can refer to it in other functions.

GET.CELL(type_number, [ref])

Returns the information about the location, contents, and formatting of the cell in the upper-left corner of *ref*. If *ref* is omitted, the function returns information about the current cell. There are 52 possible values for *type_number*, depending on what information is needed (see the Excel function manual).

GET.CHART.ITEM(x_y_index, [point_index, item_text])

Returns the vertical or horizontal position of a point on a chart item. If *x_y_index* is 1, the horizontal coordinate is returned. If 2, the vertical coordinate is returned. *Point_index* is a number specifying the point on the chart item. *Item_text* specifies which item of the chart to select.

GET.DEF(def_text, [document_text, type_number])

Returns the name for a particular area as text. *Def_text* can be a reference, value, or formula (anything you can name) in *document_text*. *Document_text* is the open worksheet or macro sheet on which *def_text* is defined. *Type_number* specifies the type of names returned (1 = Normal and default, 2 = Hidden only, 3 = All).

GET.DOCUMENT(type_number,[name_text])

Returns information about the open document named *name_text*. The type of information returned depends on the value of *type_number* (see Excel function reference for a list of these 68 numbers).

GET.FORMULA(ref)

Gives the contents of the upper-left cell of *ref* as it would appear in the formula bar. Formulas returned in R1C1 format.

Example: =GET.FORMULA(!A1) returns **5** if A1 contains 5.

GET.LINK.INFO(link_text, type_number, [type_of_link])

Returns information about the specified link. *Link_text* is the path name of the link. *Type_number* specifies the type of information desired. If *type_number* is 1, function returns **1** if link is set to automatic update. *Type_of_link* specifies the type of link you want information about:

TYPE_OF_LINK	LINK TYPE
1	n/a
2	DDE link
3	n/a
4	Outgoing NewWave link
5	Publisher
6	Subscriber

GET.NAME(name_text)

Gives the definition of *name_text* as it would appear in the Refers To text box of the Define Name command. The definition is in a text form. If the name contains references, they are returned in R1C1 style.

Example: If NET is defined as =SALES−COST, =GET.NAME(!NET) returns "=SALES−COST".

GET.NOTE([cell_ref, start_char, count_char])

Returns *count_char* characters from the note attached to *cell_ref* starting at *start_char*. Defaults to a count of all characters of the note in the active cell. Use to move the contents of a note to a cell, text box, or another note.

GET.OBJECT(type_number, [object_id_text, start_number, count_number])

Returns information about a specified object, based on *type_number*. There are 47 types of information categories defined (see the Excel function manual). *Object_id_text* is the name and number (or just the number) of the object you wish information about. *Start_number* specifies the first character you want information about, and defaults to 1. *Count_number* specifies how many characters to retrieve information about, and defaults to all.

GET.TOOL([type_num, bar_id, position])

Returns information about a tool or tools on a toolbar. *Type_num* defines the type of information you want:

TYPE_NUM	RETURNS
1	Tool id number
2	Reference of macro assigned to tool
3	Returns TRUE if tool button is down
4	Returns TRUE if tool is enabled
5	Logical value for face type (TRUE=bitmap, FALSE=default)
6	The *help_text* reference for tool

Bar_id identifies the toolbar, and *position* defines the location of the tool on the toolbar.

GET.TOOLBAR(type_num,[bar_id])

Returns information about a toolbar or all toolbars. Use this function to get information about a toolbar to edit the toolbar.

Type_num defines the type of information you want:

TYPE_NUM	RETURNS
1	A horizontal array of all tool IDs on the toolbar
2	Number designating horizontal position of toolbar in region
3	Number designating vertical position of toolbar in region
4	Number indicating width of toolbar in points
5	Number indicating height of toolbar in points
6	Number indicating toolbar position (which dock: 1 = top, 2 = left, 3 = right, 4 = bottom, 5 = floating)
7	TRUE if visible
8	An array of toolbar ID's for all toolbars
9	An array of toolbar ID's for all visible toolbars

Bar_id specifies the name or number of a toolbar.

GET.WINDOW(type_of_info,[name_text])

Returns information about the window named *name_text*. See the Excel function manual for the 25 type categories.

GET.WORKBOOK(type_number, [name_text])

Returns information about a workbook document. Type_num specifies the type of information desired: 1 = names of all workbook documents in horizontal array, 2 = name of active document, 3 = names of currently selected documents in workbook, and 4 = number of documents in workbook. *Name_text* is the name of an open workbook. If omitted, the active workbook is assumed.

GET.WORKSPACE(type_of_info)

Returns information about the workspace. See the Excel function manual for the 46 type categories.

GOAL.SEEK(target_cell, target_value, variable_cell)

Calculates the values that are necessary to achieve a specific goal. Arguments are those of the Goal Seek dialog box.

Menu Equivalent: Formula ➤ Goal Seek

GOTO(ref)

Using IF…END.IF and WHILE structures is preferable to using this function.

Directs macro to branch to upper-left cell of *ref. Ref* can be an external reference to another macro sheet.

Example: =IF(ISERROR($A$5),GOTO($C$4),) specifies that if cell A5 contains an error value, the macro should go to cell C4, otherwise go to the next line in the macro.

GRIDLINES([x_major, x_minor, y_major, y_minor, z_major, z_minor])

Controls visibility of major and minor gridlines. Arguments are logical values that correspond to check boxes in the Gridlines dialog box.

Menu Equivalent: Chart ➤ Gridlines

GROUP( )

Creates a single object from a group of selected objects. Returns object identifier for the group.

Menu Equivalent: Format ➤ Group

HALT(cancel_close)

Terminates execution of all macros. If macro is called by another macro, that macro is also terminated. If *cancel_close* is TRUE in an Auto_close macro, Excel halts the macro but does not close the document. If FALSE (or omitted), the macro is halted and the document closed.

HELP(file_text!topic_number)

Initiates help. Displays a help message specified by *file_text!topic_number*, which is a reference to a topic in a Windows help file.

Example: =HELP("HELP.TXT!99") displays Help topic 99 from the file HELP.TXT.

Menu Equivalent: Same as pressing F1.

HIDE( )

Hides the active window. Hiding windows will speed up macro execution.

Menu Equivalent: Window ➤ Hide

HIDE.OBJECT([object_id_text, hide])

Hides or displays the specified object. *Object_id_text* is the name or number of the object. If *hide* is TRUE, it is hidden. If FALSE, it is displayed.

Example: =HIDE.OBJECT("arc 1",TRUE) hides the object named "arc 1."

HLINE(number)

VLINE(number)

Scrolls the active window *number* rows (VLINE) or columns (HLINE). *Number* can be positive (forward scroll) or negative (backward scroll). *Number* should be an integer.

Example: =VLINE(9) scrolls the active window down 9 rows.

HPAGE(number)

VPAGE(number)

Scrolls the active window *number* windows horizontally (HPAGE) or vertically (VPAGE). *Number* must be an integer but can be positive (scroll forward) or negative (scroll backward).

Example: =HPAGE(1) scrolls the active window horizontally one window forward.

HSCROLL(column_number, [col_log])

VSCROLL(row_number, [row_log])

Scrolls the active window horizontally or vertically to the specified column or row. It is the equivalent of dragging the scroll box. *Column_number* and *row_number* should be either percentages less than 100 or fractions. *Col_log* and *row_log* are logical values that specify how the function scrolls. If TRUE, function scrolls to position. If FALSE, scrolls to horizontal or vertical position represented by fraction *column_number* or *row_number*.

Examples: =HSCROLL(64/256) scrolls to column BL, the 64th column (out of 256).

=VSCROLL(25%) scrolls to row 4096—because 4,096 is one-fourth of 16,384, the total number of rows.

IF(logical_test)

Use with ELSE, ELSE.IF, and END.IF in control structures (see Chapter 28).

INITIATE(app_text, topic_text)

Opens a DDE channel to an application and returns the number of the channel. *App_text* is the DDE name of the application you want to access. *Topic_text* is the name of the document or database record in the application that you want to access.

Example: =INITIATE("WORKS","BOOK") opens a DDE channel to the Microsoft Works document named "BOOK."

INPUT(prompt_text, [type, title_text, default, x_pos, y_pos, help_ref])

Displays a dialog box with title *title_text* and prompt *prompt_text,* to which the user can enter input (values, text, etc.). The box also contains the OK and Cancel buttons. When you click the OK button or press Enter, the function gives the value you entered. If you click Cancel or press Esc, the function gives the logical value FALSE. If you omit *title_text,* the title INPUT is assumed. The *help_ref* argument, if used, references a custom online help topic in a text file in the form "filename!topic_number". *Type* defines the type of value that the function returns:

TYPE	RETURNED
0	Formula
1	Number
2	Text
4	Logical
8	Reference (absolute)
16	Error
64	Array

X_pos and *Y_pos* define the position of the dialog box.

Example: =INPUT("Enter the current interest rate: ",1) displays a dialog box with the title "INPUT" and prompt, **Enter the current interest rate:** which awaits a numeric entry.

INSERT([direction])

Inserts rows or columns in the sheet. *Direction* must be a number: 1 shifts cells to the right to adjust, 2 shifts cells down, 3 shifts an entire row, and 4 inserts an entire column. If you have just cut or copied to the Clipboard, this command inserts and pastes from the Clipboard.

Example: =INSERT(1) inserts a range of cells and shifts cells to the right.

Menu Equivalent: Edit ➤ Insert

INSERT.OBJECT(object_class)

Creates an embedded object whose source data is supplied by another application. *Object_class* defines the class name as displayed in the Insert Object dialog box.

Menu Equivalent: Edit ➤ Insert Object

JUSTIFY( )

Rearranges the text of the left column of a range so that all cells in the range display text of the same width.

Menu Equivalent: Format ➤ Justify

LAST.ERROR( )

Returns the reference of the cell in which the last macro sheet error occurred. Use with the ERROR function to locate errors.

LEGEND([logical])

If *logical* is TRUE, a legend is added to the chart. If FALSE, the current legend is deleted.

Menu Equivalent: Chart ➤ Add Legend and Chart ➤ Delete Legend

LINE.PRINT(command, [file, append])

LINE.PRINT(command, [setup_text, leftmarg, rightmarg, topmarg, botmarg, pglen, formatted])

LINE.PRINT(command,[setup_text, leftmarg, rightmarg, topmarg, botmarg, pglen, wait, autolf, port, update])

Prints the active document using DOS instead of the Windows printer drivers. Included for compatibility with Lotus 1-2-3, and not recommended for general printing.

LINKS([document_text, type_number])

Returns a horizontal array of the names of all worksheets referred to by external references in *document_text* (includes path) as text values. You can then select individual names from the array for other functions using the INDEX function. *Type_number* defines the type of documents to return:

TYPE_NUM	RETURNS
1	Excel link (default)
2	DDE link
3	n/a
4	Outgoing NewWave link
5	Publisher
6	Subscriber

Example: If the chart called SALES.XLC is active and contains some data series that refer to two worksheets called SALES.XLS and FUTURE.XLS, this function will open both worksheets:

=OPEN.LINKS(LINKS("SALES.XLC"))

LIST.NAMES( )

Pastes the name list into the document.

Menu Equivalent: Formula ➤ Paste Name ➤ Paste List

MERGE.STYLES(document_text)

Merges styles from *document_text* to the active document.

Menu Equivalent: Format ➤ Style ➤ Define ➤ Merge

MESSAGE(logical,[text])

Displays the message *text* in the status bar if *logical* is TRUE. If *logical* is FALSE, the message is removed and command help text is displayed. This macro function is useful for displaying a message to the user about what a macro is doing. If *text* is omitted, the function removes any messages in the status bar.

MOVE.TOOL(from_bar_id, from_bar_position, to_bar_id, to_bar_position, [copy])

Moves a tool from one toolbar to another (see ADD.TOOL).

NAMES([doc_text, type_number], [match_text])

Returns a horizontal text array of all names that are defined in the document *doc_text*. *Type_number* defines the name types displayed (1 = Normal (default), 2 = Hidden, 3 = All). The function is like LIST.NAMES, but returns names to the macro sheet instead of the worksheet for further macro operations. *Match_text* is text enclosed in quotation marks that specifies the names to return. Wildcards can be used.

NEW(type, [xy_series], [add_logical])

Opens a new sheet, chart, macro sheet, workbook, or template. *Type* must be a number that indicates the type to open:

TYPE	OPENS
1	Worksheet
2	Chart
3	Macro Sheet
4	International macro sheet
5	Workbook
Quoted text	Template

The *xy_series* argument is used with charts to define how the data are arranged in the chart:

XY_SERIES	RESULT
0	Displays dialog box
1	First row/column is first data series (default)
2	First row/column is the category (*x*) axis labels
3	First row/column is *x* values; scatter chart is created

Add_logical specifies whether to add the active document to the open workbook. If TRUE, it's added. If FALSE or omitted, it is not added.

Example: =NEW(3) opens a new macro sheet.

Menu Equivalent: File ➤ New

NEW.WINDOW( )

Opens a new window on the current document.

Menu Equivalent: Window ➤ New Window

NEXT( )

Ends a FOR...NEXT loop (see Chapter 28).

NOTE([add_text, cell_ref, start_char, count_char])

Replaces *count_char* characters in a note attached to *cell_ref* with *add_text*, starting at *start_char*. NOTE( ) deletes note attached to active cell. Returns number of last character in the cell. NOTE("") deletes note text, but not sound.

Menu Equivalent: Formula ➤ Note

OBJECT.PROPERTIES([placement_num, print])

Determines how the selected object or objects are attached to the cells below them and if they are to be printed. *Placement_num* defines moving and sizing: 1 = moved and sized with cells, 2 = moved, but not sized with cells, 3 = not affected by moving and sizing cells. If *print* is TRUE or omitted, object is printed.

Menu Equivalent: Format ➤ Object Properties

OBJECT.PROTECTION([locked, text_lock])

Changes protection status of the selected object. *Locked* is a logical value that determines whether the selected object is locked, and is TRUE if the object is to be locked. *Text_lock* applies to objects with text (buttons and text boxes) and is TRUE to lock the text.

Menu Equivalent: Format ➤ Object Protection

ON.DATA([document_text, macro_text])

Starts the macro specified by *macro_text* whenever another application sends new data to the document specified by *document_text*. To turn off ON.DATA, omit the second argument.

ON.DOUBLECLICK([document_text, macro_text])

Starts the macro specified by *macro_text* whenever you double-click any cell in *document_text*. To turn off ON.DOUBLECLICK, omit the second argument.

ON.ENTRY([document_text, macro_text])

Starts the macro specified by *macro_text* whenever you enter any data to a cell in *document_text*. To turn off ON.ENTRY, omit the second argument.

ON.KEY(key_text, [macro_text])

Executes the macro specified by *macro_text* when key combination denoted by *key_text* is pressed. To turn off ON.KEY, omit the second argument. See Excel function manual for nondisplayed key codes list.

Example: =ON.KEY("+^R","CHART.XLM!CHART") executes the CHART macro in CHART.XLM when Shift, Control, and *R* are pressed.

ON.RECALC([sheet_text, macro_text])

Runs macro *macro_text* whenever worksheet or macro sheet *sheet_text* is recalculated. To turn off ON.RECALC, omit the second argument.

ON.TIME(time, macro_text,[tolerance, insert_logical])

Runs macro *macro_text* at *time*. *Tolerance* is the time and date (as a serial number) that defines how long you are willing to wait and still have the macro run. Use *insert_logical* to turn off a previously set TIME macro. If TRUE (or omitted), macro runs at *time*. If FALSE, the macro is turned off.

ON.WINDOW([window_text, macro_text])

Starts the macro *macro_text* whenever the window *window_text* is activated. To turn off ON.WINDOW, omit the second argument.

OPEN(file_text, [update_links, read_only, delimiter_num, prot_pwd, write_res_pwd, ignore_rorec, file_origin, custom_text])

Opens the file *file_text*. *Update_links* is used to control the updating of external references (0 = no updating, 1 = update external, 2 = update remote, 3 = update external and remote, default). If *read_only* is TRUE, changes can't be saved. Delimiter_num specifies whether values in a text file are to be separated by: 1 = tabs, 2 = commas, 3 = spaces, 4 = semicolons, 6 = nothing, 7 = custom (specified in *custom_text*). *Prot_pwd* is the password (text) to unprotect a protected file. *Write_res_pwd* is the password (text) to open a read-only file with full write privileges. *Ignore_rorec* is a logical value that controls whether the read-only recommended message is displayed. *File_origin* specifies the origin of a text file (1 = Macintosh, 2 = Windows, 3 = DOS or OS/2). *Custom_text* defines the delimiter character when opening text files.

Menu Equivalent: File ➤ Open

OPEN.LINKS(documents1_text,[documents2_text,..., read_only, type_link])

Opens the documents specified (as text) that are linked to the current document. The document names can be generated with the LINKS function. *Read_only* specifies whether the file is read only. *Type_link* specifies the type (1 = Excel, 2 = DDE, 3 = (reserved), 4 = NewWave outgoing, 5 = Subscriber, 6 = Publisher).

Example: If the chart SALES is active and refers to a sheet called SALES, this function opens the sheet:

=OPEN.LINKS(LINKS("SALES.XLC"))

Menu Equivalent: File ➤ Links

OPEN.MAIL([subject, comments])

Opens files sent via Microsoft Mail.

Menu Equivalent: File ➤ Open Mail

OUTLINE([auto_styles, row_dir, col_dir, create_apply])

Creates an outline and automatically defines settings. The arguments correspond to the Outline dialog box check boxes. *Create_apply* is a number that corresponds to the Create button and the Apply Styles button (1 = Create outline with current settings, 2 = Apply outlining styles to the selection based on the level).

Menu Equivalent: Formula ➤ Outline

PAGE.SETUP([header, footer, left, right, top, bottom, headings, gridlines, h_ctr, v_ctr, orient, paper_size, scaling], [start_num, page_order_num, color])

PAGE.SETUP([header, footer, left, right, top, bottom, size, h_ctr, v_ctr, orient, paper_size, scaling, start_num,])

The first form sets up a worksheet or macro sheet for printing. The second form sets up a chart. *Header* and *footer* must be text. *Left, right, top,* and *bottom* are numbers that specify the relevant margins. *Headings* and *gridlines* correspond to the dialog-box check boxes and are logical values—TRUE if checked, FALSE if not checked. *Size* is a number (1 = Screen size, 2 = Fit to page, and 3 = Full page). *Orient* is 1 (portrait) or 2 (landscape). *Scaling* is a percent or logical value. *Page_size* is a number from 1 to 3 (1 = screen size, 2 = fit to page, 3 = full page). Other options correspond to options on the Page Setup dialog box. For more details, see the Excel function manual.

Example: =PAGE.SETUP("Sales - 1991",Page &p,0.75,0,0.75,1,1,TRUE,TRUE,2,5) sets up a chart with the heading "Sales - 1991," page numbers in the footer, ¾" left and top margin and 1" bottom margin, to be centered horizontally and vertically on the page, and printed in landscape mode on legal-sized paper.

Menu Equivalent: File ➤ Page Setup

PARSE([parse_text, destination_ref])

Parses the input data stream. *Parse_text* is the parse line. If omitted, Excel makes a guess. *Destination_ref* defines the upper left corner of the destination for the parsed data. If omitted, the current selection is assumed. See Chapter 21.

Menu Equivalent: Data ➤ Parse

PASTE([to_ref])

Pastes from the Clipboard to *to_ref* or, if omitted, the current location.

Menu Equivalent: Edit ➤ Paste

PASTE.LINK( )

Pastes copied data into destination cells and establishes a link with the source cells.

Menu Equivalent: Edit ➤ Paste Link

PASTE.PICTURE( )

Pastes a picture of the Clipboard contents to the worksheet at the active cell location. There is no linking.

Menu Equivalent: Edit ➤ Paste Picture (with Shift held down)

PASTE.PICTURE.LINK( )

Pastes a linked picture of the Clipboard contents to the worksheet at the active cell location.

Menu Equivalent: Edit ➤ Paste Picture Link or the camera tool on the tool bar.

PASTE.SPECIAL(paste_number, operation_number, skip_blanks, transpose)

Worksheet-to-worksheet form.

PASTE.SPECIAL(rowcol, series, categories, replace)

Worksheet-to-chart form.

PASTE.SPECIAL(paste_number)

Chart-to-chart form.

PASTE.SPECIAL(data_type, [paste_link])

Application-to-Excel form.

The worksheet function pastes from a worksheet to a worksheet, where *paste_number* represents one of the following:

PASTE_NUMBER	WHAT TO PASTE
1	All
2	Formulas
3	Values
4	Formats
5	Notes

Operation_number specifies any operation desired (1 = None, 2 = Add, 3 = Subtract, 4 = Multiply, and 5 = Divide). Other arguments are logical values and correspond to the check boxes on the Paste Special dialog box.

The worksheet-to-chart function pastes data series values in rows if *row-col* is 1, and in columns if it is 2. If *series* is TRUE, the contents of the first cell of each row or column is used as the name of the data series. If FALSE, it is used as a data point. If *categories* is TRUE, the contents of the first row or column is used as the chart categories. If FALSE, it is used as a data series. *Replace* corresponds to the Replace Existing Categories check box.

When using the chart-to-chart function, *paste_number* defines what to paste (1 = All, 2 = Formats, 3 = Data series).

The application-to-Excel form pastes from another application to Excel. *Data_type* defines the data to paste from the Clipboard, and *paste_link* is a logical value that specifies if the pasted data is to be linked.

Menu Equivalent: Edit ➤ Paste Special

PASTE.TOOL(bar_id, position)

Pastes a tool face from the Clipboard to a toolbar (see ADD.TOOL).

Menu Equivalent: Equivalent to selecting a tool and choosing Edit ➤ Paste ➤ Tool Face.

PATTERNS([a_pattern, a_fore, a_back])

For cells.

PATTERNS([l_auto, l_style, l_color, l_weight, h_width, h_length, h_type])

For lines (arrows) on worksheets or charts.

PATTERNS([b_auto, b_style, b_color, b_wt, shadow, a_auto, a_pattern, a_fore, a_back, rounded])

For text boxes, rectangles, ovals, arcs, and pictures.

PATTERNS([b_auto, b_style, b_color, b_wt, shadow, a_auto, a_pattern, a_fore, a_back, invert, apply])

For chart plot areas, bars, columns, pie slices, and text labels.

PATTERNS([l_auto, l_style, l_color, l_wt, t_major, t_minor, t_label])

For chart axes.

PATTERNS([l_auto, l_style, l_color, l_wt, apply])

For chart gridlines, high-low lines, drop lines, lines on a picture line chart, and picture bar, picture column, and picture 3-D column charts.

PATTERNS([l_auto, l_style, l_color, l_wt, m_auto, m_style, m_fore, m_back, apply])

For chart data lines.

PATTERNS([type, picture_units, apply])

For picture chart markers.

All of these change the appearance of a selected object in a chart. The arguments correspond to the options in the Patterns dialog box (see the Excel function manual).

Menu Equivalent: Format ➤ Patterns

PAUSE([no_tool])

Pauses a macro. If *no_tool* is TRUE, the Resume toolbar is not displayed during the pause. If FALSE or omitted, the toolbar is displayed.

POKE(channel_number, item_text, data_ref)

Sends the data referenced by *data_ref* to the item specified by *item_text* in the application connected to channel *channel_number.* The channel number is returned by the previously run INITIATE function.

PRECISION(logical)

Sets the precision of the calculation. If *logical* is FALSE, calculations are made to full precision. If *logical* is TRUE, calculations are to the displayed precision only. Specifying TRUE may permanently alter the data.

Menu Equivalent: Options ➤ Calculation (Precision As Displayed)

PREFERRED( )

Changes the displayed chart to the default or preferred format.

Menu Equivalent: Gallery ➤ Preferred

PRESS.TOOL([bar_id, position, down])

Formats a tool so that it appears normal or depressed on the screen. If down is TRUE, the tool appears depressed. If FALSE (default), tool is not depressed. See ADD.TOOL.

PRINT([range, from, to, copies, draft, preview, print_what, feed])

Prints the sheet, chart, or macro sheet. The arguments correspond to the same arguments in the Print dialog box. *Range* is a number: 1 = Print all, 2 = Print a range of pages. *From* and *to* specify the range limits (required if *Range*=2). *Copies* is the number of copies to print. For *feed,* 1 = Continuous and 2 = Cut sheets. The *print_what* argument specifies what to print (1 = Document, 2 = Notes, 3 = All).

Example: =PRINT(1,,,1,1) prints one copy of the entire sheet as a continuous form.

Menu Equivalent: File ➤ Print

PRINT.PREVIEW( )

Previews the pages and page breaks of the document to print.

Menu Equivalent: File ➤ Print Preview

PRINTER.SETUP(printer_text)

Sets up the printer for printing. *Printer_text* name should be exactly as it appears in the File ➤ Printer Setup dialog box.

Example: =PRINTER.SETUP("HP LaserJet+ on LPT1") sets up the Hewlett-Packard LaserJet Plus printer on port LPT1.

Menu Equivalent: File ➤ Page Setup ➤ Printer Setup

PROMOTE([rowcol])

Promotes the selected rows or columns in an outline. If *rowcol* is 1 or omitted, rows are promoted. If 2, columns are promoted.

Menu Equivalent: Equivalent to clicking the promote button.

PROTECT.DOCUMENT([contents, windows, password, objects])

Turns document protection on or off, with arguments corresponding to the Protect Document dialog box check boxes. To protect a document, the first two arguments and fourth should be TRUE. To unprotect, all three should be FALSE.

Menu Equivalent: Options ➤ Protect Document and Options ➤ Unprotect Document

QUIT( )

Quits Microsoft Excel. Doesn't prompt you to save changes if error checking is turned off (ERROR(FALSE)).

Menu Equivalent: File ➤ Exit

REFTEXT(ref, [a1])

Converts the reference *ref* to an absolute reference in the form of text. Use this to operate on references with text functions. A1 is a logical value specifying A1 or R1C1 references.

REGISTER(module_text,[procedure_text, type_text,] [function_text, argument_text], [macro_type, category, shortcut_text])

NOTE
NOTE

REGISTER is an advanced function and should be used by expert programmers only.

Makes the specified dynamic link library available and returns the number identifying the code for use by the CALL and UNREGISTER functions. *Module_text* specifies the name of dynamic link library that contains the procedure you want to access. *Procedure_text* defines the name of the procedure. *Type_text* specifies the data type of the return value and the number and data types of the arguments (see the Excel function reference for details). The last two arguments define, respectively, the name of the function you are creating and its argument(s). *Macro_type* specifies the macro type (1 = function, 2 = command). *Category* specifies the function category that corresponds to the position in the dialog box. If omitted, it is assumed as user-defined. *Shortcut_text* specifies a shortcut key for a command macro.

RELREF(ref1, ref2)

Gives the reference of *ref1* relative to the upper-left cell of *ref2*. The reference is returned as text in the R1C1-style.

Example: =RELREF(A1,D4) yields R[–3]C[–3].

REMOVE.PAGE.BREAK( )

SET.PAGE.BREAK( )

Sets or removes a manual page break at the active cell.

Menu Equivalent: Options ➤ Set Page Break and Options ➤ Remove Page Break

RENAME.COMMAND(bar_number, menu_pos, command_pos, name_text)

Assigns the name *name_text* to the command in position *command_pos* on the menu *menu_pos* in the menu bar number *bar_number*.

REPORT.DEFINE(report_name, views_scenarios_array, [pages])

Creates or replaces a report definition. *Report_name* is the name of the report and *views_scenario_array* is an array of view and scenario pairs that define the report. If *pages* is TRUE (or omitted), contiguous page numbers are used for multiple sections. If FALSE, page numbers are reset to 1 for each new section.

Menu Equivalent: File ➤ PrintReport ➤ Add

REPORT.DELETE(report_name)

Deletes a report definition. *Report_name* is the name of the report to be deleted.

Menu Equivalent: File ➤ PrintReport ➤ Delete

REPORT.GET(type_num, [report_name])

Returns information about reports that are defined for the active document. *Type_num* defines the information to return where: 1 = array of reports, 2 = array of view and scenario pairs, and 3 = TRUE if continuous page numbers are used, FALSE if reset for each section. *Report_name* is the name of the report.

REPORT.PRINT(report_name, [copies_num, show_print_dlg_logical])

Prints report *report_name. Copies_num* defines the number of copies, and *show_ print_dlg _ logical,* if TRUE, shows the print dialog box for defining the number of copies to print.

Menu Equivalent: File ➤ Print ➤ Report Print

REQUEST(channel_number, item_text)

Requests an array of information specified by *item_text* from the application connected to the channel specified by *channel_number* returned by the INITIATE function.

RESET.TOOL(bar_id[, position])

Resets tool to original tool face (see ADD.TOOL).

Menu Equivalent: Equivalent to choosing Reset Tool Face on the Tool shortcut menu.

RESET.TOOLBAR(bar_id)

Resets toolbars to Excel's default set. *Bar_id* specifies the toolbar to reset (see ADD.TOOL).

RESTART([level_number])

Removes *level_number* number of RETURN statements from the stack. If *level_number* is omitted, all but one RETURN statements are omitted.

Example: Suppose that macro *C* is called by macro *B,* which in turn is called by macro *A*. Then =RESTART(1) in *C* will return execution directly to macro A when Excel encounters the next RETURN statement.

RESULT([type_num])

Defines the type of value that is to be returned by the function. The RESULT function is optional except when references or arrays are returned. If used, it must be the first function in the macro. *Type_num* defines the type of value returned:

TYPE	VALUE
1	Number
2	Text
4	Logical
8	Reference
16	Error
64	Array

Type_num can be a sum of type numbers.

Example: =RESULT(64) causes the macro to return an array.

RESUME([type_num])

Resumes a paused macro. Type_num defines how to resume with:

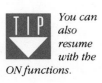

You can also resume with the ON functions.

TYPE_NUM	ACTION
1 or omitted	If paused by pause function, continue. If paused from single-step, return to dialog box.
2	Halts the paused macro
3	Continue running macro
4	Open Single-Step dialog box

Menu Equivalent: Macro ➤ Resume.

RETURN([value])

Terminates the macro execution and, optionally, returns values to the calling program or macro. If *value* is to be returned, its type is specified by the RESULT function, which, if used, must be the first function in the macro. The *value* argument can be used only with function macros.

ROW.HEIGHT([height_number, ref, standard_height, type_number])

The rows in *ref* are changed to height *height_number* in points ($\frac{1}{72}$ of an inch). *Type_number* permits you to hide, unhide, or set the height to best fit (1 = Hide, 2 = Unhide, 3 = Best fit). If *standard_height* is TRUE, *height_number* is ignored and the rows are set to the standard height.

Menu Equivalent: Format ➤ Row Height

RUN([ref, step])

Initiates a macro execution defined by *ref. Ref* should be an external reference to a macro on a macro sheet or an R1C1-style external reference on a macro sheet. If omitted, the macro function in the active cell is executed. *Step* is a logical value and, if TRUE, permits single stepping the macro. If FALSE, or omitted, the macro is run normally. *Ref* can also be a number that defines an auto macro to run:

REF	MACROS TO RUN
1	All Auto_Open macros
2	All Auto_Close macros

REF	MACROS TO RUN
3	All Auto_Activate macros
4	All Auto_Deactivate macros

Example: =RUN(MACROS.XLM!Heading) runs the macro normally, beginning at the upper-left cell of the range named "Heading."

Menu Equivalent: Macro ➤ Run

SAVE( )

Saves the current document under its current name.

Menu Equivalent: File ➤ Save

SAVE.AS([file_text, type, passwd_text, backup, write_res_pwd, read_only_rec])

Saves the sheet using the name *file_text*. *Type* is a number that defines the saved format as follows:

TYPE	FORMAT
1	Normal
2	SYLK
3	Text
4	WKS
5	WK1
6	CSV
7	DBF2
8	DBF3
9	DIF
11	DBF4
15	WK3
16	Microsoft Excel 2.*X*
17	Template

TYPE	FORMAT
18	Add-in macro
19	Text (Macintosh)
20	Text (Windows)
21	Text (DOS, OS/2)
22	CSV (Macintosh)
23	CSV (Windows)
24	CSV (DOS, OS/2)
25	International macro
26	International add-in macro
29	Microsoft Excel 3.0

Types 10, 12–14, and 27–29 are not defined. Worksheets can use all but 18, 25, and 26. Charts can use 1, 16, 17, and 29. Macro sheets can use 1–3, 6, 9, 16–26, and 29. Other arguments correspond to the Save As dialog box options. *File_text, passwd_text,* and *write_res_ pwd* are text. *Backup* and *read_only_rec* are logical values.

Example: =SAVE.AS("Sales",1) saves the file as "Sales" in the Normal format.

Menu Equivalent: File ➤ Save As

SAVE.NEW.OBJECT(object_name_text)

Saves a copy of the current object under the name you specify.

Menu Equivalent: File ➤ Save New Object (only if you are using NewWave by Hewlett-Packard).

SAVE.TOOLBAR([bar_id, filename])

Saves one or more toolbars in a specified file. Default filename, if not specified, is EXCEL.XLB. If *bar_id* is omitted, all toolbars are saved (see ADD.TOOL). *Bar_id* can be an array.

SAVE.WORKBOOK([document_text, type_num, prot_pwd, backup, write_res_pwd, read_only_rec])

Saves the workbook of which the active document is a part. For parameters, see the SAVE.AS command.

Menu Equivalent: File ➤ Save Workbook

SAVE.WORKSPACE([name_text])

Saves the current workspace—opened documents, their position on-screen and status, preferred chart formats, and workspace display settings. (Included for Microsoft Excel 3.0 compatibility only. Use SAVE.WORKBOOK in Excel 4.0.)

SCALE([cross, cat_labels, cat_marks, between, max, reverse])

Note: Category (x) axis is selected on a 2-D chart, but not an XY (Scatter) chart.

SCALE([min_number, max_number, major, minor, cross, log, reverse, max])

Note: Value (y) axis selected on a 2-D chart, or x or y (value) axis selected on a scatter chart.

SCALE([cat_labels, cat_marks, reverse, between])

Note: Category (x) axis selected on a 3-D chart.

SCALE([series_labels, series_marks, reverse])

Note: Series (y) axis selected on a 3-D chart.

SCALE([min_number, max_number, major, minor, cross, log, reverse, min])

Note: Value (z) axis selected on a 3-D chart.

All of these format the scale. The arguments match those of the corresponding Axis Scale dialog box (see Excel function reference for more details).

Menu Equivalent: Format ➤ Scale

SCENARIO.ADD(scen_name, [value_array])

Defines the specified values as a scenario. *Scen_name* is the name of the scenario. *Value_array* is a horizontal array of input values for the what-if model.

Menu Equivalent: Formula ➤ Scenario Manager ➤ Add

SCENARIO.CELLS(changing_ref)

Defines the input cells for a what-if model on the worksheet for a scenario. *Changing_ref* is a reference to the input cells for the model.

Menu Equivalent: Formula ➤ Scenario Manager ➤ Add, then editing the Changing Cells text box

SCENARIO.DELETE(scen_name)

Deletes the specified scenario.

Menu Equivalent: Formula ➤ Scenario Manager ➤ Delete

SCENARIO.GET([type_num])

Returns the specified information about the scenarios on the worksheet, where type_num is defined as:

TYPE_NUM	INFORMATION RETURNED
1	Horizontal array of all scenario names
2	Reference to the changing cells
3	Reference to result cells
4	An array of scenario values

SCENARIO.SHOW(scen_name)

Recalculates model using specified scenario and displays results.

Menu Equivalent: Formula ➤ Scenario Manager ➤ Show

SCENARIO.SHOW.NEXT( )

Recalculates model using the next specified set of input values.

Menu Equivalent: Equivalent to Formula ➤ Scenario Manager, then selecting the next scenario from the list and Show.

SCENARIO.SUMMARY([result_ref])

Creates a table showing results of all the scenarios for the model on the worksheet. *Result_ref* defines the result cells to be included in the summary report. If omitted, no result cells are included.

Menu Equivalent: Formula ➤ Scenario Manager ➤ Summary

SELECT([selection_ref, active_cell_ref])

SELECT(object_id_text, [replace])

SELECT(item_text, [single_point])

The first function applies to a worksheet or macro sheet and selects the cells referenced by *selection_ref* and makes *active_cell_ref* the active cell. *Selection_ref* should be either a reference to the active worksheet (such as !B1:B3 or !Income) or an R1C1-style reference in text form relative to the active cell in the current selection (such as "R[−2]C[− 1]:R[2]C[3]"). If you omit *selection_ref,* the selection is not changed. *Active_cell_ref* should be a reference to a single cell inside of *selection_ref* either on the current sheet or as an R1C1-style reference. If *active_cell_ref* is relative, it is assumed to be relative to the currently active cell. If *active_cell_ref* is omitted, it is assumed to be the upper-left cell of *selection_ref.*

The second function applies to selecting objects, where *object_id_text* is the text that identifies the object and *replace* is a logical value which specifies that previously selected objects are included in the selection. If TRUE (default), only the current object is selected.

The third function applies to a chart and selects the object specified by *item_text.* If *single_point* is TRUE, a single point is selected. (See the Excel function manual for *item_text* names and the use of *single_ point.*)

Examples: =SELECT(!Sales,!A5), =SELECT("Oval 1"), or SELECT("S1P2",TRUE). The third one selects the second point in the first series of a chart.

Menu Equivalent: Equivalent to selecting cells or objects with the mouse.

SELECT.END(direction_number)

Moves the active cell to the next block edge in the direction specified by *direction_number* (1 = Left, 2 = Right, 3 = Up, and 4 = Down).

Menu Equivalent: Equivalent to pressing Ctrl and an arrow key.

SELECT.LAST.CELL( )

Makes the last cell of the sheet the active cell.

Menu Equivalent: Equivalent to Formula ➤ Select Special and selecting the Last Cell option.

SELECT.SPECIAL(type_number, [value_types, levels])

Selects cells with the specified characteristics. *Type_number* identifies the dialog box option:

TYPE_NUMBER	Description
1	Notes
2	Constants
3	Formulas
4	Blanks
5	Current region
6	Current array
7	Row differences
8	Column differences
9	Precedents
10	Dependents
11	Last cell
12	Visible cells only (outlining)
13	All objects

Value_types identifies the types of constants and formulas to select (1 = Numbers, 2 = Text, 4 = Logical values, 16 = Error values).

Levels specifies how precedents and dependents are selected (1 = Direct only, 2 = All levels). It is available only when *type_number* is 9 or 10. The default is 1.

Menu Equivalent: Formula ➤ Select Special

SELECTION( )

Returns the reference of the currently selected cells or object. If an object is selected, the object identifier is returned.

Example: If the current sheet is SALES and the cells B1 to B3 are selected, then =REFTEXT(SELECTION( )) gives SALES.XLS!R1C2:R3C2.

SEND.KEYS(key_text, [wait_log])

Sends the keys specified by *key_text* to the active applications, just as if they were typed at the keyboard. *Wait_log* is a logical value that determines whether the macro should wait until actions from *key_text* are completed. If TRUE, the macro waits. If FALSE or omitted, the macro continues running without waiting for a key to be pressed (see ON.KEY).

SEND.MAIL( )

Sends the active document using Microsoft Mail.

Menu Equivalent: File ➤ Send Mail

SEND.TO.BACK( )

Places selected objects behind other objects.

Menu Equivalent: Format ➤ Send To Back

SERIES([name_ref, categories,] values, plot_order)

Represents the active data series in a chart. You cannot use it as a function in a macro sheet. To edit a series, use EDIT.SERIES. (See Chapter 19.)

SET.CRITERIA( )

Assigns the name "Criteria" to the currently selected range. (See Chapter 11.)

Menu Equivalent: Data ➤ Set Criteria

SET.DATABASE( )

Assigns the name "Database" to the currently selected range.

Menu Equivalent: Data ➤ Set Database

SET.EXTRACT( )

Assigns the name "Extract" to the currently selected range.

Menu Equivalent: Data ➤ Set Extract

SET.NAME(name_text, [value])

Defines a name on the macro sheet as a specified value. *Name_text* must be a text value for the name to be assigned. *Value* can be a number, text, logical, error value, array, or a reference. Use this function to store values while the macro is calculating.

NOTE
NOTE
If value is to be the value of a referenced cell, you must use the DEREF function.

Examples: =SET.NAME("One",1) assigns the name "One" to the value 1.

=SET.NAME("Qty",DEREF(A3)) assigns the name "Qty" to the value in A3 on the macro sheet.

SET.PAGE.BREAK( )

See REMOVE.PAGE.BREAK( ).

SET.PREFERRED( )

Sets the current chart format as the preferred format.

Menu Equivalent: Gallery ➤ Set Preferred

SET.PRINT.AREA( )

Defines the current selection as the sheet area to be printed with the File ➤ Print command. To delete the name and print the entire worksheet, use Formula ➤ Define Name, select Print_Area, and Delete.

Menu Equivalent: Options ➤ Set Print Area

SET.PRINT.TITLES([titles_for_rows_ref, titles_for_columns_ref])

Defines the referenced cells as the text that will be used as row or column titles when the sheet is printed. You can specify the row and column titles as arguments. If not specified, existing row and column titles are used. To delete the option, use Formula ➤ Define Name, select Print_Titles, and Delete.

Menu Equivalent: Options ➤ Set Print Titles

SET.UPDATE.STATUS(link_text, status, [type_of_link])

Sets the update status of a link to automatic (*status* = 1) or manual (*status* = 2). *Link_text* is the full path name of the link, as displayed in the Links dialog box. *Type_of_link* defines the type (2 = DDE, 4 = Outgoing NewWave).

SET.VALUE(ref, values)

Changes the value of the cells specified by *ref* to *values*. Formulas are not changed. Used for loop control during macro execution. *Ref* must be a reference to cells on the macro sheet. If *ref* is a range, *values* should be an array of the same size. Use to assign initial values and to store values during a macro calculation.

Example: =SET.VALUE(D5,3) sets the value in D5 of the macro sheet to 3.

SHARE( )

Places a shared view of the selection on the Clipboard.

Menu Equivalent: Edit ➤ Share (only if you are using NewWave by Hewlett-Packard)

SHARE.NAME(range_text)

Places a shared view of *range_text* on the Clipboard.

Menu Equivalent: Edit ➤Share (only if you are using NewWave by Hewlett-Packard)

SHOW.ACTIVE.CELL( )

Scrolls sheet until active cell is visible.

Menu Equivalent: Formula ➤ Show Active Cell or Ctrl-Backspace

SHOW.BAR([bar_number])

Displays the menu bar specified by the menu bar ID number *bar_number.*

SHOW.CLIPBOARD( )

Displays contents of the Clipboard in a new window.

Menu Equivalent: Equivalent to running the Clipboard from Excel Control menu.

SHOW.DETAIL(rowcol, rowcol_number, [expand])

Expands or collapses outline detail under the specified expand or collapse button. If *rowcol* is 1, the function operates on rows; if 2, on columns. *Rowcol_number* specifies the row or column to expand or collapse. If *expand* is TRUE, the function expands; otherwise it collapses. If omitted, the row or column changes state (collapsing if already expanded and vice versa).

SHOW.INFO(enable_log)

If *enable_log* is TRUE, the command activates the Info window. If the current window is the Info window and *enable_log* is FALSE, the command activates the document linked to the Info window. Close the Info window with the CLOSE function.

Menu Equivalent: Options ➤ Workspace ➤ Info Window

SHOW.LEVELS([row_level, col_level])

Displays the specified number of row and column levels of the outline. At least one of the arguments must be specified. *Row_level* defines the number of row levels to display, and *col_level* defines the number of column levels to display.

SHOW.TOOLBAR(bar_id, visible, dock, x_pos, y_pos, [width])

Displays the toolbar identified by *bar_id* (See ADD.TOOL). *Visible* is a logical values that determines if the toolbar is visible. *Dock* defines the location for the toolbar (1 = top, 2 = left, 3 = right, 4 = bottom, and 5 = floating). *X-pos* defines the horizontal position. *Y-pos* defines the vertical position in points. *Width,* if specified, is the width of the toolbar. If not specified, the last width is used.

Menu Equivalent: Options ➤ Toolbars ➤ Show/Hide

SLIDE.COPY.ROW()

Copies the selected slides, each defined in a single row, to the Clipboard. Slide Show add-in utility must be installed.

Menu Equivalent: This is equivalent to choosing the Copy Row button on a slide show document.

SLIDE.CUT.ROW()

Cuts the selected slides, each defined in a single row, and pastes them to the Clipboard. Slide Show add-in utility must be installed.

Menu Equivalent: This is equivalent to choosing the Cut Row button on a slide show document.

SLIDE.DEFAULTS([effect_num, speed_num, advance_rate_num, soundfile_text, resource])

Specifies the default value for the transition effect. See SLIDE.EDIT.

Menu Equivalent: This is equivalent to choosing the Set Defaults button on a slide show document.

SLIDE.DELETE.ROW()

Deletes the selected slides, each defined in a single row. Slide Show add-in utility must be installed.

Menu Equivalent: This is equivalent to choosing the Delete Row button on a slide show document.

SLIDE.EDIT([effect_num, speed_num, advance_rate_num, soundfile_text, resource])

Gives the currently selected slide the designated attributes. Slide Show add-in utility must be installed.

Menu Equivalent: This is equivalent to choosing the Edit button on a slide show document (see SLIDE.PASTE).

SLIDE.GET([type_num, name_text, slide_num]

Returns specified information about a slide show or slide. *Type_num* defines the information to return (1 = is the number of slides in a slide show, 2 = two-item array defining slide number range of current selection, 3 = version of add-in utility). For specific slides:

TYPE_NUM	INFORMATION
4	Transition effect number
5	Transition effect name
6	Transition effect speed
7	Number of seconds for display
8	Name of sound file associated with the slide

Name_text defines the open slide show document from which you wish information. *Slide_num* is the number of the slide for which you wish information (if *type_num*>3). Slide Show add-in utility must be installed.

SLIDE.PASTE([effect_num, speed_num, advance_rate_num, soundfile_text, resource])

This function pastes the contents of the Clipboard as the next available slide of the active slide show document. The specified attributes are assigned. *Effect_num* defines the transition effect as defined on the Effect list box in the Slide Attributes dialog box. *Speed_num* defines the speed of the transition effect and has a value from 1 to 10. *Advance_rate* defines the time, in seconds, for the slide display. *Soundfile_text* defines any sound file for the slide. *Resource* is the name of a sound resource in the sound file. Slide Show add-in utility must be installed.

Menu Equivalent: This is equivalent to choosing the Paste button on a slide show document.

SLIDE.PASTE.ROW()

Pastes any previously cut or copied slides to the current selection. Slide Show add-in utility must be installed.

Menu Equivalent: This is equivalent to choosing the Paste Row button on a slide show document.

SLIDE.SHOW([initialslide_num, repeat_logical, dialogtitle_text, allownav_logical, allowcontrol_logical])

Starts the slide show in the active document. *Initialslide_num* defines the starting slide. If *repeat_logical* is TRUE, the slide show repeats after the last slide. *Dialogtitle_text* (in quotation marks) is the title for the dialog boxes during the slide show. The default is "Slide Show". *Allownav_logical*, if TRUE, enables navigation key use during the slide show. *Allowcontrol_logical*, if TRUE, allows the Slide Show Options dialog box during the show. Slide Show add-in utility must be installed.

Menu Equivalent: This is equivalent to choosing the Start Show button on a slide show document.

SOLVER.ADD(cell_ref, relation, [formula])

Adds a constraint to the current Solver problem. *Cell_ref* defines the left side of the constraint, *relation* defines the operator (1 = <=, 2 = =, 3 = >=, 4 = int), and *formula* defines the right side of the constraint.

Menu Equivalent: Formula ➤ Solver ➤ Add

SOLVER.CHANGE(cell_ref, relation, [formula])

Changes the right side of the current constraint.

Menu Equivalent: Formula ➤ Solver ➤ Change

SOLVER.DELETE(cell_ref, relation, [formula])

Deletes an existing constraint.

Menu Equivalent: Formula ➤ Solver ➤ Delete

SOLVER.FINISH([keep_final, report_array])

Keep_final, if 1 or omitted, keeps the final solution. If 2, the final values are not kept. *Report_array* is an array argument defining the reports to create: 1 = answer, 2 = sensitivity, and 3 = limit. You can build an array to create multiple reports.

Menu Equivalent: Equivalent to choosing from the finish dialog box on a Solver completion.

SOLVER.GET(type_num, sheet_name)

Returns information about the current settings for Solver. See Excel function manual for more information.

SOLVER.LOAD(load_area)

Loads a mathematical model for Solver. Load_area defines the upper left cell of a range on the active worksheet from which you wish to load the problem specification.

Menu Equivalent: Formula ➤ Solver ➤ Options ➤ Load Model

SOLVER.OK([set_cell, max_min_value, value_of], by_changing)

Specifies the Solver parameters. The parameters correspond to those of the Solver Parameters dialog box.

Menu Equivalent: Formula ➤ Solver ➤ Options

SOLVER.OPTIONS(max_time, iterations, precision, assume_linear, step_thru, estimates, derivatives, search, int_tolerance, scaling)

Specifies the Solver options. The parameters correspond to those of the Solver Options dialog box.

Menu Equivalent: Formula ➤ Solver ➤ Options

SOLVER.RESET( )

Restores the Solver dialog box to its default values

Menu Equivalent: Formula ➤ Solver ➤ Reset All.

SOLVER.SAVE(save_area)

Saves the solver model defined by *save_area* on the worksheet.

Menu Equivalent: Formula ➤ Solver ➤ Options ➤ Save Model

SOLVER.SOLVE([user_finish, show_ref])

Solves the current model. *User_finish,* if TRUE, will not display the final dialog box. If FALSE or omitted, will display the box. *Show_ref* defines a macro to be called instead of the Show Trial Solution dialog box.

Menu Equivalent: Formula ➤ Solver ➤ Solve

SORT(sort_by, 1st_key, order1, [2nd_key, order2, 3rd_key, order3])

Sorts the specified range in the order defined by the arguments. There are two *sort_by* options:

SORT_BY	ORDER
1	Rows
2	Columns

and two orders:

ORDER	DIRECTION
1	Ascending
2	Descending

1st_key, 2nd_key, and *3rd_key* are external references to the current sheet or R1C1-style references in text. You may also wish to use the DEREF function to define a key by range name.

Examples: =SORT(1,"R12C1",1) sorts the selected rows, using R12C1 as a key, in ascending order.

If C11 on the sheet contains the text "Target," this function sorts the sheet by target values:

=SORT(1,DEREF(!$C$11),1)

Menu Equivalent: Data ➤ Sort

SOUND.NOTE(cell_ref, [erase_snd])

SOUND.NOTE(cell_ref, file_text, [resource])

Records or erases sound from a cell note (first form) or imports a sound (second form) to *cell_ref*. If erase_snd is TRUE, the sound is erased instead of recorded. *File_text* defines the file with the sounds to import. *Resource* defines a sound in the file to import. You must have a sound card with multimedia support and Multimedia Extensions installed.

SOUND.PLAY(cell_ref, file_text, [resource])

Plays a sound from a cell note or a file. See SOUND.NOTE. You must have a sound card with multimedia support and Multimedia Extensions installed. *Cell_ref* is a reference to a cell containing the sound, *file_text* is a file containing the sound, and resource is a number or name of the sound resource in *file_text* to play.

Menu Equivalent: Formula ➤ Note ➤ Play or Formula ➤ Note ➤ Import

SPELLING([custom_dic, ignore_caps, suggest_always])

Checks the spelling of the active document. *Custom_dic* defines any custom dictionary; if omitted the current dictionary is used. *Ignore_caps,* if TRUE, ignores words in total caps. *Suggest_always,* if TRUE, displays alternate words on stopping. If FALSE, Excel will wait for correct input for the spelling. If omitted, Excel retains the current spelling.

Menu Equivalent: Options ➤ Spelling

SPELLING.CHECK(word_text, [custom_dic, ignore_caps])

Checks the spelling of selected word (see SPELLING). Returns TRUE if spelled correctly, FALSE if not recognized. There is no dialog box form.

Menu Equivalent: Options ➤ Spelling on a single word.

SPLIT([col_split, row_split])

Splits the active window at *row_split* and *col_split*.

Menu Equivalent: Window ➤ Split

STEP( )

Permits running a macro one step at a time and is useful for debugging. When the STEP function is encountered in a macro execution, the calculation stops and displays a dialog box that defines the next cell to calculate and the formula in that cell. You can then click Step in this box to execute the next macro cell and stop again, click Evaluate to calculate part of the formula, click Halt to interrupt the macro, or click Continue to run the macro without single-stepping.

TABLE([row_input, column_input])

Creates a table in the selected range. Both *row_input* and *column_input* should be external references to single cells on the active sheet, or R1C1-type references in text form.

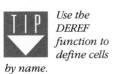

Use the DEREF function to define cells by name.

Example: In the SALES example of this book, cell D4 was used as a column input to define a table. This could also be done as follows:

=TABLE(,"R4C4")

If D3 contained the heading "Criteria" as the name for D4, you could also use the following:

=TABLE(,DEREF(!D$3))

Menu Equivalent: Data ➤ Table

TERMINATE(channel_number)

Closes the DDE channel *channel_number* set up by the INITIATE function.

TEXT.BOX(add_text, object_id_text, [start_number, number_chars])

Replaces characters in a text box with *add_text*. *Object_id_text* is the name and number (or number) of the object you wish information about. *Start_number* specifies the first character to replace, and defaults to 1. *Num_characters* specifies how many characters to replace, and defaults to all.

TEXTREF(text,[a1])

Converts *text* to an absolute reference. If *a1* is TRUE, *text* is assumed to be in the A1-style reference. If FALSE or omitted, the R1C1-style is assumed.

UNDO( )

Undoes the previous command.

Menu Equivalent: Edit ➤ Undo

UNGROUP( )

Separates a grouped object into its components.

Menu Equivalent: Format ➤ Ungroup

UNHIDE(window_text)

Unhides the specified window.

Menu Equivalent: Window ➤ Unhide

UNLOCKED.NEXT( )

UNLOCKED.PREV( )

Moves the active cell to the next or previous unlocked cell in a protected sheet.

Menu Equivalent: Pressing Tab or Shift-Tab.

UNREGISTER(register_number)

Removes dynamic link library or code resource previously registered by the REGISTER function.

UPDATE.LINK([link_text, type_of_link])

Updates a link to another document. *Link_text* defines the full path as defined in the Links dialog box. *Type_of_link* is a number that defines the type of link to update (1 or omitted = Excel, 2 = DDE, 4 = Outgoing NewWave).

Menu Equivalent: File ➤ Links ➤ Update

VIEW.3D([elevation, perspective, rotation, axes, height %])

Specifies the view of a 3-D chart. The arguments correspond to the items in the 3-D View dialog box.

Menu Equivalent: Format ➤ 3-D View

VIEW.DEFINE(view_name, [print_settings_log, row_col_log])

Creates or defines a view. *View_name* (in quotation marks) specifies the name of the view. *Print_settings_log,* if TRUE or omitted, includes the print settings in the view. *Row_col_log,* if TRUE or omitted, includes the row and column settings in the view.

Menu Equivalent: Window ➤ View ➤ Add

VIEW.DELETE(view_name)

Deletes the view *view_name* (in quotation marks).

Menu Equivalent: Windows ➤ View ➤ Delete.

VIEW.GET(type_num, view_name)

Gets information on the view *view_name* (in quotation marks). *Type_num* defines the information to get: 1 = array of views of active document, 2 = query if print settings are included, and 3 = query if row and column settings are included.

VIEW.SHOW(view_name)

Shows the view *view_name* (in quotation marks).

Menu Equivalent: Window ➤ View ➤ Show

VLINE(number)

See HLINE.

VOLATILE([volatile_logical])

Specifies that the function in which it is declared is volatile; that is, it is recalculated each time any cell in the worksheet is recalculated. In a macro, it must immediately follow the RESULT or ARGUMENT functions. If *volatile_logical* is TRUE or omitted, the function is volatile.

VPAGE(number)

See HPAGE.

VSCROLL(row_number,[row_logical])

See HSCROLL.

WAIT(serial_number)

Suspends execution of the macro until the time specified by *serial_number*.

WHILE(logical_test)

Starts a WHILE...NEXT loop (see Chapter 28).

WINDOW.MAXIMIZE([window_text])

Maximizes *window_text*. If no argument is used, active window is maximized.

Menu Equivalent: Same as Ctrl-F10 if document window isn't maximized.

WINDOW.MINIMIZE([window_text])

Minimizes *window_text*. If no argument is used, active window is minimized.

Menu Equivalent: Same as clicking the Minimize button or pressing Ctrl-F9.

WINDOW.MOVE([x_pos, y_pos, window_text])

Moves *windows_text* (or active window) to *x_pos, y_pos*.

Menu Equivalent: Document/Control ➤ Move

WINDOW.RESTORE([window_text])

Restores *window_text* or active window to its previous size.

Menu Equivalent: Document/Control ➤ Restore or Ctrl-F5

WINDOW.SIZE(width, height,[window_text])

Resizes *window_text* (or active window) to *width, height*.

Menu Equivalent: Document/Control ➤ Size or Ctrl-F8

WINDOW.TITLE([text])

Retitles active window to *text*. If text is an empty quote string, then the window title is deleted. If text is omitted entirely, the title is restored to the document name.

WINDOWS([type_number, match_text])

Returns an array of text values naming all active windows on the screen. You can then use the INDEX function to select from the array. *Type_number* specifies the types of windows to include (1 = All except add-in documents, 2 = Add-in documents only, 3 = All). The default value, if omitted, is 1. *Match_text* specifies windows whose names are to be returned, and can include wildcard characters.

Example: =WINDOWS( ) gives {"Sheet1", "Sheet2"}.

WORKBOOK.ACTIVATE([sheet_name, new_window_logical])

Activates document sheet_name. If new_window_logical is TRUE, the document is displayed in a new window. If FALSE or omitted, the document is displayed with the same size and in the same location as the workbook contents window.

Menu Equivalent: Equivalent to double-clicking document in workbook contents window.

WORKBOOK.ADD(name_array, [dest_book, postion_num])

Adds one or more documents specified by *name_array* to the workbook. *Dest_book* specifies the workbook; if omitted the active workbook is assumed. *Position_num* specifies the position in the workbook.

Menu Equivalent: Equivalent to choosing the Add button on the workbook contents window.

WORKBOOK.COPY(sheet_name, [dest_proj, position_num])

Copies *sheet_name* from one workbook into *dest_proj* and places at position *position_num*. *Sheet_name* can be an array of names.

Menu Equivalent: Equivalent to holding down the Ctrl key while dragging a document from one workbook to another.

WORKBOOK.MOVE(sheet_name, [dest_proj, position_num])

Moves *sheet_name* from one workbook into *dest_proj* and places at position *position_num*.

Menu Equivalent: Equivalent to dragging a document from one workbook to another or to a new location in the same workbook.

WORKBOOK.OPTIONS(sheet_name, [bound_logical, new_name])

Defines the workbook options. *Sheet_name* is a workbook document. *Bound_logical* specifies whether the document should be bound (TRUE) or unbound (FALSE). If not specified, the current condition is not changed. *New_name* is the document name to assign to *sheet_name*. If omitted, the name is not changed. If unbound, *new_name* must be a valid file name.

Menu Equivalent: Equivalent to selecting the Options button in the contents window of a Workbook.

WORKBOOK.SELECT([name_array], [active_name])

Selects individual or groups of documents in workbook. *Name_array* is a horizontal array of document names (in quotation marks).

Menu Equivalent: Equivalent to selecting individual or groups of documents in the workbook window. *Name_array* specifies the documents. *Active_name* specifies the sheet that should be given the focus when the selection is made; if omitted the first sheet is given the focus.

WORKGROUP([name_array_text])

Creates a workgroup, where *name_array_text* is a list of open, unhidden worksheets and macro sheets for the workgroup. If the argument is omitted, the most recently created group is recreated.

Menu Equivalent: Window ➤ Workgroup ➤ Options ➤ Group Edit

WORKSPACE([fixed, decimals, r1c1, scroll, status, formula, menu, remote, entermove, underlines, tools, notes, nav_keys, menu_key_action], [drag_drop], [show_info])

Sets the Excel workspace. The options correspond to those on the dialog box. *Underlines* is a number corresponding to the Command Underline options (1 = on, 2 = off, 3 = automatic). If *tools* is TRUE, the Standard toolbar is displayed. If FALSE, all toolbars are hidden. If omitted, the toolbar display is not changed. Menu_key_action specifies the alternate key option: 1 = Excel (default), 2 = Lotus 1-2-3 Help.

Index

Mastering Excel 4 for Windows

Worksheets on a Disk

You can order a copy of the examples in this book on an IBM-compatible diskette. Request the Excel 4 for Windows diskette from Oregon Professional Microsystems. The diskette is available in 360K 5¼" format only. The price is $19.95 postpaid to US and Canadian addresses. Send check or money order only. Make checks payable to OPM.

. . . .

OPM
4110 N.E. Alameda
Portland, OR 97212

_____
Name

_____
Address

_____
City/State/Zip

Please send me the diskette of Excel 4 for Windows worksheet examples. Enclosed is my check or money order for $19.95.

SYBEX is not affiliated with OPM and assumes no responsibility for any defects in the disk or programs.

SYBEX

FREE BROCHURE!

Complete this form today, and we'll send you a full-color brochure of Sybex bestsellers.

Please supply the name of the Sybex book purchased.

_____

How would you rate it?

____ Excellent   ____ Very Good   ____ Average   ____ Poor

Why did you select this particular book?

____ Recommended to me by a friend
____ Recommended to me by store personnel
____ Saw an advertisement in _____
____ Author's reputation
____ Saw in Sybex catalog
____ Required textbook
____ Sybex reputation
____ Read book review in _____
____ In-store display
____ Other _____

Where did you buy it?

____ Bookstore
____ Computer Store or Software Store
____ Catalog (name: _____)
____ Direct from Sybex
____ Other: _____

Did you buy this book with your personal funds?

____Yes   ____No

About how many computer books do you buy each year?

____ 1-3   ____ 3-5   ____ 5-7   ____ 7-9   ____ 10+

About how many Sybex books do you own?

____ 1-3   ____ 3-5   ____ 5-7   ____ 7-9   ____ 10+

Please indicate your level of experience with the software covered in this book:

____ Beginner   ____ Intermediate   ____ Advanced

Which types of software packages do you use regularly?

____ Accounting   ____ Databases   ____ Networks
____ Amiga   ____ Desktop Publishing   ____ Operating Systems
____ Apple/Mac   ____ File Utilities   ____ Spreadsheets
____ CAD   ____ Money Management   ____ Word Processing
____ Communications   ____ Languages   ____ Other _____
(please specify)

Which of the following best describes your job title?

_____ Administrative/Secretarial   _____ President/CEO

_____ Director   _____ Manager/Supervisor

_____ Engineer/Technician   _____ Other _____
(please specify)

Comments on the weaknesses/strengths of this book: _____

_____

_____

_____

_____

Name _____

Street _____

City/State/Zip _____

Phone _____

PLEASE FOLD, SEAL, AND MAIL TO SYBEX

SYBEX, INC.
Department M
2021 CHALLENGER DR.
ALAMEDA, CALIFORNIA USA
94501

SYBEX

SEAL